INSIDERS' GUIDE® SERIES

INSIDERS' GUIDE® TO COLUMBUS, OHIO

SHAWNIE M. KELLEY

INSIDERS' GUIDE®

GUILFORD, CONNECTICUT
AN IMPRINT OF THE GLOBE PEQUOT PRESS

The prices and rates in this guidebook were confirmed at press time. We recommend, however, that you call establishments before traveling to obtain current information.

INSIDERS' GUIDE®

Text design: LeAnna Weller Smith
Maps by XNR Productions, Inc. © Morris Book Publishing, LLC

ISSN: 1556-4479
ISBN-13: 978-0-7627-3542-6
ISBN-10: 0-7627-3542-2

Manufactured in the United States of America
First Edition/Second Printing

The Scioto River. SHAWNIE KELLEY

The Morgan House, Dublin. SHAWNIE KELLEY
Orange Johnson House, Worthington. SHAWNIE KELLEY

Sells Mansion, Victorian Village. SHAWNIE KELLEY
Buxton Inn, Granville. SHAWNIE KELLEY

Ohio Statehouse. CSRAB
Hayes Hall, The Ohio State University. SHAWNIE KELLEY

COSI. SHAWNIE KELLEY

Franklin Park Conservatory. FRANKLIN PARK CONSERVATORY

Dublin Irish Festival. SHAWNIE KELLEY
Greek Festival. CHRIS KANELLOPOULOS

Jazz and Rib Fest. SHAWNIE KELLEY
The Ohio Renaissance Festival. OHIO RENAISSANCE FESTIVAL, INC.

The Columbus Symphony Orchestra. TOM DUBANAWICH COURTESY CSO
Columbus Jazz Orchestra. JAZZ ARTS GROUP

Columbus Arts Festival. GREATER COLUMBUS ARTS COUNCIL

Via Colori. MARY MARTINEAU/SHORT NORTH BUSINESS ASSOCIATION

Grange Insurance Columbus Family Fun Fest slide. PICTURE AMERICA
Wyandot Lake Amusement and Waterpark. WYANDOT LAKE

Jack Nicklaus, The Memorial Tournament. PICTURE AMERICA

Columbus Marathon. ROD BERRY
Columbus Clippers. NICOLE ANDERSON/EXPERIENCE COLUMBUS

Ohio Stadium. OSU DEPT. OF ATHLETICS
Columbus Destroyers at Nationwide Arena. COLUMBUS DESTROYERS

Columbus skyline at night. BRAD FEINKNOPF

CONTENTS

Directory of Maps

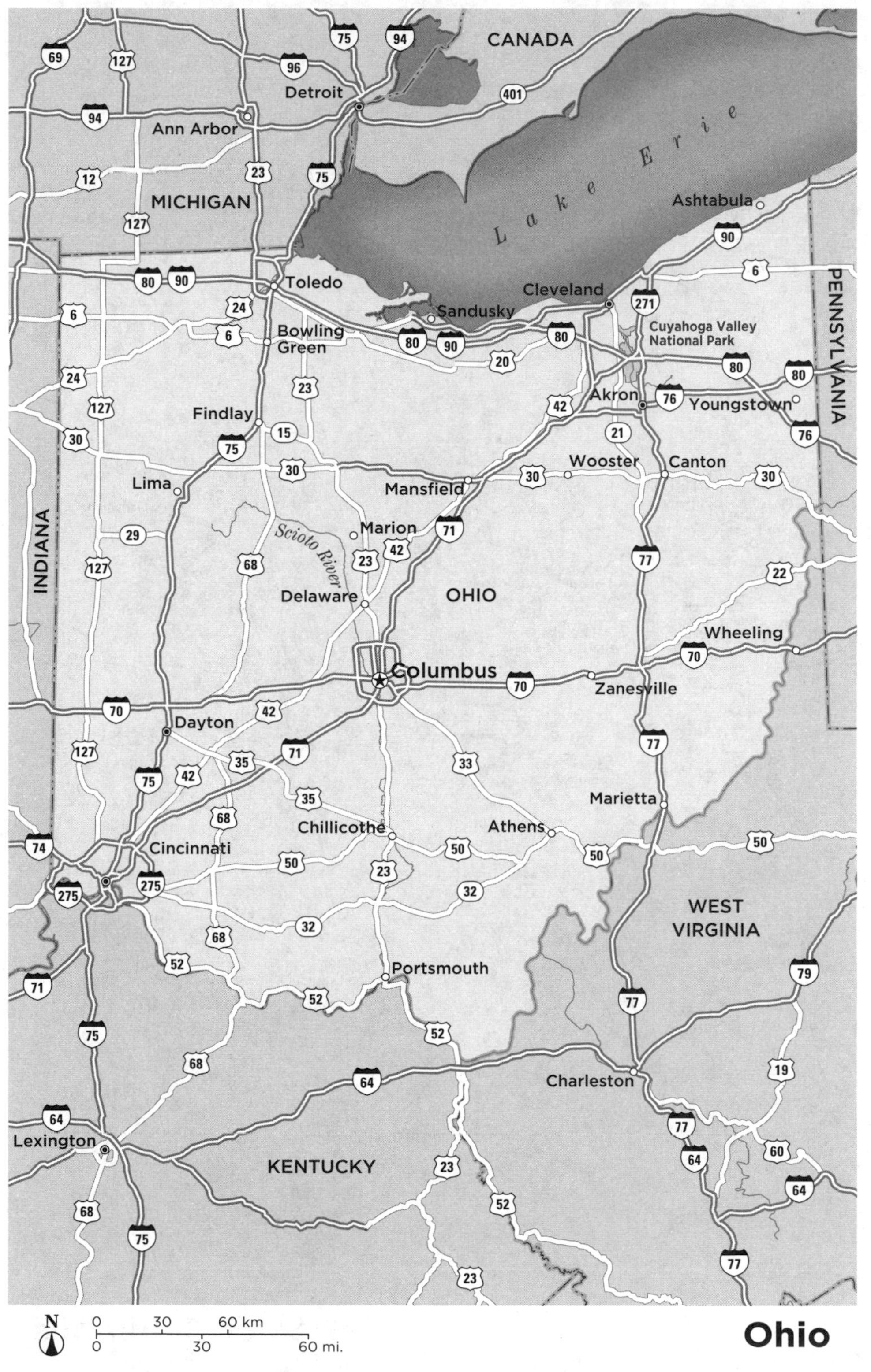
CANADA
Lake Erie
MICHIGAN
INDIANA
OHIO
PENNSYLVANIA
WEST VIRGINIA
KENTUCKY
Detroit
Ann Arbor
Toledo
Sandusky
Cleveland
Ashtabula
Cuyahoga Valley National Park
Bowling Green
Akron
Youngstown
Findlay
Wooster
Canton
Lima
Mansfield
Marion
Scioto River
Delaware
Columbus
Wheeling
Zanesville
Dayton
Marietta
Chillicothe
Athens
Cincinnati
Portsmouth
Charleston
Lexington
N
0 30 60 km
0 30 60 mi.

Ohio

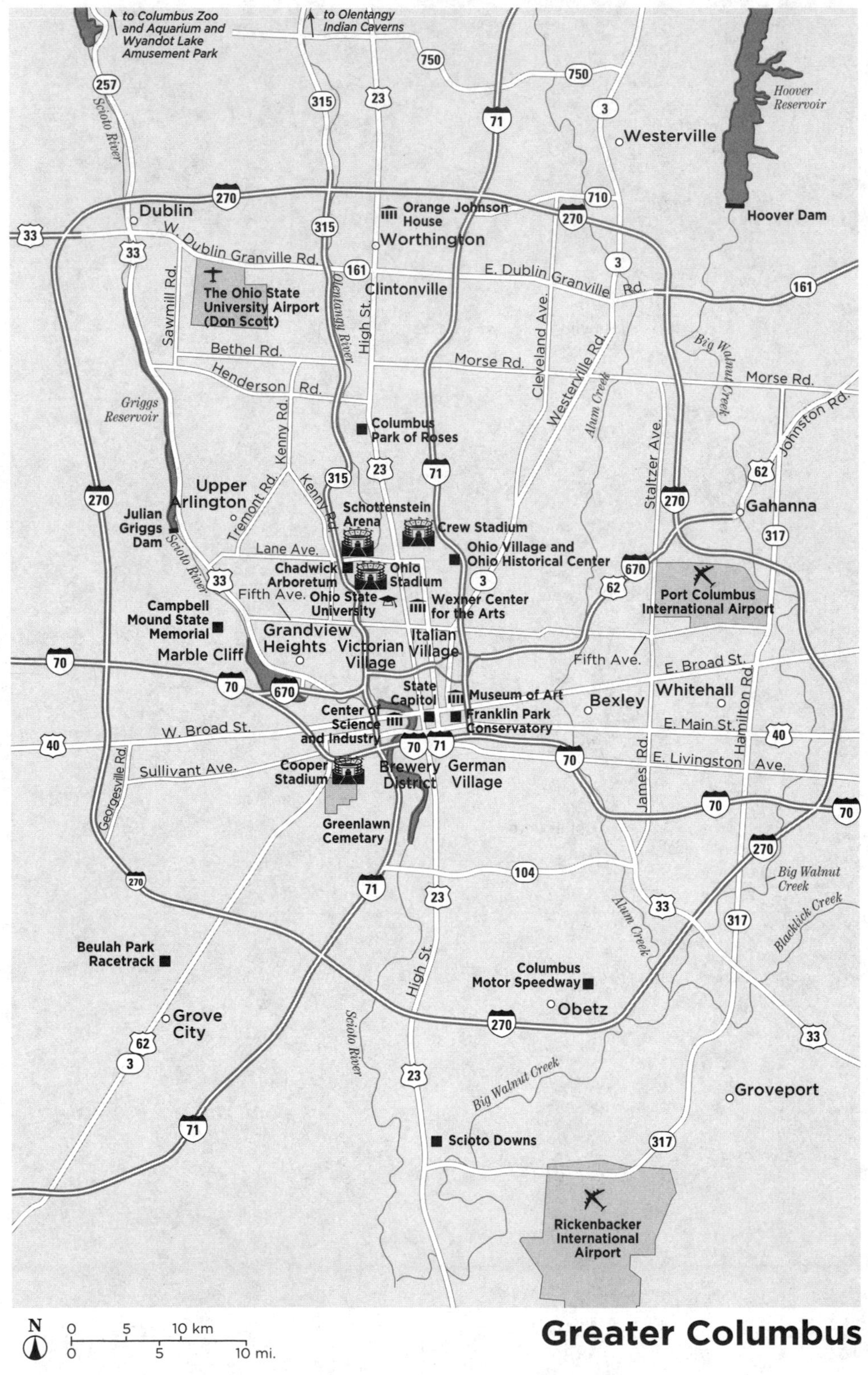

to Columbus Zoo and Aquarium and Wyandot Lake Amusement Park
to Olentangy Indian Caverns
Hoover Reservoir
Hoover Dam
Westerville
Dublin
Worthington
Orange Johnson House
Clintonville
W. Dublin Granville Rd.
E. Dublin Granville Rd.
The Ohio State University Airport (Don Scott)
Sawmill Rd.
Olentangy River
High St.
Cleveland Ave.
Westerville Rd.
Bethel Rd.
Morse Rd.
Henderson Rd.
Big Walnut Creek
Alum Creek
Griggs Reservoir
Scioto River
Kenny Rd.
Tremont Rd.
Columbus Park of Roses
Staltzer Ave.
Johnston Rd.
Gahanna
Upper Arlington
Julian Griggs Dam
Schottenstein Arena
Crew Stadium
Ohio Village and Ohio Historical Center
Lane Ave.
Chadwick Arboretum
Ohio Stadium
Ohio State University
Wexner Center for the Arts
Fifth Ave.
Port Columbus International Airport
Campbell Mound State Memorial
Marble Cliff
Grandview Heights
Victorian Village
Italian Village
E. Broad St.
Whitehall
Bexley
State Capitol
Museum of Art
Center of Science and Industry
Franklin Park Conservatory
W. Broad St.
E. Main St.
Hamilton Rd.
Georgesville Rd.
Sullivant Ave.
Cooper Stadium
Brewery District
German Village
E. Livingston Ave.
James Rd.
Greenlawn Cemetery
Big Walnut Creek
Blacklick Creek
Beulah Park Racetrack
Columbus Motor Speedway
Obetz
Grove City
Groveport
Scioto Downs
Rickenbacker International Airport
257
315
23
750
71
3
270
710
33
161
62
317
670
70
40
104
N
0 5 10 km
0 5 10 mi.
Greater Columbus

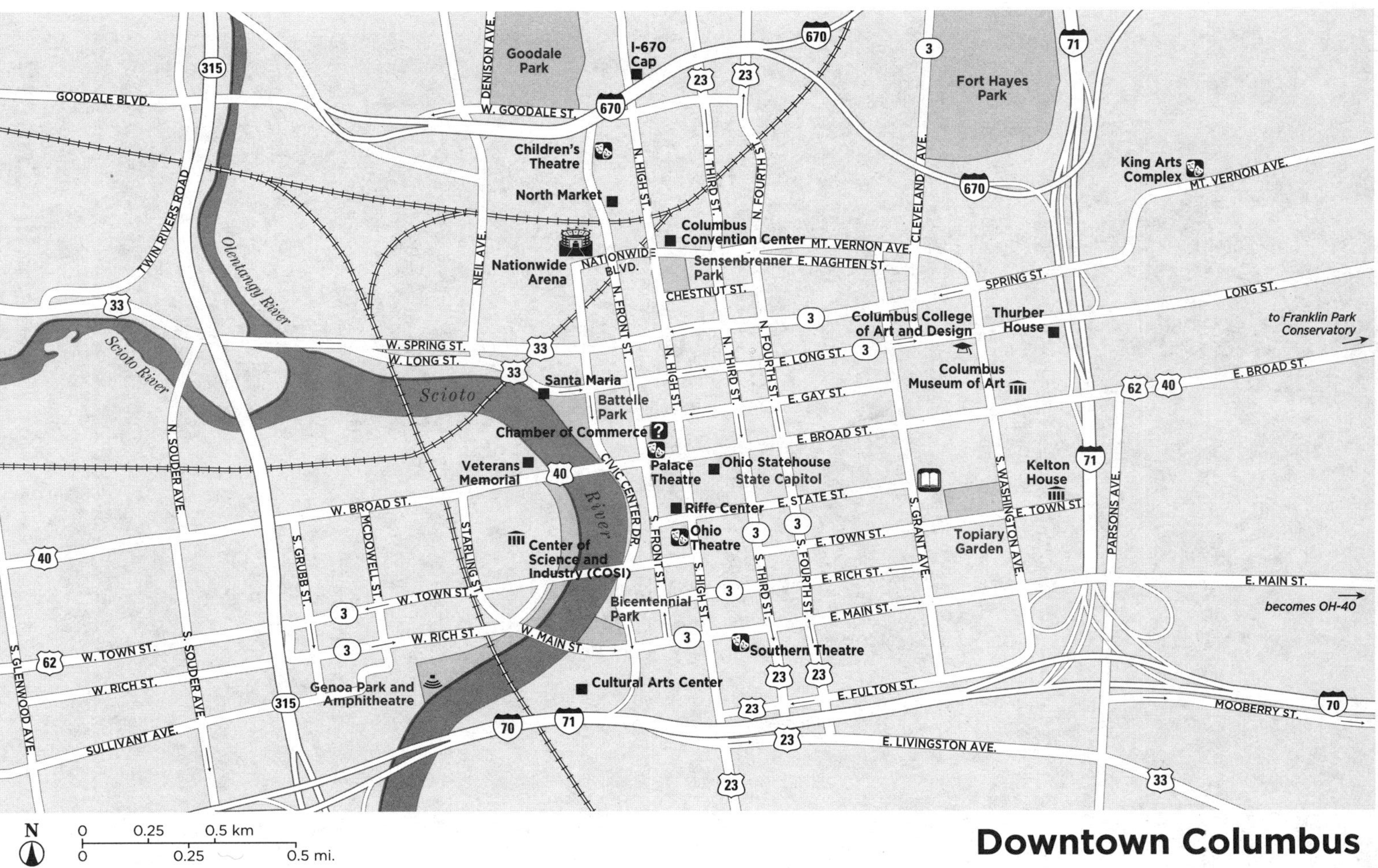

Downtown Columbus

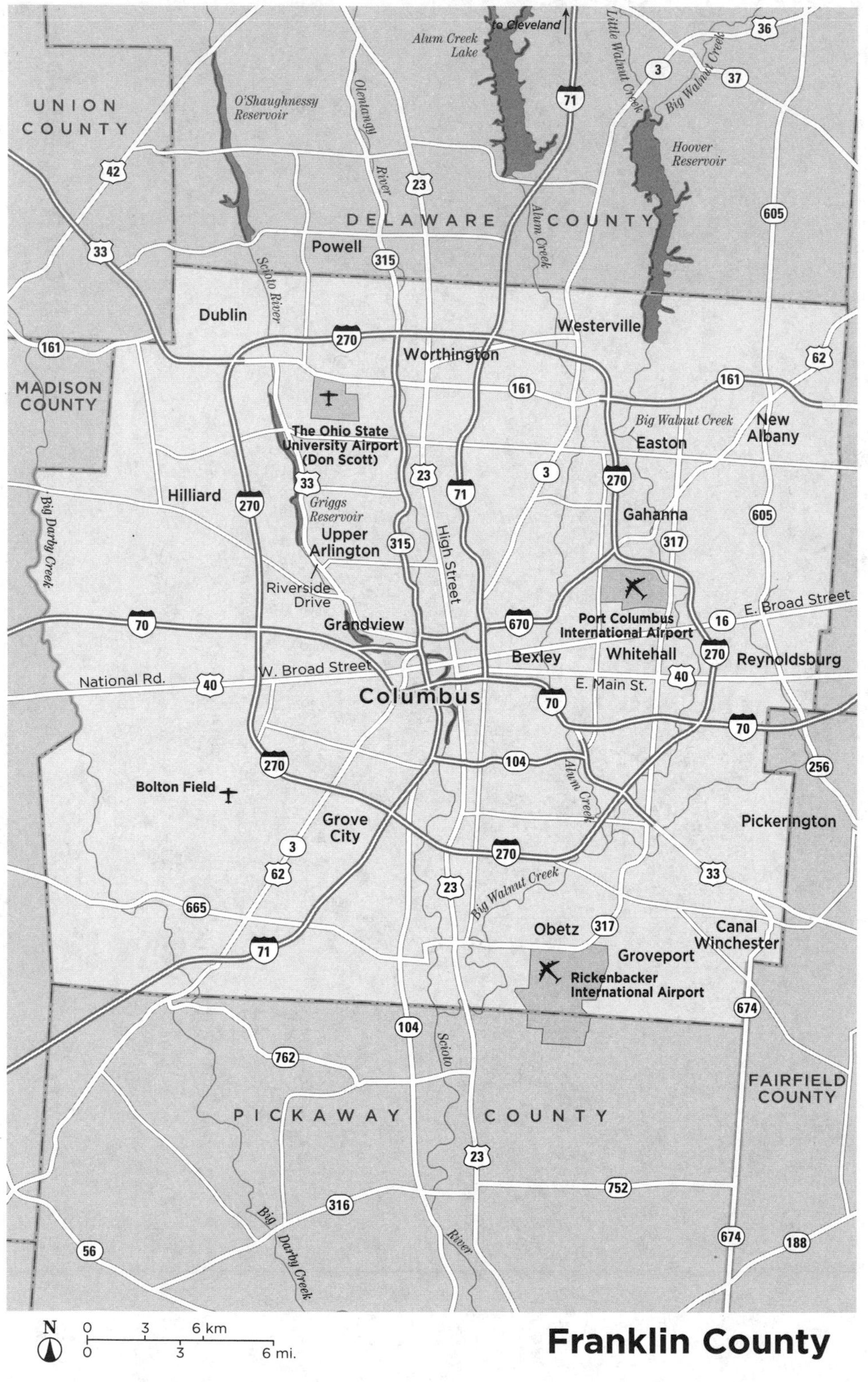

Franklin County

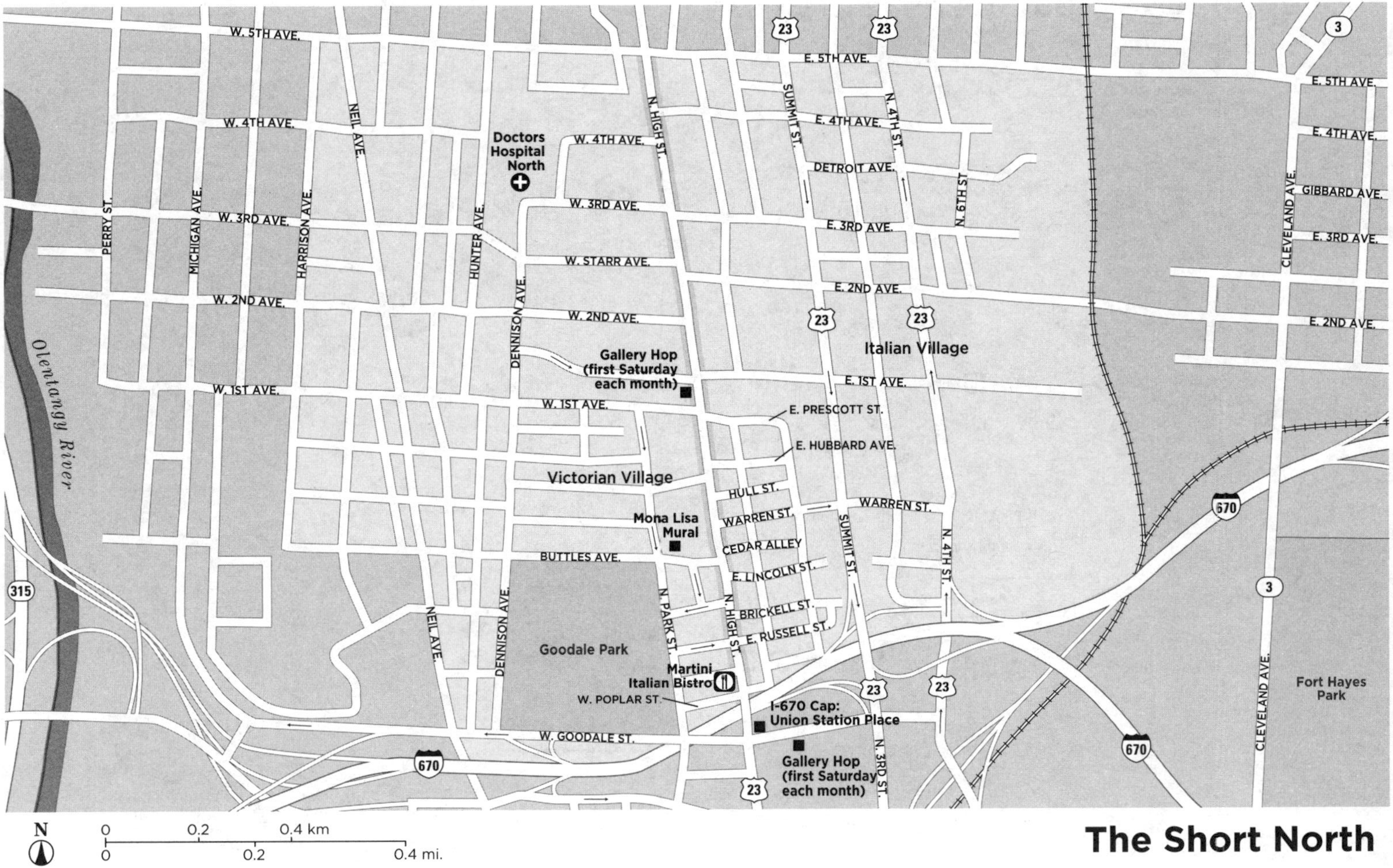

The Short North

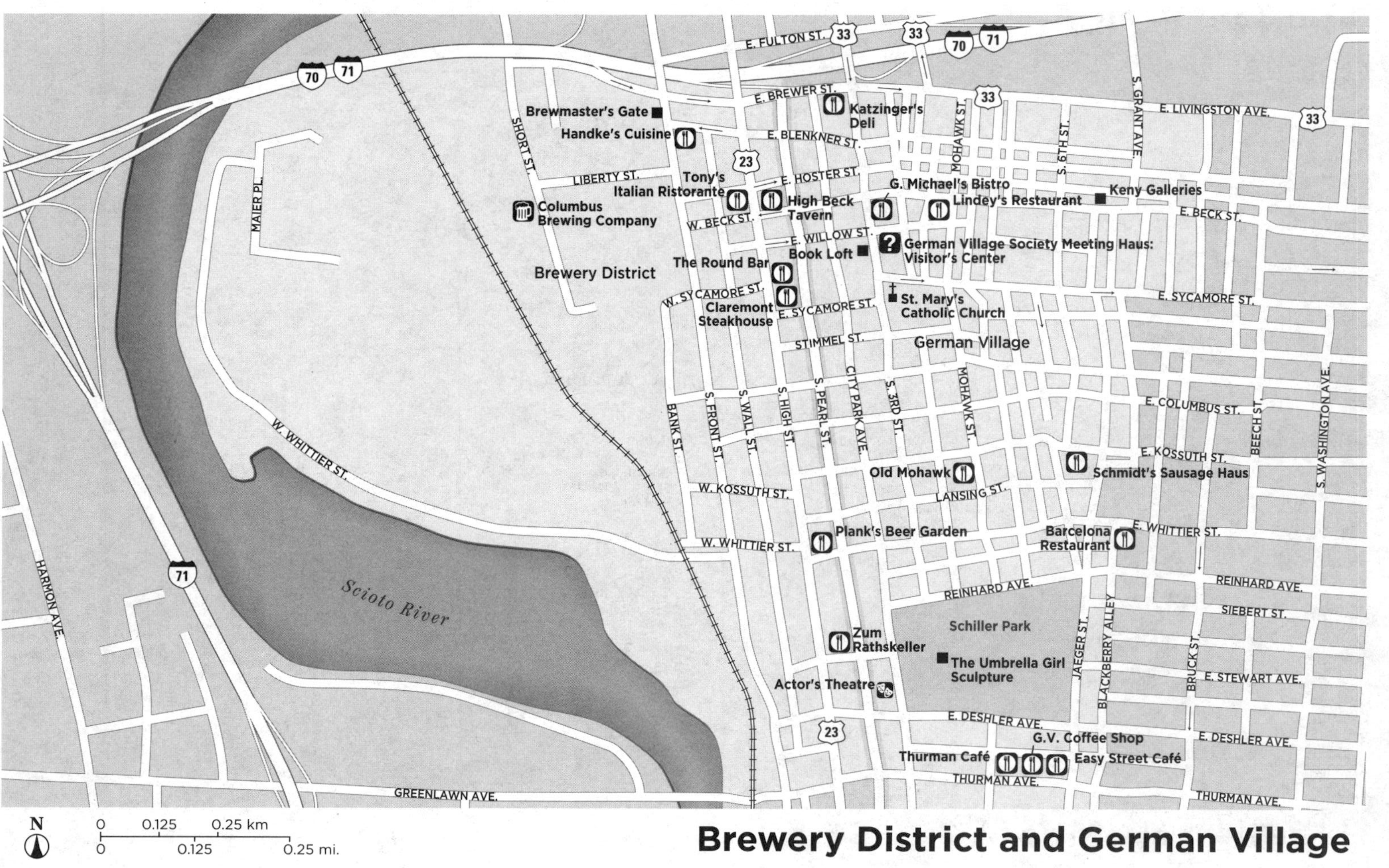

Brewery District and German Village

PREFACE

When I first moved to Columbus, I vaguely recall someone referring to it as "Cowtown" (oh wait; that someone was me!), but it didn't take very long to realize that Columbus is nothing of the sort. Interestingly enough, the only cows I have seen really do live within city limits, at the Waterman Agricultural and Natural Resources Lab, and can be found grazing in a field on the corner of a very busy intersection near the campus of The Ohio State University. Cows aside, Columbus is the antithesis of what I expected.

I was surprised to learn that Columbus, the capital of Ohio, is the 15th-largest city in the country, and it's growing fast. This is largely due to its geographical situation. Almost dead center in the middle of the state, Columbus was named the capital of Ohio in 1812 because of its centralized location. It was easy for all Ohioans to reach and made sense for it to be the legislative seat of the state. Now, almost 200 years later, the world seems a much smaller place, and Columbus is still ideally situated for travel and business as it is within a 550-mile radius (or a day's drive) of over 50 percent of the U.S. population.

Columbus is a modern, forward-thinking city. You see this in its arts community and its architecture. You see this in its business and commerce. You see this in its planning and development. Navigating the city is still manageable, given its growth spurts. Columbus was planned from conception and has two ring roads that are cut by a north-south and east-west highway, making it easy to "get there from here." I'm no Magellan, but it is difficult to get lost in Columbus—especially if you've looked at a map of the city even once.

Columbus is privileged enough to boast four proper seasons. Summers are beautiful, with billowing clouds floating lazily in the big blue sky, but they are often accompanied by sweltering temperatures and high humidity. Autumns tend to linger, warming up residential streets with flaming trees, reviving harvest festivals, and farmers' markets. Indian summer sometimes hangs around well into the holiday season. When winter finally sets in, it is crisp, cold, and often very snowy. We are frequently subjected to subfreezing temperatures, so spring is a welcome reprieve despite the rain.

Columbus is a city where neither convertible nor four-wheel-drive looks out of place. It's a city in which you can sport your woolliest winter sweaters as well as your slinkiest summer clothes. If you have the opportunity to experience the four seasons of Columbus, you'll find each offers up its own special activities.

When it comes to finding something to do, every week seems to offer some sort of festival or community event. Sports lovers can take in a Bluejackets ice hockey game, some Columbus Crew soccer, or a long list of Buckeye varsity and club sports. Art lovers have quality visual and performing arts to choose from or can take in a film at the Wexner Center. Families can spend many a day at COSI, our science center, or at the world-class Columbus Zoo. Speaking of families, Columbus is a wonderful city in which to raise kids, but it is also a great place to be solo, as Columbus was voted the No. 1 city for singles by AOL in 2003.

Once you start flipping through the *Insiders' Guide*, you'll quickly realize there is a little bit of something for everyone in the "Capital City." This guide has drawn on a wealth of information, both written and spoken, as well as personal experiences in an effort to help those just passing through Columbus make the most of a weekend, introduce those relocating to the area to the wide array of dining and shopping opportunities, and offer lifelong residents a new experience in a "new" part of Columbus. I have had a great time discovering the "Discovery City" and hope you do too.

ACKNOWLEDGMENTS

When I learned a friend was coming to work in Columbus, I attempted to purchase a travel guide as a gift for her, but there was none to be found. After a bit of correspondence with Stephanie Hester, my editor at The Globe Pequot Press, it was determined I would write *Insiders' Guide to Columbus, Ohio.* This project is very special to me for many reasons, but especially because it is the first comprehensive travel guide written about the very deserving capital of Ohio. I would like to thank Stephanie for having patience and faith in me to undertake this first, somewhat monstrous, edition.

My initial point of contact for all research was Experience Columbus. I would like to tell all the helpful people there how much I appreciated their input, contact information, and suggestions. I would also like to express my gratitude for their donation of many images in this book. They are an invaluable resource for a visitor and have been an invaluable resource for a writer.

To Kevin Foy, my partner and biggest fan, thanks for feeding me in so many ways—my mind, my heart, my creativity, and my belly. I have been able to count on you for all the important things peripheral to writing this book. Thanks for keeping the dogs and cat at bay while I typed. Thanks for being a domestic god, chauffeur, photographer and model, and for just plain tolerating me throughout the process. Thanks for sharing your great friends, who, like you, are the "true" insiders.

Amanda Kelley—my sister, best friend, and Columbus gastronome extraordinaire—you are the only person I know who has eaten at more Columbus restaurants than I have. Thanks from the bottom of my heart for so generously taking time to read numerous chapters and giving your opinion and sincere input. I hope you recognize the fruits of your efforts throughout the guide.

My brother, Jason Kelley, deserves special mention for looking over the legal contracts, giving them his blessings, and reminding me of the strict deadlines I have to meet—or else! I thank you, and Globe Pequot thanks you.

My mother, Bonnie Emery, was always ready and willing to read through chapters and tell me honestly (as an out-of-towner) if the entries made sense. I am grateful for this.

Giant thanks to my sister-in-law, Julie Kelley, for lending her expertise on Kidstuff; goodness knows she has it. Also to master shoppers Kathy Pine and Betsy Foy, for their retail connoisseurship. Dottie Foy and Ron Hoover have made invaluable suggestions, and I look forward to exploring new restaurants with you both.

I want to acknowledge the time and energy my good friends Andrew LaMoreaux and Dr. Chai Chandrasekhar have invested in "researching" various restaurants, watering holes, and festivals with us this past year. A tough job well done! Thanks also to Andy Verhage for being my sounding board and keeping me social.

One of the most exciting aspects of writing this guide is having legitimate reasons to explore new parts of town, experience new places, and talk to interesting strangers. If it weren't for so many of you taking the time to return calls, respond to e-mails, meet with me, and offer personal and professional opinions about Columbus, I would not have accumulated such a broad base of information to draw on. If it weren't for so many excited people willing to share their stories, offer guidance, or point me in the right direction, I wouldn't have been able to tackle a few daunting chapters.

ACKNOWLEDGMENTS

Special thanks go to a number of people who donated photography or let me pick their brains indefinitely: John Bizios from the Greek Orthodox Cathedral, Anne Brown with the City of Worthington, John Butterfield at the Worthington Chamber of Commerce, Kellie DiFrischia at the Columbus Dog Connection, Charles Gerard and Cheri Mitchell at BalletMet, Peg Hanley with Metro Parks, Kathy Hoke at the Ohio Historical Society, Andy Krutko with The Ohio State University's Information Services, Angie Neil at Port Columbus Airport, Jean Nemeti and Janna Buckey at WCMH, Wayne and Willa Owens at Zum Rathskeller, Chris Peterson at the Worthington Inn, and Lisa Sloan of the Columbus Metropolitan Library.

The folks at the Cincinnati Convention Center, Lily One, Ohio State Parks, The Renaissance Festival, the Quarter Horse Congress, Roscoe Village, Santa Maria, Shadowbox, and Thurber House also donated pictures, which saved me a lot of time and effort. Thank you, whether or not they are used in the book.

It has been very special indeed to have written this book, and I welcome the opportunity to learn even more about my hometown on an ongoing basis.

Insiders' Guide to Columbus, Ohio is dedicated to my two beautiful nieces, Abigail and Sarah Kelley.

HOW TO USE THIS BOOK 

When you first get a new travel guide, what do you usually do? Head straight to the history chapter to try to figure out what this place is all about? Delve into the dining and nightlife sections to figure out how much food and entertainment you can consume in one night? Or, like me, do you just thumb through, anticipating that "something special" will catch your eye? Whatever your technique, *Insiders' Guide*'s user-friendly format doesn't require reading from front to back—unless you want to, of course. *Insiders' Guide* veterans and beginners alike will find that any approach to using this guide is the right approach.

When I first relocated to Columbus, I sure could have used a comprehensive, in-depth resource like this—with the pivotal word being *used*. *Insiders' Guide to Columbus, Ohio* is the end result of a yearlong process involving a lot of research, observations, conversations, and debates. Let's not forget all the eating, drinking, and merriment that went into writing this book too. I have taken a very interactive approach to compiling this information, so my one suggestion for using this guide is to take the same approach and really *use* it. Consider this book an interactive manual to be written in, highlighted, discussed, and shared. I find it very special to have written this guide and welcome the opportunity to learn even more about my new hometown on an ongoing basis. I invite you to begin your exploration of Columbus here.

Insiders' Guide to Columbus, Ohio is written for you, the tourist. The chapters on dining, nightlife, and accommodations are organized according to neighborhood, so you can easily determine which part of town you want or need to stay in and what there is to do around the area. When passing through Columbus, this guide should help you easily find quality accommodations, good eats, and something fun to do.

First-time visitors to Columbus have been pleasantly surprised at the variety and caliber of shopping, dining, and other activities often associated with much bigger cities. Of course, we have our high-end shopping, such as Saks Fifth Avenue, Nordstrom's, and Williams-Sonoma. We have our fair share of chain restaurants, like The Cheesecake Factory and Buca Di Beppo, and can boast the original Wendy's and White Castle headquarters. As many a fine meal that can be had at P. F. Chang's China Bistro or Morton's Steakhouse, this book's objective is to bring to light the local, independent restaurants, bars, and stores offering a distinct Columbus experience.

Insiders' Guide to Columbus, Ohio is written for you, the transplant. If you are relocated, working long term, or attending college in Columbus, this guide will familiarize you with our communities, traditions, and events. The Relocation chapter describes Columbus neighborhoods, offering details about libraries, post offices, local utilities, and other practical information. Those with a family may be particularly interested in the Kidstuff and Education and Child Care chapters. Animal lovers will be happy to learn *Purina Magazine* ranked Columbus the eighth Pet Healthiest City in the United States in 2003. The Pet-Friendly Columbus chapter includes details about kennels, vets, and other animal services.

Newcomers may also want to spend a little extra time looking over the chapters unique to Columbus. Golf lovers can read up on the Golden Bear, Jack Nicklaus, and his annual Memorial Tournament. The chapter dedicated to The Ohio State University will provide students and parents with pertinent information about campus living, Buckeye sports, university facilities, and various organizations. It is here you will be introduced to the "Best Damn Band in the Land" and find out that a "weekend at Bernie's" could be as equally kooky as the movie. No chapter about OSU would be complete without an exhaustive list of campus pizza shops and watering holes. Hopefully, you will take away some fundamental information that will make your transition to Columbus a little smoother and, most of all, fun.

Finally, *Insiders' Guide to Columbus, Ohio* is written for you, the native. It is amazing how Columbus is growing and evolving. No matter how long you have lived here, there are always new experiences to be had and different parts of town to explore. You may discover your new favorite restaurant, attend an event such as The Ribs Festival or Gallery Hop for the first time and end up making a tradition of it. Permanent "insiders" may even learn a new tidbit of trivia about the "Capital City."

The chapters Attractions and Day Trips and Weekend Getaways reinforce our city's great location, and they present only a handful of the interesting places you can easily visit. History buffs can revel in bygone days at Zoar and Roscoe Villages. Sports fans cans make the pilgrimage to the Football Hall of Fame, and outdoorsy types can get back to nature in a short drive south to the Hocking Hills. Step into another world by visiting Ohio's Heartland, home to the world's largest Amish and Mennonite population. Here you can buy fine handcrafted furniture, crafts, and remarkable cheese. Read on to learn why Sugar Creek is called "Little Switzerland." Many locals don't realize there is a taste of Europe in their own backyard.

HOW THIS BOOK IS ORGANIZED

Insiders' Guide to Columbus, Ohio is not meant to be an exhaustive directory of restaurants and hotels but rather an organized guide explaining what makes Columbus "what it is." It will shed some light on the special attractions and features that make our city unique and fun. For example, where can you have a sophisticated business lunch at noon, a rowdy happy hour after work, and take in some live music at night? Lots of places! Where can you go for a fun family Friday, rock climbing on Saturday, or run off the dog's energy on Sunday? Lots of places! The format of the *Insiders' Guide* is designed to make sense of these options. It offers a logical flow to the presentation of what can often be an overwhelming amount of information.

After finding out how you can get to and around the city in the chapter not surprisingly titled Getting Here, Getting Around, take a little time to bring yourself up to speed on Columbus's history and our famous (and infamous) sons and daughters. The History chapter will explain how a little cowtown grew along the banks of the Scioto River into the cosmopolitan city it is today.

If you're new to Columbus, you may want to linger a bit in Area Overview, the chapter that introduces you to Columbus today. This is a discussion about the current state of the city, its ambience, cost of living, and people. It will offer vital statistics and information about its political atmosphere as the capital of Ohio and its diverse economy.

If you already know the basics about Columbus, it's time to dig in. Are you looking for restaurants, dance clubs, theaters, or lodging? Or perhaps you're seeking practical information about retirement or higher education. There are chapters dedicated to each. A few sections offer general discussions about media, worship, and health care, while other chapters, such as Restaurants, The Pub Crawl, and Shopping, group extensive information into neighborhoods for a more user-friendly approach. Also look for Insiders' Tip—marked with an **i**—that let you in on local secrets.

It makes sense to organize the entries geographically beginning downtown, working our way through the Arena District, the Short North, and slightly farther north to OSU's campus. The entries then move east, south, and west through the city neighborhoods, finishing up north of the city in Dublin. You will find the standardized listings provide the name, address, telephone number, Web site (if available), and price code (if applicable) for each entry, as well as a vivid description that validates its inclusion in this guide. If no town name is listed, assume the location in question is within the city limits of Columbus, unless the listing falls within a section that is entirely devoted to another town (for example, the section on Westerville restaurants does not list town names, since it is clear from the heading that they are all in Westerville). Neighborhoods within Columbus are also noted in some sections.

Each entry strives to maintain the most up-to-date information; however, if you think an entry is not accurate or feel an important tip has been left out, or you discover a secret gem of a place that deserves mention, we'll be glad to explore these suggestions for subsequent editions. Please send a note to editorial@GlobePequot.com or write to us at

The Globe Pequot Press
Reader Response/Editorial Department
P.O. Box 480
Guilford, CT 06437

Relocating can be stressful, and having to feel your way around a new city only compounds that stress. Entertaining visitors can be equally nerve-racking. No matter what your status—tourist, transplant, or lifer—*Insiders' Guide to Columbus, Ohio* is written for you. Whatever the reasons and how you decide to use this guide is up to you. It is a resource to help you discover Columbus in a fun, easy—and personal—way.

AREA OVERVIEW 

Christopher Columbus. Our namesake—but why? When researching this book, I assumed there would be some profound reason the founders chose to name the capital of Ohio after the great explorer, but there wasn't. The best (and very anticlimactic) explanation I found is that the name was arbitrarily selected. Columbus could just as easily have been Ohio City or High Bank, but they passed on both. The History chapter will go into greater detail about the original city of Franklinton being moved from the west bank of the Scioto River to higher ground on the east due to perpetual flooding. It was at this point, in 1812, that Franklinton was renamed Columbus and this same year designated the "Capital City" of Ohio.

Many people are surprised to learn Columbus is the 15th-largest city in the country, with a population of over 700,000. Along with this booming development comes big-city sprawl. Yet somehow Columbus has been able to retain a small-town, middle-America charm.

Speaking of which, not much is more American than Benjamin Franklin—another namesake—for whom the original city was named in 1797 and Franklin County established in 1803. Columbus lies in Franklin County, along with 12 other cities, 12 villages, and 18 townships. As of the 2000 census, there was a population of almost 1.1 million in Franklin County alone, making it the 33rd most populated county in the country. The other half million people live in five surrounding counties that, along with Franklin, comprise the Columbus Metropolitan Statistical Area (MSA). These five counties are Delaware, Fairfield, Licking, Madison, and Pickaway, while Morrow and Union counties have recently been added to the MSA. They were not included in the last census but are certainly accounted for in this guide.

Now that you know how we got our name, read on to learn how we got our reputation. The remaining chapter will introduce you to our city, people, and economics—the heart, soul, and lifeblood of Columbus. You can get a quick snapshot of the city by checking out the vital statistics, and you may be surprised to learn what people and ideas were born in our city.

DOWNTOWN: A 21ST-CENTURY RENAISSANCE

Columbus has one of those skylines that may not be immediately recognizable, but there are several distinct buildings that make it memorable. One can't help but be awe-inspired by the oldest skyscraper in the skyline, the LeVeque Tower, with its verticality and sculptures that scream 1930s art deco. One Nationwide Plaza is sadly reminiscent of the twin towers of New York's World Trade Center in the way they stand a solid and seemingly unmovable mass of 1970s concrete and steel. And then there is Miranova, the crescent-shaped, innovative condominiums that marked Columbus's move into the new millennium. The hazy summer vistas of city and bridges have been likened to those views up the Seine River in Paris. Romantic, indeed, but let's not exaggerate!

Downtown Columbus encompasses 1,500 acres bound by Interstate 670, Interstate 71, Route 315, and CSX Railroad. This accounts for 1 percent of the total Columbus land area. Geographically speaking, downtown Columbus is 35 percent bigger than downtown Boston and eight times larger than the Chicago loop. This area is home to 12 hotels, 7 theaters, 200 retail shops, and nearly the same number of eating and drinking establishments. A downtown residential population of 4,000 accounts for only 0.5

percent of the population, but times, they are a changin'.

A new strategic business plan was launched in 2002 by the Columbus Downtown Development Corporation, marking the start of a major revitalization effort. Beginning with a plan termed the River-South Redevelopment, the backers hope to draw new investment, recover vacant office space, create new jobs, and stimulate downtown residential living. Some $1.7 billion in public and private investments has been committed to offices, retail outlets, education, and parks since this plan was rolled out. The most recent progress report shows these improvements are well under way.

Downtown office vacancy rates have dropped in the past four quarters, and 1,400 new jobs were created or moved downtown under the Columbus Downtown Office Incentive Program. New builds will include a county courthouse and baseball stadium, while the historic Lazarus building will be renovated into the city's first green building. The Scioto Mile, a series of downtown, riverfront park systems, is also being implemented. A new nine-acre area called North Bank Park opened in May 2005, while a river-level walkway and continuous bike paths are being planned. Renovations are in store for two bridges and the existing parks, all this to make downtown Columbus a more pleasant place to work, visit, and live.

The development of these parks is essential to making downtown living attractive, but even more vital is housing. Residential development in the downtown area has remained relatively stagnant since the 1980s, but now, with 988 housing units having opened and 2,600 more in progress or planned, there will be no shortage of options for those who prefer city living. And fear not, city dwellers; there will be no need to venture to the suburbs to do "proper" grocery shopping. The Brewery District will soon be home to the first full-scale grocery store in the downtown area.

i

New downtown residents can join the Downtown Residents Association to network, attend forums, or just get to know each other at monthly meetings. You can call (614) 645-5010, or check out further information on the Web site www.downtowncolumbus.com.

Keep in mind that, with all these new plans and changes happening in downtown Columbus, this is not the only part of the city going through a renaissance. Many of the surrounding communities are undertaking their own revitalization efforts and renovations (see the Relocation chapter). Looking to the future, one can only imagine the updates that will occur in the subsequent editions of *Insiders' Guide to Columbus, Ohio*.

THE NECKLACE OF NEIGHBORHOODS

If you have the opportunity to explore the sprawling Columbus area outside the downtown area, you will find a varied landscape ranging from skyscrapers and highways to historic villages and designated scenic roads, developing suburbs to rural farmland. Barns can be found around the corner from major shopping malls and homes worth seven figures a short distance from low-income housing.

With such a variety of neighborhoods, it is nearly impossible to pinpoint an architectural style typical to Columbus. There are many pockets of Victorian homes, but even they vary in terms of their location and style. Take a drive (or a stroll) through Olde Town East or Victorian Village, and you'll see what I mean. A number of homes built between the 1850s and 1890s span the spectrum from traditional to garish. Both the Italianate and Queen Anne styles are heavily represented, but the Victorians' obsession with period revivals is evident as well. You'll find Tudor

Vital Statistics

- **Founded** by Lucas Sullivant in 1797 as Franklinton
- **Mayor of Columbus (2006):** Michael B. Coleman
- **Governor of Ohio (2006):** Bob Taft
- **Nicknames:** "Discovery City," "Capital City"
- **Population (2003):** Columbus, 711,470; Franklin County, 1,068,978; Columbus metro area, approximately 1.6 million
- **Land area:** 212.6 square miles (2.3 square miles is water)
- **Counties:** Columbus Metropolitan Statistical Area consists of eight counties: Franklin, Delaware, Fairfield, Licking, Madison, Pickaway, Morrow, and Union
- **Airports/interstates:**
  Port Columbus International Airport, Rickenbacker International Airport, Don Scott Field, Bolton Field/interstates: I-70, I-71, I-270, I-670
- **Temperatures:** Average temperature in January 28°F, July 75°F
  Average temperature (°F):

	High	Low
Winter	35	19
Spring	62	41
Summer	84	63
Autumn	65	43

- **Precipitation:** Average 37 inches of rainfall, 28 inches of snowfall annually
- **Automatic time/temperature and weatherline:** (614) 469-1010
- **Local time:** Eastern Standard Time
- **Public transportation:** COTA bus system
- **Bureau of Motor Vehicles:** (614) 995-5353; 1970 West Broad Street. There are 25 centers in Franklin County. Drivers licenses, vehicle registration, titles, and new resident information can be found online at www.bmv.ohio.gov.
- **Driving age:** 16
- The blood-alcohol level for Columbus is .08. Your license will be revoked if you are found guilty of driving under the influence of alcohol or if you refuse to take a chemical or physical test.
- If you hit a deer, you are entitled to take the carcass, but the collision must be reported to a game protector or law enforcement within 24 hours.
- **Alcohol laws:** Age 21 to purchase and consume alcohol. Beer and wine can be purchased in grocery and convenience stores, while hard liquor is sold in licensed stores Monday through Saturday.
- **Marriage:** In order to get married in Columbus, men must be 18 years of age and women 16 years of age, unless the minor has parental approval. Both parties must apply in person at the Franklin County Courthouse, 373 South High Street, 23rd floor; the cost is $40 cash.

- **Sales tax:** 6.25%
- **Columbus Chamber of Commerce:** 37 North High Street, Columbus, OH 43215; (614) 221-1321, (800) 950-1321; www.columbus-chamber.org
- **Daily newspaper:** *Columbus Dispatch*
- **Visitor center:** Downtown at Columbus City Center and at Easton Town Center
- **Major colleges/universities:** Capital University, Columbus State University, Denison University, Franklin University, Ohio Dominican University, The Ohio State University, Ohio Wesleyan University, Otterbein College, Wittenberg University, Muskingum College
- **Key business sectors in Columbus:** distribution, government, e-commerce, R&D, manufacturing
- **Top 10 employers:** State of Ohio, The Ohio State University, federal government, Columbus public schools, Nationwide, Bank One, Ohio Health, City of Columbus, Limited Brands, Franklin County

Famous and Infamous

Archie Griffin—born in Columbus, The Ohio State University; professional football player, only player to win the Heisman Trophy twice

Benjamin R. Hanby—Otterbein College; early Ohio songwriter; composed "Darling Nelly Gray" and "Up on a Housetop"

Bobby Rahal—Dennison University; race car driver and team owner; retired ranking first in career starts, second in career earnings

Branch Rickey—Ohio Wesleyan University; coach of Brooklyn Dodgers, integrated Major League Baseball by recruiting Jackie Robinson; pioneered the use of baseball statistics and batting helmets

Anne O'Hare McCormick—born in Columbus, Ohio Dominican University; first woman to win a Pulitzer Prize (1939)

Curtis E. LeMay—born in Columbus, The Ohio State University; headed World War II bomber forces; longest serving active duty general

Dr. Francis M. Pottenger—Otterbein College; pioneered cure of tuberculosis

Geraldine "Jerry" Mock—born in Columbus; first woman to fly solo around the world

Eddie Rickenbacker—born in Columbus; premier World War I combat pilot; race car driver

George Bellows—born in Columbus, The Ohio State University; Ashcan school artis

Ellen Walker Craig-Jones—born in Urbancrest; first African-American woman elected mayor of a U.S. municipality (1972)

Alice Schille—born in Columbus, Columbus College of Art and Design; America's foremost female watercolorist

Jack Hanna—Otterbein College and Capital University; director emeritus of the Columbus Zoo

Jack Nicklaus—born in Columbus, The Ohio State University; golfer, course designer, and founder of the Memorial Tournament

James Thurber—born in Columbus, The Ohio State University; writer, cartoonist

Jesse Owens—The Ohio State University; track-and-field star; first American to win four gold medals in a single Olympics at the 1936 Olympics in Berlin

John Glenn—Muskingum College; first American astronaut to orbit the earth; oldest human to go to space; Ohio senator

Mildred Elizabeth, a.k.a. "Axis Sally"—first coed at Ohio Wesleyan University to wear knickers; had tragic love affair with German soldier during World War II and returned to live out life in central Ohio

Milt Caniff—The Ohio State University; creator of comic strips "Terry and the Pirates" and "Steve Canyon"

Rutherford B. Hayes—born in Columbus; 19th president of the United States

"Woody" Hayes—Denison University and The Ohio State University; very outspoken (and very successful) OSU football coach

Revivals, Neoclassical Revivals, Georgian Revivals, and Colonial Revivals, and don't forget the abundance of eclectic homes that go unclassified.

The wealth and eccentricity of the Victorian period continue to set these parts of town apart from others, but eclectic building styles exist all over Columbus. It is no less the historic homes in Olde Worthington, the giant Georgians of New Albany, the monstrous mansions in Bexley, the tight-quartered brownstones in German Village, and the new developments in Dublin that provide a different backdrop for a unique experience in each neighborhood. If you start just south of the city and travel about 10 miles north on High Street, you'll understand.

The 1950s and '60s saw the birth of policies that would help the city avoid being strangled by prosperous suburbs during growth spurts.

HIGH STREET

As it leaves the quaint streets of German Village, High Street passes through the center of downtown Columbus, flanked by austere government buildings, modern hotels, and parking lots. Just outside the city center, the Short North, with its galleries and townhouses, has a SoHo feel to it, while a mile farther up High Street are the unmistakable signs of campus life: cheap eats, tattoo and music shops, beautiful university architecture, and not-so-beautiful off-campus housing—not to mention the occasional protest or freak show that can be seen along High Street at The Ohio State University.

At Hudson Avenue, a few-block transition is made from a university to a residential setting. Clintonville and Beechwold are the quintessential tree-lined streets, with older houses that have a lot of character and are still affordable compared with Worthington, which is the next community north. The heart of Olde Worthington, with many pubs, restaurants, and shops directly on High Street, is a good place to finish a drive.

From German Village to Worthington, a 10-mile stretch of road passes through six altogether different neighborhoods, six completely different cityscapes with six different local flavors. Keep in mind that this is just the north-south axis. If you choose to drive the east-west thoroughfare through town, you'll encounter the same thing. No matter which side of Columbus you venture to, you'll experience distinctive neighborhoods, each with its own identity and sense of community.

Encircled by this "necklace of neighborhoods," Columbus maintains a reputation for being safe and clean and offering an affordable cost of living when compared with other cities of its size. This is part of what makes Columbus a very family-friendly city. People are born and raised here, and they stay here. People move here, and they stay too.

THE EVERYMAN

When you come to Columbus, what sort of people do you expect to encounter? Well, we come in all shapes, sizes, and colors, so much so, *USA Today* called Columbus residents "The 'Everyman' of America," and it's true. Politicians woo us to no end; we are a test market for new products, a breeding ground for new restaurants and watering holes. But why?

Columbus is diverse. It is a unique population for a midwestern city, and, no matter which way you slice it, we are just not a "typical" community. Yes, Columbus is culturally, religiously, and ethnically diverse. In fact, there are more multiracial people in Franklin County than any other county in Ohio. Minorities comprise 25 percent of the population, while Franklin County has the largest number of Asians, Pacific Islanders, and Native Americans in the whole of Ohio. The past decade saw a 70 percent increase in Columbus's Asian population, but the biggest growth was the 153 percent increase in its Indian population.

Columbus has the second-largest concentration of Somalis in the country—about 30,000.

The state of Ohio might be a more representative cross section of America than Columbus, as we were rated number 65 out of 150 on Acxiom's list of cities "bearing the greatest likeness to the overall U.S. population." Maybe we aren't *their* ideal test market, but Columbus, on average, is younger and more educated with a higher disposable income than that of typical metros the same size—still making us some seriously attractive guinea pigs.

Columbus is young. We offer up the youthful demographics considered to be "risk takers" or "early adopters," meaning, if one of these atypical Columbus residents latches onto a new product or trend (or politician), there's the likelihood the vast middle of the American population will latch onto it as well. As a side note, I've also heard advertising is more affordable here than in other cities, which may add a little to our appeal.

Columbus is educated. There is a 90 percent graduation rate from Franklin County's public high schools, while the percentage of these students pursuing further education is as high as 98 percent at Upper Arlington High School, with Bexley and Worthington coming in a close second. Thirty-two percent of the region's population holds a bachelor's degree, while almost 67,000, or 8 percent, have graduate or professional degrees.

There is, however, a lot more to the Columbus population than being trendsetting, smarty-pants or making and break-

Columbus is getting younger. The median age of Franklin County has dropped from 34.3 to 32.5 in the past decade, though I have not been able to find the fountain of youth here. That would be a great Insiders' tip now, wouldn't it?

Testimony to the education of the population: Forty percent of residents carry a library card, twenty-six percent attend the ballet, opera, or theater, and nearly 707,000 are registered voters.

ing political campaigns. On the whole, we are a fun lot. We are families, and we are singles. We are gay, and we are straight. We love a good football game, and we love a good festival. We are good neighbors and responsible members of the community.

One thing that stands out about the general population is that, along with the strong sense of community, comes a tremendous love of giving. Columbus residents are social minded and community service oriented, giving back when and how we can. This can be seen in fundraisers of the most creative types for charities of all sorts. From small, nonprofit organizations for local artists to massive, corporate campaigns for the United Way, Columbus residents are very passionate about making our city a better place to live.

Revolutionary technologies and products developed in Columbus have included the Universal Product Code (UPC) system, the automated teller machine, the compact disc, and the "no-lick" self-adhesive stamp. Can't live without them!

COLUMBUS SPEAK

People of Columbus speak with a rather nondescript midwestern accent, but there are a few words that can raise an eyebrow when it comes time to actually verbalizing them. Here is a pronunciation guide for the few that cause the most grief.

Bellefontaine—For you French-speaking purists, forget about it! In the ongoing effort to butcher the beautiful French language, this town is pronounced Bell Fountain.

Jaeger Street—It's YAY-ger Street in German Village.

Morse Road—When a local says "Morse Road," it often comes out sounding like "Morris Road." Morse Road, which runs east-west, dead-ends into High Street in Clintonville, so be sure not to drive around in confusion looking for "Morris Road."

Newark—One might be inclined to pronounce this like the city in New Jersey, but this Columbus suburb's name has been condensed into one slurred syllable. Call us lazy, but we call it "Nerk."

Olentangy (River and Boulevard)—It is *not* pronounced O-len-tangy (as in a tangy sauce), but O-len-tan-gee (as in "gee"-whiz, that's how it's pronounced?!).

Riffe Building (and Theaters)—I have heard this mistakenly called the Riff Building. It is named for a longtime Columbus senator, Vernal Riffe, and rhymes with *wife*.

Scioto—This river's name has a silent *c*: Sigh-OH-tuh, not Sky-OH-tuh.

STRICTLY BUSINESS

Columbus never had the geographical advantage of being on a major water port like Cincinnati or Cleveland, so the opportunity to develop into a big industrial base was just not here. While Columbus has some manufacturing, it was during the late 20th century that the city came into its own with a booming service and distribution economy, holding true to its market town roots.

Columbus also has developed a reputation for being a leader in banking, insurance, health care, research, finance, and government and is well known for its progressive, high-tech businesses, but you will find retail and distribution being the driving forces behind the economy. Columbus is headquarters for five Fortune 500 companies and one Fortune 1000 company. It was also the launching pad for top corporations such as The Limited Brands, Wendy's International, and Nationwide. A diversified economy, as well as its outstanding workforce, is the key to the city's and region's strength. Consequently, Columbus has an unemployment rate well below the national average and has been able to endure national economic downturns.

That is, until 2001. Rather than put all of our eggs into an industrial basket, we put them in an information technology basket, and although the world did not come to a screeching halt at Y2K, IT mania certainly did. A lot of important sectors that offer business-to-business services in Columbus were negatively affected.

When Columbus succumbed to a recession (along with the rest of the country), analysts finally recognized we might not have had as diverse an economy as once thought. This was a wake-up call for the city. Action is being taken to diversify, targeting three areas of economic activity that are likely to be high-growth in the 21st century by utilizing and building on the assets that already exist in the region.

The first targeted area is advanced logistics. With a highly developed retail and distribution sector dependent on IT, it makes sense to utilize the IT-trained population and infrastructure to make distribution even more efficient. The second initiative goes hand in hand with the downtown revitalization effort. With a concentration of advertising and public relation firms, as well as several fine arts schools in the region, this seems a good opportunity to increase creative services in Columbus.

The third targeted area is life sciences. Research and development is Columbus's best-kept secret. Battelle, headquartered in Columbus, coupled with the hospitals at OSU, Children's Hospital, Roxeanne Labs, and Cardinal Health, to name a few, provides the world with cutting-edge R&D in biotechnology. Within each of these areas of growth, Columbus's location again comes into play since it is considered one of our biggest assets. Being within a day's drive of over 50 percent of the U.S. and Canadian markets, Columbus is one of the most cost-effective locations in the country to do business.

Huffman's Market, in Upper Arlington, is the first store in Ohio to be permitted carryout liquor sales on Sunday. The store may sell beer, wine, and liquor from 10:00 A.M. to midnight.

Besides being blessed with a downtown renaissance, a dynamic business environment, and great people, Columbus is committed to celebrating our diversity through fun festivals, fine restaurants, and annual cultural events. The community has access to a world-class zoo and a variety of arts and entertainment, not to mention championship college football. The information and listings in the following chapters provide more than a glimpse of what makes the quality of life in Columbus so attractive for those who choose to live here and what keeps visitors coming back again and again.

Forbes *magazine named Columbus the 10th "Best Place for Business and Careers in Metropolitan Areas with Populations of More than a Million," in May 2003.*

GETTING HERE, GETTING AROUND

On the rare occasion I have been asked, "Where *is* Columbus?" I reply, "Put your finger dead-center on a map of Ohio, and there you are." If you look at a detailed map of the city, you'll see downtown Columbus is oriented north-south along the Scioto River at a point near its merging with the Olentangy River. Easy enough! The preface to this book notes that Columbus is within a day's drive of over 50 percent of the U.S. (and Canadian) population. You can see from the mileage chart how this is the case. Many large Midwest and East Coast cities are within a humane driving distance.

GETTING HERE

Roadways

Columbus sits at the junction of two major highway intersections: Interstate 70 is the major east-west thoroughfare, and Interstate 71 is the major north-south highway through the city. Both of these roads connect to beltways around the city. Interstate 270 (Outer Belt) is the bypass loop that runs the entire way around Columbus. It connects to I-70 and I-71 from all directions. Interstate 670 (Inner Belt) rings only the downtown and provides a hassle-free route between the airport and the city center.

If you're on the road a lot, you can locate the construction zones around Columbus at www.pavingtheway.org, or go to www.buckeyetraffic.org to get the latest updates on winter roadway conditions anywhere in Ohio.

There are several roads in Columbus where the route numbers and street names are used interchangeably. Columbus, having been settled by Europeans, has a few High Streets. There is one in Dublin and another in Gahanna, but U.S. Route 23 is *the* High Street. It runs all the way north halfway to Toledo and dead-ends on the southern border of Ohio in Portsmouth. It is referred to as High Street in the 12-mile vicinity of Columbus, but farther north and south of the city the road is referred to as 23.

Broad Street, which runs east-west through the city, is slightly more confusing. Broad Street is the same as the historical U.S. Route 40 to the east of the city, but the road splits a mile to the west of Bexley where Broad Street becomes U.S. Route 16, and is referred to as such farther east of the city. The picturesque Riverside Drive, also known as 33, runs north-south along the Olentangy River. It is a nice diversion from the main drag if you have some spare time to enjoy the scenic route.

Route 315 is another important highway that runs north-south through the city and intersects all the other highways. The major exits to The Ohio State University and the Schottenstein Center are off 315. The Lane Avenue, Fifth Avenue/King Avenue exit ramps back up quickly on game days and during concerts, so be sure to allow yourself time to get through the congestion or find an alternate route during major events. When the Buckeyes are playing a home football game, you can see (and hear!) the stadium from 315—it is quite a sight.

Mileage Chart from Columbus

Baltimore	420
Chicago	311
Cincinnati	101
Cleveland	143
Detroit	204
Indianapolis	175
Louisville	210
Nashville	384
New York	589
Pittsburgh	185
St. Louis	418

The Ohio Department of Transportation has embarked on a 10-year plan to rebuild stressed roads and to address issues of congestion and high-crash areas on freeways. Needless to say, we must all get used to navigating an obstacle course of orange barrels or driving at a snail's pace through construction zones, but given the layout of Columbus, it's never difficult to find alternate routes.

Air Travel

Columbus has two international airports: Port Columbus International Airport and Rickenbacker International Airport. Their accessibility and competitive airfares are just two reasons Columbus is a very valuable choice for a business location and an affordable travel location. Check out the quick fly times—even to the West Coast.

Flying Times to/from Columbus

Atlanta	1 hour, 26 minutes
Baltimore/ Washington, D.C.	1 hour, 20 minutes
Boston	2 hours, 5 minutes
Chicago	1 hour, 7 minutes
Dallas	2 hours, 28 minutes
Denver	2 hours, 36 minutes
Houston/Dallas	2 hours, 28 minutes
Los Angeles	4 hours, 14 minutes
Miami	4 hours, 6 minutes
New York	1 hour, 52 minutes
Seattle	5 hours, 58 minutes
St. Louis	1 hour, 20 minutes

PORT COLUMBUS INTERNATIONAL AIRPORT

Port Columbus International Airport
4600 International Gateway
(614) 239-4000
www.port-columbus.com

Port Columbus International Airport is situated 15 minutes east of downtown Columbus and is easily accessible from all parts of town. In fact, this location makes it one of the most accessible airports in the country. It is also one of fastest grow-

CLOSE-UP

America's Golden Highway, U.S. Route 40

US 40 once stretched 3,200 miles between Atlantic City, New Jersey, and San Francisco, passing directly through Columbus. Some folks believe it was designated 40 because the road closely follows the 40th parallel, but this isn't the case. The highway naming system, developed in the 1920s, just happened to come up with a numerical coincidence.

US 40 became a certified highway in 1926, but its predecessor, the "National Road," was created by an act of Congress in 1806 under President Thomas Jefferson. The goal was to connect the Atlantic Ocean and the Ohio River over land, making the National Road the first federally sponsored highway. Prior to this approval from Congress, Colonel Ebenezer Zane and his brothers were anxious to start cutting their way into the Northwest Territory (now central Ohio), so, in 1796 they forged ahead with their own road, following even earlier Native American footpaths.

This important road was, at one point, rerouted to run through Columbus's business district at the request of influential businessmen and politicians. This explains its zig-zagging course through downtown near Bexley. The road was meant to link capital cities, and Dayton, feeling slighted by the road bypassing it altogether, created a misleading "alternate" route sign through the community. By the time railroads were being built in the 1830s, the National Road crossed Ohio into Indiana.

When the interstate highways were built, 800 miles of this transcontinental road were decommissioned. Ohio is fortunate to have escaped with most of the road still in use, even after I-70 was built parallel to it.

In celebration of Ohio's bicentennial, the state held a wagon trail event along US 40 from the Ohio River to Worthington and then into Indiana. If you have the opportunity to drive US 40 east of Columbus, certain parts of the road become very narrow and rural. One gains a sense of what it was like to travel along the "Main Street of America" before the road-building boom of the 1920s and '30s. A stop-off at the Zane Grey/National Road Museum along the way or viewing www.route40.net will provide further insight into America's Golden Highway history, its milestones, and other tidbits of trivia.

ing airports in the Northeast, which is reflected in the recent renovation of all concourses, the expansion of the food and retail operations, and the opening of the new air traffic control tower in 2004.

Served by 23 airlines with nearly 400 daily arrivals and departures, including 35 nonstop destinations, it is an international airport that is relatively hassle-free to fly in and out of. Despite its 35 gates and 730,000-square-foot main terminal, it is the user-friendly layout that makes Port Columbus manageable and seem more like a small-town airport. Small-town airport feeling aside, the usual big-airport security measures are in place, so you and the other 6.7 million annual passengers should allow ample time for check-in.

If you have time to kill, you can "cool your jets" at a few chain restaurants such as Max & Erma's and Damon's or at a local original such as Columbus Brewing Company. (These are some of the only places you can smoke in the airport.) You can stop in at Cup O'Joe, located on the ticketing level, for a morning coffee "on the fly" and grab those last-minute souvenirs from the PGA Tour Shop or the Big Ten Conference Shop. It is nearly impossible to leave Columbus without acquiring some sort of Buckeye paraphernalia.

Besides food and drink, Port Columbus provides other services for the weary traveler. There is an interfaith meditation room if you need to escape to peace and quiet. It is located on the baggage claim level across from carousel 6. Also on the baggage claim level is an information center, where you can pick up maps of Columbus, get visitor information, or have your party paged.

With luggage in hand, it is an easy jaunt to access ground transportation via the terminal walkway or the ground level near baggage claim. It is at ground level you can grab a shuttle to your hotel or the parking lots or hail a cab. Taxi service is offered by a number of companies, and the fare into downtown from the airport is on average around $18. It takes anywhere from 20 to 30 minutes to get into the city center, depending on the time of day.

Be advised that if you are picking up passengers (or are being picked up), you are not permitted to wait in the car outside the passenger pick-up area. Security will undoubtedly wave you on, so just keep moving. You can either park in the garage and go into the airport or just keep looping around through the arrival area until your party exits the building. It is here you find jet-lagged souls waiting with their deer-in-the-headlights gaze, examining each car as it slowly passes by—similar to travelers catatonically watching baggage glide past on the belt—until that glimmer of recognition lights up their faces when they see the familiar bag (or in this case, the car) roll up alongside them.

Major Airlines

Every major airline is represented in Columbus, and there is no one that dominates the market. This helps to keep airfare competitive. It is often easiest to go to the airlines directly to make reservations or check airfare.

Air Canada Regional—Concourse B
Reservations, baggage claim:
(888) 247-2262
www.aircanada.ca
www.aircanadaregional.ca

America West/America West Express—Concourse B
Reservations and baggage service:
(800) 235-9292
www.americawest.com

American/American Eagle—Concourse B
Reservations: (800) 433-7300
www.aa.com

Continental/Continental Express—Concourse A
Reservations: (800) 525-0280
www.continental.com

Delta/Delta Connection—Concourse C
Reservations: (800) 221-1212
www.delta.com

Midwest Express/Skyway—Concourse A
Reservations and baggage service:
(800) 452-2022
www.midwestexpress.com

Northwest/Northwest Airlink—Concourse B
Reservations and baggage service:
(800) 225-2525
www.nwa.com

Southwest—Concourse C
Reservations: (800) 435-9792
www.iflyswa.com

In 1984, the city of Columbus received the commissioned sculpture titled **Brushstrokes in Flight** *from Roy Lichtenstein. It is located inside the main terminal of Port Columbus International Airport, and you can't miss it. The 26 feet of brightly painted aluminum makes it a great meeting spot.*

United/United Express—Concourse B
Reservations and baggage service: (800) 241-6522
www.ual.com

US Airways/US Airways Express—Concourse A
Reservations: (800) 428-4322
www.usairways.com

Parking

Parking is relatively hassle-free in the attached, six-level parking garage that offers short- and long-term parking. Short-term parking is located on levels P4 and P5 and costs $2.00 per hour up to a maximum of $25. Long-term parking is on levels P3 through P6 and costs $2.00 per hour and $15 per day.

There are two outdoor, uncovered lots that offer a more economical solution to long-term parking needs, especially if you have the time to park and ride into the airport. The lots are safe, well lit, and provide a free 24-hour shuttle service to the terminal. There are covered shuttle stations in which you can wait to be picked up. The shuttles are reliable and come around every few minutes. Most important, take note of the row in which you park (for example, B14), because the lots are big, and you could spend a lot of time searching for your vehicle.

The Blue lot, which is slightly closer to the terminal and may shave a few minutes off your shuttle ride, is $6.00 per day, while the farther Red lot is $5.00 per day. These daily rates are based on a 24-hour parking period but are otherwise prorated at $2.00 for the first hour and $1.00 for each additional hour up to the maximum daily rate. A ticket is issued when you pull into the lot, and you pay at the manned tollbooth when you leave. Cash or credit card is accepted.

If you're running late or just prefer curbside service, Parking Solutions offers valet parking on the ticketing level of the terminal for $16 per day. You can even have your car ready on your arrival. Hourly rates are available. Get more details at www.parkingsolutionsinc.com/curbValet.asp.

Car Rentals

Listed below are the eight on-site car rental agencies at Port Columbus International Airport. They can be found on levels 1 and 2 of the parking garage, which is helpful in the winter, as you will not have to brave the elements to get to your car.

Alamo
(800) GO-ALAMO
www.alamo.com

Avis
(800) 331-1212
www.avis.com

Budget
(800) 527-0700
www.budget.com

Dollar
(800) 800-4000
www.dollar.com

Enterprise
(800) 325-8007
www.enterprise.com

Hertz
(800) 654-3131
www.hertz.com

National
(800) CAR-RENT
www.nationalcar.com

Thrifty
(800) 367-2277
www.thrifty.com

Airport Shuttle Service

Shuttle service into town can be arranged by calling ahead, or you can walk on spontaneously since shuttles go into Columbus about every 20 minutes. You can get a shuttle on the ground transportation level of the airport, and costs vary according to distance and number of passengers. The shuttle services listed here accept major credits cards as well as cash. Bigger hotels often have their own shuttle service, so check with them before paying extra to be transported.

Arch Express Transportation
(614) 252-2277
www.archexpress.com

Super Shuttle
(614) 252-5555 or (800) 789-3755

Urban Express
(614) 840-0411
www.urbanexpress.biz

Taxis

You can pick up a taxi at the ground transportation level of the airport 24 hours a day. The airport is one of the few places in town you can spontaneously grab a cab, as they do not cruise in Columbus. There are a number of taxi services in Columbus, but most should be contacted ahead of time for transport back to the airport—or anywhere, for that matter.

AAA Express Taxi Service
(614) 262-3333 or (800) 434-5149

Arrow Taxi Service
(614) 866-6666

i

For the frequent traveler, the EZ-Park Program is ideal. You provide a credit card number and are given an automated vehicle identification device to place in your window. This acts as an electronic key, giving access to any airport-owned lot without having to stop. Applications are on the Port Columbus Web site.

Yellow Cab
(614) 444-4444 or (800) 551-4222

Limousines and Private Cars

The rates will be more costly than a shuttle or taxi, but if you want to accommodate a large group in luxury or just prefer privacy, contact any one of the following companies to get where you are going in style. Rates will vary depending on the type of vehicle, but you can get VIP luxury cars, more traditional stretch limos, and even the trendy super-stretch Hummers and Excursions.

Arch Express Transportation
(614) 252-2277
www.archexpress.com

Supreme Limousine Service
(614) 888-9600
www.asupremelimo.com

Urban Express
(614) 840-0411
www.urbanexpress.biz

i

Fare into downtown Columbus should be around $18, and it is appropriate to tip the taxi driver 10 to 15 percent of the total fare. If you need to go outside Franklin County, both parties should mutually agree upon the rates, which should not exceed $2.00 per mile.

RICKENBACKER INTERNATIONAL AIRPORT

Rickenbacker International Airport
2241 John Circle Drive
(614) 491-1401
www.rickenbacker.org

Rickenbacker Airport, predominantly an international cargo airport, is one of the few Foreign Trade Zones (FTZ) in the United States. Rickenbacker started out as the Lockbourne Army Airbase the day after Pearl Harbor was attacked in 1941. The base grew and expanded during the Korean and Vietnam wars. In 1974, it was renamed Rickenbacker Air Force Base in honor of World War I combat pilot and Congressional Medal of Honor winner Eddie Rickenbacker, a Columbus native.

Rickenbacker has since grown into a large distribution hub, with the first development happening at Rickenbacker in 1985 with the establishment of an air cargo hub and bulk-sorting facility for Flying Tigers (now owned by Federal Express). To encourage development, Rickenbacker was established as FTZ No. 138 in 1987, and now, with 10.5 million square feet of warehouse space and trucking access, many major cargo carriers are represented: Federal Express, UPS, Polar, Evergreen, and LEP Profit.

In 2003, passenger flights began at Rickenbacker. Hooters Airline flies to Chicago and Myrtle Beach, South Carolina, while Pan Am Clipper Connection flies to sunny Florida. You can check the Rickenbacker Web site for fares and timetables.

A Foreign Trade Zone is a site within the United States legally considered outside customs territory, so goods are brought into the site duty-free and without formal customs entry. An FTZ provides users with the opportunity to lower costs and boost profits by delaying, reducing, or eliminating duties, while the entry procedures save time.

Parking and Shuttle Service

The Rickenbacker Charter Terminal is just a short drive south of Columbus. Parking rates are $2.00 for the first hour and $1.00 for each additional hour up to $5.00 per day. Taxis, shuttles, and rental cars are all available at the terminal. The same shuttle and taxi services that provide transport from Port Columbus into the city are available here. You can find their phone numbers listed with the Port Columbus International Airport information.

OTHER AIRPORTS

There are two other private fields in Columbus, so if you have the good fortune to own your own plane, or at least be able to fly one, you have options to land in Columbus.

Bolton Field
2000 Norton Road
(614) 851-9900
www.columbusairports.com/bolton

Bolton is a private airport 9 miles southwest of Columbus and has air traffic control service daily from 7:30 A.M. until 7:30 P.M. Piston, turboprop, jet aircraft, and helicopters can use this facility. Events such as fly-ins, aerobatic competitions, banner towing, and ballooning also take place on airport grounds. You can contact the general manager for more information at (614) 851-9900.

The Ohio State University Don Scott Field
2160 West Case Road
(800) 777-5488
www.osuairport.org

The Ohio State-owned Don Scott Field, named after a former OSU All-American who died in World War II, is Ohio's fourth busiest airport. It is an educational facility for OSU's School of Aviation and provides aircraft and flight services to the Columbus community. Don Scott can accommodate piston, turboprop, and single- and twin-engine aircraft. There is an array of services available to pilots, ranging from computerized weather and flight-planning facilities to room or car rental and an on-site restaurant. The Web site offers comprehensive information about the airport, ranging from arrival and departure procedures to the history of the airfield.

GETTING AROUND

If you need to get around Columbus, there is public transportation. It's reliable, but it can be tedious and time-consuming. Unless you're staying in an area where you are on a bus line or can easily walk to restaurants or attractions, I would highly recommend you rent or try to gain access to a car.

General rules of thumb in Columbus: Front-seat passengers must wear seat belts, and children under the age of four or weighing less than 40 pounds must be in a child safety seat. It is also legal to make right turns at red lights after stopping unless there are signs that say NO TURN ON RED or note specific hours during which turns are not permitted.

If you happen to need directions while exploring Columbus, people are usually friendly and willing to offer their assistance, but be prepared for them to say, "Go south on this street and east on that street." It is just the nature of the locals who may have driven Columbus's gridlike streets all their lives. For those of you who are used to using landmarks or counting traffic lights, you can easily orient yourself and find your way around if you just remember that no matter where you are, the sun always sets in the west.

Getting Around Downtown

Getting around downtown Columbus is pretty easy by car, bus, or on foot. Walking from one end of downtown to the other doesn't take more than 30 minutes, but if you don't have the time to spare, a bus can take you up the street for a nominal fee. If you're driving, downtown's roads are in pretty good shape, well marked, and uncomplicated. Like anywhere, rush hour can become frustrating, but most other times the traffic flow is good, and you can get around downtown in a matter of minutes. Traffic also tends to get clogged around the Arena District during hockey games and concerts, but this is easy to avoid if you are aware of the events.

There aren't too many idiosyncrasies to the downtown streets, but one road to watch out for is Main Street. You can take Main all the way east out of the city, but coming west it dead-ends at Grant Street and forces you to turn right (north). Like other big cities, there are a few streets, such as High and Broad, that have two-way lanes, while most of the others are only one way. The curb lanes downtown along High Street are bus and taxi lanes between the hours of 7:00 to 9:00 A.M. and 4:00 to 6:00 P.M., which means you cannot make right turns at a few major intersections during rush hour. Overall, navigating downtown Columbus is pretty straightforward.

Downtown Parking

Parking is free in most parts of the city except downtown, where there is an abundance of garages, lots, and meters. If you're lucky enough to find a meter outside rush hours (and have a surplus of

i

Be sure to watch for reduced speed limits through certain parts of town, such as Arlington, Dublin, Gahanna, and Worthington. Speed limits can decrease from 45 or 35 to 25 mph in the matter of a block or two, and police are diligent about enforcing this.

coins), you should be in good shape. Be sure to read the meter details, since there's a wide range of prices and time limits from 15 minutes to 12 hours. You do *not* have to feed most parking meters on weekdays between 6:00 P.M. and 8:00 A.M., Sundays, or holidays, but there are some exceptions to this. These meters are marked 24-hour meter enforcement, and many of them can be found in the Short North, so pay attention.

If you work downtown and prefer to park in garages near the LeVeque Tower, State House, or Nationwide, be prepared to pay premium parking rates as high as $165 per month. On average, monthly parking rates are around $100, but if you're willing to walk 5 or 6 blocks to work, you can find monthly parking for as little as $50. Daily rates at lots and garages range from $3.00 to $14.00, depending on how far you park from Capitol Square.

For a quick jaunt into town, the City Center Parking Garage will cost just a dollar if you can keep your shopping to a few hours. Be cautious at the City Center, as prices spike steeply after the first three hours to discourage all-day parking. Most parking facilities have flat weekend rates, and there are a few garages, particularly near the theaters, that have "twilight" rates. They charge around $3.00 if you enter the garage after 5:00 P.M. Here are a couple of parking options:

Columbus City Center
Main entrance on Main Street (between Third and High Streets), alternate entrance on Rich Street

$1.00 for the first 3 hours, $2.00 for each additional hour up to $9.00 maximum

Early bird rates: $5.50 if in by 9:00 A.M.

Statehouse Parking Facility
Entrance on Broad and Third Streets

$1.00 per hour

Evening rates after 6:00 P.M. are $2.00 for the first hour, $1.00 for subsequent 2 hours

Forget about parking on downtown streets at meters between the hours of 7:00 to 9:00 A.M. and 4:00 to 6:00 P.M. Violators will be towed, and it will cost $100 to get your car out of impoundment.

Buses

Central Ohio Transit Authority (COTA)
60 East Broad Street
(614) 228-1776
www.cota.com
The city bus system has 63 routes and over 4,600 bus stops. There are 27 Park & Ride facilities located around the city, so you can park for free and let someone else drive you into the city while you read the paper (or catch a few winks). There are also five Bike & Ride locations around town providing free bicycle lockers with a one-time refundable security deposit of $10.

You can view detailed maps of bus routes and timetables on COTA's Web site or by calling customer service. Weekly and monthly passes are available, but individual fares are $1.25 one-way for local buses and $1.75 for express buses. COTA LINK costs 25 cents, and transfers cost 10 cents. COTA honors the Senior Discount ID while children 49 inches to 12 years old pay 60 cents each way. Children under six ride for free.

Greyhound Bus Lines
111 East Town Street
(614) 221-2389
www.greyhound.com
Buses may not be the most comfortable form of transportation, but they're certainly one of the more economical ways to travel long distances. You can check the Greyhound Web site or call for routes and fares. There are student rates and Internet

super-saver fares. Keep in mind that Greyhound buses do not serve meals, provide blankets, or show movies, but you are allowed to carry on food and nonalcoholic beverages. Electronic equipment is permitted as long as it does not disturb your fellow travelers.

Although there is no train service in Columbus, Amtrak offers Amtrak Thruway bus connections from Columbus to Cleveland, where there are Amtrak services to Buffalo, Boston, New York, Washington, D.C., and Chicago. There is also Amtrak service out of Pittsburgh, Pennsylvania, as well. You can purchase rail and bus tickets together through Amtrak or separately from Greyhound and Amtrak.

Bike Paths

There are a number of multiuse trails throughout the city and parks. Please see the Parks and Recreation chapter for a detailed listing of the different paths.

Tours

Capital City Tours
2554 Zollinger Road, Upper Arlington
(614) 326-0942
The City Overview is Capital City's most popular tour. It lasts about two hours and is $15 per person. The "Outdoor Public Sculpture Tour" is a two-hour walking or driving tour of public sculpture in the downtown area and is also $15 per person.

Students ride the bus for free. Kids under 18 can ride free in the summer under the Summer Youth Fare Pass Program. OSU, CCAD, Columbus State Community College, and Capital University students can use their student ID to ride COTA free anywhere in the city.

The following are group tours only and require one-week notice: The "Spiritual Heritage Tour" of churches in downtown Columbus is offered Monday to Friday only. It is $22 per person and includes lunch at a church restaurant. The "Tearoom Tour" is for women only (no men or children), and the cost includes tea and transport.

The Columbus Landmarks Foundation
61 Jefferson Avenue, 2nd floor
(614) 221-0227
www.columbuslandmarks.org
The Columbus Landmarks Foundation is a group committed to preserving the city's architectural heritage. The foundation offers various guided walking tours through many historic neighborhoods, such as Capitol Square, Old Beechwold, and the Brewery District. These tours run through the summer and cost about $12 per person. There are also Halloween Ghost walks and "The Dead End Bus" tour in October and the annual candlelight tour called the "Great Hallelujah Holiday Tour of Churches" in December. You can purchase tickets online or in person.

HISTORY

Trying to sum up a city's history in just a few pages is daunting. Ohio, our nation's 17th state, celebrated its bicentennial in 2003. Though settled in its present form for only a few hundred years, much of American history and its large, colorful cast of characters have passed through the city.

As the "Mother of Presidents" and the "Birthplace of Aviation," Ohio has sent seven sons to the White House and a few into space—all of whom spent some time in Columbus. These giants of science and politics were not alone in putting the state and the city on the map. Writers, musicians, athletes, and inventors also have contributed to the city's fascinating story.

An honorable mention should go to the unnamed heroes and heroines, farmers and laborers, Native Americans and immigrants, lest we forget the folk who never made it into the history books. This faceless majority had a huge hand in shaping Columbus.

Founding father Lucas Sullivant was a forward-thinking man who had great plans for the land at what was referred to as the Forks of Scioto. By time the Capital City was established in 1812, visionary businessmen, politicians, and doctors had begun a new chapter in a story already rich with Indian and frontier history. Columbus, once at the edge of the Wild West, deep in Indian Territory, quickly became the breadbasket of America and a center of trade. The need to supply the nation with agricultural goods lured stagecoaches, the National Road, and canals to the city, making Columbus a strategic hub of transportation and distribution, which it remains to this day.

Wars, canals, and railroads came and went. Much of Ohio ended up part of the Rustbelt, but Columbus rose from the industrial ashes to become a financial and retail powerhouse. As a hub of research, development, aviation, and trade and as home to one of the nation's great universities, Columbus continues to attract visionaries. The founders' spirit of exploration and discovery has been kept alive into the twenty-first century.

This is our story.

i

Senator John Glenn, the first American to orbit the earth, is honored at The John and Annie Glenn Historic Site. His boyhood home is in New Concord, east of Columbus. Neil Armstrong, the first astronaut to walk on the moon, is also memorialized in his hometown of Wapakoneta with a lunar-shaped Air and Space Museum.

THE MOUND BUILDERS

We can thank the last ice age for Ohio's agricultural windfall. Eleven thousand years ago our state was buried under a glacier that stopped moving just short of Columbus, leaving in its wake the hills and rivers near Cincinnati. This massive chunk of ice pushed the topsoil into the central Ohio region, giving Columbus its fertile farmland and buckeye trees. As the land warmed and the ice melted away, a wide variety of prairie grass, wetlands, and deciduous trees took hold.

Several thousand years later, the vast forest that covered the region was finally able to sustain a variety of animal life. A group of people eventually emerged to become the area's first inhabitants. These ancient nomadic hunters and gatherers mastered crops and began establishing permanent villages. As society became more complex, so did their views of death and their ritualistic approach to burial.

The earliest Mound Builders, known as the Adena, Hopewell, and Fort Ancient cultures, date from 100 B.C. to A.D. 1000.

During the course of the millennium, they developed sophisticated burial and ceremonial rituals, which included the construction of a vast network of earthen mounds all over Ohio. The mounds progressively became more elaborate and sometimes reached upwards of 50 feet tall and 30 feet wide.

By the time European settlers arrived in central Ohio, there were thousands of mounds in the Ohio Valley but no sign of who built them. There is still no definitive reason why these ancient cultures faded away, but theories contend it may have been due to disease, wars, or overpopulation. It is, however, quite clear why less than 1 percent of these mounds exist today.

The early settlers attributed these extraordinary burials to everyone but the indigenous people they were displacing. Local savages couldn't possibly build something so sophisticated, and the mounds were explained away with theories of Peruvians, Vikings, and even extraterrestrial aliens. Hundreds of mounds were documented in the Columbus area alone, but by the mid-19th century most were gone, plowed over, leveled, and, in the case of the one for which Mound Street is named, used to make bricks for the first statehouse.

EARLY SETTLERS

The Native Americans who replaced the Mound Builders had established villages by the time English and French explorers arrived in the 1650s. The first documentation of Native Americans in Ohio was by French missionaries from Canada. The Iroquois, Delaware, Shawnee, and Huron people were a long way from their original homes, pressed into central Ohio by the French and British from every direction. Some tribes were acquiescent, but most wouldn't give up their lands without a fight.

By 1749, the governor of Canada had claimed Ohio for France. During the French and Indian War, both French and British frontiersmen worked their way into the Midwest to set up trading posts. It was at this time that the first written description of Franklin County was given by Christopher Gist of the Virginia Land Company.

The Buckeye State's nickname is derived from a type of chestnut tree that has been nearly eradicated from the landscape. The nut of the buckeye tree looks like a buck's eye.

While little of the French and Indian War touched Ohio, isolated incidents occurred between the Indians (French loyalists) and the British. Such was the case when Matthew McCrea was killed during an Ottawa attack on a trading post at the Forks at Scioto, making him the first person to die on the site of what was to become Columbus. England ultimately won the struggle for control of North America and banned settlement north and west of the Ohio River as a means to monopolize the fur trade. British troops were sent to suppress Indian revolts, and so began the wresting of the Northwest Territory from the Native Americans.

As a new nation emerged, little of the Revolutionary War was fought in central Ohio. By 1785, plans were made to bring the Northwest Territory into the Union, and campaigns were undertaken to negotiate (or force) treaties with the Indians. By the 1790s, villages were systematically destroyed, and the Native Americans were pushed to the northern third of the state. Shortly thereafter, the Forks at Scioto was permanently settled by Europeans.

FRANKLINTON'S FOUNDING FATHER

It didn't take long for the government to begin surveying the Northwest Territory. It was surveyed once in 1785, when township measurements were created and governing rules were put in place for when the Northwest Territory became a state. Sur-i

Many local place names are Indian words, including Ohio, Iroquois for "Great River." Other names are Wyandot, or "River at Rest," and Scioto, or "Hairy River," named for the hundreds of deer that would shed their fur on the banks of the river.

veyors were again sent from Kentucky in 1795, at which time many of the familiar streams and natural landmarks like Darby Creek were named. Among these surveyors was Lucas Sullivant, founder of Franklinton and later Columbus.

Our young country had no money to pay many of the Revolutionary War veterans or the government employees such as these surveyors, who subsequently took their pay in real estate. Lucas Sullivant took an immediate liking to the Forks at Scioto. Realizing the area near the river was on low ground and regularly flooded, he claimed thousands of acres on higher ground slightly to the west of the river, which soon became known as Sullivant's Hill.

Sullivant, an ardent admirer of Benjamin Franklin, named the new town Franklinton in his honor. In just two years, the city was planned, and attempts were made to draw people into the heart of Indian Country. The names of the earliest settlers are woven into the very fabric of the city: Dr. Lincoln Goodale, Dr. James Hoge, Pelatiah Webster Huntington, and David Deardurff, to name a few. Floods whisked the city away several times over, but Lucas Sullivant was not deterred from making his city prosper.

THE CAPITAL CITY IS BORN

By 1801, the frontier village of Franklinton was a fully functioning town, with brick homes, a church, and a jail. For forward-thinking Sullivant, his city was about the future. When Ohio became a state in 1803, Franklinton's centralized location gave Sullivant hope it would become the state capital.

The capital was originally moved between Zanesville and Chillicothe a few times, but politicians weren't thrilled with either decision. Several suggestions were made to move the capital to Delaware, Worthington (established the same year Ohio became a state), Franklinton, or the area that would soon become Dublin. The Ohio General Assembly rejected Sullivant's city simply because it was just too wet.

At this point in the state's history, the biggest industry was not agriculture or trapping, as one might think, but land. Sullivant, as a former surveyor and one of the biggest landowners, rallied four others to purchase a strip of land across the river from Franklinton. This tract was allotted to Canadian refugees from Nova Scotia who supported the American cause during the revolution. Most of the refugees were destitute and more than willing to sell their land deeds to this group.

After acquiring the Refugee Tract of land, they went about proposing this new area, which was called High Banks, to the Ohio General Assembly. The proposition was accepted on February 12, 1812, and the Capital City was born. The next dilemma: what to name the new legislative center of the state. On February 20, for whatever reasons, the General Assembly chose the name Columbus over Ohio City, in honor of Christopher Columbus.

The founders quickly planned a grid of streets that aligned with the established roads across the river in Franklinton. All that existed on the east bank of the Scioto River was the High Trail through a dense forest and a 40-foot-tall Indian mound at the corner of what is now High and Mound Streets. Ten acres each were set aside for the statehouse and a penitentiary. The capital was under way.

With the increasing stability of the economy and a growing number of people identifying themselves as Americans, the presence of British troops on American soil was challenged. Ohio, particularly

Franklinton, feared invasion by the British in Detroit, consequently putting the new capital in a vulnerable position.

THE WAR OF 1812

Coincidentally, on June 18, 1812, the day Columbus was officially established as the seat of Ohio's government and the first day of land sales, was the same day the United States declared war on Great Britain. Because of this, the capital was not physically moved from Chillicothe to Columbus until 1816.

Once again, Ohio escaped much of the war, but Columbus and Franklinton served as a mobilization and supply center for troops. A ditch was dug around the statehouse, a stockade was created, and a makeshift prison (named British Island) was built on a sandbar, which no longer exists, in the middle of the Scioto River. Future president William Henry Harrison undertook the construction of forts just north of Columbus and led a successful invasion of Detroit and Canada. He expelled the British troops at the Battle of the Thames and brought about the collapse of Tecumseh's Confederacy, marking the downfall of the Indians in Ohio.

BOOM OR BUST

Columbus saw an enormous boom between the War of 1812 and the Civil War but not without the usual postwar bust. After a period of economic hardship, flooding, and disease, many people chose to move on to other cities. In 1832, 2,000 people lived in Columbus. In just two years the city's population more than doubled to 5,000, making it the fastest growing city in Ohio. Lucas Sullivant died in 1823, but his legacy was carried on by a few friends and fellow visionaries.

As the country pushed westward and grew, so did the need for reliable modes of transportation and road systems. Enter the ruthless businessman William Neil. He recognized central Ohio's lack of water transportation and knew land was the best way to get to the capital. By the 1840s, he had acquired most of the stagecoach lines in Ohio, earning him the nickname "The Stagecoach King." Neil opened a tavern and hotel at Broad and High Streets, convenient to the statehouse. The Neil House Hotel quickly became the place to stay in downtown Columbus. He also played a part in having the National Road rerouted through Columbus's business district.

William Neil's name lived on, not in his short-lived stagecoach business or even his hotels but in what he chose to invest his money: land. He purchased a farm just north of downtown Columbus, which upon his death in 1870 became the Ohio Agricultural and Mechanical College and in turn The Ohio State University. Neil Avenue was once the private lane onto his estate.

Like William Neil, Alfred Kelley had a passion for transportation, only he was into canals. In 1816, Kelley came to the capital from Cleveland in a political capacity and remained here permanently. Seeing how the Erie Canal changed the face of American trade and commerce, he was adamant about linking Columbus to the canal system, which he did via Canal Winchester and Lockbourne.

By 1837 the canal projects were overbudget, and the state was behind in repayment. Realizing that the success of central Ohio depended on the quick distribution of Ohio's farm goods, Alfred Kelley put his house up as collateral on the

---

i

***Blue Jacket** is a dramatization of the story of a white settler adopted by the Shawnee Indians who later becomes their war chief. The action takes place on a three-acre outdoor stage. The season runs from mid-June to early September. For information, call (937) 376-4318 or (937) 427-0879.*

---

i

Lucas Sullivant, the man who transformed central Ohio, was originally buried in the Franklinton Cemetery but was moved to Greenlawn Cemetery in 1849.

unpaid interest on canal bonds. Thankfully, the legislature did not pull funding, and he kept his house. Kelley's deep integrity and unwavering belief in these modern modes of transportation began the transformation of Columbus into the hub of distribution that it is today.

In less than three decades, stagecoaches, the National Road, and canals had their heyday, then were displaced by locomotives. Both Neil and Kelley had the good sense to get involved in sponsoring the first railroad into Columbus. In 1851, a crude terminal was built on High Street, where the Hyatt Regency is now located. By 1853, locals could take the 3C train direct from Cleveland to Columbus to Cincinnati, thus ushering in a period of rail travel that lasted for 120 years.

Columbus's train traffic peaked around 1916, but it slowly declined with the increasing popularity of the automobile. Union Station fell into disrepair by the 1970s and was altogether demolished in the '80s. The only existing part of the original station is a classical-style arch that now stands in the Arena District.

THE CIVIL WAR

The Civil War left its mark on Columbus in subtle and unusual ways. A plaque commemorates a speech Abraham Lincoln gave from the south side of the statehouse on September 16, 1859, just prior to the Civil War. Within two years, Union soldiers occupied Columbus and remained here until the very end of the war.

Ohio provided more troops per capita to the Union than any other northern state, although it fell third behind New York and Pennsylvania in the total number of men who served. Ohio was represented by artillery, cavalry, and infantry units in all the major battles and campaigns, while the 5th and 27th United States Colored Troops were primarily made up of Ohioans.

Columbus was one of the major centers of mobilization and training of the Union Army. A historical marker near the Convention Center commemorates the site of Tod Barracks, one of the five military outposts located in Columbus during the war.

Named for Governor David Tod, the barracks were built in 1863 and served as headquarters for central Ohio's military administration. They ran along High Street, where the new Union Station shops are located, and could accommodate up to 5,000 soldiers. Conveniently adjacent to the train station, they also served as a recruiting depot and transfer point for soldiers on their way to new assignments.

Columbus was also home to Camp Chase, one of the Union's largest prisoner of war camps. More than 2,000 Confederate political and military prisoners from Kentucky and western Virginia died of disease and malnutrition between 1861 and the end of the Civil War. This 160-acre site was located near present-day Westgate on the West Side. Now all that exists is Camp Chase Cemetery on Sullivant Avenue. It comes as no surprise that many consider this burial ground for Confederate soldiers haunted.

One of the primary disputes of the American Civil War was slavery. When the Northwest Territory was first surveyed in 1785, a law was established making slavery illegal north of the Ohio River, thus leaving Ohio as a crucial station on the Underground Railroad. It was, however, a dangerous state for escapees.

Ohio's Black Laws, enacted in 1804, regulated and monitored the lives of African Americans, while stringent additions to the law made it nearly impossible for African Americans to settle or work in

Ohio. In 1850, the National Fugitive Slave Law was enacted, thus spurring an active manhunt of runaways. This prompted the development of the Underground Railroad, a network of safe houses and "conductors" who would help guide the escaped slaves north to freedom.

The Underground Railroad route through Ohio began at the Ohio River and passed through Chillicothe, Circleville, Columbus, Worthington, and Westerville, then north to Lake Erie and into Canada. No one was permitted to harbor slaves, and by law was required to turn them in. The Kelton family house in East Columbus is confirmed as one of these safe houses, but no written document exists. There were several others, including the Benjamin Hanby House in Westerville, but most remain as clandestine now as they were 150 years ago.

The Ohio Historical Society has extensive information about Civil War–era Columbus, and the National Freedom Center in Cincinnati is the premier place to explore the Underground Railroad. Some 500 men from Franklin County lost their lives in the Civil War, many of whom are buried in Greenlawn Cemetery.

COMING OF AGE

In the years following the Civil War, technological developments occurred, and industry began to emerge in Columbus. German immigrants established breweries. Shoe, cigar, machinery, furniture, and carriage manufacturers took advantage of the established transportation systems, an infrastructure put in place only 30 years earlier by William Neil and Alfred Kelley.

As the capital of the state, Columbus was becoming a center of education and social activity. By the late 19th century, two universities, two medical colleges, an art school, libraries, and musical societies had been established. Hospitals were also associated with these reputable medical schools, and Columbus reputedly had the largest insane asylum in the world. City records indicate that by the late 1880s Columbus had more than 50 churches and 600 saloons.

In the 1860s a single horse-drawn streetcar was pulled up and down High Street on one track, leading to the development of residential suburbs. People no longer had to live near their place of employment. By the turn of the century, horse-powered trolleys were a thing of the past. From 1905 to 1914, a system of electrified metal arches powered the streetcars, earning Columbus the nickname "Arch City."

By the close of the 19th century, Columbus saw many notable births, including World War I ace Eddie Rickenbacker (b. 1889) and the humorist James Thurber (b. 1894). The urban face of the city was changed with the addition of several towering skyscrapers, posh hotels, and theaters. Automobiles were also beginning to appear on city streets, prompting the nation's first gas station to open in Columbus on June 1, 1912.

20TH-CENTURY COLUMBUS

By the turn of the 20th century, a third of Columbus's population was of German descent, so World War I brought about a zealous move to "Americanize" the German Village part of town. A push to rename the streets and foods showed the growing sentiment against the city's German community: Sauerkraut, for instance, became "victory cabbage."

The Great War was also used as a propaganda tool to bring about Prohibition. Developments in mechanical refrigeration contributed to the increasing number of saloons, and in response to this "liquor problem," the Anti-Saloon League was formed in 1893. The organization had its first offices in Columbus and was eventually relocated to Westerville, where their primary focus was the single issue of Prohibition.

In 1913, the league announced its campaign for national prohibition through a

Columbus-born Elsie Janis was the country's first female actress and singer sent to entertain troops in France during World War I.

constitutional amendment. World War I gave the league an opportunity to develop a frenzied patriotism by associating booze with the enemy, as most brewers were German. It also purported that the resources used for alcohol production were diverted from the war effort. On January 17, 1920 the 18th amendment was passed, banning the production and consumption of alcoholic beverages.

It was during the Roaring 20s that Columbus saw the opening of the first White Castle and the construction of some of Columbus's landmarks: the LeVeque Tower, City Hall, and Central High School (now COSI). Prohibition brought about home brews, bathtub gin, and speakeasies, of which the Ringside Cafe and Larry's (on campus) still exist. This was also when Charles Lindbergh recommended Columbus as an important link for coast-to-coast air travel. The Port Columbus Airport was opened a few months before the Great Depression struck and took 15 years before turning a profit.

When the stock market crashed in 1929, over half of all Ohioans lost their jobs, but this did not affect Columbus as much as other cities because of the diversity of the local economy and its primary function as a center of government rather than industry. The lifting of Prohibition and the start of World War II breathed new life into Columbus's economy.

It was during the 1936 Olympics in Berlin that the impending threat of Adolf Hitler was felt in central Ohio. Jesse Owens, of The Ohio State University, is perhaps one of the most famous Olympians of all time. He was the first American in the history of Olympic track-and-field events to win four gold medals in a single Olympics and set records in three of the four events. Hitler refused to acknowledge Owens's accomplishment, despite his being given a standing ovation by German fans. Owens is now memorialized at Ohio State's Jesse Owens Memorial Stadium.

It was during World War II that Columbus became the modern city that it is today. It prospered through the manufacture of warplanes, particularly the Curtiss-Wright "Helldivers," and once again, Columbus became a major supply center. It was at this time that Rickenbacker Air Force Base was built. Local boy Curtis LeMay became a major war hero and retired as the armed forces' longest serving general.

In 1953, Mayor Jack Sesenbrenner coined the slogan "Come to Columbus and Discover America." Columbus was officially dubbed "Discovery City," and during the second half of the 20th century it became a leader in retail, insurance, technology, and software development and became home to the world's largest private research facility, Battelle Memorial Institute. Columbus entered the 21st century with a sound economic climate and a dynamic business community—a city, I imagine, Lucas Sullivant would be proud of.

ACCOMMODATIONS 

Whether you're in town for an extended business trip or are a weary traveler looking for a place to rest your head, Columbus offers a wide range of lodging at rates suitable to most travelers' budgets. In fact, there are over 22,000 rooms from which to choose. The goal of this chapter is to let you know where you can sleep in style, where to find basic comfort at a low price, and which parts of town offer the best values.

This chapter goes against the general rule of thumb not to include chains, but unless you stay at a bed-and-breakfast or cheap highway motel, you will find few independently owned hotels here. It just takes a quick flip through the yellow pages to realize chains are all Columbus has to offer—which isn't necessarily a bad thing. In a city this size, almost every national chain is represented. Some of the nicest hotels are affiliated with big names like Westin and Hilton, while most of the moderately priced hotels have equally familiar names.

Where to stay really depends on what you plan to do in Columbus. Hotels have been built near conference and entertainment districts, shopping areas, and the airport. The breakout of this chapter reflects these different pockets of lodging. Downtown is home to Columbus's financial and government districts. The Short North and Arena District are big convention and entertainment areas. The airport has plenty of hotels near the terminal for that quick in-and-out. The suburbs, particularly Dublin and Worthington, have big business parks offering the whole spectrum of chain hotels.

It's fair to say that some of the most expensive places are located downtown, but they are nonetheless a very good value. The most expensive room rarely exceeds $250 a night, and unlike a lot of other cities, Columbus's room rates are relatively stable throughout the year. Prices seem to spike more during conventions and annual events rather than follow a traditional "low" or "high" season.

For a purely Columbus experience, stay downtown at the historic Great Southern Hotel or the urbane Lofts. You'll be within walking distance to many restaurants, galleries, and theaters. The downtown location will allow you to easily catch a movie at the Arena Grand, shop at the North Market, and top off the evening with a meal in the trendy Short North. If you prefer to surround yourself with antiques and are looking for a taste of local history, try the Worthington Inn or the Snow House Annex in Olde Worthington. You can read more about the inn in the Close-up at the end of this chapter.

The Ohio State University has plenty of options on and near the campus. Columbus' newest upscale hotel, the Blackwell Inn, is located in the heart of OSU and is worth the splurge if you want total convenience—and a little luxury. There are, however, less expensive options just around the corner and even cheaper accommodations a few blocks northwest of campus. I have included hotels in each price range, but check out Ohio State's Web site (www.osu.edu) for links to many more options in and around the university.

Interestingly enough, many say the city's best hotel is not downtown but 10 miles east at Easton. People from the tristate area come to shop themselves silly at Easton Town Center. Many choose to spoil themselves by staying at the Hilton Columbus, but there are two other less expensive options also conveniently located on site. The three Easton hotels included in this chapter boast an 80 percent occupancy rate, so be sure to make your reservations well in advance.

If you are just passing through Columbus, you will not have any problem finding

Columbus's most comprehensive hotel information can be found at www.experiencecolumbus.com or by calling Experience Columbus at (614) 221-6623 or (800) 354-2657. Another good source is the Ohio Division of Travel and Tourism. Order free travel publications and book rooms anywhere in Ohio (including Columbus) online at www.discoverohio.com or by calling (614) 466-8844.

a quick place to layover for the night. There are clusters of fair-priced hotels and motels around the beltway (Interstate 270) and along the major highways (I-70/I-71). Unless there are unforeseen, nasty weather conditions or major festivals going on in central Ohio, you should have no problem getting a room spontaneously.

Two distinct parts of town have sprawling office developments with an endless mix of midpriced rooms and extended stay suites. The hotels around Worthington Crosswoods and MetroPlace in Dublin are newer facilities with great amenities and free parking, but nothing really distinguishes them from other run-of-the-mill mainstream lodging. One of the upshots to this explosion of suburban chain hotels is the generation of very competitive rates. You will find some of the best values in these two parts of town.

I have kept these hotel descriptions to a minimum and only note when they offer extra amenities such as complimentary Internet, breakfast, a fitness center, or swimming pool. Otherwise, you can assume that all the hotels included in this chapter have TV, cable, air-conditioning, and private bathrooms.

I have not included entries for low-priced accommodations, but it is worth mentioning that East Dublin-Granville Road (Route 161) is teeming with budget and express hotels such as Super 8, Comfort Inn, Days Inn, and Knights Inn. Many of these places charge under $50 for a room and are easily accessed from all the major highways.

Columbus does not have an excessive number of bed-and-breakfasts, but the few included here are quite charming and offer a refreshing change of pace from the chain hotel experience. What B&Bs lack in traditional hotel amenities they make up for with their homey atmosphere and charm. Whether you stay at a unique inn, a humble chain hotel, or a plush executive suite, expect to be greeted with a smile and met with the warm hospitality the Midwest is famous for.

The price code is the average RACK rate for a double room during the week. Keep in mind that most hotels have cheaper weekend rates and more expensive single rooms and suites. Many also offer romance, theater, or dinner packages and Internet discounts directly through their Web site. All the hotels listed here accept major credit cards and require plastic to guarantee the room.

$	**$50–$75**
$$	**$76–$100**
$$$	**$101–$150**
$$$$	**More than $150**

DOWNTOWN

The downtown hotels are a 15-minute drive ($20 taxi) to Port Columbus International Airport. If you are on a budget, you may want to consider staying a little farther north or east, where there are more midpriced hotels.

Best Western
Claremont Inn and Suites $$
650 South High Street, German Village
(614) 228-6511, (800) 780-7234
www.bestwestern.com

One of the better values downtown is in a primo location right at the edge of German Village. The Best Western is conveniently located 3 blocks from I-70/I-71 and is within walking distance of the great restaurants and bars of the Brewery District and German Village. This humble, pet-friendly hotel is nothing fancy, but its

60 rooms are newly remodeled and have all the basic amenities a traveler may need—and a few they may not, like free high speed Internet access, free local calls, and a heated outdoor pool (albeit overlooking the parking lot). The most attractive feature of this hotel is the lounge. The Round Bar is written up in The Pub Crawl chapter, and if that isn't enough, it's next door to one of the best steakhouses in town, the Claremont. Guests receive complimentary parking in the outdoor lot.

The Columbus:
A Renaissance Hotel **$$**
50 North Third Street at Gay Street
(614) 228-5050, (800) 417-1057
www.marriott.com

The only thing that doesn't make this a deluxe hotel is its price. Twenty-two stories and 415 rooms make The Columbus (formerly the Adam's Mark) one of the largest downtown hotels. It is perfectly situated a few blocks between the statehouse and the convention center and only 2 blocks from the Arena District. Its upscale, contemporary decor and modern amenities make it a great choice for both ambience and value. The rooms have nice extras, such as WebTV and jet tubs, and you can request Internet access in your room for a daily fee. The hotel features business, concierge, and dry-cleaning services, as well as a large fitness center and seasonal rooftop pool. Onsite parking costs $22 per day.

Crowne Plaza Hotel **$$$**
33 East Nationwide Boulevard
Arena District
(614) 461-4100
www.crownplaza.com

This first-class hotel is located on the doorstep of the Arena District and within walking distance of the restaurants, galleries, and shops of the Short North. It is known as the official hotel of the Columbus Bluejackets.

An enclosed walkway connects this 12-story facility to the Greater Columbus Convention Center, making it a very popular hotel during big conventions. Guests on business trips will appreciate the complimentary wireless Internet and business center, as well as laundry and dry-cleaning services. The Crowne Plaza was renovated in 2000 and includes an indoor pool, sauna, and fitness center. The staff speaks an impressive 10 different languages, and the hotel offers concierge and car rental services. The burger chain Max & Erma's and the upscale Morton's Steakhouse are both located on the premises, but you'd be amiss not to venture out to the fine dining establishments of the Short North. Valet parking costs $19.

Doubletree Guest Suites **$$$**
50 South Front Street at State Street
(614) 228-4600, (800) 222-8733
www.doubletree.com

The Doubletree is the only all-suites hotel in downtown Columbus and the only one with rooms overlooking the Scioto River. It is adjacent to the Huntington Bank Building and is a short walk to the Capitol building, Vern Riffe State Office Tower, and American Electric Power. The spacious, 625-square-foot suites feature a living room and bedroom separated by French doors. The rooms come equipped with a sofa bed, minifridge, microwave, two televisions, and phones. Internet access costs $6.99 per day. The Caucus Room, the full-service restaurant and bar, is open for breakfast, lunch, and dinner. Other amenities include entry to a private athletic club and complimentary weekday limo transportation within a 3-mile radius. The daily parking fee in the attached garage is $18.

German Village Inn **$**
920 South High Street, German Village
(614) 443-6506

You don't get a lot of extras at this remodeled two-story hotel, but its location 1 mile south of downtown Columbus more than makes up for that. The small, 43-room hotel is a good choice for budget travelers wanting to be in the heart of it all. The hotel is comfortable, inexpensive, and within walking distance of 30 restaurants.

Hyatt on Capital Square **$$$$**
75 East State Street
(614) 228-1234, (800) 400-5400
www.hyatt.com

Located on Theatre Row and attached to the City Center mall, this premier downtown hotel has a lot going for it—location for starters. You'll often see government figures and business bigwigs milling about the hotel, as it is in the heart of Columbus's government and financial district. A wander through the lobby will take you to the adjacent Ohio Theatre's box office.

With 400 spacious guest rooms, 13 suites, 3 Regency Club floors, and white-glove service, this Hyatt is one of only two downtown hotels to receive Four Diamonds from the American Automobile Association (AAA)—for 20 years straight. Not to mention, it has received the Consumer's Choice Award for "Best Hotel in Columbus" for seven consecutive years. The rooms are decorated with classy, cherry-veneered furniture and are specially equipped with a large personal work area. You'll find a few additional frivolities, like a second TV and third phone in most of the bathrooms. Extras such as secretarial services and express breakfasts cater to the hotel's large number of business travelers.

The concierge services are outstanding. Pamper yourself with turndown service, get tickets to a show, or schedule a massage. There is no pool on this property, but the views from the penthouse health club will help you forget about it. The fitness center is equipped with top-of-the-line exercise equipment, free weights, and a sauna.

Darby's Sports Bar is the hotel's casual watering hole, while the Plaza Restaurant offers superb dining with stunning views of the statehouse. The Plaza's decor is lavish with an Asian flair. The menu is eclectic and features seafood, steaks, and pastas. Theirs was voted the "Best Brunch in Columbus" by *Columbus Monthly* magazine readers.

The Lofts Hotel **$$$$**
55 East Nationwide Boulevard
Arena District
(614) 461-2663, (800) 735-6387
www.55lofts.com

One of (if not the most) fashionable lodging option in downtown Columbus is the boutique-style Lofts Hotel. Its 44 rooms, modeled after lofts found in Manhattan, scream designer, right down to the bathroom's fixtures and Aveda bath products. Unlike lofts in the Big Apple, they don't cost $500 or $600 per night. You'll get that big-city atmosphere for a mere $250, a small price to pay for a sophisticated dwelling steeped in history.

The Lofts are at home in the five-story Carr Building. This grand example of late 19th-century warehouse architecture is the best (and last) of its kind in Columbus. Architects have capitalized on the building's underlying industrial beauty: exposed brick walls and ductwork, wood and steel beams, curved lintels, and dramatic doorways have been given new life. The restoration of this historic landmark earned rave reviews from the architectural community when it opened in 1998.

The interior of The Lofts is at the same time urban and old world, charming and progressive, chic and cozy. Black-and-white photographs of Columbus landmarks nostalgically capture the essence of the city. The minimalist rooms are luxurious, with soft Italian leather and Frette linens, one-of-a-kind furnishings, and sleek, contemporary lines. The bathrooms boast original New York City subway tiling. Complimentary Internet access and a large workspace will inspire you.

The hotel hospitality is equally impressive. The business center, indoor pool, private fitness center, and Scandinavian sauna are top-notch. There are a lounge, restaurant, and meeting facilities on-site. Room service is available for limited hours. The Web site has a variety of well-priced packages for families and couples. This spectacular hotel is befitting the rich and interesting history of the building.

Westin Great Southern Hotel **$$$**
310 South High Street
(614) 228-3800
www.greatsouthernhotel.com
It was with great pride, on August 23, 1897, that the city was presented with The Great Southern Fireproof Hotel and Opera House. The hotel was built in response to tragic fires claiming several fine downtown hotels. This masterpiece, which is attached to the Southern Theatre, was built entirely of fire-resistant material and has survived to become the Grande Dame of Columbus. This historic hotel was restored to its original splendor by the Columbus Association of the Performing Arts (CAPA) in 1995 and remains a bastion of classic elegance and gracious service.

Ideally situated on the corner of Main and High Streets, the 196-room Westin is the southern anchor for the "Capitol South" downtown redevelopment venture. It has been tastefully updated to suit 21st-century travelers' needs while retaining its 19th-century sophistication. The Great Southern is deservingly one of two downtown hotels awarded Four Diamonds by AAA.

The French Renaissance provided inspiration for the exquisite detailing found throughout the hotel. The lobby makes quite a first impression, glowing pink and gold with marble, gilding, and cherry furniture. Original stained glass and sparkling chandeliers are a reminder that, at one time, no expense was spared on this hotel. The Great Southern has bedded many famous and fashionable people, including Eleanor Roosevelt and Presidents William McKinley, Theodore Roosevelt, and Woodrow Wilson.

The rooms are luxurious, with Queen Anne–style furniture, marble baths, and rich colors. All of the rooms (and public spaces) provide free wireless Internet access. Solo travelers might like to stay in the Victorian Cozy, a small double room equipped with all the amenities of a standard room. Twenty-three spacious suites range from a standard one-room Executive to the immaculate Thurber Suite, touted as the Crown Jewel of the Westin.

Other hotel services include a fully equipped fitness room, business center, and valet parking. Appropriately enough, the hotel's restaurant is named Theatre Cafe, while Thurber's Library Bar is the lively martini bar. You can regularly find Internet specials and weekend packages on the Web site.

THE OHIO STATE UNIVERSITY CAMPUS

There are a few hotels located directly on campus, but less expensive options, such as Red Roof Inn, Cross Country Inn, and Super 8, can be found a short distance away on Ackerman or Olentangy River Roads. Port Columbus International Airport is a 15-minute drive ($25 taxi). Don Scott Airport is five minutes away ($15 taxi). Restaurants and The Ohio State University chapters will provide information about the restaurants and bars within walking distance of these hotels.

The Roger D. Blackwell Inn **$$$**
2110 Tuttle Park Place,
Fisher College Campus
(614) 247-2110, (866) 247-4003
www.theblackwell.com
Columbus's newest deluxe hotel can be found on OSU's Fisher College of Business campus. The Blackwell serves as the executive residence for the college's Executive Education Program. With a management team pulled together by the university's Hospitality and Conference Services department, you are guaranteed to have the very best guest services and state-of-the-art technology at your disposal.

The hotel is named for renowned marketing professor and founding father of consumer behavior Roger Blackwell. He received naming rights after pledging millions to the university but is now involved in a scandalous insider-trading court case. Blackwell was found guilty, so don't be surprised if the hotel has been renamed by the second edition of this book!

There are, however, far more positive

and interesting things to focus on about the Blackwell—like its location, location, location. The hotel is directly across the street from Ohio Stadium and just a short walk from the Schottenstein Center and Wexner Center for the Arts. Many locals, forced from their homes during winter ice storms, have sought refuge here because of the convenience and quality of this hotel.

Amenities include complimentary Internet access in each room, a fitness center, concierge services, and shuttle service to the airports. Each floor has fully equipped meeting rooms and conference suites. You won't have to go far for good food and drink either. The Blackwell has a full-service lounge with its own grill menu and a separate restaurant with a respectable selection of American, European, and Asian cuisine. Guests dining at Bistro 2110 can use the hotel's complimentary valet parking.

Holiday Inn **$$$**
328 West Lane Avenue
(614) 294-4848
www.holidayinnosu.com

If you're in town for a Buckeye game or an event near OSU, you can't beat this location at the heart of the campus. Many of the 243 guest rooms in this 11-story hotel have a view of Ohio Stadium. The Holiday Inn is a 10-minute drive from the Ohio Expo Center, a 5-minute drive to the Convention Center, and just a 5-minute walk to the Schottenstein Center. This pet-friendly hotel has been awarded Three Diamonds by AAA and is a cheaper alternative to the Blackwell Inn, which is just across the street.

Guests have access to a fitness center, indoor pool, and whirlpool, as well as onsite laundry facilities. Ashley's Restaurant serves typical American hotel cuisine and hosts live jazz on select nights. Complimentary transportation is provided to the convention center, Port Columbus International Airport, and Don Scott Field. Complimentary parking is provided in the adjacent hotel garage.

University Plaza Hotel and Conference Center **$$**
3110 Olentangy River Road
(614) 267-7461, (800) 858-8471
www.universityplazaosu.com

This conference facility is not on campus but ½-mile north and is owned by The Ohio State University Endowment. The hotel has a multilingual staff, spacious guest rooms, a 24-hour business center, and a variety of meeting facilities. All of the rooms have well-lit work areas with complimentary wireless high-speed Internet access.

Other hotel amenities include an onsite restaurant and bar, dry-cleaning service, and an outdoor pool. Freebies abound in the form of complimentary passes to Bally's Total Health & Fitness, a shuttle to and from the OSU campus, and breakfast. The University Plaza is a good choice if you are attending an event at the Ohio Expo or Schottenstein or Fawcett centers. It is also 2 miles from Lennox Town Center, where you'll find a variety of shopping, dining, and entertainment options.

The historic Worthington Inn offers additional lodging at the Snow House annex on New England Avenue. Guests can choose from a standard room or three junior suites in this 19th-century home while enjoying the services and amenities of the inn, which is just across the street. For more information, call (614) 885-2600, or check out www.worthingtoninn.com.

WORTHINGTON CROSSWOODS

Located at a major intersection of I-270 and Route 23, most of the hotels in this area are ordinary chains and extended stay suites. These hotels are close to businesses including Worthington Industries, Bank One, and Polaris Amphitheatre. Worthington Crosswoods is 25 minutes from Port Columbus Airport ($25-$30 taxi) and is a safe and slightly upscale area. If you have a car, there is no shortage of complimentary parking in the huge lots. You can also enjoy a broad selection of dining and entertainment options without leaving the Crosswoods complex.

Holiday Inn $$
175 Hutchinson Avenue
(614) 885-3334
www.holiday-inn.com
The 306 guest rooms in this six-story hotel are newly renovated. Some 17,000 square feet of conference space and a new business center with Internet access makes the Holiday Inn a first-class meeting place for business travelers. In addition to a full-service restaurant and lounge, this pet-friendly hotel has an indoor pool and hot tub.

Microtel Inn $
7500 Vantage Drive
(614) 436-0556
www.microtelinn.com
You'll get the bang for your buck here. This extended stay inn offers clean, comfortable rooms at a very reasonable price. Don't expect a lot of frills, but some rooms do have oversized whirlpool tubs, and a continental breakfast is included in the price. If you stay for nine nights, you'll receive a free complimentary night. Pets are also permitted for $10 more per night.

Residence Inn $$$
7300 Huntington Park Drive
(614) 885-0799, (800) 331-3131
www.residenceinn.com
These 104 apartment-style suites come with fully equipped kitchens and are a very good value for an extended stay. The living and sleeping areas are spacious and separate from one another, and free high-speed Internet service is provided. There is an outdoor pool, spa, and fitness center. Breakfast is included, and weeknight guests can mingle at a complimentary evening social. A nonrefundable sanitation fee is charged for pets, but they are permitted.

Sheraton Suites Columbus $$$
201 Hutchinson Avenue
(614) 436-0004, (800) 325-3535
www.sheraton.com
This Sheraton is an elegant, full-service, all-suites property. There is a daily charge for Internet access in the guest rooms, but you'll find free wireless Internet access in all public spaces. Guests can dive into an indoor pool and whirlpool or get a workout in the fitness center. The outdoor pool and sundeck are open seasonally. The hotel also features limited shuttle service to the surrounding area and an onsite restaurant and lounge.

EASTON TOWN CENTER

This "city within a city" is one of the largest mixed-use developments in the country and has several lodging options, all walkable to dozens of restaurants, boutiques, and bars. The airport is only a few miles from Easton and should take about 10 minutes to reach by car ($15 taxi).

Courtyard by Marriott $$$
3900 Morse Crossing
(614) 416-8000
www.courtyard.com
This hotel is doing far better than developers had anticipated. The 126-room Courtyard is an affordable substitute for the posh Hilton without compromising location. With rooms ranging from $119 to $139 per night, they attract business people during the week and families on the weekends. Plus, it is only a few steps to the heart of Easton Town Center. The guest rooms have a few extras, such as OnCommand movie rental and complimentary Internet access. High-speed wireless Internet is available in the Business Library, along with private workstations, copiers, and fax machines. The hotel has its own cafe, where a daily breakfast buffet is served at an additional charge, and a convenience market open 24 hours a day. Parking is free.

Hilton Columbus **$$$$**
3900 Chagrin Drive
(614) 414-5000, (800) HILTONS
www.hiltoncolumbus.com

Enter the Hilton and you could be in any top-notch hotel in the world. This mammoth, seven-story hotel is located in one of Columbus's hottest shopping, dining, and entertainment districts, but you won't have to step foot inside to understand why it has been awarded a Four Diamond rating from AAA. The approach to this monumental, Georgian-style hotel is truly striking.

The Hilton is as equally magnificent on the inside as it is from the outside. High ceilings and marble floors give the vast lobby a timeless elegance. Contemporary chairs, sofas, and a sleek bar in the Lobby Lounge entice you to drop everything and indulge in a cocktail (or Starbucks coffee) while piano music wafts through the air.

The marble doesn't end at the lobby. The Hilton's 313 standard rooms are luxurious and generously sized at 400 square feet. The Italian marble bathrooms have heated mirrors and plush bathrobes, while the room features oversized beds, a large work desk, an ergonomic chair, and two phone lines. There are 68 Club Level rooms with upgraded amenities and personal concierge services. High-speed Internet access costs $9.95 per day, and breakfast is only included with Club Level rooms.

The hotel's business features include a variety of meeting rooms equipped with high-speed Internet access and a full-service business center with copiers, printers, and fax services. The Hilton is one of Columbus's premier conference locations, so it's no wonder rooms are often booked several months in advance. Recreational facilities include a complete fitness center, massage therapy room, and game room. The indoor pool is a knockout, with its soaring atrium, whirlpool, and soft lighting. The concierge can arrange tennis and golf outings at nearby facilities.

Despite the fact that there is a bevy of dining and drinking options just a few steps from the hotel, the Hilton adds two more to the mix. The stylish Dining Room serves breakfast, lunch, and dinner from an a la carte menu and buffets at breakfast and lunch. In the evening, the Easton Sports Club is an easy place to grab a beer and appetizers. The casual tavern-like atmosphere features seven plasma TVs, two pool tables, and video games.

Marriott Residence Inn **$$**
3999 Easton Loop West
(614) 414-1000, (800) 331-3131
www.residenceinn.com

This is Easton's extended stay hotel, and it is an excellent option when you want a home away from home. The inn's complimentary airport shuttle service will drop you off at the hotel, conveniently located on the west side of Easton. Each one- or two-bedroom suite provides a full range of services that echo your home: a fully equipped kitchen, furnished living and dining rooms, and complimentary Internet access. Nice touches include a complimentary breakfast buffet, free newspaper, and, possibly unlike home, daily housekeeping and a grocery service for those who want the basics picked up during a busy day. There are also a pool and fitness center on-site. Pets are allowed with a $75 nonrefundable fee, but they must be restrained or caged while housekeeping is in the room.

AIRPORT AND EAST

Looking to stay near the airport while you're in town? There are five hotels located on the grounds of Port Columbus, all providing 24-hour shuttle service to and from the terminal. Other chain hotels are located a few miles away on Taylor Road and Stelzer Road.

Concourse Hotel **$$**
4300 International Gateway
Port Columbus International Airport
(614) 237-2515, (800) 541-4574
www.theconcoursehotel.com

Staying two minutes from the airport terminal can certainly take the edge off a hectic travel day, but this 147-room hotel boasts more than a prime location. The rooms are inviting and offer guests extras, such as a microwave, refrigerator, complimentary Internet access, and free local calls. The bathrooms have some added amenities of their own: plush bathrobes, a TV, and a phone. Work off your stress at the Concourse Athletic Club, which has both an indoor and outdoor pool, or soak it away in the whirlpool. If drinking is your means to relaxation, then the Meridian Bistro should do the trick. The Concourse has 24-hour shuttle service to the airport.

Hilton Garden Inn **$$**
4265 Sawyer Road
Port Columbus International Airport
(614) 231-2869, (800) 445-8667
www.hilton.com

The 156 well-appointed guest rooms with spacious work desks, multiple phone lines, and data ports make the Hilton Garden Inn ideal for busy travelers. The hotel also features a complimentary 24-hour business center. You can relax in the whirlpool, swim a few laps, or knock out a few miles on the treadmill in the fitness center. The on-site restaurant serves breakfast every morning, and the in-house Pavilion Pantry is open round the clock.

Holiday Inn Hotel & Suites
Columbus Airport **$$**
750 Stelzer Road
(614) 237-6360
www.holidayinn.com

The newly renovated Holiday Inn Hotel & Suites Columbus Airport is located near the city's major expressways and has 210 guest rooms and suites. All rooms feature complimentary wireless high-speed Internet access, and business-class rooms have microwaves and refrigerators.

The hotel has a first-class fitness room, game room, and toddler room for the kids. The Holidome houses an atrium-style indoor pool and hot tub sure to get you itching for that tropical vacation. The hotel is a five-minute drive ($8.00 taxi) from the airport, but it also offers complimentary shuttle service to the terminal.

Stay at the Concourse Hotel, Cross Country Inn, Hampton Inn, Hilton Garden Inn, or the Comfort Suites near the airport and receive up to five days' worth of free parking. An additional $5.00 per day is collected for stays beyond five days.

DUBLIN

A whole slew of hotels and extended stays can be found in the 130-acre Metro Center Business Park and along Tuller Road in Dublin. These hotels are close to such businesses as Ashland Chemical, Cardinal Health, Honda, Nationwide, and Wendy's International. It is also close to the Columbus Zoo, Wyandot Lake Park, and the Muirfield Village Golf Club. Newer budget hotels such as the Red Roof Inn and Courtyard by Marriott can be found nearby on Post Road. This area is 25 minutes northwest of downtown Columbus. A taxi from the airport will run about $25 to $30.

Clarion Dublin **$$**
600 Metro Place North
(614) 764-2200
www.choicehotels.com

The former Wyndham has reincarnated itself as a Clarion and remains a very good value. The three-story hotel is conveniently located in Dublin's Metro Center Business Park and has 217 spacious guest rooms, which include a king- or two queen-size beds, desk, and telephone with data port. The hotel offers complimentary transportation to nearby businesses and late-night room service. Other features include a good-sized, sky-lit indoor pool and exercise facilities. The hotel has a full-service restaurant with a separate lounge, but if you are looking to get out, there's a Max and Erma's just up the road at the corner of Metro Place North and Frantz Road.

Embassy Suites Hotel **$$$**
5100 Upper Metro Place
(614) 790-9000
www.embassysuites.com

The Embassy Suites can be a bit pricey, but it's known for its consistently good service and well-appointed, extended-stay suites. You get what you pay for here. This eight-story hotel has 284 suites built around a garden-style atrium lit from above by a diamond-shaped glass ceiling. If the lobby's glass-encased elevators, lush greenery, and waterfall aren't dramatic enough, then the four-story wooden pagoda should get your attention.

Each suite has one private bedroom, living room with sleeper sofa, work/dining table, a wet bar, refrigerator, microwave, two televisions, and high-speed Internet access. The hotel amenities go beyond the complimentary breakfast and daily paper to include an evening manager's reception, a full-service business center, and babysitting services. Plenty of family fun can be had in the indoor pool, whirlpool, and fitness center. The Embassy Grille is the restaurant on site, but, for a change of scenery, Cooker Bar & Grill is right next door.

Extended Stay America **$**
450 Metro Place North
(614) 760-0053
www.extendedstayamerica.com

Budget-conscious travelers will find clean and comfortable long-term accommodations at Extended Stay America. The suites come with a microwave, refrigerator, relaxing recliner, and plenty of workspace. There are also a limited number of fully equipped kitchens. Everything you might need is here at a great price. Rooms are a good value at $260 weekly.

The closest campsite to the city of Columbus is Tree Haven Campground, located at 4855 Miller Paul Road in Westerville. It has 130 sites with water and electric, showers, and a pool. Call (740) 965-3469 for more information. You can read more about camping in the Parks and Recreation chapter.

Hilton Garden Inn **$$**
500 Metro Place North
(614) 766-9900
www.hilton.com

The Hilton Garden Inn is a new hotel located in Dublin's Metro Business Park. Each spacious guest room has a refrigerator, microwave, and 27-inch television with Nintendo and movie options. The business features of each room include a large work desk, an ergonomic chair, two phone lines, and complimentary high-speed Internet access. The hotel has a 24-hour business center, an indoor pool, whirlpool, and valet parking. You can seek out breakfast in The Great American Grill Restaurant, while the Pavilion Pantry sells a variety of sundries, beverages, microwave foods, and snacks.

Woodfin Suites Hotel **$$$**
4130 Tuller Road
(614) 766-7762
www.woodfinsuitehotels.com

Extended traveling can be a pleasure when you stay somewhere like Dublin's Woodfin Suites. There are only 18 properties in 11 states, and you'll find this one tucked on a winding road between Sawmill Road and Route 33. Each large, two-room suite has a comfortable living room, private bedroom, and full bath. The fully equipped kitchen includes a full-size range, refrigerator, microwave, and dishwasher. If you don't feel like cooking, a full breakfast is included.

Guests can swim a few laps in the outdoor pool, soak in the hot tub, or unwind at the manager's weeknight reception. Many additional services are not only available but complimentary: local calls, high-speed Internet access, daily newspaper, and a video library from which you can borrow movies to watch in your suite. Woodfin offers a 24-hour business center, free grocery shopping service, weekday shuttle service within a 5-mile radius, and complimentary use of a local health club. A limited number of suites have wood-burning fireplaces, which cost a little more but are well worth it on a wintry night.

BED-AND-BREAKFAST INNS

Guesthouses and inns offer a homelike alternative to the standard hotel. There are a handful of privately owned B&Bs scattered about town, and unlike hotels, reservations are almost always required. As their names imply, breakfast is included, and some even provide airport transportation.

50 Lincoln Inn **$$**
50 East Lincoln Street, Short North
(614) 299-5050
www.50lincoln.com
This restored 1917 brick town house is in Italian Village, just a few blocks from the Convention Center. Each of the eight rooms has decorative touches that reflect their namesakes, like Monet, Degas, and Picasso. The rooms offer a comfortable blend of antique and modern furnishings, queen-size beds, data ports, and full private baths. Local artists fill the rest of the house with an ever-changing display of works. A gourmet continental breakfast is included.

The College Inn **$$**
63 West College Avenue, Westerville
(614) 794-3090
www.bbonline.com
The College Inn has welcomed Otterbein College students and their families for the past nine years, making this one of the more established B&Bs in town. If you need to be near Otterbein, this inn is perfectly situated in the middle of historic Westerville, adjacent to the campus. The 1874 home was purchased and restored, fully intended to be a B&B. The three guest rooms have floor-to-ceiling windows, queen-size beds, and their own private bathrooms. Guests can grab a book or a game from the library and head for the drawing room or formal living room. Couch

Ohio's Bed and Breakfast Association can provide you with a list of members who have met their requirements in the Columbus area. Request this information by calling (614) 868-5567, or view all the B&Bs by region at www.ohiobba.com.

potatoes can crash upstairs in front of the TV in a more casual setting. A full breakfast is included in the cost, and airport shuttle service is available with prior arrangement. A variety of interesting weekend packages are listed on the Web site.

Four Seasons Farm
Bed, Breakfast and Barn **$$**
5490 Lithopolis Winchester Road
Canal Winchester
(614) 837-0529
www.fourseasonsfarmbbb.com
Well-behaved children, dogs, and horses are welcome at this family-friendly facility. The custom-built farmhouse is located on 34 acres just a few miles southeast of Columbus, not far from Rickenbacker Airport. Activities range from a leisurely croquet game to visiting with the farm animals, walking the grounds, and lounging in a hammock. The two large guest rooms overlook pastures and woods, but only one has a full en suite bathroom. A hearty breakfast (and other meals) is served in a formal dining room by a cozy fireplace or in the warm kitchen during winter months. Meals can be taken alfresco on the open-air patio during the summer to enjoy the sights and sounds of the property. Horses can be stabled or pastured for $15 per night, and the owner provides warm, dry kenneling for dogs in the barn. All animal boarding requires prior arrangement and proper health and shot certificates.

Harrison House Bed & Breakfast **$$$**
515 West Fifth Avenue, Victorian Village
(614) 421-2202
www.columbus-bed-breakfast.com
This 1890 Queen Anne bed-and-breakfast is

If Walls Could Talk

The Worthington Inn and its Seven Stars Restaurant is a superbly genteel operation, no matter which way you slice it. The inn is undeniably the most gracious and special accommodation in the city. The restaurant consistently rates among Columbus's top 10 and is beloved by the locals. As the second oldest operating business in Ohio, The Worthington Inn has been feeding and bedding weary travelers for over 150 years. It now ranks as one of America's most distinguished small hotels.

The story begins in 1816 when Rensselear Cowles of Connecticut came to Worthington and constructed the earliest part of this building as his residence in 1831. After his death in 1842, the property was purchased by Theodore Fuller, enlarged, and turned into a travelers' inn. From this point on, it has been a hotel of various names: the Union Hotel, the Central House, and, most recently, The Worthington Inn. What you see architecturally are various expansions of the original building, including a 1901 Victorian facade and mansard roof.

The current owners purchased and completely renovated the inn in 1982 and went to great measures to be as true to the period as possible. A hodgepodge of 19th-century architectural features and furnishings is brilliantly pulled together. People are often surprised to learn that not much more than the doors, a staircase, and a few fireplaces are original to the building. The front doors of the High Street entrance and the dining room's doors and fireplace mantels date to the original structure.

There are several other features worth noting, many salvaged from landmarks around Columbus. The rosettes on the ceiling of the Seven Stars Pub came from the former Columbus Union Train Station. The front windows of the hotel lobby (c. 1822) and the back bar in the pub are preserved from the Neil House Hotel, which was destroyed by fire in 1860. Door panels and casings from the original 1800s Franklin County Courthouse comprise the wall paneling in the pub and the Van Loon Ballroom.

Not everything is local, however. The lobby's 1830s secretary is an English piece, and the cherry registration desk was originally an 1850s store counter. The 1880s bar in the Seven Stars Pub was made in Philadelphia, and its marble countertop is used in the Wine Room's tap bar. The "dungeon door" leading into the Wine Room has traveled the farthest. This heavy bolted door came from the Bastille (the infamous French prison destroyed in 1789) in Paris.

Now, back to the future. The Worthington Inn's 26 uniquely decorated guest rooms are well priced at $125 to $150 per night. The oversized rooms are elegantly appointed with antiques and include nice extras, such as turndown service with Godiva chocolates, Frette linens, bathrobes, complimentary wireless Internet access, and a daily newspaper. Breakfast is available in the Seven Stars Restaurant, but it is not included in the

The Worthington Inn, Olde Worthington. SHAWNIE KELLEY

room rate. This should be no bother, as the hotel is right in the heart of Olde Worthington, just a few steps from several restaurants and coffee shops. You can read more about nearby eateries in the Restaurants chapter, but you do not have to leave the premises to get a good meal.

People come from all over town to dine at this venerable lodge. The carefully crafted menu with its French and Italian influences offer sophisticated "new twists on old classics." The wine list, which has been developed to match the food, has been nationally recognized with a *Wine Spectator* Award of Excellence. The chef uses locally grown and produced ingredients for his amazing scratch cooking. Even the breads and desserts are made on-site. The eclectic menu changes seasonally, but if you have the opportunity to dine here during the autumn, don't miss the very popular red oak salad with its mix of sweet, tart, nutty, and earthy flavors.

The atmosphere is refined, and the dress code is defined as "dressy-casual." The friendly staff is service-oriented but not stuffy. The inn's reputation for fine food and fine hospitality adds to the misconception that it is very expensive. The average entree is about $25 per person and well worth it. It is a shame that so many people wait for special occasions to experience the Seven Stars Restaurant at The Worthington Inn.

If you prefer a more casual ambience, the Seven Stars Pub serves food and plays host to live music on Thursday nights, during which there's a happy hour. The pub's Sunday brunch is famous for its huge offerings of shellfish, waffles, eggs, cheese, and desserts. Special buffets on holidays like Mother's Day and Easter are very busy and require reservations well in advance.

During the summer months, you can take your meals outdoors onto the front porch or brick courtyard, where everyone along High Street enjoys the live jazz and classical music. A little secret: If weather forces you indoors and you want the most romantic (or private) spot in the house, ask for table 24. It is tucked in a perfect little nook in the corner of the back dining room.

If you're looking for a place to hold a small reception, business meeting, or cocktail party, The Worthington Inn has several private rooms loaded with character. The Van Loon Ballroom, with its European crystal chandelier, can accommodate up to 120 guests and has its own private bar. The Lewis Room can accommodate up to 40 people and adjoins a lounge with a fireplace, cozy, overstuffed chairs, and a Victorian bar. The Cowles Room can hold up to 30 guests and was the master bedroom in the original private residence. The Formal Room, located at street level, was once the parlor and retains an original fireplace. It can accommodate up to 20 guests. Last, but not least, is the Wine Room, which can host up to 20 people around its bar and handmade Amish table.

Whether you stay at the hotel or are just popping around for dinner, there is no charge for parking in the lot behind the inn. Various hotel and dining packages are listed on the Web site and should be reserved by phone. Brunch is served on Sunday from 11:30 A.M. to 3:00 P.M., and the items vary from week to week. Pub fare is available in the bar or on the patio from 3:00 to 10:00 P.M. Monday through Saturday. Reservations are always recommended for dinner.

The Worthington Inn is located at 649 High Street in Olde Worthington. For reservations visit www.worthingtoninn.com or call (614) 885-2600.

located on a tree-lined residential street just a few miles north of downtown. You'll find it on the corner of Neil and Fifth Avenue within walking distance of Ohio State's campus and Battelle Memorial Institute. Like many homes in Victorian Village, it is on the National Register of Historic Places and offers guests a convenient retreat from the hustle and bustle of the city.

The Harrison House is a study in Victoriana, with its rich woodwork, lacy curtains, and big, cut-glass windows. All four guest rooms have comfortable queen-size beds, cable TV, a private phone line, and full bath. Brass or mahogany beds and rich colors add to the coziness of the rooms. A corporate apartment, replete with kitchen and separate bedroom, is available for stays of two weeks or longer. Escape to the quiet parlor with a book, or take your breakfast near the toasty fireplace in the dining room. If you prefer the great outdoors, the inn is a short walk to Goodale Park. All rooms are $119; a full breakfast is included in the price, and parking is free.

House of Seven Goebels $$
4975 Hayden Run Road, Dublin
(614) 761-9595
www.bbhost.com/7goebels

You don't have to go to New England to experience Colonial America. This reproduction 1780 Connecticut River Valley farmhouse was built in the 1970s using colonial construction methods. Purists will appreciate the attention to detail: square nails, handmade doors and latches, wide floorboards, and wooden shutters instead of curtains. The inn is a little off-the-beaten path from downtown but conveniently situated to Dublin, Worthington, and the Tuttle Mall area.

The two large guest rooms capture the early American mood, with their canopy beds, wood-burning fireplaces, and throw carpets. The Red Room has an attached bath and overlooks a meandering stream, while the Blue Room, on the north side of the house, has a detached private bath. The rest of the house is decorated with antiques and period reproductions. A full or continental breakfast is included. In the winter, breakfast is served by the fireplace in the dining room; during the warmer months, on the patio overlooking the two-acre yard and gardens.

Lily Stone Bed and Breakfast $
106 South High Street, Gahanna
(614) 476-1976

Gahanna's premier lodging is this two-story 1920s bed-and-breakfast owned and operated by the Gahanna Historical Society. It is the only one in Ohio owned by a historical society and run by a volunteer staff. The four guest rooms are decorated in the Victorian style and interestingly radiate off the landing of the staircase rather than a hallway. The room's facilities vary in that two have their own separate shower and lavatory, while two have to share. Only one room has a TV, and there is a kitchen phone for free local calls. Lily Stone is often rented out in its entirety for local events and family functions. All rooms are $65 a night and include a continental breakfast. It is well placed within walking distance of several restaurants and bars. It is also a short drive from the airport and both beltways (I-670 and I-270).

The Westerville Inn $
5 South West Street, Westerville
(614) 882-3910, (877) 816-5247
www.westervilleinn.com

This little house with its white picket fence began life as a log cabin in 1854 for a widow and her 11 children; I suppose three guest rooms now sound gloriously spacious. The bedrooms are decent sized and have a sort of country charm. The house is decorated with antiques, while the living room has a fireplace and TV/VCR for guest use. The half-acre lot has perennial and herb gardens, a fish pond, and is within walking distance of historic Westerville and Otterbein College campus.

LODGES AND RESORTS

Cherry Valley Lodge $$$
2299 Cherry Valley Road, Newark
(740) 788-1200, (800) 788-8008
www.cherryvalleylodge.com

The nation's only hotel to carry the distinction of being an arboretum and botanical garden is nestled on 18 acres 35 miles east of Columbus near Granville. This 200-room, full-service, resort-style lodge is geared toward group meetings and romantic getaways. It is a popular place for family reunions, wedding parties, and women-only weekends.

The lobby is given a rustic atmosphere with two soaring stone fireplaces, hardwood floors, and wood beam ceilings. Two beautifully landscaped courtyards and unique common areas allow for group gatherings or private moments. The oversized guest rooms have coffeemakers, refrigerators, and a VCR on which to watch complimentary videos. The 16 suites have Jacuzzi tubs, while all the rooms have dial-up Internet access.

Grab a pair of complimentary binoculars from the front desk and go wander the tranquil gardens. Check out the collection of rare heirloom and native plants that encompass some 2,000 plantings and 400 species. Birdhouses and feeders are strategically placed throughout the property to attract butterflies, bluebirds, purple martins, and hummingbirds. Fresh herbs from the Chef's Herb Garden are used in the kitchen, and the Gazebo Garden provides great photo ops.

The hotel's recreational facilities go well beyond the standard indoor and outdoor pool to include a spa, volleyball, half-court basketball, horseshoes, and shuffleboard. The game room is set up family-room style and features a pool table, video games, and a large-screen TV. Children can run off their energy in the playground and adults in the fitness room. Bicycles are also available to take out on the scenic trail system, which you can read more about in the Parks and Recreation chapter.

Deer Creek Resort and Conference Center $$$
22300 State Park Road, Mount Sterling
(740) 869-2020, (877) 677-8DEER
www.visitdeercreek.com

This beautiful resort is located 30 minutes south of Columbus in 3,100-acre Deer Creek State Park. It has just undergone $1.4 million worth of renovations. All of the lodge's 110 guest rooms have a balcony, and many overlook the lake. Resort amenities include indoor and outdoor pools (often jam-packed with people), a sauna, whirlpool, fitness room, and espresso bar. The lodge is less than 2 miles from the Deer Creek State Park Golf Course and has dining facilities on site.

Slightly more expensive lodging options include 25 two-bedroom cottages with full living, dining, and bathrooms, as well as a screened porch. The historic Harding Cabin is a spacious three-bedroom cottage once a favorite retreat of President Warren G. Harding. Its lakefront location allows for a private boat dock and full-length screened porch with a fabulous view. Cabin rates vary, and year-round packages can be viewed online.

RESTAURANTS 

This might well be the longest chapter in the book, but quite frankly, it could have easily been twice as long, given the number of wonderful restaurants in our city. Those new to Columbus sometimes struggle to see the "ethnicity" here, but the diversity of the people who live here is seen in the diversity of our restaurants. This chapter is organized according to neighborhood and aims to provide a representative and interesting cross section of the city's eateries. Writing this chapter was a lot of fun (minus the weight gained eating and drinking my way around town), but the most difficult part was picking and choosing which places to include.

Admittedly, I have not eaten *everywhere* in Columbus, but through months of research, in-depth conversations, and basic, word-of-mouth recommendations, hundreds of independently owned dining establishments have been whittled down to a selection of greasy spoons, local brewpubs, campus haunts, upscale restaurants, and comfortable coffeehouses. There are plenty of romantic places where you and your sweetheart can enjoy an intimate setting. There are the trendy spots where the "hipper than thou" crowd goes to see and be seen. There are the cheap (but good!) eats that you can find for the shoestring budget. Hopefully, after reading this chapter you will find at least a few places to tempt your taste buds.

When I first moved to Columbus, the one thing that immediately stood out was how many restaurants are located in (sometimes unattractive) strip malls, many of which have been included here. Don't let a shopping center locale scare you away. Some of the best food is hidden behind unassuming, smoked glass doors or advertised with a boring storefront sign. You'll discover über-fine dining tucked in the basement of buildings and on out-of-the-way dead-end streets.

Columbus does, however, have several trendy pockets of restaurants that should not be missed, especially if you are only visiting for a brief time. You can park your car and walk to a variety of places in German Village, the Short North, and the Arena District, but if you don't have access to a car, several buses travel along High Street, allowing you to experience the different flavors of Columbus with little effort. The more upscale chain restaurants can be found at Easton Town Center and clustered around the Polaris and Tuttle Mall areas. It takes a bit more effort to get to these places by public transportation, but at the end of the day, Smith & Wollensky and P. F. Chang's junkies can get their fix too. The "Cap" at Union Station, linking downtown and the Short North, is home to many new restaurants including Abracci, Liu Pon-xi, and a fourth Hyde Park Steakhouse.

This chapter's goal is to help you find a feast unique to Columbus—but what exactly is this? Cincinnati is known for its chili, Kansas City for its barbecue, but what is Columbus known for? Even after long interviews with restaurateurs, it is still impossible to say. Even they had a tough time nailing down a cuisine specific to our city, so for now, let's just say that dining in Columbus will satisfy any craving. Whether it's unpretentious comfort food or menus of sheer genius, we have it.

---

i

Street parking in German Village, the Short North, and the campus area can be nearly impossible on weekends. Allow yourself ample time to find a space, or take advantage of valet parking offered by many of the restaurants. It isn't always cheap, but it may be the least frustrating way to go. Some restaurants provide complimentary valet parking.

The oldest family-owned restaurant in Columbus is TAT Ristorante di Famiglia, while Whole World Restaurant and Bakery is Columbus's oldest vegetarian restaurant. The Confluence Restaurant, which sits on the banks of the Scioto River just north of downtown, has the best views of the skyline.

When it comes to fast food, we have that too—and, unfortunately, a lot of it. Columbus has one of the nation's highest ratios of national fast-food chains per capita. Besides being corporate headquarters to Bob Evans Family Restaurant, two other chains are headquartered in Columbus. White Castle, the first ever fast-food burger chain, began selling its five-cent burgers in 1921 in Kansas City. The company moved corporate headquarters to Columbus in 1934, but we consider Whiteys our golden child because the white-and-blue castle motif was conceived right here. White Castle remains privately held, and the restaurants are company-owned, not franchised, so I have made it a point to include "our" Whiteys for sentimental value, if for no other reason.

The late Dave Thomas, founder of Wendy's International, made his contribution to the weight problem of America starting right here in Columbus. The original Wendy's, which opened in 1969, is located downtown, and, after merging with Tim Horton's in 1995, the company boasts over 8,000 locations worldwide. If an international fast-food chain and square hamburgers aren't enough to immortalize a man, Route 161 (also known as Dublin-Granville Road) between Riverside Drive and Sawmill Road has been renamed Dave Thomas Boulevard. Coincidently enough, it passes Wendy's corporate headquarters along the way—imagine that!

Another local restaurateur, for whom a road is not yet named (but give it time), is Cameron Mitchell. Cameron's American Bistro in Worthington, along with his 12 other trendsetting and innovative restaurants, has propelled dining in Columbus to new levels. Rather than list them among the regular entries, I have chosen to address all of the Mitchell restaurants together in a Close-up later in this chapter.

An organization called The Columbus Originals is a group of restaurateurs who came together to promote dining at their independently owned and operated restaurants. They too are responsible for feeding a hungry Columbus, which they do with creativity and imagination. Entries for most of these restaurants (which include the likes of G. Michael's and The Elevator) are listed in their respective neighborhoods. You can also go to www.columbusoriginals.com for links to most of their Web sites or to buy a coupon book that offers discounted dining at each location. In an age of mass-marketed, franchised food joints, this is a nice way to show one's support for these fine and independently owned restaurants unique to Columbus.

What about those evenings you are not looking for innovative food and just want a simple slice of pie? I feared being laughed out of town if I didn't include some of the favorite neighborhood pizza joints, but this necessitates a disclaimer. Everyone has his or her own opinions about what makes a pizza good, but I could not include all beloved pizza shops. I have kept the descriptions of what they offer to a minimum and focused more on what the locals prefer about it. Pizza shops located on campus are listed separately in The Ohio State University chapter.

When it comes to general protocol, you can assume the restaurants accept major credit cards unless otherwise noted. Cash-only places are few and far between, but they do still exist, so I have pointed this out specifically when applicable. I have also made it a point to note when the dress code is anything more than business casual. You will find that even some of the priciest restaurants permit casual dress most nights of the week, which provides for an elegant but relaxed dining experience.

As for wheelchair accessibility, I will only point out the exceptions. Columbus is modern enough that this doesn't seem to be much of a problem as in other cities where restaurants may be located in older buildings not up to code.

A recent and controversial change that has occurred is a ban on smoking in public places. Columbus voters approved a law that prohibits all smoking in enclosed public places within the city limits of Columbus, leaving tobacco shops and some private clubs among the exceptions. Outdoor smoking areas must be at least 20 feet from an enclosed area, so say goodbye to smoking on patios at some places too. Violators of the antismoking ordinance can face civil charges and a $150 fine. Several Columbus suburbs either have passed or are considering antismoking legislation as well, so smokers beware.

Drinkers don't have it so bad. Just don't go looking for Bloody Marys before 1:00 P.M. on Sunday, as restaurants are not permitted to serve alcohol before then. Any other day of the week you can order alcohol at 11:00 A.M. Many of the restaurants included here have full-service bars, but there is often the case of that very blurry line between restaurant and pub. If you don't see your favorite restaurant-bar here, you may want to have a look in The Pub Crawl and The Ohio State University chapters.

One last but strongly recommended piece of advice on dining in Columbus is to call the restaurants before you go. Columbus has long been known as a test market for new forays into food, so it comes as no surprise that restaurants fail at a high rate in our city, but this also means some fine, fine dining is to be had when they do stick.

If to eat well is to live well, then we are living quite large in Columbus.

PRICE CODE

The following price codes are based on the average price of two entrees, excluding tax, tip, appetizers, desserts, and beverages.

$	**Cheap Eats**	**Less than $20**
$$	**Bang for the Buck**	**$21 to $35**
$$$	**Indulgent**	**$36 to $50**
$$$$	**Worth the Splurge**	**$51 and more**

DOWNTOWN

Brownstone on Main **$$**
122 East Main Street
(614) 222-3005
www.brownstoneonmain.com

N'oorlins meets Columbus, German Village style! If you want something other than the usual chicken and steak, try the Brownstone's upscale take on southern soul food. One look at the menu and you'll feel transported to the Bayou, but as you study it you'll find inventive and contemporary dishes (such as purple smashed potatoes) among the traditional southern favorites of fried catfish, jambalaya, and barbecued ribs. Caribbean flavors are also right at home with the Cajun and Creole-inspired food. The interior is as much a mix of conventional and contemporary as the menu. Three levels of traditional brownstone coziness are offset by a restrained and modern approach to the decor. Exposed brick walls, warm wood, and gentle lighting, combined with a granite bar and abstract Mark Rothko-esque paintings, make for an elegant eating environment. Intimate dining nooks provide a certain amount of privacy, allowing people to actually talk during dinner. Another option is the outdoor patio. Once you've had some good food and good wine, head downstairs for a good jam session. The Lounge at Brownstone, one of Columbus's only permanent jazz clubs, is located on the lower level. It draws a wide cultural and ethnic mix, albeit a slightly older, more mature crowd. The Lounge has all the class of a big-city jazz club but with a more relaxed ambience. You'll find live jazz and a pub menu Thursday through Saturday, but the restaurant is open seven days a week.

Confluence Park Restaurant $$$
679 West Long Street
(614) 469-0000
The Scioto and Olentangy Rivers converge at the same point a tangled mess of highways meet, so it's not surprising people whiz right by the Confluence (formerly The River Club). One might also wonder how you could miss the self-proclaimed "largest wooden structure in Columbus," but the restaurant is situated discreetly enough at the end of a long road, which can only be accessed from certain directions, so, it's possible. The wooden beams, fireplace, and exposed brick walls add to the spacious, lodge-like ambience of this restaurant, known particularly for its banquet facilities and special holiday menus. The food is good, but the views of the sparkling Columbus skyline are what make this place special. The dining room has plenty of window seating, but the patio is Columbus's only true waterfront deck. The patio draws an after-work crowd, but a more intimate mood evolves during the summer sunsets, and brick fire pits and heat lamps ease the evening chill. The cuisine is typically American, the portions are large, and the dress is casual, but no jeans are permitted. It is closed Sunday and Monday.

Elemental $$
53 Parsons Avenue
(614) 228-5700
www.elementalcolumbus.com
As the Web site says, it's hip, but not too hip. Elemental is a neighborhood restaurant in Olde Towne East that has stylish flair without trying too hard. The menu consists of American/Mediterranean comfort food with a twist. If vegetable lasagna isn't comfortable enough, the lunch menu offers a variety of hearty meals ranging from soups and salads to wraps and sandwiches. The dinner menu is broken out into Greens & Things, Sandwiches & Pastas, and main entrees. Vegetarians should have no problem finding a few items on the menu. There is also a regular change of scenery, as local artists show their work through rotating exhibitions. This is the kind of place you can carouse at the bar with friends or eat alone with a book, and neither seems strange. What you get here is a somewhat funky, urban bistro with a moderate price tag.

Elevator Brewery and Draught Haus $$$
161 North High Street
(614) 228-0500
www.elevatorbrewing.com
If your spirits need to be lifted, the Elevator is a good place to start. You can't miss the flashing sign on the side of this landmark building on High Street. What was once the historic Clock Restaurant is now a revolutionary brewpub. The only beers served, however, are the Elevator's own microbrews, but rest assured, pilsner and stout lovers alike will find something to quench their thirst. Try one by the pint, sample all 12 in flights, or choose from the extensive by-the-glass wine list. Whatever your poison, you will be drinking it in what has been touted as one of the most beautiful bars in Columbus. Everything about the Elevator screams art deco: the tiled floor, the decorative ceiling, the dark wood bar—and the glaring halogen lamps. If it seems the place is glowing blue on occasion, it could be the alcohol, but more than likely it is the aquatic blue lighting around the bar reflecting off the sky blue ceiling. The architecture isn't the only thing to rave about; the food is great too. The menu ranges from tasty tuna and savory steaks (served on hot rocks) to a gigantic portion of fish-and-chips.

If the unique bar, award-winning beer, and world cuisine aren't special enough, go gaming on the three classic dartboards and two beautifully restored billiard tables dating to 1891 and 1884. Hopefully, the Prohibition era ghosts that supposedly live here won't drain your beer when you're not looking!

Flatiron Bar and Diner $$
129 East Nationwide Boulevard
(614) 461-0033
www.flatironcolumbus.com
If you pass through downtown and notice

a triangular, tapered building and think, "Gee—that looks like the Flatiron Building in New York," well, it is. This is Columbus's version of its New York City namesake, only *this* Flatiron serves up barbecue, Cajun, and Creole food at amazingly fair prices. You will find the usual gumbo and fried oyster po'-boys on the menu, along with a not-so-usual Carolina-style pulled pork sandwich (which means no ketchup in the sauce). The colorful interior seems a bit dated, but the overall atmosphere invokes that old-school jazz and cigar-bar nostalgia that draws a faithful after-work crowd. This popular watering hole is open late on the weekends and has seasonal outdoor patio seating.

Florentine Restaurant **$$**
907 West Broad Street
(614) 228-2262
Tried-and-true Italian food is what you'll get at this Westside institution: homemade pasta, meatballs, marinara sauce, vino. Need I say more? This is the sort of place you bring the kids—and the grandparents and the aunts and uncles. Don't bother coming here if you want a fancy, quiet dinner, as the place can get lively, but what would a good, old-fashioned Italian meal be without a little noise? It's a big restaurant with multiple dining rooms, and the garish '70s wall murals are a quaint reminder that the Florentine has been around for some time. While the regulars swear by the Roman bread and ravioli Florentine, the chef will conjure up just about any combination of pasta, meats, and sauces you desire. The only thing better than the food are the prices. Most of the pasta dishes are under $10.

Indian Oven Restaurant **$$**
427 East Main Street
(614) 220-9330
www.indianoven.com
Once located on Ohio State's campus, this popular Indian restaurant went upscale downtown—and so did the prices—but you certainly get what you pay for, a fine urban dining experience. White tablecloths add a touch of class to the open and airy dining room. The streamlined, stainless steel bar is a classy after-work meeting place, while the patio permits dining outdoors during the summer months. The usual curries and tandoori dishes are available in whatever degree of spice you can handle, while more sophisticated house specialties have been added to the menu. The Indian Oven offers plenty of vegetarian entrees and turns out a wonderful selection of breads from the open kitchen.

Jack's **$**
52 East Lynne Alley
(614) 224-3655
Jack's old-fashioned diner has been serving home-cooked meals since 1922 and expects payment the old-fashioned way—cash on the barrel, folks. The menu is straight from Grandma's kitchen: fried bologna, bean soup, and pecan pie. Top it off with a strawberry malt or some hand-dipped ice cream, and you'll be ready for a nap. No alcohol is served and no reservations are taken, but when you're looking for that double cheeseburger on the fly, call Jack's and they'll have lunch ready for pickup in 10 minutes. This quick-service diner caters to you busy nine-to-fivers, so they are open bright and early for breakfast and lunch but closed on weekends.

Saigon Palace **$$**
114 North Front Street
(614) 464-3325
High-end Vietnamese fare is served in a modest but vibrant setting. The Palace is known for its "happy pancakes" (rice crepes and crisp veggies), which makes for a nice, light meal. The restaurant has been around for years, but it's located far enough off the beaten downtown path that many locals have never heard of it. If you like Asian food, this is certainly worth a try. It's closed Sunday.

White Castle **$**
111 South High Street
(614) 444-8661
www.whitecastle.com
The burger phenomenon has been around since the early 1920s and was regarded as "poor folks' food." Fast food isn't necessarily cheap or fast these days, but good old Whiteys keep their Slyders priced at about a half dollar, making theirs more affordable than most. At a time when people are hugely concerned with health issues, one might think Slyders "slide" down your throat because of grease, but this is not the case. White Castle steam-grills burgers on a bed of onions, making it less greasy than a lot of others. Convinced of the misnomer? You can also order the Slyder-sized chicken, fish, and sausage sandwiches, which are, along with most other side dishes, properly deep-fried. The coffee is good enough to be carried in grocery stores. This inaugural location is open 24 hours a day.

Meat rationing during World War II forced White Castle to sell hot dogs and eggs rather than burgers. An impressive list of firsts includes being the very first fast-food chain, the first to use industrial-strength spatulas, the first mass-produced paper hat, the first to sell a million and a billion hamburgers, and the first frozen fast food to be carried in stores.

GERMAN VILLAGE/ BREWERY DISTRICT

Barcelona **$$$**
263 East Whittier Street
(614) 443-3699
www.barcelonacolumbus.com
Barcelona was an instant German Village favorite, and their consistently good food and service keep it popular, but don't let the name fool you. Barcelona's menu leans more toward general Mediterranean food than Spanish, but there are also wonderful paella and a beautiful assortment of tapas. The unique antipasto appetizer is large enough to be a small meal in itself or serve several people as a starter.

The dining area is elegant, and the caliber of food could justify a far stuffier atmosphere, yet it remains casual and comfortable. It's the outdoor patio, however, that brings something truly special to this restaurant. Enclosed with lush greenery, old-fashioned street lamps, and tiny white lights, it feels trés European and quickly became one of the city's most desirable alfresco options. I have also bestowed it the honor of most romantic patio in Columbus. Barcelona has live music two days a week and weekday happy hour specials. Reservations are recommended on the weekends, and valet parking is available.

Claremont Restaurant **$$$$**
684 South High Street
(614) 443-1125
This old-time steakhouse retains a red meat menu and a solid reputation as one of the best restaurants in town. Not much has changed in the Claremont's nearly 60-year existence, including its signature dishes: a classic pepper steak and a bacon-wrapped filet mignon. Though known primarily for its steaks, several seafood and pasta specialties have been added to the menu, along with the occasional specials that are "served until they're gone." But the one dish people can't seem to get enough of is the Provimi liver and onions. Who knew?

Likewise, the decor has remained about as unchanged as the menu. One can eat at the not-meaning-to-be-retro-cool bar or in the minimally updated dining room, while listening to live piano music. Some of the wait staff has even worked here for decades, not to mention the regulars who have become permanent fixtures. Some things are best left unchanged. It's open seven days a week, with limited dinner hours on Sunday.

Easy Street Cafe **$$**
197 Thurman Avenue
(614) 444-3279
www.wedeliver2you.com
Easy Street is a pretty easygoing restaurant with a bar. The friendly service and laid back ambience compliments the affordable menu. Enjoy a full steak or pasta dinner at simple wooden tables, or the budget-minded can opt for chicken wings, salads, or soup. With no fewer than 10 types of chicken sandwiches, 8 types of gyros, and a bunch of burgers, one might say they are heavy into sandwiches. They are also heavy into memorabilia—just check out the walls. Eric Clapton has frequented Easy Street as he passed through Columbus (proof is on the wall). The kitchen closes at midnight, making it a good place for a late-night snack.

G. Michael's American Bistro & Bar **$$$**
595 South Third Street
(614) 464-0575
www.gmichaelsbistro.com
Another one of German Village's "hot spots" serves a contemporary fusion of American and Italian cuisines. The menu changes seasonally, but there are always creative pasta and seafood dishes to choose from. Salmon filet is the best seller, while the lasagna appeals to the masses.

The variety of dining atmospheres will leave you with no doubt that this vibrant bistro was once a fine German Village town house. If you're feeling social or want a view of every person who walks in the door, you'll probably not make it past the long, mirrored bar, where one can drink from an extensive wine list and dine off the full menu while listening to live music on certain nights. Proceed into the main dining area, where it is well lit and equally lively. Rich velvet hangings separate the back room for an even cozier setting. The intimacy of the dining room is surpassed only by the privacy of the patio, which has six tables in the shade of a big tree. Romantic, indeed, but be sure to make reservations, particularly if you want to dine outdoors.

Handke's Cuisine **$$$$**
520 South Front Street
(614) 621-2500
www.chefhandke.com
Columbus is fortunate enough to be home to one of the world's 68 officially designated master chefs. German Chef Hartmut Handke brings 40-plus years of culinary expertise to every aspect of your dining experience at his highly acclaimed restaurant located in the basement of the former Schlee Bavarian Brewery. Handke's reeks of class and exclusivity, despite being underground. The massive stone walls and the heavy vaulted ceiling of this 19th-century rathskeller are as unique a setting as any you will find in Columbus. It deservedly serves as the impressive backdrop to some seriously exquisite food.

Have you ever looked at the cover of a gourmet magazine and wondered where you could find a dish that photogenic? Well, bring your camera! Alaskan sable fish, Chilean sea bass, and buffalo tenderloin are part of a menu that will please the most worldly of palates. Dessert lovers should definitely save room for a symphony of sweets, including a sampling of five sinful delights.

Before heading into the lower levels for dinner, take a peek at the display case full of national and international awards and trophies. It doesn't take long to learn that *Zagat's* isn't the only one to give Chef Handke's food top ratings. It's a true testimony to the magic one will encounter in the wine cellar of this former brewery. Reservations are recommended, and the dress code is about as formal as it gets in Columbus. Handke's is closed Sunday.

Katzinger's Delicatessen **$**
475 South Third Street
(614) 228-3354
www.katzingers.com
This German Village institution is open for breakfast, lunch, and dinner seven days a week. People come from all over to what is possibly the best deli in town. Even Bill Clinton stopped in, but apparently the

president couldn't find his favorite deli combo among Katzinger's 80-odd sandwiches. This 1994 visit resulted in the creation of a sandwich called, creatively enough, "President Bill's Day at the Deli": corned beef with Swiss cheese and spicy mustard on pumpernickel. Given their outstanding selection of deli meats, cheeses, and breads, it's surprising they didn't have that combination already.

Create your own sandwich; go for one of the absolutely monstrous Reubens, or order off the vegetarian and vegan menus. Throw in some garlic pickles, potato salad, and rugelach for dessert, and your takeout out is officially gourmet. You can eat outdoors if you are quick enough to get a street-side table, but if you'd rather eat in, the bustling and ever-friendly atmosphere is unpretentious, and the service is the same. Katzinger's is also a specialty store that carries Jewish, kosher, and other ethnic foods.

Lindey's **$$$**
169 East Beck Street
(614) 228-4343
www.lindeys.com

Lindey's has been voted one of Columbus's top-10 restaurants 18 years in a row, and with reason: the charming location, chic atmosphere, and innovative food.

A restored 1850s brownstone is a natural home for this bistro-like interior that harks back to the turn of the 20th century. The high ceilings are intricately decorated. Bentwood chairs, polished brass railings, chandeliers, and hardwood floors give the bar area an Edwardian feel. Of the three separate dining areas, the front room is the liveliest and is often a stage for the movers and shakers of Columbus.

The exceptional kitchen turns out old familiars, such as grilled chicken and pesto and rack of lamb, as well as more creative dishes, like pecan-crusted tilapia and Hunan-glazed pork chops. Be sure to leave room for the dessert appropriately called "Post Mortem": coffee ice cream topped with Kahlua hot fudge sauce.

Lindey's has two of the more coveted alfresco dining options in Columbus: a tranquil ground-level terrace and a patio perched on the rooftop. The latter offers decent views of the city skyline. Reservations are a must on any weekend, particularly for outdoor dining.

Plank's Cafe & Pizzeria **$$**
743 Parsons Avenue
(614) 443-6251

Columbus residents loves their Buckeyes, and it's obvious at Plank's. The walls of this sports-themed, family-friendly restaurant are a shrine to OSU, but there is a strong showing of Blue Jacket, Clippers, and Crew memorabilia. It will be a stretch, but if you can't find your college pennant tacked up somewhere on the overloaded walls, bring one in, and you will be reimbursed for it.

As for the food, they've been in the same digs since 1939, if that says anything. Plank's serves full breakfasts, lunch, and the usual pizzeria fare, such as burgers, brats (as in bratwursts), subs, and pickled-tongue sandwiches (for real). The pizza crust is sweeter than usual, which makes it a popular favorite in the neighborhood. Expect to be welcomed with open arms and a very friendly and accommodating staff. If you must stay at home to watch the football game, this is one of the only places in Columbus that delivers everything on the menu. Plank's Cafe is not to be confused with Plank's Biergarten, which is listed in The Pub Crawl chapter.

Schmidt's Restaurant und Sausage Haus **$$**
240 East Kossuth Street
(614) 444-6808
www.schmidthaus.com

This German Village landmark is located in a historic brick livery stable and serves traditional German-American fare in a classic (touristy) beer hall setting. The Schmidts began sharing their recipes with Columbus from a concession stand at the Ohio State Fair in the 1920s (currently the second oldest food booth at the fair). The restaurant is actually part of a family-owned business started in 1888, so it's not surprising to learn some of the restaurant's recipes have been in the Schmidt family for over 100 years.

Their hospitality does the homeland proud as you are bid "Guten Essen!" and pointed toward the buffet by Bavarian costume-clad servers. If table service is your preference, order the popular Bahama Mama sausage from the menu. And what would a German restaurant be without a fine selection of beers? Probably not German! Schmidt's is open seven days a week and has live music Wednesday through Saturday.

Progressive eaters will find the Arena District, the Short North, and Easton afford you the luxury of parking in one place and walking to a large selection of restaurants. The parking garages are free in Easton, but many meters are enforced 24 hours in the Short North. Parking in German Village can be cutthroat, so valet parking is recommended.

Tony's Italian Ristorante **$$$**
16 West Beck Street
(614) 224-8669
www.tonysristorante.net

Forget Italian fusion; this is the real deal—straightforward, upscale Italian food in a straightforward, upscale setting. There is no escaping the historic brick buildings of the Brewery District, and Tony's is located in yet another one. The timeless decor is kept simple and elegant, with white tablecloths, pastel colors, and a baby grand piano. Arches break up the space and give the dining area intimacy and privacy. Even the TV over the bar is as subtle as one could be. There is no arguing the number of excellent house specialties on the menu, but some say Tony's serves the best veal in central Ohio. You be the judge. I do, however, recommend leaving your younger children at home unless you can reserve the veranda. It's a nice outdoor dining option in good weather—with or without the kids.

Zum Rathskeller **$$**
966 South High Street
(614) 444-3531
www.maennerchor.com

Zum Rathskeller recently opened its doors to the public, but this once-private restaurant is by no means "new," as it has been the private dining club for the Maennerchor (German men's choir) for more than 60 years. Thankfully, they have chosen to share Zum Rathskeller with Columbus, and it was voted one of the city's best new restaurants in 2004.

Once inside, you may be surprised at how large this place really is. The Konzert Hall, on the upper level, is a banquet hall that can be rented for parties. The coziness and character of this upper room carry over into the lower levels, which house the bar, restaurant, and a few more private rooms. One of the most striking features of Zum Rathskeller is the big old, mirrored bar lined with top-shelf alcohol and tall bar chairs.

Appropriately enough, the walls are painted with sheet music and the coats of arms of different German cities. The deep and well-documented heritage of this restaurant is seen not only in the decor but, most tangibly, in the number of commemorative plaques and trophies on display throughout the building.

While the ambience is definitely one of old-world charm, the cuisine, paradoxically, is quite modern. Zum Rathskeller's talented chef comes direct from Stuttgart. So yes, he can conjure up a pile of traditional brats if that's what you really want, but you'd be absolutely amiss not to try some of the more contemporary dishes on the menu. One doesn't normally think of duck being a German entree, but you'll find a full page of dinners that have a continental tinge to them.

Zum Rathskeller is open for both lunch and dinner and offers entertainment by way of live piano music in the restaurant and a big-band orchestra in the

Konzert Hall. If you want to experience a true piece of German Village history or have been looking for a unique dinner setting, Zum Rathskeller will provide you both. If German food really, truly isn't your thing, just come for the beer.

ARENA DISTRICT

Abracci Steaks and Italian **$$$**
511 North High Street
(614) 224-2373
From the owners of R. J. Snappers comes an upscale Italian bistro in the "Cap" at Union Station. The spacious restaurant and Bellini Bar is elegant and modern. The menu features dry-aged steaks and pasta and the chef makes fresh mozzarella each day. Abracci opened to immediate local acclaim and was named one of Columbus's best new restaurants of 2004. Valet parking is available around the corner on Swan Street.

Japanese Steak House **$$**
479 North High Street
(614) 228-3030
This restaurant is exactly what Americans have come to expect from a Japanese hibachi house: eight people sitting around a table watching a show of chopping, dicing, and flying knives, while heaping piles of chicken, steak, and shrimp are grilled right before their eyes. Some folks prefer the fried rice or salads, and there is also a limited sushi menu, but it is safe to say everyone comes for the entertainment. If it's your birthday, you will, at the urging of management, receive a side-grabbing performance of "Happy Birthday" from everyone in the vicinity. Reservations are recommended on weekends and for larger groups.

Kooma **$$**
37 Vine Street
(614) 224-3239
One doesn't normally use the words *industrial* and *cozy* in the same breath, but Kooma is definitely both. The minimalist, stripped down approach to the decor of this tiny restaurant is given an element of warmth with its earth tones and friendly staff. The trendy fusion of Korean and Japanese cuisine is a perfect fit with the trendy atmosphere. Sushi fans can belly up to the bar for an artful chirashi or any number of traditional rolls. The regular menu includes creative noodle and hibachi dishes, but leave room for the fish ice cream: a vanilla ice cream cone shaped like a fish. Techno music is played until midnight on the weekend, so expect to encounter the trendiest of trendies at this time.

i

Dine and park for $3.00 in the Arena District's Marconi Garage at 245 Marconi Boulevard. Dine in an Arena District restaurant, and present your receipt (of $15 or more) to the parking attendant within two hours of entering the garage and pay only $3.00. You will pay the hourly rate for parking in excess of two hours.

SHORT NORTH

Benevolence A Cafe **$**
41 West Swan Street
(614) 221-9330
www.benevolencecafe.com
This throwback to the '60s era of vegetarian cafes lives up to its name, as donations from this "conscientious cuisine" go toward the Highland's Nature Sanctuary. Besides, what vegetarian could turn up a nose to earthy salads, soups, and bread made from scratch? The daily offerings are posted on a board, and many of the ingredients used are organic. The bread alone is a meal, but save a hunk to sop up some hearty soup. Dining is laid back and communal, so "Peace, love and happy eating!"

Betty's Fine Food and Spirits **$$**
680 North High Street
(614) 228-6191
www.bettysfoodandspirits.com
Betty's is eclectic the whole way around.

The patrons are as varied and interesting as the West Coast–inspired menu and decor. This is one place a sailfish leaping across the back wall doesn't seem out of place. A bevy of Betty Boop and animal figurines live above the bar, while retro-chic girlie posters adorn the walls. But make no mistake: Betty's is named for the owner and not Miss Boop.

The menu's unique pastas, hearty sandwiches, and vegetarian dishes are well priced for the budget minded. The mac and cheese is divine, the meatloaf is filling, and the burgers have people talking. A word of advice: There are only about a dozen tables, so there may be a long wait on busy evenings. This should be no bother, seeing as you can pass the time at the bar sampling the large selection of odd microbrews on draft or opt for a refreshing Betty Ford Clinic Special: lemonade with a shot of Finlandia vodka.

Haiku Poetic Food and Art $$$
800 North High Street
(614) 294-8168

Feeling poetic? Art abounds in several forms at this Japanese restaurant. Changing exhibitions of local artists grace the walls. If this isn't enough to inspire you to write your own haiku, then perhaps the food is. The menu has 15 types of noodle dishes and other pan-Asian fare, but regulars come here for the fish. The sushi bar is larger than most in Columbus and has individual tables, with a flat-screen TV playing underwater scenes. The small dining room is elegant and Zen-like, with both traditional low benches and regular seating. A polished wait staff serves the inventive and artistic fish dishes. The partially covered outdoor patio faces High Street and hosts live music during the summer months, while jazzy electronic-type music is played inside on weekends. Haiku has an overall hip and laid-back vibe to it.

The Happy Greek Restaurant and Pub $
660 North High Street
(614) 463-1111
www.happygreek.com

If the architectural details around the bar and the wall murals don't give away the Mediterranean theme of this restaurant, the menu with 25 specialties from all over Greece will. The pita sandwiches are very popular, as are the Greek salads. The restaurant serves traditional kebabs, moussaka, and several interesting vegetarian dishes in a casual and relaxed setting. It's no surprise the wine list features Greek wines. Sit at a table in the front window and gawk at passersby on High Street, or spend time gawking at the beautiful dessert case. You can't go wrong with either. Some say this is Columbus's Greek food at its best.

L'Antibes Classic French Cuisine $$$
772 North High Street
(614) 291-1666
www.lantibes.com

The French take their eating seriously, and it's no different here. Classic French fare such as foie gras, escargot, lamb, and seasonal contemporary dishes come together on this Francophile's dream menu. The chef is known, however, for his veal sweetbreads. With extremely high ratings in the *Zagat's* survey, L'Antibes lives up to every expectation, as does the wine list, which received an award of excellence from *Wine Spectator*.

The lacquered art deco–style chairs and subdued colored walls give the restaurant a restrained, modern elegance. The menu and atmosphere are a true demonstration of "less is more." Don't wait for a special occasion to indulge in a brilliant French dinner in one of Columbus's most romantic settings. The small size of this restaurant (about 15 tables) allows for very personalized service but also necessitates advance reservations. L'Antibes is closed Sunday and Monday and offers valet parking.

Lemongrass an Asian Bistro $$
641 North High Street
(614) 224-1414
www.lemongrassbistro.net

East meets West meets NYC at this industro-funky restaurant. A big-city, modern ambience serves as the setting for the American-Thai fusion cuisine. Popular options include pad thai, sate with peanut sauce, and an extensive selection of sushi. Vegetarians love Lemongrass for their meatless entrees, while the Lemongrass salad comes highly recommended by everyone. In keeping with the artsy spirit of the Short North, exhibitions are rotated through the restaurant on a monthly basis, and live music is regularly offered in the piano court. The stylish bar is a little claustrophobic but a good locale for people watching—when you can get a seat.

Northstar Cafe **$$**
941 North High Street
(614) 298-9999
www.thenorthstarcafe.com
Focusing on locally grown, organic products and healthy preparation, Northstar serves the healthiest, albeit nontraditional, brunch in town. Among the more popular offerings are the Cloud-9 pancakes with ricotta and Ohio maple syrup and the smoked turkey hash. Brunch and lunch may require a bit of a wait, but this only speaks to Northstar's booming popularity. It is also open for dinner and offers a limited selection of alcoholic beverages. With floor-to-ceiling windows and a generous outdoor patio, this cafe is no greasy spoon—so don't anticipate greasy spoon prices. As one of Columbus's best new restaurants in 2004, you *can* expect a vegetarian-friendly menu that supports local farmers and tastes great too.

R. J. Snappers Bar and Grill **$$$**
700 North High Street
(614) 280-1070
www.rjsnappersrestaurant.com
R. J. Snapper's motto, "Seafood with Imagination," speaks to its inventive menu, making it *the* place to get seafood in the Short North. A few menu items are pricey, but if you love seafood, you are guaranteed a memorable meal—especially if you splurge on the lobster Savannah. It's not often one can have all the meat from a pound and a half lobster without having to work for it. Even the most basic fish dishes are served up with some ingenuity.

Meat eaters are accommodated with a nice selection of aged steaks, lamb, and chicken, and the "wow" factor is not lost on these nonseafood dishes. The bar is pretty small and seems more a place to wait for your table than a bar to stay and drink all night. But if you choose to hang out at the bar, the people are friendly, and the wall murals alone are enough to hold your interest. They are painted to simulate stucco buildings with balconies and stone walls, reminiscent of an Italian seaside village. There is a definite nautical theme running throughout the restaurant, but the inhabitants of the fish tank are not on the menu. A nice touch is the complimentary valet parking.

Rigsby's Cuisine Volatile **$$$**
698 North High Street
(614) 461-7888
www.rigsbyscuisinevolatile.com
Rigsby's has been creating edible art since 1986 and is consistently rated among the top handful of restaurants in Columbus. Innovation has been present here from the start. The open kitchen behind the marble bar was the first of its kind in Columbus, while the evolving menu consists of intriguing, cutting-edge American cuisine with Italian and French overtones. Rather than offering one or two signature dishes, Rigsby's creates critically acclaimed signature *food.*

There is always something on the menu for both the curious and the less adventuresome, but when forced to pick a standout, the seafood cioppini is a brilliant house specialty that gets rave reviews. The classic bouillabaisse is always on the menu and contributes to Rigsby's outstanding ratings from *Zagat's.* The Eleni-Christina Bakery provides the bread, of which the sourdough is particularly popular. Rigsby's draws crowds for both the power lunch and sophisticated dinners, so dress for a chic and classy dining experience. There is live music on the weekends, and complimentary valet parking is provided.

VICTORIAN VILLAGE

Basi Italia **$$**
811 Highland Street
(614) 294-7383
www.basi-italia.com
This little gem of Victorian Village is deceivingly simple as you enter from an alley-like street, but what was formerly Pizza Pete's is now an intimate little trattoria serving knockout Italian food. The attention is not to decor but to food and service. It is upscale food without the stuffiness associated with fine dining—perhaps the Italian hospitality takes the edge off. The menu is wide-ranging, but the more popular items are grilled ribeye, spaghetti puttanesca, and, of course, the gelato. Some say they serve the best margherita pizza in town. Basi Italia is worth seeking out, but it's closed Sunday and Monday.

Cafe Apropos **$**
443 West Third Avenue
(614) 294-5282
This unassuming corner shop is a classy little cafe with its own is micro-roaster on site. They roast just enough coffee for a few days, so you are guaranteed a fresh cup of joe to go with that bagel or muffin. There's a small selection of snacks, and customers are provided with wireless Internet, so you'll often find tables full of diligent folk hammering away at their computers. If you're looking for adult beverages, there's a wine shop on-site, but alcohol isn't served in the cafe.

Dragonfly neo V Cuisine **$$**
247 King Avenue
(614) 298-9986
www.dragonflyneov.com
Colorful, bold, daring, and *flavorful* are a few of the words used to describe Dragonfly's strictly vegetarian menu. In fact, *USA Today* rated it one of the 10 best vegetarian restaurants in the country. Do not come expecting a hippie, tofu-eating crowd. The menu is exactly as the name implies: neo v(egan) cuisine, so nonvegetarians are pleasantly surprised to find complex and inventive flavors not normally associated with vegetarian and vegan dining.

Mushroom Wellington and jerk vegetable pizza are just two reasons you won't miss the meat here. The owners use organic ingredients from local sources, and even the wine and beer are organic. The menus change seasonally but remain ever fresh and inventive. The daring food is coupled with a serene and somewhat enchanting ambience. The annex hosts changing exhibitions by local artists.

Estrada's Mexican Restaurant and Cantina **$**
240 King Avenue
(614) 294-3065
With its colorfully painted walls, this cheery eatery is less Americanized than a lot of other Mexican restaurants in Columbus. You'll find students and local denizens throwing down monster burritos and overindulging in Coronas and pitchers of margaritas. It's extremely crowded on weekends and on the patio during summer months, but this (and plastic palm trees) only adds to the festivities. Though near campus and very popular among students, the restaurant instructs patrons in certain "behavioral" and "cleanliness" rules to ensure a jovial but civil dining experience. If you don't mind furnishings that are a bit rough around the edges, you'll find that the food and friendly atmosphere more than make up for the tattered furniture and springs poking through your seat. Estrada's accepts the student BuckID.

Spinelli's Deli **$**
767 Neil Avenue
(614) 586-0408
www.spinellisdeli.com
Forget the Golden Arches! Go for the more personal touch with fresh-baked pastries, breads, and bagels seven days a week at this simple Victorian Village neighborhood deli. Along with a creative deli sandwich, you will get a good dose of per-

sonality. It's open for breakfast and lunch, and there are fun seasonal menu options.

THE OHIO STATE UNIVERSITY AREA

Alana's **$$$**
2333 North High Street
(614) 294-6783
www.alanas.com

Adventurous diners, rejoice! Slightly north of campus is a truly edgy and innovative restaurant with a lot of "Shock factor." The Alana Shock factor, that is. This chef (and co-owner) opened Alana's Food and Wine in 1999 after developing her art form at several reputable restaurants, including Emeril's in New Orleans.

Alana's menu has cleverly named dishes, such as "paprika smitten tiger shrimp seared with lemon, sherry and love," which sounds straight from a romance novel. Fearless types leave themselves open to the whims of the master chef by ordering the degustation, a series of small courses paired with the appropriate wines. Alana's self-proclaimed "food of love" is ever changing and has a diverse, global panache to it.

Like the menu, the decor is eclectic and sophisticated. Tight table placement, dark wood, and fun artwork lend a definite French brasserie quality to the dining room and bar (which is small). A European-style cafe is also readily felt outdoors on the multileveled patio. The upper area is covered with an awning for outdoor dining in iffy weather, while the open street-level patio has a privacy wall covered in plants and white lights. It's difficult to nail Alana's down in words, so just try it out for yourself. It's closed Sunday and Monday.

Bento Go-Go **$**
1728 North High Street
(614) 298-8817
www.bentogogo.com

Eat in or grab and go from this industro-modern campus eatery. It's also located close enough to the Oval and many academic buildings to squeeze in a proper lunch between classes. Bento Go-Go is one of the few places on campus with an outdoor patio. It's an entertaining spot to indulge in a healthy lunch and watch people along High Street. The noodle dishes and wraps are affordably priced, and the bento boxes and sushi are the most popular menu items. They serve beer, sake, and a refreshing Thai iced tea. The BuckID is accepted here.

Blue Danube **$**
2439 North High Street
(614) 261-9308

This local institution, the "Dube," as it is affectionately known, might draw "Dube"ious looks at first glance. It's a bit grungy, cigarette smoke has settled into the very fabric of the building, and the music can get quite loud, but it is a campus dining experience through and through. The Dube has been open since 1940 and draws a mixed crowd of Ohio State students, gothic types, and neighborhood locals looking for mostly American-Greek comfort food at decent prices.

Blue Nile Ethiopian Restaurant **$**
2361 North High Street
(614) 421-2323
www.ethiopiancuisine.com

Super hospitality greets you at the door of the Blue Nile, allowing one's first Ethiopian dining experience to be far less intimidating than it might seem. Upon entering this storefront restaurant, one quickly learns another language and culture. You will be asked if you prefer to sit at an American table or around the *mosseb,* a low table accommodating a community platter. It should be known that eating from the same plate is socially significant, as it creates a bond of loyalty and friendship.

Order the injera (spongy crepe-like bread) to gather up chicken or lamb cooked in Berber sauce (spicy red pepper sauce) and gomen (collard greens and potatoes). Then, forget all the rules about not eating with your hands. It is traditional to scoop up the food with your bread and eat this hearty cuisine with your fingers. Ethiopian pictures and instruments decorate the walls, while understated Ethiopian music plays in the background. There is also a lunch buffet with a variety of meat and vegetable dishes to choose from.

El Vaquero **$**
3230 Olentangy River Road
multiple locations
(614) 261-0900
www.elvaquerorestaurants.com
The mostly Mexican/Spanish speaking staff has fooled many a local into thinking this restaurant is a "mom and pop" shop, but the fact that it is corporate owned does not diminish the quality and authenticity of the (authentically Americanized) Mexican food. You can find every combination of tortillas, tacos, burritos, meat, beans, and rice you can dream of somewhere in the 160 menu options. Be careful not to fill up on the complimentary chips and salsa, as the servers will diligently replenish the baskets as they pass by. This classic Mexican fare comes at rock-bottom prices, but definitely divert your savings into the house margarita. It is well worth the extra money. The two other El Vaquero locations are in Upper Arlington and Worthington.

Jack & Benny's **$**
2563 North High Street
(614) 263-0242
The exterior of this hash house is no more than a basic storefront with a small sign, but the packed booths and throngs of hungry (often hung over) people willing to wait outside on the sidewalk for a table is a sign of what is inside: friendly service and friendly food. This greasy spoon is the campus favorite for pancakes, omelets, and a la carte breakfasts for the shoestring budget. Good luck getting a table; all I can suggest is patience. Lunch is served after 11:00 A.M. during the week.

Moy's Chinese Restaurant **$**
1994 North High Street
(614) 297-7722
It is a consensus among OSU students that Moy's is the best Chinese food on campus. This authentic restaurant has been operated for 30 years by a couple from Hong Kong and is always packed with students, faculty, and locals who know about the great food at takeout prices. The service is consistently good and the place is clean, given its prime location on the main drag of America's largest university campus.

Tajmahal **$$**
2247 North High Street
(614) 294-0208
www.tajmahalcolumbus.com
Some 20 years ago Tajmahal Indian and Pakistani Cuisine became Columbus's first Indian restaurant. After a recent proliferation in South Asian eateries, it has maintained its position as one of the most beloved. Tajmahal reopened in 2004 as a strictly vegetarian restaurant while its sister, Taj-II, just up the street at 2321 North High Street, serves the gamut of meat and vegetarian dishes. Taj-II also has a daily lunch buffet and generous outdoor patio. Tajmahal's location, just north of campus, looks a little run-down, but it is safe and worth the trip. Call ahead for reservations, as it is small and seating is limited. Also, give yourself time to find street parking. This is campus, after all.

CLINTONVILLE/BEECHWOLD

Aladdin's Eatery **$**
2931 North High Street
(614) 262-2414
www.aladdinseatery.com
This quiet, casual eatery, just north of campus, draws a student crowd as well as neighborhood regulars. Aladdin's serves healthy, inexpensive Middle Eastern food, so healthy, you won't feel guilty racing for the amazing dessert case as soon as you finish your meal. Hummus, tabouli, and falafel are among the standard fare, while pita pockets filled with just about anything are the house specialties. Aladdin's serves freshly squeezed fruit juice and has

one of the most extensive tea lists in town. "Eat healthy. Eat good" is its motto, and one can do both in this environmentally friendly restaurant. A second location is on Grandview Avenue.

Dante's Pizza **$**
3586 Indianola Avenue
(614) 268-5090

This well-known local pizza parlor is found in an unassuming, outdated strip mall, but the homemade pasta and thin, crispy pizza make it the unofficial-official favorite among Clintonville residents. You can taste wine in the sauce and garlic in the sausage. 'Te's, as it is affectionately nicknamed, also serves the usual, fried pub grub. Don't expect much in the way of atmosphere. You can eat in and have drinks at one the few tables, but the paneled dining area is small and practically indistinguishable from the kitchen. There's nothing fancy about Dante's, which is probably why the locals like it so much.

Nancy's Home Cooking **$**
3133 North High Street
(614) 265-9012

This hole-in-the-wall has been a Clintonville landmark since the 1960s and the prices (and decor) haven't changed much either. The only thing that changes is the menu—daily. It's a homey place where you take a seat at the cramped counter (or small booths) and chow. Regulars sometimes serve themselves their own beverages. There is some semblance of a breakfast menu painted on the wall, but most likely you're eating whatever is being served.

Regular breakfast items are French toast and the garbage omelet. Lunch is equally simple, typically no more than two, home-cooked entrees to choose from, like meatloaf or burgers. People come here for the conversation and camaraderie—and the chicken noodle soup, so don't be surprised if it runs out. *Zagat's* has rated Nancy's as a top value restaurant, not to mention it has been highlighted on television shows and in national newspapers and magazines. It's common for both students and locals to frequent this diner.

Rube's Diner **$**
4408 Indianola Avenue
(614) 261-9846

In this health-crazed day and age, it's refreshing to find a good old-fashioned diner: linoleum floors, the smell of grease in the air, ceiling fans circulating secondhand smoke. It could well be the greasiest of all greasy spoons, but you gotta love it. Rube's is open only for breakfast and lunch and is a throwback to the days when cholesterol, fat, and smoking at breakfast were perfectly acceptable. The weekend service is usually quick and good, but take heed if you want something special, as your request might be met with a raised eyebrow.

Unless you order water, you will find nothing diet about this place. Clean freaks probably shouldn't come here either, as the decor is a bit "charming"—in a beat-up, lived-in sort of way. There is no question, however, that you will be served excellent home-style food at really good prices. The emphasis is on eggs, with an endless list of omelets and variations on the fried or scrambled. So, take a deep breath and go clog some arteries!

Talita's **$**
2977 North High Street
(614) 262-6000

Columbus's first Mexican restaurant is a small, family-owned shop with an emphasis on good food and personable service. The dining room is casual, with its tables, booths, and hodgepodge of stuff from south-of-the-border hanging around. The menu has the usual Mexican fare, as well as pastas and sandwiches. They also serve beer and mixed drinks. Talita's might well be the cheapest Mexican restaurant in town, with most meals averaging about $6.00, while takeout gets you an additional 10 percent discount.

Turkish Cuisine $
2653 North High Street
(614) 447-9222
Just north of campus is yet another ethnic eatery of the Mediterranean type. This modest but well-maintained storefront restaurant offers a menu laden with reasonably priced Turkish cuisine. Turkish starters, kebabs, pastries, and coffee are among the offerings. Even the stuffed cabbage is given a Turkish twist. The service is very friendly and the food is a great value, enough so *Columbus Monthly* included it among its best new restaurants in 2004.

Villa Nova Ristorante $$
5545 North High Street
(614) 846-5777
Villa Nova has been a Clintonville staple since the 1970s, and the proof is in the food, which remains an assortment of old-time Italian entrees and bar food. The restaurant is family-friendly, as are the prices. They offer good happy hour specials with a complimentary food buffet for those who patronize the bar. The nosh may be good, but this place is more about ambience—and, boy, do you get it. The walls are packed with enough memorabilia to cause a sensory overload. License plates, posters, and copper pots are among the eclectic and continuously growing collection. It's just a fun neighborhood place where the line between restaurant and bar is blurry—especially after happy hour.

Whole World Pizza and Bakery $
3269 North High Street
(614) 268-5751
This is not a place to go when you are in a hurry. Columbus's oldest vegetarian restaurant is a bustling little cafe where healthy New Age types can be found enjoying a broccoli burger or tofu scramble served at a very leisurely pace. A number of different pizza toppings allow for creative combinations, and the Greek spinach pizza is a favorite among regulars. Vegan dishes are on the regular menu and turn up as an occasional daily special. But fair warning, not everything listed on the menu is available everyday, so have a backup selection ready, just in case. Their soups and sandwiches come highly recommended.

WORTHINGTON

Anatolia Cafe $$
1097 Worthington Woods Boulevard
Worthington Crosswoods
(614) 781-0700
www.anatoliacafe.net
If you have kebabs on the brain, this cozy Turkish restaurant will suit your needs. The menu has over a dozen different types to choose from, such as gyro, shish, chicken, and lamb, as well as hummus, grape leaves, and other Mediterranean delights. Checkered tablecloths and hanging rugs add a lot to the interior ambience of this simple yet well-reviewed storefront eatery.

Bravo! Cucina Italia $$
7470 Vantage Drive, Worthington Crosswoods
(614) 888-3881
The faux columns and painted plaster may only simulate Roman ruins, but the food is 100 percent Italian. Bravo! is not unlike an authentic Italian bistro. It is a spacious, active restaurant with good service, reflecting how well staffed it is. The large bar is a popular place for the over-40s of Columbus to mix and mingle and is a fun people-watching place.

People travel far and wide for Bravo's pasta and wood-fired pizzas. There is no shortage of pine nuts, sundried tomatoes, and mushrooms on the menu. Wine racks are stacked to the ceiling, showing off the nice selection of bottles, and there's a seasonal outdoor patio. Though Bravo is a local franchise, with restaurants popping up in other states, it's an inspired place. The other location, Bravo! Italian Kitchen, at 3000 Hayden Road, (614-791-1245), carries the same menu and has an outdoor patio.

CLOSE-UP

Cameron Mitchell: Redefining Columbus Dining

No one can pass through Columbus without encountering the name Cameron Mitchell. This ambitious restaurateur has taken dining in Columbus to new levels beginning in 1993 with Cameron's American Bistro. The Mitchell empire has grown to include 22 restaurants in 11 different cities. This book typically does not include chains, but with 13 restaurants located here in Columbus, a great disservice would be done not to include the Upper Arlington native in this chapter. Even more importantly, you will not be disappointed with the individuality of each place and the consistently high quality of food and service.

Cameron's American Bistro $$$
2185 West Dublin-Granville Road
Linworth
(614) 885-3663

Cameron Mitchell's flagship restaurant remains innovative even after 12 years. The atmosphere around the art deco bar is intimate and cozy, while the restaurant is romantic and comfortable. If you visit the newer Mitchell restaurants, Cameron's may seem a bit passé, but one look at the menu and you'll know there is nothing outdated about this place. There's a nice wine list, and it's popular with the over-30 set.

Cap City Fine Diner & Bar $$
1301 Stone Ridge Drive, Gahanna

1299 Olentangy River Road
Grandview Heights
(614) 478-9999, (614) 291-3663

Despite the high-back booths, shiny chrome, and mirrors, these diners are no greasy spoons. Bright colors and pop art murals give the Finer Diners an updated retro ambience. As for the food, who knew meatloaf would ever be considered fine dining? Leave it to Cameron Mitchell to make the most sophisticated of comfort food.

Columbus Brewing Company $$
525 Short Street, Brewery District
(614) 464-2739

Wood-fired pizzas, hefty sandwiches, and ale-friendly fare are among the choices at Cameron Mitchell's Brewery District restaurant. Catch a glimpse of the microbrewery in action from the wood-paneled dining room, or enjoy one of their seasonal brews on the open-air patio. The bar service is usually pretty quick, and unlike most other Mitchell Restaurants, they have good happy hour specials. Tours of the Columbus Brewing Company are available upon request.

Columbus Fish Market $$$
1245 Olentangy River Road, Grandview

40 Hutchinson Avenue, Worthington Crosswoods
(614) 291–3474, (614) 410–3474
Spongebob Squarepants doesn't have anything on the aquatic-inspired decor in Mitchell's two casual seafood restaurants. Blue underwater murals grace the walls around the bar, while wooden booths and lobster tanks gives them a distinct New England–style chowder house flair. Though casual in nature, the Fish Market is not cheap. You will, however, find one of the biggest selections of fresh seafood that Columbus has to offer, as well as a little bit of everything else on the menu, including steaks and pasta. Like many of Mitchell's restaurants, an understated Asian theme runs throughout the menu.

M $$$$
2 Mironova Place, downtown
(614) 629–0000
Talk about a first impression! Luxurious, dramatic, and upscale are a few words that come to mind when you first enter Mitchell's marquee restaurant, M. It is located on the first level of the Miranova building and has views of the Scioto riverfront and the Columbus skyline. M is sophisticated and trendsetting in both its decor and menu. Sheer fabric and funky, kinetic lighting make for a theatrical atmosphere, but its ambience is upstaged by a truly cutting-edge global cuisine that has earned the restaurant critical acclaim in its brief existence. A night out at M can be painful to the pocketbook, but you are paying for an experience you can't have anywhere else in Columbus. M typically attracts the "style set," posttheatergoers, and on Saturday evenings it becomes Columbus's premier late-night lounge.

Martini Italian Bistro $$$
445 North High Street, Arena District

1319 Polaris Parkway, Westerville
(614) 224–8259, (614) 844-6500
Martini's is a flashy sort of place that lures the fashionable types in after a hard day's work, the downtown location particularly. Its art deco bar is full of carousing professionals pounding hard liquor, while the Westerville location is a bit more subtle. The wine list is extensive, and, as the name suggests, they serve nearly 20 kinds of martinis. The food isn't bad either. The menu includes contemporary Italian dishes and is often among the top-10 Italian restaurants in Columbus.

Mitchell's Steakhouse $$$$
45 North Third Street at Gay Street downtown

7619 Huntington Park Drive, Worthington Crosswoods
(614) 621–2333, (614) 888–2467
Cameron Mitchell's New York–style steakhouses are a class act and can hold their own next to any big-city chophouse. The downtown location is in a beautiful, renovated bank building, and its subtle lighting,

burnished wood, and soaring ceilings provide one of the most atmospheric settings in town. The Crosswoods location has more of an elegant supper club ambience, with sunken floors and live piano music. Both have equally impressive menus loaded with dry-aged and prime steaks, lobster, and a wine list to die for. After one experience you'll understand why so many local carnivores say Mitchell's Steakhouse is their favorite restaurant.

Molly Woo's Asian Bistro **$$**
Polaris Fashion Place
(614) 985-9667
Who knew a restaurant with a mall location could be voted Columbus's Best Asian Restaurant? Cameron Mitchell, no doubt. His Asian-themed Molly Woo's is very Oriental, to say the least. Giant red lanterns hang from the industrial ceilings, and Chinese sculpture and ceramics fill in all the nooks and crannies. This spacious, bamboo-accented restaurant is filled with businesspeople at lunch and shoppers at dinner—and with good reason. The food is artistic and tasty. Sushi and firecracker chicken are among the menu items, but the spring roll was voted Best in Columbus in 2004. Patio and bar seating are also available.

The Ocean Club **$$$**
Easton Town Center
(614) 416-2582
Mitchell's upscale seafood restaurant is totally nautilus, from the cobalt blue floor to the shell ceiling and optic lighting. You'll have an underwater experience from the moment you set foot in the door. The bar is partially enclosed in glass, fishbowl style. Most of the menu consists of inventive seafood dishes and exotic fish flown in from all corners of the world. The Ocean Club offers a dining experience that shouldn't be rushed, and with this attitude, the somewhat slow (but impeccable) service can be overlooked. The Ocean Club is a must for any seafood lover visiting Columbus.

China Dynasty **$$**
1930 East Dublin-Granville Road
(614) 523-2008
www.chinadynasty-cmh.com
This award-winning restaurant serves high-end Hunan, Cantonese, and Szechuan cuisine and has been voted Columbus's number 1 Chinese restaurant every year since 1999. Traditional Chinese fare can be found alongside more creative dishes. Favorites include crispy shrimp with walnuts and General Tso's chicken, while lo mein noodles, a symbol of longevity in China, are among the more popular dishes. Everything here is made from scratch and there is a strong emphasis on presentation.

You will be served pretty food in a pretty atmosphere, as intricate screens, fresh greenery, and rich colors add elegance to the ambience. This restaurant is a great option for the family, as there are set combination meals that will feed several hungry people at a good price. The other location is in the recently renovated Lane Avenue Shopping Center (614-486-7126) in Upper Arlington, and the Sunday buffet is a steal.

Hunan House Gourmet Chinese Dining **$$**
2350 East Dublin-Granville Road
(614) 895-3330
Szechuan, Hunan, and Mandarin dishes are the specialties turned out at this extremely popular Chinese restaurant. This sophisticated sit-down restaurant has marble lions keeping guard over the large, elegant dining room and is the antithesis of the typical fast-food Chinese joint. Menu favorites are Szechuan and Hunan anything, but the overall quality and magnificent presentation of the food draw people from all over central Ohio. There are two other locations called Hunan Lion, one in Gahanna and the other on Bethel Road, which are just as good.

Hyde Park Prime Steakhouse **$$$**
55 Hutchinson Boulevard, Worthington Crosswoods
(614) 438-1000
www.hydeparkgrille.com
The Hyde Park Group's attempted "go" at seafood, the Metropolitan Seafood Grill, has metamorphosed into another steak lover's paradise. They kept some of the Metropolitan's more popular seafood dishes on the current menu, but when it comes to red meat, Hyde Park tops the list of steakhouses in Columbus.

You'll find daily specials as well as the standard Hyde Park selection of beef dishes named for Ohio sports figures. One of the longtime favorites is Steak Kosar (filet mignon topped with lobster, béarnaise sauce, and vegetables), while Steak Tressel (New York strip with roasted garlic and mushrooms), which has come onto the menu more recently, is also popular. The a la carte side dishes are portioned large enough to serve two, and the sides are more interesting than the usual baked potato or rice.

This is the third Hyde Park in Columbus, but as they say, three's a charm. Anyone familiar with the other two will notice this steakhouse is a lot larger but has the same comfort and offers the same fantastic service. You can pick from about 75 wines by the glass, but if you can't decide on just one, get a flight. You shouldn't wait until a special occasion to try out any one of the Hyde Park restaurants.

La Chatelaine French Bakery and Bistro **$**
627 High Street, Olde Worthington
(614) 848-6711
Some might consider the casual bistro food "French Dining 101," but the pastries and breads are masterful. If you have ever been to Paris, you have probably stood with your nose pressed against a bakery window, gazing in awe at the rows of edible art. You'll do that here. Newcomers "oooh" and "ahhh" at the fruit-topped tortes and bulging eclairs, while regulars drive out of their way to have La Chatelaine's baked goods.

It isn't at all unusual to find people munching only a baguette along with a cup of coffee or sharing intimate conversation over a bottle of wine. Full breakfasts and lunches are served cafeteria style, while a refined dinner menu and table service add a formal touch to the otherwise light and airy, French countryside-inspired bistro. There's an outdoor patio, which is open seasonally, as well as a second location on Lane Avenue in Arlington that also has a patio.

Pasta Petite **$**
6096 Boardwalk Street, just off Busch Boulevard
(614) 436-4066
Mamma mia! This is a classic example of the strip-mall pastaria serving good, solid Italian food from a simple storefront eatery. It's all about options here. They serve a huge selection of pastas and pizzas, which can be ordered by the slice or full pie and is available in three different crusts. Salads also come in three different sizes to suit your appetite, while wraps satisfy the carb-conscious. Even the bruschetta comes in a variety of options. The pasta is al dente, and the service is

friendly. Order at the counter, and the food is served at your table. Eating in should be the first option, but they will make anything to go.

Spain Restaurant $$
888 East Dublin-Granville Road
(614) 840-9100
Who knew a restaurant in a Best Western hotel could serve the most authentic Spanish (not to be confused with Mexican or Latin) food in town? And it's good! The chef is from Spain and highlights dishes from the Galician region, which means garlic and saffron fill the air. The menu has a few pasta dishes but is meat and seafood intensive. Wash down the acclaimed paella and exceptional veal with some Spanish or Portuguese wine. For you thirstier types, try a pitcher of the homemade sangria before trying your hand at salsa. The weekends bring sexy dancers to the dance floor for Latino Nights.

The Worthington Inn
and Seven Stars Restaurant $$$
649 High Street, Olde Worthington
(614) 885-2600
www.worthingtoninn.com
This four-star inn and restaurant is highlighted in a Close-up near the end of the Accommodations chapter. The venerable Seven Star Restaurant is consistently ranked as one of Columbus's favorite dining spots and serves highly imaginative food in an intimate and friendly atmosphere. This is truly a one-of-a-kind dining experience in Columbus.

WESTERVILLE

Carsonie's Restaurant $
6000 Westerville Road
(614) 899-6700
Bocce, anyone? Carsonie's is about as well known for its bocce court as for its strombolis. Once you satisfy your hunger with huge portions of pasta or the unusual Italian fries, you can satiate your competitiveness with a game of bocce on the fenced-in patio. This family-friendly restaurant even has an outdoor sandbox for the kids.

Nazareth Restaurant & Deli $
5663 Emporium Square,
Cleveland Avenue and Route 161
(614) 899-1177
www.nazarethdeli.com
It may take some effort to find this out-of-the-way storefront deli, but it's definitely worth seeking out for its authentic Middle Eastern food and genuine hospitality. Don't let the baseball bat-brandishing proprietor scare you off! He's a friendly fellow—really—and you will not have to lie when he comes around (bat in hand) asking how the food is. They serve up (above average tasting) traditional fare such as hummus, falafel, tabouli, and shawarma for lunch and feature grape leaves and kebabs in several different sizes for dinner. The tables and booths are comfortable, and the ambience is pleasant. It can be busy at lunch, so call ahead for takeout, and be patient with the service.

Pasquale's Pizza & Pasta House $
14 North State Street
(614) 882-6200
Westerville's answer to pizza pie lies just around the corner and in the somewhat evasive side door of this building. Just follow the arrow painted on the window. The popularity of this pizzeria lies in the details. The sweet sauce-covered crust is loaded with toppings. The staff is service oriented and well known for their ability to get special orders right the first time. The restaurant is casual and homey feeling. It's well suited for a family dinner; well priced for one too. They offer both delivery and takeout.

Polaris Grill $$
1835 Polaris Parkway
(614) 431-5598
www.polarisgrill.com
The defunct 55 Restaurant group has semi-reincarnated itself as Polaris Grill and still serves some of 55's popular menu

items alongside newer, more innovative American dishes. Pasta, grilled chops, and blackened chicken are among the entrees, while barbecued rib tips and Aztec chowder are the newer appetizers.

In keeping with 55 tradition, the belly-busting Sunday brunch offers the usual carving stations, Belgian waffles, and a variety of fruits, breads, and brunch-type foods. Similar to the original 55, it's a casual restaurant with spacious booths and tables. It is often filled with business people during the week, giving it a dressier atmosphere than it has on the weekends.

Udipi Cafe **$**
2001 East Dublin-Granville Road
(614) 885-7446

This strictly vegetarian restaurant is generally packed full of Indians, which is a telling sign of the southern Indian fare being served. The well-worn carpeting and plain leather booths give the restaurant a lived-in look, but the staggering number of dosa options will quickly divert your attention away from the simple decor.

The dosa, a thin crepe filled with potatoes and onions, is Udipi's specialty. One will also find above-average dal and curries on the menu. Although milk and butter are used in many dishes, no meat, fish, or eggs are to be found here. The reasonably priced lunch buffet is a good time to sample a variety of soups, curries, and vegetable offerings.

Westerville Grille **$**
59 South State Street
(614) 794-1900

This is yet another popular greasy spoon open for early breakfasts and catering to an ever-growing list of regulars. Sit in a cozy booth or belly up to the counter for the popular breakfast burrito, or fill up on the $5.00 blue-plate specials at lunch. The 'ville Grille serves a variety of home-style dinners such as Yankee pot roast and lumpless mashed potatoes, but the big seller is the fish-and-chips.

EASTON

Upscale chain restaurants such as Smith & Wollensky, the Cheesecake Factory, and Restaurant Hama abound at Easton Town Center, but there are a few locally owned restaurants that can hold their own next to these giants. Cameron Mitchell's extremely popular Ocean Club is also located here and is discussed in the Close-up earlier in this chapter.

Bon Vie Bistro & Bar **$$$**
4089 The Strand East
(614) 340-4222
www.bon-vie.com

Oh-la-la! As part of the Brio-Bravo-owned restaurant group, you know you will experience the "good life" here. The zinc-topped bar, tile floors, and tin ceilings give the restaurant an open and airy feeling, but it's the white table linens on intimately spaced tables that create a convincingly Parisian bistro ambience. A true Francophile, however, will realize the decor is far more French than the menu (aside from offering a plat du jour—special of the day).

Catering to a mainstream American palate, the menu draws inspiration from French cuisine, but that's about where it ends. The sauces and main entrees aren't quite as sophisticated or robust as true French cooking, but with this in mind, do come prepared for incredible French-influenced American food in a convivial Parisian atmosphere.

A few traditional dishes such as vichyssoise, salade Niçoise, and chicken cordon bleu are on the menu. There's a fine wine list, and Wednesday night is martini night. Bon Vie has been given the title of best martini in town. It also has a sidewalk cafe-style terrace that overlooks Easton's Central Park fountains for al fresco dining in the summer months.

Brio Tuscan Grille **$$$**
3993 Easton Station
(614) 416-4745
www.brio.com

Escape to the Tuscan countryside for a

few hours and find *la dolce vita* (the good life) at Brio. The innovative menu includes not only the heavy, red-sauced cuisine so often associated with Italian restaurants but also lighter grilled and seafood dishes inspired from all regions of Italy. Brio is as much a purveyor of steak and seafood as pastas.

The wood-fired ovens are used to roast steaks, fish, and chops as well as turn out gourmet pizzas and flatbreads. The ovens were actually imported from the homeland, and the decor simulates a sprawling Tuscan villa. Arches, columns, and palm trees break up the dining area, which is quite large, while mosaics, plaster walls, and earthy colors lend it intimacy. This upscale version of Bravo! Italian Kitchen opened in 1999, and like Bravo!, it rarely disappoints. Brio continues to leave an impression on Columbus visitors and locals.

Cafe Istanbul **$$**
3983 Worth Avenue, across from Nordstrom's
(614) 473-9144

Outstanding Turkish cuisine can be found in the part of Easton with the least amount of foot traffic. You'll enter into what resembles a Turkish bazaar and forget you are anywhere near the Easton sprawl. The red-and-white striped arches and iron chandeliers are most striking. Carpets, brass, and ceramic decorations scream of the Arabesque.

The bar is modern and minimalist, while the waiting area has traditional low tables at which to enjoy a glass of wine or Turkish coffee. Aside from the chic decor, the authentic and inspired food is what sets Cafe Istanbul apart from the dozens of other Mediterranean inspired restaurants in Columbus. The gastronomically curious will not be disappointed with anything on the menu, but there's also an extensive range of the familiar: hummus, falafel, and kebabs, just to name a few. The restaurant features Turkish wines, coffees and teas, and an outdoor patio.

NEW ALBANY/ GAHANNA AREA

Asian Gourmet and Sushi Bar **$$**
1325 Stone Ridge Drive
(614) 471-8871
www.asiangourmetandsushibar.com

Formerly known as China Gourmet, the restaurant moved and the name has been changed to reflect the addition of Thai, Korean, and Japanese cuisine, as well as a sushi bar. The chef's specials range from General Tso's, teriyaki, and sesame chicken to Thai curries. In terms of sushi, there's a wonderful selection of nigiri, sashimi, and more than a dozen types of rolls. The atmosphere is modern but comfortable for both individuals and families who can be accommodated at large tables. There's also a traditional tatami room for private dining.

Eagle Pizza **$**
2 North High Street
(614) 855-7600

Renovation to the exterior has classed up this family-style pastaria in typical New Albany fashion, with rich brick, stone sculptures, and a new roof, but New Albanyites still consider this the best deal in town. The casual atmosphere is seen in the fact that there are no regular menus, just a posting by the entrance. The fare is simple: pizzas, subs, and the very popular twice-baked spaghetti. It's a neighborhood eatery where patrons likely know one another and their children work here. The table service is good, but keep in mind they do not accept credit cards.

Gahanna Grille **$**
82 Granville Street
(614) 476-9017

So what if you have to fix a wobbly table with a few matchbooks under the leg, or the decorations consist of laminated advertisements for local businesses and pictures of people who have put away a Double Beanie burger? Locals don't come here for the ambience (or even the slow but friendly service). They come for the company of others who just like to hang out in a modest neighborhood restaurant—and they come for the burgers.

Those who live in these parts will swear on their lives the Gahanna Grill makes the best burgers. They certainly make one of the biggest! The Beanie burgers, loaded with toppings and slaw, are nothing compared to the Double Beanie, while the faint of heart can wimp out with the smaller Academy version. If you finish off a Double Beanie, you will get a free T-shirt and a picture of your mug on the wall. They also serve regular fried pub grub, soup, and salads, as well as a whole gamut of meat and seafood entrees.

Gahanna Pizza Plus **$**
106 Granville Street
(614) 428-9878

If you want some pizzazz in your pie, look no further. Taking first in the 2003 Mid-America Pizza Pizzazz and first in the 2002 Columbus Pizza Challenge, the Gahanna Pizza Plus crew must be doing something right. Their competitive costs and baker's dozen of specialty pies keep them popular among Gahanna and New Albany residents, so popular they've won first place three years in a row at the Taste of Gahanna. The crust is bready, and the tart sauce is visible through a thin layer of cheese. The most popular specialty pies are the mega meat and three mushroom pizzas, but there are more than 35 high-quality toppings to choose from if you prefer to create your own. If blue-ribbon pizza isn't your craving, subs and salads are also available. You can find discount coupons on the Web site.

Gibby's New Albany Grille **$$**
29 South High Street
(614) 775-0270

A more toned-down, family-oriented version of the popular Gibby's bars located in the former Olivia's. The building has been renovated to include booths, televisions, and a video-game room for the kids. New Albany village mementos adorn the walls and the menu has been tweaked to include a dozen new sandwiches and entrees. Gibby's is open seven days and week and the bar stays open late most nights.

BEXLEY

Bexley's Monk **$$$**
2232 East Main Street
(614) 239-6665
www.bexleysmonk.com

Bexley's Monk doesn't sit directly on Main Street. Use the Drexel Theatre as a landmark to find it in the adjacent shopping plaza. The restaurant has a parking lot, but if you're averse to walking 20 paces to the front door, valet parking is an option. The Monk draws the more mature, well-quaffed, heavily perfumed types looking for good food and good fun. The wood-paneled dining room is a warm and inviting place to have a quiet, romantic dinner, yet it exudes an air of formality. In contrast, the energetic bar, with its brass rails and tiled floor, is more spacious and has a bistro/jazz club atmosphere.

It is well known that people come here to be seen and to rendezvous, hence the recognition as one of the most romantic bars in town. Whether eating in the dining room or carousing at the bar, one has high visibility—especially if you take the stage on Mondays for open mike night. Don't worry, most nights of the week they leave the entertainment to the professionals. People come from all over town for the jazz and cigar smoking.

They come here to eat too. Bexley's Monk has topped Columbus's food critics' list every year since they opened in the early 1980s. The food is exemplary. Lots of pastas, lots of salads, creative seafood dishes like horseradish-encrusted scallops, and gourmet pizzas show a versatile and diverse kitchen. The Caribbean spiced shrimp appetizer is a favorite with regulars, while racks of lamb and filet mignon are some of the popular entrees. Full-course meals are served in the bar, and there's a wonderful selection of wines by the glass and top-shelf liquor.

Bexley Pizza Plus **$**
2540 East Main Street
(614) 237-3305
This family-owned carryout has been a Bexley staple for over 20 years. Bexley residents say it's the thick and chewy handmade crust, topped with tangy sauce, that makes this pizza so good. But it may also be the head-spinning number of toppings and gourmet combos such as Greek pizza. The pizza comes in two sizes, 12 and 16 inches, at dinner, and an 8-inch individual pie is another option at lunchtime. Subs, garlic bread, and salads are also available.

Fisherman's Wharf Pier I **$$$**
2143 East Main Street
(614) 236-0043
It's all in the name. If Fisherman's Wharf doesn't tell you what is served at this Bexley favorite, the nautical decor will. The mounted fish, model ships, and nautical gear that bedeck the entrance and a prow-shaped bar give this restaurant a smart, East Coast ambience. The tables are cozy and tightly placed, so don't expect privacy during dinner conversation. There's no water in sight, but in fishbowl fashion, the glass windows of the dining room face Main Street for clientele to watch the passersby—or vice versa.

Patrons aren't the only ones under observation; so is the chef. The entrees, which go well beyond the basic fish-and-chips, can be seen made from scratch in the open kitchen. The selection from under-the-sea ranges from shrimp and scallops to snapper and tuna. More unusual fish entrees include arctic char and Dover sole, and the Mediterranean-tinged chicken, lamb, and beef dishes give away the Greek owner's heritage. The Wharf is consistently ranked among Columbus's top restaurants.

Giuseppe's Ritrovo **$$**
2268 East Main Street
(614) 235-4300
The incredibly rich southern Italian cuisine is a telltale sign of the owner's roots in Calabria, and the creative (and occasionally fancy) daily specials clue you in to his days as a chef on a cruise liner. Ritrovo, which means "gathering place," is a storefront eatery that captures the essence of Italy with its black-and-white photography on the walls and the homemade food. Egg pasta is handmade daily using traditional Italian techniques, and the sauces are varied. The spinach rollati (rolled lasagna noodles stuffed with spinach and four cheeses) is the house favorite. The interior is cozy, and the bar is friendly. There's outdoor seating on a small sidewalk patio. Giuseppe's is an interesting place to try out unique pasta at a reasonable price.

The Top **$$$**
2891 East Main Street
(614) 231-8238
www.thetopsteakhouse.com
The black-and-white-striped awning with the Top logo is a landmark on East Main Street. Although Bexleyites lay claim to this old-school steakhouse, you will find a diverse clientele, from old-timers who frequented the Top since it opened in the 1950s to the 20-somethings dressed to impress.

After you allow your eyes to adjust to the dimly lit, cavernous interior, you will find the ultimate timeless steakhouse—fireplace, copper-topped bar, black Naugahyde booths, and all. The decor remains unchanged. The menu is timeless and extensive. The clientele is unwavering. The bar is perfectly campy. All this makes for a true supper club experience where you can envisage Rat Pack crooners slinging martinis with Hitchcockian blondes.

The menu features all sorts of fine cuts of beef, pork, and lamb. The seafood options are equally impressive, but the hefty surf and turf goes unmatched. The Top is closed on Sunday.

WHITEHALL

Butch's Italian Cafe **$$**
4720 East Main Street
(614) 864-7300
www.butchsitaliancafe.com
This Italian restaurant is well reviewed and commands a loyal following. Traditional pastas make up most of the menu, but the variations seem endless. Pick your pasta, then select from eight sauces and a laundry list of veggie and meat toppings. Even the lasagna comes with several options. Those with a smaller appetite can opt for a half portion, then wash it all down with some Chianti or Peroni beer. You may want to save room for dessert, imported all the way from Carnegie Deli in New York City. The wood-paneled dining room is accented with red vinyl chairs, giving this restaurant an old-school charm.

Pho Little Saigon **$**
885 South Hamilton Road
(614) 231-7357
A Vietnamese couple suggested I include this restaurant. The aromas may draw you into this small storefront eatery, but don't let the menu (which is in Vietnamese) scare you away. Translations and brief descriptions in English are included, but it may be easier to just order by number. The specialty is a variety of beef noodle soups that have a very fragrant broth, but you'll also find the familiar: General Tso's chicken, wor sue gai, and a variety of chow mein noodle dishes. For something different, try one of the several types of Vietnamese-French coffees. You have the option to eat in or carry out.

TAT Ristorante di Famiglia **$$**
1210 South James Road
(614) 236-1392
www.tatitalianrestaurant.com
This east side restaurant has been serving homemade Italian dinners to Columbus since the late 1920s, officially making it the oldest family-owned restaurant in the city. Over the years, they have moved a few times but have retained that old-school Italian restaurant ambience. Pastel colors and twinkly lighting, along with cushy booths and packed tables, give off the image of one big family in one giant dining room. Unlike the decor, the menu has been updated a few times to reflect the city's changing tastes. One can have American, Chinese, and vegetarian dishes, as well as their trademark Italian. Favorites include the wedding soup, chicken cacciatore, and baked lasagna. If you come before 6:00 P.M., you can take advantage of early bird dinner specials, but this restaurant can be quite busy most days of the week. It's closed on Monday.

REYNOLDSBURG/ PICKERINGTON AREA

City BBQ **$**
5979 East Main Street, multiple locations
(614) 755-8890
www.citybarbeque.com
Thought you had to go to Kansas City to get good barbecue? Well, think again. City BBQ's goals are simple: to make the best barbecue anywhere and to share this great American food with Columbus. According to the most discriminating barbecue lovers, they *are* putting Columbus on the map with their extraordinary (secret) sauce and pure smoked meats. The menu features ribs, beef brisket, pork, and chicken. The sides are scratch-made southern dishes like baked beans, corn pudding, and hush puppies. A sandwich and side dish can be plentiful, but don't leave without trying the peach cobbler. The service is nothing fancy; it's more or less an indoor picnic. You order at a counter and eat at crammed tables. The four other locations in Upper Arlington (the original), Gahanna, Powell, and Westerville offer the same great menu and communal dining.

Scali Ristorante **$$**
1901 State Route 256
(614) 759-7764
www.scaliristorante.com
This family-owned operation is the far east side's place for classic Italian done well. This strip mall restaurant serves straightforward pastas in a dining room brightly painted with Italian scenes. The white table linens add a touch of class, and the service adds a touch of warmth. The wine list offers more than 10 Chiantis; it is the food, however, that explains the parking lot full of cars and the dining room full of people.

The usual antipasti, salads, and pastas are on the menu, and the bread is homemade. Regulars suggest the veal with wild mushrooms but say you can't go wrong with any of the daily specials. Scali's has a small bar, a refrigerated case full of beer, as well as the aforementioned wine list. Weekend reservations are recommended, as one can wait upwards of 45 minutes for a table.

HILLIARD

Mark Pi's China Gate **$$**
3641 Fishinger Boulevard, Mill Run
(614) 527-8582
Mark Pi's might be better known for various express takeout shops around town, but this sit-down restaurant carries upscale Chinese food in a casually elegant setting. The spacious dining room has booths and tables arranged around the centerpiece fishpond (but don't feed the fish!). There's also a full-service bar with a television. The menu ranges from appetizers to meat and seafood entrees to combination dinners for groups. You'll also find a nice selection of vegetarian dishes. The service is generally fast and friendly.

Starliner Diner **$**
5240 Cemetery Road
(614) 529-1198
This Cuban-fusion restaurant is a kitschy, colorful place to experience cuisine that's just a little different in a setting that's just a little different. The furniture doesn't match. The murals and wall decorations are kooky. One's senses are overloaded with fragrant aromas, festive music, and Spanish talk. Fun and affordable is the best way to describe a dining experience here.

Many locals don't realize this eatery has been around for 10 years, but Starliner Diner has developed quite a loyal following that swears by the Cajun jambalaya. The food ranges from southwestern to Cajun to Caribbean, but the menu has a mostly Cuban slant to it. The Cuban-style pizza bread salad, with its beautiful presentation, is popular among those looking for something dietesque. Pasta lovers go for the fettuccini caliente, while vegetarians opt for the pan-roasted vegetables with black beans and rice. Often overlooked are the desserts (which come in epic portions), so save plenty of room for the famous flan. They also serve a hearty breakfast, including huevos rancheros. Don't blink or you might drive right by the tiny strip mall set back off Cemetery Road.

Taj Palace **$$**
3794 Fishinger Boulevard, Mill Run
(614) 771-3870
www.tajpalacecolumbus.com
You will find this restaurant on the corner of the shopping plaza at Mill Run. Just look for the colorful beaded curtains in the front windows. The food is consistently good, and the menu runs the gamut of curries and tandooris. There's a nice selection of breads and vegetarian dishes, as well as a full-service bar featuring Indian beers and many different wines by the glass. The lunch buffet features a fantastic selection of 25 meat and vegetarian items at a great price, but come early for a table. It can be quite busy around noon. A full dinner buffet is offered Monday night, while Tuesday night's buffet is a strictly vegetarian combination of northern and southern Indian dishes. The service is unhurried, but attentive and friendly.

The Yard Club **$$$**
4065 Main Street, Old Hilliard
(614) 771-1400
www.yardclub.com

The Yard Club has been named in *Zagat's* as one of Columbus's top 10 restaurants. It is a public restaurant that offers a private membership to bolster the community and develop friendships among the locals. This Irish-themed restaurant is located in an 1883 landmark building in Old Hilliard, where the Irish heritage is rich. The atmosphere is clubby, with dark wood paneling and sectioned off dining rooms.

Some of the fare is distinctly Irish, such as the creamy Limerick chowder and fish-and-chips but meat eaters particularly will leave quite content. The Irish pot roast is a favorite among regulars, and you will not be disappointed with any of the Angus beef entrees. The portions are huge, and the quality of meat is topnotch. The pasta and seafood dishes are equally fine and filling.

The bar is large and carries a number of imported and domestic beers on draft, but not as many as you would expect from a true Irish pub. The Yard Club focuses on quality rather than quantity. Reservations are recommended, particularly on the weekends.

GRANDVIEW

Barley's Smokehouse,
Ale House No. 2 **$**
1130 Dublin Road
(614) 485-0227
www.barleysbrewing.com

The Smokehouse is not to be confused with Barley's Brewpub in the Arena District. They serve the same beers but have very different menus. The focus here is on barbecue, burgers, and pit-smoked meats. The plank floors, high wooden booths, and multiple televisions around the bar give it a casual sports bar feeling. The dining room proper has plank floors and wooden tables and is separated from the bar. There is also an area with pool tables, dartboards, and video games. Barley's is a casual place to hang out with your friends and have a few drinks, but it's also comfortable and affordable enough to take the whole family. They offer happy hour and game day specials.

If you're looking to participate in Scotland's annual celebration of its poet laureate, Barley's Smokehouse holds an annual Robert Burns dinner sometime around January 25. They pipe out the haggis (but you don't have to eat it!), toast with a wee dram of scotch, and tap the Robert Burns Scottish Export Ale.

Braddock's Grandview **$$$**
1470 Grandview Avenue
(614) 487-0077

A recent fire forced a facelift to the interior of this popular Grandview restaurant, but their Low Country southern fare remains the same, with a few steak and seafood additions. Drawing inspiration from the refined cooking styles of Charleston, South Carolina, and Savannah, Georgia, the menu is popular among local food critics. The cracker jack mahimahi and shrimp and grits are seafood favorites, while the Vegetarian Tower certainly provides above and beyond your daily intake of veggies. Meat eaters should not overlook the surf and turf. The new interior has a weathered seashore look to it and retains the same old comfortable atmosphere. The sidewalk garden patio is open during the summer months.

Eastern Bay **$$**
2055 Riverside Drive (Route 33)
(614) 487-1198

From the shape of the building, one might recognize this McDonald's from a past life, but the inside of this Asian bistro is far from fast food. The fine Chinese fare that is found here is not undermined by the comfortable and casual ambience. Cozy booths afford couples a quiet, intimate dinner, while larger groups can choose to share their meals across big, round tables. Now, about the food: It looks good, it tastes good, and it always comes out piping hot. If you come here a handful of times, you will be recognized and acknowledged. The service is prompt and courteous, even on the busiest of days. The main entrees may not be as cheap as some Chinese restaurants, but this is good quality Asian cuisine, and you get what you pay for. The lunch and Sunday buffets are a great deal. Priced below $10 per person, the buffets are a great way to sample a variety of the fine fare.

Figlio Grandview **$$**
1369 Grandview Avenue
(614) 481-8850
www.figliopizza.com

This lively and noisy gourmet pizza place is where residents come from surrounding neighborhoods to get their carb boost. Figlio is pizza and pasta all the time. The menus are simple but varied. The designer, wood-fired pizzas have been carefully crafted with toppings that range from kung pao shrimp to wild mushroom. The owner has even taught classes on how to make the perfect pizza dough. Pasta selections are just as varied and lovingly created. Hands down, the most popular dish is the spicy chicken diablo, but you're bound to be happy with any of the sauces, which are the main attraction.

The interior is bistro like, with its tiled floor and intimate table spacing. It's cozy, to say the least. If you're claustrophobic or expecting to have a private conversation, this is not the place for you. Some have said Figlio is too crowded and noisy, but it's just a very social place where people gather to talk and enjoy their designer carbs. There is an outdoor patio open during the summer months, which provides people watching along Grandview Avenue. It's closed Sunday.

Panzera's Pizza **$**
1354 Grandview Avenue
(614) 486-5951

Often rated at the front of the pizza pack, Panzera's has been creating addicts since 1982. Some say it's the thin, crispy crust, while others claim it's the fruit-flavored sauce, and still others love the sharp, greasy cheese. Whatever it is, the dough and sauce are freshly made, and the pepperoni is thick and salty, quite bacon-like. The menu also includes subs and pasta, but don't forget to grab a bundle of homemade pizelles for dessert. This Grandview staple has a seasonal outdoor patio, otherwise you have to get your pie to go.

Paul's Fifth Avenue **$**
1565 West Fifth Avenue
(614) 481-8848
www.paulsonline.com

Paul's has two different personalities under one unassuming roof. Down-home cooking is served for breakfast and lunch, while gourmet fare is turned out at dinner. For 35 years this Grandview tradition has filled local bellies with pancakes and eggs for breakfast and burgers and lasagna for lunch. The morning hours bring in the greasy spoon crowd looking for home fries, while the afternoon will attract local business people wanting a salad and "sammich" (yes, it's spelled that way on the menu). The evening brings out a more sophisticated and affordable menu of seafood and meat, or you can build your own pasta. There are nightly chef's specials and a decent wine list.

Rotolo's Pizza **$**
1749 West Fifth Avenue, multiple locations
(614) 488-7934
www.rotolospizza.com

This is not just another Grandview pizzeria. Folks from Grandview Heights have been calling Rotolo's meaty, cheesy pizzas a tradition since 1976. The rest of Columbus seems to like it too, as it has claimed numerous awards throughout the years. Lovers of thick-crust pizza will enjoy the pliable crust. It is lightly covered with a sweeter sauce and loaded with lots of mozzarella. The pepperoni is small, thick, and crispy but there's a bevy of high-quality ingredients to pile on—and that they do! The menu also features subs, salads, and a handful of pasta entrees. Keep in mind this is takeout only. Rotolo's does not deliver and does not have a dining room.

Shoku **$$**
1312 Grandview Avenue
(614) 485-9490

As soon as you enter, you will realize this is not a traditional Japanese restaurant. Shoku, which means "to eat" in Japanese, is a trendy place where the young and hip tend to congregate. It may look modest on the exterior, but the interior is bold and contemporary. The wait staff, clad in black, scurries around the dining room, and techno-world beat music thumps in the background. Steel and chrome provide a modern feel, while the golden-glazed walls give it an almost rustic look.

The decor at this eclectic pan-Asian restaurant may be minimalist, but the food certainly is not. The menu is a hybrid of Korean, Thai, Japanese, and Chinese cuisines and consists mainly of satays, noodles, wraps, and house specialties. The dumplings stand out as an appetizer, while the Korean-influenced Shoku beef is a house specialty. The sushi is fresh and the presentation artistic, but the prices lie at the more expensive end for sushi. You have the option of eating in the dining room, in a separate bar area, at the sushi bar, or outside on the patio overlooking Grandview Avenue.

Spagio **$$**
1295 Grandview Avenue
(614) 486-1114

Spagio's has paved the way for more upscale, metropolitan dining in Columbus, and some have argued it's the best restaurant in town. They certainly have some of the best desserts, which you can't help but notice when being marched right past the case on the way to your table. If you resist the temptation to dive straight into the tiramisu, you will find a menu full of inventive "spa" food ranging from wood-fired pizzas to gourmet pastas, from paella to elk (yes, I said elk). Brunch is offered on Saturday and Sunday, and there's a limited late-night menu after 11:00 P.M.

The decor is as eclectic as the menu. All sorts of umbrellas and other bits and baubles dangle from the ceiling, while vintage posters and murals cover the walls. There are two very different bars at which to take in the surroundings. The front bar is small and offers a bird's-eye view of the comings and goings of patrons (and that darn dessert case). The back room has a larger, island-style bar in the middle of the dining room. The whole restaurant is good for people watching, and it's a fun social place. Just about everyone in Columbus seems to come here. Tuesday nights are fun to pop around for a glass of wine and some live jazz. Spagio's has a small outdoor patio and is adjacent to Spagio Cellars, which is listed in The Pub Crawl chapter.

Trattoria Roma **$$**
1447 Grandview Avenue
(614) 488-2104
www.trattoria-roma.com

Trattoria Roma is *the* upscale Italian restaurant of Grandview, and it doesn't get more intimate than a few cozy tables with white linens nestled in a deep red dining room with the likes of Dean Martin crooning in the background. The fare is Old Country cuisine from central and northern Italy. The menu falls somewhere between traditional and adventuresome. You can have fresh handmade pasta in a rich cream sauce or a simple marinara, but the kitchen is known for its slow-roasted osso bucco and amazing rotolo di pasta. Regulars concur that the service is impeccable, and the sidewalk patio is truly romantic. There's a small bar, and the restaurant is open for dinner seven days a week.

UPPER ARLINGTON

Alex's Bistro on Reed **$$$**
4681 Reed Road
(614) 457-8887

For 18 years, Arlington Square Strip Mall

has been home to this unpretentious, upscale French bistro. The menu is posted outside, so you can see what you're getting yourself into: duck, salmon, filet mignon. Does classic French fare sound good? Then entrez vous!

The dimly lit, dark wood and brass bar is a great place to have a cocktail before dinner, and as someone put it, it's the sort of place to meet your mistress. Mirrored walls and white tablecloths continue the bistro-style decor through to the dining room, where you will be spoiled with escargot and creamy pate, trout and lamb. The menu changes seasonally, but you will always find crepes in the mix. All the items served are hormone-free, free-range, and/or organic. End your night sweetly with Alex's ever-famous crème brulée or chocolate mousse. Wines are available by the glass, bottle, or half-carafe, and there is occasional live entertainment in the bar.

Big Ten Subs **$**
3051 Northwest Boulevard
(614) 326-2410

So it's a sub shop, but as an official licensee of the Big Ten athletic conference, the parent company will donate a percentage of sales to scholarship funds at member universities. This flagship eatery is decorated with college memorabilia and is located close to the OSU campus. They have TVs showing different events and cater (and often host) pregame tailgate parties. The subs are big, and the salads come with a surprising list of toppings like oranges, raisins, sunflower seeds, and Chinese noodles.

Chef O'Nette **$**
2090 Tremont Center, between Tremont and Redding Road
(614) 488-8444

The Chef-O is a total time warp. This is no throwback diner—it's the real deal. Seats have been swiveling at the counter since 1955, making the Chef-O an Upper Arlington tradition for three generations. The menu is full of old-time comfort food like fried chicken and fish sandwiches, but the mainstays of the menu are the Hangover Sandwich and the Chef-O-burger. Some people go just for the soda fountain malts and shakes. They offer full-service takeout and have an antiquated drive-through window.

El Vaquero Mexican Restaurant **$**
2195 Riverside Drive (Route 33)
(614) 486-4547
www.elvaquerorestaurants.com

Most people living west of the Olentangy will say to go to El Vaquero for good authentic Mexican food, thinking this corporate-owned restaurant is a mom-and-pop shop. The decor is nothing fancy, and though there are some piñatas and blow-up Corona bottles hanging from the ceiling, it's not as garish or contrived as some Mexican chains. The Spanish-speaking wait staff is very attentive, and your refillable basket of chips and spicy salsa will seem bottomless. The food never fails to come out very fast, as if Speedy Gonzales himself made it. It will probably take you longer to figure out what you want from the 160-plus menu options than to actually get your food. Be careful, because the plates and the food arrive steaming hot, and the refried beans are like liquid lava at times.

Figlio Arlington **$$**
3712 Riverside Drive (Route 33)
(614) 459-6575
www.figliopizza.com

Similar to the Grandview location, this upscale eatery (pronounced FEEL-ee-oh) serves designer wood-fired pizzas and creative gourmet pastas in a casual and lively dining room. It's a very popular neighborhood gathering place, and often half of Upper Arlington seems to be in the dining room, which is probably what gives Figlio its noisy vibrancy. This is an easy place for a relaxing but quality dinner. The bar is small and classy. The pleasant fenced-in patio is popular for alfresco dining in the summertime.

Hyde Park Grille **$$$**
1615 Old Henderson Road
(614) 442-3310
www.hydeparkgrille.com

I hesitate to call anything the "best," but I will go out on a limb here and say one should come to this dark, clubby steakhouse with high expectations. Valet parking is complimentary, and one could say the caliber of cars parked outside reflect the caliber of dining you will find inside. A friendly host will guide you past the bar, where cigar smokers and the over-30 set look equally at home, into one of the cozy, wood-paneled dining rooms.

The menu is loaded with top-quality cuts of meat, which can be enhanced with any of the gourmet sauces named for Ohio sports celebrities. Steak Rahal (as in Bobby) is a bacon-wrapped filet mignon with caramelized Dijon hollandaise sauce. The house favorite is Steak Kosar (named for the Browns' Bernie Kosar). This huge filet is topped with lobster and served in bordelaise sauce. Seafood lovers won't be disappointed with classics such as oysters Rockefeller, lobster tails, and king crab. Like the other Hyde Park restaurants, the side dishes are varied and come portioned for two. The quality of service matches the food—world-class. Hyde Park Chop House on Frantz Road in Dublin has very similar ambience, service, and menu.

Iacono's Pizza & Restaurant **$**
4452 Kenny Road, multiple locations
(614) 451-0234

Iacono's serves Italian food just like Grandma made. This storefront pizzeria offers full-service takeout, limited delivery, and a cozy eat-in dining room that is extremely family-friendly. The sauces, meats, and pizza dough are made without preservatives from recipes that have been passed down through the family. Alcohol is served in the dining room, and there's a nice selection of six-packs to carry out. Locals love the airy, thin-crusted pizza with its tangy sauce and crispy pepperoni. The pastas and the handmade egg noodles stand out. People will drive across town for the spaghetti and meatballs. That says it all. The two other Columbus locations are in Hilliard and on Sawmill Road.

Kaya Grill and Sushi Bar **$$**
4710 Reed Road
(614) 326-2551

Kaya serves a variety of Japanese, Thai, and Korean cuisine, with the latter being the specialty. There's a small sushi bar, which gets mixed reviews, but almost everyone agrees the Korean barbecue is top-notch. One can sit at regular tables in the dining room or at booths with built-in grills. Kaya's tableside grilling is unique in Columbus and features a wide selection of grillables such as meats, seafood, shrimp, and scallops. Korean delicacies like monkfish with vegetables, cooked Japanese fare, and noodle dishes are also on the menu. The ambience is serene, and a double-sided fireplace adds to the tranquility.

Kikyo Japanese Restaurant **$$**
3706 Riverside Drive (Route 33)
(614) 457-5277
www.geocities.com/kikyo_sushi

Kikyo isn't obvious, as it sits back in a somewhat dated strip mall off Route 33, but this is one of Columbus's tried-and-true traditional Japanese restaurants and sushi bar. The decor is restrained, and the sushi bar is smaller than it looks. It seats about 10 people comfortably, so call ahead to reserve a place if you really like to watch the edible art being made. The dining room is slightly larger and is a mix of tables and booths, while a private room is available for larger groups. There's a decent selection of wine, beers, and sake. Kikyo is closed on Monday.

Moretti's of Arlington **$$**
2124 Tremont Center, between Tremont and Redding Road
(614) 486-2333

First-rate, zesty southern Italian food is served in a modern setting in this storefront restaurant located in a part of town where strip malls are called "plazas." Behind the smoke-colored glass door is a small but lively bar leading into a small but festive dining area. The walls are deep red. The paintings of Florentine bridges are colorful and glossy. The room is lit by track lighting, but the fire in the fireplace is faux. Once you settle in to the (lived-in) chairs, you may not be able to get up after stuffing yourself with the sumptuous, hand-rolled pasta piled with meats and cheese. Though one will find hearty classics and pizzas on the menu, the kitchen turns out some very sophisticated dishes and nightly specials. Moretti's is open for dinner only and closed on Sunday.

Restaurant Japan **$$**
1173 Old Henderson Road, Kenny Center
(614) 451-5411
This casual strip-mall restaurant has a very traditional, understated elegance. The dining room is large and unpretentious; the sushi bar is small and always busy. There isn't anything trendy about this place, but the sushi menu is extensive, and the fish is very fresh and well prepared. If you are struggling to decide what to get, order the Columbus Box, which comes with a selection of just about everything. There are Korean selections alongside the cooked Japanese fare. Tempura, deep-fried tofu, and udon noodles are house favorites. Sushi lovers claim this is the best Japanese restaurant because of the portions, price, and atmosphere.

Sher-e-Punjab **$$**
1140 Kenny Square Mall, off Kenny Road
(614) 538-9790
Located in the same shopping center as many other ethnic eateries, this casual restaurant is known primarily for its northern Indian vegetarian buffet on Tuesday night. The daily lunch buffet isn't too shabby either. The staff is very friendly, and they serve high-quality food in a roomy dining area. Vegetarians are generally pleased with the selections. Depending on the day of the week, there are two different doors you can enter through. If one is locked, try the other.

Spiro's Scioto Inn **$**
3140 Riverside Drive (Route 33)
(614) 481-8448
This hybrid Greek cafe/American diner, once located on Trabue Road, now calls Upper Arlington home. Spiro's opens early for breakfast, and in keeping with the Greek theme, you can order an omelet with feta and tomatoes or, if you prefer American greasy spoon, a breakfast sandwich. A whole gamut of Mediterranean and American food can be had for lunch and dinner, but the house favorites are gyros and the pastitsio (pasta and meat covered with cream). The dining room and bar areas are both spacious, and the decor is restrained. There are several large-screen TVs to catch the games, as well as pool tables and live music. The bar is most lively on Saturday nights as it plays host to a karaoke party. The clientele is diverse and spans every age group, so 20-somethings and 70-somethings will feel right at home. Spiro's has a small outdoor patio that overlooks Riverside Drive.

Thai Taste **$$**
1178 Kenny Square Mall, off Kenny Road
(614) 451-7609
The aroma of coconut and curry greets you at the door of this very casual storefront eatery. The dining room has a makeshift "islandy" feel, with umbrella tables, a waterfall of flowers, and a few fish tanks, but the food is a true taste of Thailand. The cold Thai salad gets great reviews, as does several red snapper dishes. A few Chinese entrees are included for the more mainstream. Thai Taste is open every day but closed between lunch and dinner.

Tommy's Pizza **$**
1350 West Lane Avenue
(614) 486-2969
Some locals will go to their graves swearing that Tommy's makes the best pies in the universe. They're cheesy, the pepperoni curls up at the edges, and the crust is crispy, not too thick, not too thin. You will,

however, have to pick up your pizza (or eat in), as they do not deliver. Tommy's menu includes subs, salads, and full dinners. This restaurant is totally family-friendly, which adds to the appeal for those who live in the neighborhood.

DUBLIN

Chile Verde Cafe **$$**
4852 Sawmill Road, Carriage Place Shopping Center
(614) 442-6630
You will be taken aback if you come expecting cookie-cutter Americanized Mexican food. The fare here is northern New Mexican (as in the state of New Mexico), and it is far spicier than typical Mexican cuisine. The salsa is homemade, and the portions are huge. This family-friendly restaurant is small and often packed. There's no bar, but you can choose from a nice selection of Mexican beers and really good margaritas. Chile Verde does not accept reservations, but it's worth the wait for a Santa Fe experience.

Kihachi Japanese Restaurant **$$$**
2667 Federated Boulevard
(614) 764-9040
The pearl of Sawmill Shopping Center, Kihachi is the most authentic Japanese dining experience you will find in Columbus; its predominantly Japanese clientele and the occasional long wait for a table speaks to this. The focus here is not on sushi, but on exquisitely executed dishes—both traditional and adventurous. For a true taste of Tokyo, try the 10-course dinner. Reservations are highly recommended.

La Scala Italian Bistro **$$**
4199 West Dublin-Granville Road
(614) 889-9431
www.lascalaitalianbistro.com
This restaurant, named for the La Scala opera house in Milan, has been family owned since 1972, and the decor will certainly give away its '70s origins. You'll enjoy classic Old World Italian entrees in an elegant ambience that the older generation of Columbus seems to be attracted to. La Scala's has live piano music midweek and other entertainment on the weekends.

Oscar's **$$**
84 North High Street, Old Dublin
(614) 792-3354
This pleasant restaurant, located in historic Dublin, has a bunch of small dining rooms, hard wood floors, and stained glass, giving it a "historic house" sort of atmosphere. It's a lunchy sort of place, and the dress is casual. The menu is somewhat small but gourmet. All the items seem to have a global flair to them, from Thai stir-fried calamari and Jamaican jerk quesadilla to Louisiana crab cakes and plain old burgers. The bar is cozy, and the outdoor patio is very quaint. It's closed on Sunday.

The Riverview Restaurant and Bar **$$$**
6125 Riverside Drive (Route 33)
(614) 717-9325
www.riverviewcolumbus.com
The exposed beams, stone walls, and working fireplace of this big restaurant give the interior a retro, lodge-like feeling, while wonderful views of the Scioto River are provided from the dining room and large outdoor patio. The dining room has a lot of atmosphere and is situated between the semi-open kitchen and large windows facing the river. This is one of the most scenic places to dine alfresco in Columbus, and full menu service is provided on the patio. The owners of Bexley's Monk recently acquired the Riverview, so there is no doubt they know their food. The menu is contemporary and offers creative seafood dishes, salads, and sandwiches. It is far from pub grub, and so are the prices. The bar area is big and lively, and the reputation of being a "pick-up" place among the 40-something set hasn't been shaken with new ownership. There's live music on select nights.

Taste of Bali $$
2548 Bethel Road, Carriage Place Plaza
(614) 459-7230
www.tasteofbali.com
The sign for Columbus's only Indonesian restaurant is easily overshadowed by the neighboring theater's marquee, but if you are looking for something totally unique in Columbus, you'll find this family-owned eatery tucked in the elbow of a big shopping plaza. One might say Indonesian cuisine is somewhat akin to Thai food. The sauces can be sweet or fiery; coconut and peanuts flavor a lot of the dishes, which are large enough to be shared between two people. If it is your first time, try the rijsttafel (Dutch for "rice table"), a combination of appetizers and entrees. With Indonesian music playing in the background, the atmosphere is inviting and comfortable, and the decor is certainly striking.

DUBLIN-WORTHINGTON/ DUBLIN-ARLINGTON AREAS

Hoggy's Roadside Grille $
2234 West Dublin-Granville Road
(614) 431-6465
www.hoggysrestaurants.com
"Do it Hoggy-style." That's what it says on the T-shirts for this local chain of casual barbecue restaurants. Each shop is different in size, ambience, and decor, but the menu and high-quality of food remain the same. Pulled pork sandwiches and ribs are the specialties. The sides are totally fun (and filling) and provide many alternatives for vegetarians. Forgo the usual French fries for the greens and hoppin' john or a bowl of mac and cheese. You can smell Hoggy's smoking a mile away—and they smoke everything right down to the potatoes. Other locations can be sniffed out in Dublin, Grandview, Gahanna, Grove City, and Westerville.

Hunan Lion
Gourmet Chinese Dining $$
2038 Bethel Road
(614) 459-3933
Surprise! Another good restaurant in a shopping center! There is something for every palate among the 120 Szechuan, Hunan, Mandarin, and Thai dishes listed on the menu. With nearly two dozen appetizers and soups and all the usual classics, a few surprises do pop up on the menu. Several people have mentioned the shark fin soup as being exceptional, and you don't see New Zealand green-shell mussels in black bean sauce or Thai red curry duck everyday. The dining room is large, with wall murals and carpets, while velvet seating and ceramic vases add an air of sophistication.

Lido's Pizza and Restaurant $
2540 Bethel Road
(614) 459-5858
This little mom-and-pop storefront eatery is popular with neighborhood families, with its takeout window for pizzas and small, casual dining room. The menu is full of Italian comfort food, subs, and salads. Lido's is a great value, especially on Monday nights, when they offer an all-you-can-eat buffet full of pizza, pastas, and salad. There's a small selection of alcohol, and you can get a half-carafe of Chianti for a very reasonable price.

Moretti's $$
5849 Sawmill Road
(614) 717-0400
This is one instance where not judging a book by its cover would serve you well. One might drive right by this less-than-attractive strip mall and miss out on some of Columbus's best Italian food. Moretti is a family name synonymous with fine Italian dining. A disproportionately large number of people say this is by far their favorite restaurant in Columbus. The interior is plain, Old World Italian decor (with a few Greek statues thrown in), and the cuisine is 100 percent authentic. The menu consists of old reliables, like four types of lasagna, traditional pizzas, chicken cacciatore, and veal parmigiana. Don't expect frozen breaded cutlets. Everything here is made from scratch, and you'll know it.

The Refectory Restaurant $$$$
1092 Bethel Road
(614) 451-9774
www.therefectoryrestaurant.com

I could probably end this entry right here with a laundry list of awards—*Wine Spectator*'s Grand Award and Best of Award of Excellence, AAA Four-Diamond Award, DiRona Award for Distinguished Restaurants of North America, and five stars locally—but there is so much more to say about this landmark of great dining.

The Web site has a very detailed history of this unique and distinguished building, which began as a church in the 1850s and took its place as Columbus's premier French restaurant in 1982. The spirit of the past can be felt in the hand-hewn wooden beams of the high ceilings and exposed brick walls, while the stained-glass windows are a reminder of the spiritual place this once was.

Whether you love classic or contemporary French fare, "spiritual" is a good way to describe a dining experience here. It begins with a candlelit dining room and ends with a symphony of desserts. In between, an exquisite meal prepared with flair is served from a seasonally changing menu. The attention to detail is staggering, and the service is superb. In the tradition of true French dining, nothing is hurried. You are not supposed to eat your dinner; you are supposed to experience it.

The original schoolhouse is now the lounge. Give your eyes a moment to adjust, and you'll see it's a cocktail bar and small bistro in one. There's a separate bistro menu, which offers three courses for under $20. The mirrored bar is long and traditional, with high-backed stools. The fireplace blazes forth in the winter.

Wine lovers will be pleased to know The Refectory has a Cruvinet wine preservation system, allowing them to sample eight fantastic wines by the glass from its world-class wine cellar. The Refectory is one of only 95 restaurants worldwide to receive the prestigious award from *Wine Spectator* for its cellar, which encompasses more than 700 selections.

Reservations are strongly recommended well in advance of the holidays. Aside from the main dining room, The Refectory offers alfresco dining in the courtyard during the summer months and a private room in the wine cellar, which is loaded with character and allows you to dine among the bottles. The Refectory is closed Sunday.

---

i

As customary in France, The Refectory offers a prix fixe menu. This usually includes a starter, entree, dessert, and coffee. It's a good way for the budget-conscious to enjoy dining at one of Columbus's top three restaurants. Eating in the lounge off the bistro menu is another option.

Siam Oriental Restaurant $$
855 Bethel Road
(614) 451-1109

Siam is one of Columbus's longest-operating Asian restaurants (1983) and is tucked in a shopping center between a grocery store and a computer superstore. Who knew this storefront restaurant, which is much bigger than it looks from the outside, would serve some of the city's best Thai and Chinese cuisine? The comprehensive menu is broken out into Thai and Chinese dishes, while the lunch buffet is a great way to sample both. The Sunday brunch is still wildly popular after all these years. The interior is basic shades of pink and cranberry, while lacquered chairs give it that hint of the Orient. The dining room is open and dotted with white tablecloth-clad tables, while booths around the perimeter provide cozy conversations.

COFFEE AND TEA SHOPS

Caffeine junkies can get their fix quite effortlessly in Columbus. With no fewer than 25 Starbucks and a dozen Caribou Coffees, you might be surprised at the other options you have for a caffeinated experience. Starbucks aficionados may want to try out some of the fine, independently owned coffee shops around town, many of which are found in shopping centers or in various residential areas. However, there seems to be a disproportionately large number of them along High Street.

Columbus has the ultramodern coffee shops and the greasy spoons. We have places for intimate conversations on overstuffed sofas. There are well-lit coffee shops in which to study the night away, knowing your next jolt of caffeine is just a few steps away. Many of the places listed here, such as Scottie MacBean and Kafe Kerouac, have wireless Internet access, while others have changing exhibitions of art and photography. Most carry some sort of food or snacks. Whether you want tea or coffee, you can have it in any sort of environment you want and well into the night.

Brenen's Cafe & Catering
1860 North High Street, OSU Campus
(614) 291-7751

Cafe Corner
1105 Pennsylvania Avenue, Victorian Village
(614) 294-2233

Cafe Mozart
4490 Indianola Avenue, Clintonville
(614) 262-9601

Coffee Table
731 North High Street, Short North
(614) 297-1177

Cup O' Joe Lennox
1791 Olentangy River Road, Lennox Town Center
(614) 291-1563

Cup O' Joe and Mo-Joe Lounge
600 North High Street, on the Cap
(614) 225-1563

Drexel Radio Cafe
2256 East Main Street, Bexley
(614) 231-0498

German Village Coffee Shop
193 Thurman Avenue, German Village
(614) 443-8900

Heavenly Cup
25 North State Street, Westerville
(614) 523-3306

Kafe Kerouac
2250 North High Street, OSU Campus
(614) 299-2672

Latte 2A Tea
247 East Main Street, New Albany
(614) 855-0666

Pochi Tea Station
2060 North High Street, OSU Campus
(614) 299-9460

Scottie MacBean
660 High Street, Olde Worthington
(614) 430-8648

Stauf's Coffee Roasters
1277 Grandview Avenue, Grandview
(614) 486-4861

ZenCha Tea Salon
982 North High Street, Short North
(614) 421-2140

THE PUB CRAWL 

Columbus, like any other big city, has the whole gamut of drinking possibilities. Pick your poison, and pick your people. It's likely you'll find something that tickles your fancy. There are noisy pubs for the rowdy and sophisticated wine bars for the restrained. There are sports bars and pick-up bars. There are places you can hunker down all night and areas you can bar hop until your coach turns into a pumpkin. All you need to know is what you enjoy.

For the restless soul who likes a change of scenery throughout the course of the evening, there are a few areas with a concentrated number of bars and pubs within a few blocks' radius. Grandview and the Short North are good neighborhoods to park and walk to multiple locations. Grandview is quainter (and a little more residential) than the trendy Short North, but both have equally established watering holes that cater to a wide range of thirsts and budgets. You will notice a large number of entries concentrated in these two neighborhoods, as well as the Brewery and Arena Districts.

The Arena District is loaded with chain restaurants and bars, such as Gordon Biersch, Red Star Tavern, and Ted's Montana Grill. The Brewery District has Claddagh Irish Pub, while Easton has Bar Louis, Adobe Gilas, and yet another Irish chain, Fado's. You can catch your favorite sporting events at bars like Champps and Damon's. Each of these chains has an upside, but the objective of this chapter is to focus on Columbus's homegrown bars, pubs, and bistros.

This chapter will not list every watering hole in town, but instead pinpoints the tried-and-true drinking establishments unique to Columbus and popular within different age groups. For consistency, the bars are listed in their respective neighborhoods, while The Ohio State University chapter has its own section dedicated to the pub crawl. I apologize if your favorite haunt is not included, but I have not imbibed at every bar in town. ("Whew!" says my partner.)

You may notice the drinking chapter is not as long as the dining chapter. This is due to that blurry fusion of restaurant and bar. Some of you may define these places a little differently than I do. Many of the restaurants in the previous chapter have full-service bars and are frequented more for their beverages than their food. Likewise, many of the bars in this chapter can satisfy your hunger, but the entries do not go into great detail about the food unless they offer something special.

Basically, if the word *pub* or *tavern* is in the name, it's in this chapter. If the bar is well known for tailgating or game day specials, it's in this chapter. There are several places in Columbus that have outdoor patios with happy hour deals, music, and activities during the summer months. They too are included here.

Hopefully, this cross section of drinking establishments will prove the abundance of carousing that is to be had in our city. Normally, one can carouse till 2:00 A.M., but some bars stay open later, while a handful close a lot earlier. Special note has been made when this is the case.

I would like to disclaim all the fun beer talk about to ensue with a few last words.

---

i

Pub crawlers never look out of place in Grandview, nor do they in the Short North during the Gallery Hop. The Hop, which happens the first Saturday of each month, becomes more of an urbane pub crawl. There is something permissible about planning your evening around art for art's sake, then sticking around to drink for art's sake.

Whatever your capacity to imbibe, do so with responsibility. As anywhere, drinking while driving is prohibited and strictly enforced. Please see the Area Overview for alcohol-related statistics and laws. If you happen to overindulge, remember that Columbus taxis do not "cruise" but can easily be called from any bar (or restaurant, for that matter). Just let the hosts or bartenders know, and they will gladly call a cab.

DOWNTOWN

Downtown Columbus tends to close down a little early, but things should change as revitalization efforts draw local businesses in this direction. The bars listed here are long-established watering holes. Of course, all the major hotels have their own bars, but they have not been included here, as their entertainment options are mentioned in the Accommodations chapter.

Club 185
185 East Livingston Avenue
(614) 228-3904
This friendly neighborhood bar was established in 1954, but after recent renovations it now attracts trendier, young professionals in the 20 to 30 age group. In typical German Village style, the bricks are exposed, the bar is dark, and the ceiling is tin. Mirrors give it an almost bistro-like quality, while couches offer a certain amount of coziness. The atmosphere is convivial, but there's no escaping the noisiness of the place. When it comes to food, it's known for their beef-on-weck and cheeseburgers and serves food till 1:00 A.M.

The Jury Room
22 East Mound Street
(614) 224-7777
The former Courthouse Pub & Grill has reverted back to its original name and is under new ownership, but it is still not a late-night bar. In fact, the Jury Room only serves dinner until 8:00 P.M. It's not a pick-up bar, and you'll find no live music either. It is, however, the watering hole frequented by the judicial arm of Columbus, and you'll find lawyers hashing out the details of their cases over lunch. Though located downtown, it has a true neighborhood bar atmosphere. Come here when you want to toss back a few at happy hour, have a conversation over a pint, and, maybe, encounter a few ghosts. According to the proprietor, this 173-year-old landmark pub is haunted. The small outdoor patio overlooks Mound Street.

The Ringside Cafe
19 North Pearl Street
(614) 228-7464
This 100-year-old tavern, once a speakeasy during the prohibition, is arguably Columbus's oldest sports bar. This dark bar, full of antiques and weary business folk, is tucked in a little alley between all the big buildings. There are decent happy hour prices, and the menu consists of sandwiches and burgers named for famous boxers. The Ringside is more of a happy hour spot and closes around 8:00 P.M. It is not open on weekends.

GERMAN VILLAGE/ BREWERY DISTRICT

The brick streets and cramped brownstones are a reminder that this historic district is home to some of the oldest taverns in Columbus. Parking can be a nuisance, but you are never a far from a popular watering hole. If you choose to park and walk, this area is safe.

The High Beck Corner Tavern
564 South High Street
(614) 224-0886
This lively (and dark) bar is one of the oldest watering holes in town. The clientele is unpretentious. A small patio out front overlooks High Street, allowing you to watch everyone coming and going. There's live music on select nights. The

menu is available for lunch and dinner, and food is served almost until closing.

The Olde Mohawk
821 Mohawk Street
(614) 444-7204

The casual and friendly Olde Mohawk is known for its horseshoe-shaped bar, great service, and hearty, rib-sticking food. It's been a popular German Village hangout for over 60 years. As one of the village's oldest pubs, the Olde Mohawk has acquired all sorts of savory regulars, ranging from mayors to yuppie couples to young kids in shredded jeans. Reubens don't get any fresher than corned beef pulled right off the bone, while the walls, plastered with pictures, will give you a sense of the neighborhood's history. Legend holds this was once a brothel.

Plank's Biergarten
888 South High Street
(614) 443-4570

This old-fashioned beer garden opened in 1960 and is known as much for its pizza as its large selection of beers and microbrews. Most of Columbus is familiar with the Plank family's name, but this sports bar is not to be confused with nearby Plank's Cafe (same family). The atmosphere is casual, and the exposed brick walls and wooden floors are typical of German Village. One can veg out in front of the big-screen TV with "The Works," a pizza loaded with every available topping, then wash it down with one of the 10 beers on tap or choose from the 40 bottles. During summer months, move your party outside to the patio, where there are picnic tables and several televisions. Plank's Biergarten has live music on selected nights, and they deliver year-round.

Round Bar
650 South High Street
(614) 461-9010

It's attached to a Best Western hotel, but who cares? It's round! Booths line the curved walls of this unconventional bar, giving enough privacy to people who want to converse but offering good views the entire way around the room. A nice selection of top-shelf liquors and vintage drinks are served from a central, circular sunken bar. The muted pastel colors can't hide the retro bar that it is.

In the spirit of drinking responsibly, phone numbers for taxi services have been included. It might be wise to program them into your cell phone: Acme Taxi (614-777-7777), German Village Taxi (614-221-2222), Yellow Cab (614-444-4444). Fares between downtown and neighborhoods like Dublin and Worthington may cost a little more, but it's worth it.

Thurman Cafe
183 Thurman Avenue
(614) 443-1570

Thurman's began as a pub in 1937, so it has had almost 70 years to gather the eclectic memorabilia that covers the walls. The worst thing about Thurman's is the wait for a table. Its fun and casual atmosphere attracts people from all around Columbus, and most will agree that Thurman's offers not only the best burger in town but also one of the biggest (if you consider 28 ounces big). Vegetarians will, no doubt, take pleasure in the great steak fries. Food is served until 1:00 A.M., making it a great stop for a late-night snack and drinks.

Victory's Bar
543 South High Street
(614) 224-0693
www.victorys.com

Victory's is obviously doing something right, as it has outlasted some of the trendier places that have come and gone during its 20-year existence. This weekend party spot has shaken its reputation as the ultimate place to meet Mr. or Ms. Right, but it could just be that the clientele has grown up a bit. It hosts modern rock and cover bands and has a dance floor on which the 20- to 30-somethings shake their groove thing. For a different sort of entertainment, you'll find pool, pop-a-shot basketball, and pinball. You can also just grab a slice of pizza and relax on the large, multilevel outdoor patio during the warmer months.

ARENA DISTRICT

The newest entertainment district is 1 block west of the Greater Columbus Convention Center and was built up around Nationwide Arena. Parking options include lots, garages, and street meters.

Barley's Brewing Company, Alehouse No. 1
467 North High Street
(614) 228-2537
www.barleysbrewing.com
The godfather of Columbus microbrewing, Scott Francis, has been serving Barley's traditionally brewed ales, stouts, and seasonal beers since 1992. A rare, gas-fired brew kettle caramelizes the malt for MacLenny's Scottish Ale, a must for beer lovers. Virtually everything is worth tasting here. A firkin cask of "real ale" is tapped each Friday and is served till it's gone (and it goes fast). Barley's is considered one of the best brewpubs in town, but ironically, it is not located in Columbus's historic Brewery District.

Barley's is situated across the street from the convention center, making it a convenient meeting point from all parts of town. The spacious oak bar and dining room have a lot of seating, televisions, and a few dartboards. Be advised, when a band is playing, it becomes crowded and very loud. The menu is varied and consists of reasonably priced American and British food. Mildred's sauerkraut balls and the pile-high nachos top the list of popular appetizers. You can also take home a jug of your favorite Barley's brew, refillable as quickly as you can drink it.

Brother's Bar & Grill
477 North Park Street
(614) 221-0673, (614) 232-9020
During the week, Brothers draws more of an after-work crowd with its TVs, pool tables, and happy hour specials, but come weekend think spring break. It seems everyone in Columbus who has recently turned 21 winds up here. Aside from the attractive 20-something crowd, the dance floor is the other big draw. With the summertime comes an outdoor patio for dining and drinking under the stars. The adjacent Taswërks draws a slightly older crowd, but is under the same ownership.

Frog, Bear and Wild Boar Bar
343 North Front Street
(614) 621-9453
www.frogbearbar.com
This place with all the animals in its name is a big bar with loud music and a lot of elbows being bumped. It's primarily an evening venue, but it has become quite popular with the downtown crowd at lunch. Could it be the view overlooking Nationwide Courtyard or perhaps the all-day $1.50 domestic beer special? Maybe it's the impressive assemblage of upscale bar food on the menu. Evenings bring about the mid-20 to mid-30 set, and the gigantic outdoor patio is packed all summer till the wee hours of the morning. Expect to pay hefty cover charges on some nights. Live local and regional bands play on Thursday, and a deejay cranks out dance music on weekend nights.

O'Shaughnessy's Public House
401 North Front Street
(614) 224-6767
www.ospub.com
Located just a stone's throw away from Nationwide Arena, O'Shaughnessy's is a popular stopover for those going to games or concerts. Food is served in a dining room and loft area separate from the bar. It's open for lunch and dinner, and the corned beef sandwich gets rave

reviews. Games are shown on a few TVs, while energetic Irish musicians provide live entertainment. The atmosphere can be festive and the bar a bit claustrophobic before and after events.

SHORT NORTH

This SoHo-style neighborhood is a safe, fun place to people watch and stroll around. Who would believe this melting pot of the alternative and trendy, casual, and upscale was once a crime-ridden, run-down area?

Blazer's Pub
1205 North High Street
(614) 299-1800
www.rascalnut.com/blazers
Every night is ladies' night, but anyone is welcome at this primarily lesbian bar. You will find good drinks at a good price in a very friendly setting. There's karaoke on Thursday, which will help you tap into your inner star, and if karaoke isn't your thing, they also have pool and darts. Happy hour goes until 8:00 P.M.

Brian Boru's Pub
647 North High Street
(614) 221-1250
Yes, Brian Boru was for real, and there is a mammoth mural of this Irish king galloping across the back wall of the pub. Other than that, this is the Short North's answer to an Irish pub, but don't expect too much authenticity beyond a good selection of beer. The gold margaritas are very popular with regulars. You can take a seat out front on the outdoor patio, or you can stay inside and play pool and darts.

Burgundy Room
642 North High Street
(614) 464-9463
www.burgundyroom.net
This is Columbus's one and only wine and tapas bar, but you don't have to be a connoisseur to recognize why people flock here. A wine menu the size of a phone book with 60-plus wines by the glass says it all. But it's not just the consumables that set this place apart from other bars. The ambience definitely lives up to its smooth-sounding name. The Burgundy Room exudes a traditional wine bar ambience, with its wooden floors and long, narrow bar. Autumnal colors warm up the space a bit, but it could just be the wine.

The menu makes it easy to pair wine with food, as it is separated into white and red. Try not to come with a huge appetite, as the tapas are "European-sized," which basically means they are small portions. Try the beef carpaccio or the Manhattan clam chowder, a rarity on Columbus menus. The staff is knowledgeable and enthusiastic. The Burgundy Room is a must for all wine enthusiasts, but they also have a fine selection of imported beers, scotches, and vodkas.

Mac's Cafe
693 North High Street
(614) 221-6227
Mac's has the inviting nature and atmosphere of a true Scottish pub, not to mention a huge selection of imported and domestic beers. The walls are decorated with paraphernalia from the British Isles and golf towels from various courses. Wooden floors and booths give the place a publike warmth, while a piano player bangs out tunes on certain days. Bring your best mate along for a Scotch egg or cottage pie, then shoot a game of pool in the back room.

Novak's on High
479 North High Street
(614) 224-8821
You have to climb a long flight of narrow stairs up to this dark bar, past a doorman who will card you if you look under 30. Novak's is a late-night favorite among young professionals looking for a stiff drink. The bar is often full, but the best seats in the house are next to the windows overlooking High Street. There are a few pool tables, but the crowds will sometimes hinder the game.

Short North Tavern
674 North High Street
(614) 221-2432
This Short North institution is often voted the best neighborhood bar. It's been serving up soups, subs, chili, and pasta for ages, and no doubt many a grandfather has tied one on here. There are dartboards and live music several nights a week, with a small cover charge. If you happen to like one of the paintings hanging on the walls, it can be yours—if the price is right. All the art by local artists is for sale.

Union Station Video Cafe
630 North High Street
(614) 228-3546
www.columbusnightlife.com
Dozens of TVs buzzing with music videos line the walls of this predominantly gay bar. *Friends, Queer Eye,* and OSU games are piped in on a weekly basis, while show tunes take over on Sunday. This preclubbing hot spot serves a full range of home-cooked entrees, pastas, and burgers in a relaxed, nonthreatening atmosphere. A great happy hour runs seven days a week.

Zola Dining Lounge
782 North High Street
(614) 291-3463
www.zoladininglounge.com
Art and imagination are what this restaurant/late-night lounge is all about. Wood-fired gourmet pizzas, unique seafood specials, and other fusion cuisine are served until 10:00 P.M., after which a late-night menu kicks in until 2:00 A.M. In keeping with an enchanted yet sophisticated atmosphere, the bar glows with red lighting, and the wine list is inspired. This comfortable, urbane lounge, named for writer Emile Zola, is open 7 days a week until 2:30 A.M. It showcases artwork by students from the Columbus College of Art and Design. A professor from CCAD, Dawson Kellogg, made the stunning chandelier. Zola's was rated one of the best new restaurants of 2004 by *Columbus Monthly.*

VICTORIAN VILLAGE

B. Hampton's
West Third Avenue and Harrison
(614) 299-6999
From the outside, this may look like a fancy bistro, but once inside you'll find a very different story: loud music, unassuming decor, people of all ages hanging out at the long, wooden bar. The clients are a mix of locals who can walk from their Victorian Village homes and college students who manage to create their own dance floor between the tables. This popular bar serves a versatile and affordable mix of pub grub and pasta entrees. You'll also find very good happy hour specials.

Victorian's Midnight Cafe
251 West Fifth Avenue
(614) 299-2295
www.victoriansmidnightcafe.com
This self-proclaimed "hub of weirdness" falls somewhere between a coffeehouse and a bar, though one might be inclined to lean toward the latter, as they stock around 40 beers, serve a wide range of food, and have live entertainment. An open mike seems to attract a varying degree of talent looking for their 15 minutes, while onlookers lounge around on sofas and church pews. The violet walls, pink detailing, and antique-shop decor add to the individuality of this cafe. Vegetarians and vegans are catered to, but comfort foods, such as chili and "big fat subs," are also available.

Zeno's Victorian Village
384 West Third Avenue
(614) 294-9158
A little bit of trivia: This friendly neighborhood pub lays claim to the city's second-longest bar. This is a fun, casual place, with dancing, billiards, and a dining room that serves pizzas, sandwiches, and the usual late-night nosh. The clientele is a mix of locals and students of all ages.

CLINTONVILLE/BEECHWOLD

Dick's Den
2417 North High Street
(614) 268-9573

This cool neighborhood dive is a favorite for jazz among the over-30 group. The bar has been around for decades, and the decor is a friendly reminder of this. Time-worn bar stools, picnic tables, and a jukebox that plays only vintage soul and jazz create a '60s "Beat" atmosphere, which is only enhanced by jazz-backed poetry readings and regular tributes to Jack Kerouac.

Ledo's Lounge
2608 North High Street
(614) 263-1009

This simple neighborhood bar on the corner of High and Duncan draws both a Clintonville and campus clientele. Ohio State students converge on the place later in the evenings, when females can partake in a weekly hula-hoop contest atop the bar while anyone can participate in Pogo-Stick Mondays. How smart is it to have people bouncing on pogo sticks with a belly full of beer? You are also guaranteed plenty of drunken, sing-a-long songs. Ledo's has a small outdoor patio, and free pizza is provided during happy hour on Friday.

Oldfield's on High
2590 North High Street
(614) 784-0477
www.oldfieldsonhigh.com

Not quite a dive campus bar but still bordering on grungy, Oldfield's draws more of a postgraduate crowd, with its proximity to campus, happy hour specials, pool tables, and TVs. There is live entertainment and dancing many nights of the week.

Patrick J's
2711 North High Street
(614) 784-0660

Patrick J's is a tried-and-true neighborhood bar, with TVs, tables, and good food, the latter creating that fuzzy line between restaurant and bar. At the end of the day, it is just a comfortable gathering place for locals and a post-college-aged crowd. The menu items are named after local streets and attractions. The Park of Roses Reuben and Arden Road roast beef dip are particularly popular, while vegetarians might prefer the Broadway veggie burger. There are also drink specials, plenty of bar food, and a nice selection of salads. The restaurant was refurbished after a 2002 accident involving a fire truck crashing into the building, so have a look at the photos on the wall—it's rather shocking. The outdoor, fenced-in deck has a dozen tables, and an occasional acoustic or blues band will play at Patrick J's.

WORTHINGTON

Kacy's Sports Bar & Grill
480 East Wilson Bridge Road
(614) 847-0780

Kacy's is all sports, all the time. If video games, Golden Tee, and dartboards don't create a festive enough environment, perhaps the karaoke will. The menu consists of basic entrees, appetizers, and sandwiches with sports-related names. There are also daily happy hour specials. During the summer, you can play bocce ball and listen to live classic rock on the patio.

P. K. O'Ryan's Restaurant & Pub
666 High Street, Olde Worthington
(614) 781-0770

If you're in the mood for some blarney, you'll get it here along with a pint of ale and some good Irish stew. The restaurant, located in the front of the building, is a classy little place with a small bar, but don't be disappointed. The pub proper is in the back of the building and accessed through a different side door. They both use the same kitchen and share the same menu. Since the restaurant side closes early, the pub offers a full range of nosh and spirits well into the evening. With a bit of luck, Worthington has been bestowed this lively Irish pub whose owners have thoughtfully decorated the dark walls with treasures brought from across the pond.

Feeling Fishy?

Ask anyone in the city where to get the best fish-and-chips, and most likely they'll say The Bag or The Bucket. The Old Bag of Nails Pubs are a charming group of English-style taverns that have become an institution throughout the Columbus community. The Rusty Bucket Corner Taverns are more of a hybrid pub-bistro that, likewise, commands a faithful following. Diehard aficionados and true veterans of English pubs might find both of these establishments a bit contrived or too Americanized, but there is no denying their fish-and-chips are as good as any you'll find in England.

If you have ever ventured across the pond to London and wandered beyond Buckingham Palace, chances are you have encountered the Bag's namesake. Many Columbusites make the pilgrimage to the Motherhouse, which is also where Paul McCartney met his first wife, Linda Eastman.

Of the six Bag of Nails locations, the flagship pub in Olde Worthington is the closest to an authentic pub and is aptly named, as it was once part of the neighboring hardware store. Its dark, tight quarters are often two or three people deep at the bar. Unless you show up early for one of the half-dozen tables, you may end up waiting upward of an hour to be seated, especially on weekends. Never mind, though; the bar is more the focal point of this pub. The drink menu offers a long list of imported beers and has one of the best selections of scotch around. It's a good atmosphere in which to have a pint of Guinness, but not with a large group.

The five other locations are more accommodating to larger groups and have similar atmospheres. Separate bar and dining areas give off a more restaurant-like vibe, but the Bag of Nails in Grandview and Gahanna have a lively neighborhood pub feel to them, especially at happy hour. They are popular meeting places for groups, and the wait for a table isn't nearly as long as it would be in Worthington.

If you prefer a more family-oriented atmosphere, the Bag of Nails in Upper Arlington, Bexley, and Powell offer the same pub menu in a more spacious restaurant setting. Cozy booths and big tables give families the option of dining away from the bars. These three are definitely the most restaurant-like of them all. One should not come here expecting an authentic pub experience, but they can get a bit rowdy on weekends and during OSU football games.

The booze ban has been lifted in uptown Westerville, and another Bag will soon be opened to those folks living in the northeast. No matter where you are, you're never far from a Bag of Nails Pub. Any one of them is worth seeking out for their signature fish-and-chip and deep-fried pickles.

The Rusty Bucket Corner Taverns can, quite literally, be found on the corners of a few upscale shopping plazas. They are by no means pubs in the purest sense of the word. They are spacious and gleaming, with a lot of light wood. They are

A happy patron at the Old Bag of Nails Pub, Upper Arlington. SHAWNIE KELLEY

open and airy and have plenty of big-screen TVs around the bar area. In fact, the Rusty Buckets are more akin to a glossy Parisian bistro than an English tavern, but who cares? They make a mean fish-and-chips, not to mention killer burgers. Families are as much at home in these restaurants as single guys watching the game at the bar. Weekends can become crowded, but the regulars find it well worth the wait for a table.

Speaking of waiting, if you have never tried Marino's Seafood Fish and Chips in Grandview Heights, you best go get in line. While it may seem like a glorified Long John Silver from the outside and the spartan interior is a bit bland, fast food is taken to new heights at this seafood joint. You can't ask for better value and quality for under $7.00. They'll load you up on fried fish, chips, and hush puppies, but also offer healthier items such as poached, baked, or stuffed fish, seafood linguine, and soups. Marino's has a handful of booths at which you can eat in, but most people carry out. There is a reason their fish-and-chips are regularly voted best in Columbus, and that's because they are just downright good. Marino's Seafood is located at 1216 West Fifth Avenue, and its phone number is (614) 481-8428.

Old Bag of Nails Pubs
663 High Street, Olde Worthington
(614) 436-5552
www.oldbagofnails.com

63 Mill Street, Gahanna
(614) 337-9430

2102 Tremont Center, Upper Arlington
(614) 486-6976

1099 First Avenue, Grandview Heights
(614) 299-7211

18 North Nelson Road, Bexley
(614) 252-4949

1993 Hard Road, Powell
(614) 764-2233

24 North State Street, Westerville

Rusty Bucket Taverns
180 Market Street, New Albany
(614) 939-5300

1635 West Lane Avenue
Upper Arlington
(614) 485-2303

6644 Perimeter Loop Road, Dublin
(614) 889-2594

7800 Olentangy River Road, Worthington
(614) 436-2626

WESTERVILLE

Wendell's Pub
925 North State Street
(614) 818-0400
Tucked in the back of a small strip mall, this unpublicized pub can be a little evasive, but it's worth searching out when you are on this side of town. They serve up really good fish-and-chips in a bistro-like atmosphere. The bar is large, and there's a nice selection of draft beers and wines by the glass. You may eat in the bar area, the dining room, or on the outdoor patio, which is quite pleasant in the summertime, despite overlooking a parking lot.

NEW ALBANY/ GAHANNA AREA

Flanagan's Pub
3001 Reynoldsburg-New Albany Road
(614) 855-7472
www.flanaganspub57.com
At first glance, you may mistake this green, box-shaped building for a garage, but inside it's a friendly, casual bar that has been keeping men out of their wives' hair since 1957. Anything more than jeans and T-shirts seems overdressed, and anyone with a penchant for racing will take pleasure in the memorabilia covering the walls. The ambience is familiar and cozy. Many locals on this side of town swear by Flanagan's burgers.

Gatsby's
151 North Hamilton Road
(614) 476-0088
Come here only if you are feeling rowdy and in the mood to have a good time. This compact place is surprisingly equipped for dancing, karaoke, sand volleyball, and fantasy NASCAR racing. There are two outdoor patios and live music on many nights.

Signatures Bar & Grille
94 Mill Street
(614) 475-2220
This bar-restaurant fills up rather quickly on weekends, as many of the live bands draw a faithful crowd from all over town. The whole gang can be accommodated at wooden tables, and the food is above-average pub grub. The outdoor patio is one perk, and NTN trivia is the other.

GRANDVIEW

Brazenhead Pub
1027 West Fifth Avenue
(614) 737-3738

Like its mother house in Dublin (Ohio), Brazenhead's features an authentic Irish setting complete with wood paneling, brass fixtures, and a fireplace. The building is multistoried, so if the ground floor gets crowded (and it does), head to the bar downstairs. Tables are tucked in cozy little nooks, called snugs, and there are a dozen different beers on tap.

The large, fenced-in patio faces Fifth Avenue, but people watching more than makes up for this unexciting scenery. Brazenhead can be crowded on Wednesday evenings because of the appealing happy hour specials. In the summertime, Irish bands pack the patio on Thursday. They have a commendable lunch and dinner menu, which includes the popular Guinness-battered fish-and-chips.

Buckeye Hall of Fame Cafe
1421 Olentangy River Road
(614) 338-6412
www.halloffamecafes.com

You don't have to bleed scarlet and gray to appreciate the quality and sheer volume of historic Ohio State sports paraphernalia that lines the walls of this cafe. Star-shaped tiles set in the Walk of Fame immortalize Buckeye superstars in Hollywood fashion. Autographed footballs, basketballs, photos, game stubs, and uniforms are among the items in the changing displays, and one of Archie Griffin's two Heisman Trophies is permanently exhibited.

This large facility is broken into the Trophy Room, with its big, open bar area and separate dining room, and the Arena Room, with its big-screen TVs and interactive video games. The upscale menu ranges from appetizers and burgers to filets and pasta. The Buckeye Cafe hosts a variety of social events, including live music, a dinner theater, and tail-gating parties. It also offers a preconcert "Shuttle to the Schott" to spare you the grief of parking. The student BuckID is accepted here.

With British-style pubs popping up all over Columbus, one might be interested to know that pub is short for "public house." It is commonly held that as Romans conquered Britain, pubs were built as safe stopover points along the inhospitable roads. It was the industrious medieval monks who first served home-brewed ale at their public guesthouses.

Byrne's Pub
1248 West Third Street
(614) 482-4722
www.byrnespub.com

Byrne's is an Irish pub in every aspect—a dark wooden bar, friendly bartenders serving up a bit o' blarney, and pints of frothy Guinness—the proper way. There is even Irish music on the jukebox. Byrne's does not serve food, but you are not expected to drink on an empty stomach. Fill up on free popcorn, or order grub from Granddad's Pizza right across the street. The outdoor patio is festive, and traditional Irish bands entertain Monday night patrons. Visit often enough and you might be in the running for Patron of the Month.

Gibby's
1433 West Third Avenue
(614) 488-3711
www.gibbysbarandgrill.com

This cozy restaurant is a popular gathering place in the heart of Grandview. Sports fans come for the half dozen TVs showing football games and golf tournaments. Foodies come for the award-winning chicken wings and the seafood gumbo. Belly up to the bar or take a seat on the full-service patio in the summertime. A fireplace warms the spacious dining room in the winter. Gibby's offers daily food specials, a Sunday brunch, and an inexpensive happy hour Monday through

Friday. A second location is in the Arena District at 51 Vine Street (614-221-5550).

The Grandview Cafe
1445 West Third Avenue
(614) 486-2233
www.grandviewcafe.com
The Grandview Cafe doesn't have that "mom and pop" ambience their home-style food might imply. It has more of a reputation for being a pick-up joint among the mature singles, but it retains a calm, relaxed environment. A large bar and booths fill the ground level, while a bar and stage dominate the second floor. Local bands play on the weekends, when it becomes very crowded. Patrons can spill over onto an outdoor patio in the summer months. People tend to meet and eat at this convenient spot before pub hopping across Grandview.

The Knotty Pine
1765 West Third Avenue
(614) 488-8878
Though recently renovated, non-Grandview denizens might be surprised to learn that this modern pub has been serving the neighborhood since 1935. Described as a bar that serves food, the dining rooms take on a family atmosphere at mealtimes, but the evenings attract patrons from the surrounding area looking for a casual, friendly drinking environment. It is a nice blend of retro woodwork and understated modern decor. A big front patio is open seasonally, and the bar features flat-screen TVs.

Red Door Tavern
1736 West Fifth Avenue
(614) 488-5433
This oasis among trendy eateries has remained unchanged since it opened in 1964. The Grandview landmark has a wood-paneled dining room, antiques, plenty of bar stools, and, of course, a red door. Those who wear jeans and drink domestic beer will feel right at home here.

The Rose & Thistle
1200 Chambers Road
(614) 486-1990
An out-of-the-way location can make this old English-style pub a little difficult to find. The pub is in the lower level of the building, but you'll know you're in the right place when you encounter farm equipment and a carriage on display in the entry. Stained glass and memorabilia-covered walls give the Rose & Thistle a casual, pubby feel. There's a large selection of ales and single-malt scotches, but the menu consists mostly of American favorites. There's also outdoor patio seating.

Spagio Cellars
1291 Grandview Avenue
(614) 486-1114
www.spagiocellars.com
Spagio Cellars is a cross between a wine bar, cigar lounge, gift shop, and wine emporium. Peruse the shelves for that perfect bottle to uncork and enjoy at one of the tables, or take it home with you for later. Spagio's carries gourmet food items, international cheeses, stemware, and several thousand premium wines, including those hard-to-find bottles. The limited menu serves food from the adjacent Spagio restaurant.

UPPER ARLINGTON

Arlington Billiard & Cafe
1975 West Henderson Road
(614) 538-0008
Just look for the OSU flag as big as the American flag next to it, and you've found the Arlington Cafe. There is a little bit of something for everyone here, which is why it's regularly voted Columbus's top sports bar by local magazines. People of all ages are drawn to the pool tables and TVs showing games and reality shows. The 20-somethings are usually found wiggling around on the dance floor to '70s and '80s music. The menu is loaded with appetizers,

salads, and pizzas. One can escape the rowdiness of the Arlington Cafe to its adjacent, mellower sister bar, Cazzie's.

Pockets Sports Bar & Grill
4510 Kenny Road
(614) 442-7665
www.pocketssportsbar.com
Pockets is a sports bar that prides itself in showing a comprehensive range of sporting events. Check out the Web site, or pick up a calendar listing all the football, baseball, basketball, hockey, golf, NASCAR, and pay-per-view sporting events shown on their 21 televisions (6 big screens). The bar is pool table intensive but also has video games, NTN trivia, and a new outdoor patio. The menu offers good-value pub grub and daily, college-priced happy hour specials.

DUBLIN

The Bogey Inn Lounge & Restaurant
6013 Glick Road
(614) 764-1727
www.bogeyinn.com
This clubby bar sits on the edge of Muirfield Village Golf Club and draws celebrities and golf greats when they are in town for the Muirfield Golf Tournament. It's no surprise there is a golf mural on the wall and stained-glass panels of famous courses in the skylight. The dining room is warm, with mahogany tones and exposed brick, while the bar is relaxed and surrounded by flat-screen TVs. The huge patio plays host to summer volleyball tournaments and outdoor dancing.

Brazenhead Pub
56 North High Street, Old Dublin
(614) 792-3738
What can a million dollars get you? In this case, an authentically reproduced, character-ridden Irish pub in historic Dublin (Ohio). Sparing no expense on the handmade interior, it was installed by carpenters brought direct from the Emerald Isle. Three floors of snugs (private nooks) offer intimacy and privacy. Fireplaces on each floor and a lot of dark wood enhance the coziness; antique Guinness signs, imported brew, and Irish-themed nosh comes across more Irish than a real Irish pub. Contrived or not, there is a lot of atmosphere here. Irish bands play on the outdoor patio during the summer.

Dublin Village Tavern
27 South High Street, Old Dublin
(614) 766-6250
www.dublinvillagetavern.com
This 115-year-old, ivy-covered building has served as a stagecoach stop, post office, and hardware store. It now serves the community in a different way, with tavern-style fare and daily drink specials. Regulars come for the burgers and congeniality. George Killian Lett, the great-grandson of the founder of Killian's Brewery in Ireland, even made a personal visit shortly after they opened.

Flannagan's Dublin
6835 Caine Road,
at Sawmill Road and I-270
(614) 766-7788
www.flannagans.com
Who says you have to live in California to play beach volleyball? Flannagan's attracts a young, fun crowd with its sand volleyball courts, live music, and, oh yeah, drinks. You'll find a large selection of bottled and draft beer at cheap prices. The massive outdoor patio has a full-service bar, televisions, and pool tables for those on the sidelines. A variety of live local and national bands pass through these doors. Flannagan's serves typical pub grub for dinner only.

Mary Kelley's
7148 Muirfield Drive
(614) 760-7041
www.marykelleys.com
This Dublin favorite is both a bar and a restaurant serving American fare. The lodgelike dining room is separated from

the Boarshead Pub by a double-sided, fieldstone fireplace. It is an open and spacious bar with live music on select nights. As a side note, their pies get rave reviews.

DUBLIN-WORTHINGTON/ DUBLIN-ARLINGTON AREA

Coaches Bar & Grill
1480 Bethel Road
(614) 457-3353
This popular sports bar has a very homey feel to it and, despite its location in a big strip mall, has all the qualities of a local, neighborhood bar, such as big-screen TVs, super-friendly service, and the occasional summertime cookout. The outdoor patio has three TVs and provides a quieter setting to catch that big game. Coaches sponsors softball teams and tends to draw the postgame crowd, drinking in victory or drowning their sorrows.

Fitzgerald's Sports Tavern
2640 Bethel Road
(614) 457-3489
Plenty of food and drink specials, a dance floor, pool tables, and karaoke contests draw a mixed bag of people to this sports bar/dance club. The menu includes the usual pub fare, along with appetizers and dinner entrees. A big-screen TV and sports memorabilia offer a good setting to catch a variety of sporting events. When the weather is nice, take your drinking outdoors, where there are four televisions on a big patio.

NIGHTLIFE

When the sun goes down, do you go out? I am not going to try and fool anyone into believing that Columbus's nightlife is anything like New York City or Chicago, but not much is. While researching this chapter, I was surprised at how many people said, "There's nothing to do" or "The options are limited," but one might better understand their sentiments after learning they just moved here from Las Vegas and New York. At the end of the day (and, hopefully, by the end of this chapter), the night owls of Columbus can find enough to keep them busy until the wee hours of the morning.

Those of you who have not yet retired your dancing shoes will be happy to know there are a handful of nightclubs to satisfy the "serious clubber" in you and countless bars with dance floors for the not-so-serious. More and more pubs and clubs that cater to Columbus's large gay population are cropping up in the downtown and Short North areas. Rather than create a separate listing singling them out, I have chosen to integrate them here and into The Pub Crawl and Restaurants chapters. Effort has been made to mention the alternative scene when appropriate.

As for live music, Columbus has loads of venues, ranging from formal concert halls and amphitheaters to dedicated blues bars and neighborhood taverns featuring national and local acts. Once again, the Brewery District, Arena District, and the Short North are the premier, late-night entertainment districts where one can park and walk to some of the most popular live music venues in the city. The entries here will focus on those specific areas, while the clubs on campus are listed in The Ohio State University chapter.

If it's the theater arts you prefer, Columbus boasts five major downtown venues at which the city's arts organizations perform year-round. The Ohio State University and Otterbein College each have their own campus theaters, while several communities and high schools put on annual productions. You can read more about Columbus's performing arts in The Arts chapter, but they should not be overlooked as a fun night out on the town.

An alternative to a sophisticated evening out at the theater might be a raucous night of risqué *Saturday Night Live*-style skits and music at 2Co's or the Shadowbox Cabaret. Those looking for entertainment of an even more "adult" nature usually know where to find it, so I am only going to make the passing comment that strip clubs, gentlemen's clubs, after-hours clubs—what have you—are plentiful in Columbus, so just check the yellow pages. They are not listed here. Live music, comedy, and improv can be had almost any night of the week, but your best bet is to check out *The Other Paper,* a weekly entertainment publication, for the goings-on around the city.

Movie lovers have a variety of options, ranging from movies at mainstream multiscreened cineplexes, foreign and alternative flicks at the smaller independent Drexel Theatres, or avante-garde film festivals at the Wexner Center. Columbus can also brag a monstrous, state-of-the-art movie screen at the science center and an old-fashioned drive-in just south of the city.

For the more caffeinated types, some coffee shops are open well into the early morning, and bookworms will find many of the bookstores stay open long past a lot of people's bedtimes. And don't forget the bowling alleys, which are listed in the participant sports section of the Parks and Recreation chapter; some of these joints are open 24 hours a day and serve food and beer long into the night.

If, after reading through this introduction and the entries in this chapter, you can still find nothing to do after dark in

Columbus, my final suggestion is to just go to bed.

CINEMAS

Several multiscreened AMC theater complexes, conveniently located around Columbus, offer the most recent releases of mainstream movies. There are 18 theaters at Dublin Village (Sawmill Road and Interstate 270), a whopping 30 at Easton Town Center, and 24 screens at Lennox Town Center (Kinnear Road). You can call (614) 429-4262 to hear the movie times at any of these three theaters or prepurchase tickets. Movies-16 at 329 Stoneridge Lane in Gahanna (614-471-7321) is another option for those of you on the East Side.

If you are not concerned about seeing the film the week it's released, then a discount theater may be the way to go, especially if you plan on hauling the whole family. Entrances may range from 50 cents to $4.00 at the following theaters: Cinemark Movies-12 theaters are located at 2570 Bethel Road in Carriage Place Plaza (614-538-0400) and in Mill Run Plaza off Fishinger Road (614-777-1010).

Arena Grand Theatre
174 West Nationwide Boulevard
(614) 469-5000
www.arenagrand.com

The owners of the Drexel Theatres have redefined going to the movies. Columbus's newest state-of-the-art theater shows independent and first-run films in a first-rate setting. Take advantage of a unique service that allows you to reserve luxurious leather reclining seats on the balcony level, super-rise level, or in an intimate "studio-style" screening room up to a week in advance. Arena Grand has eight screens, 1,700 seats, and a full-service menu and bar. Take your drinks into the theater, or dine on the terrace level while watching the movie. Parking in the Arena Grand garage is only $1.00 with a validated ticket.

If you are a student or senior, be sure to show your ID for discounted admission to most of the movie theaters listed in this chapter. Matinee showings (movies before 6:00 P.M.) are also generally cheaper.

Drexel Theatres-Bexley
2254 East Main Street
(614) 231-9512
www.drexel.net

If you prefer foreign-language films and artsy documentaries to Hollywood blockbusters, this is one of the only places to find them in Columbus (aside from OSU). The historic theater is atmospheric and old-fashioned, so the picture can be a little dim when compared to high-tech cinemas. Ginger Rogers even attended the opening of this theater. The attached Radio Cafe serves coffee, beer, wine, and snacks and has its own street-side entrance.

Drexel Theatres-Grandview
1247 Grandview Avenue
(614) 486-6114
www.drexel.net

This Grandview landmark is Columbus's other offbeat independent movie theater. Like its sister in Bexley, it shows alternative flicks on one big, old-fashioned screen. The ticket booth is literally a booth. The Drexel Theatres are a true celebration of film and have regular cinematic events, like runs of *Monty Python, Casablanca* night, and science-fiction marathons.

John Glenn Theatre at the Center of Science and Industry (COSI)
333 West Broad Street
(614) 221-2674
www.cosi.org

Educational and scientific movies are shown Wednesday through Sunday on the seven-story extreme screen. These monstrous, head-spinning films about volcanoes, space, and world culture run about 40 minutes. General admission to COSI is not required, but discounts are given to science center ticket holders.

South Drive-In
3050 South High Street
(614) 291-3297
The last traditional drive-in in Columbus is not going anywhere anytime soon because it's not in the most desirable part of town for developers. Tuning into the radio might be the better alternative to the old-fashioned speakers, as they don't work very well (we are probably just spoiled with high-tech theaters). It's open seasonally.

Wexner Center for the Arts
1871 North High Street
OSU campus
(614) 292-3535
www.wexarts.org
As part of The Ohio State University, this is Columbus's foremost venue for contemporary and independent film and video. It sponsors several film series throughout the year that feature atmospheric international movies, classics, and documentaries on alternative and artsy topics. Visiting filmmakers will sometimes speak before the showing of their film. The theater is located in the film/video theater in the Wexner Center Building on OSU's campus.

CONCERT VENUES

Most of Columbus's major concert venues are located right in the heart of the city, so you'll never have to go far, but that's not to say you won't sit in traffic for hours. Some of these venues play host to an array of sporting and entertainment events aside from concerts. Tickets can be purchased at the individual box offices, Kroger Ticket Master Outlets, or by contacting Columbus Ticket Master directly at (614) 431-3600 or at www.ticketmaster.com.

Columbus Music Hall
734 Oak Avenue
(614) 464-0044
www.columbusmusichall.com
This restored Victorian-era firehouse, located just east of Broad Street, is home to an intimate concert hall featuring live jazz, contemporary folk, classical, Latin, and country music. There are also regular, ongoing programs. Tickets can be purchased at the door or in advance by calling.

Germain Amphitheater
2200 Polaris Parkway, Westerville
(614) 431-2200
Also known as Polaris Amphitheater, this is Columbus's premier outdoor concert venue. Some 20,000 people can be packed into general and reserved seating to see big-name acts like the Dave Matthews Band, Jimmy Buffett, and Aerosmith. Most of the reserved seats are under a covered pavilion, while lawn seats have no protection from the elements. Lawn seats are the cheapest tickets and can be the most fun for big groups. Food and alcohol are available. Give yourself ample time to sit in concert traffic on Polaris Parkway and Route 71.

Nationwide Arena
200 West Nationwide Boulevard
(614) 246-2000
www.nationwidearena.com
When the Bluejackets aren't playing on their home turf, the Arena becomes a major concert venue for acts like U2, Elton John, and the Rolling Stones. You will also find a mixture of unusual events like rodeos, ice performances, and monster truck jams. Tickets may be purchased at Nationwide Arena's ticket office or through Ticket Master.

Newport Music Hall
1722 North High Street, OSU campus
(614) 294-1659
www.newportmusichall.com
America's longest continually running rock club is located right in the heart of America's biggest university. Newport can hold up to 1,700 people, but most seats have good views of the stage, as it was once a theater. As old as it is, it shows no sign of slowing down and is still the venue where

up-and-comers take the stage. Jefferson Airplane and the Grateful Dead played here back in the day, while more recently Three Doors Down and The Killers graced the stage. Though some college students might find the prices a bit steep, it is still one of the more affordable concert venues in the city.

PromoWest Pavilion
405 Neil Avenue, Arena District
(614) 461-5483
www.promowestpavilion.com
This indoor/outdoor facility caters to concertgoers who prefer a smaller, more intimate venue accommodating anywhere from 500 to 3,000 people. General admission tickets to the indoor concerts translate to "standing room only," as most of the seating is reserved. There is no covered area outdoors, but there are a limited number of reserved seats down front. A majority of the outdoor seating is on the lawn. PromoWest brings in newer, bigger names and emerging talent in comedy, rock, jazz, and country music. The likes of David Gray, George Clinton, and Marilyn Manson have played here.

i

Park in the Buckeye Lots (off Ackerman Road), and the Quick Schott shuttle will provide pick-up and drop-off service to the Schottenstein Center's front door beginning 90 minutes before and for an hour after the event. It also operates during men's basketball games. Call (614) 688-3939 to see if it's running.

The Jerome Schottenstein Center
555 Arena Drive, just off Lane Avenue OSU campus
(800) GO-BUCKS
www.schottensteincenter.com
Affectionately referred to as "The Schott," the Value City Arena is home not only to The Ohio State University's basketball and hockey teams but also to big-name concerts like Bruce Springsteen and Usher. This modern facility can accommodate up to 21,000 for concerts. Tickets can be purchased during normal weekday business hours at the Schottenstein Box Office in the southeast rotunda or any time through Ticket Master.

Veterans Memorial
300 West Broad Street, downtown
(614) 228-5421
www.fcvm.com
Built in 1955 and recently renovated, this is the largest auditorium in Columbus. It can seat nearly 4,000 people and is ideal for small concerts, conferences, and graduations. David Bowie, Bob Dylan, and even "The King" played Vets Memorial, and the annual Arnold Schwarzenegger Classic (see Annual Events and Festivals) brings some of the world's most prestigious bodybuilders to this stage.

GROUP ENTERTAINMENT

This section includes a variety of amusement places that can entertain individuals as well as couples and larger groups.

2Co's Cabaret
790 North High Street, Short North
(614) 470-2267
www.shadowboxcabaret.com
This intimate warehouse-theater in the heart of the Short North is owned and operated by Shadowbox Cabaret. It offers dramatic theater, light theater, monologues, poetry, and live music. The shows run about two hours, Thursday through Saturday, and there's a full menu and bar service. In between skits, the performers dole out drinks and food, so be sure to leave them a great tip for their doubly hard work. Reservations are strongly recommended, as tickets are sold at the door on a first come, first served basis.

Cloak & Dagger Dinner Theatre
1048 Morse Road, Worthington Area
(614) 842-2583, (800) WE-KIL-4U
www.cloakdagger.com

A four-course meal, along with murder, mystery, and mayhem, is served up in between scenes by the characters from these ever-changing performances. You'll be treated to talented singing and dancing while you sit back and try to figure out "whodunit." The price, which runs about $40, includes the meal and show. Performances are on Friday and Saturday, and prepaid reservations are required.

The Funnybone Comedy Club and Cafe
145 Easton Town Center
(614) 471-5653
www.columbusfunnybone.com
National and local comedians give live performances seven nights a week at this Easton staple. Drew Carey, Jerry Seinfeld, and Ellen Degeneres are among the biggest names to have played here. Food and alcohol are served, and if you are on the mailing list, you will occasionally get discount coupons and free passes.

Gameworks
165 Easton Town Center
(614) 428-7529
www.gameworks.com
This is no arcade. High-tech shooting, racing and flying games, virtual boxing, and dance machines are but a few of the video games you will find in this two-story game center. You'll also find pool and ski-ball, but there's no Ms. Pacman here. There are two full-service bars and a full menu with upscale bar food. Just make sure you ride the virtual roller coaster *before* you eat! Gameworks is state-of-the-art fun for teens, adults, and groups. There is no cover charge to enter.

Shadowbox Cabaret
164 Easton Town Center
(614) 265-7625
www.shadowboxcabaret.com
Saturday Night Live-style comedy sketches, theatrical shorts, and live rock music make for a unique (and hilariously risqué) alternative to traditional theater. There is no age limit on entrance, but these shows are not for the easily offended. They are given an R rating for adult language and content. A full-service bar and pub grub are served up by the performers between skits. Tickets can be purchased on a first come, first served basis at the door, but it is recommended you prepay and guarantee yourself a spot. Tables seat four, so chances are couples will be seated together if the show is a sellout. Student tickets are discounted for certain performances.

Speeds Indoor Kart Racing
3651 East Main Street, Whitehall
(614) 236-5050
www.speeds.cc
Feel the need for speed? Speeds is Ohio's first indoor go-kart track. This European Grand Prix–style racetrack has 18 high-speed karts that can reach up to 40 mph on the ½-mile track. Individuals 15½ years and older with a driver's permit can get behind the wheel after signing a release. You receive a printout after each race to see where you ranked in the heat. Appetizers and sandwiches are available, and there's a pub on-site, which is open late.

LIVE MUSIC AND DANCING

Downtown

Fahrenheit Nightclub
283 East Spring Street
(614) 224-9972
www.fahrenheitclub.com
Fahrenheit is a multilevel, energetic, wild dance club that draws in a young college crowd. The music varies, as do the patrons. Country music, mechanical bull riding, and line dancing are offered Thursday nights while Friday is theme night. The deejay spins techno, top-40, and hip-hop on Saturday, and thanks to a powerful sound system (and lots of female skin), Saturday has been voted the top night to get your groove on. Fahrenheit also has pool tables and an outdoor patio with a bar. There are open select nights for teens ages 13 to 18; otherwise, you must be over 18 to get in. A

modest cover is charged. Free parking is available all around the club.

Long Street Entertainment
40 East Long Street
(614) 222-3000
www.longstreetclubs.com
Six bars and clubs form this block-long compound located just off Long Street. It consists of Global dance club with its fenced in patio; the International Room and the Mambo Room, which is a Miami-style dance club, retractable roof and all; Long Street Live, which features local and regional bands and has a small patio out back; Fabric, a martini lounge; and the Barfly, a lounge with an outdoor patio. Poor college students will be pleased to learn the cover for all six places is only $5.00 on Friday and Saturday nights, but you have to be at least 21 to get in. Those 18 and older are allowed entrance on Thursday nights.

The Red Zone and Standard Lounge
303 South Front Street
(614) 621-0416
www.redzone-club.com
This staple of the Columbus club scene has three different areas to choose from. Patrons, varying in age from 18 to their late 30s, can trance dance on two huge dance floors, while those 21 and over can escape to a quieter lounge. The Zone has a great sound system and LightJockey lighting system. Nationally and internationally known deejays come here to spin, so expect to drop a bundle, as there is a steep cover charge and drinks are expensive.

Wall Street Nightclub
144 North Wall Street
(614) 464-2800
www.wallstreetnightclub.com
This cavernous, industrial dance club is the grandest of downtown lesbian and gay hangouts, but it's not so outrageous that conservative types would feel uncomfortable. Wednesdays attract the men. The music ranges from thumping techno and hard trance dance to country line dancing. Wall Street also has zany events like Off-the-Wall Comedy nights and drag shows. You must be 21 to enter the TGIFF (Thank God It's First Friday) parties; otherwise 19 and older are admitted.

German Village/ Brewery District

Brewmaster's Gate
495 South Front Street
(614) 228-4283 (GATE)
www.228gate.com
This 18,000-square-foot, multilevel indoor-outdoor pavilion shares "The Gate" entertainment complex with The Green Room (formerly Ludlow's). It spans 6 square blocks of brick buildings preserved from the historic Hoster's Brewing Company. The facility has a 15-by-18-foot video board, state-of-the-art sound system, huge dance area, and two big bars. Entertainment ranges from local bands and national acts to the *Survivor*-like "Gate Wars." The clientele is diverse, depending on what's going on. This over-21 venue is open Friday and Saturday, with a 99 cent happy hour every Friday.

C.B.R.'s
503 South Front Street
(614) 224-8155
www.cbrbar.com
Listen up, single men—C.B.R.'s three indoor bars and large dance floor have become all the rage among bachelorette parties. Aside from top-40, blues, and reggae, this Chicago-style bar offers live local entertainment several nights a week. You will find the entrance to this friendly, unpretentious nightclub at the back of the building behind CD-101. C.B.R.'s has a small outdoor patio and is closed Sunday through Tuesday.

Pearl Bar
560 South High Street
(614) 621-1213
Pearl Bar was Barrister Hall in a previous incarnation, but well-dressed jazz junkies

can still find live jazz, rhythm and blues, and the occasional poetry reading six nights a week at this classy, dark wood bar. Fridays always feature blues and R&B, while Saturdays feature jazz. Be advised that it gets quite crowded, and consequently, the service can get lost in the shuffle.

Arena District

Blue's Station
147 West Vine Street
(614) 884-2583
www.bluesstation.net
Columbus's premier live blues venue gives you a little taste of the Big Easy. The horseshoe-shaped bar and colorful decor have a funky art deco flavor. The menu features southern-style food, but what exactly does one drink with a deep-fried peanut butter and jelly sandwich? The fenced-in, outdoor patio provides good people watching along Vine Street. You can have the blues Tuesday through Saturday, while happy hour specials run daily from 4:00 to 7:00 P.M.

Carlisle Club and Grill
445 North High Street
(614) 464-2582
The young and the cool seem to congregate at this swank but claustrophobic nightclub. The upper lounge is crowded with a diverse mix of 20- to 30-somethings (and the occasional 40-something slips in) sipping fancy and somewhat expensive cocktails. The basement-level dance club thumps with loud, hip-hop/techno music. They charge a cover and ID just about everyone.

Fat Eddie's Bar
391 Neil Avenue
(614) 224-2430
www.fateddiesbar.com
Fat Eddie's is adjacent to and owned by the PromoWest Pavilion, so it makes sense that they advertise themselves as "the place to be before and after Arena District events." There are TVs, video games, air hockey, and pool. The menu is basic pizzas and pub grub, and local bands play on Thursday night. The outdoor patio on Neil Avenue overlooks the Arena and provides good views of concertgoers.

Little Brothers
1100 North High Street
(614) 421-2025
www.littlebrothers.com
If you like live music in an intimate venue, Little Brothers is your place. Local and national acts take the stage seven nights a week. The Red Hot Chili Peppers and John Lee Hooker played here in the '80s, and a whole host of musical genres have been represented in the 25-year history of this club. Columbus is exposed to the rising stars of rock, reggae, blues, Celtic, and country music here. You must be over 18 to get in, and prices are reasonable, ranging from $2.00 to $20.00. Tickets can be purchased at the door and in some cases through Ticketmaster.

Short North

Axis Nightclub
775 North High Street
(614) 291-4008
www.columbusnightlife.com
Axis gained its popularity as a gay dance club, but it is becoming a staple of Columbus nightlife for gay and straight, men and women alike. The weekend crowd is still predominantly sweaty, shirtless dancing men. This minimalist, industrial dance club has several bars and a cabaret-style lounge. The deejays spin "intelligent" techno on Wednesday and high-energy trance music on Friday and Saturday. Axis hosts outrageous drag shows and other fabulous events like *The Rocky Horror Show* and way-off-Broadway performances by the Reality Theatre troupe. Serious clubbers say Axis can hold its own next to the big-city clubs. It gets great

reviews from everyone. It doesn't open until 10:00 P.M., and there's a cover.

Havana Video Lounge
862 North High Street
(614) 421-9697
This is Columbus's ultracool gay, lesbian, and bisexual club, but many a straight person has professed a comfort level at this upscale lounge. Big screens show videos, the dance floor is energetic, and the drinks are strong. Alternative mixed with popular dance is the music of choice, while a perfectly poured martini is the drink of choice. Grab a cigar and head for a table outside, or stay indoors to check out all the tight T-shirt-clad patrons checking out each other. There are drag shows and male revues on select nights.

Surrounding Neighborhoods

Andyman's Treehouse
887 Chambers Road, Grandview
(614) 294-2264
www.andymanstreehouse.com
The name is derived from CD-101 deejay Andyman and a tree around which the club is built. Yes, there is a big, old oak tree right in front of the stage. Kick back on a sofa or hang out on the deck-style patio and listen to some good live music. This adult tree house seems to attract the clientele whose bedtimes are well after midnight. No cover is charged on Tuesday and Wednesday, and Andyman's is closed on Sunday.

Slapsy Maxie's Pub
1019 Mediterranean Avenue, off Busch Boulevard
(614) 433-0077
www.slapsymaxies.com
This rock 'n' roll bar is named for boxer "Slapsy Maxie" Rosenbloom and carries on his tradition of "laughter, good times, and friendly people." It is located in the Continent near Worthington. Enjoy electronic darts, foosball, and pool tables. When bands aren't playing, the jukebox never gets a rest. The crowd is young, and summertime features a weekly midnight cookout.

Stoly's Bar and Billiard
154 North Hamilton Road, Gahanna
(614) 476-5250
Situated in an old grocery store in a strip mall, this dance club is a lot bigger than it looks from the outside. They draw a youngish crowd on the weekends and have great happy hour specials throughout the week. They also have TVs and several pool tables.

Thirsty Ear Tavern
1200 West Third Avenue, Grandview
(614) 299-4987
www.thirstyeartavern.com
If you thirst for consistently good, live music, this neighborhood tavern is a favorite. You will find local, regional, and national acts performing rock and country, but most often they'll be singing the blues. Good taste abounds at the Thirsty Ear. Many of the 18 draft beers are imported and microbrews, but you will find whatever you want among the 120 bottled beers. They carry *all* the small-batch bourbons, a dozen single-malt whiskeys, and two dozen vodkas. The owner's diverse tastes are seen not only in the huge drink selection but also in the display of collectible records and posters in the bar. The menu offers reasonably priced sandwiches and appetizers. Wednesday is open stage night, and the Ear is closed Monday.

SHOPPING

To say shopping in Columbus is plentiful and varied is an understatement—we have been referred to as a retail powerhouse. It's probably stretching it a bit to say that Columbus and shopping are synonymous, but if you are new to the city, it won't take long to realize that you do not have to hop a plane to Chicago to do some good shopping (though it sounds fun!).

In the past 10 years, Columbus has experienced a retail building boom, but only the major malls have been included here. Downtown revitalization efforts hope to breathe new life into the once unparalleled Columbus City Center. The newly renovated Shops at Lane Avenue and the Mall at Tuttle Crossing continue to attract shoppers to the northwestern parts of Columbus, while the newer Polaris Fashion Place engulfs half of Westerville. The innovative Union Station Place shops in the Short North are now open for business, while Easton maintains its position as Columbus's shopping mecca.

This chapter, like most others, focuses on the independently owned shops, but unlike them, it is written from a top-down perspective. It begins with the major, general shopping areas, briefly pointing out the suburban malls, some of which are becoming outdated as new shopping concepts are introduced to the city. It then categorizes the different types of boutiques, markets, and discount shopping available.

The section titled "Specialized Shopping" organizes entries by category rather than neighborhood. They range from antiques shops and booksellers to wine and garden shops. Clothing shops have not been included because there are just too many, nor has every cool and trendy boutique been mentioned. Most of the shops included here have been around for quite some time and seem to have staying power—which is impressive in a test-market city like Columbus.

I won't even begin to list the department stores that have a presence in Columbus, but Filene's, Saks Fifth Avenue, Kaufmann's, and J. C. Penney will no doubt strike a familiar chord with out-of-towners. One will also find Macy's replacing the homegrown Lazarus stores in just about every major mall. Founded in 1851 by Simon Lazarus, the store has been around for as long as Columbus has been a modern city. A one-room boutique grew into the city's major department store chain, which is now owned and operated by Macy's.

Columbus is also home to one of the most successful retail chains and largest retailer of women's clothing in the world: The Limited. This Columbus-based chain was started by Leslie Wexner in 1963 with a single store. By 2000, The Limited had upward of 4,000 stores and had changed the face of retailing through vision and meticulous attention to store planning, presentation, service, and distribution.

Who hasn't heard of Victoria's Secret or Bath & Body Works? What teenage kid hasn't coveted a pair of Abercrombie & Fitch jeans or scooped up seasonal sale items at Express and Structure? These are just a few of The Limited's retail businesses, as are Henri Bendel, Penhaligon's, Lane Bryant, and Lerner New York—most of which are represented in Columbus at one shopping center or another.

Columbus might have a slew of suburban strip malls and shopping centers, but there is plenty of unique, offbeat shopping to be found all over town. Like the restaurants, many of these independently owned boutiques are clustered in the old downtowns of a few neighborhoods. German Village, Grandview, and Worthington are all good places to have lunch and leisurely stroll from store to store. The old-fashioned shopping experience is not lost on the ultra-hip Short North. High Street is lined with stylish boutiques and artsy galleries, all very walkable to one another.

Of course, Columbus didn't earn the nickname "Cowtown" for nothing. Its location in the heart of prime farmland means there are some fine farmers' markets that come to town each summer. The section "Markets and Specialty Food Shops" includes full-service gourmet food markets and fresh-food markets and highlights the historic North Market in a Close-up near the end of this chapter.

Stores in Columbus do not go out of business nearly as often as restaurants do, but to be on the safe side, I suggest calling to make sure they are still open—especially if you have to drive across town. Hours of operation have not been included since they vary, but generally, most of the bookstores are open until 10:00 or 11:00 P.M. throughout the week, and the malls typically close around 9:00 P.M. You will have no problem finding somewhere in Columbus to spend your hard-earned dollars.

SHOPPING CENTERS

Columbus City Center
111 South Third Street, downtown
(614) 221-4900, (800) 882-4900
www.shopcitycenter.com

The City Center has anchored downtown shopping since 1989, but business has waned as the focus has shifted to suburban malls and Easton Town Center. The City Center is still touted as the premier downtown shopping destination, but it's really the only downtown shopping venue. This three-floor, enclosed mall has about 90 national and local retail shops and restaurants. It is connected to the Hyatt on Capitol Square and Ohio Theatre.

The City Center is anchored by Kaufmann's Department Store, and, though many of the shops have relocated to suburbia, some of The Limited boutiques, like Express Men, Victoria's Secret, and Lane Bryant, remain. Several chain shoe and sporting good stores are represented, as well as a variety of mobile phone shops. People can often be found lounging in the amphitheater-style grand court, listening to live music, or milling about the food court. Parking is available in the attached garage and at meters along the surrounding streets.

Easton Town Center
160 Easton Town Center, Easton
(614) 337-2200
www.eastontowncenter.com

The shopping mecca of Columbus is located about 7 miles northeast of downtown, just a few minutes from the airport and New Albany. The Limited developed this outdoor, boutique-style complex as a response to consumers' seeming boredom with traditional, indoor malls. It's a very European concept to stroll and shop, so Easton Town Center has created a pristine, Old World atmosphere, with Georgian architecture, plenty of greenspaces, fountains, and individual, store-front boutiques.

Easton's retail and office space encompasses more than 2.9 million square feet, making it one of the nation's largest mixed-use complexes—and it's only half developed. Needless to say, Easton isn't your quick in-and-out. It's a bit of a shopping commitment, but at least it's easy to get to. An interchange off Interstate 270 leads right to its front door, providing easy access from all parts of town.

It's the sort of place you can be lured into for days on end; in fact, more than 30 million visitors per year make Easton one of Central Ohio's most popular attractions. Statistics maintain that half of central Ohio visits Easton at least once a week in a 90-day period. And what's all the hubbub about? Eating, drinking, living, working, and shopping! There is so much to do here, it isn't funny. You can read about Easton's dining options in the Restaurants chapter and hotels in the Accommodations chapter. This entry focuses on Easton as a retail adventure.

Several department stores are located in Easton, including a flagship Lazarus-

Macy's and Nordstrom's. Easton has also attracted many upscale clothing boutiques like Ann Taylor, bebe, and BCBG. The young and hip will enjoy J. Crew, Banana Republic, and Benetton. Eclectic and luxury home goods are sold at shops like Anthropologie, Yves Delorme, Williams-Sonoma, and Sur La Table. Of course, many of The Limited stores are represented here, alongside a variety of shoe stores, jewelry shops, and children's boutiques.

If you prefer not to shop or run errands with three kids in tow, Villa Keyus is a reputable drop-in play care service where you can leave your children ages 2 through 12 for up to four hours. This family-owned day care center charges an hourly rate for the upscale learning and exploring environment. You can feel comfortable leaving your children while you have dinner or run some errands, but beware—the kids may not want to leave!

Developers tried to avoid parking spaces in front of the buildings, and on Friday nights you might think they forgot about it altogether, but parking does exist. The three large garages attached to the mall are free. The four surface lots, located near Barnes & Noble, Johnny Rockets, Lifetime Fitness, and The Container Store, are also free. There is no charge to park at either department store, but the one-hour street-side meters are enforced. However, a portion of the coins (and parking tickets) goes to charity.

Shops on Lane Avenue
1585 West Lane Avenue, Upper Arlington
(614) 481-8341

If you haven't been to this mall in a while, it may be worth a return trip. The old Lane Avenue Shopping Center got a facelift, a new name, and a few new tenants. Some oldies but goodies like Larson's Toys and Games and China Dynasty are still around, while newer, more upscale clothing boutiques like Ann Taylor Loft, White House/Black Market, and Coldwater Creek have taken up residence. Replenish your shopping batteries at the new Rusty Bucket or Wolfgang Puck Express. Free parking is available in lots in front of and behind the plaza.

If you are visiting Easton Town Center from at least 50 miles outside the city, you are entitled to a special coupon booklet. Just present your ID with a form that can be printed from Easton's Web site or filled out in person at the Guest Services Desk inside the mall, and you'll receive the discount book.

Lennox Town Center
Olentangy River Road and Kinnear Road, Grandview

This open-air complex is located just off Route 315, slightly west of the OSU campus. It is a popular place with students, and the retail options are a reflection of this. You'll find Target, Staples, Old Navy, World Market, and Barnes & Noble Booksellers, as well as an AMC 24-screen movie theater. Lennox is usually very busy on the weekends, and parking can become somewhat cutthroat.

Polaris Fashion Center
1500 Polaris Parkway, Westerville
(614) 846-1500
www.polarisfashionmall.com

This sprawling indoor mall opened in 2001 on the north side of Columbus, just off I-71. It is anchored by several large department stores, including Saks Fifth Avenue, The Great Indoors, Kaufmann's, Sears, and J. C. Penney. The mall features over 150 specialty stores, including Coach, J. Jill, and Cole Hahn, a day spa, and three sit-down restaurants and an upscale food court. Mall amenities include valet parking and a fun children's play area designed in conjunction with the Columbus Zoo. Parking in the outdoor lot is free.

The Mall at Tuttle Crossing
I-270 and Tuttle Crossing Boulevard Dublin
(614) 717-9604
www.shoptuttlecrossing.com

Tuttle opened in 1997, when the shopping focus shifted from the downtown City Center to this suburban mall. You can see this sprawling complex from I-270, but it is more discreet when entered from Hayden Run Road. The mall is anchored by Kaufmann's, Sears, J. C. Penney, and Macy's. It features 140 specialty stores, such as Pottery Barn, Ann Taylor, and EB Games.

Parents, bring your kids along for COSI Tuttle Tuesdays, during which the children's play area is filled with themed science experiments, activities, book readings, songs, and a chance to win free COSI passes.

Union Station Place
North High Street, Short North
The innovative, pioneering project that came to be known as "The Cap" is one of the Short North's crowning jewels—literally. The recently christened Union Station Place is located atop the bridge that crosses over Interstate 670, linking the Short North with downtown both visually and literally. The barren bridge was once an eyesore and presented a disheartening walk from the Arena District to the Short North.

Now 27,000 square feet of retail and restaurant space totally eliminates the view of the interstate from High Street and actually encourages foot traffic between downtown and the Short North. People don't even realize they are crossing over a highway. The concept of retail shops built along a bridge is modeled after pedestrianized bridges in 16th-century England and Italy. Its architecture echoes the former train station, which once stood nearby, arches and all. Similarly European are the covered colonnades under which sidewalk cafes and patios afford views into downtown. The shops are definitely trendy and reflect the hip, urbane nature of the Short North and the Arena District.

Worthington Square Mall
150 West Wilson Bridge Road
Worthington
(614) 841-1110
This enclosed mall is located near I-270 and High Street (Route 23). It services north Columbus, and its mainstays have been high-end clothing shops such as Godfrey's and Godfrey's Women's Clothier, Acorn, Ann Taylor and Jos. A. Bank Clothiers. Like many of the smaller suburban malls it's hanging in there.

SPECIALIZED SHOPS

Antiques

American Primitive
1251 Grandview Avenue, Grandview
(614) 488-2040
This little storefront shop deals in Americana, if you didn't gather that from the name, and you get the real deal here, patina and all. Early American furniture, clocks, and decorative arts are among the interesting inventory.

Bexley Antiques
2353 East Main Street, Bexley
(614) 231-7719
Bexley Antiques has been dealing European antiques for almost 30 years. You'll find a broad selection of silver, English, French, and continental furniture, as well as the largest collection of Oriental porcelain and English Staffordshire in the area. During the holiday season, they carry Venetian glass, 19th-century cut glass, and Christmas items.

German Village Antiques
716 South High Street, German Village
(614) 443-2511
If you don't have anything specific in mind or are just enjoy browsing through a general hodgepodge of the old and eclectic, you'll like this shop. It carries a little bit of everything.

Greater Columbus Antique Mall
1045 South High Street, Brewery District
(614) 443-7858
www.greatercolumbusantiquemall.com
Columbus's first (and largest) antique mall is located in a period building in the historic Brewery District. Five floors of antiques fill this 11,000-square-foot building, so give yourself some time to work your way through room after room of glass, furniture and collectibles.

Sōbō Style
3282 North High Street, Clintonville
(614) 447-8880
www.sobostyle.com
Shabby-chic is how the home furnishings at Sōbō are described. This boutique is not exactly an antiques shop, but rather a treasure trove of new household items mixed with vintage and retro furniture. Some of the pieces are even constructed of salvaged wood or old barn siding. It's a neat place if you are looking for that unique, country-painted piece.

Bakeries and Goodie Shops

Eleni-Christina Bakery
641 North High Street, Short North
(614) 461-0021
If you've ever had the bread at Rigsby's in the Short North, then you've already experienced Eleni-Christina Bakery. They supply this top-rated restaurant with much of its baked goods. During the holidays they specialize in rum-soaked stollen bread and a full range of Christmas cookies, including gingerbread men. It also sells a Friday-only challah.

Juergen's Traditional Bavarian Bakery and European Cafe
525 South Fourth Street, German Village
(614) 224-6858
This unassuming German Village institution has been around for 30 years and is open for breakfast, lunch, and dinner. It is a great place to get your fill of traditional German food. Weiner schnitzel and kaesespaetzle can be washed down with a drink from the bar. They also serve a variety of coffees and have a bakery that carries a superb selection of European pastries, breads, and tortes.

Just Pies
5525 North High Street, Clintonville
(614) 888-0021
www.just-pies.com
This specialized bakery carries over 25 varieties of award-winning pies and has received national attention from Oprah and the Food Network, but what makes them so good? The fruit pies are stuffed with strawberries from California and raspberries from Oregon. Meringue and whipped cream are made daily from scratch, but secretly, it's all in the crust. You'll never eat another pie once you have one of these. They've opened a second location in Westerville, and Just Pies are carried at local markets like Huffman's, Weiland's, and the Hills Market.

Krema Nut Company
1000 West Goodale Boulevard
Grandview
(614) 299-4131
www.krema.com
While shopping, try not to miss some of the local businesses that have become Columbus institutions. The city is home to the nation's oldest commercial peanut butter manufacturer, the Krema Nut Company, where you can take a tour and see how peanut butter is made. They have been working with nuts since 1898 and specialize in the production of gourmet nuts, trail mix, hand-dipped chocolates, and all-natural peanut butter. Krema's second retail location in the convention center has a gourmet PB&J sandwich store.

Pistachio
680 North Pearl Street, Short North
(614) 220-9070
www.pistachiosweets.com
Offering the total dessert experience, this

sweet kitchen turns out some of the city's most beautiful and artisanal desserts. The menu includes an ever-changing selection of biscotti, cookies, tortes, pies, and cheesecakes. Decisions will be difficult given the 50-plus options to choose from. The shop is closed on Sunday.

Tremont Goodie Shop
2116 Tremont Center, Upper Arlington
(614) 488-8777
www.tremontgoodieshop.com
Though some people come here for fresh quiche and chicken potpie, dessert is always the main course. Glass cases are lined with colorful frosted cookies, cupcakes, and fruit squares. Kids love the frosted, flavored bubble gum, and everyone loves the buckeyes. The nonyeast, salt-rising breads are a must, but the most popular temptation is the cinnamon sticks. Made with butter, cinnamon, and butterscotch, they double as breakfast or dessert.

Book and Music Sellers

Barnes & Noble
3685 West Dublin-Granville Road, Dublin
(614) 798-0077

4005 Townsfair Way, Easton
(614) 476-8480

1735 Olentangy River Road
Lennox Town Center (OSU Area)
(614) 298-9516

1285 Polaris Parkway, Westerville
(614) 985-0283

3280 Tremont Road, Upper Arlington
(614) 459-0921

Book Loft of German Village
631 South Third Street, German Village
(614) 464-1774
www.32rooms.com
As the Web site suggests, this 1863 historic building has 32 rooms chock-full of coffee table books, cookbooks, general fiction, and hard-to-find titles, making this one of the largest independent bookstores in the country. As you mosey through the maze of rooms, it may feel like a used bookstore, but everything is new—even some of the most recent best sellers are heavily discounted. Looking for something specific? A map breaking out the building into wings may prove helpful, but those preferring to wander will find the rooms nicely labeled according to special interest, and you may just encounter the resident cat snoozing on a shelf. Claustrophobic people should probably not shop here.

Books on High
1124 Goodale Avenue, Grandview
(614) 299-9985
www.booksonhigh.com
Books (no longer) on High is still the same friendly neighborhood bookstore, only in a new location. You'll find a wide selection of art and general interest books, but there are also collectibles and children's lines, like early editions of *Nancy Drew* and *Hardy Boys.*

Borders
6670 Sawmill Road, Dublin
(614) 718-9099

4545 Kenny Road, Upper Arlington
(614) 451-2292

Half Price Books, Records and Magazines
1375 West Lane Avenue, Upper Arlington
(614) 486-8765
New and used books are sold at discounted prices, sometimes even more than half off. The building is a lot bigger than it looks from the front. Several rooms are crammed full of fiction, nonfiction, business, and children's books. A limited selection of magazines, calendars, used music, and videos is also available. There are two other locations on 2660 Bethel Road and 2656 Brice Road.

Magnolia Thunderpussy Records
1155 North High Street, Short North
(614) 421-1512
www.thunderpussy.com

You'll find a great inventory of vinyl, along with DVDs, posters, video games, and T-shirts at this indie rock record store. You won't have to wrestle for parking, as it has its own lot next to the store.

Village Bookshop
2424 West Dublin-Granville Road
Linworth
(614) 889-2674
Independent booksellers are a rare breed these days, so you shouldn't miss this historic church-turned-bookstore. This white clapboard building is easy to find, as it is located along Route 161 in Linworth, between Worthington and Dublin. You can get lost for hours on the two floors of overstock, out-of-print, and used books. They are particularly strong in art, history, and cookbooks.

Crafty Galleries

Cowtown Art
668 North High Street, Short North
(614) 228-7690
www.cowtownart.com
Just when we thought we shook the Cowtown image . . . As you walk along High Street, you may notice a rusted sculpture of a dog begging for money (for alcohol research) with a few beer cans strewn about; this Barstool Dog is made from recycled material and is just an inkling of the quirkiness you'll find inside. This fun, funky gallery really dispels the Cowtown myth, with its affordable modern art and contemporary home decor. The gallery supports local artists who work in a variety of media.

Global Gallery
682 North High Street, Short North
(614) 621-1744
www.glblgllry.com
As part of the Fair Trade network, this boutique's goal is to help people in third world and developing countries by paying their artisans living wages for the crafts they produce. These objects, which include jewelry, wood carvings, ceramics, and textiles, may seem a bit kitschy, but the money is for a good cause. The gallery also hosts changing exhibitions of local artists and has a second location in Easton.

Golden Hobby Shop
630 South Third Street, German Village
(614) 645-8329
www.columbusrecparks.com
This consignment shop is located in a two-story 1864 schoolhouse and carries handmade items by Columbus residents ages 55 and older. You will find beautiful, one-of-a-kind items such as paintings, furniture, quilts, and birdhouses. The "Golden Age Hobby Show" has been featuring senior handicrafts for over 50 years now.

Helen Winnemore's
Contemporary Craft Gallery
150 East Kossuth Street, German Village
(614) 444-5850
This contemporary craft gallery has become a landmark in German Village over the past 60 years. Seven rooms are loaded with a variety of handcrafted items, functional art, jewelry, and sculpture. It is considered one of the oldest stores of its kind in the nation. And you thought this was just a house on the corner!

Eclectic Boutiques

A La Wiskets
2800 Fishinger Road, Upper Arlington
(614) 451-1235, (800) WISKETS
www.wiskets.com
If you're looking for that one unusual decorative piece to complete a room, this is your place. This eclectic store carries everything from candles and Christmas ornaments to hard-to-find home accessories. It also has floral design and unique gift baskets, which can be shipped nationally.

Accent on Wild Birds
1390 Grandview Avenue, Grandview
(614) 486-7333
www.accentonwildbirds.com

This very unique wildlife store carries general items like science toys and craft arts, but it specializes in rare fossil, insect, and meteorite shell and mineral specimens. The accent on birds comes in the form of feeding and housing supplies. This wild store also carries Harmony Kingdom figurines and an enormous selection of Woodstock wind chimes.

Byzantium
1088 North High Street, Short North
(614) 291-3130
www.bigbead.com

Though predominantly a bead store, this gift shop carries artsy crafts from around the globe. The walls and shelves are decked with African baskets, Indian blankets, and Muslim prayer rugs. Cases filled with African trade beads, Czech glass, and gemstone, wood, ceramic, and vintage beads line the walls. Byzantium can even hook you up with collectable and Swarovski crystal beads. Nowhere in Columbus tops this place for jewelry-making supplies. Classes are occasionally held on-site.

Curio-A-Go-Go
861 North High Street, Short North
(614) 280-0780

This is probably one of the most fun and eclectic stores in Columbus. Who wouldn't get a laugh from faux-fur postcards or eau de toilette named Dirt and Cucumber? The painfully hip staff will slice off a sliver or a slab of fruity handmade soap. The ambience has a bit of a girlie tinge to it, but, overall, the wild and creative gifts are perfect for that fabulous friend in your life.

Curio Cabinet and Christmas Village
679 High Street, Olde Worthington
(614) 885-1986
www.curiocabinet.com

Curio Cabinet is a fitting name for a shop that carries just about every line of dust collector you can imagine. Whether you collect the Wee Forest Folk, Madame Alexander dolls, Herend porcelain, or Lladro figurines, the Curio Cabinet has them. The year-round Christmas Village carries exclusive Christmas ornaments and nutcrackers, and is a Dept. 56 dealer. It is also one of only 16 stores in the country that is a designated Starlight Store, carrying the complete line of Christopher Radko ornaments and collectibles. Radko groupies can rub elbows with him at scheduled times during the year.

Etc. Gifts
542 South Drexel Avenue, Bexley
(614) 235-6921

If you are tired of the same old stuff, check out this women's accessory boutique in downtown Bexley. The infamous handbag room has designer, imported, and trendy purses from everywhere. The owner brings in independent designers and carries a popular Israeli line. Both the handbag and jewelry lines change a few times a year, so you'll never see the same things.

The Flag Lady's Flag Store
4567 North High Street, Clintonville
(614) 263-1776
www.flagladyinc.com

Don't step foot in here unless you're proud to be an American—or at least a Buckeye. You'll find every size and type of indoor/outdoor American, state, military, and historical flag. You want the Betsy Ross or Spirit of '76 flag? You got it! Flagpoles, seasonal banners, sport and college pennants are also stocked. In the spirit of democracy, The Flag Lady doesn't limit you to just OSU flags. Yes, you can get a Michigan flag if you must. In fact, almost two dozen university banners are available, as are custom-made flags. The Flag Lady oozes with so much patriotism that First Lady Laura Bush made an appearance here.

Fortin Welding & Ironworks
944 West Fifth Avenue, Grandview
(614) 291-4342
www.fortinironworks.com

Known for its ornamental ironwork, this family-owned iron and metal manufacturer has been designing, making, and standing behind its wrought-iron products since 1946. Step into the impressive showroom to see the variety of driveway gates, fences, railings, and trellises available. There are also a few lines of indoor and outdoor furniture and sporting equipment, like soccer and lacrosse goals. Whether you want small decorative pieces or large fences, you're guaranteed quality craftsmanship.

Fritzy Jacobs
635 High Street, Olde Worthington
(614) 885-8283
www.fritzyjacobs.com
This incredibly bright and cheery store is packed with unique designs and quirky decor for the home. You'll find everything from pillows to stationery to things for the garden. They carry a whimsical line of Cath Kidson's aprons, oven mitts, and handbags and have a room brimming with ideas for the wee ones. This is the sort of place girlfriends buy gifts for girlfriends.

Lily One
39 West New England Avenue
Olde Worthington
(614) 781-1433
www.lilyone.com
Named for the owners' grandmothers, Lily One is located in the Worthington Inn's original carriage house. This charming boutique is spilling over with vintage furniture, beautiful linens, unforgettable baby gifts, and distinctive lighting devices. Like a Parisian flea market, the inventory is ever-changing. Despite being located on a side street, this shop is a true standout in Olde Worthington.

Loot
641 North High Street, Short North
(614) 221-5668
www.lootstyle.com
A blend of modern lines and European country antiques makes this boutique a favorite among lovers of the shabby-chic style. Apart from distressed furniture, lacy linens, and country-cottage fabrics, Loot also carries a frilly collection of vintage-style clothes and jewelry. It's a great place to find a gift for the "girly-girl" in your life.

Morgan House Gifts
5300 Glick Road, Dublin
(614) 889-0037
www.morganhse.com
The Morgan House, built in the 1860s and set on six acres, is both a restaurant and a gift shop that carries reproduction furniture and home accessories. It also has a wonderful gourmet food shop and full-service restaurant on-site. Visitors can watch creative artisans making the wares sold in the gift shop.

On Paper
737 North High Street, Short North
(614) 424-6617, (800) 286-6617
www.onpaper.net
Those who appreciate fine stationery and high end writing instruments, or who just have a penchant for communicating the old-fashioned way—by handwriting—will be in their glory here. On Paper carries an extensive selection of gift wrap, personalized stationery, and envelopes. You'll find handmade papers embedded with flowers and embossed leather journals. On Paper also stocks an assortment of antique pens and desk accessories. This shop is a must for anyone wanting unique invitations, announcements, seals, or embossers.

Wooden Putter
1439 Grandview Avenue, Grandview
(614) 488-7888
www.woodenputter.com
The golfer who has everything will love the distinctive gifts, apparel, and memorabilia at this Grandview boutique. You'll find anything from antique clubs and knickers to golf art and display cabinets. Also interesting is the golf-themed furniture, barware, and classy desk accessories. The Wooden Putter has a changing selection of Bobby Jones sportswear.

Wren House Gifts
695 High Street, Olde Worthington
(614) 848-8442
www.wrenhousegifts.com
Here is yet another eclectic shop in Olde Worthington that specializes in furniture, decorative accessories, garden accents, and seasonal merchandise. A quick look around and you might suffer a sensory overload. Two floors are packed tight with country-cottage and primitive furniture, folk art, lamps, and many one-of-a-kind decorations. One sniff of the air and you'll know they are in the candle business as well.

Yankee Trader
463 North High Street, Short North
(614) 228-1322
www.yankeetraderonline.com
Here's a kooky place and most definitely the "funnest" store in town! To say they specialize in party supplies will not do the Yankee Trader justice. You will find all the makings for great themed parties: Luau, Mardi Gras, and, of course, scarlet and gray Buckeye supplies. They also carry the best selection of Halloween, theatrical, and holiday costumes in Columbus. If life-sized celebrity stand-ups don't spice up a party, then perhaps piñatas, gag gifts, or wigs will do the trick. It isn't unusual to walk in and find people wearing Viking helmets and feather boas sword-fighting in the aisles.

i

Oakland Nursery opens satellite Christmas tree lots around Columbus during the holidays. They carry a variety of live trees, pine wreaths, and swags.

Nurseries and Garden Shops

Connells Maple Lee Flowers & Gifts
615 High Street, Olde Worthington
(614) 885-5350, (800) 790-8980
www.cmlflowers.com
You'll find a most beautiful and colorful selection of fresh flowers, plants, and silk arrangements in this small shop founded in 1946. Strolling along High Street, there is no question about which storefront it is—just look for the brick building covered with hanging baskets in the summer and pumpkins in the fall. They also carry stuffed animals and seasonal and novelty gifts.

Garden Smiles
1493 Polaris Parkway, Westerville
(614) 847-3660, (800) 225-1178
www.gardensmiles.com
Ohio sculptor George Carruth fills his studio with unique garden and home accessories, in a variety of media, created by him and other locally and nationally recognized artists. Some 200 cast stone images, personalized plaques, stepping stones, and free-standing statues are among the garden accessories to choose from. Quirky benches, door knockers, and rain gauges are also available.

Oakland Nursery
1156 Oakland Park Avenue, Columbus
(614) 268-3511
www.oaklandnursery.com
Green thumbs swear by this award-winning nursery. Central Ohio's premier landscaping center, founded in 1940, encompasses 17 acres of competitively priced gardening products. You'll find all of your gardening needs and then some, including mulch, trees, exotic plants, birdseed, and water-gardening accessories. Aside from having the largest plant selection in Ohio, Oakland Nursery has the largest selection of roses in the Midwest. They run seasonal specials such as an annual spring fling in March and have a second location in Delaware.

Strader's Garden Center
5350 Riverside Drive, Dublin
(614) 889-1314
www.straders.net
Columbus's other garden center has four locations in the city, but this one is the primary nursery. The greenhouse carries a

wide variety of fresh plants, trees, and herbs, as well as a nice selection of gardening tools and fertilizer. Bigger outdoor equipment, like lawnmowers, snowblowers, and grills, is sold seasonally.

Wine and Cigars

Barclay Tobacco & Cigar
2673 Federated Boulevard, Dublin
(614) 764-0300
Put this in your pipe and smoke it—1,500 square feet of retail space, a 300-square-foot enclosed humidor, and cigar storage lockers available for monthly rental. This store is the larger of two locations; the original Barclay Pipe and Tobacco can be found in the Shops at Lane Avenue in Arlington (614-486-4243). Both Barclays carry their popular estate pipes and a full line of smoking merchandise.

Carnardo Wine & Cheese
1735 West Lane Avenue, Upper Arlington
(614) 486-7474
Carnardo's location off to the side of The Shops at Lane Avenue is not terribly obvious, but it's definitely worth seeking out for the personalized and knowledgeable service, as well as the interesting selection of wines from around the world. It also carries a select number of microbrews and imported beers and has scheduled wine tastings.

Gentile's Wine Sellers
1565 King Avenue, Grandview
(614) 486-3406
www.gentiles.com
For 70 years Gentile's has been providing Columbus with fermented favorites from around the world. This full-service wine shop doesn't mess around. It stocks 2,000 different wines and premium beers and carries the largest selection of Diamond Creek in the country. There is a wine bar on-site, which is a good thing, because the store hosts over 150 wine tastings a year. The King Avenue location has a small art gallery with changing exhibitions and a Mama Mimi's Take'n Bake Pizza shop on-site. A second location is at 6867 Flags Center Drive in Westerville.

SherBliss
274 South Third Street, German Village
(614) 221-9636
www.sherbliss.com
Is there anything better than chocolate and wine? I think not. You'll find over 200 varieties of wine, domestic and imported beers, wine paraphernalia, and cookware. All this vino is complimented by hand-dipped candies and a signature line of Maramor chocolates. Even diabetics can find something to love about SherBliss, as they have a large selection of "safe" truffles, bridge mix, caramels, and turtles. Treat yourself!

Stewart Wine Shop
1816 West Fifth Avenue, Grandview
(614) 488-6113
The service at this small mom-and-pop wine shop is outstanding! Mr. Stewart will point wine lovers to a perfect vintage, and he'll point beer lovers to the back of this shop, where a small selection of domestic microbrews and imports hide in the coolers. It's a great place to learn a few things about wine.

The Wine Gallery
1500 Polaris Parkway, Westerville
(614) 846-1110
Despite its location in the middle of a sprawling suburban mall, this classy little wine shop offers up some of the finer things in life: cigars, cutters, Riedel glassware, and, of course, wine. The knowledgeable owner stocks the place with interesting reds, whites, and ports and is quick to offer helpful advice. Wine tastings are held all day, every day. A second location is now open in Easton.

The Wine Shoppe & Bistro
7178 Muirfield Drive, Dublin
(614) 799-9222
www.thewineshoppe.com
Eat, drink, and be merry seems to be the

motto at this wine shop, located in the middle of an upscale strip mall near Muirfield. One part of the store is devoted to retail and the other to consumption. You can peruse the great selection of international wines for a few bottles to take home or settle down at a table to do a little sampling. There is a chic wine bar and small dining area, where you can order light fare and have wines properly paired with the food. It offers regular wine tastings and classes.

MARKETS AND SPECIALTY FOOD SHOPS

Bellisari's Italian Market
2124 Arlington Avenue, Upper Arlington
(614) 487-8530
www.bellisaris.com
Specialty oils, fine wines, pastas, and gourmet canned goods line the shelves of this upscale neighborhood market, but if you don't have time to cook, Bellisari's has a full line of premade appetizers, entrees, and sandwiches, including classics like lasagna, eggplant parmesan, and meatballs. Their deli cases are full of meats and imported cheeses, while their fresh breads, pastries, and pizzas make the decisions even more difficult. There are an outdoor patio and a small, informal eating area in which to sit back with an espresso and ponder which of their cooking classes to take.

Caprianno's Italian Market
6500 Riverside Drive, Dublin
(614) 761-1266
www.capriannos.com
Located in a strip mall at the corner of Routes 161 and 33, this market is Dublin's alternative to the major chain grocery stores. This grocer specializes in fine cuts of meat, international and domestic wines, and gourmet foods. They also have a catering service.

Carfagna's
1405 East Dublin-Granville Road
Worthington
(614) 846-6340
This little, family-owned Italian grocery store has been in business since 1937 and continues to hold its own next to the giant chain stores. You'll find a great selection of Italian meats, cheese, and pastas here, along with a good selection of olive oils.

Europia Gourmet Foods
672 North High Street, Short North
(614) 460-3000
www.europiagourmet.com
This is the Short North's answer to a local market: pâté, smoked salmon, fine mustards, and specialty pastas. You know how all neighborhood markets have a humidor with Cohiba and Monte Cristo cigars! Europia also serves as a takeout for the convention center and hotel across the street and puts together fun gourmet gift baskets that can be shipped anywhere. Wander downstairs and do a little wine tasting. Europia carries over 300 fine wines, sake, mixers, and barware.

The Hills Market
7860 Olentangy River Road, Worthington
(614) 846-3220
www.thehillsmarket.com
Food hobbyists and lovers of fresh seafood go to the Hills. This upscale, full-service grocer carries a great selection of specialty foods, wines, and high-end staples. It's known for its meat department, but with daily fresh fish shipments, its seafood selection is equally good, particularly the organic salmon and live lobsters, which they'll steam if you're a bit squeamish about that. The deli features cheese from around the globe, 35 varieties of Mediterranean olives, and a constantly changing menu of prepared foods. The Hills often hosts wine tastings and has a Value Wall, which carries a nice selection of wines for under $15. At the end of the

day, the staff takes a lot of pride in their service and knowing who you are and remembering what you like.

Huffman's Market
2140 Tremont Center, Upper Arlington
(614) 486-5336
www.huffmansmarket.com
This neighborhood market is most popular among Arlington residents, but come Sunday, people from all parts of town are likely to turn up, as Huffman's is the first store in Ohio since Prohibition to sell liquor on Sundays. This full-service grocery store carries all your basic cooking needs, as well as a variety of gourmet and specialty foods, fresh meats, and "heat and eat" ready-made meals. One of the more unique products is My House Wine, with custom-designed labels. Huffman's holds a weekly wine tasting every Friday from 2:00 to 6:00 P.M., and the store features a delivery service on Monday, Wednesday, Friday, and Saturday. With a minimum order and small delivery charge, you can have your groceries delivered to your doorstep—let's see Giant Eagle do that!

Patel Brothers
1170 Kenny Square, Upper Arlington
(614) 273-1376
Having the right spices and grains is terribly important for Indian cooking, and you will find everything you need right here, along with other odds and ends from India including Bollywood movie rentals. This shop is tucked in a small strip mall off Kenny Road, but this is where most of my Indian friends suggest shopping for both the basics and more complex Southeast Asian recipes.

Penzeys Spices
4455 Kenny Road, Upper Arlington
(614) 442-7779, (800) 741-7787
www.penzeys.com
If you've ever driven across Kenny Road and wondered what that weird round building is across from Iacono's Pizzeria, well, it's a spice store. With just a handful of shops in the Midwest, Penzeys is a mom-and-pop-type business where you can mail-order unusual spices from a catalogue, or if you are lucky enough to have a shop nearby, you can buy them in person. Penzeys carries all sorts of interesting herbs, spices, meat rubs, and unusual seasonings at reasonable prices.

Rife's Market
1417 West Fifth Avenue, Grandview
(614) 488-7151
You can't miss this tiny market, which looks like a garage on the busy corner of Grandview and Fifth Avenue. You will find most of your basic cooking needs somewhere on the shelves, but people generally shop here for the fresh seasonal produce and particularly fine meat department.

Seafood Japan
1167 Old Henderson Road
Upper Arlington
(614) 451-6002
Next to Restaurant Japan is this Japanese grocery, where you will find all the makings for your own sushi as well as high-quality, premade sushi. Fish aside, you'll find a great selection of soy sauces, rice, noodles, and soups. The frozen selection of fish, appetizers, and entrees is comprehensive. Most of the product labels are in Japanese, but the staff speaks English and can help with questions. There's also a small produce section, and the store carries Asian beverages and miscellany from the Far East, like hair supplies and holiday decorations.

Shane's Gourmet Market
447 East Livingston Avenue
German Village
(614) 358-5555
www.shanesgourmetmarket.com
The main focus at this gourmet market is preparing the highest quality meals for takeout; you have the option to eat in, eat outdoors, or carryout a wide variety of creative dishes and sushi. It also carries an interesting variety of hard-to-find market

CLOSE-UP

The Historic North Market

The North Market (www.northmarket.com) is located at 59 Spruce Street in the Arena District, but this wasn't always the case. Local butchers, bakers, and farmers began selling their goods to the public in 1876 from a building at 29 Spruce Street, once the site of the city's public cemetery.

Though not in its original location, North Market is the only one of Columbus's four public markets to survive. The Central Market at Town and Fourth Streets was torn down due to urban development. The Boys and Girls Club on South Gift Street was once the West Market, while the East Market at Mt. Vernon and Miami Avenues burned down in 1947.

After fire gutted the North Market in 1948, the city decided not to rebuild. Merchants pooled their money and purchased a temporary building to house the market, while the city maintained ownership of the property. Three decades later, after hitting rock-bottom and watching the old building fall apart at the seams, Nationwide Insurance sold the turn-of-the-century Advanced Thresher warehouse to the North Market Development Authority. Columbus once again rediscovered its market roots and opened the doors of the current market in 1995.

On any given day, 35 regular merchants fill the indoor stalls. Just like the good old days, you'll find fresh meat, seafood, cheese, and flowers. Bluescreek Farms Meats carries hormone-free meat and handmade sausages direct from its Marysville farm. If you are after more exotic game, have a look at North Market's Poultry and Game's selection of rabbit, elk, bison, and alligator. Bob the Fish Guy doesn't do alligator, but he does sell some of the freshest seafood in town.

You'll find beautiful mixed bouquets and exotic plants at Market Blooms, a fabulous selection of wine and beer at Grapes of Mirth, and unusual fruits and veggies at North Market Produce. Curds and Whey's 300 types of imported and domestic cheese makes it one of central Ohio's best sources, not to mention its interesting collections of caviar, fancy vinegars, and honey.

When it comes to prepared food, the North Market is becoming increasingly

items, olive oils, pastas, and cheeses. Shane's will meet all your condiment needs with fancy vinegars, mustards, dipping oils, and salsas. It has an extensive selection of wines, champagne, sake, and beer, but the little half-bottles of wine are of particular note.

Vincenzo's Convenient Elegance
6393 Sawmill Road
Dublin-Worthington Area
(614) 792-1010

The amazing smells that waft through this bustling market will send you into a food frenzy, even if you aren't hungry. Shelves ethnic in its offerings. Mediterranean, Indian, Chinese, Vietnamese, and Japanese food items are among the options. Many of the stalls not only serve premade meals but also carry ingredients and groceries for cooking at home. Jose Madrid's award-winning salsa is made on-site and is carried at several of the local markets, like Huffman's. If traditional fare is more your speed, then try the "Best Corn Beef Sandwich West of the Hudson River" at Barry's New York Style Deli, a grilled panini from the Best of the Wurst, or huge slices of hand-tossed pizza from Sarefino's.

A million people annually visit the North Market to eat, shop, or just people watch. It is once again one of Columbus's most beloved landmarks. You'll find the market conveniently nestled between downtown and the Short North. It is within a short walking distance of most downtown hotels and easily accessible from High Street and I-670. On-site parking is available at an hourly rate, which is discounted with validation from one of the market vendors. Be certain to add the North Market to your list of must-sees if you are visiting Columbus for the weekend.

The Historic North Market. SHORT NORTH BUSINESS ASSOCIATION

and counters are lined with pastas, baked chickens, marinated and roasted veggies, and heaps of olives. While some people get their dinners to go, others linger to shop for bread, cheese, and spiced meats. Vincenzo's is not a deli, so don't expect to pop in and grab a cheap sub to go. This is gourmet meal replacement.

Weiland's Gourmet Market
3600 Indianola Avenue, Clintonville
(614) 267-9878
www.weilandsgourmetmarket.com
Where to start with this place? Weiland's is the whole package: specialty food retailer, meat, seafood, and produce market, destination wine shop, caterer, and friendly

neighborhood grocer. This 40-year-old market is located in a run-down, nondescript strip mall between Worthington and the OSU campus, but people flock here from all corners of town. Oddly enough, as one of Columbus's premier markets, there is nothing fancy or pretentious about Weiland's. They just sell great food.

Carnivores drool over the cases of deli meats, tenderloins, chops, and sausages. Lost children can usually be found hovering near the lobster tank, while Mom and Dad wander through rows of marinades, salad dressings, ethnic foods, and prepackaged side dishes. It's almost cruel having so many cheeses to choose from. Fresh produce, breads, and baked goods round out the meal. Wine lovers are always pleased they don't have to make another stop, as Weiland's stocks more than 1,200 labels. Let's not forget a fresh bouquet of flowers for the table. This is top-notch, one-stop shopping.

Wild Oats Natural Marketplace
1555 West Lane Avenue
Upper Arlington
(614) 481-3400
www.wildoats.com
Albeit a chain, I can't leave out one of Columbus's premier organic and natural food shops. This full-service grocer carries everything from nuts to soup and has a number of tables and booths in a dining area for eating in. This particular Wild Oats has a coffee and dessert bar, premade sushi, gourmet sandwiches, and a totally organic salad bar. The cheese and wine selections are extensive, as are the deli options. The store also carries organic produce, health products, and healthy living magazines. These vibrant stores are dedicated to the environment and fair trade.

FARMERS' MARKETS

I have listed a few of the more popular markets to which farmers from all over Ohio bring their fruits, vegetables, plants, and baked goods throughout the summer. The days and times vary.

North Market Farmers' Market
59 Spruce Street, Short North
(614) 463-9664
www.northmarket.com
A free outdoor farmers' market takes place every Saturday during the growing season. Local farmers sell homegrown fruits, vegetables, flowers, plants, and herbs. The market also has music and activities for children. It is open from early April through November.

Pearl Alley Farmer's Market
Pearl Alley and Broad Street, downtown
(614) 645-5001
This bazaar is open 10:30 A.M. to 2:30 P.M. on Tuesday and Friday, from May through the end of October. Along with fresh produce and baked goods, merchants sell a variety of products ranging from ethnic crafts and clothing to books, handbags, and jewelry.

Worthington Farmer's Market
High Street, Olde Worthington
Booths and stalls are set up along High Street in Olde Worthington between 9:00 A.M. and noon every Saturday throughout the summer. The season extends through October, or later, depending on how the crops did. You'll find everything from herbs and fresh-cut flowers to corn and pumpkins. No admission is charged, but you do have to park away from the town center and walk in.

DISCOUNT AND OUTLET SHOPPING

There are no big shopping outlets in Columbus, but the Prime Outlets at Jeffersonville are an easy 45-minute drive south on I-71, while the Lodi Outlets are north on I-71, closer to Cleveland. There are more than a few Sam's Clubs, Wal-Marts, and Targets in every corner of the city.

Eddie Bauer Warehouse Store
4599 Fisher Road, Columbus
(614) 278-9281
www.eddiebaueroutlet.com
This warehouse is located on the West Side of Columbus and offers inventory 25 to 70 percent off retail prices. The outlet carries casual, sport, and rugged outdoor clothes, as well as home decor and other accessories like watches, backpacks, and mugs. It's open seven days a week.

Schottenstein Department Store
3251 Westerville Road, Westerville
(614) 471-4711
www.rvi.com
If you don't mind digging through all sorts of random brands and various quality clothing, you can find some good deals at this discount department store. There are several stores in Columbus, so just check the phone book for the one closest to you. Schottenstein sells everything from name-brand coats, shoes, sportswear, and home decor to bins and racks full of clearance items. Diligent shoppers can sometimes find things for as little as $1.00, but don't be surprised if you encounter aggressive shoppers on occasion.

Southland Expo Center
3660 South High Street, Columbus
(614) 497-0200
This flea market features about 200 stalls each week. It is open on Friday from noon to 6:00 P.M. and weekends from 10:00 A.M. to 6:00 P.M.

THE OHIO STATE UNIVERSITY

It's official; The Ohio State University (OSU) is the biggest university in the country. The fall 2004 enrollment stood at 58,365, bumping the University of Minnesota from its first-place position by a handful of students. At last count, OSU has more than 26,000 full-time employees, property encompassing more than 15,000 acres, and a budget of $3.06 billion—bigger than some small countries. The main campus alone has 50,995 students, making this the largest single campus in the country, but don't the let size put you off.

According to *U.S. News and World Report* annual college rankings, OSU is rated the best public university in the state of Ohio and 22nd among public universities in the country. It is particularly noted for its linguistics department and colleges of education, engineering, and business. In fact, the *Financial Times of London* placed Fisher College's MBA program 40th in the world in its 2004 international rating of business schools.

Despite fine academic reviews, the idea of being just "a Social Security number" at such a monstrous university scares more than a few students away. It's important, however, to recognize that one of the upshots to attending such a large public school is the amount of academic, athletic, and research resources available to students and faculty.

Upward of $528 million in funding from external sponsors has helped The Ohio State University earn a reputation as one of America's preeminent research institutions. With over $100 million coming from the National Institutes of Health, it's no wonder the medical school rates in America's top 25 research schools and the College of Medicine and Public Health ranks 44th.

Ranking 12th among public universities in overall research expenditures, Ohio State is well on its way to becoming one of the world's leading research universities, and it helps that their facilities and curriculum can support whatever it is that students need to do. For example, the OSU library system is ranked 12th strongest among public universities in the country by the Association of Research Libraries.

Ohio State's course offerings are as extensive as it gets, the sports programs are world class and many of the facilities are brand new and top-notch, but the college experience isn't just about the academics. The February 2003 issue of *Rolling Stone* magazine named Columbus the "#10 City in the Nation for Campus Scenes that Rock." And rock it does—sometimes to the dismay of the parents footing the bill.

The university receives high scores with students for social and nightlife. No matter which way you slice it, OSU is a party school. All of its social offerings can be a distraction, of course, but it also offers those students who can afford to eat out and the older crowd who can legally imbibe in alcohol a lot of variety.

The campus area has no shortage of ethnic eateries, 24-hour pizza joints, and cheap watering holes, some of which have been campus institutions as far back as Prohibition. Entries for pizza shops are listed here, while campus-area restaurants are covered in the Restaurants chapter. This chapter also includes a few of the drinking establishments that are identified with the Ohio State experience. You can't visit OSU without buying a dirt-cheap pitcher of beer at the Out-R-Inn or basking in the shadow of the Horseshoe at the Varsity Club during a football game.

It doesn't take long to realize many of Ohio State's more popular traditions revolve around Buckeye sports, football in particular. Tailgating is a huge fact of campus life. Lane Avenue is blocked off while partyers spill onto the streets all around the stadium. Locals gladly partake of the pre- and postgame mayhem, which can leave quite an impression on out-of-towners—especially if you're from Michigan.

Anyone vaguely familiar with college sports understands the seriousness with which schools take their rivalries. Very few can match the animosity between The Ohio State University and the University of Michigan, which seems to grow stronger once you graduate. While this rivalry is dealt with later in the chapter, mention must be made of the infamous disturbances that followed the 2002 Ohio State–Michigan game, causing the university to clamp down on the excessive sports-related drinking.

Stringent open-container laws are now enforced on football Saturdays. No more wandering across Lane Avenue with your open can of beer. No more verbally abusing Michigan fans slinking back to their cars for the drive north. While many of the responsible game goers are disappointed with these restrictions, it's all in an effort to curb offensive fan behavior.

For 150 years, OSU academics, traditions, and landmarks have become synonymous with Columbus. While not everyone is a Buckeye fan, it is impossible to separate the university from the city. Whether the Buckeyes win national titles or CNN highlights our "enthusiastic" rioting fans (after a win, no less), whether scandal rips through various departments or OSU students find a cure for cancer, what goes on at The Ohio State University is a total reflection of our city and often defines Columbus in the eyes of the rest of the country.

The school is often referred to as Ohio State or OSU, but the proper name, when used as a noun, is* The *Ohio State University—as named in 1878.

The goal of this chapter is to provide general information and dispel some myths about America's largest university, offer pointers on how to get around and manage the campus sprawl, and make some sense of why so many locals are Buckeyes to the bone. We begin with a brief history of the university but you can read more about William Neil, the man who donated the land, in the History chapter. "Campus Today" includes an overview of the student population, faculty, academics, and facilities. This is followed by a discussion about the Buckeyes and their traditions. The chapter ends with a listing of campus shops, pizza places, and the quintessential pub crawl.

HISTORY

President Abraham Lincoln's revolutionary Land Grant Act of 1862 laid the foundation for college education to be within reach of all high school graduates. Congress granted federally controlled lands to the states in order to establish institutions to teach the general population agriculture, mechanics, and military tactics. In 1870, the Ohio General Assembly established the earliest school that was to become what we now know as The Ohio State University.

The Ohio Agricultural and Mechanical College was first established on farmland bequeathed by Columbus businessman William Neil. As the name suggests, this college intended to matriculate students strictly in agricultural and mechanical disciplines. It opened its doors for classes in September 17, 1873, when 24 students met at the old Neil farm, 2 miles north of Columbus.

The college's curriculum was disputed among just about everyone. Some wanted to keep it devoted solely to agriculture, while others wanted to broaden the scope to include classical studies. In 1878, a vote was passed to include English and classical and foreign languages. It was at this time the college changed its name to The Ohio State University. Six of the men who began in the first class graduated this same year, while the first woman graduated from The Ohio State University in 1879.

CAMPUS TODAY

Faculty and Academics

The diverse range of studies envisioned by the first board of trustees at The Ohio State University continues to this day. Students have 174 undergraduate majors, 122 master's degrees, and 94 doctoral degrees to choose from. Over 12,000 courses are offered in 200 fields of study. The original board would be proud.

Current president Karen A. Holbrook and provost Barbara R. Snyder oversee the 18 different colleges and schools that make up The Ohio State University. The colleges range from architecture to engineering to veterinary sciences, and each has its own application and admission requirements. Just have a look at the homepage of the department you are interested in, and you will find comprehensive faculty, admission, and departmental information.

Admission criteria vary for each school, but three primary factors are considered in the competitive review process: completion of a college preparatory curriculum in high school, grade point average, and SAT or ACT scores. The outlying regional campuses in Lima, Mansfield, Marion, Newark, and Wooster have their own standards of admission and deadlines. Links to each campus can be found on Ohio State's main Web site.

The student-to-faculty ratio is 13:1. Contrary to popular belief, only 6 percent of the first-year classes have more than 100 students, while 89 percent have fewer than 50. The advanced undergraduate classes are even smaller, so that the ratio becomes even more realistic during junior and senior years. Yes, freshman might have a few auditorium-sized classes, but there are pointers on the Web site about how to make the most of this situation.

Many parents and students tend to forget about or overlook the esteemed faculty The Ohio State University employs. In classes with 100 or more, students may have trouble appreciating that these professors come from all parts of the world and from highly respected universities. They not only teach classes but conduct cutting-edge research, spearhead innovative discoveries, and create new art and technologies along with their students. Just read the laundry list of faculty members who have received the highest awards and honors within their fields.

Seven Ohio State faculty members have received the rank of fellow from the American Association for the Advancement of Science, eight have received the prestigious Guggenheim Memorial Fellowship for humanists, and we can't forget to mention the dozen or so Fulbright scholars, a Sloan fellow, and three faculty members elected recently to the Academy of Arts.

Like all big public schools, the undergraduate program at OSU receives its share of negative publicity, but like anywhere, an education becomes what you make you of it. It is the graduate schools, however, that have put The Ohio State University on the map. Between 1999 and 2003, Ohio State was ranked 8th in the nation for granting doctoral degrees. Nearly 3,000 graduate students taught 10,000 undergraduate students during the 2003–2004 academic year. In this case, OSU has size going for it, making it a leader in graduate education.

For complete information, check out The Ohio State University Web site at www.osu.edu, or call (614) 282-OHIO. For undergraduate application information, contact the admissions office at (614)

292-3980. For graduate information, contact the graduate admissions office at (614) 292-9444.

Students and Alumni

The current student population is made up mostly of Ohioans, with an almost even breakout of men and women. One third of the entering freshmen in the fall of 2004 ranked in the top 10 percent of their graduating high school class, while two thirds ranked in the top 25 percent. Thirty-seven percent were admitted into arts and sciences, while engineering and business came in a close second at 16 and 11 percent, respectively.

The annual tuition for a full-time undergraduate student in 2005-06 was around $8,100 for residents and $19,300 for nonresidents. The average room and board is about $8,000. The tuition and fees were increased 12.1 percent for the 2005-2006 academic year due to cuts in state funding and an increase in utilities and employee benefits. This is not cheap for a public school education, but scholarships and federal and state financial aid are available.

Single full-time students entering college directly from high school are required to live on campus their first year, unless they are staying with parents and commuting. Living on campus certainly has its advantages both academically and socially. Ohio State's 31 resident halls are convenient to classes and within walking distance of athletic and art facilities, fraternity and sorority houses, and the restaurants, bars, and shops of High Street.

All of the dormitories have laundry facilities, and many have weight rooms, TV rooms, and computer labs. All of the dorms and suites have cable hook-up and come furnished with a refrigerator and microwave. In addition to regular coed residential halls, the university has specialized living for African Americans, same-sex residences, halls for upper classmen only, and study-intensive environments for honors students.

Once you settle into your new home, getting around this sprawling campus can seem daunting, especially if you have to walk from class to class in a short period of time. The best suggestion to incoming students is to spread your classes out, allowing enough time to get from point A to point B. Also, keep a map of the campus buildings handy when scheduling, so you can see how realistic it is to make it to your next class on time. Many of the academic buildings are clustered around the Oval, so this generally isn't a big problem.

The Campus Area Bus Service (CABS) has several routes that services the campus and beyond. The Campus Loop North and Campus Loop South each make about 20 stops throughout their respective sides of campus from 6:50 A.M. until just after midnight. The bus stops are well marked and obvious. The East Residential heads toward Indianola Avenue, east of High Street, while the Commuter Express services the Buckeye Lot west of campus. You can contact CABS at (614) 292-6122, or check out the Web site (www.tp.ohio-state.edu) for detailed information about the routes.

Those who like to cycle will find plenty of bike racks outside most buildings. This is undeniably the best and quickest way to get around campus. It will also save you the hassle and expense of parking.

Driving and parking on campus can be tough at peak times. The general rule of thumb is the higher your student status, the better your parking options. There are surface lots, parking garages, and shuttles that go between central campus and west campus lots. Rates vary depending on where you want to park, but the closer

Ohio State's student identification card is called the BuckID. It functions as the official university photo ID, library card, and meal plan card, and, with appropriate funds, is a debit card accepted at many locations on and off campus.

i

Parking meter violations will cost you $25, and nonregistered vehicles are fined $50 for parking in a permit lot. Pay attention to the time allotment on the meters because they vary from 45 minutes to 2 hours.

you are to central campus, the more expensive it becomes.

Short-term, single-day, and visitor permits can be purchased for $3.00 per day at 160 Bevis Hall. The parking garages charge a varying hourly rate for nonpermit holders. Students and visitors alike should be warned: OSU takes parking seriously. In 2004, campus security wrote almost 80,000 citations and raked in almost $1 million in parking violations. Students cannot graduate or register for classes until their parking violations are paid or disputed and settled. Check out the link to the Transportation and Parking Services, or call (614) 292-9341 or (877) OSU-PARK for information on how to purchase a parking permit and the different options.

If students need a little extra academic support, there are a variety of options. The Academic Learning Lab (614-688-4011), located at 1640 Neil Avenue in the Younkin Success Center, is a "one-stop learning shop" where students can be tutored in time management, improve study skills, and learn how to take better notes. Free walk-in tutorial assistance is also available at the Mathematics and Statistics Learning Center (614-292-4975), while personal tutors at the Writing Center (614-688-4291) will help students of all levels with their writing projects. It is located in 485 Mendenhall Lab, and tutoring is by appointment only.

The Office of Student Affairs (614-292-9334) can provide information related to anything outside of the classroom, from on- and off-campus housing, food service, and health issues, to recreational activities. Its Web site (www.studentaffairs.osu.edu) has links to all of the student organizations and services. A student resource guide is available online that includes diversity initiatives, intramural groups, campus technology services, and the student code of conduct.

A good place for students to begin looking for a job is the Office of Residential Life (614-292-8266), one of the largest employers of undergraduate students on campus. The office helps students find jobs that work around their class schedules. The Financial Aid Office (614-292-0300, 800-678-6440) can also assist eligible students in finding jobs through the federal work-study program. There are plenty of places to look for nonuniversity jobs, such as the classified ads in the *Columbus Dispatch* and the *Lantern,* OSU's campus newspaper. Employment and other classifieds are sometimes posted on bulletin boards in most of the academic buildings.

A variety of alumni services is available to those who survive their coursework, pay all their parking tickets, and go on to graduate: career services, networking, alumni clubs, and societies, to name a few. Rumor holds that somewhere in the world an Ohio State alumni meeting is taking place every nine hours. It is fair to say you can go anywhere in the world and bump into one of OSU's 310,000 living alumni.

A quizzical eyebrow might be raised when you visit a remote island and encounter someone wearing a "Buckeye Dad" T-shirt or when you spot an "O" ballcap in a Beijing market, but it should never be surprising. Take it from a former OSU student: No matter where you end up, once a Buckeye, always a Buckeye.

Diversity

The range of Ohio State's minority and international student body adds another dimension of diversity and culture to both the school and the city of Columbus. It also generates unique needs, so the university has focused on creating a campus environment that recognizes, respects, and appreciates cultural differences. This is important since more than 4,100 international and 8,100 minority students are enrolled across all of the campuses.

The Office of Minority Affairs (614-292-8732) is a good place for minorities to find scholarship services, tutoring programs, and graduate or professional recruitment. The office is located at 1030 Lincoln Tower, 1800 Cannon Drive. It also provides information about the extensive minority student organizations, such as the All-Ethiopian Student Association, Chinese Student Association, and Turkish Student Association.

As part of the university's Diversity Action Plan, a multicultural center was established to provide intellectual, cultural, and support programs for minority students, faculty, and staff. Located on the fourth floor of the Student Union, individual offices focus on academics, advocacy, and community development for American Indian, Asian-American, African-American, Hispanic, Gay, Lesbian, Bisexual, and Transgender students. The center also houses the Rape Education and Prevention Program and Men's and Women's Student Services.

With nearly 2,000 staff and faculty members who are veterans, Ohio State is the only university in the nation with a dedicated Veterans Affairs office to assist their employees. This office also serves as a focal point for veterans' advocacy, referrals, financial aid, and activities for students and staff alike.

Ohio State isn't just tooting its own horn. Outside sources are recognizing the university for its ongoing commitment to multiculturalism. *Black Enterprise* magazine rated The Ohio State University 44th in their annual ranking of the country's 50 best colleges for African Americans. The Frank West Hale Jr. Black Cultural Center, located in the heart of campus at 153 West 12th Avenue, is open seven days a week. It hosts social, cultural, and educational programs focused on the African-American culture and houses an impressive collection of artwork depicting the African-American experience. The Black Studies Library can be found on the second floor of the main library.

The Ohio State University is among the top five higher education institutions for granting doctorate degrees to African Americans and in the top 20 for Hispanic students.

A final testimony to OSU's diversity plan is the newly created Kirwin Institute for the Study of Race and Ethnicity. This center brings together scholars from around the world to deliberate issues such as race, poverty, housing, and ethnic and religious conflicts. To learn more about diversity, affirmative action, and access for the disabled at The Ohio State University, you should read the diversity reports on the Web site. Contact the Diversity Services Office by calling (614) 688-4394 or stopping in at 154 Denney Hall, 164 West 17th Avenue.

Student Organizations and Activities

Being a student on campus or just being a resident of a large university town can be rewarding. Both students and the community reap the benefits of the endless number of campus programs available. The entire city can experience up-and-coming athletes, new artists, and fresh ideas turned out through various campus media. With 750 registered student organizations to choose from, you can find pretty much any activity you would want to be involved with.

OSU offers all the traditional college activities, like choral groups, musical ensembles, and a homecoming committee. Political types may become active in one of the three student governments. There are almost 50 honor societies, as well as numerous local and national service and awareness organizations.

OSU students can ride COTA buses for free anywhere in the city by showing their red BuckID.

If you are looking for intramural sports or physical activity of some sort, there are hundreds of possibilities: ballroom dancing, ice hockey, bowling, and skiing, to begin with. There are too many to list here, but the Parks and Recreation chapter includes information and contact details of the more popular intramural and club sports offered at OSU. You can also check out the link to Campus Life at www.undergrad.osu.edu.

From a social standpoint, one can understand the appeal of joining a fraternity and the sense of camaraderie it can create for a person who might otherwise feel lost at such a big school. Five percent of the undergraduate men and 6 percent of the women are part of Ohio State's Greek life. In order to receive a membership invitation to any one of the 37 fraternities and 21 sororities, students must earn a GPA of 2.25 and have 12 credit hours under their belt.

While Greek life is most closely associated with partying and slacking, it also provides opportunity for community involvement and creates lifelong friendships. Statistics have shown that the overall GPA of OSU's Greek community (3.07) was higher than the overall university GPA (3.02). Who knew?

There are almost 50 religious or spiritual organizations on campus. Many take advantage of the free meeting space in the Ohio Union, which also has a designated Muslim Prayer Room. The Campus Crusade for Christ is the largest religious organization and draws between 600 and 800 students to its weekly meetings. Other spiritual groups focus on Catholic, Jewish, Coptic, Sikh, Pagan, and a variety of Christian religions.

Those looking to be involved in university news and media have plenty of options. The student-produced yearbook, *The Makio* (614-292-8763), can be purchased for $50. *The Buckeye Net News* publishes daily e-mail news bulletins for students, and *OSUToday* publishes them for the faculty. The *Black Horizons* magazine is a student-run publication, and *Mosaic* is the undergraduate arts and literature magazine.

The *Ohio State Lantern* (614-292-2031; www.thelantern.com) is the university's official student newspaper. Established in 1881, the *Lantern* is one of Ohio's oldest newspapers and is currently the 15th largest paper in the state. It is published every weekday when classes are in session and twice weekly during the summer quarter. The *Lantern* also partially serves as a laboratory for journalism students and is consistently rated as the best daily student newspaper in the country by the Society of Professional Journalists.

Ohio State operates a public television station, WOSU channel 34, which began broadcasting in HDTV format in 2003. It has two public radio stations, 820 AM (NPR) and 89.7 FM, both with the call letters WOSU. The university has a short-range student radio station called The Underground. If you live in the dorms, you can pick it up on cable channel 4, or go to www.underground.fm and listen to the broadcast live via RealPlayer.

This is just a sample of what the university has to offer. Check out the link to Campus Life at www.undergrad.osu.edu for a complete listing and links to the different organizations.

CAMPUS BUILDINGS AND FACILITIES

Many OSU students come from Smalltown, USA, and are initially overwhelmed with the sprawling campus—understandably so. Who wouldn't be intimidated by a campus with over 300 buildings, a medical center, satellite communications center, supercomputer, polar research center, airport, wildlife preserve, and dairy farm? Situated on more than 1,700 acres, the school is as big as it sounds.

The Ohio State University is comprised of the main campus in Columbus and six regional campuses. In all, Ohio State has over 850 buildings, 26 of which are residence halls and 4 that are on the National Register of Historic Places. This doesn't include all the shops, services, and restaurants that line High Street; the school's occasionally dilapidated and always interesting main drag.

If campus wasn't already big enough, don't worry, it's growing. Students who attend OSU after 2005 will never know the "old" High Street, thanks to the South Campus Gateway project. The area along High Street between 9th and 11th Avenues is being developed by the Campus Partners. The Gateway is not a mall. It serves more as a transition into the university area and includes office space, rental housing, parking, and 40 retail, dining, and entertainment venues. The development, anchored by Barnes & Noble College Bookstores and an eight-screen Drexel cinema, opened in fall 2005.

Apartment buildings in Gateway South are available for occupancy and Panera Bread, Ugly Tuna Saloona, and Potbelly Sandwich Works are just a few of the food shops now open. Eddie George's Grill and Skye Bar are among the businesses slated to open throughout the winter and spring.

No matter how much time you spend wandering the grounds and getting to know the campus, it never gets smaller, only more manageable. This section will provide a brief overview of the primary facilities only on the main campus. After a few visits and with a little familiarity, functioning in this 1,700-acre "city within the city" will become less intimidating. I promise.

Academic and Conference Buildings

Computer centers (614-292-8400) operate all over campus on a first come, first served basis and are open long hours. The labs that have both Windows and Mac computers are located at 590 Baker Systems Engineering Building, 171 Haggerty Hall, and at the main library. In addition, labs can be found in Page Hall, Ohio Union, the Central Classroom Building, and the Math Building.

The Faculty Club (614-292-2262; www.ohio-statefacultyclub.com) is a private club for OSU faculty, staff, graduate students, and alumni. A one-time initiation fee is charged, and it is open to members for lunch and dinner. The Faculty Club also hosts special events like art exhibitions and receptions.

Fawcett Center (614-292-1342; www.fawcettcenter.com) is one of the largest state-of-the-art conference facilities in the country and serves as a prototype for conference centers on large campuses. It is located at 2400 Olentangy River Road, northwest of campus, and is home to the WOSU stations and The Ohio State Development offices.

Drake Union (614-292-3222; www.theatre.osu.edu) is home to Ohio State's Theater Department, as well as conference and banquet facilities. It sits along the banks of the Olentangy River at 1849 Cannon Drive.

Hayes Hall (614-292-7481; www.history-of-art.osu.edu) was built in 1893 and is one of the historic landmark buildings on campus. It is home to the history of art department, art studios, and the John C. and Susan L. Huntington Archive of Buddhist and Related Art.

Hopkins Hall (614-292-5171; www.arts.osu.edu) is located on the north side of the Oval and is home to the College and Department of Arts and many art studios. Its galleries feature changing exhibitions of student artwork.

The Main Library (614-292-6154; www.library.osu.edu), formally known as the William Oxley Thompson Library, was built in 1913 and towers over the Oval. It is undergoing a $99 million renovation, which will make it one of the nation's best public university libraries. OSU's library system has upward of two dozen libraries and an equal number of specialized collections, which include architecture, fine arts, and science and engineering libraries. The Moritz Law Library, business library, and medical libraries are among the graduate and professional libraries on campus.

The Ohio State University Medical Center (800-293-5123; www.medicalcenter.osu.edu) encompasses a college of medicine and public health, 5 hospitals, 2 free-standing research institutes, and 30 community-based facilities. Located directly on campus are the University Hospital Clinic and the James Cancer Clinic, a leading cancer research institute as well as research and teaching facilities.

Ohio Union (614-292-7924; www.ohiounion.com) is the primary gathering place for students, faculty, and staff. This building houses the Undergraduate Student Government, many student organizations, conference ballrooms, a theater, and a food court with televisions and plenty of seating. The building sits between High Street and 12th and College Avenues. Woody's, a full-service restaurant and bar, is located in the Union. Plans are in place to begin building a new student union in 2007; the services in the current building will be relocated until the new Ohio Union opens in 2009.

Orton Hall (614-292-2721; www.geology.ohio-state.edu), home to the Department of Geological Sciences, is one of the oldest buildings on campus. Built in 1893, it's on the south side of the Oval and is supposedly haunted by its namesake, Edward Orton. This building's stone turret is one of the most recognizable landmarks on campus, and the bells chime every day, reminding you how late you are for class. Its geological museum is worth a look.

The Student Visitor Center (614-292-3980; www.campusvisit.osu.edu) is located in Enarson Hall, which is named for Ohio State's ninth president, Harold Enarson. The building was completed in 1910 and was the first student union on a state university campus and the fourth established in the United States. It is located at 154 West 12th Avenue and has been renovated eight times in the past 90 years.

Veterinary Hospital (614-292-1171; www.vet.ohio-state.edu), located on the west side of campus, is both a research and teaching hospital. It also serves as a primary pet care facility for the campus and Columbus community.

The Wexner Center for the Arts (614-292-3535; www.wexarts.org) is a multidisciplinary contemporary arts center and museum. It features a broad range of art exhibitions, film and video screenings, and music, dance, and theater performances in the Mershon Auditorium. Read more about the Wexner Center and its intriguing architecture in the Close-up in The Arts chapter.

Athletic Facilities

OSU can boast one of the most comprehensive collegiate sports programs in the country. It offers 16 men's sports ranging from baseball, basketball, and football to fencing, golf, and hockey. OSU has 17 women's collegiate sports teams, including, lacrosse, softball, and volleyball, and three coed teams. The department operates on a budget in excess of $80 million and has spent $300 million on upgrades to existing facilities and new-builds.

The best source of information about Ohio State athletics is the athletics department homepage, www.ohiostatebuckeyes.collegesports.com. Links to all the various facilities and sporting opportunities can be found in this section. Information has been included only for Ohio State's primary athletic buildings, but there are a dozen more not included here.

Bill Davis Stadium (614-292-1075) is the home of OSU's men's baseball and women's softball teams. It is located on the west side of campus near the Schottenstein Center just off Lane Avenue. Tickets to the games can be purchased at the gate.

The Golf Club (614-459-GOLF; www.ohiostatebuckeyes.com) is located 2 miles northwest of the campus at the intersection of Kenny and Tremont Roads. The Golf Club was established in 1938 and can boast two of the country's finest collegiate golf courses, the Scarlet and the Gray. National tournaments are held here, and anyone affiliated with the university can play either course. Its restaurant, overlooking the Scarlet golf course, is open to the public.

Jesse Owens Memorial Stadium, opened in 2001, is one of the newest additions to OSU's state-of-the-art athletic facilities and is arguably the finest multisport facility in the country. The stadium hosts track-and-field, lacrosse, and soccer events.

Jesse Owens Recreation Centers (614-292-7671) are located on the north, south, and west sides of campus. They provide students with cardio equipment, free weights, and exercise machines. Outdoor basketball courts, tracks, and baseball diamonds are also available for pick-up games and recreational leagues. The West Center is the only place on campus to play indoor tennis.

Larkins Hall, OSU's old recreation center, has been leveled to accommodate the Recreation and Physical Activity Center—a new, state-of-the-art facility being built in four phases. The first phase consists of the Adventure Recreation Center and the Outdoor Adventure Center, located at Kenny Road on Woody Hayes Drive. Students have access to wall-climbing, outdoor equipment rental, and planned excursions. The Rec Main building provides students with 25,000 square feet of fitness space, basketball and racquet courts, indoor tracks, and locker rooms. Additional amenities include athletic and personal trainers, massage therapy, babysitting, and dining options. Phase III, the McCorkle Aquatic Pavilion, includes lap pools, leisure pools, a spa, and sauna. The final phase will house the School of Physical Activity and Educational Services, basketball courts, and an indoor golf station and putting green. Membership fees are built into students' costs. Faculty and staff can pay a $100 quarterly membership fee to use the facilities and may purchase membership for their family. RPAC is located on West 17th Street.

The OSU Ice Rink (614-292-4154) is located at 390 Woody Hayes Drive, right next to St. John's Arena. The facility is home to the ice hockey varsity and club teams and includes a warming room, locker rooms, training room, and pro shop.

The Schottenstein Center (614-292-2624; www.schottensteincenter.com) opened in 1998 and is the home of the OSU men's and women's basketball and hockey teams. This distinct-looking arena is located off Lane Avenue, just west of campus. You can read more about "The Schott" as an entertainment venue in the Nightlife chapter.

St. John Arena (614-292-7572) is home to the wrestling team and men's and women's volleyball and gymnastics teams. The building was erected in 1956 and ushered in Ohio State's golden era of basketball. The basketball teams now play at the Schottenstein Center.

LANDMARKS

The Lane Avenue Bridge is a new state-of-the-art suspension bridge crossing the Olentangy River, making it easier to get from High Street to Route 315 on the west side of campus. This cable-stayed bridge, opened in 2003, has six 12-foot-wide traffic lanes flanked by 12-foot-wide walking lanes. It is not only a beautiful addition to campus but a necessary one.

Mirror Lake is Ohio State's oldest landmark. It was originally fed by a natural spring, which figured prominently in the site being chosen for the university. Several landmarks in their own right surround mirror Lake Hollow: Browning Amphitheatre, Bucket and Dipper Rock, the Faculty Club, and Pomerene Hall. Don't be shocked to see drunken students taking a dip each Michigan week.

The Oval is the heart of Ohio State's campus, but it's really more of a quadrangle. Buildings, pathways, and trees line this grassy hub of activity. Because of its centralized location, the Oval makes a great meeting point and is often the site of protests or rallies. In the summer months you'll see loads of college kids basking in the sun—with their books, of course.

The Ohio Stadium transcends athletic facilities. Its unique horseshoe configuration makes it one of the most recognizable stadiums in all of college athletics, hence its inclusion here under landmarks. With a capacity of more than 101,000 fans, Ohio Stadium is currently the second largest in the Big Ten and the third largest college stadium in America. Even if you aren't a football fan, you can't overlook the nostalgia this building invokes.

Stadium plans were announced in 1919, and architect Howard Dwight Smith was hired. The animal husbandry department surrendered a pasture west of Neil Avenue in exchange for facilities west of the Olentangy River, which was later straightened and diked to prevent flooding. Ground was broken for Ohio Stadium on August 3, 1921, and completed in time for the 1922 football season. Its dedication game was held against Michigan on October 21, 1922, and the stadium was paid off a few months before the stock market crashed in 1929.

"The Shoe," the home of Ohio State football, retains its original U-shape and is on the National Register of Historic Places. It underwent $200 million worth of renovations between 1999 and 2001 and hosted its largest crowd (105,565) on September 10, 2005, against the Texas Longhorns. Ohio Stadium, where the notorious OSU–Michigan game continues to happen every other year, is a must-see when you visit Columbus.

BUCKEYE TRADITIONS

It all begins Welcome Week, when incoming freshmen catch the Scarlet Fever. It doesn't take long to learn the fight songs and be sucked into the world of Brutus Buckeye, and the deep-rooted spirit doesn't stop at graduation. Even locals who attended other universities are often die-hard Buckeyes. Why? Because few schools boast the successful sports history that the Ohio State Buckeyes can, and few have such deeply rooted traditions associated with it.

A century and a half of time-honored traditions is engrained in the very fabric of our city. All true Buckeye fans will know who Woody Hayes, Eddie George, and Brutus Buckeye are. They know where Block-O and the Buckeye Grove are located. They bemoan the loss of the Neutron Man and revel in the sound of the Victory bell. They defensively remind you that the school colors are scarlet and gray. Not red, burgundy, or silver; scarlet and gray. This section will clue you into the most popular Ohio State traditions so you don't make these kinds of mistakes.

"Across the Field"

Also known as "Fight the Team," this is the Buckeye fight song you hear played throughout the games by "The Best Damn Band in the Land."

The Best Damn Band in the Land (TBDBITL)

Founded in 1878, The Ohio State University Marching Band is a cornerstone of the university and has been dubbed by the fans as TBDBITL, or "The Best Damn Band in the Land."

Block-O

This student cheering section has been around since 1938 and is OSU's largest and most recognizable student organization. Well known for their noisy antics during the football games, they have had an increasing presense at the men's basketball games (perhaps the women's basketball team should get a visit from the NutHouse). Block-O has its own Web page, www.blocko.org.ohio-state.edu, which counts down the days, hours, minutes, and seconds until the next football season.

Brutus Buckeye

The school mascot is a nut! Brutus is one of the more visible and lovable symbols of Ohio State athletics. In 1965, an art student designed and introduced the first Brutus, while the name was chosen in a contest.

Buckeye Football

Where to begin? Baby Buckeyes are born everyday. These fledgling Bucknuts quickly develop into full-grown football fanatics who will follow their team to the ends of the earth. Why? Because The Ohio State football team gives us something to cheer about.

OSU has one of the most storied football programs in the country. In the past 50 years, they have won over 400 games, including five national championships: 1942, 1954, 1957, and 1968, and, most recently, in 2002, under head coach Jim Tressel. To learn more than you've ever wanted to know about the team, you can go to the OSU Web site or visit the countless number of unofficial Web sites dedicated to the Buckeye mania.

Buckeye Grove

Ohio State All-Americans are honored by having a Buckeye tree planted in their name at the south side of the stadium.

Buckeye Leaves

In 1968, Woody Hayes started the tradition of placing Buckeye Leaves on the Ohio State helmets when they make a good play. When you see a sticker-covered helmet, you know you're seeing a good player.

"Carmen Ohio"

"Carmen Ohio" is the stirring alma mater of The Ohio State University. It is the oldest school song still in use. It was written by OSU freshman Fred Cornell in 1902 after a loss in Ann Arbor and can bring a tear to the eye of even the rowdiest of football fans.

Dotting the *i*

The grand finale of the band's famous "Script Ohio" is when a senior sousaphone player prances out of formation to "dot the *i*" in a most theatrical manner. The *i* dotter will kick, turn, and bow, causing the crowd to go completely giddy. A trumpet player first dotted the "Script Ohio" *i* on October 10, 1936. Decades later, this honor is familiar throughout the world but is typically relegated to band members. The few honorary nonband "*i* dotters" have included Bob Hope and Woody Hayes, and, on the 50th anniversary of "Script Ohio," members of the 1936 OSU marching band "dotted the *i*" en masse.

Gold Pants

A gold charm in the shape of football pants is given to players and coaches following wins over Michigan. The tradition began in 1934, when Coach Francis Schmidt was asked how OSU would deal with its arch-nemesis from Ann Arbor, and he replied that Michigan players "put their pants on one leg at a time just like everybody else." The Buckeyes then went on to shut out Michigan four consecutive times, prompting a group of businessmen to create the "Gold Pants Club," awarding these charms to all players who beat the Wolverines.

"Hang on Sloopy"

To an Ohio State fan, this song is much more than just a 1965 hit by the McCoys—it's synonymous with OSU football. "Sloopy" made its debut October 9, 1965, at the OSU–Illinois game and was a firmly rooted tradition by the end of that season. TBDBITL will break into riffs of "Sloopy" whenever something goes our way. It is also the official state "rock song." I wonder if Bruce Springsteen knew this when he played "Sloopy" at his last concert here and the crowd instinctively interjected the "O-H-I-O" chant.

The Neutron Man

Orlas King is perhaps the best-known Buckeye fan in history. Decked out in team colors and a scarlet-and-gray beret, he was the man you would see dancing wildly in the stands to the song "Neutron Dance" by the Pointer Sisters. The Buckeyes even created a special scoreboard graphic for their unofficial mascot. He attended most of the home games since the mid-1970s but passed away in October 2004.

If you are thinking about buying a football ticket from a student, don't. As of last season, a BuckID must accompany all student tickets, which are scanned for validity. So, a fake ID won't work. Student tickets can be passed along to their parents—for a fee, of course.

OH-IO

What is the proper response to someone yelling "O-H" with their hands up over their heads like a ballerina? "I-O," of course. There is no limit as to where and when you can shout this chant during football season. You'll hear it echoed down the streets, between strangers at bars, and even over the telephone.

The Ramp Entrance

One of the band's most famous traditions dates back to 1928. Band members and football fans let out a roar as the band parades down the ramp onto the field. The drum major struts triumphantly across the field and stops to execute the traditional back bend, touching his plume to the ground and sending the crowd into a frenzy. After a few rounds of "The Buckeye Battle Cry," a drum major baton performance, and a salute to the opposing school, the band performs the pregame show.

The Rivalry with the State Up North

Die-hard Buckeye fans can't even bring themselves to say the name "Michigan." They prefer to leave it at "the state up north." OSU and Michigan played their first game in 1897, and the annual Ohio State-Michigan football game was ranked No. 1 on a list of the "10 Greatest Rivalries in Sports" compiled by ESPN.com. The whole week before the Michigan game is devoted to mustering up school spirit. There simply is no greater rivalry in college athletics.

Scarlet and Gray

Scarlet and gray have been Ohio State's official school colors since 1878 and were chosen by three students because "it was a pleasing combination . . . and had not been adopted by any other college."

Script Ohio

The most famous tradition at The Ohio State University is the band's trademark "Script Ohio." After performing Carmen Ohio in a triple O formation, the band, led by the drum major, begins scrolling single file into a cursive spelling of the word *Ohio*. The "Script Ohio" formation was first performed during the 1936 season and takes three and a half minutes to complete.

Victory Bell

The Victory bell is located in the southeast tower of Ohio Stadium and is rung after every Ohio State victory. It was a gift of the classes of 1943, 1944, and 1945. On a calm day, it is said the bell can be heard 5 miles away.

Woody Hayes

I won't even try to sum up this former coach in one paragraph, other than to say he still embodies Ohio State football for many people today. His legendary temper ultimately cost him his job, but the football team enjoyed the best (and worst) of times while he was coach (1950–1978). He was known for his love of competition and history and his hatred of Michigan and losing. Whether people liked or disliked him, his name is immortalized around campus.

SHOPPING

There are a number of retail clothing stores, secondhand shops, and pharmacies located along High Street. Printing services such as Kinko's and video rental from Blockbuster and North Campus Video are also convenient to campus.

Buckeye Corner
1677 West Lane Avenue
(614) 486-0702
www.collegegear.com
You'll be seeing red when you enter this mothership of all things Buckeye. You can find everything, from Ohio State clothing to tailgating paraphernalia, including marching band CDs, jewelry, and flags. It is definitely a well-organized and high-stocked store, but it's a bit more expensive than its campus competition. There is another location in Easton.

College Traditions
286 West Lane Avenue
(614) 291-4678
www.collegetraditions.com
This campus store has a huge selection of Ohio State gift and sportswear. You'll find limited-edition artwork, bobble heads, and national championship memorabilia. Even Fido will find something he likes. This is a great place for die-hards to find yard decorations and bedroom ensembles.

Conrad's College Gifts
316 West Lane Avenue
(614) 297-0497, (888) GIFT-OSU
www.conrads.com
This is the original Ohio State concept store and has the reputation of carrying the most complete line of Buckeye products. You can find the smallest sizes for your Buckeye baby and clothing up to XXXL for your big Buckeye.

The Ohio State University Bookstore
1598 North High Street, the Gateway
(614) 247-2000, (888) 678-5664
www.ohiostate.bkstore.com
After 100 years as a family-owned bookstore and campus institution, Campus Partners purchased Long's, and it is now operated by Barnes & Noble College Bookstores. As one of the country's largest academic bookstores, students will find everything they need from textbooks

to computer supplies. It also carries a large selection of computer software, clothing, and dorm supplies.

The Ohio State University Shops
Various locations on campus
www.osustores.com
Several stores, such as The Chemistry Store and the Corner Store, exist to meet the needs of different colleges and departments. Students can find everything from zinc oxide to Mac computers. Check out the different locations and hours on the Web site. The OSU Bookstore can be reached at (614) 292-2991, or visit www.ohiostate.bkstore.com.

Singing Dog Records
1644 North High Street
(614) 299-1490
www.singingdog.com
The Dog opened in 1980 and is always in the top 2 or 3 "Best Record Stores" in Columbus, particularly for alternative and urban music. It buys, sells, and trades mostly CDs and cassettes. You can get cash or credit for just about anything the owners feel they can resell.

University Flower Shop
243 West 11th Avenue
(614) 421-1600, (800) 494-2900
www.osuflowers.com
This florist is right in the heart of campus and will deliver to all student housing areas as well as the major hospitals. It carries fresh flowers, silk arrangements, balloons, and specialty baskets. This full-service FTD florist has another location at 1878 North High Street.

CAMPUS PIZZA PLACES

Just make your way along High Street or Lane Avenue, and you'll eventually come across the standard pizza chains. Pizza Hut, Domino's, Donato's, and Papa John's are all represented somewhere in the vicinity of campus. So are plenty of good sub shops like Quizno's and Penn Station East Coast Subs. This section will suggest a handful of the more popular pizza places directly on campus. Most of them are open late and accept the BuckID.

Adriatico's New York Style Pizza
265 West 11th Avenue
(614) 421-2300
This tiny pizza shop makes a big Siçilian pizza. The crust is thick, and the sauce is rich and garlicky. Though you can find cheaper pizza on campus, this is one of the favorites. The dine-in crowd is more the professor or graduate student types having pizza and beer. It also has a steady inflow of customers from residents of nearby Victorian Village. The tiny shop is located on the corner of Neil and 11th, across from the freshman dorms. They deliver and accept the BuckID.

Catfish Biff's
75 West 11th Avenue
(614) 421-7421
No fish—just pizza. Down the street from Adriatico's is the exact opposite type of pizza: thin and crispy. Catfish Biff's is a no-brainer among hungry students. The pizza is good and cheap, not to mention you can have a pack of smokes delivered with your pie. They provide carryout and delivery only, but BuckID is accepted here.

Flying Pizza
1812 North High Street
(614) 294-1011
The pie found here stands above the competition, according to some campus pizza connoisseurs, but everyone agrees they have the best Italian ice. This hole-in-the-wall on High Street has about a half-dozen tables, canned soft drinks, and pizza that some New Yorkers say is as close to NY pizza as it gets. The crust is thin, hand-tossed, and comes round or square. The selections are pretty basic, but you can add veggies for a little extra or buy pizza by the slice. You might even get a good dose of NY-style attitude

thrown in for free. It's a really homey place. Flying Pizza does not deliver but accepts BuckID.

Hound Dog's Three Degree Pizza
2657 North High Street
(614) 261-4686
If the motto "Pizza for the People" isn't a dead giveaway that this campus institution dates back to the psychedelic '60s, then the wall murals of a pooch smoking and drinking will. Despite ancient bathroom graffiti, the place is clean and the ambience can be quite acceptable at three in the morning. Aside from several kinds of pizza, this sit-down restaurant serves edible pub grub, typical pizza shop fare, and beer. Expect to see a mix of young Abercrombie & Fitch–Urban Outfitters–Old Navy types hanging around the jukebox. Hound Dog is open 24 hours a day, every day, except major holidays, and accepts BuckID.

Mama's Pasta & Brew
23 Campus Place
(614) 299-7724
Located in the self-proclaimed "world's worst location" is this kitschy campus institution that has been filling students' bellies with pizza, pasta, and beer since 1983. This grungy-looking building without windows is tucked in an alley between 14th and 15th Avenues, but don't let that scare you off. Mama's has a loyal following of students and alumni who take part in annual raft trips and golf scrambles. Good Italian dinners for $6.00 are hard to come by, unless it's at one of the great campus dives of all time. They even accept BuckID.

Tommy's Pizza
174 West Lane Avenue
(614) 294-4669
Tommy (well, at least an oil painting of him) greets everyone at the door. The full-service menu includes consistently good pizza that many say is the best in the entire world. The menu runs the gamut from subs to sandwiches to full Italian dinners. The place is decorated with Big Ten memorabilia on wallpaper covered with Ohio symbols, buckeyes, and footballs. Tommy's does not accept BuckID.

THE PUB CRAWL

Bernie's Distillery
1896 North High Street
(614) 291-3448
Half dingy eatery and half dingy bar, Bernie's has been a campus haunt since 1976. A descent below High Street will take you to a dark, dank bar with possibly the worst bathrooms ever. The lack of windows is offset by the amount of graffiti and advertisements covering the walls. None of this deters the campus population from Bernie's cheap beer and edible food. The restaurant is open all day, serving sandwiches and vegetarian selections. The bar opens in the afternoon. With such good drink prices, it's no wonder everyone leaves this place smelling like a distillery! This is also a live music venue featuring local and regional indie rock and alternative acts on a stage the size of a king bed. Despite it's "underground" atmosphere, Bernie's draws a mixed campus crowd. Skaters and jocks mingle with ease. If you can overlook the leaky water pipes and brain-blowing music, you'll have a great time. The deli, Bernie's Bagels, accepts BuckID.

Bristol Bar
132 East Fifth Avenue, at Summit Street
(614) 291-0552
www.bristolbar.com
Somewhere between OSU's campus and downtown, a historic building was renovated into this chic and cozy martini bar. The candlelit interior is totally metro—uncomfortable barstools, well-dressed, cocktail-guzzling, upwardly-mobile types and all. No food is served, but the drink menu is loaded with unique and innovative martinis, excellent bottled beer and champagne, and fine cigars. Valet parking makes up for its location in a somewhat "transitional" part of town.

Four Kegs Bar & Grill
12 East 15th Avenue
(614) 298-8000
Cheap brews and a big patio are this bar's claim to fame. Consistency is not. This has had three or four different names over the past seven years, and you have to wonder why. It has a fantastic location at the corner of High and 15th, and provides some of the best people watching. Even when classes are finished and college mating rituals have ceased for the summer, the view of the Wexner Center isn't so bad. With one of the only outdoor patios on campus, it overflows with people on sunny days. During inclement weather there are pool tables and televisions inside. The menu has the usual pub grub, and the jukebox has over 100,000 tunes to pick from. Kegs does not accept BuckID.

J. R. Miggs
1630 Neil Avenue
(614) 421-1306
www.cateringconceptsbyjrmiggs.com
There can be a lot of brainpower in this little neighborhood bar when Ohio State students invade. Too bad it all turns to mush with such good beer prices! It's quite the "collegiate" thing to do—drink beer by the pitcher in a dive bar, but Miggs offers a fine selection of imported bottles for a good price too. The menu consists of great tasting bar food as well as an assortment of sandwiches. If you land one of the few outdoor tables, it's a good place to enjoy the late afternoon sun—and don't be surprised to see your professors strolling by. BuckID is accepted here.

Larry's Bar
2040 North High Street
(614) 299-6010
www.larrysbar.com
Poetry over pints—does it get any better than that? Intellectuals, students, artists, philosophers, and OSU faculty are drawn to one of the oldest watering holes on campus. They have been since 1923. During Prohibition, it is rumored that Larry's was a speakeasy. Campus remained dry long after Prohibition, but Larry's was one foot north of OSU property, making it the closest spot to campus to have a drink. On slow nights at Larry's people actually come here to study. Wednesday's—"hump day"—get busy, and the regulars come out of the woodwork on the weekends. Well-behaved dogs are even permitted in the bar.

The Library Bar
2169 North High Street
(614) 299-3245
This is an appropriate name for a campus bar located on the barhopping strip along High Street. The place has a lot of character, and two generations of Ohio State students claim fond memories of this bar. With a laid-back atmosphere and friendly staff, it gets very crowded, making it almost impossible to get a seat at the bar. But who goes to a campus bar to sit down? The upper level is lively with pool tables, foosball, and shuffle bowling. The lower level has darts and pinball, and the booths make this area a little quieter. It is well known that the Library has some of the best happy hour prices on campus. Live music and televised football games are the other draws.

Out-R-Inn
20 East Frambes Avenue
(614) 294-9183
This campus institution has been a gathering place since 1980 and continues to be for those who can't leave their college days behind. It's basically a two-floor house-turned-bar with two different outdoor spaces. Grab a table on the front porch or a picnic table out back, where there is a full-service bar and televisions on the fenced-in patio. There are pool tables and dartboards, and, after expanding to the adjacent building, pizza can be had, along with cheap pitchers of beer. Out-R-Inn is a campus mainstay and provides the absolute quintessential college-bar experience.

Skully's Music Diner
1151 North High Street
(614) 291-8856
www.skullys.org

Situated in that transitional area between the Short North and Ohio State's campus is this eclectic dance-and-music venue that plays host to live alternative music on the weekend. It draws a diverse crowd, and the interior is funky, with a focus on leopard print. Two bars, a dance floor, and a pool table will keep you entertained, but if you prefer to just hang out, there are sofas and tables inside and a small outdoor patio on High Street. Skully's has a full menu with daily specials and great happy hour prices, and serves food till midnight on weekends.

The Thirsty Scholar
2201 Neil Avenue
(614) 298-9805

Old-timers remember this place as the Black Forest Inn. This two-story bar was totally renovated and opened as The Thirsty Scholar in 1997. The upper bar may seem a little small, but there is an entire lower level with pool tables, foosball, and a big-screen television. This place can be a little evasive, but you'll spot its neon sign on the side of the white "house" just north of Lane Avenue. It is very close to the Horseshoe and St. John's Arena and makes a great meeting place before and after sporting events. There are daily happy hour specials (as if the regular prices aren't cheap enough!). The menu is limited to sandwiches and appetizers, but the prices are great, and the food tastes good too.

Varsity Club & Pizza
278 West Lane Avenue
(614) 299-6269, 299-5029

You know you're in Buckeye territory the moment you walk through the VC's door, or perhaps even sooner. This scarlet-and-gray painted building, which is pushing 50 years as a campus institution, sits in the shadow of the historic Ohio Stadium. One has to wonder how many times the jukebox here has cranked out "Hang on Sloopy" or people have shouted "O-H," "I-O" across the bar. Everything at the Varsity Club, from the menus to the decor, celebrates Ohio State sports—including the patrons. Don't even think about getting a seat here before or during a football game unless you come very early, and even then it will be a matter of luck. The usual pub nosh, along with pastas and subs, is on the menu. The food is quite affordable, as are the drinks.

Woody's Place
The Ohio Union
1739 North High Street
(614) 292-3397

Located in the heart of campus, Woody's is a casual place to grab a sandwich and a drink (alcoholic or non), catch a game on the big screen TV, or see a local band. It is usually closed during the summer quarter, but accepts both BuckID and the university meal plan. Be sure to take a photo ID if ordering alcohol; everyone is carded.

GOLF

Many people do not realize that Columbus not only has a very rich golf history but also is quickly becoming a golf destination for travelers. Yes, you heard me right: People come to Columbus to golf. It could well be because Columbus is consistently home to four of the world's top 100 golf courses. According to the May 2005 issue of *Golf Digest,* which ranks America's top 100 courses, Muirfield Village Golf Club (Dublin) came in the highest at No. 18, Scioto Country Club (Upper Arlington) ranked No. 59, The Golf Club (New Albany) is No. 51, while the Double Eagle Club (Galena) placed No. 68.

Don't let these stats scare you away. Columbus courses range from superexclusive country clubs with elite golf courses to the not-so-exclusive private clubs, but rest assured you need not have membership anywhere in order to play golf on a critically acclaimed, demanding, or picturesque course. Columbus has one of the best samplings of "daily fee" golf courses in the country. There is the Irish-inspired Golf Club of Dublin, with its sod-lined bunkers and low stone walls, and the very popular Phoenix and New Albany Links courses, and one shouldn't overlook the several inexpensive municipal courses where novices don't have to feel as if they are holding up the game while they hone their skills. Take it from me, these are great places to learn the game without losing a load of balls in water and woods.

i ***Tom Weiskopf was one of the designers of the breathtaking Loch Lomond Golf Club in Scotland, making him, and his partner, Jay Moorish, the first American architects of a course in golf's Motherland.***

Somewhere in between country club and public course falls Longerberger Golf Club. One of the most exclusive public golf courses in the Midwest and one of the best public golf courses in the nation is just a short drive from the city. In 2000, *Golf Digest* named Longerberger "America's Best New Upscale Public Course" and, in 2004, *Golf* magazine ranked it 39 on America's "Top 100 You Can Play" list. Do not translate this into a readily available tee time, as Longerberger has one of the more coveted tee times for a public course. If you are truly desperate to play this course, rumor has it you can occasionally find a tee time on eBay.

Columbus has long been a breeding ground for golfers. Just check out the roster. The Ohio State University golf team has nurtured the likes of Jack Nicklaus and Tom Weiskopf, both of whom were instrumental in bringing Ohio-born John Cook back to his old stomping grounds to attend OSU. No golf fan (especially not from Columbus) will forget local boy Ben Curtis bringing home the Claret Jug from across the pond after his low-key win at the 2003 British Open. Curtis is believed to be the first person since Francis Ouimet at the 1913 U.S. Open to win a major championship in his first go. Funny, Curtis was so under the radar, many a Brit mistook his residence of Kent, Ohio, for Kent, England. And then there was Jack . . .

OHIO STATE PARK GOLF COURSES: A GOOD DEAL

Golf packages with optional lodging and meals are available through six of Ohio's state parks. They provide championship quality, 18-hole public courses with golf cart rental and pro shops on-site. The state parks are an affordable place to get away for a day or a weekend or to hold a tournament. Season passes and gift certificates are also available. You can contact each one for individual information, or check out the Web site www.dnr.state.oh.us/parks/facilitiesmaps/ohiogolf.htm.

Deer Creek State Park: (740) 869-3088
Hueston Woods State Park: (513) 523-8081
Maumee Bay State Park: (419) 836-9009
Punderson State Park: (440) 564-5465
Salt Fork State Park: (740) 432-7185
Shawnee State Park: (740) 858-6681

DRIVING RANGES AND GOLF INSTRUCTION

While many of the golf courses have their own practice areas, these facilities are dedicated driving ranges and provide various levels of instruction on-site.

Ables Golf on Avery
5300 Avery Road, Dublin
(614) 529-9650
www.golfables.com
This 30-acre practice facility and teaching center is managed by two professionally certified golf instructors. It is lit for evening sessions and offers 110 grass tees, 30 heated and covered tees, and short-game greens and sand bunkers. Group lessons and one-on-one instruction are available, as are junior lessons and girls-only clinics. You can drop your kids off at their 18-hole miniature golf course while you brush up on your swing, or you can take a parent-child lesson together. The extremely reputable Ables is open year-round.

Four Seasons Golf Center and Dome
5000 East Broad Street
(614) 322-3663
www.fourseasonsgolfcenter.com
This 64-acre golfing facility is open everyday, March through December, weather permitting. You will find the largest number of grass tees in the area and 40 covered lighted tees so you can hit balls until well after sundown. Your game need not suffer in the winter, as there are 48 hitting stations on two levels inside the domed complex. There's also a challenging 18-hole outdoor miniature golf course for the rest of the family. Instructors are on hand for fine-tuning your swing.

For more information on golf in Ohio, course information, or golf instruction, check out www.ohio-golf.com.

Golf Center of Dublin
6720 Riverside Drive
(614) 889-8585
There's nothing pretentious about this driving-range formerly known as Bash. It's open seasonally, with outdoor and covered tees, and golf instruction is available.

The Golf Center at SportsOhio
6100 Dublin Park Drive
(614) 791-3002
www.thegolfcenteratsports-ohio.com
Open seven days a week year-round, this facility has over 100 grass tees, 60 artificial tees, and a two-story area with 36 covered, heated tees. You can perfect your short game in the chipping areas, sand traps, putting greens, and target greens. The facility also boasts a par 3 and miniature golf course, pro shop, snack shop, and concession area. There is plenty else to do at SportsOhio, so read on about the batting cages and ice-skating on-site for the nongolfers or children in your life in the Kidstuff chapter.

Guaranteed Golf
(614) 457-GOLF (4653)
www.guaranteedgolf.com
In 1982, professional golfer Dave Christensen developed an eight-week golf school in conjunction with The Ohio State University, and it has since become one of the Midwest's leading golf schools. The classes are taught by the top local golf instructors and are held at a variety of

CLOSE-UP

Jack Nicklaus: A Legend in His Spare Time

Few names are more synonymous with golf than Columbus-born and-bred Jack Nicklaus. When Tiger Woods was toddling around in diapers, our Golden Bear-turn-Buckeye was dominating the major championships like no one before. Born January 21, 1940, and raised in Upper Arlington, Jack's father took him to the golf course, when at age 10, he shot a 51 on his first nine holes. At 13, he broke 70. In 1959, at age 19, he became the youngest player in 50 years to win the U.S. Amateur. He won his second amateur two years later, and, after claiming he wouldn't turn professional, Jack left Ohio State in 1961. The Golden Bear became the Golden Boy!

Like Bobby Jones, Nicklaus was a golf prodigy. Taking inspiration from his hero, and more specifically, from Bobby Jones's 1926 U.S. Open (or PGA) win at Scioto Country Club here in Columbus, Jack gave it his best to win the Grand Slam year after year. It was 1972 that provided a very special opportunity for Nicklaus to take the four great tournaments as they were being played at what he claimed were "good courses" for him. Good is an understatement when it came to his ability to play the courses at Augusta, Pebble Beach, Oakland Hills, and Muirfield in Scotland. It was at these four courses that some of the most famous shots of his career took place, putting him in the ranks alongside his hero.

Besides playing the game famously, the Nicklaus name is identified with all aspects of golf: course design, golf academies, real estate, clothing, golf equipment, and now a museum—Not to mention the annual Jack Nicklaus Memorial Tournament, which draws the world's most famous golfers to Columbus for a week around Memorial Day.

With 20 major championships (18 Grand Slams and two amateur events), 100 worldwide professional victories, an international conglomerate, and an annual tournament, Jack's renowned achievements go unparalleled. Bobby Jones himself recognized his talents when he said of Nicklaus's 1965 Masters win: "Nicklaus played a game of which I am not familiar." Jack's legendary status was once again confirmed when the PGA named him Golfer of the Century in 1988, but Juan "Chi Chi" Rodriguez summed it up brilliantly when he called Jack Nicklaus "a legend in his spare time."

The Jack Nicklaus Museum
2355 Olentangy River Road
(614) 247-5959
www.nicklausmuseum.org

Golf fans and museum goers alike can immerse themselves in Jack Nicklaus's passion for the history and game of golf by visiting the museum, which is located between the OSU campus and the university golf course. There are exhibitions dedicated to the legends of golf and the decades Jack Nicklaus transcended the game. There is a Memorial Tournament Gallery and Nicklaus Art and Design Galleries, as well as exhibitions about Ohio State's golf programs and the university's Turf Science and Management Program. Golf devotees can also host a party or business event in this shrine.

The Jack Nicklaus Memorial Tournament
5760 Memorial Drive
(614) 889-6700
www.thememorialtournament.com

It makes sense that Jack Nicklaus would conceive a golf tournament in the hometown where his legendary game got its start. His desire to create an annual tournament that brings the world's best golfers together once a year was realized in May 1976. The tournament is played the weekend during or after Memorial Day at the Muirfield Village Golf Club in Dublin, a suburb of Columbus.

Nicklaus designed the Muirfield golf course, and it comes as no surprise that it is named for a most revered course on which he won his first of three British Opens in 1972 at Muirfield, Scotland. Jack's Muirfield was dedicated two years before the first Memorial Tournament on May 27, 1974, with an exhibition game between two former Buckeyes, Jack Nicklaus and Tom Weiskopf. The 220-acre course, which has been tweaked and its holes remade by the perfectionist, includes an 11-acre driving range, seven lakes, and streams winding through lush, manicured property (at least during tournament time) lined by homes that comprise one of Columbus's more affluent areas.

The general public can buy badges for the full week of events, which includes practice rounds for three days prior to the actual tournament. For those of you who may not be able to afford the full week, badges for just the practice rounds cost about $30. It's not nearly as crowded as during the tournament, so it lacks a bit of energy and excitement, but you can still catch a glimpse of Ernie, Tiger, and Retief doing what they do best. Keep in mind the golfers are not the only ones who make out financially during this tournament. Some of the money benefits charitable organizations in the central Ohio area. Since the tournament's inception, over $5 million has been raised for Columbus Children's Hospital, the Memorial's primary beneficiary. This is once again a testimony to the giving nature of Columbus folk.

The Memorial Tournament, which remains one of the more popular stops on the PGA tour, is a reflection of Nicklaus's love and respect for the game, and it honors the memory of deceased and living golfers who distinguish themselves in the game. This is Jack Nicklaus's legacy to golf—and to Columbus.

golf and sports centers around Columbus. Call or see the Web site for registration and location details.

Tee'd Up Indoor Golf
7542 Pingue Drive, Worthington
(614) 846-9222
Tee'd Up is unique in the sense it teaches with golf simulators and offers a special opportunity to virtually "play" some of the world's greatest golf courses. The facility has other virtual games, such as soccer, baseball, and football. It is available for private parties and conferences.

For you lady golfers who may find the intimidation factor a bit much on the ever male-dominated course, a new six-week program called "Bridge to Golf Ohio" is aimed at helping women learn the jargon and etiquette through classroom time, develop their game with the use of a golf simulator, and create the confidence to stick with it. The National Golf Foundation is tracking these efforts. Instruction is offered at the Tee'd Up Indoor Golf facility.

Westerville Golf Center
450 West Schrock Road, Westerville
(614) 882-9079
www.westervillegolf.com
The 120 lighted tees for nighttime practice, 80 grass tees, 40 covered heated tees, chipping greens, sand bunkers, and a putting green coupled with two 18-hole miniature golf courses (and eight batting cages) make this is the largest driving range and family entertainment center in central Ohio. The facility is open year-round, golf clubs are available to rent, and there is no dress code. PGA-licensed instructors are also available by appointment.

The Executive Women's Golf Association offers women the opportunity to learn, play, and enjoy golf through golf instruction, clinics, outings, and leagues. Lady golfers can join the Columbus chapter via the Web site www.ewgacolumbus.com, or call (614) 470-EWGA (3942).

GOLF COURSES

The following courses are located in Franklin, Delaware, and Licking counties, and the executive-length courses are marked with an (E) after the name. Assume the courses are 18 holes, par 72 unless otherwise noted.

Public Courses

FRANKLIN COUNTY

Airport Golf Course (par 70)
900 North Hamilton Road
(614) 645-3127
www.nn.net/golf

Blacklick Woods Golf Course
7309 East Livingston Avenue
Reynoldsburg
(614) 861-3193
www.metroparks.net

Bridgeview Golf Course
2738 Agler Road
(614) 471-1565

Champions Golf Course (par 70)
3900 Westerville Road, Westerville
(614) 645-7111
www.nn.net/golf

Gahanna Municipal Golf Course
(9 holes, par 35)
220 Ridenour Road, Gahanna
(614) 471-0579

Golf Club of Dublin
5805 Eiterman Road, Dublin
(614) 792-3825
www.golfclubofdublin.com

Grovebrook Golf Club (par 71)
5525 Hoover Road, Grove City
(614) 875-2497

Homestead Springs Golf Course
5888 London-Lancaster Road, Groveport
(614) 645-3050

Mentel Memorial Golf Course
6005 Alkire Road, Galloway
(614) 645-3050
www.nn.net/golf

Minerva Lake Golf Course (par 69)
2955 Minerva Lake Road, Westerville
(614) 882-9988
www.minervalakegolf.com

New Albany Links
7000 New Albany Links Drive
New Albany
(614) 855-8532
www.newalbanylinks.com

Phoenix Golf Links
3413 Jackson Pike, Grove City
(614) 539-3636
www.phoenixgl.com

Raymond Memorial Golf Course
3860 Trabue Road, Hilliard
(614) 645-3276
www.nn.net/golf

Thorn Apple Country Club
1051 Alton-Darby Road, Galloway
(614) 878-7703

Turnberry Golf Course
1145 Clubhouse Road, Pickerington
(614) 645-3100
www.nn.net/golf

Walnut Hill Golf Course (9 holes, par 36)
6001 East Livingston Avenue
(614) 645-3100
www.nn.net/golf

Westchester Golf Course
6300 Bent Grass Boulevard
Canal-Winchester
(614) 834-4653
www.westchestergolfcourse.com

Wilson Road Golf Course
(9 holes, par 30) (E)
1900 Wilson Road, Hilliard
(614) 645-3221
www.nn.net/golf

DELAWARE COUNTY

Arrowhead Lakes Golf Course
(9 holes, par 36)
580 North Walnut Street, Galena
(740) 965-5422
www.arrowheadlakesgolf.com

Bent Tree Golf Course
8665 Route 37, Sunbury
(740) 965-5140
www.benttreegc.com

---

i

There are only a few entry points to the Memorial Tournament. No cell phones, cameras, or outside food or beverages are allowed on the grounds. You are able to buy souvenirs, food, and alcoholic and nonalcoholic beverages from vendors once on the grounds.

Big Walnut Golf Club (9 holes, par 32) (E)
6683 Route 61, Sunbury
(740) 524-8642, (614) 267-4844

Blackhawk Golf Club (par 71)
8830 Dustin Road, Galena
(740) 965-1042
www.thehawkgolfinc.com

Hidden Valley Golf Course
(9 holes, par 28) (E)
580 West Williams Street, Delaware
(740) 363-1739

Mill Creek Golf Club
7259 Penn Road, Ostrander
(740) 666-7711
www.millcreekgolfclub.com

Oakhaven Golf Club
2871 Route 23 North, Delaware
(888) 504-6281, (740) 548-5636
www.oakhaven.com

Royal American Links
3300 Miller Paul Road, Galena
(740) 965-1215
www.americangolf.com

Safari Golf Club
10245 Riverside Drive, Powell
(614) 645-3444

Shamrock Golf Club (par 71)
4436 Powell Road, Powell
(614) 792-6630
www.shamrockgc.com

Sunbury Golf Course (9 holes, par 35)
1349 Golf Course Road, Sunbury
(740) 965-5441

Tanglewood Golf Club
1086 Cheshire Road, Delaware
(740) 548-6715

Twin Oaks Golf Club (9 holes, par 36)
7931 Harriott Road, Dublin
(614) 873-8511

LICKING COUNTY

Broadview Golf Course (9 holes, par 35)
5694 Headleys Mill Road SW, Pataskala
(740) 927-8900

Burning Tree Golf Course (par 71)
4600 Ridgley Tract Road SE, Newark
(800) 830-4877, (740) 522-3464
www.burningtreegolfcourse.com

Clover Valley Golf Club
8644 Route 37, Johnstown
(740) 966-5533
www.clovervalleygolfclub.com

Cumberland Trail Golf Course
8244 Columbia Road SW, Pataskala
(740) 964-9336
www.cumberlandtrailgolf.com

Forest Hills Golf Course (9 holes, par 36)
811 Forest Hills Road, Heath
(740) 323-4653

Granville Golf Course (par 71)
555 Newark Road, Granville
(740) 587-0843
www.granvillegolf.com

Harbor Hills Country Club (9 holes, par 36)
225 Freeman Memorial Drive, Hebron
(740) 928-3596

Hillcrest Golf Course (9 holes, par 34) (E)
8866 Sportsman Club Road, Johnstown
(740) 967-7921

Indian Hills Golf Course (9 holes, par 36)
4663 Columbus Road SW, Granville
(740) 587-0706

Kyber Run Golf Course
5261 Mink Road, Johnstown
(740) 967-1404
www.kyberrungolf.com

The Legends at Locust Lane
1345 Watkins Road, Alexandria
(740) 924-2316
www.legends.com

Licking Springs Golf Club (par 71)
2250 Horns Hill Road, Newark
(740) 366-7328
www.lickingspringsgolf.com

The Links at Echo Springs
5940 Loudon Street, Johnstown
(740) 587-1890
www.echosprings1.com

Longerberger Golf Club
One Long Drive, Nashport
(740) 322-5588
www.longaberger.com

Raccoon International Golf Club
3275 Worthington Road SW, Granville
(740) 587-0921
www.raccooninternational.com

St. Albans Golf Club (par 71)
3833 Northridge Road, Alexandria
(740) 924-8885
www.golfus.com/stalbans

Village View Golf Course (par 73)
210 South Main Street, Croton
(740) 893-4653

Top Teachers

According to www.ohio-golf.com, 5 of the top 10 golf instructors are in the Columbus area. Based on annual teaching volume, they are as follows:

#1. Dave Christensen at Guaranteed Golf, Columbus
#4. J. R. Ables at Ables Golf, Dublin
#7. Bob Brokaw at Westerville Golf Center, Westerville
#8. John Fridley at Guaranteed Golf, Columbus
#9. Hank Oakes at The 235 Golf Center, Dayton

Willow Run Golf Course (par 71)
Routes 310 and 161, Alexandria
(740) 927-1932

Private Courses

FRANKLIN COUNTY

Brookside Golf and Country Club
2770 West Dublin-Granville Road
Worthington
(614) 889-1758
www.brooksidegc.com

Columbus Country Club
4831 East Broad Street
(614) 861-1332
www.columbuscc.com

Country Club at Muirfield Village
8175 Muirfield Drive, Dublin
(614) 764-1714
www.tccmv.com

Eagle Eye Golf Course (9 holes, par 35)
3990 East Broad Street
(614) 692-2075

The Golf Club
4522 Kitzmiller Road, New Albany
(614) 855-7326

Heritage Golf Club
3525 Heritage Club Drive, Hilliard
(614) 777-1690
www.heritagegc.com

Hickory Hills Golf Club (par 71)
3344 Georgesville-Wrightsville Road
Grove City
(614) 878-1057
www.hickoryhills.com

Jefferson Golf and Country Club
1415 Reynoldsburg-New Albany Road
Blacklick
(614) 759-7784
www.jeffersoncountryclub.com

Little Turtle Country Club
5400 Little Turtle Way, Westerville
(614) 882-5940
www.littleturtlecc.com

Muirfield Village Golf Club
5750 Memorial Drive, Dublin
(614) 889-6740

New Albany Country Club
5757 Johnstown Road, New Albany
(614) 939-8520
www.nacc.com

Oakhurst Country Club
3228 Norton Road, Grove City
(614) 878-3223
www.americangolf.com

Ohio State University Golf Club
3605 Tremont Road, Upper Arlington
(614) 459-4653
www.ohiostatebuckeyes.com

Riviera Country Club
8205 Avery Road, Dublin
(614) 889-2395

Scioto Country Club (par 71)
2196 Riverside Drive, Upper Arlington
(614) 486-1039
www.sciotocc.com

The Willows
1005 Richardson Road, Groveport
(614) 836-5874
www.willowsgc.com

Winding Hollow Country Club
6140 Babbitt Road, New Albany
(614) 855-8600
www.windinghollowcc.org

Worthington Hills Country Club
920 Clubview Boulevard, Worthington
(614) 885-9128
www.worthingtonhills.com

York Golf Club (par 71)
7459 North High Street, Worthington
(614) 885-5459

DELAWARE COUNTY

Dornoch Golf Club (par 71)
3329 Columbus Pike, Delaware
(740) 362-2582
www.dornochgolfclub.com

Double Eagle Club
6025 Cheshire Road, Galena
(740) 548-5454

Kinsale Golf and Fitness Club
3737 Village Club Drive, Powell
(740) 881-6500
www.golfkinsale.com

The Lakes Golf and Country Club
6740 Worthington Road, Westerville
(614) 899-3080
www.lakesclub.com

The Medallion Club
5925 Medallion Drive E, Westerville
(614) 794-6988
www.medallionclub.com

Rattlesnake Ridge Golf Club
1 Rattlesnake Drive, Sunbury
(740) 965-6255
www.rrgolfclub.com

Scioto Reserve Golf Club
7383 Scioto Parkway, Powell
(740) 881-9082
www.sciotoreserve.com

Tartan Fields Golf Club
10416 Concord Road, Dublin
(614) 792-0900
www.tartanfields.com

Wedgewood Golf and Country Club
9600 Wedgewood Boulevard, Powell
(614) 793-9610
www.wedgewoodcc.com

LICKING COUNTY

High Lands Golf Club
10391 Hollow Road SW, Pataskala
(740) 927-3966
www.hlgc.net

Moundbuilders Country Club (par 71)
125 North 33rd Street, Newark
(740) 344-9431

PARKS AND RECREATION

Parks and green spaces, along with an endless number of recreational and leisure activities, enhance the overall quality of life in Columbus. Several studies have concluded that natural settings reduce stress, stimulate good health, and elicit positive feelings, so it is safe to say you can find health and happiness *somewhere* in the 17,000 acres of parks in the Columbus area. Whether you like to swim, cycle, canoe, or go bird watching, you can do it here. And you can do much of it for free.

For those who like a good stroll in the park, Columbus has a variety of gardens, lake and riverside scenery, and an extensive city park system, including 14 Metro Parks, herb gardens, rock gardens, and the brilliant Park of Roses. Columbus also holds annual festivals dedicated to roses, violets, and tomatoes.

The active types who prefer cycling, roller blading, or running to a leisurely amble have plenty of opportunity to burn off energy in a number of places. One of this chapter's close-ups will bring to light several multiuse biking and hiking trails throughout the city. A general listing of parks and community centers will suggest where to swim or play tennis. Also included are phone numbers and links to a variety of organized sports leagues and guided outdoor tours and activities.

Getting outdoors can make you smarter too. The Columbus Department of Parks and Recreation, the Department of Natural Resources, and the state parks all offer educational classes that will get you back to nature. Go on a free guided canoe trip with an expert who can interpret the local flora and fauna, or take a walk through one of the nearby nature preserves to find rare species of plants and animals. Several parks have nature and environmental study centers, where you can watch for wildlife or experience hands-on learning.

Rather than passively enjoying the Columbus landscape, you can get down and dirty too. If "dirt therapy" is your thing, there are a number of garden clubs and horticultural societies from which to learn the secrets to gardening in zone 5, or seek advice from the experts at OSU's Chadwick Arboretum. The Department of Natural Resources offers youth and adult educational gardening and nature programs, not to mention the numerous volunteer opportunities to help keep Columbus beautiful.

You don't have to be a landlubber to enjoy the outdoors here in Columbus. Despite being landlocked, there is a lot of water to be had in the tricounty area. Two of Ohio's 11 designated Scenic River systems are in the Columbus area. Some 22 miles of the Olentangy River and 82 miles of Big Darby Creek, along with its tributary, Little Darby Creek, flow through the gently rolling Ohio River Valley.

Parts of the Olentangy River are flanked by dramatic shale banks, while the Darby Creek watershed is known for its

---

i

The state of Ohio has wonderful natural resources. At least 20 of the 74 state parks and about a third of the 82 public nature reserves are within an hour's drive of the city. View maps and read more about the facilities, educational programs, and local wildlife at the Department of Natural Resources Web site: www.dnr.state.oh.us.

---

abundance and diversity of aquatic and terrestrial plants and animals. The Darby is not only a State Scenic River but also a National Scenic River. To help keep the Darby ecosystem flourishing, a building moratorium and a push to block future building are under way.

This chapter is by no means exhaustive of all the activities that are available in Columbus, but read on to learn how much there is to do. It will discuss the popular parks, expound on many of the participant sports and leisure activities, and provide some practical information for boaters and bikers. I have no doubt there is something to tickle everyone's fancy in the following pages.

PARKS AND URBAN GREEN SPACES

All parks listed here are free of charge and open from dusk until dawn, year-round, unless otherwise noted.

Schiller Park

This 23-acre oasis in the middle of German Village has been a park since the early 1800s. After changing hands (and names) a few times, the villagers donated a statue of German poet-philosopher Friedrich Schiller in 1891, and the name stuck. The Huntington Garden Promenade was installed in 1993, and Schiller's quotes are etched into the granite as a tribute to the park's namesake. The perimeter of Schiller Park is lined with the Victorian homes that German Village is known for. It is a great place to take a walk and enjoy the architecture, do a garden tour, or let your children run loose in the playground. The newly renovated Schiller Recreation Center offers arts and crafts classes, weight training, and other exercise and dance classes. Contact the center at (614) 645-3156 for program information.

In 1872, Canova's statue of the Greek goddess Hebe was installed in Schiller Park. It served a variety of functions, from drinking fountain to rain shield, until it mysteriously disappeared in the early 1950s. The sculpture* Umbrella Girl, *an updated replacement of the Hebe statue, was a labor of love by local artist Joan Wobst and was dedicated in 1996.

Bicentennial Park

Bicentennial Park was dedicated on Independence Day 1976 and is conveniently located downtown along Civic Center Drive. There are pools, a fountain, and benches that make for a nice break from the office. This is also the place to be for major summer festivals or to just sit back and enjoy the views along the Scioto River.

Battelle Riverfront Park

Like Bicentennial Park, Battelle is located in downtown Columbus along Civic Center Drive. They are practically extensions of each other and will eventually be linked by a promenade as part of the Scioto Mile development of the old and new riverfront parks. The replica of Christopher Columbus's ship, the *Santa Maria,* is berthed here, and several sculptures and memorials are incorporated into this park. It makes a great starting point for a walking tour of Columbus's outdoor public art.

Confluence Park

This cleverly named park sits at the confluence of the Olentangy and Scioto rivers. Offering commanding views of the city's skyline, Confluence Park is home to

Columbus's only waterfront restaurant of the same name. This is just one of the prime locations from which to watch the fireworks during the Fourth of July.

Goodale Park

On the edge of Victorian Village, Goodale Park is Columbus's oldest park and one of the earliest urban public green spaces in the United States. The 35 acres of land was granted to the Columbus community in 1850 by Dr. Lincoln Goodale and is now overseen by the Columbus Department of Parks and Recreation in conjunction with the Friends of Goodale Park. With majestic trees and lovely views of the skyline, Goodale Park is only a short walk from High Street, away from the hubbub of the Short North.

The park plays host to Columbus's Com-Fest and provides the backdrop for free concerts throughout the summer. Goodale is also a pet-friendly park, has an extensive playground area, tennis courts, a pond, and a gazebo, but park goers mostly come here to escape to peace and serenity in the middle of the city.

METRO PARKS—THE OASIS IN THE SUBURBS

The Columbus and Franklin County Metropolitan Park District, known as the Metro Park system, was created in 1945. The district's commitment to conserving central Ohio's natural resources and providing the community with public parks and educational programs can be seen in the 14 beautiful and unique parks encompassing 22,500 acres in 7 different counties. Each park has its own facilities, lodges, picnic areas, nature trails, activities, and rules.

The Metro Parks are all located within or very close to Columbus city limits. Most of them are situated off Interstate 270 (the Outer Belt) and are well marked with brown ATTRACTION signs. They are not operated by the Columbus Department of Parks and Recreation, nor should they be confused with city parks. You can view a map and learn more about each individual Metro Park at www.metroparks.net.

Battelle-Darby Creek Metro Park, Galloway

The view across Big Darby Creek as it meanders through this park is breathtaking. Both Big and Little Darby creeks are home to several species of fish and freshwater mussels, some of which are listed as endangered or threatened. Battelle-Darby Park holds one of the largest areas of land in the surrounding watershed. The unique aspects of this park are its 10 prairie habitats and five wetland sites that have been replanted in recent years.

Activities include basketball, canoeing, cross-country skiing, sledding, and hiking. There are facilities for environmental studies and shelters with picnic and playground areas. Pets are welcome on the 1.6-mile trail, but they must be kept on a leash at all times.

Blacklick Woods Metro Park, Reynoldsburg

Blacklick Woods, the first Metro Park, has been a park since 1948. It has since grown to include 632 acres and provides city dwellers an opportunity to see wildlife in forest and wetland settings right at their doorstep. Aside from a mixture of grassland, forest, and seasonal swamp pools, there's the 54-acre Walter A. Tucker Nature Preserve. This area is a National Natural Landmark and has been designated an Ohio Watchable Wildlife site. You can view nature without disturbing it by watching through a panoramic one-way window that opens to the forest and pond. If you must have a closer look, there

CLOSE-UP

Whetstone Park: Coming up Roses

A sprawling 105-acre park is tucked conveniently off North High Street in Clintonville and runs along a very scenic part of the Olentangy River. The Olentangy was originally named Whetstone River by the early settlers because of the type of whet stones found in the area. The city bought this farmland in 1944 to turn it into what it is now: a free public park. It includes the Whetstone Herb Garden and the Whetstone Park of Roses, one of the largest municipal rose gardens in the country.

Thirteen acres is dedicated to the cultivation of over 11,000 rosebushes of more than 350 varieties. At the center of the garden is a beautiful fountain, but the focal point is really all around it. Roses in every color of the rainbow create a sensory overload from the moment you enter the park. Rose lovers come from all over to attend the annual Rose Festival every June, but bloom time runs for several months. Your senses can feast on fresh sights and smells through September.

The Park of Roses also contains a few specialized rose gardens, a daffodil garden with more than 1,200 varieties, and an herb and perennial garden. Call (614) 645-3222 for information about the monthly tours or to volunteer to help maintain the gardens.

The Whetstone facilities include a small yet photogenic wedding pavilion and clubhouse that can be rented for events. Free concerts are held during the summer months on the stage in the Park of Roses. Bleacher-type seating is situated around the pavilion, but many people bring along a blanket or lawn chair to sit back and enjoy the entertainment, which ranges from the traditional classical and jazz to the odd (calliope music). Whetstone also has soccer fields, a softball diamond, tennis courts, and a picnic area with a playground and shelter. Several paved bike paths pass through the park, and hiking paths meander along the banks of the river. Whetstone Park is the pride of Clintonville and shouldn't be missed.

is a 4-mile boardwalk and bike trail that weave through these woodlands.

Activities include basketball, cross-country skiing, sledding, and educational programs. There is a lodge and picnic and playground areas. If you are a golfer with an environmental conscious or an environmentalist who likes to golf, the course at Blacklick Woods is the place for you. It won membership in Audubon's Cooperative Sanctuary Program for Golf Courses because of its environmental design.

Blendon Woods Metro Park, Columbus

Blendon Woods Metro Park opened in 1951 and contains another one of Ohio's 80 Watchable Wildlife sites. Bird-watchers have year-round access to two observation shelters overlooking the 11-acre Thoreau Lake, which sits within the 115-acre Walden Waterfowl Refuge. No fishing is permitted in this lake. The trails will lead you through the same maple and oak-hickory forests, open fields, and stream-cut ravines that once led the local Native Americans.

Activities include cross-country skiing, ice-skating, and educational programs. Facilities include shelters and picnic and playground areas, as well as a 3,500-foot disk golf course, youth group camp sites, and a nature center. Goldenrod Trail is the 1.2-mile pooch path. Dogs must be leashed at all times.

Chestnut Ridge Metro Park, Carroll

Unfortunately, the native chestnut forest that was once here vanished due to a deadly fungus that was introduced years ago, but you can walk the Homestead Trail located high atop the ridge and see remains of Far View Farms, with its original fruit trees planted by the family.

Activities include cross-country skiing, fishing for those under age 15, and educational programs. Facilities include picnic and playground areas. There are two docks from which the lake and neighboring wetlands can be appreciated and where fishing events are held. There is also an observation deck that offers vistas across the trees into downtown Columbus. The foliage is quite a sight in the autumn.

Clear Creek Metro Park, Rockbridge

With nearly 5,000 acres, Clear Creek is the largest of the Metro Parks and was opened in 1996. Park naturalists teach cultural programs that are focused on the prehistoric, Native American, and European history and settlement of the area. You will find over 800 species of plants and 40 species of ferns, many of which are endangered, while hiking the unimproved trails of this park's valleys, ridges, and sandstone cliffs.

A nature preserve is not the same as a state park, nor is it a recreational area. Some preserves are situated within parks (such as Blacklick Woods) but contain special wildlife, unusual plants, or unique geological formations that deserve an extra level of protection. More than 28,000 acres in Ohio is classified as protected nature preserve.

Prairie Warbler Trail is appropriately named for the prairie warblers that nest here. Clear Creek is stocked with trout, and the cold, tumbling water in certain parts of the creek makes great conditions for fly fishing. Fishing is permitted in Clear Creek, but bag limits allow 12-inch minimums and a maximum of two trout. Fishing rules are posted throughout the park.

Glacier Ridge Metro Park, Plain City

The newest Metro Park is a work in progress yet abounds with outdoor activities. Hiking, biking, and horseback riding trails wind throughout the 1,000-acre park just northwest of Dublin. The park is currently undergoing wetland and prairie restoration. A unique feature in the landscape is a working windmill that generates power for the park.

Heritage Trail Metro Park, Hilliard

This 87-acre Metro Park, which opened in 2002, is the trailhead for the 7-mile Rails-to-Trails multiuse path that runs from Hilliard to Plain City. The walking/jogging/bike path in this park is paralleled for 4 miles by a horse trail. You can read

Inniswood Gardens Etiquette: In-line skating and jogging are not allowed in the gardens, nor are food and beverages, but there are benches and tables at the entrance where you can enjoy your refreshments. Shirts and shoes must be worn on the grounds, and keep to the trails in the natural areas.

more information about the Rails-to-Trails conservancy program in Columbus in one of this chapter's Close-ups.

Highbanks Metro Park, Lewis Center

Highbanks Metro Park opened in 1973 and was designated a National Natural Landmark because of the beautiful 100-foot shale bluffs that tower high over the banks of the Olentangy River. The 206 acres of Highbanks are also protected as the Edward F. Hutchins Nature Preserve. Take advantage of the observation deck to get a great view of the ravines and bluffs, or check out the Indian earthworks at three locations along the trail.

Activities include canoeing, fishing, cross-country skiing, sledding, and educational programs. Facilities include shelters and picnic and playground areas, as well as the Environmental Study Center, a butterfly and hummingbird garden, and a nature center, at which you can see fossils from the park and learn about the Adena Indians who once inhabited the area. There are two paved bike trails, Big Meadows Path and Oak Coves Path, for bikers and runners. A primitive walking trail leads out to a large wetland area with a bird-viewing center. Dogs must be kept leashed while on the 3.5 miles of unimproved trail. Be advised that this trail is closed to hikers and pets when snow arrives in order to provide undisturbed ski tracks for cross-country skiers.

Inniswood Metro Gardens, Westerville

Active sports are not permitted at this park-within-a-park. Inniswood, one of the more manicured Metro Parks, is tucked inside a nature preserve, so hiking is the main activity that goes on here. Streams, woods, and wildflowers make up only part of this 121-acre park, which was opened in 1984. Inniswood's claims to fame are its collection of 2,000 species of plants and many themed gardens.

There are several feature gardens, such as a rose garden, a cutting garden, a white garden, and an herb garden with themed "rooms." There is also a 2.8-acre children's garden and a prairie garden that highlights species native to Ohio. The Memorial Garden caters to shade-loving plants, while the Woodland Rock Garden is a peaceful, natural area of waterfalls with woody and perennial species.

Three miles of paved trails run throughout the park, but leashed pets and bicycles are permitted only on Chipmunk Chatter Trail, which can be accessed at Sunbury Road. Several horticultural and natural history programs are available on-site. Inniswood Garden Society and volunteers do an outstanding job keeping up with the seasonal maintenance of the gardens so that everyone can enjoy beautiful grounds and natural areas year-round. Garden lovers shouldn't miss Inniswood.

Pickerington Ponds Metro Park, Canal Winchester

Bird lovers, grab your binoculars and head over to Pickerington Ponds. This Metro Park, which opened in 1989, protects a wetland and woodland area ideal for sighting some of the 260 bird species that have been spotted here. You can call for a daily recorded message of bird sightings, or go have a look for yourself. This Metro Park is a Watchable Wildlife site and has two observation decks offering views of Ellis Pond, from which you might spot songbirds, hawks, owls, and many other waterfowl. Hike along an uncovered boardwalk and trail to get a more personal wildlife viewing.

Prairie Oaks Metro Park, Hilliard

Some of Columbus's oldest nature can be found in one of the newest Metro Parks. Opened in 2000, Prairie Oaks is a diverse natural area near Big Darby Creek. The 30-acre Oak Savannah runs along the edge of the original forest, while 230 acres of native grasslands and prairie have recently been planted. The Potland Wetland Restoration area allows for some interesting species of sandpipers, plovers, waterfowl, and butterflies to be observed.

Activities at Prairie Oaks are fishing, cross-country skiing, hiking along unimproved trails, and educational programs. Facilities include shelters and picnic and playground areas and a newly installed bridle trail. Leashed pets are welcome on the Sycamore Plains Trail only.

Sharon Woods Metro Park, Westerville

Sharon Woods' 761 acres is enough to shelter you from the two major highways that pass nearby. You can hike, bike, jog, or just wander along the winding trails through wetlands and woodlands. The park contains a 3.8-mile multiuse trail, an observation deck overlooking an 80-acre field, and two sledding hills, one for children under age 10 and the other for teens and adults.

Activities include fishing, in-line skating, sledding, and educational programs. The facilities include a lodge, shelters, picnic and playground areas, and four fishing docks for children under age 15.

Slate Run Metro Park and Historical Farm, Canal Winchester

The early settlers mistakenly named this park for the black sheets of rock found throughout the landscape, which they thought were slate. It should actually be called "Shale Run," but Slate Run it is. The park and living museum at Slate Run opened in 1981 and offer a glimpse into what family life was like on an 1880s farm. As the season changes, so do the farm chores. Volunteers dressed up in period clothing manage the household, but visitors are more than welcome to participate in harvesting or canning produce when the season calls for it.

The park has a 2-mile hiking trail through woodlands and fields. There is also a 2.5-mile horse trail with a parking lot that has hitching posts and can accommodate horse trailers. The activities at Slate Run include in-line skating, fishing for children ages 15 and under at Buzzard's Roost Lake, educational programs, and youth group camps. The facilities include shelters, picnic and playground areas, and boardwalks with observation decks running throughout the 156 acres of wetland. One of the more unique features at Slate Run is Blackburn Bridge, a fully restored historic covered bridge.

Three Creeks Metro Park, Groveport

The Alum, Big Walnut, and Blacklick Creeks converge in this 1,300-acre park appropriately named Three Creeks. Once an illegal dumping ground, this Metro Park is now home to deer, mink, wood ducks, and other varieties of wildlife. Opened in 1999, the park provides a 9-mile, paved multiuse trail for those who want to run, bike, or in-line skate through grasslands and wetlands, past ponds and streams. With a name like Three Creeks, it isn't surprising the activities here include canoeing and fishing, as well as educational nature programs. Picnic facilities are available, and leashed pets are permitted on the trails. Just be sure to clean up after them!

GARDEN CLUBS AND SOCIETIES

There are numerous garden clubs in the Columbus and central Ohio region, but only a few are listed here to highlight a cross section of what is available. They range from Columbus chapters of national societies to specialized, local gardening clubs.

The Central Ohio Rose Society
(614) 846-9404

Columbus Rose Society
(614) 895-1801
www.buckeyerose.com

Ohio State University
Chadwick Arboretum
(614) 688-3479
www.chadwickarboretum.osu.edu

Columbus African-Violet Society
(614) 444-6315
www.avsa.org

Worthington Hills Garden Club
(614) 885-9516
www.worthingtonhills.org/gardenclub

Greater Columbus Dahlia Society
(614) 471-7268
www.midwestdahliaconference.org

The Audubon Society meets every month (May–September) at various parks around Columbus. The phone number for the local chapter is (740) 549-0333, and its Web site is www.columbusaudubon.org. There are two 24-hour hotlines for bird sightings: Dial-A-Bird and (614) 221-WREN.

Botanical Society of America
(614) 292-0501
www.botany.org

Columbus Bonsai Society
(614) 237-5572
www.columbusbonsai.v-space.org

Columbus Horticultural Society
(614) 276-1728

Herb Society of America,
Central Ohio Unit
(614) 888-4247
www.herbsociety.com

Inniswood Garden Society
(614) 895-6216
www.metroparks.net/inniswood.htm

COLUMBUS DEPARTMENT OF RECREATION AND PARKS

The folks at the Columbus Department of Recreation and Parks (614-645-3300; www.columbusrecparks.com) seem to do it all! They keep us healthy and happy and playing outdoors through city parks, boat docks, golf courses, and bike trails. They provide the community with athletic, artistic, and cultural classes, as well as facilitate gatherings of families and friends at picnic shelters, swimming pools, and softball diamonds.

Columbus has 28 neighborhood recreation centers, and each facility offers a variety of services designed to meet the needs of children, adults, and families. These programs range from social programs, such as CRPD Therapeutic Recreation for the disabled community and the City's Free Summer Lunch Program, which provides meals for children, to leisure activities such as after-school projects and sports leagues. Some of these classes are free, while others are fee-based. There are also adult and senior athletic, exercise, and art programs.

There is no residency requirement to participate in programs offered by Colum-

bus Recreation and Parks. However, the recreation departments of individual neighborhoods may have different requirements, such as resident and nonresident fees.

You can check the Columbus Department of Recreation and Park's Web site for a full list of centers and programs. The city also operates seven golf courses, which are listed in the Golf chapter. As you will see from the range of parks, recreational facilities, participant sports programs, and cultural activities, there is no age limit to enjoy a stroll in the park or to take a class for personal enrichment.

There are a lot of volunteer opportunities at the Department of Recreation and Parks. If you have the time to teach an art class or aerobics class or give guided nature walks, call (614) 645-6640. Camp counselors and volunteers for golfing events and park clean-ups are also needed.

Community and Sports Centers

Many of the neighborhood community centers have adult leagues for a variety of sports. The Columbus Department of Recreation and Parks has adult leagues for football, basketball, softball, and volleyball. See its Web site for further schedules, fees, and online registration forms: www.crpdsports.org.

Berliner Park Sports Complex
1300 Deckenbach Street
(614) 645-3366
www.columbusrecparks.com
Maintained by the Department of Recreation and Parks, the indoor sports complex has four basketball and four volleyball courts, while the outdoor facility has 31 well-kept diamonds for softball and baseball, and areas for football, rugby, soccer, and walking. It is the largest softball facility in the United States and is located south of downtown Columbus off I-71 and Greenlawn Avenue.

Dublin Community Recreation Center
5600 Post Road, Dublin
(614) 410-4550
www.dublin.oh.us/dcrc/index.html
Voted the best suburban community center in 2003 by *Columbus Monthly* magazine, the center is a central point for community gatherings. The center has two swimming pools, a gymnasium, fitness area, and jogging and walking track, extensive programming, such as aerobics classes, personal fitness, and swimming instruction, and an open gym, sports leagues, theater, and community hall for meetings and classes. The fees are determined according to resident/nonresident status.

Westerville Community Center/
Westerville Sports Complex
325-350 North Cleveland Avenue
(614) 901-6500
www.ci.westerville.oh.us/parkshome.asp
This 96,000-square-foot facility has become the heart of Westerville's parks and recreation department. With a leisure pool and lap pools, tracks, fitness center, gymnasium, climbing wall, supervised room for children, lounge, and indoor playground, this facility caters to individuals and families alike. There are daily admission fees, or you can purchase individual and family PASSports. Keep in mind that nonresidents are charged a little more. Those who work full time in the Westerville area can take advantage of Westerville resident rates and attend no-sweat lunchtime exercise programs or squeeze in a quick workout before going home.

The Worthington Community Center
345 East Wilson Bridge Road,
Worthington
(614) 436-2743
www.worthington.org/city/center.cfm
People who work full time or live in Worthington can use this facility at a reduced

rate. The center offers two indoor swimming pools, a hot tub, fitness center, jogging/walking track, and art and child care rooms. Individual and family passes are available, or you can purchase punch cards good for 10 or 20 individual visits.

PARTICIPANT SPORTS AND LEISURE ACTIVITIES

Ballooning

For a bird's-eye view of Columbus and the surrounding area, you can call Above It All Balloons at (614) 879-6523 or Flying Colors Hot Air Balloon at (614) 447-8684. True balloon enthusiasts can check out the Central Ohio Balloon Club at www.cobc.00go.com.

Boating

Boating, water skiing, and tubing in Columbus can be a blast, but you have to make sure your vessel is legal before you can have a boatload of fun. All boats, including kayaks, canoes, rowboats, and pedal boats, must be registered through Ohio's Bureau of Motor Vehicles; licenses are valid for three years. The fees range from $12 to $93 and help support Ohio's boating programs. Registration can be renewed online at the Ohio Department of Natural Resources Web site: www.dnr.state.oh.us.

Once you have all the paperwork in place, there are three marinas at which you can dock your boat for under $500. The Columbus Department of Recreation and Parks operate Griggs Reservoir, O'Shaughnessy Reservoir, and Hoover Reservoir. Powerboats can take advantage of Griggs' and O'Shaughnessy's 40 mph open zones, while sailing and pontoon boats are more common on Hoover because of the 10 mph speed limit across the entire lake. Dock season runs from early May through late October, and a public lottery is held each spring for those wishing to dock at one of the marinas. Leaseholders are given first dibs to renew their space from year to year, but you can apply for dock space any time in the season.

There are also a few private boat club options around Columbus. Leatherlips Yacht Club (614-889-8997), Hoover Yacht Club (614-882-6980), and Scioto Boat Club (614-876-4937) are all membership-based private clubs. See the Sailing entry for more information, and don't forget the endless boating opportunities two hours north at Lake Erie. Read up on the lakefront and Erie island activities in the Day Trips and Weekend Getaways chapter.

The Columbus Sail and Power Squadron
6345 Sawmill Road, Dublin
(614) 798-0223
www.usps.org/localusps/columbus
The CSPS is the local unit of the world's largest nonprofit boating organization. With over 500 members in Columbus, it sponsors a wide range of boating activities, events, and educational and safe boating classes and does free vessel safety checks. You must be at least 18 years of age to gain membership.

Bowling

Palace Lanes
57 Forest Hills Boulevard
(614) 895-1122
www.palacelanes.com
If you are looking for the "country club of bowling," look no further than Columbus Square Bowling Palace. There is casual and league bowling, while regional and national tournaments are also held here. Open 24 hours a day with 64 lanes, a sit-down restaurant, sports bar, game room, and "Power Rail," which is an automatic bumper bowling system for kids, bowling junkies can get their fix anytime of day here.

There are quite a few bowling alleys around Columbus, but here is a short list.

AMF Sawmill Lanes
4825 Sawmill Road, Dublin Area
(614) 889-0880

Holiday Lanes
4589 East Broad Street
(614) 861-1600

Western Lanes
500 Georgeville Road
(614) 274-1169

BOWLING ASSOCIATIONS

Columbus Women's Bowling Association
(614) 237-3924

Greater Columbus Bowling Association
(614) 237-3716

Camping

The city of Columbus no longer operates public campgrounds, but the state runs campgrounds to accommodate all types of tents and trailers. At a minimum, campgrounds provide drinking water, restrooms or latrines, pads for parking a car or trailer, picnic tables, and fire rings. Campsites range from no-frills, walk-in tent sites to full-service sites for recreational vehicles with electrical and water hook-ups. Pets are allowed on designated grounds and must be kept on leashes at all times.

KOA camping is another option that can accommodate primitive tents or the big rigs up to 85 feet. There are 15 cabins on-site, a swimming pool and showers, and cable, telephone, gas, and firewood can be had for an extra charge. KOA is conveniently located off of I-70, and Buckeye Lake is right next door. Call (800) 562-0792. or go to www.koakampgrounds.com to make your reservations.

Canoeing and Kayaking

The Columbus Department of Recreation and Parks offers group canoe trips on the Scioto River, which launch from Indian Village and can be integrated into weekend camping getaways. If you have your own canoe or kayak, there are launches along the Scioto and Olentangy rivers. If not, you can rent a kayak from the marinas at Alum Creek, Hoover Reservoir, a little farther north at Delaware State Park, or to the east at Buckeye Lake. If you don't mind a short drive south of Columbus, Scioto Trail State Park has two small lakes with tranquil waters excellent for canoeing and kayaking. Many of the state parks also have canoeing/kayaking packages that include lodging.

As for guided tours, let Morgan's Ft. Ancient Canoe Livery put you in a canoe and take you on a one-day river trip or a camping weekend. You can check out the canoe/kayak tours at www.morganscanoe.com, or call (800) WE CANOE. Hocking Hills Canoe Livery (740-385-0523) also has boating trips of different lengths for all skill levels. It offers an interesting Moonlight Canoe Ride on the Hocking River. You leave at sunset and canoe back by the light of the moon—after which you can have your fill of marshmallows around a bonfire.

Climbing

Vertical Adventures (614-888-8393) gives climbers of all skill levels over 4,000 square feet of varied terrain on which to practice top roped climbing, bouldering, and leading, which is the most advanced climbing at this facility. It offers climbing courses and monthly seminars, and there's a complete pro shop on-site. Check out the Web site www.verticaladventuresohio.com for rates, hours, and lessons.

CLOSE-UP

Happy Trails to You!

Central Ohio affords cyclists and mountain bikers of all levels a pedal through some of Ohio's most beautiful scenery. Blacklick Woods and Sharon Metro Parks each have 4 miles of trails while Three Creeks Metro Park has 9 miles. Highbanks Metro Park does not have any mountain biking trails, but it does have two paved paths for cyclists. Several Columbus communities, including New Albany and Dublin, maintain integrated bike paths throughout neighborhoods.

Twelve miles north of Columbus, beginners will enjoy the fun twists and turns along a 10-mile network of bike paths at Alum Creek State Park. East of the city is the 14.3-mile paved Thomas J. Evans Trail, which begins in Newark and winds along Raccoon Creek to Johnstown, Ohio. The 10-mile Panhandle Trail also leaves Newark but runs the opposite direction to the east. From this local trail you can connect to the scenic Blackhand Gorge Bikeway, one of the Rails-to-Trails paths.

The Rails-to-Trails conservancy program is creating a nationwide network of bike trails out of former rail lines, and many miles pass through Columbus. You can learn about the program, purchase guides, and see an exhaustive list of trails at www.railtrails.org. Detailed information about each Columbus trail can be found at www.traillink.com.

Blackhand Gorge Bikeway, named for the outcroppings of bedrock called blackhand sandstone that occurs in this area, is located southeast of Columbus in Newark. It is a 4.26-mile asphalt path weaving through beautiful Ohio scenery. It passes through thick woods, crosses streams, and runs along the river. Keep your eyes open for cool rock formations.

Heritage Rail Trail is a 6.1-mile trail beginning in the historic district of Old Hilliard and ends close to Plain City.

Interstate 670 Bikeway is a 3.5-mile asphalt pathway leading from the airport, through the city, and ending at Cleveland Avenue. It is recommended more as a commuter bikeway than a recreational path, because it follows the highway, and there are curbs, bridges, and busy crossings to contend with.

Olentangy-Scioto Bike Path was Ohio's first rail trail. Established in 1969, this asphalt trail runs 17 miles right

Another option is Columbus Outdoor Pursuits (614-442-7901), which has its own climbing facility as part of a rock-climbing program. Equipment is provided at no extra charge, but it is recommended you bring your own shoes.

Put your climbing skills to use in the great outdoors by heading to either Hocking State Forest or John Bryan State Forest. You are allowed, by permit, to rappel and rock climb in designated areas established within the parks. If you prefer guided tours, take a trip with Outdoor Adventures (740-380-0902; www.climbhocking.com).

through the heart of Columbus. The Olentangy/Scioto Trail mile marker 0 is located at Broad Street, and the miles are marked north and south of this point with either wooden posts set next to the trail or half-mile "ticks" on the pavement. Maps tend to divide this path into four sections: Upper and Lower Olentangy and Upper and Lower Scioto trails.

Beginning at Frank Road, it passes through Berliner Park in German Village and heads north through downtown Columbus and the OSU campus. It passes through Clintonville and several parks before ending in Worthington Hills. This is definitely one of the more popular multi-use trails in the city. You will see bikers, joggers, walkers, and cross-country skiers (only in the winter, of course).

Westerville Bikeway is a short and sweet 2.2 miles. It begins at Cherrington Road and ends at Maxtown Road. This Rails-to-Trails bikeway is part of the Ohio Erie Trail, which will eventually run continuously from the Ohio River at Portsmouth in southern Ohio north to Lake Erie in Cleveland.

For those who are not familiar with biking etiquette, a few pointers for trail usage could never hurt. Keep right, and pass on the left. More considerate cyclists have bells (or some sort of audible signal) to warn they are coming up from behind. The speed limit is 15 mph, and no motorized vehicles are permitted on any trails. Alcohol is strictly prohibited. Pets are permitted on the trails, but they must be leashed at all times. Happy trails to you!

Thomas J. Evans Bike Trail. SHAWNIE KELLEY

Cricket

There are several active cricket clubs in the central Ohio region, but most of them are student organizations. They are at Wittenburg University, Ohio Wesleyan University, Wooster College, and The Ohio State University. The cricket club of The Ohio State University is open to students, alumni, and members of the community. The team plays other universities and clubs, so members must be willing to travel to surrounding states for matches. There is no coach, but there are three officers who are responsible for managing the team. Fees are $50 for students and

$100 for nonstudents. Contact Ohio State's Department of Recreational Sports at (614) 292-7671 for further information.

Cycling/ Mountain Biking

Under Ohio law, bicycles are defined as vehicles, and cyclists are obligated to adhere to the same rules as motorists. Bikers can be sited for speeding, drunk or reckless driving, and riding against traffic. The use of a horn, bell, or some sort of audible device is required, as is a light after dark. Some communities enforce their own rules, such as requiring helmets or limiting cyclists to dedicated bike paths. Just be conscientious of the rules if you plan to ride on a road shared with other vehicles.

If you prefer to keep your riding to the trails, read the Close-up on bike paths in this chapter for specific multipurpose trails in and around Columbus. The Ohio Department of Transportation publishes a brochure titled "Ohio's Bikeways" that can be requested at (614) 752-4685 or online at www.dot.state.oh.us/bike. There are about 15 cycling clubs in Columbus, and the Web site www.ohiocycling.info will direct you to the individual club links and provide contact details.

Field Hockey

The United States Field Hockey Association has men's, women's, and coed club teams in Columbus. The Columbus Field Hockey Club and The Ohio State University club teams are open to players who are college age and over. These local club teams compete with others on a regional and national level. Go to www.usfieldhockey.com/clubs for specific contact information.

Fishing

The locals fish everywhere, from the Olentangy and Scioto Rivers to the streams and ponds in some of the Metro Parks to the lakes and reservoirs surrounding Columbus. Large- and smallmouth bass, trout, and crappies are among some of the fish inhabiting central Ohio waters. The muskie, which is native to Ohio, is the largest of the Ohio game species. One of the best muskie resources is the Ohio Muskie Club and can be linked through the Department of Natural Resources, one of the more comprehensive fishing guides to the region: www.dnr.state.oh.us/wildlife.

Fishing licenses are $19 for those between ages 16 and 65. Those over 65 can reap the benefits of being a senior and get a license for a mere $10. Fishing licenses are not required for those under age 16 or when fishing in private ponds and lakes. Contact the Division of Wildlife at (614) 644-3925 with specific questions.

Folf/Disk Golf

There are two Frisbee golf courses in the area: one at 2933 Riverside Drive on the east side of Griggs Reservoir and one on the east side of Hoover Reservoir on Central College Avenue. There is no cost to play; you can contact the Columbus Department of Recreation and Parks for further information. Blendon Woods Metro Park also has a dedicated disk golf course.

Golf

See the Golf chapter for a listing of courses and driving ranges.

Horseback Riding

Columbus isn't the Wild West, but there are a number of horse breeders, dealers,

boarders, and academies in the area. Conveniently located near Dublin, Liberty Farm (614-279-0346; www.libertyhorse farm.com) offers hunter and jumper instruction for people of all ages and has showing programs and an interscholastic riding team. A few of the Columbus Metro Parks have integrated horse trails, which are noted in the Close-up in this chapter.

The following is a list of a few more stables at which you can board your horses, take lessons, or go on guided tours:

Arrow Riding Stable, Orient
(614) 877-3443

Dublin Stables, Powell
(614) 764-4643

5-Star Equestrian Center, Grove City
(614) 875-8582

Glenbarr Oaks Equestrian Center
Westerville
(614) 855-7696

Pamela Graham Hunters & Jumpers
New Albany
(614) 855-0919

You can also check out www.horse rentals.com/ohio.html for a comprehensive listing of stables, boarding, and lessons in the state.

Ice Hockey

Ice hockey has really taken off in Columbus. Men and women over the age of 18 can get involved in year-round adult recreational ice hockey leagues at one of the Chiller ice facilities. They host special events, tournaments, playoffs, and championships, and the Columbus Blue Jackets Hockey School holds adult ice hockey and goalie camps at the Chiller rinks. People of any skill level can sign up as an individual or as a team, so contact the league commissioner at (614) 791-9999, or have a look at the Chiller Web site: www.thechiller.com to register.

Columbus Outdoor Pursuits (614-442-7901) is a nonprofit organization with outdoor programs for youths and adults. It offers basic and intermediate canoe and kayaking schools, low-budget boating trips, caving, rock climbing, hiking, backpacking, and bicycling programs, as well as winter activities such as cross-country skiing. You can view the courses or register online at www.outdoor-pursuits.org.

Chiller Dublin (614-764-1000) has two NHL-sized rinks and has one of the largest learn-to-skate and junior ice hockey class programs in the country. Chiller Easton (614-475-7575) also is a dual-rink facility. It has one NHL regulation-size rink and the only Olympic-size rink of its kind in Ohio. Chiller North (740-549-0009) is located in Lewis Center and features two NHL-size rinks and a pro shop. You might even be able to catch some curling going on here. The CoreComm Ice Haus (614-246-3380), which is located inside the Nationwide Arena, is the practice rink for the Columbus Bluejackets. All four facilities offer skate rental, locker rooms, a party and meeting room, and concessions. See the Kidstuff chapter for information regarding youth ice hockey.

The Ohio State University has men's and women's club ice hockey teams, open only to OSU students. If you can't get enough of the stuff, go watch them play at the OSU Ice Rink. Learn more about the men's team, get contact details, and view their schedule at www.osuclubhockey.com and the women's team at www.geocities .com/osuclub.

Kayaking

See the Boating and Canoeing and Kayaking entries for details.

The Adaptive Adventure Sports Coalition (TAASC) offers people with physical or mental disabilities the opportunity to pursue outdoor activities, such as kayaking, sailing, and skiing. Call (614) 293-4963 for program information, registration, or volunteer information.

Kickball

The Columbus division of the World Adult Kickball Association (WAKA) plays Wednesday and Thursday evenings at Berliner Park Sports Complex. The fee is $63 per player and includes all games and T-shirts. Call (614) 645-3366 for details, or go to www.worldkickball.com to register online.

Lacrosse

Lacrosse in Columbus is not quite a way of life as it is in, say, Baltimore or Long Island, but it is very popular here. If you are interested in playing in an adult lacrosse league, have a look at the Ohio Lacrosse Foundation's Web site: www.ohlax.com. This chapter of USLacrosse provides links to regional club teams for adults, information regarding high school and college teams, and clinics and tournaments. The men's Columbus Club team is part of the Midwest Club Lacrosse Conference. The Ohio State University has men's and women's varsity teams and club teams open to students, as do several of the other universities in the area, such as Denison University, Ohio Dominican, Ohio University, Ohio Wesleyan University, and Wittenberg University.

Parachuting

For thrill seekers who want to try skydiving, the AerOhio Skydiving Center (800-726-3483) is a good place to start. Weekday tandem jumping must be scheduled in advance, but walk-ins are welcome on the weekends. First-time jumpers have the options of accelerated freefall, tandem, or static line jumps, and for the experienced divers there are even more options. Learn how to "dive right the first time" at Skydive University (www.aerohio.com).

Polo (Equine)

The United States Polo Association has a chapter here in Columbus. The Columbus Polo Club plays every Sunday afternoon (June-September) at the Bryn Du Polo Field in Granville. View the Web site at www.columbuspolo.com, or call the club hotline at (740) 967-7529.

The Ohio State University Polo Club (614-291-3216) is a coed sports club welcoming players of all skill sets at different levels of membership. Active students can join the junior or varsity teams, while alumni who are no longer eligible for collegiate play can still use the club-owned horses and play on the club team. Social and associate memberships are available to nonstudents.

Pools

Swimming pools are located in the community centers listed in this chapter, as well as some of the city's recreation centers. The Department of Recreation and Parks operates a dedicated aquatic center (614-645-3129) with swim classes for ages 6 months and up. Open swim sessions cost only $1.00 for admission. Many neighborhoods also offer fee-based membership to community pools, so check if there is a pool near you.

Racquetball and Handball

A good place to start is the Racquetball Club of Columbus, which is located at 1100

Bethel Road. The club has five Terstep panel racquetball courts, including two with glassed-in viewing, 10 Novacrylic tennis courts, and a fitness center. There are programs for men, women, and children. For membership rates or information on lessons and leagues, call (614) 457-5671, or view the Web site: www.racquetclub1.com.

Many private gyms and athletic facilities in Columbus have racquetball and handball courts, so contact the gym directly before joining. The Ohio State University has about 20 racquetball courts available to students and those who hold a Recreational Sports Activity pass.

Rowing

If you want to learn the art of sculling, sweep rowing, or coxing, you should join the Greater Columbus Rowing Association. No experience is required, as members are divided into categories of novice, intermediate, and advanced. Membership includes use of the boathouse, which is located on the Scioto River, and equipment. The association requires 5 hours of boathouse volunteer service. You can contact the GCRA at (614) 777-4003 or www.columbusrowing.org. Members can also get involved in competitive rowing and regattas.

If you prefer your crisp mornings on land, you can watch The Ohio State University crew practice on the Olentangy River or go cheer on one of the high school crew teams from Dublin, Upper Arlington, Wellington, or Westerville High Schools.

Rugby

Not only does Ohio breed some amazing football players, but we churn out some good rugby players too. More than 72 American and Canadian teams converge on Columbus every year for the Ohio Rugby Classic, which is held at Berliner Park. Men's and women's collegiate teams and high school teams compete in this round-robin tournament. The Ohio State University Rugby Football Club takes part in this tournament on top of their regular season schedule.

If you need a little extra help around the house, why not Rent-A-Rower? For $50 (you provide supplies) you can put a club rower to work for four hours doing odd jobs around the house, cleaning, or minor painting. If you need to get some yardwork done or windows washed, call (614) 470-3980 and support the OSU rowing team.

The Scioto Valley Rugby Club spun off from the OSU Rugby Club in the 1970s and is no longer directly tied to the university. Their home field is at Whetstone Park in Clintonville, and membership is open to the community. The SVRC can be reached at (614) 989-9764 or online at www.sciotorugby.com.

Ladies, rugby isn't just for men these days! Information regarding the Scioto Valley Women's Rugby Football Club (once lovingly referred to as the "Iron Ovaries") can be viewed at the same Web site, or call the SVWRFC hotline at (614) 470-3036.

Running/Walking

The community and recreation centers listed in this chapter have paved or indoor tracks around which you can walk or run. If you are interested in walking through scenic areas rather than circling a track, read the "Happy Trails" Close-up about various multiuse trails located throughout Columbus.

Sailing

There are a handful of sailing options around Columbus. You can get details about the sailing school at the Ohio Division of Watercraft by calling (614) 265-

6652. Those of you who captain your own ship should have a look the Alum Creek Sailing Association (www.alumcreeksail ing.com). It has a marina with launch ramps and a carry-on launch area for beach craft, picnic areas, and shower facilities. The association sponsors races and offers both social and instructional programs. ACSA can be reached at (614) 846-3666.

The Hoover Sailing Club (614-898-9248), located at Hoover Reservoir, holds races every Sunday afternoon and Wednesday evening. The club offers sailing instruction for adults and youth and plays host to annual regattas. More links and general information can be found in the Boating entry.

Scuba Diving

A.S.K. Scuba Center
6522 Riverside Drive, Dublin
(614) 889-2822
www.askscubacenter.com
A.S.K. provides a wide range of aquatic training, from simple swimming lessons to PADI, SDI, TDI, MDEA, and Scuba Ranger certifications. The center sells and rents scuba equipment and puts together dive trips.

The Central Ohio School of Diving
2355 West Dublin-Granville Road
(614) 889-5677
www.divecosd.com
COSD offers both private and small-group diving lessons in an indoor heated pool, but you must provide your own mask, fin, wetboots, and snorkel. It also sells diving equipment and organizes dive trips.

The Underwater Connection
1177 West Third Avenue
(614) 298-9777
www.underwaterconnection.com
The Underwater Connection is a PADI five-star IDC center, where you can get certified in open-water diving, scuba instruction, and everything in between. Members of the scuba club receive discounts in the store and perks such as free airfills and equipment rentals. The club also organizes social events as well as local and international dive trips.

Skating

IN-LINE SKATING

All you have to do is show up to be a member of the Columbus Inline Skating Club (www.columbusinline.com). There is no membership fee, and weekend skates are held on various trails and safe country roads around Columbus.

ICE SKATING

Public skating sessions are held at the three Chiller ice facilities. Information can be viewed online at www.thechiller.com. Chiller Dublin (614-764-1000) has two rinks and hosts up to 13 public skating sessions per week. It also has one of the largest learn-to-skate programs in the country. Chiller Easton (614-475-7575) also is a dual-rink facility, one of which is the only Olympic-size rink of its kind in Ohio. The CoreComm Ice Haus (614-246-3380), which is located inside the Nationwide Arena, is the practice rink for the Columbus Blue Jackets and is open for public skating. All three facilities offer skate rental, locker rooms, a party and meeting room, and concessions.

The Chiller Figure Skating Club, an organization helping skaters, coaches, and judges develop their skills, is a member of the U.S. Figure Skating Association. The club holds clinics, exhibitions, and competitions. The Web site is www.chillerfsc .com, and the phone number is (614) 475-7575.

The Ice Rink at The Ohio State University also has public skating sessions, with adult and youth lessons. Skate rental and private lessons are also available. Call the rink at (614) 292-4154 for the skating schedule.

Skateboarding

Skateboarders will be in concrete heaven in Dodge Skate Park at 667 Sullivant Avenue (614-645-8151) on the west side of Columbus. There are three in-ground bowls at 3, 4, and 6 feet deep, as well as a quarter pipe, bank ramp, and fun box. Membership is $10, and the park is open from April to November. Skaters must wear helmets. A few communities such as Upper Arlington, Worthington, Gahanna, and Bexley have installed smaller skate parks in the neighborhoods.

Skiing

Mad River Mountain
Bellefontaine
(937) 599-1015, (800) 231-SNOW
www.skimadriver.com
Mad River Mountain, a full-service ski resort, is located at Ohio's highest point, an easy drive from Columbus on Route 33. There are slopes for beginners and some new trails of varying difficulty for seasoned skiers. Ski lessons and lift passes are among the services to check out online. A variety of food and drink is available at the base lodge, while Friday and Saturday night feature a "midnight madness" ski party that goes from 10:00 P.M. until 3:30 A.M. for you night owls. If you partake of these festivities, make note that there is no lodging at this facility. There is also a ski and snowboard rental shop, gift shop, game room, and children's zone on-site.

Soccer

Adult men's and women's soccer programs are available at most of the recreation centers operated by the Columbus Department of Recreation and Parks. Call (614) 645-3300 to find out where the soccer leagues and organized practices meet and how to join. Youth soccer programs are listed in the Kidstuff chapter.

Information regarding Columbus's top-flight soccer league can be found at www.premierleague.hypermart.net. The Premier League, which is affiliated with the Southern Ohio Adult Soccer Association, the United States Soccer Association, and the United States Soccer Federation, has two divisions of men's teams.

Softball

Columbus is crazy for softball! It seems that every community, every business (big or small), and even the tiniest neighborhood bars all have softball teams. There are teams for slow-pitch, fast-pitch, beer drinkers, men, women, youth, gay, and lesbian, the physically and mentally challenged—you name it, there is probably a league for it here. Just ask around to find out about teams in your community, or check with your place of employment. It won't take much legwork to find a team that's a perfect fit for you.

The Columbus Department of Recreation and Parks has both adult and youth softball leagues that play springtime through the fall. If you are interested in playing in a city league, see the Web site at www.crpdsports.org for schedules and league options. Parks and Recreation also sponsors several tournaments throughout the year. Another resource for adult slow-pitch softball is the Columbus National Softball Association at www.columbusnsa.com, or call (614) 895-2253 for more details.

i

The Columbus Ski Club is an adult coed sporting league that reaches beyond the slopes. Check out www.columbusskiclub.org for adult leagues in soccer, golf, volleyball, tennis, bowling, billiards, darts, rock climbing, canoeing, horseback riding, and, of course, skiing. Call (614) 481-SNOW to find out more about the different activities.

Squash

Joining the Columbus Squash Racquets Association also gets you membership in its parent organization, the United States Squash Racquets Association (USSRA). The Web site www.squashclub.org/csra offers information about local events, tournaments, and leagues and can help connect you with other squash players in Columbus.

There are a few gyms, such as Lifetime Fitness in Easton (614-428-6000), and other private athletic facilities that have squash courts. The Capital Club hosts an annual tournament in January, which draws squash players from all over the region. It is the premier place to play squash in Columbus, but one must be a member to use the squash courts. The Ohio State University also has 25 courts for racquetball, handball, squash, and wallyball, all located in OSU's Recreation and Physical Activity Center that are accessible to students, faculty, or anyone holding a current BuckID.

Tennis

Public tennis courts are common in Columbus. Most neighborhoods have courts, and many of them are lit so you can play in the evenings. Most of the parks and community centers listed in this chapter have tennis courts, so you may want to just call the park to learn if there are any special rules or policies.

The Ohio State University's Department of Recreational Sports has club teams for skiing, martial arts, field hockey, ice hockey, rugby, and even paintball. All club teams are open to OSU students, but some are open to alumni and the general community. See www.ohiostate recsports.org for specifics, or call (614) 292-7671.

The "Tennis in the Parks" program is put on by the Columbus Department of Recreation and Parks. It offers free lessons for adults and youths at various tennis courts around the city, but you must provide your own racquet. The city also sponsors adult tennis leagues and lessons for those with varying skill levels. Check out the department's Web site, or call (614) 846-7517 for information regarding the tennis program.

If you're looking for private or group tennis lessons, you may want to contact your local community center or high school to find out if there are tennis instructors. There are also a number of private clubs in Columbus that have their own tennis courts and leagues and offer lessons.

Volleyball

The Ohio Valley Region of USA Volleyball is an amateur athletic sports association that gives players the chance to play in local, regional, and national competitions. The Web site has a comprehensive listing of programs, leagues, and tournaments. Links to juniors, men's, and women's teams, as well as general volleyball news and headlines, can be found at www.ovr.org. Another good place to inquire about adult leagues is the Columbus Department of Recreation and Parks. Call (614) 645-3300 to find out how to join. Volleyball enthusiasts can also get on an e-mail list at www.volleyball.org to receive e-mail about local classes, clinics, tournaments, leagues, open games, and pick-up games and keep tabs on professional and collegiate volleyball events in the area.

If it's sand courts you're after, check out many of the state parks, or contact Capital City Sports at (614) 921-0188 (www.capitalcitysports.com) about summer sand leagues. It is not unusual to see a rowdy, fun-loving crowd playing sand volleyball at a handful of bars around town, such as Gatsby's in Gahanna and Flannagan's in Dublin.

PET-FRIENDLY COLUMBUS

We love our animals here in Columbus. The May 2003 issue of *Purina* magazine named Columbus the No. 8 Pet Healthiest City in the country, and we do what we can to keep it that way. Park goers shouldn't be surprised to find man's best friend running alongside his master on one of the trails or playing catch in many of the parks. But, given the large number of green spaces in Columbus, it is a bit surprising (and a little disappointing) that there aren't more dedicated dog parks for our canines to frolic. While Columbus City Council is addressing this issue, the section titled "Dog Parks" will point out a few places where owners tend to congregate, some with designated times for dogs to run free.

Speaking of running free, the city of Columbus has no leash laws (rottweilers being the exception), but they do exist and vary throughout the parks. A spirited dialogue is under way about drafting stringent laws, but until then most of Columbus's city parks are, at minimal, dog friendly. Some of the city-operated parks expect you to have your dog under verbal control only, while others require they be kept on a leash of 6 feet or less. The rules are usually posted at park entrances.

Certain neighborhoods have mixed verbal and leash laws. Upper Arlington, Worthington, Bexley, Whitehall, and Grove City are among the Columbus communities with some sort of animal control laws beyond the state code. The smartest thing to do is call ahead to confirm the rules at the park, or just take a leash along and check for signage.

This pet-friendly section will clue you in on where to go to adopt or track down your lost pet. One thing you may notice is that many of the rescue organizations work together in the best interest of all the homeless animals of Columbus, not just those in their own shelter. They pool their resources and facilities and cross-reference one another on their Web sites. If you can't find a pet that suits your household at one shelter, there is always the chance you are only a link away, so keep looking. Maybe pay a visit to one of the shelters; Internet pictures don't always do justice!

Once you have that new family member, you will not be disappointed to learn that Columbus has the highest vet-to-pet ratio in the country and a wonderful veterinary program and hospital at The Ohio State University. It's no wonder preventive health care is at the top of the awareness agenda. With Fido or Fluffy home and healthy, it's time to spoil them rotten.

Columbus has its fair share of Petland, PetsMart, and Pet People chain stores, but there are plenty of locally owned boutiques where you can indulge your four-legged foodie's gourmet palate and haute couture style. See the section that lists the specialty stores for that extra-special something. You will find that many of the pet stores are animal-friendly, so take them along for the shopping spree.

i

All dogs three months of age and older must be registered annually by January 31 and immunized against rabies by a licensed veterinarian. The current year's license tag must be displayed on a dog's collar or harness at all times, even while the dog is on the premises of the owner.

SHELTERS AND RESCUES

Columbus, like many other cities, has a severe overpopulation problem with cats and dogs. If you want to give a home to an animal, consider adopting from one of the many shelters to help reduce the euthanasia of thousands of cats and dogs every year. A good place to start is the Columbus Dog Connection (614-637-1342), which is a network of dog enthusiasts who alleviate some of the burden from shelters by providing foster homes for the animals until a permanent home can be found. The Web site www.columbusdogconnection.com has pictures of homeless dogs and cats, information about adoption, awareness events, and links to all the central Ohio rescues and shelters.

Another networking group to have a look at is Animal Outreach, based in Dublin. You can view the Web site at www.animal-outreach.org or call (614) 473-WAGG for links to shelters, veterinarians, and information about Animal Outreach's Spay Neuter Assistance Program, which helps to subsidize the cost of a pet's spay or neuter surgery if you are unable to afford it.

Capital Area Humane Society
3015 Scioto-Darby Executive Court
Hilliard
(614) 777-7387
www.cahs-pets.org

A state-of-the-art shelter with quality staff and volunteers makes this a safe haven for the many unwanted animals that come through their doors. Images of dogs, cats, rabbits, and pocket pets, such as hamsters and gerbils, can be found online. Keep in mind that not all are able to be photographed and displayed on the Internet, so make a trip to the Humane Society to see if your pet is waiting. There's also bingo nights every Sunday and Monday, with some of the proceeds going to the Humane Society. The doors open a few hours early so you can come and visit the animals beforehand.

---

i

Mingle with our Mutts is an adoption event held at the Franklin County Animal Shelter on the third Sunday of each month from noon until 2:00 P.M. This event is coordinated in conjunction with the Columbus Dog Connection. You can find out more by calling either facility or viewing their Web sites.

Cozy Cat Cottage
62 Village Pointe Drive, Powell
(614) 336-8510
www.cozycatcottage.com

The Cozy Cat Cottage is a nonprofit, no-kill cat adoption center, though there is one permanent shelter dog to make sure the felines are exposed to canines. The center relies on donations, adoption fees, fundraisers, and boutique sales to help maintain this center for abandoned and abused cats. The adoption fees range from $65 to $100 and include medical testing, vaccinations, and spaying or neutering. Senior citizens can adopt a cat for free. They accept monetary donations and have a wish list of supplies on their Web site for those who can donate goods. If you prefer to donate your time, any talent you have will be put to good use. Another special need is adopters who want to provide hospice care for terminally ill cats.

Franklin County Dog Shelter
1731 Alum Creek Drive
(614) 462-4360
www.franklincountydogs.com

Open seven days a week, this shelter lets you adopt a dog in less than an hour. There is a cash-only nonrefundable adoption fee of $78, but this ensures your dog is spayed or neutered and has all its shots. Other services provided by the shelter are dog mixers, awareness programs, rabies clinics, and pet therapy. The shelter accepts donations in the form of money, dog food, carriers, blankets, and towels. If you are an animal lover but can't adopt, then sign up for some volunteer work.

Animal Control works in conjunction with Franklin County Dog Shelter, so

check here if your dog goes missing. Unfortunately, they are not able to accept cats at this shelter but are working with other shelters and dog facilities toward becoming a no-kill facility. Definitely do not overlook the Franklin County Dog Shelter as a place to find your next pet.

Friends for Life Animal Haven
Canal Winchester
(614) 837-6260
www.theanimalhaven.org
The Animal Haven is a no-kill animal rescue organization that takes in cats, dogs, kittens, and puppies. The rescues are placed in foster homes or live at the shelter in a homelike, open environment, as none of the animals are caged. The adoption fee, which includes a thorough examination, spay or neuter, worming, and up-to-date vaccinations, is $109 for dogs/puppies and $60 for cats/kittens. Sponsor a pet or volunteer your time. A special program at this shelter is the Forever Foster Program. You provide TLC and a foster home for a senior dog or cat to live out the rest of its life, and the Animal Haven will pick up the veterinary costs.

PetPromise
(614) 878-8281
www.petpromise.org
PetPromise is a nonprofit, no-kill animal rescue organization that focuses its adoption efforts on stray, abandoned, homeless, or abused cats and dogs. PetPromise functions solely on donations and the generosity of volunteers and foster parents. They do not yet have a shelter, though an effort to raise $90,000 for one is under way. Until then, pets are placed in foster homes until permanently adopted.

Pets Without Parents Columbus
4522 Indianola Avenue
(614) 459-7297, (614) 267-PAWS
www.petswithoutparents.net
This nonprofit, no-kill shelter accepts all breeds of dogs and cats. All pets are spayed/neutered and given their shots before going to their new home. Also onsite is the Faux-Paws Gift Shop. Animal lovers will see their money put to work, as proceeds from every purchase go to the shelter to help make it a better place for pets-to-be. Donations by way of money or supplies are always welcomed, and you can view a wish list at the Web site. Volunteering your time or any other talent is another wonderful way to contribute if you can't take a cat or dog home with you.

i

The Capital Canine Connection is a therapeutic visitation group whose teams of humans and dogs visit Children's Hospital, nursing homes, and rehabilitation centers. If you have a well tempered, well-mannered, friendly dog that loves attention and gives attention, you may want to share your dog's affection with others who might need it. Call (614) 777-7387 ext. 291, to get involved.

Other Rescues

Cat Welfare Association
741 Wetmore Road
(614) 268-6096
www.catwelfareohio.com

Citizens for Humane Action
3765 Corporate Drive
(614) 891-5280
www.chaanimalshelter.org

Cool Cats
(614) 475-8111

i

If you have a physical or cognitive disability, contact Canine Companions for Independence to get involved with a free program to be partnered with a highly trained dog to enhance your self-reliance. The North Central Regional Training Center of this national nonprofit organization can be contacted at (740) 548-4447 or www.caninecompanions.org.

Forgotten 4-Paws
Lancaster
(740) 687-9244
www.forgotten4-paws.org

EMERGENCY AND VETERINARY SERVICES

The following lists just a select few of the many animal hospitals around Columbus. Most of them have referral services, which can direct you to a specialist or a vet in your area.

Animal Medical and Emergency Hospital
2527 West Dublin-Granville Road
(614) 889-2556
www.drdonn.com

Easton Animal Hospital
2959 Stelzer Road, Westerville
(614) 476-0000

Gahanna Animal Hospital
144 West Johnstown Road, Gahanna
(614) 471-2201

MedVet Associates, Ltd.
300 East Wilson Bridge Road
Worthington
(614) 846-5800
www.medvet-cves.com

The Ohio State University
Veterinary Hospital
601 Vernon Tharp Street, OSU Campus
(614) 292-3551
www.vet.ohio-state.edu

Shearer Pet Hospital
1383 Bethel Road
(614) 457-5991
www.shearerpethospital.com

Willow Wood Animal Hospital
5891 Zarley Street, New Albany
(614) 855-3855

KENNELS, BOARDING, AND DAY CARE

When it comes to boarding your four-legged friends, it seems there are nearly as many kennels as there are vets in Columbus. This chapter provides just a handful of lodging options, but plenty more can be found in the yellow pages. If you feel better leaving your beloved family pet in familiar surroundings, you may want to start by checking with your veterinarian or contacting some of the animal hospitals listed, as many of them have on-site kenneling.

Canine Social Club
1103 Dublin Road, Grandview
(614) 488-3647
www.caninesocialclub.org
The CSC comes highly recommended for the value and level of service provided to your pup. Day care dogs are monitored by a dedicated staff in an open atmosphere at this indoor facility. There is no outside space due to city ordinances, but this doesn't detract from the fun to be had and the romping to be done. CSC offers kenneling and has a do-it-yourself dog bath on-site as well. What sets this day care apart from others is that the staff works with Franklin County Dog Shelter to provide foster care for dogs until they are permanently adopted. Volunteers will also drop off and pick up Franklin County shelter dogs at the facility as a way to get them out of the shelter for a day and to allow interaction and playtime with day care dogs.

Cheryl's Doggie Daycare
4712 Trabue Road, Hilliard
(614) 527-1158
www.cherylsdoggiedaycare.com
If your dog suffers separation anxiety or you just want your dog in an environment where it can play and interact while you are at work, drop it off at Cheryl's Doggie Daycare. All dogs must be 12 weeks or older, spayed or neutered, on a flea control program, healthy and up to date on all

shots, nonaggressive, and able to play well with other dogs and people. As a member of the North American Dog Daycare Association and Pet Sitters International, your dog will be well looked after by the professional staff certified in pet first aid. You can also contact Cheryl's for pet sitting in your home.

Doggie Business
(614) 218-1305
www.doggiebusiness.com
An affordable alternative to kenneling your dog may be to have professional, insured care providers check in on your pets, take them for a walk in familiar territory, and give them a little lovin' while you are out of town. The rates for their services vary depending on the amount of time, but it is reasonably priced enough to permit people within a broad economic range to use these services. In fact, they have the lowest rates in town, which is why they are attracting young professionals with pets. The co-owners of Doggie Business not only are animal lovers but are creating an environmentally friendly business by using 100 percent biodegradable waste bags and limiting business to places they can easily access by public transportation or bike. This means their current territory is limited to German Village, Victorian Village, the Short North, Clintonville, and the OSU campus area.

The Pet Resort at Willow Wood
5891 Zarley Street, New Albany
(614) 855-4800
www.petresortatwillowwood.com
The Pet Resort at Willow Wood isn't cheap, but if your pampered pooch requires a vacation while you are on vacation, then look no further. The Pet Resort is the Ritz-Carlton of kennels. Besides a variety of accommodations, other services such as grooming, "pet"icures, training, massages, and one-on-one cuddle time can be had for a fee. For the dogs, there are runs of various sizes, deluxe suites, playtime, and doggie day care. Where else will your dog be walked several times a day, then bedded down to watch Animal Planet in the privacy of its own room? Cats too can have their own deluxe suites and climb the trees in the kitty playrooms. On top of all the good care they will receive here, you can sleep soundly knowing Willow Wood Animal Hospital is in the adjacent building.

For a list of pet-friendly hotels in the Columbus area, have a look at www.pets-allowed-hotels.com/us/ohio/Columbus. The Web site provides links to hotels and their policies. Most are chain hotels and allow one pet less than 50 pounds. Pet-friendly cabins at Lake Erie and the Hocking Hills are noted along with their Web sites in the Day Trips and Weekend Getaways chapter.

Wizard of Dogz
(614) 747-4407
www.wizardofdogz.com
If in-house pet sitting is your preference, call the Wizard of Dogz. Sitters will come to your home and do all they can to keep your pet as close to its regular schedule as possible. It will be fed, loved, and taken for its usual walk. As an added service, they will bring in the mail, water plants, and take out trash as instructed. Insured, bonded, and licensed by several pet-sitting organizations, they can also provide pet massage, puppy training, behavior modification, and personal pet consultations.

DOG PARKS

One of the more popular parks to take your pet is Antrim Park in Worthington, where frolicking dogs have been known to retrieve a stick or two from the lake. Despite the word on the street, all Worthington parks permit dogs off-leash at all times, as long as they are under verbal control of the owner. Control of one's dog is often a matter of opinion, but none the less remains at the owner's discretion. As long as you are courteous to the nondog people by cleaning up after Fido and keeping your four-footed family member relatively contained, good harmony can be maintained within the parks.

Dogs are permitted off-leash before 8:00 A.M. and after 8:00 P.M. during daylight savings time at all parks in Upper Arlington. During these off-leash hours a pet owner must be able to demonstrate that the dog is under direct control. You can also read a little more about the well-attended dog park at Goodale in Parks and Recreation, while the residents of German Village similarly converge on Schiller Park each evening. Jefferson Park in Bexley, however, is one of the few that do not permit pets at any time, but there are plenty of city parks nearby, most of which are well marked with animal regulations.

There are waste bag dispensers at certain parks such as Whetstone, but be sure to take your own just in case. If you don't clean up after your pet in a public place, it could result in his impoundment. We can't have the hound in the pound!

Alum Creek Dog Park
(740) 548-7600
www.neighborhoodlink.com/org/alumcreekdogpark

Alum Creek State Park is developing a four-acre, pet-friendly park along Alum Creek Reservoir. This beachfront area will be a fenced-in, leash-free zone, giving your pooch walk-in access from the beach. Other amenities will include a dog wash station, drinking water for pets (and their people), waste disposal bags for the dogs, and facilities for the humans.

Bark Park
Powell
www.barkpark.org

The only negative thing about Bark Park is that the wait list is a mile long! Bark Park is a nonprofit, all-volunteer organization that was established at a private home to raise money for Columbus's homeless animals. With 10 fenced acres, a pond, an agility course, and a load of dog toys, your pooch can run off its energy, then get a good scrub at the dog wash. Records of vaccinations and spay/neuter from your veterinarian are required upon membership, and the dog must be socialized with adults, children, and other dogs of all sizes. Bark Park is held on Saturday from 10:00 A.M. to 4:00 P.M., May through October. There is an awareness table, a dog wash, and a concession stand (for humans) set up by a different humane organization each week. You are charged a one-time seasonal membership fee of $75.00 and $5.00 each time you enter the park. Concessions and dog baths are extra, but well worth it, as 100 percent of all proceeds go to the rescue of the day.

Bark Till Dark Park
Hills-Miller Road, 18 miles north of Worthington
www.barktildarkdogpark.com

This new dog park is located 3 miles north of downtown Delaware off Route 23. It is a membership-based social club for dogs. Amenities include a swimming pond for the dogs and picnic area for their people. Little dogs can play in a protected, fenced-in area, and times can be reserved for "play dates." It is open seven days a week and provides a fenced-in area where dogs can romp off-leash. Full membership costs $30 a month and gives access to the park seven days a week. Weekend membership (Saturday and Sunday only) is $25 a month.

Westerville Bark Park
708 Park Meadow Road

The city of Westerville created an off-leash dog park in May 2005. A one-acre park is available for larger dogs, and a one-quarter-acre gated area is provided for smaller dogs. Both feature drinking fountains and hydrants. The Westerville Convention and Visitor's Bureau, along with Capital Area Humane Society, sponsors an annual event called the Dog Days of Summer, which includes adoption efforts and a Mutt March.

SPECIALTY PET SHOPS

True animal lovers spare no expense on their furry friends, and there is no shortage of pet supply stores for any budget in Columbus. For that extra-special something—a matching collar and leash set, organic bagels, or a special "Woofday" cake—look no further than the places listed here. All the boutiques listed are pet-friendly, so pack up your pets and get shopping.

Heidi's Bakery
1409 Grandview Avenue, Grandview
(614) 481-8329, (877) PETSNACK
www.heidisbakery.com
Heidi's Homemade is the piece de résistance of health food stores for cats and dogs. Working with nutritionists and pet specialists, the owners created a diet of raw and organic foods for both cats and dogs as an alternative to subjecting their dog to rigorous cancer treatments. As soon as you enter the door, it is obvious from the yummy smells that everything in the store is homemade. All food and treats are made from scratch, with no preservatives, sugars, or by-products, and many of the treats contain all natural, healing ingredients, such as chamomile and peppermint for cats and garlic for dogs. You can treat your puppy to a birthday cookie that reads "Happy Arfday!" or pop in for special holiday treats. The *Whole Dog Journal* listed Heidi's as approved whole pet treats, meaning the food you buy here is not only tasty but good for pets too. A portion of its proceeds goes to charitable animal organizations, and fundraisers are often held at the store.

Lula's Pet Place
6518 Riverside Drive, Dublin
(614) 792-6666
www.lulaspetplace.com
This boutique, conveniently located in Village Square Shopping Center at the intersection of Riverside Drive and Route 161, is chock full of interesting and eclectic bits and bobbles for your four-legged companion. If you want to find a funky dog bed, furry playthings for your cat, unique collars, and animal-inspired artwork or indulge in over-the-top treats for your pet, browse around Lula's. It is impossible to leave this place without buying something!

Posh Pets
743 North High Street
(614) 299-PETS
www.poshpetsboutique.com
This is the place to go for all those unique dog and cat accoutrements you don't need but must have. Cozy beds, fun toys, premium foods, and high-end treats are among some of the "necessities." You can find an assortment of bejeweled and faux furred collars here, and remember the only real fur you will encounter at Posh Pets is on the pets you bring along. If you spare no expense for your furry friends, then a Swarovski crystal collar from Fox and Hounds or a Burberry coat might fit the bill. And why not indulge in a "Canine Cuban," a cigar-shaped treat for dogs, while they lounge on their red velvet chaise from Poochie of Beverly Hills? Despite the fancy name dropping that can be done in this boutique, the staff is particularly nice.

SPECTATOR SPORTS 

With no major league football, baseball, or basketball teams, Columbus has forever been a college football town. There is no doubt Ohio State football is still the biggest draw, attracting crowds in excess of 100,000 to the games, but the city is now more than a one-sport town. If you want to watch professional teams play without having to leave Columbus, there are a few options.

The Columbus Blue Jackets play ice hockey teams from across the National Hockey League at the Nationwide Arena. The Columbus Crew hosts national and international soccer teams in their namesake stadium. The Columbus Clippers, the minor league affiliate of the New York Yankees, calls Cooper Stadium home. Scioto Downs features live harness racing, while Beulah Park, Ohio's first thoroughbred racetrack, is just a few minutes outside the city.

Columbus can also boast two relatively new sports arenas that double as entertainment venues: Nationwide Arena, featuring the Columbus Blue Jackets, and the Schottenstein Arena, hosting Buckeye basketball and a variety of national tournaments. The Ohio State University has a number of new and recently renovated athletic facilities that host men's and women's sporting events. Tickets are typically available to the public; more information can be found in The Ohio State University chapter.

While the Buckeyes reign supreme, a few other local universities have sports programs open for public attendance, some of which are quite good. The men's lacrosse team at Ohio Wesleyan University (740-368-3340) is looking to win its third consecutive North Coast Athletic Conference. The OWU men's basketball and soccer teams and women's soccer team have recently snagged four NCAA Division III national championship titles between them. Another Division III school, Capital University, has basketball teams we need to keep an eye on in upcoming years.

With all this talk of college sports, what do the locals do when they need an NFL, MLB, or NBA fix? Unfortunately, they have to go to Cleveland or Cincinnati. They're not far, but it's just far enough to have to make a day of the event. Columbus natives seem to have split loyalties between the Cleveland Browns, Cavaliers, and Indians and the Cincinnati Bengals and Reds. On some occasions you might even find Pittsburgh fans in the mix. Because of Columbus's close proximity to these cities, sports fans will probably never see a major league football, basketball, or baseball team established here.

History buffs might get a kick out of going to an Ohio Village Muffins or a Lady Muffins match. The 19th-century-style baseball teams are made up of Ohio Historical Society volunteers who wear authentic uniforms, while a commentator talks spectators through the game of base ball (historically two words), using the original rules from 1860. The Muffins' long season lasts from April to October, and their home field is at Ohio Village at the Ohio Historical Society. Contact the Ohio Village at (614) 297-3000, or check out the Web site www.ohiohistory.org to purchase tickets or to participate.

For an up-to-date schedule of sporting events in the city, check out www.experiencecolumbus.com. Information about teams and athletic facilities in Cleveland and Cincinnati can be found in the Day Trips and Weekend Getaways chapter, while the legendary Buckeyes are covered in both The Ohio State University and Parks and Recreation chapters. Columbus is big on participatory sports—golf, softball, and soccer—but read on for a listing of the spectator sports the city has to offer.

Beulah Park
3663 Grant Avenue, Grove City
(614) 871-9600
www.beulahpark.com
Built in 1923, Beulah is Ohio's first thoroughbred horse racing track and is located just 15 minutes southwest of Columbus. In 1983, it was the first track in Ohio to offer Simulcast wagering on the Kentucky Derby, and in 1993, it was the first in Ohio to offer telephone betting on national games. Racing purists who can't make it down to Horse Country for the Derby find Beulah to be an acceptable substitute. You will not, however, find big hats or refined gentry here. It is a completely casual environment, with imported beer and mixed drinks at best.

Beulah offers live racing from February to May and September to December, and year-round satellite broadcasting of national thoroughbred and harness races. The facility features an enclosed clubhouse overlooking the track, indoor/outdoor seating, and an outdoor plaza. Despite the gambling and drinking, this is a family-friendly place and often holds family-oriented events and concerts. General admission is $2.00, and parking is $1.00. Whatever more you spend is up to you.

Columbus Blue Jackets
Nationwide Arena
200 West Nationwide Boulevard
(614) 246-3350
The Columbus Blue Jackets Is one of the National Hockey League's newest teams and is based at Nationwide Arena. The Blue Jackets, in fact, are the only NHL team to play its games in the same facility in which they practice. The team's nickname was voted on by fans, and a cartoon-like bee is their logo and mascot. The Blue Jackets lost their first game against the Chicago Blackhawks on October 7, 2000, and since then, they've had average seasons. They have yet to make the playoffs, but at this point, most fans are just happy to have hockey.

The Blue Jackets play from September through April. Individual tickets can be purchased through Ticketmaster at (614) 431-3600 or the Blue Jackets office at (614) 246-PUCK. Individual ticket prices vary depending on where you want to sit in the 18,000-seat arena, but the average cost of a single ticket is around $59. This inspired arena is so well-designed, there isn't a bad seat in the house, even if you're stuck in a $40 seat up in peanut heaven.

Columbus Clippers
Cooper Stadium
1155 West Mound Street
(614) 462-5250
www.clippersbaseball.com
Columbus has had a professional baseball team since the turn of the 20th century, but the Jets pulled up stakes and moved away in 1971. After doing without baseball for six years, a push by Franklin County Commissioner Harold Cooper brought about a new minor league baseball team. The Clippers were originally affiliated with the Pittsburgh Pirates, but it has been the triple-A affiliate of the New York Yankees since 1979. *Baseball America* magazine recognized the Clippers as the top minor league franchise in its 20th-anniversary edition. The Clippers play at Cooper Stadium on the west side of the city, but a new stadium is in their future. Individual tickets cost anywhere from $3.00 for general admission to $9.00 for box seats. Season tickets to all 72 homes games cost $375 per seat.

---

i

Two adults and up to four children can attend a Sunday Columbus Clippers game for $10.

Columbus Comets
Whitehall Yearling High School
Whitehall
(614) 322-0568
www.columbuscomets.com
The Columbus Comets are part of the National Women's Football Association and play by the exact same rules as the NFL, except with a slightly smaller ball.

They have a lot going for them, including one of the league's toughest defenses and the No. 1 punter—not to mention their own cheerleaders. The goal is simple: Rise to the top of the 40 team heap to become the next NWFA champs. The Comets play an eight-game season at the Whitehall Yearling High School field. Individual tickets cost $10, while season tickets are only $35.

Columbus Crew
One Black and Gold Boulevard
(614) 447-CREW
www.columbus.crew.mlsnet.com

The 1994 World Cup was held in the United States, and Major League Soccer was born. MLS is the fifth major professional sports league established in America, and Columbus's very own Black and Gold was one of the first 10 inaugural clubs. Crew Stadium, built in 1999, is unique in that it is the country's very first stadium built specifically for soccer. It is located very close to The Ohio State University and can be seen and accessed from Route 71. Tickets to see "Columbus's Hardest Working Team" are still a great value. Individual tickets range from $16 to $35, while flexible season tickets cost between $49 and $558. The Crew Games are broadcast in English on 103.9 FM and in Spanish on 1550 AM.

Columbus Destroyers
Nationwide Arena
200 West Nationwide Boulevard
(614) 246-HITS, (877) COLS-AFL
www.columbusdestroyers.com

In 2003, the Buffalo Destroyers Arena Football team was relocated to Columbus. The team plays an eight-game season at Nationwide Arena throughout April and May. Former Buckeye and new head coach Chris Spielman made his coaching debut in January 2005. Year two saw the unveiling of a new logo and uniforms. Arena football tickets are one of the better values around town. A season subscription will run you anywhere from $99 to $234, while individual tickets cost between $11 and $30. The Destroyers games are broadcast live on their own six-station network, including 107.1 FM and 1270 AM in nearby Marysville.

Mid-Ohio Sports Car Course
7721 Steam Corners Road, Lexington
(800) MID-OHIO
www.midohio.com

One of the nation's top road-racing tracks is located 60 miles north of Columbus. This 2.4-mile track hosts a variety of motor sports, such as motorcycle racing, CART, and Vintage Grand Prix, as well as the largest amateur car race in the world. General admission tickets for a three-day weekend give access to the entire area except the grandstand and paddocks. Prices range from $25 to $50. Individual day tickets will run about $15 to $35. Children 12 and under are admitted free to the grounds and paddock areas, but tickets must be purchased for grandstand seating. Tent camping and motor home camping passes are sold on a first come, first served basis, and cost varies depending on the event.

National Trail Raceway
2560 National Road SW, Hebron
(740) 928-5706
www.nationalraceway.com

Every summer, you will inevitably notice an excessive number of vehicles towing hot rods and motorcycles along Interstate 70. More than likely, they are heading to National Trail Raceway near Buckeye Lake. Just 20 miles east of Columbus is a National Hot Rod Association championship drag-racing track. Throughout the summer, hard-core drag racers converge on central Ohio for a variety of events, including super gas races and the popular Night Under Fire, an event full of jet cars and trucks with fire exhaust and fireworks. The facility can accommodate crowds up to 120,000. General admission prices and gate times vary depending on the event, but a spectator will typically fork over $10 to get in, while racers will pay anywhere from $20 to $65.

Scioto Downs
6000 South High Street
(614) 491-2515
www.sciotodowns.com
One of Ohio's four harness tracks is located just 2 miles south of Route 270 on Route 23 (South High Street). Live harness racing is in season from May through September. The grandstand has the best view of the homestretch and can accommodate up to 3,500 fans, while the clubhouse is a full-service dining room and likewise provides good views of the track. When the weather cooperates, the outdoor patio puts you as close to the race as you can get. Simulcast of harness and thoroughbred racing is offered in the Penthouse Racebook, where there is a light menu and a full bar. Scioto Downs has a family-friendly atmosphere and can accommodate large groups with minimal notice. General grandstand admission is $1.50, and parking is $1.00. Admission into the clubhouse, patio, or penthouse is an additional $3.00.

THE ARTS

In the past 25 years, Columbus has seen a proliferation of cultural organizations and an explosion of art galleries, theatrical troupes, and community-based cultural events. The city's steady growth and the influx of transplants have led to many positive outgrowths within the arts community: the diversification of audiences, new venues in which to experience all sorts of music, opportunities to hear authors discuss or read from their works, exhibitions by international artists, and world-class theater and dance.

Columbus's arts scene is full of local talent and offers its residents access to emerging artists and famous traveling exhibitions. The performing arts take on a global and avant-garde perspective that one might not expect to find in the heartland of America. This is attributed partly to the young, growing, and highly mobile population of Columbus.

One of the drawbacks to this young, hip population is, when compared to places like Cleveland or Cincinnati (which are not growing), Columbus's arts seem to suffer a lack of regular subscribers and support on a community level. A survey by ArtsMarket Consulting has shown that Columbus residents are not completely aware of the quality and variety of arts opportunities that are available to them. This chapter's goal is to show the depth and breadth of Columbus's rich art scene to both visitors and residents alike.

Newcomers and the less informed will find valuable information at www.columbusarts.com. The Columbus Arts Web site maintains a sophisticated and updated database of various art activities in the region. It provides contact details, hours, and links to the Web sites of literary, theater, dance, and visual arts organizations, as well as links to body art, sacred art, and graphic designers. A good source of event information is the Experience Columbus Web site, as mentioned throughout this guide.

Columbus supports a number of visual arts venues, including an eclectic concentration of retail galleries in the Short North. You can get a festive overview of these shops during the popular Gallery Hop, which takes place the first Saturday of each month. Restaurants and shops stay open late, and many of the art galleries coordinate exhibitions and receptions around these weekends. It also is a great way to meet many of the artists whose work they promote.

Art hounds looking to admire rather than purchase will find everything from sculpture and painting to photography and glass on display somewhere in the city. Dolls, railroad equipment, and early televisions are the focus of a few small, specialized museums. The Impressionist and German Expressionist collections at the Columbus Museum of Art are outstanding. The museum does not have very many Old Masters, but lovers of all things modern will appreciate the visual arts in Columbus.

When it comes to the performing arts, Columbus is home to the Columbus Symphony Orchestra, BalletMet, Opera Columbus, jazz and chamber music ensembles, and a recent flood of professional and amateur theater groups. Many of them have formal seasons followed by a casual summer series. The more popular seasonal series have been included in this chapter.

A majority of performances are held at one of the three historic, downtown venues: the Palace Theatre, the Ohio Theatre, and the Southern Theatre. The newer Capitol Theatre at the Riffe Center and the Columbus Performing Arts Center offer more intimate settings for smaller and local productions.

While traditional performing and visual arts are well represented, Columbus's contemporary art scene is thriving. The city's youthful demographics and reputable art schools provide both a breeding ground and a good audience for cutting-edge art forms.

The Ohio State University and the Columbus College of Arts and Design are good places to watch for emerging artists. They host student and faculty exhibitions throughout the year and keep the local art scene interesting. Capital and Franklin Universities also have their own art galleries. Likewise, one shouldn't overlook the colleges as a source of quality affordable theater. Otterbein College Theatre is quite reputable and offers subscriptions to nine shows.

An increasing collaboration between the different art forms can be seen in the types of venues being developed. The Wexner Center, which is discussed in a Close-up later in this chapter, offers an interdisciplinary approach to contemporary art. Rather than limiting itself to one specific art form, the center has exhibition galleries, performance spaces, and film theaters. Grandview's Art Annex and MadLab are multiuse spaces where artists push the definition of art beyond their limits. The King Arts Complex is another example of a multidisciplinary venue with space for dance, visual arts, and educational programs.

Almost every major arts organization in the city has some sort of youth or adult art program. The Greater Columbus Arts Council Web site is the best place to search for community classes. A few adult programs have been mentioned here, but children's cultural activities are addressed in the Kidstuff chapter.

Ultimately, the best approach to Columbus arts is to check out the suggested Web sites or weekly calendar of events in free papers like *Alive!*, *The Short North Gazette*, and *The Other Paper*—and go experience art.

i

Columbus's flourishing and vibrant arts community earned the No. 12 spot in **American Style** ***magazine's annual "Top 25 Arts Destinations" in 2003.***

ART ORGANIZATIONS

Columbus Association for the Performing Arts (CAPA)
55 East State Street
(614) 469-0939
www.capa.com

Diverse musical programming makes CAPA one of the country's premier presenters of national and international artists. The various series cover a diverse mix of pop, folk, jazz, classical, and country entertainment. Comedy and theatrical performances are also given. Performances are held at all the major downtown venues and the Columbus Zoo Amphitheatre. CAPA's popular summer movie series includes classics like *Funny Face* and family flicks like *E.T.* All movies are held at the Ohio Theatre, and tickets are $3.50 for adults and $3.00 for seniors.

The Columbus Foundation
1234 East Broad Street
(614) 251-4000
www.columbusfoundation.org

In 2005, this community foundation gave $895,000 in grants to many of central Ohio's arts organizations. This unique organization provides financial support not only to the larger art institutions but also to the small, grassroots arts groups, where funds might be limited. The Community Arts Fund provides lesser grants to the small and medium-sized organizations that bring performance opportunities and art education to the community. Some of these recipients are Glass Axis, Chamber Music Columbus, and The Actor's Summer Theatre Company.

Dublin Arts Council
37 West Bridge Street, Dublin
(614) 889-7444
www.dublinarts.org

This local council offers high-caliber community classes in the performing, literary, and visual arts. Art shows, performances, and cultural events are held throughout Dublin, while changing art exhibitions take place in the gallery at 7125 Riverside Drive. A variety of programming is available to adults, teens, and children.

Greater Columbus Arts Council (GCAC)
100 East Broad Street
(614) 224-2606
www.gcac.org

The Greater Columbus Arts Council can be thanked for its role in stabilizing and advocating the arts in Columbus beginning in the early 1970s. Originally responsible for managing only the Columbus Arts Festival and a calendar of events, the GCAC recognized the city's rich art scene and developed a long-range plan to promote Columbus through its cultural activity.

Realizing the economic impact the arts have on Columbus, City Council developed a funding partnership with GCAC that currently distributes more than $2 million annually between 70 organizations. This funding goes to support individual fellowships, grants, community arts education, business arts partnership programs, public art initiatives, and so much more.

Throughout its 30-year history, the GCAC has become one of the most highly regarded local arts councils in the country. Its Web site is a great place to look for information on grants, community arts education and the Columbus Arts Festival.

Ohio Arts Council
727 East Main Street
(614) 466-2613, (888) 243-8622
www.oac.state.oh.us

This state agency supports the arts throughout Ohio by providing financial assistance to artists and art organizations. Funding comes from the Ohio General Assembly and the National Endowment for the Arts. Programming is focused on art access, innovation, and learning. The OAC's Riffe Gallery in downtown Columbus features changing exhibitions of Ohio artists and state museum collections.

Ohio Art League (OAL)
954 North High Street
(614) 299-8225
www.oal.org

This nonprofit organization has been supporting and representing Ohio artists across all disciplines for nearly a century. The OAL introduced George Bellows and Roy Lichtenstein to the world. It promotes the arts through workshops, lectures, and publications. A prestigious biannual juried art exhibition, held at the Columbus Cultural Arts Center, attracts the best of local artists. Joining the OAL is a good way to stay abreast of the Ohio arts scene. Membership starts at $35.

Worthington Arts Council
777 High Street, Worthington
(614) 431-0329
www.worthingtonarts.org

This not-for-profit organization has been promoting and supporting community arts and cultural activities for almost three decades. Their programming includes educational outreach, student exhibitions, and professional opportunities for local artists.

PERFORMING ARTS

BalletMet
Palace Theatre
34 West Broad Street, downtown
(614) 229-4848
www.balletmet.org

I have heard the word *intelligent* used to describe BalletMet's storytelling ability; the desire to sit through intermission to discuss a brilliant performance is testimony to this. The company's 28 dancers are known for their commitment to technique and the ability to handle the challenging and innovative choreography of artistic director Charles Gerard.

The troupe's repertoire includes classic, contemporary, and original choreography. The BalletMet season consists of six programs in addition to free performances, which are part of the summertime Rhythm on the River series. Their annual "Nutcracker" is new and improved.

In 1989, BalletMet made its international debut in Cairo, Egypt, and continues to entertain audiences beyond Columbus. As one of only 18 dance companies selected to perform at the Joyce Theatre in New York in 2004, their debut performance received rave reviews. BalletMet currently ranks among the top 12 companies in the country, while its dance academy and outreach programs are ranked fifth in size. Tickets usually range between $25 and $75, and additional discounts are given to students with a valid ID.

Columbus Symphony Orchestra
Ohio Theatre
55 East State Street
(614) 228-8600
www.columbussymphony.com
Central Ohio's oldest, largest, and most visible arts organization calls the historic Ohio Theatre home. The symphony performs more than 110 concerts a year and reaches an audience of 450,000 with live and broadcast performances. The CSO is on the hunt for a new music director but is temporarily under the artistic direction of Maestro Günther Herbig.

The regular season includes classical music that can be subscribed to in a variety of packages. Two hours prior to the show, students with a valid ID can purchase the best available tickets for only $8.00. During the regular season, concerts begin at 8:00 P.M. on Friday and Saturday and 3:00 P.M. on Sunday. The summertime series, which is slightly cheaper and more casual than the regular season, includes Picnic with the Pops and Popcorn Pops, a more family-oriented concert series.

Chamber Music Columbus
Various venues
(614) 267-2267
www.columbuschambermusic.org
This all-volunteer organization is one of Columbus's oldest and more inspired arts organizations. CMC has been showcasing national and international chamber music artists and ensembles for half a century. The season runs from October through May, and the concerts are held at Southern Theatre and various campus auditoriums. Many of the concerts are broadcast on WOSU-FM's *Music in Mid-Ohio* at a later date. The shows are a great value at $5.00 to $12.00.

The Columbus Bach Ensemble
Pontifical College Josephinum
7625 North High Street, Worthington
(614) 225-1685
www.columbusbachensemble.com
This is central Ohio's only Baroque orchestra and chorus, specializing specifically in the works of J. S. Bach. Most of the eight-concert series is performed in the beautiful, gothic-looking St. Turibius Chapel at the Josephinum, but a few are held at other venues.

Columbus Gay Men's Chorus
177 Naghten Street
(614) 265-7477
www.cgmc.com
This choir supports mainly gay men, but it is open to all individuals regardless of race, gender, or color. Year-round concerts are held at various venues, but the choir has recently moved to the Capitol Theatre in the Vern Riffe Center. Membership is by audition, and tickets can be purchased through Ticketmaster or directly from the chorus box office at (614) 228-CGMC.

Columbus Jazz Orchestra
33 Warren Street
(614) 294-5200
www.columbusjazzorchestra.com
This is the jazz lover's ticket to swing, jazz, and blues performed in a big-band

setting. The CJO plays music of the legendary greats: Gershwin, Duke Ellington, Count Basie, and Ray Charles, among others. The orchestra has toured Europe and features guest artists throughout the season. Performances take place primarily at the Southern Theatre and sometimes the Palace. Ticket packages vary in price and can be purchased through Ticketmaster or at the theatre box offices.

Opera Columbus
Mershon Auditorium
Wexner Center for the Arts, OSU campus
(614) 469-0939
www.operacolumbus.org
In 1981, Opera Columbus broke away from the Columbus Symphony Orchestra, then merged with Columbus Light Opera in 2001 to form an independent opera company. Beginning with the 2005-2006 season, the operas will be performed in grand style at the Mershon Auditorium on the OSU campus.

Opera Columbus maintains a traditional fall-winter season, with five heavier performances like *Tristan und Isolde* and *Don Giovanni.* Summertime brings lighter musical performances. Never fear, English subtitles are projected onto the screen above the stage. There is also no dress code for the opera, unless you feel like dressing up. We keep it casual in Columbus. Season subscriptions vary in price and can be purchased through the box office or Ticketmaster.

ProMusica Chamber Orchestra
Southern Theatre
21 East Main Street, downtown
(614) 464-0066
www.promusicacolumbus.org
This professional chamber orchestra was founded in 1978 and has earned a reputation as one of the top chamber orchestras in the country. It plays Baroque masterpieces, global music, and works specifically composed for small orchestras. Collaborations with other arts organizations throughout the city, traveling to schools and holding open rehearsals for seniors, have helped broaden its audience. Various series and special events are offered throughout the season. The subscription packages are well priced, and individual tickets cost around $20.

THEATER

The Actor's Theatre
(614) 444-6888
www.theactorstheatre.org
With Shakespeare as their focus, this troupe brings outstanding public theater to central Ohio. They provide outdoor theater to the community on a "free-will donation" basis, which provides locals who may not have the means to go to a formal theater with the opportunity to experience fine acting at a price they can afford—free. The season runs from May through September, and donations are accepted during intermission. There is no seating, so be sure to bring a blanket or chairs for theater alfresco at Schiller Park in German Village.

BlueForms Theatre Group
(614) 975-FROG
www.blueforms.info
According to *American Theatre* magazine, BlueForms is one of "a dozen young, American companies you need to know." This exciting new theater group emphasizes works that question society and culture. They reexamine existing plays and perform original pieces in an enlightening and entertaining way. Tickets are well priced at $10.00 and only $5.00 for students. Anyone under 18 can attend for free. They perform at various small venues and the Columbus Fringe Festival.

Broadway in Columbus
(614) 224-7654, (800) 294-1892
www.broadwayacrossamerica.com
Fifth-Third bank sponsors 8 to 10 national touring Broadway productions in Columbus each year. Shows like *The Producers, Phantom of the Opera,* and *The Lion King* are typically held at the Palace and Ohio Theatres. Prices vary. Tickets can be pur-

chased from Ticketmaster or Broadway Across America.

Capital University Theatre
2199 East Main Street, Bexley
(614) 236-6011
www.capital.edu
Capital's theater department puts on four productions a year and works in conjunction with the Conservatory of Music to stage the occasional musical. Plays include classics, Shakespeare, and contemporary scripts. Parking is free at the university.

Center Stage Players
(614) 306-0447
www.centerstageplayers.com
Central Ohio's only all-musical performance troupe is an all-volunteer organization and puts on campy cult classics like *The Rocky Horror Picture Show* and *The Best Little Whorehouse in Texas*. Performances are sometimes held at Buckeye Valley High School or Millennium Nightclub, but Axis Nightclub is this alternative group's home venue.

Columbus Theatre League
(614) 975-3764
www.theatresummit.net
This organization consists of five groups: BlueForms Theatre Group, MadLab, Pantheatrics, Out of Our Heads Improv, and Warehouse Theatre. The goal is to stimulate theater-going habits through awareness about the theater scene and various cross-promotional discount programs.

Contemporary American Theatre Company (CATCO)
77 South High Street
(614) 469-0939
www.catco.org
A dynamic ensemble of players makes up Columbus's premier professional theater company. Scripts range from American classics like *Cat on a Hot Tin Roof* to off-Broadway hits. Quirky, modern scripts by David Mamet and international plays are also part of the repertoire. This diverse theater company, which is becoming one of the nation's major regional theaters, can be seen in Studio One at the Riffe Center for the Arts. A variety of flex-ticket options and subscription packages vary in price for the seven-show season.

Broadway in Columbus tickets can be purchased as part of a "Dinner and Broadway" package at any of the downtown Cameron Mitchell restaurants. This includes a preshow dinner or matinee lunch and the best available tickets, which are delivered to your table during the meal. Call (614) 621-FOOD, or make your reservations online at www.cameronmitchell.com.

Curtain Players
5691 Harlem Road, Galena
(614) 470-4809
www.curtainplayers.com
This award-winning not-for-profit theater group was established in 1943 and has been performing in a 78-seat church-turn-theater since 1981. It is the only community theater with a paid artistic director and boasts six high-quality productions per season. Shows have included *Cash on Delivery, Angel Street,* and *The Last Night of Ballyhoo.* Prices range from $8.00 for individual tickets to $50 for the season.

Otterbein College Theatre
Campus Center Theatre
100 West Home Street, Westerville
(614) 823-1109
www.otterbein.edu
Otterbein offers individual tickets or subscriptions to the theater department's six annual productions. The theater is newly renovated, and the performances range from Neil Simon plays to musicals like *Jesus Christ Superstar.*

Red Herring Theatre Ensemble
(614) 469-0939
www.redherring.org
This semiprofessional theater group performs a variety of critically acclaimed, off-

Broadway-style plays and focuses on ensemble production work. Its home venue is in the Riffe Center at 77 South High Street. Individual tickets range from $10 to $26, and a season subscriptions cost between $34 and $85.

Warehouse Theatre Co.
(614) 488-9119
www.warehousetheatre.org
Formed in 2002, this troupe undertakes plays that are culturally significant to our generation and the new century. Shows are performed in the Van Fleet and Shedd Theaters at the Davis Discovery Center, 549 Franklin Avenue. Tickets vary in price, and students are given discounts with an ID.

WETCo
(614) 299-6774
www.wetco.org
The Women's Explosive Theatre Company was established in 2002 by six Ohio State University theater graduates frustrated with the number of good roles available to women. Their ambitious and eclectic productions earned them the 2004 runner-up spot for Best Live Theatre Company in *Columbus Alive*'s reader's poll. Shows are held at the Jewish Community Center, 1125 College Avenue. Tickets vary in price.

Women at Play
2990 Shadywood Road
(614) 457-6580
www.womenatplaysite.com
A group of female playwrights collaborate to produce their own original works that focus on women's issues or perform existing productions that address women's experiences and relationships. Many plays are site specific—the conservatory, gallery, or beauty salon—while a few are performed at the Davis Discovery Center. Tickets range from $10 to $20.

SEASONAL SERIES

CAPA Summer Movie Series
The Ohio Theatre
55 East State Street
(614) 469-1045
www.capa.com
During the summer, the historic Ohio Theatre reverts to its original function for CAPA's summer movie series. Classics like *The Godfather* and family films like *Indiana Jones* are shown in the air-conditioned theater on the big screen. Tickets are $3.00 to $3.50 and can be purchased at the kiosk.

Music in the Air
Various venues
(614) 645-7995, (614) 645-3800
www.musicintheair.org
Throughout the summer, free outdoor performances by local, national, and international acts are sponsored by the Columbus Department of Recreation and Parks. The concerts take place at various parks around the city. Rhythm on the River is held at the downtown Riverfront Amphitheatre on Friday nights during July and August. The Short North Sunday Jazz series brings favorite local jazz musicians to the Goodale Park Gazebo Sunday at noon, June through August. Call or check the Web site for a listing of free concerts held at Whetstone, Goodale, Franklin, and Topiary parks. Just be sure to bring your blanket or lawn chairs, as many of these concerts offer lawn seating only.

Picnic with the Pops
Olentangy River Road
(614) 228-8600
www.PicnicWithThePops.com
The Columbus Symphony Orchestra performs a variety of pop concerts out under the stars on the lawn of Chemical Abstracts throughout June and July. Highlights have included tunes by the Commodores, Broadway under the Stars, and a special performance by the Ohio State Marching Band. The tickets are cheaper and the performances more casual than

the formal season. Discounted lawn tickets are also available.

Shakespeare in the Park
Schiller Park, German Village
(614) 444-6888
www.theactorstheatre.org
Every summer since 1982, The Actor's Theatre Co. has taken the stage at Schiller Park Amphitheatre for the annual Shakespeare in the Park. Just bring a blanket and stretch out under the stars for a free dose of the bard's wit and wisdom. Schiller Park is located at 1069 Jaeger Street, and the plays begin around 8:00 P.M. Families are welcome, but it is suggested to keep the little ones under wraps, and turn your cell phones off.

VENUES

Capitol Theatre
Vern Riffe Center for the Government and the Arts
77 South High Street
(614) 460-7214
www.oac.state.oh.us
This intimate performance hall is located on the third floor of the Riffe building at the corner of High and State Streets. It is managed by CAPA, and smaller performances by BalletMet, local theater troupes, and touring productions like *Riverdance, Stomp,* and *Peter Pan* are held here. With seating for fewer than 1,000 people, there isn't a bad seat in the house.

Columbus Zoo Amphitheatre
9990 Riverside Drive, Powell
(614) 645-3550
www.colszoo.org
This intimate outdoor stage sits on the banks of the Scioto River and is a great place to catch a performance by the Columbus Children's Theatre or one of the CAPA-sponsored concert series. Parking is available on the zoo grounds for $2.00, and it is suggested guests bring chairs or blankets for lawn seating.

MadLab
105 North Grant Avenue
(614) 470-2333
www.madlab.net
Just slightly north of downtown, this alternative venue welcomes all types of artistic disciplines. Hosting highly experimental art forms, like Japanese noise art and avant-garde dance, this innovative arts facility has the capacity to support multimedia theater, music, dance, visual arts, and any other "undefined" art form. Traditional theatergoers may find the productions a little weird, but the culturally advanced just might like the group's daring and progressive approach to the arts. This former garage is a small, intimate theater that suits local productions' budgets and need for flexibility.

Martin Luther King Jr. Performing and Cultural Art Complex
867 Mount Vernon Avenue
(614) 645-5464
www.thekingartscomplex.com
This multifaceted facility is called the King Arts Complex for short. Built in 1925, it is on the National Register of Historic Places and is the only historic building in Columbus designed by an African-American architect. Its cultural and artistic programs focus on the African-American heritage and experience. Programming encompasses dance, music, and literary and visual arts. The Elijah Pierce Gallery showcases local and national artists, and there is ample free parking in the vicinity.

The Ohio Theatre
55 East State Street
(614) 469-1045
www.capa.com
A "palace for the average man" was built in the Spanish Baroque style in 1928. It was originally designed as a Loews movie house and seats nearly 2,800 people. This beautiful building is located across from the state capitol and is on the National Register of Historic Places. The Ohio was saved from the wrecking ball in 1969 and was subse-

Wexner Center for the Arts

You're wandering along High Street and notice a huge skeletal, disjointed-looking building sprawling across OSU campus. You stop and say, "What is this?"

Well, it's a lot of different things: a museum, a theater, a studio, and a library, but most importantly, it is a conversation piece. This experimental building is doing exactly what it was intended to do—make you think and talk.

The Wexner Center for the Arts is a multidisciplinary arts center conceived as a laboratory for contemporary visual and performing arts and film. The center opened in November 1989 after an unprecedented $225 million fundraising campaign. Leslie H. Wexner, chairman and founder of The Limited, Inc. and one of America's top 50 art collectors, footed a large portion of the bill. His contribution earned him the naming rights, so the building is dedicated to his father, Harry L. Wexner.

The design of the building was selected through an international competition, after which architects Peter Eisenman of New York and Richard Trott of Columbus were chosen. Their goal was to create a revolutionary structure that forces people to look at the world in a different way. They were indeed successful. The building itself is an embodiment of what is inside. The architecture often generates the same (sometimes hot) debate as the art it houses. Both challenge us to look at new forms and consider what is art or, in this case, architecture.

The Wexner Center's location serves as an entry point to the university. It is situated where The Ohio State University intersects the community—both literally and philosophically. In some ways, it links Columbus to the rest of the world through its promotion of international art and ideas. The entry plaza lines up directly with the runway at the Port Columbus airport, symbolizing artists coming from around the globe.

Architecturally, the building is full of symbolism. To put it simply, the slightly off-kilter nature of the building echoes the pattern of the campus's uneven street grid. Its scaffolding-like passageway represents the Wexner Center as an "unfinished" building, ready and willing to embrace new art. An effort to symbolically link the past with the future is seen in the castle-like towers on the south end of the facility. They are a visual reference to the turrets of the "Armory," a former campus building that once stood on the site of the Wexner Center.

The center has recently undergone two years' worth of renovations, which included infrastructural changes and improvements to the climate control systems. These upgrades greatly increased the flexibility and function of the gallery space through which exciting exhibitions revolve. The 12,000 square feet of gallery space has the capacity to handle all sorts

The Wexner Center for the Arts. SHAWNIE KELLEY

of traditional and nontraditional media. The Wexner Center has featured everything from sculpture and photography to multimedia and video installations.

Music, dance, and theater offered by the Wexner Center are as equally wide ranging and innovative as the visual arts. Performances take place on a variety of stages around campus, but the Mershon Auditorium is its primary venue. Built in 1957, the Mershon was renovated into a world-class theater in 1996. Seating around 2,500, it features a generous stage with a 75-seat orchestra pit and, like many European opera houses, has a concert-quality pipe organ. Thrilling contemporary artists, classical musicians, pop stars, and even OSU graduates have graced the Mershon stage.

This strong and challenging facility requires strong artists and artwork able to hold its own. Since its inception, the Wexner Center has hosted a long list of emerging artists, contemporary masters, and cultural pioneers. The exhibition/show archive reads like a "Who's Who" list: Twyla Tharp, Merce Cunningham, Roy Lichtenstein, Julie Taymor, and on and on. Visiting filmmakers have also been known to introduce their own films prior to screening.

The Wexner Center offers year-round films and videos that you won't find anywhere else in the city. Everything from cinematic classics and rare documentaries to independent and international films has turned up on the movie schedule. Annual film festivals and themed series are also part of the programming. Screening takes place in the Wexner Center for the Arts' Film and Video Theatre.

The Wexner Center for the Arts has been a building shrouded in controversy since the beginning, from the selection of the controversial architect (chosen for that very reason) to the current $14 million renovations to the art the center represents. It has gained notoriety for its groundbreaking architecture and put The Ohio State University on the cultural map with cutting-edge art. Whether you love it or hate it, the Wexner Center is like any worthwhile piece of art—it gets a reaction.

The Wexner Center offers the community wonderful public programming and lectures. It encourages artistic experimentation through a variety of student residencies and fellowships. Everything you need to know about the Wexner Center is somewhere on the extensive but user-friendly Web site: www.wexarts.org. Contact the information desk at (614) 292-3535, or visit in person at 1871 North High Street. You can't miss it!

quently purchased and restored by CAPA. Today it is home to BalletMet, the Columbus Symphony Orchestra, and the Broadway Series and hosts over 100 classical, theatrical, and comedic acts per year.

The Palace Theatre
34 West Broad Street
(614) 469-9850

The sumptuous Palace Theatre first opened as a vaudeville house and cinema in 1926. Over the years, all the big names in entertainment have taken the stage, making the Palace the most active live-show theater in Columbus. Although this theater never faced the same potential fate as the Ohio and Southern, it was likewise purchased by CAPA in 1989 and is now home to Opera Columbus. The Palace hosts a year-round schedule of performances by all of Columbus's major performing arts organizations and CAPA-sponsored shows and concerts. Parking is available directly behind the Palace Theatre in the LeVeque Tower garage for $3.00.

The world-renowned architect Thomas Lamb designed both the Palace and the Ohio theaters. The sweeping grand staircase of the Palace is proof of the inspiration drawn from the palace of Versailles, near Paris.

The Southern Theatre
21 East Main Street
(614) 340-9698
www.capa.com

The Southern Theatre opened in 1896 as part of the Great Southern Fireproof Hotel and Opera House. Its fireproof construction ensured structural longevity, but by 1979, the theater was in dire straights and closed. Like the Ohio Theatre, a public campaign saved the building, which was subsequently purchased and gifted to CAPA in 1986. A 14-month overhaul brought Columbus's only 19th-century theater back to life in a magnificent way. The intimate interior is striking, with its gold gilding, soft lighting, and electric blue curtain. The Southern is home of the Columbus Jazz Orchestra, ProMusica Chamber Orchestra, and Columbus Gay Men's Chorus and hosts several touring productions throughout the year. Its inclusion on the National Register now ensures the great Southern the legacy it was intended to have. Suggested parking is in the City Center garage on Main Street.

VISUAL ARTS

Museums

Columbus Museum of Art
480 East Broad Street
(614) 221-6801
www.columbusmuseum.org

The museum, established in 1878, is located 4 blocks east of downtown, and you'll know you've found it when you see the big bronze Henry Moore sculpture in front of the Broad Street entrance. With more than 9,000 works, the museum houses an outstanding collection of late-19th- and early-20th-century American and European modern art. Works by Degas, Monet, Matisse, Picasso, and Ernst make up an exceptional collection of modernism.

The two names one encounters repeatedly associated with the museum collections are Howald and the Siraks. The museum can thank Ferdinand Howald, an important collector of early-20th-century American and European art, for his contribution of 280 works in 1931. Sixty years after this gift, Howard and Babette Sirak gave their personal collection of 78 pieces of European impressionism and expressionism a new home at the CMA.

The Museum of Art is particularly well known for its superb regional collections of Columbus's very own Elijah Pierce and George Bellows. The museum boasts the largest public collection of woodcarvings by folk artist Elijah Pierce. It also acts as repository for the world's biggest collection of paintings and lithographs by George Bellows, one of the finest American artists of his time.

Other highlights include pieces by Edward Hopper, Norman Rockwell, and Georgia O'Keeffe. Frederick Schumacher gifted his collection of 17th- and 18th-century works to the museum in 1957. The outdoor sculpture garden has a substantial collection of 20th-century pieces, while "Eye-Spy: Adventures in Art" is an interactive display for children and families.

Visitors can dine at the Palette Cafe and browse the Children's Shop or the Museum Gift Shop. The museum charges $6.00 for adults and $4.00 for students and seniors. Sunday is free for everyone. CMA is closed Monday and stays open until 8:30 P.M. on Thursday. Parking is $3.00, but admission and parking are free for members.

Meet Me @ the Museum is a social event held at the museum every Thursday from 5:30 to 8:30 P.M. It features gallery tours, light food, a cash bar, and local musical entertainment. The cost is regular admission, and parking is free after 5:30.

The lively Gallery Hop is held the first Saturday night of each month. Restaurants, bars, shops, and galleries stay open late and host special exhibitions and entertainment.

Early Television Museum
5396 Franklin Street, Hilliard
(614) 771-0510

The free museum displays a fantastic collection of early television sets. Highlights include mechanical sets made between 1929 and 1932 and early color television from 1954. It is open only on weekends.

Ohio Craft Museum
1665 West Fifth Avenue, Grandview
(614) 486-4402
www.ohiocraft.org

This museum houses a permanent collection of contemporary crafts and hosts small changing exhibits and five major exhibitions per year. The Craft Research

Library is on-site, and educational workshops are offered. The museum is closed on Saturday, and admission is free.

Ohio Railway Museum
990 Proprietors Road, Worthington
(614) 885-7345
www.ohiorailwaymuseum.org
One of the oldest railway museums in the nation is here. This museum was founded in 1948 and houses a collection of 30 pieces of vintage railway equipment. Take a demonstration ride on one of the museum's streetcars or interurbans, and learn the history of electric transportation. It is open Memorial Day through Labor Day, and a small admission is charged.

Old Rectory Doll Museum
50 West New England Avenue
Worthington
(614) 885-1247
Nineteenth-century dolls and toys are on rotated display at this small specialized museum operated by the Worthington Historical Society. Highlights are American, French, German, and Parisian bisque fashion and milliners' dolls. Docent-guided tours may be arranged, otherwise tours are self-guided. The museum is closed Sunday and Monday but open year-round. A small admission is charged.

Riffe Gallery
Vern Riffe Center for the Government and the Arts
77 South High Street, downtown
(614) 644-9624
www.oac.state.oh.us
This free gallery features changing exhibitions by Ohio artists and collections from state museums. The exhibits are organized by guest curators striving to present the breadth, depth, and vision of Ohio arts. Located in the same building as Capitol Theatre, this open and airy gallery is a nice place to browse before a concert. It closes at 4:00 P.M. most days but remains open until 8:00 P.M. on Wednesday and Saturday. It is closed Monday.

RETAIL GALLERIES

Several art and photography galleries are clustered in the Short North Arts District, but much of the gallery scene is spattered around the city. You can park and walk to a variety of long-established galleries in Bexley and German Village, while newer ones are popping up around Clintonville and Grandview. Many galleries will send out invitations to their opening exhibitions to those on their mailing lists. ColumbusArts.com has a somewhat exhaustive listing of galleries and links to their Web sites.

A Muse Gallery
996 West Third Avenue, Grandview
(614) 299-5003, (877) 299-5003
www.amusegallery.com
This unique gallery represents over 40 contemporary artists who work in a variety of mediums and are collected and shown around the world. The underlying tone of the pieces and the soft ambience of the gallery space are one of sensuality. Owner Caren Petersen provides corporate and private art consulting services as well. Her second location, 2Muse, is at 855 Grandview Avenue in the new Global Living building.

Art Access Gallery
540 South Drexel Avenue, Bexley
(614) 338-8325
www.artaccessgallery.com
This fine-arts gallery, located in the heart of Bexley, was once a post office. It specializes in regional artists and carries an eclectic mix of oil and acrylic paintings, pastels, gouache, lithography, and sculpture. Exhibitions change each month.

Gallery 3131
3131 North High Street, Clintonville
(614) 327-4800
www.gallery3131.com
This storefront operation serves as owner Chris Niswanger's graphic design firm and gallery space. While the identity of this new gallery is being developed, the pri-

mary goal is to make art more accessible to the general public and to debunk the myth that art is elitist. The gallery shows works in a variety of styles and medium by local professional and amateur artists.

Gallery V
694 North High Street, Short North
(614) 228-8955
www.galleryv.com

As one of the most respected galleries in Columbus, Gallery V has been featuring regional, national, and international artists since opening in 1993. Director Lynne Muskoff is the only one of the original five owners to have stuck it out in the Columbus art scene—and we're grateful she did. This place is a class act. It may look intimidating when you walk by, but beginners and collectors are made to feel equally welcome. Works by Han Xin and Barbara Vogel are among the 35 artists currently represented. The gallery can be rented for private parties that are catered by Rigsby's Volatile Cuisine.

Glass Axis Studio & Gallery
1341-B Norton Avenue, Grandview
(614) 291-4250
www.glassaxis.org

This nonprofit arts organization was established in 1987 as a place where students and members of the community can come together and exchange ideas about the medium of glass. This unique full-service studio has grown to include a cold shop and hot shop, and flame- and kiln-working facilities. Membership is offered to experienced students at discounted rates, allowing them use of the facilities, while members of the community can register for all levels of glassblowing classes. Demonstrations and fundraising events are also held on-site.

Hammond Harkins Galleries
2264 East Main Street, Bexley
(614) 238-3000
www.hammondharkins.com

This fine-arts gallery features contemporary painting and sculpture. Among its premier landscape painters are Paul Hamilton and David Jewell. Sculptors Joan Wobst and Tony Davenport are also represented. A second location is on Summer Street in Edgartown, Massachusetts, on Martha's Vineyard.

Hawk Galleries
153 East Main Street, downtown
(614) 225-9595
www.hawkgalleries.com

Making the move from the Short North to a downtown location doesn't seem to have mattered. *Columbus Monthly* readers voted Hawk Galleries the Best Art Gallery in Columbus in 2004. This open and airy gallery features original blown-glass art and 3-D art. It also carries contemporary ceramics, crystal, and metal sculpture. Director Tom Hawk believes collecting studio glass is the best value in fine arts today. His gallery represents an impressive list of 40 artists, including 2 of the world's foremost living glass artists: Dale Chihuly and Lino Tagliapietra.

Keny Galleries
300 East Beck Street, German Village
(614) 464-1228
www.kenygalleries.com

The brothers Keny have a treasure trove of American artworks packed into a quaint German Village town house. They deal in historic American paintings and 19th- and 20th-century folk art, but specialize in master watercolors by big names, like Winslow Homer and Alice Schille, as well as prominent Ohio artists like Edward Potthast and George Bellows. You'll also find works by contemporary folk artists and the great folk masters such as Elijah Pierce and William Hawkins. The prices are reasonable, considering the Kenys have been known to sell pieces to major museums, such as the National Gallery of Art.

Kiaca Gallery
941 North High Street, Short North
(614) 298-0028

Owner Talle Bamazi has brought the best of contemporary African art to Columbus in an innovative and philosophical way.

The gallery, which opened in 2003, features both national high-profile artists and talent indigenous to Columbus. Art offerings range from free-standing sculpture and mixed media paintings to photography. Bamazi, an award-winning painter and graduate of the New York Academy of Art, teaches painting classes to children and adults at Kiaca.

Lindsay Gallery
986 North High Street, Short North
(614) 291-1973
www.lindsaygallery.com
This comfortable gallery is situated on the northern most end of the Short North and features American folk and outsider art. Wondering what exactly outsider art is? Just pop in and ask Duff Lindsay. The owner is more than happy to oblige you with a definition by pointing out the pieces hanging on the wall. Given the vision and creativity, it's hard to believe most of the artists represented by this dealer are self-taught or have no formal training. There is a little bit of everything at this gallery; just take a peek in the back room!

Rebecca Ibel Gallery
1055 North High Street, Short North
(61) 291-2555
www.rebeccaibel.com
Working with emerging and mid-career artists, this gallery has been exhibiting contemporary painting, sculpture, and photography in Columbus since 1993. Ibel recently opened a second location in the ultramodern Two Miranova Place, downtown.

The Roberts Gallery
539 South Drexel Avenue, Bexley
(614) 236-1245
www.robertsgallery.com
This cozy, sophisticated art gallery deals in a variety of paintings, prints, and engravings. Many of the paintings, old or new, tend to be impressionistic in style. Despite its high-rent location in downtown Bexley, the atmosphere is laid back, and the owner, Brian Roberts, makes you feel right at home whether you are looking to buy some artwork or have it appraised. The gallery also provides restoration and framing services.

Roy G. Biv
997 North High Street, Short North
(614) 297-7694
This nonprofit public art gallery was started by a few Columbus College of Art and Design students and is considered one of the edgier galleries in town. It can afford to take more risks, because government subsidization alleviates the need for pressure sales. Roy G. Biv features many different types of media, including paintings, ceramics, mobiles, and sculptures, encompassing a variety of genres. Exhibitions change monthly.

Sherrie Gallerie
937 North High Street, Short North
(614) 298-8580
One way to alleviate art's intimidation factor is to throw a little jewelry in the mix. Sherrie Hawk's new gallery focuses primarily on individual ceramic artists but lures passersby in with one-of-a-kind, handcrafted jewelry. The gallery features ceramic sculpture, wall hangings, dinnerware, and blown glass. The occasional collection of wearable art is thrown into the exhibition mix.

ATTRACTIONS 

Columbus isn't exactly a mecca of tourism, but if you are here to see the sights, you'll find it an easy and unintimidating city to explore. We have plenty of unique attractions that rate high with out-of-towners. Our world-class zoo and the seven-story building shaped like a Longerberger basket are two of the sights visitors (and longtime residents) should make the effort to see.

Consider the city's namesake and pay a visit to the *Santa Maria,* an authentic replica of Christopher Columbus's flagship. Then consider the Native Americans and check out one of the ancient Indian mounds located in and around Columbus. I have included only one in this chapter, but you can contact the Ohio Historical Society at (614) 297-2300 or www.ohiohistory.org for a full listing of mounds, earthworks, and Native American sites in Ohio.

Some of Columbus's attractions are located downtown (or close by), while the rest are scattered about the city. This chapter's entries are divided into three categories reflecting this division: "Downtown," "Surrounding Neighborhoods," and "Farther Afield," meaning within an hour's drive.

Major public monuments are included here rather than The Arts chapter because they have a broad appeal to a variety of people and are often located on public grounds. Amusements and attractions catering specifically to children have been listed in the Kidstuff chapter, while places of interest over an hour away can be found in Day Trips and Weekend Getaways.

Columbus has activities in all prices ranges. Admission to most of the attractions included here are under $10 per person. Rather than assign price codes, only the exceptions will be noted. Not much is free in Columbus, so if you live here or frequent the city, consider joining your favorite organization or taking out a membership that gives additional benefits and ongoing free entry.

As a final note, two of the best sources of information on attractions in Columbus are the yellow pages and *Experience Columbus.* The front of the phone book has a very general listing of the major attractions and their contact details. *Experience Columbus* has a more comprehensive list of sites and events. The Web site www.experiencecolumbus.com has a search function allowing you to sort by location and date, or you can call (614) 221-2489 or (866) EXP-COLS for further information.

DOWNTOWN

Center of Science and Industry (COSI) Columbus
333 West Broad Street
(614) 228-COSI, (888) 819-2674
www.cosi.org

This hands-on science museum is currently celebrating its 40th anniversary and has shuffled more than 17 million visitors through its doors to discovery. Aside from being one of the most popular attractions in Columbus, it is one of the more well-respected science centers in the country. COSI is currently located in what was once the Central High School, but the grand classical architecture makes it look more like a majestic state building sitting along the banks of the Scioto River.

This living museum provides hands-on, discover-based exhibits, where kids of all ages (and parents) can explore how things work in the world around them. There are eight exhibition areas called "learning worlds," many with interactive displays allowing visitors to conduct their own underwater experiments, explore space, or try their hand at the country's only high-wire unicycle.

Separate admission is charged for the outdoor Big Science Park and the iWERKS Extreme Screen Theatre, where mind-boggling scientific and cultural movies are shown several times a day. Admission for adults (13 and older) is $12.00, for children $7.00. Combination passes to the science center and theater are $17 and $12, respectively. Children under 2 are admitted free of charge. The annual membership levels vary in cost. The science center is closed Monday and Tuesday.

Greater Columbus Convention Center
400 North High Street
(614) 827-2500, (800) 626-0214
www.columbusconventions.com

The Greater Columbus Convention Center is located in an area that was once Columbus's major railroad terminal. Architecturally, it strives to reflect this in the shape and pastel coloring of the rectangular buildings that, from the air, look like boxcars. This multipurpose facility straddles the Short North and downtown.

The center plays host to many of Columbus's biggest conferences, competitions, and expositions. It is conveniently located near the major entertainment districts and within walking distance of several reputable hotels and restaurants. It also has its own food court and shops.

Ohio Statehouse
Broad and State Street
(614) 728-2130, (888) 644-6123
www.statehouse.state.oh.us

The symbolic center of the city encompasses 10 acres called Capitol Square and is the country's eighth oldest working capitol building. The statehouse, interchangeably referred to as the Capitol, has been used by legislators since 1857 and is recognized as a National Historic Landmark.

After the first statehouse on this site burned down, the current building was constructed of Columbus limestone in the Greek Revival style between 1838 and 1861. Prison labor from the penitentiary was used to construct the ground level of the building. An 1840s rumor held that all good stone masons had to be very wary of the law. Otherwise, they would end up in jail for the silliest thing and forced to use their talent on the statehouse.

Nathan B. Kelly was the architect responsible for the design of the lavish center rotunda and cupola, along with other architectural improvements, such as installing a heating and ventilation system. Building resumed in the 20th century, with the judiciary annex finished in 1901, and an atrium, built in 1993 connects the statehouse and Senate Building. Both buildings were restored to their original beauty in 1996.

Among the sights not to miss are the statehouse rotunda's lavish marble floor and stained-glass skylight; the reproductions of original desks, carpets, and chandeliers in the House of Representative and Senate chambers; the marble map of Ohio in the Map Room; and the original mosaic tile floor of the Grand Staircase in the Senate Building.

The statehouse is open seven days a week between 7:00 A.M. and 7:00 P.M. A free 45-minute guided tour gives an in-depth look at the history, architecture, and functions of the building. Information can be obtained in the rotunda, accessible from High Street, or the information desk at the Third Street entrance. The visitor center, which includes a cafeteria and gift shop, is located on the ground floor of the building.

Santa Maria
Battelle Riverfront Park
Marconi Boulevard
(614) 645-8760
www.santamaria.org

This full-size replica of Columbus's flagship offers a museum-quality look at the lives, games, and navigational tools of 15th-century explorers. Costumed interpreters dramatize the events of the mission on this 98-foot wooden cargo ship. Tours last about 45 minutes and run from May through October. The *Santa Maria* ends the season with a haunted ship event around Halloween. There is a mod-

Ohio Statehouse Monuments

There are several interesting monuments located on the grounds of the statehouse, making for a nice walking tour. The following is a quick explanation of the more interesting sculptures and their location.

Cannons: The four cannons, which consist of two Napoleon 6-pounders and two 12-pounders, were made of cast bronze at the Miles Greenwood foundry in Cincinnati, Ohio, in 1864.

Christopher Columbus Discovery Plaza: This statue, located on the south side of the statehouse, was made for the Pontifical College Josephinum by Alphons Pelzer in 1892. When the Josephinum moved to Worthington in 1932, it was gifted to the state.

McKinley Monument: On the west side of the statehouse is the 1906 monument to assassinated President William McKinley made by H. A. MacNeil, of New York.

Mount Vernon Sundial Replica: The Daughters of the American Revolution erected this sundial in 1932 on the north side of the statehouse.

Ohio Veterans' Plaza: This veterans' memorial was designed by Schooley Caldwell Associates in 1998 as a reminder that our government could not exist without the sacrifices of our veterans. It is dedicated to all Ohio men and women who have served in the armed forces since World War II. It also serves as the east entrance to the statehouse and features a drive-through, drop-off area.

Ohio World War Memorial: World War I American infantrymen are honored in this 1930 sculpture designed by Arthur Ivone. It is located on the west stairs of the statehouse.

"Peace" Statue: In 1923, the Women's Relief Corps of Ohio erected this statue by Bruce Wilder Saville on the north side of the statehouse in honor of Civil War soldiers.

"These Are My Jewels" Statue: The oldest monument on the statehouse grounds was designed by Levi Tucker Scofield of Cincinnati for the World's Columbian Exposition of 1893. Portrayed in the statues are Cabinet members Edwin M. Stanton, secretary of war, and Salmon P. Chase, secretary of the treasury; Presidents James A. Garfield, Rutherford B. Hayes, and Ulysses S. Grant; and Generals William Sherman and Phillip Sheridan. The female figure is Cornelia. It was moved to the capitol in 1894 and is now located at the northwest corner of the statehouse.

est admission fee, and the tall ship can be rented for overnight programs and special events.

Thurber House
77 Jefferson Avenue
(614) 464-1032
www.thurberhouse.org

One of America's greatest humorists, James Thurber, and his family lived in this house during his college years at The Ohio State University (1913–1917). It has been lovingly restored as a literary center, museum, and bookstore and is on the National Registry of Historic Places. Literary pilgrims can tour several rooms of early-20th-century period furnishings and may even bump into a few ghosts. Highlights include the typewriter Thurber used when working for the *New Yorker* magazine.

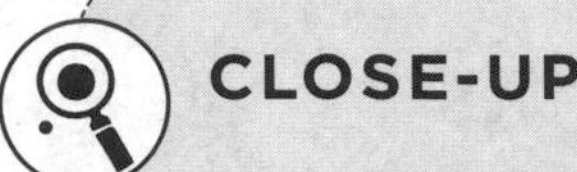

A Little Monkey Business

A handful of animals were donated to the Columbus Zoological Park (now the Franklin Park Conservatory) in 1927, setting the direction for a fully planned zoo. Its current location swallows up nearly 600 acres of land and houses 700 species and 7,800 specimens of animals. Some 2.5 million visitors now pass through the grounds of this world-class zoo each year.

Construction of buildings and the acquisition of animals occurred throughout the 1940s and 50s. The 1970s brought about the implementation of an education department designed to promote awareness of human relationships to the natural world. It was in the '80s and '90s that the Columbus Zoo came into its own. Director Emeritus Jack Hanna built national recognition for the zoo through frequent television appearances. Most people will remember him on *Late Night with David Letterman*. Hanna, however, was not the zoo's first celebrity.

The year 1956 saw the birth of the world's first captive-born gorilla, Colo. She celebrated her 48th birthday in 2004 and has been the cornerstone of a ground-breaking gorilla breeding program. This event foreshadowed the revolutionary facility the Columbus Zoo would become as a leading breeder of many endangered species. It is known worldwide for breeding lowland gorillas, cheetahs, polar bears, and 40 species of turtles. The zoo has reintroduced West Indian manatees, Mexican wolves, bald eagles, and Atlantic loggerhead and Pacific green sea turtles into the wild.

The zoo is broken up into various regions that simulate the natural environment of the animal's native continent. Educational signage is displayed throughout the exhibits. The North American Region is the largest. It features bears, wolves, bison, moose, and cougars. The African Forest exhibits animals native to both the lowlands and the Congo: bonobos, lions, chimpanzees and leopards, to name a few. The Voyage to Australia and the Islands of Southeast Asia feature not only orangutans, kangaroos, and komodo dragons, but also a boat ride through the islands.

There are exhibition areas dedicated to specific species of animals. The Flamingo/Alligator Exhibit houses colorful birds native to the southeastern United States and the Caribbean. The Humboldt Penguin exhibition provides underwater views of these birds who think they are living on the west coast of South America. The Discovery Reef is a 100,000-gallon aquarium designed to simulate a coral reef from a scuba diver's perspective. Colorful fish, stingrays, and sharks call this home.

When it comes to one-of-a-kind exhibits, the Columbus Zoo is one of only a few in the country that permanently houses koalas. It has the world's largest display of pachyderm and a collection of reptiles also among the largest of its kind.

Discovery Reef at the Columbus Zoo and Aquarium. COLUMBUS ZOO AND AQUARIUM

The Columbus Zoo is one of only three facilities outside Florida to exhibit the rare West Indian manatee.

The zoo is an incredibly interactive and hands-on place to take your family. Habitat Hollow is an educational exhibit focused on habitat preservation. Wings, Stings, and Play Things Park is a giant kids' insect-themed playground. There is a petting zoo, train, and pony rides, as well a 1914 vintage carousel with all 52 of its original horses. There are programs and special events year-round for adults and children. Several food courts and gift shops can be found throughout the grounds.

The zoo is located at 9990 Riverside Drive in Powell (614-645-3550 or 800-MONKEYS). It is open every day of the year. Admission is $12.00 for adults and $7.00 for children. Children 2 and under are free. Senior admission is $3.50 on Tuesday and Franklin County residents (with ID) receive 50 percent off regular admission on Wednesday. Membership will get you reciprocation to other zoos throughout the country. Parking is $3.00. For more information visit www.columbus zoo.org.

Abraham Lincoln visited the statehouse three times. A plaque commemorates a speech he gave to Ohioans shortly after the Lincoln-Douglas debates in 1859. He addressed the legislature in 1861, and his final visit was on April 29, 1865. Lincoln lay in state for a day in the rotunda as his casket was transported to its final resting place in Illinois.

The gallery presents book-related exhibitions and year-round programs, which include writing classes for children, author readings, and Thurber celebrations. Thurber House programming goes beyond Columbus city limits by sponsoring the Thurber Prize for American Humor and an adult writer-in-residence. The bookstore carries all of Thurber's books in print. The museum is open daily from noon to 4:00 P.M., and admission is free. Guided tours are offered on Sunday for a small fee.

Topiary Garden
Old Deaf School Park
480 East Town Street
(614) 645-6640
www.topiarygarden.org

This clever garden art is modeled after French artist Georges Seurat's late-19th-century painting titled *A Sunday Afternoon on the Isle de la Grande Jatte.* This postimpressionist landscape painting is translated into a real landscape and is the only such re-creation in the world. The ensemble consists of 54 topiary people, 8 boats, 3 dogs, a cat, and a monkey, making it one of the nation's largest topiary gardens.

The garden is best viewed from the east, as the artist conceived the painting from a hill in the east overlooking the Seine River. This project was conceived by James Mason, an instructor at the Columbus Recreation and Parks Department's Cultural Arts Center. The topiary is maintained by the department, and the museum shop, which funds the garden, is located in the gatehouse and open April through December. Entrance to the garden is free.

SURROUNDING NEIGHBORHOODS

"Field of Corn" Sculpture
Dublin and Rings Road, Dublin

In celebration of Dublin's agricultural heritage, this display of public art was commissioned by the Dublin Arts Council in 1994. Columbus artist Malcolm Cochran cast 109 6-foot ears of white concrete corn that stand upright in rows at the intersection of two major roads. On closer look, the layout resembles the white grave markers in Arlington National Cemetery. Osage orange trees and office buildings serve as the backdrop, but from certain angles this is quite a photo opportunity.

Franklin Park Conservatory
1777 East Broad Street, Columbus
(614) 645-8733, (800) 214-PARK
www.fpconservatory.org

Three miles east of downtown is a classic turn-of-the-century conservatory listed on the National Register of Historic Places. A plant house has been on this site since 1895. The conservatory showcases more than 400 species of plants from a variety of climate zones. Highlights include large bonsai and orchid collections and the country's largest public display of poinsettias during the holidays.

The conservatory encompasses 28 acres and includes sculptures, fountains, a Japanese garden, and an outdoor amphitheater that hosts summer concerts. Special events, such as an annual living butterfly display and changing art exhibitions, are held throughout the year. Admission is $6.50 for adults and $3.50 for children. Students and seniors are given discounts with proper ID. It is closed Monday.

Leatherlips Sculpture
Scioto Park
7377 Riverside Drive, Dublin
The Dublin Arts Council commissioned this 12-foot limestone sculpture in 1990 as the first in its Art in Public Places program. Each piece relates to Dublin history. This portrait memorializes Wyandot Native American Chief Leatherlips. Local history holds he was executed by fellow tribesmen near Scioto Park. Climb up into the open head and you'll get a great view of the river and amphitheater. *Leatherlips* was created by Boston artist Ralph Helmick and is located in Dublin's Scioto Park, just off Route 257.

Motorcycle Hall of Fame Museum
13515 Yarmouth Drive, Pickerington
(614) 856-2222
The headquarters of the American Motorcycle Association is located just 15 miles east of downtown Columbus and houses the Motorcycle Hall of Fame Museum. On display are historical and classic through present-day bikes. There are also plaques with information about the inductees to the Hall of Fame. The museum is open regular business hours daily, and a small admission is charged. Seniors get a discount, and children 18 and under are free.

Ohio Expo Center
717 East 17th Avenue
(614) 644-3247, (888) OHO-EXPO
www.ohioexpocenter.com
The 150-year-old Ohio Expo holds over 200 events year-round. This huge 360-acre facility is home to 6 of the 12 major events held in Columbus, the Ohio State Fair and Quarter Horse Congress being the two largest. Other events range from horse, cattle, and dog shows to the monthly Scott antiques show and the annual Sugarloaf Crafts Festival.

There are 20 buildings in the complex, with ties for 2,000 cattle and the capacity to seat up to 20,000 people. The center is located just off Route 71, a few minutes from downtown and near the OSU campus. Parking rates vary per vehicle, depending on the event. Traffic becomes very congested in this area before and after events.

Shrum Mound
Campbell Park
McKinley Avenue, Hilliard
(614) 297-2630
It is held that this ancient mound was built by the Adena Indians sometime between 800 B.C. and A.D. 100. Shrum is the last remaining conical burial mound in Columbus and is maintained by the Ohio Historical Society. Visitors are sometimes disappointed to see it is "just" a 20-by-100-foot mound of grass with stairs leading to the top, but it is the ancient and sacred nature of the site that makes it special. Entry is free.

"Watch House" Sculpture
Coffman Park
5600 Post Road, Dublin
Symbolism abounds in this 1998 sculpture created by Columbus artist Todd Slaughter. A symbol of the connection between Dublin's past (the native culture) and present (the contemporary culture) is seen in a copper house that sits atop an earthen Native American–inspired mound. Prairie grass and sunflowers refer to the garden crops of Ohio's first farmers. The windows cut out of the planetarium-like dome represent the expanding and changing nature of the landscape, people, and universe. Admission is free.

FARTHER AFIELD

Dresden Village and
Longaberger Homestead
5563 Raiders Road, Dresden
(740) 322-5588
www.longaberger.com
Dresden was a tiny village when the Longaberger family first came to Ohio in 1896, but it is now headquarters to one of the Forbes Top 500 private companies in America, the famous handmade basket company started by Dave Longaberger in

1976. Pictures don't do justice to the Longaberger Company's home office near Newark. The building is a replica of the Longaberger market basket, only 160 times larger. Tours of this basket building are available seven days a week.

The nearby Homestead shares the Longaberger story and traditions. Tourists are shuttled in by busloads. The faithful pilgrimage to this state-of-the-art basket-weaving facility and to see the world's largest apple basket. They tour a replica of the founder's home, weave their own baskets, and shop till they drop.

Longaberger also has an 18-hole golf course of tournament caliber, accommodating every skill level with five sets of tees. You can read more about the golf course in the Golf chapter. A magnificent clubhouse features a restaurant and golf shop. The Place Off the Square is a 117-room hotel owned and operated by the Longaberger Company. It has two more restaurants, an indoor pool, gift shop, and banquet facilities.

A whole calendar of events encompassing craft and quilt shows, heritage days, and holiday events can be found online. Hours of operations and cost vary, depending on what you want to do and the season, so it is best to call ahead.

Ohio Caverns
2210 East State Route 245, West Liberty
(937) 465-4017
www.ohiocaverns.com

The largest of Ohio's caverns is open regular business hours, year-round, and are located beneath the grounds of a 35-acre park with shelters and picnic areas. Visitors are guided through the colorful stalactite and stalagmite formations on a 45-minute, mile-long tour. The path is level and paved, but you should wear sturdy walking shoes. Regardless of the outdoor weather, the interior of the caverns remains a constant 54° Fahrenheit, so bring a jacket. Admission is charged.

Olentangy Indian Caverns
1779 Home Road, Delaware
(740) 548-7917
www.olentangyindiancaverns.com

Beautiful limestone passages were formed millions of years ago by underground rivers cutting their way through solid rock. They were used by local Native Americans and rediscovered in 1821 by J. M. Adams, a member of a westbound wagon train. Today, guided tours are offered through the winding maze of underground rooms integrated with stories of ancient Indian lore. The tour features a "Council Rock" used by the Wyandottes for tribal ceremonies.

Artifacts and geological exhibits can be seen at the on-site museum, and goods can be purchased at the gift shop. Tours are offered April 1 through October 31, and there is an admission fee of $8.00 for adults and $5.00 for children ages 7 to 15. Those under 7 are free. A 25-foot climbing wall, 18-hole miniature golf course, petting zoo, and picnic areas are also located on the grounds.

The Wilds
14000 International Road, Cumberland
(740) 638-5030, (866) 444-WILDS
www.thewilds.org

Can't afford a safari? A day at the Wilds is nothing short of a trip to Africa! This 10,000-acre wildlife conservation park, tucked in the hills of Ohio, is the largest facility of its kind in North America. Guided tours in open-air buses will allow you to see large groups of rhinos, giraffes, Asian wild horses, red wolves, mountain zebra, gazelle, and many other species. Bird lovers come to spot some of the 150 bird species documented here.

The safari-style tours allow for spectacular photography and wildlife sightings, while the observations decks along Lake Trail Mini-Park and the Outpost offer extended viewing areas. Dine in the Overlook Cafe and shop in the Gift Market, or better yet, stay on the property in The

Lodge at the Wilds. A special Sunset Safari, which includes a twilight dinner and guided tour, is offered seasonally.

The Wilds is open Wednesday through Sunday, June through August, and Saturday and Sunday in May, September, and October. Adult admission is $12.00, and children are $7.00. Annual memberships are available. The Wilds is located 20 miles southeast of Zanesville, about an hour east of Columbus.

HISTORICAL SOCIETIES

History buffs will be excited to learn there are several preserved or restored 19th-century homes in and around the city, many of which are operated by local historical societies. Included here are just a few of Columbus's active and better known societies. Some of them maintain their own collections or work out of interesting landmark buildings. Most put on annual holiday events, offer walking tours, and are dedicated to preserving their neighborhoods' cultural and architectural heritage.

Gahanna Historical Society
101 South High Street, Gahanna
(614) 475-3342
This society sponsors the annual May Herb Festival and offers a 1-mile walking tour of Olde Gahanna's 16 historic landmarks, which include the Log House and two historical churches.

German Village Society
588 South Third Street
(614) 221-8888
www.germanvillage.org
The society is housed in the historic German Village Meeting Haus and offers the most comprehensive tours of the neighborhood. The visitor center has a short video, maps, and books about the area. Other souvenir items and information about the village are also available. They organize the annual Haus und Garten Tour the last Sunday in June.

Victorian Village Society
120 West Goodale Boulevard
(614) 228-2912
www.victorianvillage.org
The Victorian Village Society promotes restoration, preservation, and maintenance of this historic district. It is a nonprofit civic association that sponsors social events in the Victorian Village area. It hosts the annual Victorian Village Tour of Homes each September.

Worthington Historical Society
50 West New England Avenue
Worthington
(614) 885-1247
www.worthington.org/history/society.htm
Working out of the Old Rectory, this society preserves the history and heritage of the community and operates historic properties such as the Orange Johnson House. They organize annual home and garden tours, reenactments, and special holiday events.

HISTORIC HOMES

Some of the homes included here are dedicated to interpreting 19th-century life in Ohio. You will find museum-style displays ranging from "old stuff" laid out on tables to period rooms with changing exhibits. Some provide costume-clad docents, and others have self-guided tours, but each gives you insight into a little piece of Columbus history.

Fletcher-Coffman Homestead
6659 Coffman Road, Dublin
(614) 764-9906
This 1860's homestead, listed on the National Register of Historic Places, features guided tours through period rooms full of 19th-century furniture. The restored barn has a display early Ohio farm machinery and barn furnishings. The Heritage Gardens have interesting heirloom and antique interpretive plantings of the late 1800s.

CLOSE-UP

Living in the Past: The Ohio Historical Center and Ohio Village

Ohio's history can be explored through a dynamic panorama of displays at the Ohio Historical Center. More than 60,000 people annually climb the sprawling staircase into this hovering mass of concrete. The 250,000-square-foot building houses the Ohio Historical Society (OHS), Historic Preservation Office, archives, library, and museum collections. The Historical Society has amassed more than 1.6 million artifacts related to Ohio's history, natural history, and archaeology since its foundation in 1885.

OHS is known for having one of the country's most significant collections of artifacts from Native American cultures. The first Ohioans exhibit features the famous Adena Pipe. This human-shaped smoking tube was carved by prehistoric natives and found just south of Columbus. Weapons, tools, crafts, and a re-created Indian village offer a chronology of Ohio's prehistoric and historic Indian cultures.

Another permanent exhibit focuses on Ohio's history between 1770 and 1970. Exhibits show how the state has developed into a microcosm of the nation during two centuries of change. They document industrial progress through a variety of dioramas, an 1880s carriage shop, vintage cars, and 1920s newsreels that continuously run. A few of the galleries feature outstanding 18th- and 19th-century furniture and decorative arts. The Christopher Collection of interior furnishings and Currier and Ives lithographs are must-sees.

Other highlights from the permanent collections include the Conway Mastodon, a skeleton of an ice age elephantine animal, and the race car in which local boy Bobby Rahal won the 1986 Indianapolis 500.

The archives contain historical documents, publications, census data, and records related to Ohio's state and local government. The library holds 142,000 volumes of books and more than 15,000 maps. The reading room is open Wednesday, Thursday, and Saturday, and research assistance is available in the reading room. The archival department offers the occasional genealogical workshop and maintains the online collection catalog.

Adjacent to the center is Ohio Village, a re-creation of a 19th-century Civil War–era town. The village is open for school groups and signature events throughout the year. Musicians will perform on summer weekends and during the Christmas season. Just check out the Web site for the calendar of events. The Colonel Crawford Inn will serve traditional midday meals when the village is open.

The Ohio Historical Center is located off Route 71 along 17th Avenue near the Ohio Expo Center. OHS can be contacted at www.ohiohistory.org or (800) OLD-OHIO. Admission costs $7.00 for adults and $4.00 for children. Parking costs $4.00 but is free for members. There is a gift shop on-site that carries history and Ohio-related items.

There are 19 historic districts and 34 buildings on the Columbus Historic Registry. The landmark areas include East Town Street, Iuka Ravine, Hamilton Park, and Old Beechwold Historic Districts. Structures of architectural significance include Eddie Rickenbacker's boyhood home, the LeVeque Tower, and Orton Memorial Laboratory at The Ohio State University.

Hanby House
160 West Main Street, Westerville
(614) 891-6289, (800) 600-6843

The Benjamin Hanby House State Memorial is maintained by the Westerville Historic Society. This former home of composer Benjamin Russell Hanby, known for his songs "Darling Nellie Gray" and "Up on the Housetop," was built in 1846. Furniture and personal items of the Hanby family, who occupied the home from 1853 to 1870, are on display. Highlights include a walnut desk made by Hanby, the original plates for the first edition of "Darling Nellie Gray," and a large collection of sheet music. The Hanby house was also a station along the Underground Railroad. It is only open weekends, and a small admission fee is charged. Members of the Ohio Historical Society receive free admission.

Heritage Museum
530 East Town Street, Olde Town East
(614) 228-6515

This exceptional Italianate-style home was built in 1852 by Philip Snowden and is on the National Register of Historic Places. It was once the home of Ohio governor David Tod, but it is now a museum and serves as the international headquarters for the Kappa Kappa Gamma fraternity. The rich history of the home and the organization is documented in several restored Victorian-period rooms. Tours are available weekdays, and a small admission is charged.

Kelton House Museum
586 East Town Street, Olde Town East Historic District
(614) 464-2022
www.keltonhouse.com

Lovers of all things Victorian should make it a point to stop in at this 1852 Greek Revival-style home located just east of downtown. Restored by the Junior League of Columbus, this was once the home of a prominent merchant family from 1852 to 1975.

The museum conveys the story of 19th-century urban Columbus through period rooms and collections of lavish furnishings, decorative arts, and personal items from three generations of the Kelton family. Some of the highlights include a Duncan Phyfe lyre card table and a grandfather clock made circa 1790.

The Kelton family house was one of several Underground Railroad safehouses along East Town Street. Pearl Hartway, an escaped slave from Virginia, took refuge with the family for 10 years until she married Thomas Lawrence, a free black carpenter from Cadiz, Ohio. An Ohio Underground Railroad Association plaque on the museum grounds commemorates these events.

The Kelton House is only open on Sunday and for holiday events. The entrance fee is minimal, and there's a museum shop on-site.

Orange Johnson House
956 High Street, Worthington
(614) 885-1247

The oldest restored house in Franklin County began in 1811 as a pioneer cabin built by Aurora Buttles. Five years later, it was purchased by Orange Johnson, "the most prominent and prosperous businessman in Worthington." In 1819, a Federal-style wing was added, and the family resided here until 1863. The home is beautifully restored and features furniture of the Federal period, some connected to early Worthington families. The kitchen has a working fireplace, where cooking demonstrations are given. The O. J. House is open Sunday, at which time guided tours are offered. A small admission is charged.

HISTORIC TOWNS

Several restored villages and sites are within an easy drive of the city. Many provide costumed interpreters and craft demonstrations.

Clifton Mill
75 Water Street, Clifton
(937) 767-5501
www.cliftonmill.com

At one time there were approximately 100,000 mills in this country, but now, fewer than 100 are still in original operating condition. Forty-five minutes southwest of Columbus is one of the largest water-powered grist mills still in existence, around which the village of Clifton grew. Clifton Mill was built in 1802 on the Little Miami River to take advantage of the concentrated water funneled through the gorge. A tour provides insight to one of America's earliest industries and explains the mill's involvement in the Civil War.

The Millrace Restaurant offers beautiful views overlooking Clifton Gorge and serves home-cooked meals for breakfast and lunch. The pancake and cornbread mix is made on-site, and those who tour the mill receive a free sample bag. The gift shop carries wheat and corn meal, while the gallery displays a collection of 300 flour bags from different mills. The mill, gorge, and grounds are decorated with over 3.2 million lights each year to create a spectacular holiday illumination and waterfall of lights.

Historic Lyme Village
5001 State Route 4, Bellevue
(419) 483-4949
www.lymevillage.com

Historic Lyme Village was started by a group of individuals dedicated to "preserving yesterday for tomorrow." Many of the structures were moved to Lyme Village in the 1970s and '80s. Pop into the visitor center for a map before touring the town's 16 19th-century buildings, which include log houses, barns, stores, and a one-room school house.

The Victorian Wright Mansion, built in 1882, houses the museum, and the 1836 Seymour House was the first building in the village. Events such as Victorian Tea, Pioneer School, and Civil War Reenactments are held throughout the year. Church services are held on Sunday at the New England-style Lyme Church. The Sunday school is the oldest continuous organization in Ohio.

Malabar Farm
3954 Bromfield Road, Lucas
(419) 892-2055
www.malabarfarm.org

This 900-acre working farm and hostel is located on Malabar Farm State Park. The 32-room mansion was once the home of Pulitzer Prize-winning author and highly acclaimed agriculturalist, Louis Bromfield. Year-round guided tours of the "Big House" provide insight to Ohio's farming traditions, as well as Bromfield's life and philosophies. The admission fee is around $2.00. Seasonal wagon tours of the farm are offered for an additional fee.

Twelve miles of hiking, horse, and cross-country ski trails assure there is plenty to do on the property, which is owned and operated by the state. Regular events include square dances, a maple syrup festival, Heritage Days, and wildlife weekends. The 19-bed hostel offers dormitory-style lodging in a 1913 Sears, Roebuck Catalog House. Malabar Inn Restaurant is located in a restored 1820s stagecoach inn and is open Tuesday through Sunday, May 1 to October 31, and on weekends in March and April.

Roscoe Village
381 Hill Street, Coshocton
(740) 622-9310, (800) 877-1830
www.roscoevillage.com

Roscoe Village was established in 1817 as Caldersburgh by James Caulder. It was renamed for abolitionist William Roscoe in 1830 and grew into the fourth-largest wheat port with the advent of the Ohio-Erie Canal. The prosperity of Roscoe declined with the demise of the canal industry in the early 20th-century. Historic preservation began in the 1960s, and today, Roscoe Village is a living museum—women with hoop skirts and all!

This charming restored 1830s canal town offers quaint shops filled with crafts, books, candles, and gourmet foods. Stroll the brick sidewalks, and explore pocket gardens and 19th-century buildings. Artisans such as blacksmiths, weavers, and broom makers offer live demonstrations, while visitors can learn the art of candle dipping or tin punching for themselves. A fee is charged for seasonal guided tours of the gardens and the 45-minute horse-drawn canal boat ride. "Living History" tickets can be purchased at the visitor center.

Overnight guests can stay in the relaxed environs of the Inn at Roscoe Village. Dining options include the more upscale King Charley's Dining Room and Tavern at the Inn or a more casual atmosphere at Captain Nye's Bakery.

Roscoe Village has a calendar full of events year-round, such as Apple Butter Stirrin', arts and crafts festivals, Civil War reenactments, and Christmas candle lightings. The village's Johnson-Humrickhouse Museum has collections of American Indian artifacts and 18th- and 19th-century Asian, European, and American decorative arts. There is a small entrance fee for this surprisingly fine regional museum.

Sauder Village
22611 State Route 2, Archbold
(419) 445-2231, (800) 590-9755
www.saudervillage.org

Forward-thinking Erie J. Sauder (1904–1997) turned his love of Ohio's history into a living museum. The dozens of buildings at Sauder Village are authentic 19th- and early-20th-century structures, disassembled and moved from their original locations around northwestern Ohio to create this village. The buildings, along with collections of agricultural equipment, textiles, and household furnishings, relate the story of how Ohio's earliest settlers transformed the Great Black Swamp into fertile farmland.

A costumed staff reenacts life in various historic settings and offer demonstrations such as spinning or old printing techniques and food preparation. Children will enjoy the hands-on activities at Little Pioneers Homestead. There is a general store, quilt shop, and gift center, as well as the AAA-rated Barn Restaurant on-site. The Barn offers a buffet and family-style dinners, while the Doughbox Bakery sells pies Grandma would be proud of. There is both a campground and an inn at the village. The village is open seasonally, but the restaurant, inn, and bakery are open year-round.

i

Escaping to the country was considered the highest form of sophistication among the 1940s New York smart set. Bromfield's good friends Humphrey Bogart and Lauren Bacall were married at Malabar Farms on May 21, 1945. Exhibits related to their nuptials make this one of the most popular tourist attractions in northern Ohio.

Zoar Village
Zoar, 3 miles southeast of I-77
www.zca.org

Zoar Village was founded in 1817 by a group of peace-loving German Separatists escaping religious persecution in their homeland. This self-sufficient community was one of the few experiments in communal living in the United States that actually succeeded. With the passing of the Zoarite spiritual leader in the 1850s and the increasing influence from the outside world, the community voted to disband in 1898.

Today, you will find a mixture of privately owned homes and restored buildings operated by the Ohio Historical Society. The gardens are beautifully maintained and serve as a focal point in the village. Architectural highlights include a cupola-topped Assembly House, School House, Town Hall, Meeting House, and The Number One House.

Zoar Tavern and Inn was built as House Number 23, the original home of the village doctor. The inn is located on Main Street and is now a functioning restaurant and guesthouse. The tavern serves fine seafood, pastas, and steaks in a relaxed and casual ambience. The guest-house is a modern, cozy four-unit lodge located behind the Zoar Post Office. More information can be found at www.zoar-tavern-inn.com.

VINEYARDS

Ohio is one of America's top 10 wine producing states and turns out more than 500,000 gallons every year. The state has a rich winemaking history, which began in Cincinnati in the early 1800s. Three vineyards in the Columbus area have maintained that long tradition of growing flavorful grapes for quality wines. Check out www.ohgrapes.com, or call (614) 728-4216 for a brochure about all the Ohio wineries.

Slate Run Vineyard Winery
1900 Winchester-Southern Road
Canal Winchester
(614) 834-5757
www.slaterunwine.com
Slate Run Vineyard is a small farm winery situated amid four acres of vineyards 19 miles from downtown Columbus. Wines are made from grapes grown at Slate Run and fruits from other orchards. Highlights include fruit wines and German and Burgundy-style wines. There are also a cozy tasting room, gift shop, informal tours, and picnicking. Informal tours are offered Monday through Saturday.

Willow Hill Vineyards
5460 Loudon Street, Johnstown
(740) 587-4622
Willow Hill Vineyards, one of Ohio's smaller wineries, is located on 93 acres east of Columbus, near Granville. Willow Hill uses French and German hybrid and Native American grapes. This small farm winery overlooks a beautiful four-acre lake and is open seasonally.

Wyandotte Wine Cellars
4640 Wyandotte Drive
(614) 476-3642
www.wyandottewinery.com
Gourmet fruit wines and award-winning table wines are made at the sister winery of William Graystone Winery in German Village. Along with grape wine, raspberry and cranberry wines are their specialty. Tours are given Tuesday through Saturday. There is a tasting room and gift shop at this country winery, while the downtown Graystone cellars is available for private events.

TOURIST INFORMATION AND VISITOR BUREAUS

Figuring out what to do while you're in Columbus couldn't be easier. These visitor centers can be contacted for further tourist information about each neighborhood. I have included the city or chamber of commerce contact details when there is not a specific visitor's bureau.

Bexley Area Chamber of Commerce
2242 East Main Street, Bexley
(614) 235-8694
www.bexleyareachamber.org

Convention and Visitors Bureau of Worthington
579 High Street, Worthington
(614) 841-2545, (800) 997-9935
www.worthington.org

Dublin Convention and Visitors Bureau
9 South High Street, Dublin
(614) 792-7666, (800) 245-8387
www.dublinvisit.org

Gahanna Convention and Visitors Bureau
116 Mill Street, Gahanna
(866) 424-2662, (866) GAHANNA
www.visitgahanna.org

The City of Grandview Heights
1016 Grandview Avenue, Grandview
(614) 488-3159
www.grandviewheights.org

City of Hilliard
3800 Municipal Way, Hilliard
(614) 876-7361
www.cityofhilliard.com

New Albany Area Chamber of Commerce
220 Market Street, New Albany
(614) 855-4400
www.newalbanychamber.com

Upper Arlington Area Chamber of Commerce
2120 Tremont Center, Upper Arlington
(614) 481-5710
www.uachamber.org

i

Discover Ohio (www.discoverohio.com) provides comprehensive visitor information, travel packages, state agency information, and events for the entire Buckeye State. Experience Columbus (formerly the Columbus Convention and Visitors Bureau) is located at 90 North High Street. An exhaustive guide to events and attractions in Columbus can be viewed at www.experiencecolumbus.com or by calling (614) 221-6623 or (800) 354-2657.

Westerville Visitors and Convention Bureau
28 South State Street, Westerville
(614) 794-0401, (800) 824-8461
www.visitwesterville.org

KIDSTUFF

Ask 10 different kids what they like to do in Columbus, and you'll get 10 very different answers. The input from parents is as equally varied, but one thing can be agreed on: Columbus is a great place to rear a family. Many of Columbus's most popular family activities have already been listed in the Attractions chapter, but it is good to remember places like the zoo, the Center of Science and Industry (COSI), and the Columbus Conservatory, though catering to a broad audience, have extensive educational programs for kids. This chapter will present a variety of activities that target specific age groups, ranging from toddler to teen. They are broken out into categories that are relatively self-explanatory.

The "Kid Culture" section focuses on classes and shows developed especially for youth by Columbus's performing and visual arts organizations. Some are free, while others require enrollment, audition, or limited financial commitment, such as buying tickets. Two good places to start looking for any arts information, including children's activities, is Columbus Arts (www.columbusarts.com) and the Greater Columbus Arts Council (GCAC) (614-224-2606; www.gcac.org).

In 1993, the GCAC developed the "Children of the Future" program, an innovative model of arts programming targeting at-risk youth. The program works in conjunction with Columbus public schools, the city, and major arts organizations to provide after-school art activities at drop-in sites around the city. This is a great opportunity for inner-city or latchkey kids to explore their creative sides (and stay out of trouble!) while Mom and Dad are still at work. Contact the GCAC for a list of sites and activities.

Events created specifically for children have also been included here, but many of the festivals listed in the Annual Events and Festivals chapter have booths dedicated to kids' activities. Stalls at the Columbus Arts Festival allow children to create their own works of art, while the Dublin Irish Festival has a whole area dedicated to the wee folk. Some families enjoy special interest events, like the annual train show, while others live for the Quarter Horse Congress. This is just a reminder not to overlook other chapters as a source for family fun.

The "Kid Play" section focuses on amusement and seasonal activities, and "Kid Science" on fun educational programs, while "Kid Sport" lists some of the more popular athletic camps and youth leagues. The city of Columbus places heavy emphasis on public green spaces, so there are plenty of options to get the family outdoors and active. The Parks and Recreation chapter includes information on bike trails, skiing, and a range of sports the whole family can participate in.

Popular family-friendly restaurants have been listed in the "Kid Eats" section. Who wouldn't dig the biggest McDonald's in the country or oodles of noodles heaped on a plate? "Kid Shop" will point out some of the more interesting toy stores and kiddy boutiques however, the selection has been limited to a few key places. You'll have no problem finding chain toy and clothing stores, such as Abercrombie Kids, Gap Kids, Limited Too, and Toys-R-Us, in most of the malls.

At the end of the day, it is just a matter of what you and your children like to do and how you define family fun. This chapter provides a kid's-eye view of the more popular activities, many of which come with recommendations from the younger crowd.

PARENT STUFF

A good place to find out what's going on in the Columbus area is *Columbus Parent*. This free monthly publication is full of informative articles and advertisements targeting parents with toddlers through teens. It is carried at 700 locations in central Ohio, including Kroger grocery stores, but for $20 a year you can have it delivered to your door. Subscribe by calling (614) 438-8100 or online at www.columbusparent.com.

MOMS Clubs are a wonderful way to meet other stay-at-home moms while socializing the kids. This national nonprofit organization holds weekly play groups, and provides support services, babysitting, and social opportunities. MOMS Club events and contact details are listed in the back of *Columbus Parent*. Branches are currently located in Bexley, Powell, Westerville, and northwestern Columbus, which services Clintonville, Upper Arlington, and Worthington.

Stay-at-home dads haven't been forgotten, either. Columbus Dads meet several times a week at various locations around town, and like the MOMS Clubs, they provide fathers with adult interaction and children with play group time. The Columbus chapter can be contacted via e-mail at columbusdads@wideopenwest.com or by calling (614) 791-8271.

When it comes to children's haircuts, forget the intimidating barbershop experience and take them to a kids-only salon, where they'll experience the "funnest" haircuts in town. Cookie Cutter (www.haircutsarefun.com) and Snip Buzz Bangs (www.snipbuzzbangs.com) are Columbus's two premier children's salons, each having multiple locations. They've traded in barber chairs for planes, trains, and automobiles. Toddlers can sit in fun, animated seats while watching their favorite cartoon or film on their own TV. Polaroid pictures, along with a lock of hair, are included to commemorate baby's first haircut.

There are three Cookie Cutter locations in Columbus: Arlington (614-451-5437), Hilliard (614-876-7700), and Polaris Parkway (614-846-5610). The three Snip Buzz Bangs are in New Albany (614-428-9999), Pickerington (614-522-0220), and Dublin (614-792-BUZZ).

KID CULTURE

Performing Arts

BalletMet
322 Mount Vernon Avenue, downtown
(614) 229-4848
www.balletmet.org
Columbus's premier ballet company offers an extensive list of educational and academy classes. Children as young as 4 can enroll for beginner ballet, while a varied curriculum offers youth ages 6 and up everything from modern, jazz, and tap to Irish step, Pilates, and advanced movement. The YouthMet performs at special events, and the price of tuition ranges from $315 to $800.

The Chamber Music Connection
242 Sinsbury Drive North, Worthington
(614) 848-3312
www.cmconnection.org
The CMC is a local organization providing all levels of chamber music education for students of all ages and abilities. The classes are small, and the programs are geared primarily for string, wind, and piano instrumentalists. The CMC sponsors four major programs for school-age students: two 9-week programs in the fall and winter, a weekend Spring Festival in May, and a weeklong Summer Festival in July.

Columbus Children's Choir
Broad Street Presbyterian Church
760 East Broad Street, downtown
(614) 761-9588
www.columbuschildrenschoir.org
Auditions are held annually for this

independent, community-based children's choral program. Children in second through seventh grade are placed according to their grade and musical skill in one of nine different ensembles. For those who make it, enrollment lasts an entire season, and tuition costs between $350 and $475. They rehearse on a weekly basis throughout the school year, and members must reaudition each year.

Columbus Children's Theatre
512 North Park Street, Arena District
(614) 224-6672
www.colschildrenstheatre.org

Columbus Children's Theatre, founded in 1963, is the oldest and largest children's theater in central Ohio. The academy introduces kids ages 5 through 15 to all facets of the theater arts through creative drama classes. The classes cost between $70 and $100. Aside from teaching young actors, CCT presents the community with fun live performances such as *Alice in Wonderland, Sleeping Beauty,* and other plays geared toward family audiences.

Educational activities abound at the local libraries. For example, Grandview Heights, Upper Arlington, and Westerville libraries have free puppet shows, movies, and story times for toddlers. Barnes & Noble bookstores also have free children's activities and book clubs for 'tweens.

Columbus Symphony Youth Orchestra
55 East State Street, downtown
(614) 228-8600
www.columbussymphony.com

The symphony has been helping Columbus's youngest musicians find their inner maestro for 50 years now. Some 300 children grades 3 through 12 make up the four different youth orchestras. Junior Strings encourages the development of young string players in grades 3 through 6, while the Chamber Strings Orchestra is made up of talented players in grades 6 through 9. Both hold at least three concerts per season. The Cadet Orchestra is comprised of students grades 7 through 10, who also perform three concerts per season.

One hundred young musicians in grades 9 through 12 form the primary Youth Orchestra, which has been nationally recognized and recently held their first European tour. It is a big commitment to be involved in any of these orchestras, as members must take private lessons, participate in their school band, and attend weekly rehearsals. Tuition is $300 per season.

Columbus Youth Ballet
5076 North High Street, Clintonville
(614) 433-7090
www.columbusyouthballet.com

CYB is a nonprofit, children's performing ballet company. Dancers ages 12 to 18 perform classic and contemporary ballets at an affordable family price; tickets usually are $16 to $18. A summer workshop for advanced ballet techniques, modern and jazz dance, and pantomime is available for students ages 10 and older with a minimum of three years of ballet training.

Historic Dramas
Various locations

Make learning history a little more fun by taking the family to the region's three 90-minute outdoor historical dramas: *Johnny Appleseed, Blue Jacket,* and *Tecumseh!* The latter two are not recommended for children under the age of 5 or 6.

Johnny Appleseed is performed in the heart of Johnny Appleseed Forest in Ashland. The captivating story of John Chapman is played out under the stars to beautiful music. Tickets, which range in price from $8.00 to $21.00, can be purchased by calling (800) 642-0388 or online at www.appleseedoutdoordrama.com.

Blue Jacket, the story of the legendary frontiersman adopted by the Shawnee Indians, is a tale of friendship, loyalty, family, and honor. This impressive play features professional actors, a herd of galloping horses, and reproduction Revolutionary War cannons. It is performed at Caesar's Ford Park Amphitheatre in Xenia, and tickets range from $6.00 to $15.00. The box office phone number is (937) 376-4318, and the Web site is www.bluejacketdrama.com.

The epic struggles of Shawnee leader Tecumseh are brought to life at Sugarloaf Mountain Amphitheatre in Chillicothe each summer, from June through September. Everything about *Tecumseh!* is top-notch: The script was written by Pulitzer Prize-nominated and Emmy-winning author Allan W. Eckert, the haunting music was recorded by the London Symphony Orchestra, and the story is narrated by Native American actor Graham Greene. It's no wonder this drama has received international acclaim during its 33-year run. Tickets range from $8.00 to $18.00 and can be purchased by calling the box office at (866) 775-0700 or online at www.tecumsehdrama.com. Backstage tours are available, and the free Mini Museum houses ancient Indian artifacts from the region. The on-site buffet-style restaurant is very casual but requires reservations.

Opera Columbus
177 East Naghten Street, downtown
(614) 469-0939
www.operacolumbus.org

Students of all ages are welcome to explore the world of music and operatic theater at two- or four-week summer camps, which include activities such as singing, movement games, and the production of an original opera. The youth Opera Residency programs teach students to create an opera from start to finish, including the costumes and sets. The Master Class Series help the more serious students in grades 9 through 12 hone their musical skills and develop stage presence and proper vocal technique. The Columbus Opera Youth Chorus is yet another ensemble that performs in various productions.

Students in sixth grade through college can take advantage of Opera Columbus's discounted dinner theater package. The evening includes dinner, a ticket to the opera, a preopera lecture, and the program guide. Contact Opera Columbus at (614) 469-0939 for more details.

Visual Arts

Columbus Museum of Art
480 East Broad Street, downtown
(614) 221-6801
www.columbusmuseum.org

The Columbus Museum's kid-friendly programming is extensive. The museum collections include "Eye Spy: Adventures in Art," an interactive exhibition for children, and the "Acoustiguide" audio tour, which features talking paintings and sculpture.

Every Saturday, from 1:00 to 3:00 P.M., families with school-aged children can participate in the museum's walk-in Doodle program. Each month highlights a different theme, such as landscapes or abstraction, through which kids are introduced to a variety of artistic styles and processes. Children ages 6 and older can explore the museum's collections and special exhibitions through self-guided art activities. Doodles require no preregistration or fees beyond general admission.

The museum also has free, hands-on art activities for very young children. Adults can bring kids ages 3 to 5 for free workshops from 10:00 A.M. to 12:30 P.M. on the first Saturday of each month. The weekly WOW Art! program is a combination of stories and activities for preschoolers that costs $30 for four weeks.

Full- or half-day summer camps are also available for children in first through eighth grade, during which they learn about drawing, painting, sculpture, photography, and more.

Dublin Arts Council
7125 Riverside Drive (Route 33), Dublin
(614) 889-7444
www.dublinarts.org
Toddlers and preschool-aged children have a chance to learn about the art on display at the gallery and work on age-appropriate activities through the ARTventures series. Parents are encouraged to leave their 3- to 5-year-olds, but they must accompany children ages 18 through 36 months. You can pay for individual sessions or subscribe by the half or full year. Summer ARTcamps provide youths ages 6 through 16 the opportunity to explore techniques like printmaking, sculpture, and dance through a variety of workshops ranging in price from $65 to $180.

Teen Arts Fusion
Wexner Center for the Arts
The Ohio State University
(614) 688-3986
www.wexarts.org
Summer programming at the ultramodern Wexner Center offers teens ages 14 to 18 the chance to explore their creativity through contemporary art forms, such as video, digital, sound, performance, and other alternative media. Sign up for various one- or two-week themed workshops, from digital documentary and video art to experimental photography and robotic sculpture. The cost ranges from $55 to $130 for the week.

PAINT YOUR OWN POTTERY

There are several places adults can go to paint their own ceramic pieces, but not all welcome toddlers. Marcy's Clayground in Powell (614-932-9000; www.marcysclayground.com) is one that does. The Mom and Me program, held the second Monday of every month, is designed for moms and preschool-aged toddlers. However, the wee artists are welcomed at all times. Summer camps are also available.

Color Me Mine (614-761-1153; www.dublin.colormemine.com) is a franchised paint-your-own-pottery studio in Dublin that holds Tuesday story time and paint sessions for toddlers and their parents. Color Your World (614-418-9225) at Easton Town Center does not necessarily cater to children but offers a few summer camps for kids.

Coolabah Clay Studio, at 7077 Duncan's Glen Drive, Westerville (614-794-9371), invites children ages 4 to 13 to make their own masterpieces from a lump of clay. Four sessions cost around $50 and are held once a week.

Special Programs

CAPACITY Studios
1002 East Livingston Avenue
near Bexley
(614) 372-1822
www.ecapacity.org
Teens are invited to showcase their talents at free arts workshops sponsored by the Columbus Association for the Performing Arts (CAPA) and funded with major grants from local businesses. Arts professionals lend guidance in the fields of music, dance, poetry, painting, graphic design, and more. The studios hold regular open mike nights and sponsor Dine-In Discussions, which allow teens to voice their opinions on various topics. All programs are available to youth ages 12 to 19.

"High Five" Program
(614) 675-5555
www.high5cols.org
Students ages 13 to 18 are eligible for $5.00 tickets to Columbus arts and cultural events at various venues. Check out the High Five calendar on their Web site, or call the hotline to hear a listing. Reserve a spot ahead of time online or by calling. A voucher will be issued to redeem a ticket at the box office (or venue). All you need is $5.00 cash, the voucher, and an ID proving you are between the ages of 13 and 18. A school or recreation center ID, driver's license, bus pass, report card, or birth certificate will do the trick.

Kaleidoscope Youth Coalition
751 Chambers Road, Grandview
(614) 294-7886
www.kaleidoscope.org

KYC is a drop-in center for lesbian, gay, bisexual, transgender, or questioning youth in the central Ohio area. This community center offers a supportive environment in which games, activities, special events, and a theater program help kids develop a positive self-image. There are also a library with Internet access, discussion and support groups, and the occasional pizza party. The center is located in the Lennox Center next to Sabo's Camping and is open to youth under the age of 20. Walk in daily, Monday through Friday, from 4:00 to 9:00 P.M.

Music in the Air
(614) 645-7995
www.musicintheair.org

The Columbus Department of Recreation and Parks sponsors free outdoor performances by local, national, and international acts. The concerts are held throughout the city parks. Magical Music Mornings are free concerts directed toward the youth at various parks, such as Whetstone in Clintonville. View the Web site, or call the 24-hour information line at (614) 645-3800 for an updated listing.

Popcorn Pops
2540 Olentangy River Road
(614) 228-8600
www.picnicwiththepops.com

As part of the Columbus Symphony's Picnic with the Pops series, these special performances are intended for families with young children and are held on the lawn of Chemical Abstracts. There are free pre-concert activities, and the shows have included music from *Harry Potter, The Wizard of Oz,* and Disney movies. Birthday party packages and group discounts are available.

KID EVENTS

Buckeye Central Scenic Railroad
Byesville, south of I-70 and I-77 junction
(800) 579-7521

All aboard this vintage locomotive for a 3.5-mile train ride between Byesville and Derwent. This historic train travels the longest straight stretch on the Marietta & Pittsburgh Railway (built 1871-1873) and crosses over two bridges built in 1898 and 1907. It operates late May through late October, and tickets cost between $5.00 and $7.00. Special runs include a Train Robbery, a haunted Halloween ride in late October, and a Santa Express the first two weeks in December.

Buckeye Quarter Midget Racing
Ohio Expo Center
717 East 17th Avenue, OSU campus
(614) 402-6227
www.buckeyequartermidget.com

Kids ages 5 to 16 can competitively race quarter midget cars. These scaled-down versions of actual midget race cars have full four-wheel, independent suspension and roll cages, so needless to say these are not go-karts. The Buckeye Quarter Midget Racing Association is based at Columbus Motor Speedway, just outside the city in Obetz. The racing schedule includes events throughout the summer and fall, and the Buckeye Indoor Series is held at the Ohio State Expo Center in the winter.

Christmas at Ohio Village
1982 Velma Avenue, just off I-71
(614) 297-2666, (800) 686-1541
www.ohiohistory.org

---

i

The Columbus Youth Commission is a group of 21 young adults from across greater Columbus, ages 13 to 21, who advise the mayor and city council on youth issues. The commission helps provide leadership in the development of priorities and a comprehensive agenda for the city's youth.

Families enter the world of Charles Dickens at the Ohio Village's Victorian Christmas celebration. Characters from his stories come to life as carolers wander the streets of this re-created 19th-century Civil War-era village, and readings are done by candlelight. Buggy rides, refreshments, and Victorian holiday traditions are among the offerings. Check with the Ohio Historical Society later in the year to get the specific dates and themes of the holiday festivities.

Easter egg hunts are held in various communities, as well as the Columbus Zoo (614-645-3550). Contact the Department of Recreation and Parks (614-645-3300) for dates and times.

Creepside Festival
Creekside Park, 123 Mill Street
Gahanna
(614) 342-4250
www.gahanna.gov
All the little goblins come out one night around Halloween for a spooktacular family adventure. Gahanna Parks and Recreation puts on this free event for children of all ages, and while most kids come for the candy, some do come for the hayrides, music, and other activities.

Family Days at Sunwatch
Sun Watch Indian Village and Archaeological Park
2301 West River Road, Dayton
(937) 268-8199
www.sunwatch.org
This reconstructed 800-year-old village is a National Historic Landmark. It hosts a summer solstice festival honoring American Indians and a Kids Dig Archaeological Festival. On the first Saturday of each month (March through December), families with children can explore Native American culture through themed demonstrations, activities, reconstructed buildings, and gardens.

Family Fun Fest
Genoa Park, Riverfront Amphitheatre
Washington Boulevard
(614) 645-7995
www.musicintheair.org
This interactive, family-friendly festival brings together fun and education. Children will find artistic adventures at the Kid's Creative Studio and Oodles of Noodles. They can explore their dramatic side at the Puppet Theatre or scale Mount Scioto, the rock-climbing wall. Entertainment has included performances by canine hotshot Air Bud and "Jungle Jack" Hanna. Rides, food, fireworks, and river excursions will keep Mom and Dad entertained.

Hayes Easter Egg Roll
Rutherford B. Hayes Presidential Center
Hayes and Buckland Avenues, Fremont
(419) 332-2081, (800) 998-7737
www.rbhayes.org
Children between the ages of 3 and 10 are invited to participate in an old White House tradition started by President Hayes in 1878. There is no entry fee; just bring three hard-boiled colored eggs for various races across the lawn. Prizes are awarded in several age groups, and an egg-decorating contest is also held. Children can visit with the Easter Bunny and receive passes to tour the Hayes Home and Museum.

Kidzapalooza
Veterans Memorial
300 West Broad Street, downtown
(614) 221-4341
www.610wtvn.com/kidzapalooza
This annual festival of kid fun is held at the end of January. Activities are geared mostly toward children 12 and under. Music, magic, and carnival rides are found, along with hands-on exhibits by COSI and activities sponsored by Magic Mountain. Tickets cost $5.00 at the door, and kids under 2 are free.

New Albany Classic
Wexner Residence, off Kitzmiller Drive
New Albany
(614) 939-3026
www.thenewalbanyclassic.com
The New Albany Classic Invitational Grand Prix and Family Day is one of Columbus's more unique fundraising events. World-class equestrian sports, carnival rides, live entertainment, hometown heroes, a petting zoo, and a variety of arts organizations come together to raise money for the Columbus Coalition Against Family Violence. One hundred percent of the proceeds goes to various institutions advocating and supporting family causes. Admission is a great value at $15 per person or $25 for two adults. Children ages 16 and younger are free, but all tickets must be purchased in advance or through Ticketmaster. It goes on rain or shine in late September.

TeenFest
Creekside Park
123 Mill Street, Gahanna
(614) 342-4250
www.gahanna.gov
This one-of-a-kind central Ohio festival is a great opportunity for teens to show off their talents. Creekside Park is the backdrop for an evening of games, dance contests, music, and art geared toward the teens in the community. This free event runs all day on a Saturday in July until 11:00 P.M.

Ye Old Mill Ice Cream Festival
11324 State Route 13, Utica
(740) 892-4339, (800) 589-5000
www.velveticecream.com
Central Ohio has been celebrating America's favorite dessert for 30 years at the home of the Velvet Ice Cream Company, just east of Columbus. Operated on the site of an 1817 mill, this fourth-generation, family-run business has been cranking out the creamy confectionery since 1914. Tours of the mill are available May through October.

The Ice Cream Festival, held in late May, is kicked off with a parade and includes heapings of children's activities like balloon tosses, wheelbarrow races, and a Magic Tent. Daily ice cream–eating contests are sure to ruin their appetites, as will the Root Beer Float Tent, but with such temptations like Olde Tyme vanilla, raspberry fudge cordial, and mint chocolate chip, how could you not let them indulge in dessert all day? Foods, arts, crafts, and classic cars are also exhibited. Admission and parking are free.

KID PLAY

Amusement

Gameworks
Easton Town Center
(614) 428-7529
www.gameworks.com
This high-tech arcade features two levels of shooting, racing, and flying games, virtual boxing, and dance machines. Manual games such as pool and skee-ball are available for the video game challenged, but you can't leave without riding the virtual roller coaster at least once before you eat. Gameworks is state-of-the-art fun for teens, adults, and groups. There is no cover charge to enter. You just pay as you play, and game cards can be purchased at various price increments. Gameworks has a full menu and a great happy hour for adults.

Magic Mountain Family Fun Centers
East Center, Brice Road and I-70
Polaris Center, Polaris Parkway and I-71
(614) 844-4FUN
www.magicmountainfuncenter.com
Both entertainment complexes have a mix of 11 indoor and outdoor attractions that appeal to all age groups. Arm yourself

Toddlers can run off energy at three free indoor play areas in Tuttle Mall, Polaris Fashion Place, and the Graeter's Ice Cream store at 2555 Bethel Road.

with a phaser in a game of laser tag, or program your own virtual roller-coaster ride—loops, corkscrews, and all. Wee adventurers can navigate through a sea of balls or jump around in Kids Gym Playland. The whole family can challenge each other at bumper cars, video games, Adventure Golf, go-karts, and batting cages. Once you work up an appetite, pig out at The Magic Buffet (only at the Polaris location), which features 14 different types of pizzas and a huge salad bar. Kids six and under receive admission for one dollar on Toddler Tuesday.

Pump-It-Up
8200 Business Way, Plain City
(614) 873-7271, (866) 325-9663
www.pumpitupparty.com
If you're looking for a unique way to entertain your children (and 24 of their closest friends), look no further than this giant, inflatable play land. The facility has no less than a dozen different blow-up structures to jump, box, slide, and play around in. Though primarily a party zone for private rentals, parents can bring children ages 5 and under every Wednesday from 10:00 to 11:00 A.M. during the school year.

SportsOhio
6314 Cosgray Road, Dublin
(614) 792-1630
www.sports-ohio.com
SportsOhio has several different facilities in one complex, including an award-winning miniature golf course, batting cages, and Can-AM Track Racers. Children under 58 inches tall can ride with Mom and Dad or go it alone in the Rookie Track Racers. The Midwest Gymnastics and Cheerleading Facility, the Chiller Ice-Skating Rink, and Soccer First are also located within this park. Each has its own schedule of summer camps, weekend clinics, and youth leagues. See the Kid Sport section for further information and contact details.

WOW Family Fun Center
4900 Evanswood Drive
I-71 and Morse Road
(614) 846-5626
www.wowfamilyfun.com
This particular location features a wooden rink for roller and in-line skating, as well as a designated skate area for beginners and toddlers. Skate rental is available, while the Roller Cafe serves up typical rink snacks and drinks. The primary customers are ages 5 to 15, and though skating is the main attraction, toddlers will enjoy the Big Fun Playhouse, where they can climb a three-story jumbo gym or play in the Bouncy Toy Area. Older kids (and adults) can compete at laser tag in a black light arena or play popular video games at Treasure Island Arcade.

Wyandot Lake Amusement and Water Park
10101 Riverside Drive (Route 33), Powell
(614) 889-9283
www.sixflags.com
Wyandot Lake is a combination amusement and water park owned by Six Flags and features more than 45 rides, water slides, and attractions. Most of the parks nonwater entertainment, such as the Sea Dragon wooden coaster, appeals to the younger set, as do the watery gadgets on Christopher's Island. A family favorite is the "Dive-In Movies" shown every Friday night in July, at which time the wave pool is transformed into a giant movie theater showing family flicks. Those seeking thrills should stick with the water rides. The 445-foot drop down Zuma Falls or plunging through rushing water on Shark Attack is sure to get a few screams. An inner tube float on Canoochee Creek is perfect for a lazy summer day.

Park hours vary depending on month and day. Admission ranges from $20 to $26, but regulars may wish to get the season pass. At $50, it pays for itself after two visits. Season pass holders and Columbus Zoo members can use their membership cards for free parking at

Wyandot Lake. Public picnic areas are provided in both parking lots.

Summer Camps

If your children love the great outdoors, they may be interested in the programs offered at most of the Metro Parks. The Budding Naturalist (ages 6 to 8) and Junior Naturalist (ages 9 to 12) series allow children to explore fields, streams, forests, and ponds with Metro Park professionals. Blossoming green thumbs, ages 6 to 12, can learn a thing or two about horticulture through the Junior Gardeners program at Inniswood Metro Gardens. The two-hour sessions highlight plant and animal life, their habitats, and, of course, gardening.

Metro Parks also offer year-round interactive classes that introduce preschoolers to nature through story time and hand-on activities. Weeklong summer camps at different parks are another option for children in preschool through ninth grade. Campers participate in age-appropriate activities, games, and crafts while learning about nature. Prices for the weekly camps range from $60 to $160, and children must bring a packed lunch. Find out more about the programs, campfires, and Friday night movies by calling (614) 891-0700 or looking online at www.metroparks.net.

The Columbus Department of Recreation and Parks offers a selection of summer camps for kids of all ages. Camp Buckeye is held at Tuttle Recreation Center just north of the OSU campus, where campers ages 6 to 12 join in a variety of sporting activities, such as tennis, softball, basketball, and hiking. The kids will create works of art and finish each day off with a swim at the Tuttle pool.

Children ages 6 to 12 learn about Native American folklore and culture, study nature, do arts and crafts, and explore caves during 10 weekly summer camps held at Indian Village. Just look for the teepees on the west side of the Scioto River off Fishinger Road, and you've found the village. Parents will appreciate the high-energy recreation offered here. After a day full of fishing, canoeing, swimming, and boating, the kids will certainly come home tuckered out!

i

P.L.A.Y. grants are available to financially challenged families. There is a specific registration process, but scholarships for $50 toward fall, winter, and spring classes and $80 toward one-week summer camps are available. Call (614) 645-3325, or see the Columbus Parks and Recreation Web site for the application.

Indian Village also has a state-of-the-art multipurpose Indoor Recreation Center (614-645-5972), with a high ropes course, portable climbing wall, traverse wall, and fidget ladder. The facility, including teepees, is available for group outings, campouts, workshops, parties, and other educational programs.

Teens too old to attend Indian Village but not ready to give up their camping days can volunteer to be a counselor in training and share their knowledge with the younger kids. Application can be made through the Department of Recreation and Parks. Another option is the Teen Outdoor Adventure Camp. Each day begins in Franklin Park at the Indoor Adventure Center at 1747 East Broad Street, Bexley. Campers between the ages of 13 and 17 will be transported to various locations, such as Hocking Hills and Indian Village, for canoeing, orienteering, hiking, and rock climbing.

Youth of all ages will enjoy the Great Art Getaway. Children and teens can explore their creative side in a beautiful natural setting at Smith Farms Parkland, near Groveport. These weeklong sessions tap into the children's creativity and observation of nature through a series of art projects. Younger kids (6 to 12) will learn how to make silk screens, design T-shirts, fire ceramics, create sculpture, and put on theatrical productions. Teens will participate in additional activities, like macramé, mural painting, and bead work. Also on the agenda are tours of the farm, a water slide, and camping out. Parents have the option of transporting their children directly to the farm or dropping them off at several points around the city.

Each of the aforementioned camps costs around $75 to $85 per child per week, but there are many others to choose from. You can view the camp schedule and register online at www.columbusrecparks.com or by calling (614) 645-7000. Summer activities are also provided at many of the city's 55 neighborhood playgrounds, which are staffed with professional summer program leaders.

U-Pick Farms

As the seasons change, harvest activities start cropping up around Ohio—literally. Farms and orchards will throw open their gates to visitors wanting to pick their own fresh fruits and vegetables or take a tractor ride. There are a few small local places that are open for picking: Doran's Farm Market at 5462 Babbitt Road in New Albany (614-855-3885) and Hoffman's Farm Market at 800 Rome-Hilliard Road (614-878-5161) both offer green beans and tomatoes. Fifteen miles south of Columbus along Route 23 is Renick's Family Market (740-983-3096), where you can pick your own pumpkins, wander through a corn maze, or set the kids lose in the L'il Farmer's Play Yard while you shop the market. West of Columbus, on 6010 Converse Huff Road in Plain City, is Yutzy's Farm Market (614-873-3815), where you can not only pick strawberries and corn, but also purchase Amish cheese and Ohio grown products. The selection of bulk dry goods and spices is impressive.

Lynd Fruit Farm in Pataskala (740-927-1333; www.lyndfruitfarm.com) is a seventh-generation, family-owned orchard and is the place to pick no less than a dozen types of apples and pumpkins. Wagon rides, a giant corn maze, and several interactive children's programs make this a great place for quality family time.

One of the most popular places for that annual hayride in the Columbus area is Circle "S" Farms (614-878-7980; www.circlesfarm.com), just off London-Groveport Road in Grove City. Both summer and autumn are great times of the year to visit this family-friendly farm. You can pick your own strawberries and raspberries in the summer and pumpkins in the fall. The Fall Fun Days offer a laundry list of activities, such as a six-acre corn maze, scarecrow cave, petting zoo, and puppet shows. There is no shortage of traditional fall events like hayrides, bonfires, tractor rides, and markets.

KID SCIENCE

4-H Club
2120 Fyffe Road, OSU campus
(614) 292-4444
www.ohio4h.org

This nonformal educational youth development program was started in 1902 in nearby Clark County as a way to teach school-age kids about agriculture and science through hands-on learning. 4-H now offers classes in more than 200 subjects that encourage youth to learn leadership, citizenship, and life skills.

Children ages 5 to 19 have the opportunity to experience organized activities, such as camping, workshops, and field trips, or get involved in specialized programs about flight, animal science, photography, and much more. Teens can develop their leadership and communication skills, travel abroad, or enter competitions at the Ohio State Fair. Project books have been developed for families, so that parents can engage in activities with the kids.

The new Nationwide and Ohio Farm Bureau 4-H Center is located on the west campus of The Ohio State University, but there are branches in all 88 of Ohio's counties, as well as regional and OSU extension offices. 4-H membership is free, but you should check with each individual county about fees for certain classes or workbooks.

COSI
333 West Broad Street, downtown
(614) 228-2674, (888) 819-COSI
www.cosi.org

COSI offers a range of programming for children and their favorite adults. Preschool workshops have been developed for children age 3 to 5 that introduce our youngest scientists to things like balloons, animals, and liquids. COSI Academy gives high school students the opportunity to meet monthly to discuss science issues and to develop their own scientific skills with professionals in various science fields.

Camp COSI offers themed weeklong day camps from June to August. Engaging hands-on activities are designed for age groups 3 to 14. The camps cost between $165 and $260. Baby Einsteins will learn about fish and dinosaurs, while slightly older space cadets can explore the solar system, solve crimes, or dig for fossils. The oldest kids make overnight treks to caves or Lake Erie, while astronaut wannabes can attend Space Academy and talk to Kathy Sullivan, the first American woman to walk in space.

The entire family can join in Family Friday Nights. The last Friday of every month, from 5:00 to 9:00 P.M., COSI hosts special activities, movie previews, and a dance party in the atrium. All exhibition areas and theaters, including the Extreme Screen, are included in the $7.00 admission fee.

Franklin Park Conservatory and Botanical Gardens
1777 East Broad Street, Bexley
(614) 645-5921, (800) 214-PARK
www.fpconservatory.org

Summer youth programs combine fun and education into half-day workshops. Children ages 4 to 14 will learn how to garden, investigate bugs, and try their hand at a variety of garden-inspired art forms. All camps cost $75 to $85 and meet for five days. Family Fun Days, held the second Saturday of each month, feature music, educational programs, and crafts that are included in the regular price of admission.

The Ohio State University

The Entomology Department offers tours of the conservatory (614-688-5593) and Insectary (614-292-9634) located at 322 West 12th Avenue. Children can get a close look at over 130 species of insects, from tarantulas to hissing cockroaches to walking sticks. The conservatory features a tropical house, desert house, and over 1,200 other plant species. Tours, which cost only $2.00, must be scheduled a few weeks in advance, as this is an active research facility.

The Waterman Agricultural and Natural Resources Laboratory, on the corner of Lane Avenue and Kenny Road, offers guided tours of this working dairy farm. Kids can meet the 140-cow herd, tour the barns, and learn about various chores, such as milking cows and making cheese. Adults may be interested to learn about quality control, artificial insemination, and consumer issues. Your children just might leave knowing that chocolate milk does not come from brown cows! Call (614) 292-6759 to schedule a tour of the complex.

Orton Geological Museum
Orton Hall
125 South Oval Mall, OSU campus
(614) 292-6896

Built in 1893, Orton Hall is one of the oldest buildings on Ohio State's campus and is home to the university's geology department. What many people don't know is that the first floor of this building also houses a small museum with one of the largest fossil collections in the Midwest. As you enter, the skeleton of a giant ice age ground sloth greets you. This free museum displays prehistoric turtle shells, dinosaur eggs, and mastodon teeth. It also highlights Ohio's geologic history and exhibits one of 12 meteorites found in

Ohio. OSU's first president, Edward Orton, donated the collection. Guided tours are available upon request.

KID SPORT

If your children want to be involved in Little League baseball, softball, or football, you should check with city, school district, or community centers, as there are just too many to list here. The Columbus Department of Recreation and Parks offers a range of athletic summer camps at reasonable prices ($60 to $90 per week). For details about youth leagues and summer camps, call (614) 645-7000, or register at www.columbusrecparks.com using the online forms.

The Football Camp held at Barrack Recreation Center (614-645-3610) on 580 East Woodrow Avenue in southeast Columbus gives boys and girls ages 11 through 14 the opportunity to learn the fundamentals of defensive and offensive football strategies while practicing all team positions.

The instructional Gymnastics Camp at Franklin Park Adventure Center, 1755 East Broad Street, is not for beginners. Boys and girls between the ages of 7 and 14 participate in daily apparatus rotations, conditioning, and stretching. Girls must be at levels 4, 5, and 6 and boys at levels 5, 6, and 7, as the focus is on vault, parallel bars, beam, and floor.

In June, kids ages 7 to 12 can sign up for a week of tennis instruction, drills, and games at Whetstone Tennis Courts in Clintonville. This tennis camp is appropriate for beginners and intermediate players. Novices are taught basic skills, while advanced players develop on-court strategies. Nontennis activities, like wall climbing and picnic games, are offered during lunchtime.

Coed track-and-field camps are offered a few times in June at various locations for kids ages 9 to 14. They focus on sprinting, distance running, hurdles, jumps, throws, and relays. Participants will have the opportunity to compete in a track meet at the end of the month.

The city has also developed therapeutic recreation camps (614-645-5648), which are modified to meet the needs of individuals with disabilities. Weekly sessions are held at Schiller Park in German Village and Franklin Park in Bexley. The inclusive camps make every effort to accommodate a variety of special needs. Campers have the opportunity to take part in ball sports, arts and crafts, and photography and explore the great outdoors at various park systems. Some of the other fun events include picnics, parades, talent shows, and an overnight camp.

One of the advantages to having a major league soccer team in Columbus is access to great soccer camps and academies held throughout the summer. National and international professionals teach the Crew Soccer Camps during five-day sessions held at various locations throughout the city. Campers of all skill sets are welcome to learn drills and develop ball skills. The classes are well priced, at $125 to $145 per week. More information is available at (614) 447-CREW or www.columbus.crew.mlsnet.com.

Children can learn the art of "footie" at another camp coached by licensed English, Scottish, and Welsh instructors. The Challenger British Soccer Camp, sponsored by the Columbus Department of Recreation and Parks, is held at Antrim Park and Big Walnut Park. The focus is on developing foot skills. Each camper takes part in technical and tactical practices and scrimmages. The hourlong mini-soccer camp is for 4- and 5-year-olds, while the

i

All types of kites are welcome at the Fun Fly, sponsored by the Columbus Kiters the second Saturday and fourth Sunday of each month. It is held from 10:00 A.M. to 5:00 P.M. at the Ohio School for the Deaf, 550 Morse Road, Clintonville. Just tell the guard at the gate you are there to fly kites.

half- and full-day camps are offered to age groups 6 to 14. Register for this camp by calling (614) 645-7000. The cost ranges between $50 and $140. Fees include a hand-stitched soccer ball, camp shirt, and skills evaluation from the coach.

Children ages 2 and up will receive top-notch soccer instruction at Soccer First, one of Ohio's finest indoor/outdoor soccer facilities, located at SportsOhio in Dublin. Ten outdoor fields, three professional-size indoor fields, training areas, and state-of-the-art equipment ensure a good starting point for new players and a premium environment for competitive players. KinderTots, KinderKickers, and Kickers have programs, which focus on the 2 to 10 age group, while leagues and the academy cater to all age groups. Other leagues, instruction, and camps in lacrosse, flag football, and field hockey are offered at Soccer First. Get further information by calling (614) 793-0101 or going to the Web site, www.soccer-first.com.

Also at the SportsOhio complex is the Midwest Gymnastics and Cheerleading facility (www.midwestgymandcheer.com), where programming is available to children as early as preschool. Classes range from fundamental gymnastics skills to extensive training in all Olympic gymnastic events for boys and girls. All-around instruction is available for individual and competitive cheerleading squads, as are various summer camps. Call (614) 764-0775 for further information.

Ice hockey has taken off in Columbus since the Blue Jackets came to town in 2000. The Junior Jackets Hockey Program is a great way for children and parents to learn the basics of skating, stick handling, and shooting, while the Stick and Puck youth program is an opportunity for young hockey players ages 6 to 17 to practice their art.

There are four Chiller Ice Rinks, where hockey leagues, camps and clinics are offered throughout the year. One is located at the SportsOhio Complex in Dublin (614-764-1000), and the others are at Easton (614-475-7575), Lewis Center (740-549-0009), and the Ice Haus at Nationwide Arena (614-246-3380). You can view the Web site for youth programs and the schedule of public ice-skating sessions at www.thechiller.com, or call each individual rink.

KID EATS

Buca di Beppo
60 East Wilson Bridge Road, Worthington
(614) 848-8466
www.bucadibeppo.com
Hearty Italian cuisine is dished up in American-size portions—one entree is large enough to feed four to six people. Buca has a setting in which even the noisiest of families feels comfortable. If you want the best seat in the house, ask for the table in the kitchen. That will keep the tribe entertained! There's a second location in the Arena District.

Chuck E. Cheese
2711 Martin Road, Dublin
(614) 791-9480
www.chuckecheese.com
Chuck E. Cheese, the giant mouse, has been entertaining (or terrifying) little kids for over 25 years—and they still love him! The food here is not the big attraction, but the electronic puppet show, games, tickets, and prizes are. Kids play skee-ball, pop-a-shot, and video games for strips of tickets redeemable for some seriously junkie stuff, but who cares? It's all in fun. There are three of these pizzeria-style restaurants in the Columbus area, and all of them are open until 10:00 or 11:00 P.M., so the kids can run amok way past their bedtimes.

Cozymel's Coastal Grill
6100 Park Center Circle, Dublin
(614) 717-0448
www.cozymels.com
This is a family favorite for food from south of the border. A lot has to do with its bustling atmosphere, but no one can complain about the food—not even the kids, who have their own Mexican menu. Servers

make fresh guacamole right at your table, and there's a list of fun, tropical (adult) drinks. Go ahead and indulge! The kids won't know the margarita slushy machines aren't serving Slurpees. They'll be too busy watching the energetic staff.

Dave & Buster's
3665 Park Mill Drive, Hilliard
(614) 771-1515
www.daveandbusters.com
This Dallas-based entertainment complex has been included for its sheer entertainment value. The huge building is split up into a dining room, bar, billiards and shuffleboard room, and amusement area, with games ranging from skee-ball and basketball to racing and shooting. Virtual simulators sit side by side with some of the earliest arcade games, like Ms. Pacman and Donkey Kong. Bust a move on dance machines or take a swing at Madden Golf. This is the sort of place parents, teens, and tots can all find something to do. And, unlike the madhouse Chuck E. Cheese can be, children must be accompanied by an adult at all times. The food isn't bad either. They have two full-service bars and an extensive adult menu, with steaks, seafood, and salads. The children's menu has the usual suspects: grilled cheese and chicken fingers.

Johnny Rockets
Lennox Town Center
1787 Olentangy River Road, Grandview
(614) 291-8239
www.johnnyrockets.com
This All-American diner is a throwback to days when food was less complicated and the jukebox cost 5 cents. The food is fast, the service is friendly, and, yes, the tabletop jukebox will belt out a song for a nickel. The must-have menu items are burgers, cheesy fries, and the best hand-dipped malts in town. Kid's meals come with a small-size portion of fries and a drink, but many prefer to just get ice cream and swivel around at the counters. Every half hour the servers dance around to oldies, and, if prodded, they might even tell your child the secret to getting ketchup out of the bottle. There is a second location at Easton.

McDonald's Restaurant
The Strand West, Easton Town Center
(614) 416-4508
www.mcdonalds.com
At 11,500 square feet, this one-of-a-kind, family-themed McDonald's is one of largest in the country. While most of the interior looks like an outdoor park, the main counter resembles the original 1950s McDonald's. Another interesting feature is a separate McTreat dessert counter, with ice cream, cookies, and pastries, and a coffee bar serving specialty coffee, espresso, and cappuccino.

There are specific areas designed for family, kids, 'tweens, and adults. The children's area is a mini-McDonald's complete with drive-through, where children can pretend they are working the restaurant or ride in toy cars to place their orders. Outside this restaurant is a play land with giant, overstuffed equipment shaped like items from a Happy Meal. The space for 'tweens has a computer game station, regular board games, and a karaoke station, where they can record their own music. Some tables even have listening domes, where kids can select their own music. Parents can sneak away to a quieter area to read the paper or gather for adult conversation.

KID SHOP

Build-A-Bear Workshop
Easton Station, Easton Town Center
(614) 473-8888
www.buildabear.com
Kids will love picking out their own furry friend to stuff, recite the "bear promise," and take home. The store has a selection of more than 25 animals (bears, monkeys, dogs, etc.) in the $10 to $25 price range to choose from, as well as hundreds of outfits and accessories. Once assembled, the kids can name it, personalize a birth

certificate, and add a recorded message. The store has a fun, interactive atmosphere for kids and parents.

Club Libby Lu
The Strand West, Easton Town Center
(614) 337-9080
www.clublibbylu.com
If you have a VIP (Very Important Princess) in your family, then this adorable shop is the perfect place for her to find a few fabulous accessories and get a super-duper makeover. The makeover specialist will transform her into a rocker chick, an enchanted princess, or a Hollywood starlet for $20. The makeover includes all the accessories for "the look," as well as a few extra treasures she can pick out for herself. Libby Lu is appropriate for girls as young as 3 and hosts special Mom and Me makeovers as well as sassy birthday celebrations.

Discovery Channel Store
Gramercy Street, Easton Town Center
(614) 478-9125
www.discoverychannelstore.com
This store is built around the Discovery Channel's educational success, and their products expose shoppers to science and technology, travel, and exploration. This store carries a variety of state-of-the-art gadgets, captivating games, home accessories, and clothing, but the best sellers are kid-related items. Globes, telescopes, remote-controlled dinosaurs, and science kits are among the top sellers. Several of the Discovery toys, such as the DNA Explorer Kit and the 3-D Space Projector, have won various awards for their educational value.

The Doll House
109 North High Street, Gahanna
(614) 471-8484
www.boydsbearshop.com
This quaint boutique is located in a 100-year-old house in Olde Gahanna and is central Ohio's largest dealer of Boyd's Bears. Stuffed animals aside, The Doll House also sells the Vera Bradley collection, Lee Middleton dolls, and a nice selection of candles and general home decor.

Larson's Toys & Games
Shops On Lane Avenue, Upper Arlington
(614) 486-2885
www.larsonstoys.com
This old-fashioned, family-owned toy store carries just about anything children like to play with, and when you are at a loss, the staff is quick to make suggestions. Classics include things like wagons, art easels, wooden blocks, and traditional board games. You'll find popular lines of toys, dolls, and stuffed animals, including Thomas the Tank Engine, Lego kits, and Madame Alexander dolls. The art kits and educational activities are great for older kids. Larson's has a second location in the Worthington Mall and offers free wrapping for all purchases.

The Laughing Ogre
4258 North High Street, Clintonville
(614) A-MR-OGRE
www.thelaughingogre.com
Columbus is a vibrant comic and cartoon community, so it should come as no surprise that the city is home to one of the country's best and most small-press-friendly retailers. This comic book shop in Clintonville is a treasure for comic lovers and carries everything from mainstream to small-press comic books. You'll also find a huge selection of graphic novels, mini-comics, and trade paperbacks. The Ogre holds in-store signings and legendary preconvention parties that attract fans and professionals.

Science 2GO!
333 West Broad Street, downtown
(614) 228-2674, (888) 819-COSI
www.cosi.org
This little shop of wonders is located in COSI and carries science- and technology-related toys, books, and hands-on activities.

You'll find merchandise for people of all ages, but children particularly like the fossils, astronaut food, and bug kits. Parents can appreciate these toys, which spark creativity and stir children's imagination.

The Train Station
4430 Indianola Avenue, Clintonville
(614) 262-9056
www.trainstationohio.com

The name is a friendly reminder that this store is exclusively for model railroad enthusiasts. It carries full lines of model railroad and train products, books, videos, magazines, scenery, and paints. The Train Station is an authorized dealer of brass model importers, including Overland, Glacier Park, and Sunset Models, and is also a Lionel Authorized Value Added Dealer and LGB Authorized Train Stop.

ANNUAL EVENTS AND FESTIVALS

We love our festivals. Columbus celebrates everything from diversity to beer. According to a National Endowment for the Arts' survey, Ohio ranks second in the nation for attendance at festivals, and no doubt, Columbus contributes a huge chunk to these numbers. Every weekend brings warm weather celebrations or winter expos, not to mention the countless number of church festivals, community days, and charity events held on a local level.

The venues, entry fees, and size of the festivals vary dramatically. Certain events, such as the Wendy's International Cycling Classic and the Rose Festival, draw a select crowd, while everyone in Columbus seems to turn up for the Dublin Irish Festival and Oktoberfest in German Village. Thousands of people pass through the doors of the convention center and fairgrounds for huge annual events that have been going on, in some cases, for over a century.

Not every event has been included in this chapter, but major marathons, ethnic festivals, and holiday celebrations are listed alphabetically in the calendar month they occur. Also included here are a few neighborhood arts festivals and street fairs that attract visitors from all over the state.

Smaller, more specialized events, such as music, home, and garden shows, can be tracked down at the convention center or expo Web sites. Various walks held by national charities can be found on city calendars, as well as the specific charity Web site. One-time events and exhibitions are listed in *The Other Paper* and *The Short North Gazette,* while the seasonal series sponsored by Columbus's performing arts organizations are mentioned in The Arts chapter.

Gallery Hop is a popular, ongoing monthly event held in the Short North the first Saturday of each month. Art galleries stay open late and often feature new or special exhibitions. Restaurants and bars host live entertainment, and the area remains festive well into the night, particularly in the summer.

The city's Web site (www.columbus.gov) has a limited calendar of events, and the Web site for Experience Columbus (www.experiencecolumbus.com) provides a comprehensive listing with short descriptions of upcoming events in and around the city. This chapter will point you in the right direction for planning your weekend or holiday itinerary in Columbus.

JANUARY

Columbus Golf Show
Veterans Memorial
300 West Broad Street
(614) 221-4341

Columbus is focused on its golf game, even in the dead of winter. Over 20,000 people come to see hundreds of vendors and golf-related exhibitions at this three-day exposition. Putting greens and indoor driving ranges will get you itching for that next golf trip. Admission is $8.00; children under 12 are free.

Martin Luther King Jr. Day
The King Arts Complex
867 Mount Vernon Avenue
(614) 645-0642

This annual birthday celebration is held at Columbus's leading African-American arts and cultural institution. It features a variety of performances, activities, and events commemorating the life of the late civil rights leader. A breakfast is held in his honor. The price of admission is a nonperishable food.

FEBRUARY

Arnold Fitness Weekend
Greater Columbus Convention Center
400 North High Street
(614) 431-2600
www.arnoldfitnessweekend.com

Columbus's Jim Lorimer and Arnold Schwarzenegger are the driving forces behind the world's largest fitness weekend. What began as the Mr. World Contest in the 1970s has evolved into a world-class sporting event offering hundreds of thousands of dollars in prizes.

Some 12,000 athletes converge on Columbus in late February for 20 different sporting competitions, 8 of which are represented in the Olympics. Anchoring the weekend are the Arnold Classic and Ms. International bodybuilding competitions, but a short list of other events include the Martial Arts Festival, the Cheerleading and Dance Team Championship, the Arnold Gymnastics Challenge, and the 5K Pump and Run.

The Arnold Classic is held at Veterans Memorial, and most other events are held at the convention center, where the Arnold Fitness Expo features 600 booths of clothing, fitness equipment, nutritional information, and autographed merchandise. Ten dollars gains you admission to anything in the hall, including certain preliminary rounds. Children under 10 are free. Tickets to the finals vary in price and can be purchased in advance through Ticketmaster or at the venue the day of the event.

Easy Rider's Annual Bike Show
Veterans Memorial
300 West Broad Street
(614) 221-4341
www.easyriders.com

This trade show is wall-to-wall choppers. The show features the finest custom motorcycles in the world, vendors, roadwear fashions, and door prizes. Adult admission ranges from $15 to $20, and entire weekend passes are available. Children over 5 cost $7.00; those under 5 are free.

Great American Train Show
Ohio Expo Center
717 East 17th Avenue
(614) 644-3247
www.greatamericantrainshow.com

Over the course of 20 years, this Chicago-based touring model train show has become America's largest. The show promotes the hobby of model railroading and features local and national sellers, hobby shops, train specialists, and several operating train layouts. A highlight is the tiny "Magic Scale" trains that fit in the palm of your hand. Admission is $8.00; children under 12 are free.

Sugarloaf Crafts Festival
Ohio Expo Center
717 East 17th Avenue
(614) 644-3247
www.sugarloafcrafts.com

This expo is not a country craft or home craft show; rather it focuses on fine art and contemporary crafts. Industry publications rank Sugarloaf Crafts Festival in the top 100 craft shows in the United States. Admission is $7.00; children under 12 are free.

MARCH

Columbus International Auto Show
Greater Columbus Convention Center
400 North High Street
(614) 799-2232
www.columbusautoshow.com

The 51st year of the auto show saw record-breaking attendance. Last year, nearly 500,000 visitors passed through the convention doors to see what's new in the automobile industry. Exhibitions include classic cars, luxury cars, and alternative fuel vehicles. Major prizes are given away, and an activity center will keep the kids busy with a giant slide and moon bounce. The show lasts about 10 days, and the cost for admission is under $10.

St. Patrick's Day Parades
Downtown Columbus and Dublin
The city of Columbus's St. Patrick's Day parade begins downtown after mass at St. Patrick's Church and ends at Veterans Memorial.

The suburb of Dublin fittingly goes all out for its patron saint. The Grand Leprechaun leads the parade from Metro Center to High Street in Old Dublin. A free Blarney Bash, with food, drink, musicians, and dancers, is held in the parking lot of the Dublin Clarion Hotel until 11:00 P.M. Storytellers, crafts, and activities abound in a separate heated tent for the wee ones.

APRIL

Capital City Half Marathon
Downtown Columbus
www.capitalcityhalfmarathon.com
Capital City Half Marathon is held in early April. The 13.1-mile marathon begins and ends at PromoWest Pavilion in the Arena District. Runners wind through scenic and historic areas of downtown Columbus, German Village, the Short North, and Victorian Village. A 2-mile lap through the OSU campus and around Ohio Stadium has been added.

Pooch Parade
High Street, Olde Worthington
(614) 888-3494
www.poochparade.net
This all-day event, held the fourth Saturday in April, culminates in one of the biggest dog parades in the country. There are a number of fun activities to share with your pet. Prizes are given for the best float and different categories like "Best Costume" and "Dog Who Looks Most Like His/Her Person."

Rescue Row provides awareness information and is a great way to meet dogs available for adoption from more than 30 rescue groups. Dog-related items can be found in booths along Vendor Row. There is no charge to participate in the parade, but donations are split between rescue organizations.

MAY

African American Heritage Festival
OSU campus
(614) 688-8449
www.osuheritagefestival.com
These weeklong events include cultural dancers, storytelling, and dinners. Student organizations, BET (Black Entertainment Television), and nationally acclaimed speakers help celebrate African-American history and culture with free events held throughout campus. A few of the formal dinners and parties charge for admission tickets.

Asian Festival
Franklin Park
1777 East Broad Street
www.asian-festival.org
Fifteen Asian-American groups are represented at this festival celebrating the rich heritage of various Asian cultures. More than 100,000 people attend this free festival held around Memorial Day weekend. Enjoy traditional stage performances, authentic cuisine, and shopping the Asian Market. Learn more about diverse cultures through hands-on activities and fascinating cultural booths. Parking is free, but there is a shuttle provided between Columbus State Community College and the park.

Dandelion Festival
Breitenbach Wine Cellars
Old Route 39, between Dover and Sugar Creek
(330) 343-3603, (800) THE-WINE
www.breitenbachwine.com
The first weekend in May is the annual Dandelion Festival at Breitenbach Wine Cellars. It's everything dandelion, from cookbooks to wine. Those of you with the

gift of culinary genius should try out your skills in the dandelion cook-off.

May Herb Festival
The Gahanna Historical Society
101 South High Street, Gahanna
(614) 475-2509
www.visitgahanna.com
The Gahanna Historical Society celebrates spring with an herb and crafts show featuring fresh herbs, quilts, and various demonstrations. Learn medicinal and culinary uses and get answers to gardening questions. You'll leave knowing why Gahanna was named the "Herb Capital of Ohio" in 1972. No admission fee is charged.

JUNE

Columbus Arts Festival
Downtown Columbus Riverfront
(614) 224-2606
www.gcac.org
This huge arts fair, organized by the Greater Columbus Arts Council, ushers in the summer for four days in early June. More than 300 artisans and craftspeople sell their wares from booths along the Scioto River. Continuous art activities keep the children (and adults) busy, while nonstop entertainment on two stages keeps your toes tappin'. Admission is free, but do expect to pay event parking prices.

Columbus Rose Festival
Whetstone Park of Roses
3923 North High Street, Clintonville
(614) 645-6640
Everything's coming up roses during this weekend festival in mid-June. Events including the Columbus Rose Club's Annual Rose Show, lawn and garden vendors, entertainment, and workshops are located throughout the 13-acre park. General admission is free.

Creekside Blues and Jazz Festival
Creekside Park, Gahanna
(614) 418-9114
www.gahanna.gov
This free festival, which showcases blues and jazz music, is Gahanna's premier summer event. Aside from the music, you'll find arts and crafts, classic cars, children's activities, and the usual festival fare. Its location in Creekside Park allows for some interesting contests: frog jumping, fishing contests, and canoe races. It is held the third Saturday in June.

Festival Latino
Downtown Columbus Riverfront
(614) 645-7995, (614) 645-3800
www.festivallatino.net
Spice up your weekend at Ohio's largest Hispanic/Latino event. International and regional artists perform on three different stages. Authentic cuisine, arts, crafts, and educational activities celebrate the diversity of Latin American cultures. Shop at the market place, learn the meringue, and help your children make copper bracelets. Admission is free, and the festival is held all day Friday and Saturday until midnight.

German Village Haus und Garten Tour
588 South Third Street
(614) 221-8888
www.germanvillage.com
Residents of German Village open their doors and gates for visitors to appreciate the design and restoration of a dozen homes and gardens. Admission is $15 in advance and $20 the day of the tour. Tickets can be purchased through the German Village Society.

Ohio Scottish Games
Lorain County Fairgrounds
Junction of State Routes 58 and 18
www.ohioscottishgames.com
Kilt up and head to this traditional Scottish Festival, where you will see hammer throwing and Highland dancing at its best. Aside from professional and amateur athletic competitions, awards are given in various dance, harp, and fiddle categories. Explore your heritage at the genealogy tent, or find your family plaid on Tartan Days. And what's more Scottish than bagpipes and golf? These hallmarks of Scot-

tish culture are celebrated with a golf outing and a tattoo performance. The festival is sponsored by the Scottish-American Cultural Society of Ohio.

Pride Parade and Festival
Goodale and Bicentennial Parks
(614) 299-7764
www.stonewallcolumbus.org
More than 55,000 visitors from the tri-state area attended the Midwest's largest gay pride festival last year. Stonewall Columbus, an organization that serves the central Ohio gay, lesbian, bisexual, and transgendered community, hosts a series of events at the end of June that help raise awareness and celebrate gay pride. The festival begins with a rally for gay rights and ends in a Mardi Gras–style parade with a rainbow of floats and people. Expect to see costumed marchers and dancing in the streets.

Worthington Arts Festival
Village Green, Olde Worthington
(614) 885-8237
www.owba.net
This two-day juried arts-and-crafts show draws artists from all over the country. Works in a variety of media, ranging from clay and paint to metal and wood, are featured, along with jewelry and photography. The show is held Saturday and Sunday, and admission is free.

JULY

Doo-Dah Parade
Goodale Park, Victorian Village
www.shortnorth.com
This zany Fourth of July tradition is a celebration of free speech, political satire, inspired (and sometimes stupid) lunacy, and opinionated people wanting to be noticed. It's the only Independence Day parade in the city of Columbus, and it's free to all. Join in if you have a daring, silly, funny, and/or good idea. Actually, a bad idea might be even better for this parade full of bad taste, weird bicycles, Marching Fidels, Gandhi on skates, and the occasional pot-bellied pig.

Jazz and Rib Fest
Downtown Columbus Riverfront
(614) 221-1321, (800) 950-1321
www.columbus.org/jazz
The largest free rib festival in the nation straddles both sides of the Scioto River for three days in June. Nearly 30 ribbers from nine states serve tons of mouthwatering ribs to the smooth beats of top local and national jazz artists.

Pickerington Violet Festival
Victory Park
Off Lockville Road, Pickerington
(614) 834-2717
www.violetfestival.org
Pickerington celebrates the area's sweet floral ground covering with an annual festival that includes an arts-and-crafts show, rides and entertainment, a violet parade, and the crowing of Miss Violet Festival.

Red, White, and Boom
Downtown Columbus Riverfront
(614) 421-BOOM
Independence Day begins with entertainment, food, and a parade. It ends with the largest (and many say the best) synchronized music and fireworks display in the Midwest. The heart of the event is on the west side of the Scioto River near COSI, but the fireworks can be seen as far away as Ohio State's campus. There is no rain date and no charge for this event, but be prepared to wrestle with a hundred thousand people for parking spaces.

Wendy's International Cycling Classic
Various parts of Columbus
www.wendyscycling.com
Every summer, around the same time as the Tour de France, several dozen riders gather in Columbus for a four-stage race through various parts of the city. Top teams are represented, and the courses can be viewed online. There is no charge to cheer on the cyclists from the sidelines.

CLOSE-UP

The Ohio State Fair: Americana-on-a-Stick

Almost half the state of Ohio is considered prime farmland, and one in seven people are employed in some aspect of agriculture. It's no wonder the state fair, which attracts over a million visitors, is among the largest in the country. For two weeks in August, a mix of special competitions, exhibitions, entertainment, rides, and thousands of animals showcase Ohio's agriculture and farming industry in an educational and fun way.

The fair began over 150 years ago, and, despite its evolution, many of its early traditions have been preserved. The earliest fairs focused entirely on agriculture, but they quickly came to include food and entertainment. In 1896, Ohio's was the first fair in the country to be lit by electricity. The annual butter sculptures were first exhibited in 1903 and remain a popular attraction today. An All-Ohio Boys Band began performing in the 1920s, and its descendants, the All-Ohio Band and State Choir, are the fair's veteran performers.

The schedule is packed with horse, dog, and livestock shows and cattle, pig, and poultry competitions. Big names like Clay Aiken and Brooks and Dunn take one of the five stages. Other attractions include tractor and truck pulls, 70 amusement rides, square dances, and people's choice awards, not to mention the food. Almost 200 vendors sell every type of fair fare imaginable, while three air-conditioned restaurants provide options other than deep-fried everything-on-a-stick.

The Ohio State Fair is also home to the largest Junior Fair in the nation. Thousands of youngsters exhibit everything from livestock to ponies, to photography and candy. When the kids aren't competing and showing, there are magicians, a petting zoo, a farm animal delivery room, and several rides allowing parents to accompany younger children.

State fairs have long been a part of American culture, and in keeping with the U.S. spirit of diversity, the Ohio State Fair has added a permanent celebration of

AUGUST

Brew at the Zoo
Columbus Zoo and Aquarium
9990 Riverside Drive, Powell
(614) 645-3581, (800) 666-5397
www.columbuszoo.org

This after-hour's fundraiser supports conservation efforts while guests enjoy food, beverages, and entertainment in a wild setting. This adults-only event is held on a Friday night, and tickets cost around $25.

Dublin Irish Festival
Coffman Park
5200 Emerald Parkway, Dublin
(614) 410-4545, (877) 67-GREEN
www.dublinirishfestival.org

The Ohio State Fair. OHIO STATE FAIR

Hispanic culture called Fiesta Ohio. Additionally, a different culture will be honored on a changing basis each year as a reflection of the growing variety of ethnicities represented in the area.

The fair is held for 15 days at the Ohio Expo Center (formerly the Fairgrounds), located at 717 East 17th Avenue. Call (614) 644-FAIR, or check out the Web site www.ohiostatefair.com for a full schedule of events. Adult admission is $8.00, and seniors and children (ages 5 to 12) cost $7.00. Children under 5 are free; bigger families can save some money during Family Value Days. Parking is $5.00 per vehicle.

As one of the largest and most popular Irish festivals in the country, the American Business Association named the Dublin Irish Festival as one of the top 100 events in North America for 2005. Six stages feature national and international Celtic bands. The cultural area includes genealogy booths, dance instruction, and music workshops. Visitors can enjoy the Irish art of storytelling or learn the traditions of an Irish wake in the Spoken Word Tent. Families can pay a visit to Brian Boru's Ireland in a re-created 10th-century village or partake of traditional arts and crafts in the Wee Folks area.

With over 70 stalls of unique imported goods, the expansive Marketplace is like an Irish arts festival unto itself. Vendors serve

Irish beer along with authentic food from the British Isles. Festivities go on until midnight Friday and Saturday. Sunday is kicked off with three different masses: an Irish mass in Gaelic, a traditional mass, and an interdenominational service.

You don't have to be Irish to compete in the contests for reddest hair, greenest eyes, and most freckles. A highlight of the festival is a 25-ton sand sculpture carved during the course of the weekend. All entertainment and most activities are covered under a general admission ticket, which costs between $8.00 and $20.00 for adults. Entry is $5.00 for seniors.

SEPTEMBER

Columbus Italian Festival
St. John the Baptist Church
720 Hamlet Street
(614) 294-8259
www.columbusitalianfestival.com
Italian or not, you'll feel like part of the family at this festival that has been giving Columbus a carb boost for more than 25 years. There's no shortage of pizzas, home-style pastas, and Italian cookies. The whole family will enjoy the live entertainment and open-air market. Admission is $4.00 per person; children under 12 are free. A weekend pass is available for $10 per person.

German Village Oktoberfest
South Grant and East Livingston Avenue
(614) 221-8888
www.germanvillage.com
Locals have been donning their lederhosen for over 40 years as German heritage and culture is celebrated for three days right in the heart of historic German Village. Plenty of beer, brats, and bands can be found till the wee hours of the morning. Festival favorites include the Kinderplatz for children and the Marketplatz for everyone else. Admission is $8.00 for adults, with discounts for seniors. Children under 12 are free.

Greek Festival
Greek Orthodox Cathedral
555 North High Street, Short North
(614) 224-9020
www.greekcathedral.com
Labor Day weekend brings about a celebration of Greek heritage and the Orthodox Christian faith. Greek Festival dancers in full traditional costumes entertain guests as they indulge in Mediterranean food, pastries, and drink. Highlights include a replica of a traditional Greek village home, cooking demos, tours of the cathedral, and exhibitions of iconography and calligraphy. Admission is $3.00, $2.50 for seniors. Children 12 and under are free.

The Little Brown Jug
Delaware County Fairgrounds
(740) 362-3851, (800) 335-3247
www.littlebrownjug.com
The Little Brown Jug, held the third Thursday after Labor Day, is the Kentucky Derby of harness racing. The race, held during the Delaware County Fair, is part of the Triple Crown of the famed Grand Circuit. This pacing classic for three-year-olds is the most attended harness race in the country. The tailgating events have been called "the biggest cocktail party in the state of Ohio," but you might want to save your sunhats and seersucker suits for the Kentucky Derby. People dress casually for this event. Tickets cost from $20 to $200.

Ohio Renaissance Festival
2 miles off I-71 on Route 73
Harveysburg
(513) 897-7000
www.renfestival.com
If you were born 400 years too late, fear not! For two months every autumn, you'll be transported to 16th-century England, where you can rub elbows with royalty, banter with fools, and feast like nobility on turkey legs. This authentically re-created medieval village is a sprawling 30 acres of Renaissance cottages, craft shops, vendors, and stages.

Hundreds of costumed performers, storytellers, and musicians mill about the bustling lanes of the open-air marketplace and perform on 12 stages. Full-armored jousts, swordsmen, and an action-packed pirate show set the crowds cheering. People of all ages are entertained by games of skill and human-powered rides. Try your hand at archery, or rescue the damsel in distress from the castle tower.

Every weekend has a different theme, such as the Highland Fling or Feast of Fools, so no matter how often you go, it's never the same. Tickets are $17, and children over the age of 5 cost $10. Tickets are cheaper if purchased online, and students are given discounts on certain weekends. The festival runs from mid-August through the end of October.

Ohio Swiss Festival
Downtown Sugar Creek
(330) 852-4113
www.sugarcreekohio.org
Some 100,000 people attend this four-day festival at the end of September in Sugarcreek, Ohio's "Little Switzerland." There's plenty of cheese to go around, as well as polka bands, alpine horn players, and a yodeling contest. Other highlights include parades, a quilt auction, and the crowning of Little Swiss Miss. The festival features two traditional Swiss athletic events: the Steinstossen, where men and women heave a heavy boulder as far as they can, and the Schwingfest, the Swiss version of wrestling. Admission is free.

Reynoldsburg Tomato Festival
Civic Park
6800 Daugherty Drive, Reynoldsburg
(614) 866-2861
www.visitreynoldsburg.com
Interested in tasting tomato fudge? Well, you can at this five-day festival celebrating the juicy fruit. Tomato exhibits, contests for the biggest tomato, and the crowning of the Tomato Queen are just a few of the highlights. Admission is free, but parking is $5.00.

Upper Arlington Labor Day Arts Festival
Northam Park
(614) 583-5310
www.ua-ohio.net
The Upper Arlington Labor Day Festival features almost 200 local, regional, and national artists in a variety of media. It is considered one of the best one-day arts festivals in the state and offers activities and entertainment for the whole family. There is a silent auction that supports the Cultural Arts Division of Upper Arlington, art activities for children, and a stage offering music, dance, and storytelling. Admission is free.

The state of Ohio is the country's leading producer of Swiss cheese, making about 64 million pounds annually. Sugar Creek is the center of Ohio's Swiss cheese industry, and Guggisberg is the home of the original Baby Swiss.

Via Colori
Short North Arts District
Goodale Avenue and Park Street
(614) 228-8050
www.shortnorth.org
Professional and amateur artists from all over Ohio create original chalk works of art directly on the city streets in gridded squares. This Italian street painting festival is unique in that you can watch the artwork evolving over the course of a weekend. If the artists aren't entertainment enough, there is a performance stage, as well as food, drinks, and vendors.

Victorian Village Tour of Homes
Victorian Village
(614) 228-2912
www.victorianvillage.org
The tour offers you an inside look at a dozen beautiful Victorian Village homes and gardens in various states of renovation. The event benefits the Victorian Village Society. Tickets cost $10 in advance and $15 the day of the tour.

Via Colori is the centuries-old tradition of street painting. It was practiced by Italian war veterans of the early Renaissance period who painted religious icons in the courtyards of the great cathedrals.

OCTOBER

All-American Quarter Horse Congress
Ohio Expo Center
717 East 17th Avenue
(740) 943-2346
www.oqha.com

With more than 16,000 horse show entries, the All-American Quarter Horse Congress is the world's largest single-breed horse show and the second-largest event held at the Ohio Expo. Over the course of three weeks, the congress attracts 650,000 people to the Columbus area, bringing more than $110 million to the local economy.

The daily schedule features horsemanship, roping, and racing events, as well as collegiate and 4-H/FFA horse judging contests. Other highlights include a Congress Queen contest, a youth tournament, and a horse bowl. Lectures and demonstrations provide educational information about the care and management of the American quarter horse. Commercial vendors sell western and English wear, towing vehicles and trailers, equine-related art, and jewelry.

The cost is $20 per vehicle for one-time admission and $60 for the entire show. There is no additional admission charge on top of this fee. There are additional charges for the Professional Bull Rider tour and the Freestyle Reining Performance.

The All-American Quarter Horse Congress contracts with several hotels in the Columbus area for discounts during the congress. The hotel reservation line is (740) 943-3906 and operates regular business hours. Reservations begin early April and end mid-September.

Circleville Pumpkin Show
Downtown Circleville
(740) 474-7000
www.pumpkinshow.com

Have you ever seen a 950-pound pumpkin? If so, chances are you have attended the Circleville Pumpkin Show. Called "The Greatest Free Show on Earth," over 400,000 people travel 45 minutes south of Columbus, making this the sixth-largest festival in the country.

The show had its humble beginnings in 1903, when the mayor of Circleville invited the local farmers to exhibit their corn fodder and pumpkins in front of his office. A century later, the promotion of premium agricultural pursuits has been maintained. You will see some of the biggest pumpkins on earth, not to mention indulge in edibles, such as (in the voice of Bubba Gump) pumpkin pie, pumpkin burgers, pumpkin bread, pumpkin ice cream, pumpkin waffles, pumpkin fudge, pumpkin pizza . . .

Pumpkin delicacies aside, the entire city center is blocked and converted into a mecca of arts, crafts, and specialty stalls and vendors selling the usual fair fare (corndogs, fries, and funnel cake). No alcoholic beverages are served on the streets.

You don't have to be a pumpkin connoisseur to have fun here. There are plenty of rides and games, parades, pie-eating contests, and musical concerts to keep everyone occupied. You can even witness the crowning of Miss Pumpkin. Whatever level of pumpkin passion you may exude (or not), it is certainly worth a look at Ohio's oldest festival. It takes place the third Wednesday through Saturday in October. Admission is free, but parking rates vary depending on proximity to the fair.

Columbus Marathon
Downtown Columbus and surrounding suburbs
(614) 421-RUNN
www.columbusmarathon.com

More than 5,000 runners turn up for the flat, fast, and fun Columbus Marathon. It is onsistently ranked as one of America's op 20 marathons by *Runner's World* and one of the top 10 fall marathons by *USA oday.* The Children's Run for Fun and the Columbus Marathon Relay are also part of this nationally renowned marathon.

NOVEMBER

Columbus International Festival
Veterans Memorial
300 West Broad Street
(614) 487-1300
www.unacol.org

he Columbus chapter of the United Nations Association celebrates the many faces of the city with 150 exhibitions and two stages of continuous cultural entertainment. A Parade of Nations is held each afternoon, while 60 countries are represented through food, crafts, folk dancing, and educational materials. Admission is $7.00; seniors and students pay only $5.00. Children ages 6 to 12 cost $2.00, and those under 6 are free. You will receive a "passport" upon entry, which can be stamped by the various exhibitors as you "travel the globe."

Scott Antique Shows
Ohio Expo Center
17 East 17th Avenue
(614) 644-3247, (740) 569-2800
www.scottantiquemarket.com

he Scott Antique Shows are the largest indoor shows in the country and have become the Midwest's most important egular antiquing event. The weekend shows are held on a monthly basis from November through April. The season opens in November with 1,000 booths in two huge buildings. The subsequent shows draw a "mere" 800 vendors.

For a non-scary alternative to traditional Halloween events, the Enchanted Forest at Aullwood Audubon Farm in Dayton allows you and your family to meet fairies and costumed animals during guided walks and stories around the campfire. The farm is located at 1000 Aullwood Road and can be reached at (937) 890-7360.

Admission is free, but parking at the Expo Center cost $4.00 a day.

DECEMBER

Westerville Fantasy of Lights
Alum Creek State Park
www.alumcreek.com

This drive-through light show runs seven days a week from mid-November until the end of December. Top off your drive through the park with free hot chocolate and cookies at Santa's house. Entry costs $10 per vehicle on weekdays and $15 on weekends.

First Night Columbus
Various downtown venues
(614) 481-0020
www.firstnightcols.com

This affordable, alcohol-free community-oriented celebration features hundreds of entertainers and art exhibitions at 30 venues across the city; a teen dance is held at COSI, and a hunt for art installations will send you scavenging the city. The main performance stage is at the City Center, while the other activities are held at COSI and city hall. Festivities continue from late afternoon, ending with a countdown to a midnight fireworks extravaganza.

Souvenir admission buttons are $8.00 in advance and $10.00 the day of the event. Children 5 and younger are free. The buttons give you access to all First Night activities at all venues. Trolleys travel between downtown venues begin-

America's largest outdoor holiday light show is just under a two-hour drive east of Columbus on Route 88 in Wheeling, West Virginia. Ogelbay Resort has been hosting this 6-mile drive through its spectacular wonderland of lights since 1985. The show remains fresh by adding a few new designs each year and special exhibits. For more information, call (304) 243-4000.

ning at 6:30 P.M. and are free for anyone wearing a "First Night" admissions button. Tickets go on sale at COSI, Fifth Third Banks, and Giant Eagle grocery stores in December. They can also be purchased online.

Holiday Lights Parade and Festival
Granville to Mill Street, Olde Gahanna
(614) 342-4250
www.visitgahanna.org

More than 100 lighted floats and marching bands will get you into the holiday spirit Gahanna-style. Highlights include Clydesdale horse-drawn carriages and free post-parade activities and entertainment.

Wildlight Wonderland
Columbus Zoo
9990 Riverside Drive, Powell
(614) 645-3581, (800) 666-5397
www.columbuszoo.org

Each November, Columbus Zoo transforms itself into an illuminated wonderland and has been dubbed one of the top 10 holiday light shows in the country. A winter stroll through the zoo is enhanced with two million sparkling lights, carolers, and live reindeer. Other activities include ice skating on the frozen lake, horse-drawn wagon rides, and an appearance by Santa Claus. During the festival, the Columbus Zoo also pays tribute to Kwanzaa with an evening full of crafts, dancing, and music honoring African-American heritage.

Don't worry; the animals are not forgotten. You can watch Santa Paws pay the animals a visit with specially wrapped treats in early December. Admission is $9.00, seniors $7.00, and children $5.00. Admission is free for zoo members. Wildlights is closed the evenings of Thanksgiving, Christmas Eve, and Christmas Day.

DAY TRIPS AND WEEKEND GETAWAYS

If it's a change of scenery you're looking for, you'll be amazed at what you can experience within a few hours' drive of Columbus. Walk in the footsteps of an escaped slave along Ohio's Underground Railroad, or discover how the Amish maintain their simple way of life in this rapidly changing world. Ride the world's tallest roller coaster, or eat at a haunted inn. No matter which direction you drive, you are assured to find a good time outside Columbus.

This chapter is focused on one-tank day trips all within the Buckeye State. If you're not familiar with Ohio, you might be surprised at how varied the terrain and towns are. You don't have to leave the state to find hills or valleys, lakes or beachfront, big cities or small villages. This chapter includes favorite perennial getaways, ranging from amusement and cultural attractions in nearby cities to a weekend on the Lake Erie Islands.

In two hours, you can be at the Rock and Roll Hall of Fame or lying beachfront by Lake Erie. North on Interstate 71 is the most direct route to Cleveland, but it isn't the most inspiring landscape. You'll undoubtedly have a more scenic journey if you get off the highway and take the side roads running through Ohio's heartland. Spend a day (or a weekend) in Holmes County, home to the world's largest Amish population; a visit here is like stepping back in time.

The drive south on I-71 is equally uninspiring, but once you hit the southern border of Ohio, everything changes. Lovely hills embrace Cincinnati, which is situated along the Ohio River. Here, you can take in one of the country's oldest zoos or catch a game at Great American Ball Park.

If you fancy the great outdoors, check out the Parks and Recreation chapter for details about state parks and camping information. Historic towns such as Roscoe Village and Zoar are listed in the Attractions chapter, but this is not to say you shouldn't stay the night. The same goes for Cleveland and Cincinnati. Both are only a short drive from Columbus and make equally good day trips or weekend getaways. Some of the cities included here have their own *Insiders' Guide*. So, if you are itching to explore beyond the surface, grab a guide, gas up, and get going!

DAY TRIPS

Ohio's Heartland

Holmes County Chamber of Commerce and Tourism Bureau
35 North Monroe Street, Millersburg
www.amish-heartland.com

One of the easiest and more unique day trips from Columbus is a visit to Ohio's heartland, also known as Amish Country. A leisurely drive through Holmes, Wayne, or Tuscarawas counties will take you

---

i

Get to the heart of Ohio's Heartland by requesting a Holmes County map or the* Amish Lanes and City Lights *vacation guide from the Holmes County Info Center at (330) 674-3975, www.holmescounty chamber.com. Other Web sites that may prove helpful are www.visitamish.com, www.visitamishcountry.com, www.sugar creekohio.org, www.millersburgohio.com, and www.discoverohio.com.

Some fundamental observances when visiting Amish communities are to drive slowly and be cautious of the horse and buggies sharing the narrow roads. Respect people's privacy when taking pictures, or at least ask permission if you think they might be in your photo. Finally, some businesses are open on Sunday but may have limited hours. Be sure to check beforehand.

through numerous towns established in the 19th century by German and Swiss religious separatists such as the Amish and Mennonites. Known for their work ethic and peaceful existence, they shun most of the conveniences of the modern world. Horse and buggies carry them to church. Windmills power their homes. Crops are harvested the old-fashioned way—by hand. It doesn't take long to see how the world's largest Amish population (which equates to about 40,000) maintains their religious beliefs into the 21st century through their simple ways of life. Whether for a day or a weekend, it is worth the 80-mile journey back in time for a piece of cheese or a piece of tranquility.

If you are interested in being chauffeured through the scenic back roads, there are a few companies offering personalized tours of the countryside. Contact Amish Country Tours of Ohio at (330) 674-4448, www.amishcountrytoursofohio.com, and Amish Culture Tours at (330) 893-3248, www.buggytrailtours.com. Both operate year-round. With names like Charm, Berlin, Walnut Creek, and Sugar Creek, you'll not want to miss any of these delightful villages—no matter who does the driving!

ATTRACTIONS

Alpine Hills Museum and Information Center
16 West Main Street, Sugar Creek
(330) 852-4113, (888) 609-7592

There is no missing this colorful museum in downtown Sugar Creek. Three floors of exhibits and audiovisual displays explain the Swiss and Amish heritage, cheese making, and farms of the area. A fun time to visit is during the Ohio Swiss Festival on the last Friday and Saturday in September.

Amish and Mennonite Heritage Center
5798 County Road 77, Berlin
(330) 893-3192

Make this your first stop in Amish Country. The 265-foot cyclorama, one of only three in America, interprets the Amish-Mennonite history through a series of pictures. There is also a video presentation, pioneer barn, Conestoga wagon, and information center on-site.

Breitenbach Wine Cellars
Old Route 39, between Dover and Sugar Creek
(330) 343-3603; (800) THE-WINE
www.breitenbachwine.com

As you enter the property to this award-winning winery, it seems you've turned the corner into a little Swiss village. The rolling hills of Breitenbach Valley provide lovely views if you choose to sip your wine on the patio, while an indoor tasting station allows you to sample before buying. Fred's BBQ is in session every Saturday from May through October. Peruse the gift and cheese shop, grab a bottle of wine, and enjoy some grilled food in a tranquil setting.

Guggisberg Cheese Factory
5060 State Route 557, Millersberg
(330) 893-2500, (800) 262-2505
www.guggisberg.com

If you thought Baby Swiss cheese came from Switzerland, think again. After years of experimentation, the original Baby Swiss was born here in Millersberg. Guggisberg is now one of the largest manufacturers of Swiss cheese in the country. The factory has over 40 varieties of cheese, as well as Swiss chocolates and cuckoo clocks. You can even watch the cheese being made. It's open Sunday.

Rolling Ridge Ranch
3961 County Road 168, Millersburg
(330) 893-3777
This petting zoo is a great place for animal lovers to get up close and personal with more than 400 animals and birds from around the world. There are a gift shop and restaurant on-site, but most interestingly, you can feed the animals from a guided horse-drawn wagon until 5:00 P.M. or from your own car until 6:00 P.M.

Schrock's Amish Farm and Home
Route 39, 1 mile east of Berlin
(330) 893-3232
www.amish-r-us.com
As one of Holmes County's top 5 attractions, there is something for everyone on this Amish homestead. You can take the kids on buggy rides, tour an Amish home, or pet the animals. Shoppers can get lost in Gramma Fannie's Quilt Barn, Dutch Heritage Woodcrafts, or the 15,000-square-foot Antique Mall.

SHOPPING

Shopping in Amish country is an attraction in its own right. If you are looking for one-of-a-kind gifts or handmade furniture to serve as family heirlooms, you will find an enormous variety of Amish (and "English") goods. You will also find a large number of gift barns, craft malls, and furniture outlets that have several rooms and floors full of shopping.

Apple Creek has Coblentz Furniture, and Loudonville has Amish Oak Furniture Co. There is Sol's Palace in Berlin, Swiss Village Craft Mall in Sugar Creek, and the Country Craft Mall in Charm. You get the idea! There is often a lot of shopping under one roof. In fact, the Holmes County Amish Flea Market near Walnut Creek has more than 500 booths in 3 buildings and is the No. 1 attraction in Holmes County.

Carlisle House Gifts
4962 Walnut Street, Walnut Creek
(330) 893-2535
www.carlislegifts.com
Shoppers are greeted at the door of this Victorian home with fragrant aromas, while pleasant music entices them to explore the three floors of gifts, home furnishings, and the Thomas Kinkade showcase gallery. A separate store called Global Crafts carries handmade gifts by third world artists.

Coblentz Chocolate Company
4917 Route 515 at Route 39
Walnut Creek
(330) 893-2995, (800) 338-9341
Fudge fanatics and caramel connoisseurs will be in heaven at this old-fashioned candy store. Wooden floors and candy jars lining the walls invoke a nostalgic sensation, while the cases full of chocolate cause a mouth-watering response. Even those with sugar-restricted diets will find a variety of sugar-free candies at Coblentz.

Grandma's Alpine Homestead
Route 62, between Wilmot and Winesburg
(330) 359-5454
www.alpinehomestead.com
The Alpine Swiss Village carries the second largest selection of cuckoo clocks in North America, ranging in price from $25 to $2,500. Find the ticker of your dreams or, perhaps, one made by the world's oldest cuckoo clock manufacturer, Anton Schneider. One dollar will get you a look at the *Guinness Book of World Records'* largest cuckoo clock, also on the Homestead site.

Heini's Cheese Chalet and Country Mall
Route 62, 1 mile northeast of Berlin
(330) 893-2596, (800) 253-6636
www.heinis.com
Eight decades later and still having local products delivered by horse and buggy, Heini's Cheese isn't just a cheese shop; it's a cheese *chalet*. You can sample 50 different types of cheese, test out Heini's famous yogurt cheese, or indulge in some hand-dipped ice cream. It's open on Sunday.

Ohio produces more cheese than any other state (including Wisconsin) and provides the nation with a third of its Swiss cheese. The number of cheese shops that are located in Ohio's heartland is testimony to this fact. Fifteen cheese shops in Sugar Creek alone make more than 10 million pounds of cheese annually.

Kauffman's Country Bakery
4357 Route 62, 1 mile north of Berlin
(330) 893-2129

This is the place to come for your holiday stollen bread. For more than a decade, the Kauffman brothers have been turning out over 20 varieties of breads, strudel, cookies, and pies daily from old-fashioned stone hearth ovens. They also carry a large selection of jams, jellies, and apple butter. Kauffman's is open seven days a week.

Lehman's Hardware and Appliances
One Lehman Circle, Kidron
(330) 857-5757, (888) 438-5346
www.lehmans.com

Move over, Wal-Mart! This Amish "superstore" carries the world's largest selection of authentic historical products for those seeking a simpler life. Since 1955 Lehman's has been preserving the past for the future. People like the Amish, environmentalists, homesteaders, and anyone who seeks items to lead a more self-sufficient lifestyle shop here.

Lehman's carries everything from buckets to board games. If you need a lantern, fireplace, or wood-burning stove, you'll find it here. You will also find all your cooking essentials, from the butter churn to the dinner bell. Lehman's products uphold the store's slogan: "More than a store, it's a way of life." Lehman's has a second store in Mount Hope, and both are closed on Sunday.

Miller's Drygoods
4500 Route 557, Charm
(330) 893-9899
www.millersdrygoods.com

Holmes County's first quilt shop has a large selection of handmade Amish quilts, rugs, pillows, and wall hangings. It carries over 8,000 bolts of fabric and has an outlet in the basement. Anyone interested in quilting or sewing should definitely have a look here.

'Tis the Season
4363 Route 39, 1 mile east of Berlin
(330) 893-3604
www.amish-r-us.com

You can have Christmas any time of the year at Ohio's largest year-round Christmas store located on Schrock's Amish Farm. You will find three floors of holiday collectibles and over 200 decorated trees. Ornament collectors spend hours searching through thousands of ornaments for that special one. 'Tis the Season carries Lenox, Old World Christmas, Loony Tunes, and a huge selection of Christopher Radko ornaments.

Walnut Creek Cheese
2804 Route 39, Walnut Creek
(330) 852-2888
www.walnutcreekcheese.com

Get a serious taste of Holmes County. Walnut Creek Cheese carries the Amish area's largest selection of cheese, meats, and bulk foods. You'll find cookbooks, canned vegetables, and the exclusive Uncle Mike's smoked meats here. One might think this a popular place because they fulfill any cooking need, but I suspect it's the ice-cream parlor's giant ice-cream cones.

World Crafts
Olde Millstream Plaza, Kidron
(330) 857-0590

This interesting shop is a demonstration of Mennonites practicing what they preach. The store was conceived as a way to aid people in need, so it carries fairly traded merchandise such as jewelry, fabric, baskets, ceramics, toys, and wood items by artisans from 35 developing countries, including Bangladesh, the West Bank, Kenya, Peru, Vietnam, and Haiti. It is managed and staffed entirely by volunteers, and the net profits are put back into projects, which directly or indirectly help others in need.

DINING

There's nothing like a home-cooked meal in these parts, and trust me when I say there is no shortage of buffets or spacious, family-style restaurants. Most of the restaurants listed here have what is called the "Amish family-style" or "sampler" options on their menus, meaning you can select two or three meats to accompany vegetables, *real* mashed potatoes, and an all-you-can-eat salad bar. With words like *Alpine* and *chalet* in many of the restaurant names, you'll probably succumb to the Wiener schnitzel, but don't plan on washing it down with a German beer. Most family-style restaurants are dry.

Another unique aspect to the dining experience is that many restaurants are part of a larger complex with gift shops, an inn, or a general store, or at least within easy walking distance of such. Entries have been included for several places that will afford you this "one-stop shopping": food, stores, and lodging, all on the same premises. Many restaurants in Amish country are closed on Sunday, so it is important to call ahead if you are visiting during the weekend.

Alpine Homestead Restaurant
Route 62, between Wilmot and Winesburg
(330) 359-5454
www.alpinehomestead.com
How often do you get to use the word *smorgasbord?* You can use it here every day if you want. Sixty items on an all-day buffet certainly constitutes a smorgasbord, but you can also order off a set menu. You name it, they have it: noodles, salad, ice cream, three-dimensional murals of the Swiss Alps, and, oh yeah, the biggest indoor cuckoo clock in the world. Sneak a peek for free if you are eating in the restaurant; otherwise, it costs $1.00.

Amish Door Restaurant and Village
1210 Winesburg Road, Route 62, Wilmot
(800) 891-6142
www.amishdoor.com
The village complex includes the family-style Amish Door Restaurant, Amish Door Shoppes, Barn Shops, and the Inn at Amish Door. You will find everything from wooden toys to bulk fabric in the Amish Village. It is possible to spend hours (or days) here if you like to eat and shop.

Beachys' Country Chalet
115 Andreas Drive, Sugar Creek
(877) 852-4644
www.beachyrestaurant.com
Choose from specifically Amish or Swiss specialties and 15 types of homemade pies; the best sellers are the peanut butter cream and rhubarb, and you can take home your favorite pie from the on-site bakeshop. The gift shop also carries handmade quilts.

Chalet in the Valley
Route 557, near Charm
(330) 893-2550
www.chaletinthevalley.com
Everything's Swiss here, not just the cheese, from the chalet-style building overlooking Doughty Valley to live Swiss music on weekends. You are served by traditionally clad wait staff and will, no doubt, leave yodeling. The Chalet has a broad menu, with Amish, Swiss, and Austrian specialties. Closed January, February, and Monday year-round.

Der Dutchman Restaurant
4967 Walnut Street (Route 515), Walnut Creek
(330) 893-2981
www.dhgroup.com
If you don't mind sharing the place with buses full of tourists, you will not be disappointed. Despite the throngs of people, you will find consistently good food and service here. The dining room has a beautiful view of Genza Bottom Valley, and the

restaurant is situated amid the shops on the main drag in Walnut Creek.

Dutch Valley Restaurant & Shops
Route 39, Sugar Creek
(330) 852-4627
www.dhgroup.com
This huge complex houses not only a family-style restaurant and bakery but also Dutch Valley Furniture, Dutch Valley Gift Market, with its three floors of home and garden accessories, and Dutch Creek Foods (www.dutchcreekfood.com), which carries fresh meats, cheese, jams, and candies. Everything is closed on Sunday.

LODGING

Ohio's heartland has plenty of chain hotels near the cities of Wooster and New Philadelphia, but you will have a much more personalized experience if you stay at one of the privately owned country inns or bed-and-breakfasts. Keep in mind there are dozens of guesthouses in the tricounty area, so check out individual city Web sites, or request vacation brochures to learn of other options. It's best to call for reservations since some Amish-owned facilities do not have the Internet. Most places are open year-round and accept major credit cards. Listed here is a small sampling of unique accommodations, their contact details, and Web sites when available.

Bed-and-Breakfasts

Garden Gate Get-A-Way Bed & Breakfast
6041 Township Road 310,
off Route 39 in Millersburg
(330) 674-7608
www.garden-gate.com
Garden Gate's four rooms are a reflection of its country charm, and the garden is brought indoors with guest rooms named the Briar Patch Room and Rose Garden Room. All have private baths but share a common area with kitchen facilities and lounge. Escape to the solitude of a porch swing or socialize with other guests around a crackling evening fire in the outdoor pit.

Gilead's Balm Manor Bed & Breakfast
8690 County Road 201, Fredericksburg
(330) 695-3881, (888) 612-3436
This English Tudor-style manor is located on five landscaped acres and nestled alongside a scenic two-acre lake. Every suite has a private bath, two-person Jacuzzi, fireplace, and equipped kitchenette. If you prefer to stay indoors, you'll find satellite TV, VCR, and board games. Five suites lead onto a private deck, while the sixth has a view of stay woods. Whether you walk the grounds, feed the catfish, or hang out in the gazebo, it's a great place to get back to nature and sleep in style.

Grandma's Homestead
3135 County Road 135, 1.5 miles southwest of Walnut Creek
(330) 359-5454
www.millerhaus.com
Kick back in a rocking chair and take in the stunning views of the surrounding farms from one of the highest points in Holmes County. This Amish-style home has 10 rooms with private bath and air-conditioning. Quilts and antiques add cozy touches to the rooms, and the homemade French toast is heavenly.

Hotel Millersburg
35 West Jackson Street, Millersburg
(330) 674-1457, (800) 822-1457
www.hotelmillersburg.com
Located near the well-preserved town square, this interesting Victorian hotel has been welcoming visitors since 1847. The 24 rooms have private baths and offer old world charm alongside modern-day amenities. There are a restaurant and tavern on-site.

Springhouse Bed and Breakfast
10903 State Route 212 NE, Bolivar
(330) 874-4255, (800) 796-9100
www.springhousebnb.com
A discreet location off Route 212 only adds to the charm of this 1857 Greek Revival inn. The dedicated owners haven't missed a detail in any one of their four rooms or

third-floor suite. Visitors find themselves in themed rooms, individually decorated with antique and modern furnishings, pampered with plush bathrobes, scented soaps, and chocolates. Guests have full access to the common area of the house and an outdoor, private, two-person hot tub. Breakfast is gourmet, so don't miss it. Seclusion on five and a half acres and the proprietors' wonderful hospitality make the Springhouse a revitalizing escape from the bustle of city life. The personal touch at this bed-and-breakfast is just one of the many things that keep the regulars coming back over and over again.

Cabins and Lodges

Coblentz Country Cabins
Berlin Area
(877) 99-SLEEP
www.amishcountrylodging.com
These two log cabins can accommodate anywhere from four to eight people per unit, making this a great group getaway. Linens, towels, and television make it feel like home, but the cathedral ceilings, hardwood floors, lofts, and game room give it a country lodge feeling. It's spacious enough for a large family to spread out, while the Jacuzzi, fireplace, and peaceful surroundings provide romance for couples as well.

Donna's Premier Lodging
Berlin Area
(330) 893-3068, (800) 320-3338
www.donnasofberlin.com
Indulge yourself in pure luxury at any one of the cabins, villas, bridal suites, chalets, and honeymoon cottages. All accommodations come with fully equipped kitchens, Jacuzzi, fireplace, TV/DVD, and outdoor grill. Those looking for a Poconos-style retreat do not have to drive eight hours to get it. Look no further than the "Romancing the Stone" cabin, with its indoor waterfall, mood lighting, and remote control gas logs in a massive stone fireplace. If you prefer "city dwelling," the villas are Cape Cod-style units that are within walking distance of downtown Berlin.

Landoll's Mohican Castle
561 Township Road 3352, Loudonville
(419) 994-3427, (800) 291-5001
www.landollsmohicancastle.com
This 1,100-acre estate is fit for a king with its luxury cottages, log cabins, and, yes, castle. King-size beds, hardwood floors, gothic carved doors, fully equipped kitchens, Italian baths with heated tile floors, Jacuzzi, and fireplaces will leave you feeling majestic. If that isn't enough, rent a golf cart and explore the 30 miles of trails that run through your royal forest. Pamper yourself in elegant solitude, or indulge in winter skiing only 90 minutes from Columbus.

Country Inns

Country inns are independently owned hotel/motel facilities, usually located in or near the more popular towns, such as Berlin, Charm, and Walnut Creek. The rooms are set up hotel style, with private bathrooms and cable television, and often have indoor swimming pools and include breakfast. These are always a nice, affordable choice for families.

Amish Country Inn
Routes 39/62, 1 mile west of Berlin
(330) 893-2862, (800) 935-5218
www.amish-r-us.com

Berlin Village Inn
5135 Route 39, Berlin
(330) 893-2861, (800) 869-7571
www.berlinvillageinn.com

Carlisle Village Inn
4949 Walnut Street (Route 515)
Walnut Creek
(330) 893-3636, (877) 4CARLISLE
www.carlislevillageinn.com

Guggisberg Swiss Inn
5025 Route 557, Charm
(330) 893-3600, (877) 467-9477
www.bbonline.com/oh/guggisberg

Swiss Village Inn
206 South Factory Street, Sugar Creek
(800) 792-6822
www.swissvillageinn.com

Canton

Canton/Stark County Convention and Visitors' Bureau
222 Market Avenue N, Canton
(330) 454-1439, (800) 533-4302
www.cantonstarkcvb.com

As the birthplace of the National Football League and home to the Professional Football Hall of Fame, Canton holds a special place in the heart of sport fans, but be assured the city is more than just a shrine to America's favorite past time. Canton is the birth and burial place of 25th president William McKinley, and an imposing hometown memorial serves as a tribute. Canton can boast five arts organizations and three times as many golf courses in the area. "Sweeping changes" began here with the advent of the Hoover (electric vacuum) Company. If you appreciate sports, fine performing arts, or unique historical sites and museums, a visit to Canton is worth the 90-minute drive.

ATTRACTIONS

Canton Classic Car Museum
555 Market Avenue
(330) 455-3603
www.cantonclassiccar.org

Housed in the 1915 showroom of a Ford-Lincoln dealership, this little museum has a lot of nostalgia. Among the 50 antique and classic cars, you'll find a 1901 Olds Surrey, a bulletproof gangster car, and Johnny Carson's 1981 DeLorean.

Cultural Center for the Arts
1001 Market Avenue N
(330) 452-4096

This is one of the few centers in the country that houses all the city's major art disciplines under one roof. The Canton Museum of Art (www.cantonart.org) has seen its share of high-profile exhibitions in its 70 years. The permanent collections focus on American watercolors and contemporary ceramics. The Canton Ballet (www.cantonballet.com) offers public performances three times a year, while the Canton Symphony Orchestra (www.cantonsymphony.com) gives more than 60 concerts annually. The Canton Civic Opera (www.voci.com) has been performing for over 50 years, and the Canton Players Guild Theatre (www.playersguildtheatre.com) is one of the nation's oldest and largest community theaters.

First Ladies' National Historic Site and Education and Research Center
331 Market Avenue S
(330) 452-0876
www.firstladies.org

The center is housed in two historic buildings and serves as a tribute to the achievements and contributions of each first lady and other important American women. The Bank Building will become the National First Ladies' Library Educational and Research Center, with a replica of the first White House library. The Saxton House is the physical home of the library and has been restored to its original Victorian splendor. It is worth a look for the authentic period furniture and recreation of President McKinley's study.

Harry London Candies
5353 Lauby Road
(330) 494-0833

Canton has yet another Hall of Fame dedicated to another of America's favorite pastimes—chocolate. The Chocolate Hall of Fame is located at one of Ohio's largest chocolate factories. Take a tour to learn how these gourmet chocolates are made, then shop for a mouth-watering souvenir from the Midwest's largest chocolate store.

MAPS Air Museum
2260 International Parkway
(330) 896-6332
www.mapsairmuseum.org

The Military Aviation Preservation Society (MAPS), located on the west side of the

Akron-Canton Airport, is dedicated to preserving historical aircraft. This hangar-turned-museum houses permanent collections of vintage war birds and civilian aircraft. Learn the history of aviation and its impact on society through the displays of fighter, bomber, and transport aircraft, or observe restoration in progress. Watch the historical birds in flight at the Aero Expo, which is held each June.

Pro Football Hall of Fame
2121 George Halas Drive NW
(330) 456-8207
www.profootballhof.com
Did you know football was born on November 12, 1892? You can see its "birth certificate" in the form of the payment voucher to William "Pudge" Heffelfinger for $500 to play in a single game. Since then, football has become the most popular sport in the United States, and this 83,000-square-foot shrine is dedicated to the great game and its great players. You can learn general football and team-by-team history here or watch National Football League footage in Cinemascope at GameDay Stadium, the state-of-the-art turntable theater.

The Hall of Fame is a complete chronicle of football and is ever changing with new exhibits and mementos, and don't forget the annual induction ceremony held every August. A weekend full of events, culminating in the Hall of Fame football game, is a good time to rub elbows with the full spectrum of NFL alumni. This world-class museum is open every day of the year except Christmas, and the gift shop is the only one in the country that carries merchandise from all 32 NFL teams.

DINING

The 356th Fighter Group Restaurant
4919 Mt. Pleasant Road N
(330) 494-3500, (800) 994-2662
www.356fg.com
Dine amid World War II memorabilia while listening to 1940s music. Request a window table for views of the Akron-Canton Airport runways. Headphones are available to listen to the airport control tower.

Bender's Tavern
Second Street SW and Court Avenue
(330) 453-8424
www.bendersrestaurant.com
Bender's has been around since 1902 and lays claim to the title of Canton's oldest restaurant. Aside from the TVs (and women being allowed in the bar), some things have not changed in 100 years. Locals swear by the quality and consistency of Bender's food, and it's no wonder—fresh seafood has been flown in from Boston and Maine since 1932.

Mulligan's Pub
4118 Belden Village Street NW
(330) 493-8239
This popular watering hole serves a variety of dishes, ranging from pastas to burgers to vegetarian dishes. It also serves food until closing, which makes it a favorite place for that late-night snack.

Cincinnati

Greater Cincinnati Convention and Visitor's Bureau
511 Walnut Street
Fifth Third Center, Fountain Square
(513) 621-2142, (800) CINCY-USA
www.cincyusa.com
Cincinnati is only an hour south of Columbus, but it couldn't be more different. Nestled in a scenic bend of the Ohio River, the city's riverfront location held a pivotal role throughout history. From the inception of the city, through its steamboat, pork-packing, and industrial heydays, the river brought prosperity to its residents. It also brought freedom to thousands of slaves who crossed over into the free states of the North.

The river is the natural boundary between Ohio and Kentucky, but Greater Cincinnati straddles the two states. The airport is on the south side of the river, so

You can't leave the "Chili Capital of America" without trying its signature dish: spicy ground beef ladled over a plate of spaghetti. Order a "three-way" and you'll get mounds of shredded cheddar; throw in some onions, and it's a "four-way." Add beans, and it's a "five-way."

don't panic when you fly into Cincinnati and see a WELCOME TO KENTUCKY sign. As you cross into Ohio, you're greeted by the city's beautiful skyline and the neighborhoods oozing into the surrounding hills.

The downtown area has been undergoing a renaissance for several years, which means entertainment districts have been developed, the arts are flourishing, and riverfront stadiums have been built. The city has plenty of riverboat cruises, cultural events, and attractions to keep you busy for a day or a week.

This section focuses only on the Ohio side of the city, including Mount Adams, a lively hub of dining and nightlife with fantastic views of downtown Cincinnati. For more information, pick up an *Insiders' Guide to Cincinnati*, or request the official visitor's guide from the Visitor's Bureau listed at the beginning of this section. If planning to explore the city, you can park below Fountain Square in a 24-hour lot that charges $1.00 for the first two hours or $15.00 for the entire day.

ATTRACTIONS

Cincinnati boasts groundbreaking attractions and offers plenty of year-round family fun and sporting events. The Delta Queen Steam Boat Co., America's oldest continuously operated cruise line, is based in New Orleans but makes regular stops in Cincinnati. You can learn more about the overnight packages on these paddle wheels by calling (800) 543-1949 or checking out www.deltaqueen.com.

Cincinnati Art Museum
953 Eden Park Drive
(513) 721-ARTS
www.cincinnatiartmuseum.org

The Cincinnati Art Museum opened in 1886 and is one of the country's oldest visual arts institutions. Collections span the globe and represent 6,000 years of world civilization. The museum has a display of Cincinnati's own Rookwood pottery, carved furniture, and paintings from the city's golden age (1830–1900). European artworks include old masters such as Titian, Rubens, and Gainsborough, as well as modern masters Picasso, Braque, and Chagall. The American galleries show works by Copley, Wyeth, Hopper, and Rothko. The museum is not downtown, but rather up a winding hill in Eden Park. The museum is free to everyone on Saturday and closed Monday.

Cincinnati Museum Center
1301 Western Avenue
(513) 287-7000, (800) 733-2077
www.cincymuseum.org

This is the first place hotel concierges suggest to visitors with families. The complex is located in the historic 1933 Union Terminal and houses six different museums. Detailed re-creations of Cincinnati's heritage tell the city's story at the Cincinnati History Museum. Kids can explore the world at CINergy Children's Museum. Step into Ohio Valley's ice age in the Museum of Natural History and Science, or check out the free African American Museum of the Arts on the lower level. The facility also has an OMNIMAX theater and houses the Cincinnati Historical Society Library.

Cincinnati Zoo and Botanical Gardens
3400 Vine Street
(513) 281-4700, (800) 94-HIPPO
www.cincinnatizoo.org

The world famous Cincinnati Zoo and Botanical Gardens is the No. 1 attraction in the city and consistently ranks among the top zoos in the country. It is internation-

ally known for its successful protection and propagation of endangered animals such as rhinos and cheetahs. Opened in 1875, this is the nation's second-oldest zoo, and the 1905 Elephant House is a national landmark. The zoo is open every day. Cash only (no credit cards) for admission.

Harriet Beecher Stowe House
2590 Gilbert Avenue
(513) 632-5133
The author of *Uncle Tom's Cabin* lived in Cincinnati for 19 years, and her home-turned-museum displays family photos, journals, manuscripts, and artifacts from African-American history.

Paramount's King's Island and Boomerang Bay
6300 King's Island Drive, King's Island
(513) 754-5700
www.pki.com
Many recognize the Midwest's premier theme park from the episode of *The Brady Bunch* that was filmed at King's Island when it first opened. Owned by Paramount Communications, many of the rides are themed around Paramount movies: *Top Gun, Lara Croft: Tomb Raider*, and *Face Off,* to name a few. But, it's "The Beast" that has continued to thrill people of all ages since 1979. This wooden roller coaster was named the number one classic coaster of all time by *USA Today,* and now its offspring, "Son of Beast," is breaking all the wooden coaster records.

Kids will enjoy Hanna Barbera Land and Nickelodeon Splat City and can spend time with SpongeBob and Dora the Explorer. More adventurous children can have a go at "The Beastie," a mini version of the big coaster. The whole family can beat the heat at Boomerang Bay, a new Aussie-style water park with over 50 water rides, including water funnels, lagoons, and a water fortress. The park is open daily spring through Labor Day and weekends only through October. If you plan to go more than once in a summer, consider getting season passes, which range from $90 (for adults) to $300 (for a family of four). Children under 3 are free.

Taft Museum of Art
316 Pike Street
(513) 241-0343
www.taftmuseum.org
A small yet superb art museum is located in one of the finest examples of Federal architecture in the Palladian style. The landmarked 1820 Baum-Longworth-Taft house contains 700 works of art encompassing European masters, exceptional Chinese ceramics, early American painting, and furniture. Closed Monday.

William Howard Taft National Historic Site
2038 Auburn Avenue, Mt. Auburn
(513) 684-3262
www.nps.gov/wiho
The restored birthplace and childhood home of the 27th U.S. president and 10th chief justice of the Supreme Court, William Howard Taft, commemorates his life and career in four period rooms and various exhibits. The Taft house is open seven days a week, and admission is free.

PERFORMING ARTS

Cincinnati is home to some of the oldest and most respected performing arts organizations in the country. The mid-February Fine Arts Sampler Weekend is a great way to get an overview of what the "Queen City" has to offer.

The Aronoff Center for the Arts (513-977-4150; www.cincinnatiarts.org) is located in the heart of downtown Cincinnati at 650 Walnut Street. This state-of-the-art facility has three stunning performance spaces and features the Weston Art Gallery. It hosts Fifth Third Bank's Broadway in Cincinnati. Call (513) 241-2345, or view www.broadwayacross america.com for more information about touring productions. The Cincinnati Ballet (513-621-5219; www.cincinnatiballet.com), one of the country's top 10 professional companies, performs a repertoire of clas-

CLOSE-UP

The Road to Freedom

Nearly 150 years ago, 100,000 enslaved African Americans sought freedom through the Underground Railroad. The symbolic name was given to the north-bound route slaves followed to gain their freedom. A clandestine network of safe houses, operated by abolitionists, whites, free blacks, and Native Americans, helped runaways make their way as far north as Canada. Whispers of the Underground Railroad became reality when escapees crossed the Ohio River from Kentucky, first stepping foot on free soil in southern Ohio.

With one of the most important Underground Railroad stations in nearby Ripley, Cincinnati is a befitting place for the National Underground Railroad Freedom Center. This cultural icon stands as the nation's newest celebration of freedom and is the largest museum dedicated to the Underground Railroad. It opened August 24, 2004 (the day the United Nations celebrates the international abolition of slavery) to rave reviews and promises to quickly become a national treasure.

African-American architect Walter Blackburn of Indianapolis designed the distinctive center. The three buildings symbolize the cornerstones of freedom: courage, cooperation, and perseverance. The curved architecture echoes the winding river and philosophically reflects the precarious, changing path to freedom. During construction, representatives from worldwide freedom organizations added containers of soil from their sites to symbolically represent the free soil the slaves struggled to reach. The center sits between the Great American Ball Park and Paul Brown Stadium, overlooking the Ohio River toward Kentucky. Visitors can stand on an open deck and imagine the perilous escape thousands of slaves made across the river.

Through interactive exhibits and simple storytelling, this museum uses the power of the past to convey a simple yet profound message promoting human rights and freedom for all. See and touch the walls of a slave jail dismantled and moved from Kentucky. This emotional centerpiece served as a pen for slaves prior to being taken south for human auction. Other artifacts of interest include a first edition of *Uncle Tom's Cabin* and male slave trousers made of "Negro cloth," a coarsely woven cotton cloth purchased in large quantities by plantation owners.

The Freedom Center also highlights Ohio's position and unique historical contribution to the Underground Railroad. It brings to life the struggles for freedom

sic, neoclassic, and contemporary dance at the Aronoff Center more than 30 times annually.

The Music Hall, built in 1878, is the grande dame of Cincinnati arts venues (513-744-3344; www.cincinnatiarts.org). This landmark building is well known for its colorful history, stunning architecture, and fine acoustics. Located at 1241 Elm Street, the hall is the home of the coun-

The National Underground Railroad Freedom Center. FEINKNOPF PHOTOGRAPHY

not only in our country but also around the world and throughout history, including the present day. "The Struggle Today" spotlights the legacy of the Underground Railroad and freedom movements in contemporary society. The Hall of Heroes honors 100 people, ranging from those who helped American slaves in the 1800s to those who are currently fighting Asian sex slavery. Appropriately enough, the Freedom Center plans to host seminars on teaching cultural diversity in schools.

This 19th-century freedom movement challenged the way Americans viewed slavery and human rights. You will not leave this place without examining your own attitude about freedom in the past, present, and future. And like the Underground Railroad, the Freedom Center's effect will be felt far beyond Cincinnati. For more information regarding hours and admission, call (513) 333-7500 or (877) 648-4838, or view the Web site at www.freedomcenter.org.

try's second-oldest opera company and fifth-oldest orchestra. As one of the nation's leading opera companies, the Cincinnati Opera (513-621-1919; www.cincinnatiopera.org) puts on four productions a year in June and July. The Cincinnati Symphony Orchestra (513-381-3300; www.cincinnatisymphony.org) performs under the direction of Paavo Järvi, and the season runs from September to May.

SPORTS

If you don't know much about Cincinnati, you've still probably heard of the Bengals and the Reds, or at least know of Pete Rose. This section will focus on the two great American sports born right here in Ohio: football and baseball.

Cincinnati is home to the oldest franchise in professional baseball and the newest ballpark. The Cincinnati Reds' new home, the Great American Ball Park (513-765-7000; www.cincinnatireds.com), pays tribute to the city's great riverboat history with a set of stacks that shoot off fireworks after home games. It also pays homage to the Reds' rich past with statues of famous players, famous-date banners, and the Reds' Hall of Fame and Museum. Fans are treated to interactive displays and exhibits offering a comprehensive look at baseball's development, beginning with the first professional team, the Cincinnati Red Stockings of 1869.

Portable radios are permitted in the stadium, provided the volume does not disturb your neighbor. Guests are welcome to bring cameras and keep foul balls, and encouraged to try the deep-fried Twinkie. No alcohol is sold after the seventh inning. Daily tours run from early April to the end of the season.

Cincinnati has been treated to a new football stadium as well. Rather than move the Bengals to Baltimore, fans overwhelmingly voted to increase the sales tax in order to build a new football-only facility and keep the franchise at home. In 2004, the Bengals began playing in their new waterfront home, Paul Brown Stadium (513-455-4805; www.bengals.com).

This modern stadium has 56 concession stands, the Bengals Museum, and a FieldTurf playing surface and is open at the end zones, providing views into the city and over the river. The plaza located on the southeast corner of the stadium hosts a three-hour pregame event with music, food, and drinks in the Jungle Zone. Cameras and handheld radios with earpieces are permitted, but not video equipment. Tours are available on Tuesday through Thursday, during the summer months.

DINING AND DRINKING

Foodies will be excited to learn that Cincinnati has more award-winning restaurants per capita than any other U.S. city. You'll find a concentration of diverse restaurants in the Backstage District around the Aronoff Center and around the Main Street District.

Ambar India Restaurant
350 Ludlow Avenue, Clifton
(513) 281-7000
www.ambarindia.com

Meat lovers and vegetarians alike rave about Ambar India Restaurant. The authentic northern Indian cuisine wins the "best of" polls year after year. Known for savory tandoori oven dishes and adventurous curries, this restaurant is worth venturing outside downtown for.

Arnold's Bar & Grill
210 East Eight Street
(513) 421-6234
www.arnoldsbarandgrill.com

Cincinnati's oldest tavern, established in 1861, is located in a quirky old building and retains some of its 19th-century decor. The historic eatery has long been one of Cincinnati's finest saloons, and legend holds that, during Prohibition, the second-floor bathtub was used to make gin. The walls of this spirited place are covered with paraphernalia, while the menu features traditional Italian and American cuisine.

Campanello's Restaurant
414 Central Avenue
(513) 721-9833
www.campanellos.com

This family-owned restaurant is a local landmark and has been one of the most popular Italian restaurants in Cincinnati for 25 years. Only "3 blocks from the beach," it is located within walking distance from all downtown hotels, as well as the convention center. The restaurant gained national fame during the 1990 Reds championship season. World Series MVP Jose Rijo ate his pregame meal at Campanello's before every home game. During the World Series, Campanello's sent his pregame meal (lasagna, Italian salad, and cappuccino) via Federal Express to the Reds' hotel in Oakland.

Havana Martini Club
580 Walnut Street at the corner of Sixth
(513) 651-2800
Grab a stogie from the walk-in humidor and kick back in plush comfort at Cincinnati's premier cigar venue. The drink bar features perfect accompaniments to that perfect cigar: handcrafted martinis, single-malt scotches, and an extensive selection of premium liquors. Havana has live entertainment and is closed Sunday.

Maisonette
114 East Sixth Street
(513) 721-2260
www.maisonette.com
Mobil Travel Guide has awarded the Maisonette five stars for an unprecedented 40 consecutive years, making this the longest running five-star restaurant in the country. Traditional French cuisine is complemented by an extensive wine list, which has been bestowed its own honor, the *Wine Spectator* Grand Award Top 100. You can't beat this place for romance! A tie and jacket are required for men, and no denim is permitted for anyone. Be sure to make reservations three to four weeks in advance if you plan to go on a Friday or Saturday night.

Fewer people realize this distinguished French restaurant shares a kitchen with a casual chophouse called La Normandie Steak, Seafood & Spirits (513-721-2761; www.maisonettegroup.com). This famous, cozy bar has been right next door at 118 East Sixth Street for 70 years. It offers the same quality experience as the Maisonette, but at a third of the cost.

Montgomery Inn at the Boathouse
925 Eastern Avenue
(513) 721-7427
www.montgomeryinn.com
Montgomery Inn's famous ribs and sauce are a Cincinnati institution. There are several locations throughout the city, but the Boathouse sits just east of the city and provides beautiful views of the Ohio River and northern Kentucky.

Mt. Adams Fish House
940 Pavilion Street, Mt. Adams
(513) 421-3250
www.mtadamsfishhouse.com
If you love seafood and have money to burn, this is some of the best in Cincinnati. The dining room has an upscale-casual atmosphere and a small sushi bar. The signature dish is Nova Scotia salmon, and all the fish is flown in daily. Meat eaters should look elsewhere, as the menu is predominantly seafood.

Nicola's Ristorante Italiano
1420 Sycamore Street
(513) 721-6200
www.nicolasrestaurant.com
The contemporary and spacious Nicola's, once a car barn for incline trolleys in the 19th century, is one of the most beautiful restaurants in the city. The menu is sophisticated and refined, the atmosphere is dressy casual, and there's an outdoor patio for dining alfresco. This is a great place to kick off a theater night, as it is just a few minutes away from the Aronoff Center and the Music Hall.

Rookwood Pottery Bistro
1077 Celestial Street, Mt. Adams
(513) 721-5456
For a unique experience, dine in the kilns of historic Rookwood Pottery. Three huge brick kilns occupy the main floor of this Tudor-style building. Two have dining alcoves that need to be requested upon arrival, as they do not take reservations. The atmosphere and menu are casual, fea-

turing everything from gourmet burgers to steaks and seafood, but I sense people come here more for the ambience than the food.

Teak Thai Cuisine and Sushi Bar
1049 St. Gregory Street, Mt. Adams
(513) 665-9800
www.cincinnati.com/dining/teakthai
This award-winning Thai restaurant comes highly recommended for its noodle dishes, outstanding sushi bar, and tremendous views of downtown Cincinnati. The restaurant has patio dining and is open seven days a week.

ACCOMMODATIONS

Cincinnati is an easy day trip from Columbus, but if you decide to spend the night, you'll have no problem finding bed-and-breakfast inns, historic hotels, and an endless number of chain hotels. Downtown is home to the historic Hilton Netherland Plaza and the huge Millennium Hotel, while the area just north of the city is loaded with midpriced hotels servicing King's Island. Listed here are a couple of the more reputable and interesting options downtown.

Cincinnatian Hotel
601 Vine Street
(513) 381-3000
www.cincinnatianhotel.com
This landmark, four diamond/four star hotel, built in 1882, is the only small luxury hotel in the city. It has been rated by *Condé Nast Traveler* magazine as one of America's top 25 hotels. Guests are showered with royal treatment, so it's no wonder the likes of Ronald Reagan, Tom Cruise, and the Rolling Stones stayed here. Armoires, spacious dressing rooms, sitting areas, and writing desks give the 147 guest rooms more of a residential feel. You do, however, pay for Cincinnati's foremost address. As the most expensive hotel in town, expect to spend upward of $170 a night.

Vernon Manor Hotel
400 Oak Street
(513) 281-3300
www.vernonmanorhotel.com
Convenient to both "Pill Hill" (the hospital district) and the University of Cincinnati, this uptown manor offers competitive rates for its 177 rooms and suites. This charming reproduction of an English manor house was built in 1924 and is a member of the Historic Hotels of America. The unique rooms are decorated with antiques, and the rooftop garden provides guests views of the city.

Cleveland

Greater Cleveland Convention and Visitor's Bureau
(800) 321-1001
www.travelcleveland.com
It's a nondescript, two-hour drive north to Cleveland, bearing in mind traffic on I-71 is often thick and congested, but once you get there, the journey will be well worth it. Cleveland extends 100 miles along the southern shore of Lake Erie, making it the largest lakefront metro area in the country. Geographically speaking, Lake Erie is the country's largest freshwater resource and provides year-round entertainment for mariners and landlubbers alike. Marinas, yacht clubs, restaurants, and museums take advantage of the lakefront views.

A few things can easily be packed into a one-day trip, but it is always tempting to stay the weekend. More akin to Pittsburgh than Columbus, Cleveland has all the trappings that come with having once been a great manufacturing and steel city: a rich, 200-year history, old money, interesting architecture, a thriving arts community, professional sports teams, and multicultural neighborhoods, many with their own distinct heritage and lots of good eating! Whether you come to shop at the West Side Market, take in a show at Severance Hall, or go to a Browns' game, there is plenty that will keep you returning to Cleveland.

ATTRACTIONS

Check out Cleveland by land or sea. Take a narrated tour of the city on Lolly the Trolley with Trolley Tours of Cleveland (216-771-4484), or schedule a guided tour with Walking Tours of Cleveland (216-575-1189). The *Nautica Queen* (800-837-0604; www.nauticaqueen.com) offers panoramic views of the city and sunset dinner cruises on Lake Erie.

African American Museum
1765 Crawford Road
(216) 791-1700
www.aamcleveland.org
America's first museum dedicated to the African-American experience offers four core exhibits reflecting on black life in Cleveland, scientists and inventors of African descent, and civil rights moments. It offers a glimpse into the African-American role in the United States by exploring the past and present. It is open Tuesday through Friday, and admission is $4.00.

Cleveland Botanical Gardens
11030 East Boulevard
(216) 721-1600
www.cbgarden.org
The 10 acres of landscaped gardens include an award-winning children's garden, Japanese garden, and a new, one-of-a-kind glass house featuring two of the world's most delicate ecosystems: the desert of Madagascar and the cloud forest of Costa Rica. Fifty species of butterflies, birds, and insects are also exhibited. The gardens are open daily. Admission is $7.00 for adults and $3.00 for children.

Cleveland Metroparks Zoo and The Rainforest
3900 Wildlife Way
(216) 661-6500
www.clemetzoo.com
This 168-acre zoo is home to 3,300 animals, of which 84 are endangered species. It also has the largest collection of primate species in North America. The zoo features Wolf Wilderness, Australian Adventure, and the two-acre indoor Rainforest. It is also a botanical garden.

Cleveland Museum of Art
11150 East Boulevard
(216) 421-7340, (888) 262-0033
www.clevelandart.org
This highly acclaimed museum has more than 40,000 works of art spanning 6,000 years. The 70 galleries feature ancient Egyptian and Roman sculpture, Renaissance armor, and Impressionist paintings. Be sure to venture out the back door to see Rodin's most famous sculpture, *The Thinker.* The CMA's collections of pre-Columbian and Asian art are unrivaled. Admission is free; the museum is closed on Monday.

Cleveland Museum of Natural History
Wade Oval Drive
(216) 231-4600, (800) 317-9155
www.cmnh.org
Explore the earth and beyond at Ohio's largest natural history museum. Discover prehistoric Ohio through dinosaur exhibits, gawk at the impressive collection of rare diamonds in the Gallery of Gems and Jewels, and track planetary movements and lunar events at the new Shafran Planetarium. This outstanding museum is open daily. Admission is $7.00 for adults, $4.00 for children.

Great Lakes Science Center
601 Erieside Avenue
(216) 694-2000
www.glsc.org
Learn about the Great Lakes, science phenomena, the environment, and technology at one of America's largest science museums. The center covers some 250,000 square feet, housing hundreds of hands-on exhibits and an OMNIMAX theater. The waterfront building is located between the Rock and Roll Hall of Fame and the Cleveland Browns' Stadium. The science center is open daily, and parking is available (for a fee) in the attached garage.

Peter B. Lewis Building
Bellflower Road and Ford Drive
(216) 368-6339
www.weatherhead.case.edu
Just look for the dramatic, cascading steel ribbons on the campus of Case Western Reserve, and you've found the most advanced management school facility in the world. Public tours of this stunning Frank Gehry building are available on weekends.

Rock and Roll Hall of Fame
1 Key Plaza
(216) 781-7625, (800) 764-ROCK
www.rockhall.com
Cleveland has always been a major force in music history and is the site for the Rock and Roll Hall of Fame. I. M. Pei's spectacular building rises above Lake Erie and boldly expresses rock's raw power. Permanent collections of music artifacts and changing exhibitions tell the story of the musical forces that have shaped our lives. The hall hosts annual inductions, music festivals, and traveling exhibitions. It is open daily. Admission is $20 for adults and $11 for children. Kids under 8 are free.

University Circle
(216) 791-3900
www.universitycircle.org
The cultural center of Cleveland is located 4 miles east of downtown on the campus of Case Western Reserve University. University Circle is an attraction unto itself, having more cultural and performing arts institutions packed into 1 square mile than anywhere else in the country. Cleveland's major museums and several performance halls are located within walking distance of one another through a beautiful park setting.

ENTERTAINMENT DISTRICTS

The Flats
www.cleveland.com/flats
Located along the east and west banks of the Cuyahoga River in what was once the industrial heart of Cleveland, this riverfront district is home to more then 50 restaurants, bars, adult clubs, and microbreweries. The party is taken outdoors onto the boardwalk and patios in the summer months.

Historic Warehouse District
www.warehousedistrict.org
Downtown's oldest commercial center now features trendy restaurants, wine bars, and live music venues. Some of the city's hottest restaurants, jazz bars, and lounges are found in converted warehouses in this area just east of the Flats. It is also home to art galleries, boutiques, and funky coffee shops.

THEATER

Playhouse Square Center
1501 Euclid Avenue
(216) 771-4444
www.playhousesquare.com
Five beautifully restored theaters are at home in Playhouse Square Center, making this the nation's second largest performing arts center. The Allen, State, Ohio, Palace, and Hanna host most of Cleveland's major performing arts organizations. Tickets for the Cleveland Opera, dance, ballet, and Broadway can be purchased directly through the Playhouse Square Web site or at the box office.

The Cleveland Playhouse, located at 8500 Euclid Avenue in University Circle, is recognized as America's longest running regional theater. Call (216) 795-7000, or go to www.clevelandplayhouse.com for tickets. The Cleveland Orchestra (800-686-1141; www.clevelandorchestra.com) performs at the architecturally stunning Severance Hall, also in University Circle.

SPORTS

Cleveland is home to several professional sports teams, but baseball is one of the city's oldest traditions, dating to 1869. The Cleveland Indians (866-48-TRIBE; www.indians.com) have played at Jacobs Field since 1994. This urban ballpark was built as part of the Gateway Sports and Entertainment Complex, which also includes Gund Arena, home of Cleveland's professional basketball team, the Cavaliers. You can purchase Cavs' tickets by calling (216) 420-2100 or online at www.nba.com/cavaliers.

The Cleveland Browns (888-891-1999; www.clevelandbrowns.com) have a pretty confusing team history. To the heart-wrenching dismay of the fans, this football franchise was moved to Baltimore in 1996, but the city of Cleveland rallied to keep the name, colors, and history of the Browns in their city. The team has since returned to the shores of Lake Erie and plays at the new Cleveland Browns Stadium.

The official tailgate party takes place before and after each game in the "Buzzard Barking Lot" on the north side of the stadium, but the party continues throughout the game in the rabid, fan-filled "Dawg Pound." Be prepared for a lot of barking and drastic mood swings when things don't quite go fans' way. Bone-chilling wind blows off the lake, so dress very warm for games. Stadium tours are available April through December.

DINING

Downtown Cleveland is full of stylish restaurants, bistros, and microbreweries, particularly in the historic Warehouse District and the Flats. Stuff yourself on cannoli and biscotti in Little Italy or kielbasa and pierogies in Slavic Village. Whatever you want is on the menu somewhere in Cleveland.

Blue Point Grill
700 West St. Clair Avenue
(216) 875-STAR
Located in the historic Warehouse District, the Blue Point lives up to its aquatic name in both cuisine and decor. You'll dine on the city's best raw and cooked seafood in blue-swathed ambience. It is regularly voted Cleveland's best overall restaurant and is a great place for a power lunch or romantic dinner.

Great Lakes Brewing Company
2516 Market Avenue, Ohio City
(216) 771-4404
www.greatlakesbrewing.com
The GLB Co., founded in 1988, was the first microbrewery in Ohio. The brewers craft their beer in an environmentally responsible manner, recycle through their Zero Waste Initiative, and purchase organic, locally grown ingredients to support local business. The menu is loaded with upscale American pub food, and if their lofty social practices aren't enough, pints of beer are only $3.00 during happy hour.

Johnny's Downtown
1406 West Sixth Street
(216) 623-0055
This contemporary and sometimes rowdy restaurant is a popular spot among the movers and shakers, celebrities and theatergoers. Beefeaters will be pleased with the variety of steak options on the menu. The ambience is eclectic but chic.

John Q's Steakhouse
55 Public Square
(216) 861-0900
Cleveland's most popular steakhouse has reigned supreme for 20 years with its melt-in-your-mouth Angus steaks and prime rib. The rich wood and brass fixtures give this a classic steakhouse ambience, but private booths offer a more romantic setting.

Little Bar and Grill
614 Frankfort Avenue
(216) 861-2166
This little bar is tucked in a cozy historic brick building off Sixth Street and has been serving award-winning cheeseburgers since 1956. The atmosphere is casual, and it can get quite crowded, especially during games.

Pickwick & Frolic Restaurant
2035 East Fourth Street
(216) 241-7425
www.pickwickandfrolic.com

Flatbread pizzas and comfort food are served in a modern, publike restaurant that is part of a larger entertainment venue. For a British-themed meal, try the fish-and-chips or ham and cheddar ale soup, then slip down to Kevin's Martini Bar for more drinks. Dinner/theater packages are also available at Frolic Cabaret and Frolic Comedy Club.

Tommy's
1824 Coventry Road, Cleveland Heights
(216) 321-7757
www.tommyscoventry.com
You'll find the biggest and best selections of healthy foods in the funky Coventry part of Cleveland Heights. Tommy's offers a great selection of vegetable and "meatless" pies. The changing menu always has something new and unusual to tempt your vegetarian taste buds. Regulars swear by the vegetarian French onion soup.

Trattoria Roman Garden
12207 Mayfield Road
(216) 421-2700
Frank Sinatra tunes and red wine flow in the three dining rooms and outdoor patio of this Little Italy institution. It's not a fancy place, but folks line up at the door for the eggplant parmesan. Parking is nearly impossible in this area, but the food is worth the effort.

ACCOMMODATIONS

There are a variety of lodging options in downtown Cleveland, ranging from mid-priced hotels such as the Comfort Inn and Hampton Inn to the Embassy Suites for extended stays. The two hotels included here are Cleveland's most reputable, but they are also the most expensive.

Renaissance Cleveland Hotel
24 Public Square
(216) 696-5600, (800) 468-3571
www.marriot.com
This magnificent 15-story hotel, built in 1918, is a designated Historic Hotel of America and is located right in the heart of the city. It has an indoor pool and is connected to Gund Arena and Jacobs Field by indoor, climate-controlled walkways. The hotel's Sans Souci restaurant serves classic French and Mediterranean fare in a truly ritzy setting.

Ritz Carlton
1515 West Third Street
(216) 623-1300, (800) 241-3333
www.ritzcarlton.com
Cleveland's only four star/four diamond property features 208 luxurious guest rooms and suites with scenic views of downtown and Lake Erie. This first-rate hotel is adjacent to the Tower City shopping center and connects via an enclosed walkway to Gund Arena and Jacobs Field. It is within walking distance of the Rock and Roll Hall of Fame and all lakefront attractions. The Century at the Ritz is the hotel's elegant restaurant and sushi bar, which is open to the public.

Dayton Area

Dayton Convention and Visitors' Bureau
(800) 221-8235
www.daytoncvb.com
One of the easiest day trips from Columbus is the 45-minute pilgrimage west to Dayton, home of the Wright brothers and the "Birthplace of Aviation." The area's premier attractions are mostly flight-related, but history and art buffs may be pleasantly surprised at what else Dayton has to offer.

Antiques lovers may want to stop off along the way at the Heart of Ohio Antiques Center in Springfield (937-324-2188; www.heartofohioantiques.com). Some 650 dealers from over 20 states are represented at this huge mall conveniently located off Interstate 70.

When you make your way to Dayton, you can get your fill of flight at a bunch of places. Start off at the historic Wright

Cycle Company (937-225-7705), located at 22 South Williams Street. It is here that Orville and Wilbur Wright managed a bicycle and print shop. In addition to antique bicycles, visitors can view machinery and see where the first flight tests were held.

Next stop: Wright Patterson Air Force Base. The National Museum of the U.S. Air Force (937-255-3286; www.wpafb.af.mil/museum) houses hundreds of aircraft, ground vehicles, flight equipment, and missiles, making this the world's largest aviation museum. Also at WPAFB is the National Aviation Hall of Fame (937-256-0944; www.nationalaviation.org), where America's air and space pioneers are honored in exhibits spanning the dawn of flight through the current space age. The more popular highlights include early Wright brothers' models and the plane that dropped the atomic bomb on Nagasaki, Japan, in 1945.

It seems that the Wright brothers were interested in more than just flight. They were also among the founding patrons of the Dayton Art Institute (937-223-5277; www.daytonartinstitute.org). This surprising little gem of a museum houses an impressive collection of 12,000 works ranging from early American furniture to Italian Baroque paintings to 1970s pop art.

For more information about Dayton, contact the Visitors' Bureau or the Chamber of Commerce at 1 Chamber Plaza (937-226-1444; www.daytonchamber.org).

Granville

Village of Granville Council
141 East Broadway Street
(740) 587-0707
www.granville.oh.us

Located just 30 minutes east of the city, this quaint village is practically a suburb of Columbus. Anyone who has visited the small, charming town of Granville will understand when I compare it to the town in *It's a Wonderful Life.* You almost expect to see Jimmy Stewart running madly around the streets. The village is full of restored 19th-century homes, quaint boutiques, and little pubs. It is also home to the very picturesque Denison University.

New Englanders from Granville, Massachusetts, and Granby, Connecticut, settled Granville in 1805. The Granville Historical Society at 115 East Broadway Street (740-587-3951; www.granvillehistory.org) is a good place to learn about local history. The Robbins Hunter Museum is located at 221 East Broadway in the historic 1842 Avery-Downer home (740-587-0430). The museum features 11 furnished rooms with 18th- and 19th-century American, European, and Asian antiques, paintings, sculpture, carpets, and furniture.

The Buxton Inn, located at 313 East Broadway Street (740-587-0001; www.buxtoninn.com), is Ohio's oldest continuously operated inn in its original building. This former stagecoach stop dates to 1812 and has a fascinating history—and possibly a few friendly ghosts. The restaurant offers mostly French and American cuisine in an Old World setting, while the separate tavern has its own lighter menu.

The inn's 25 guest rooms, with private baths and period antiques, are located in four restored homes, all connected to the inn by formal gardens and walkways. Rooms range in price from $70 to $90 a night. One interesting piece of trivia is that Presidents William Henry Harrison, Abraham Lincoln, and William McKinley all spent the night here, and all died in office. Coincidence? Most likely.

The Granville Inn (740-587-3333; www.granville.com) is just across the street, at 314 East Broadway, likewise offers fine dining and accommodations. This English country manor-style building was built in 1924. The inn recently came under new ownership, bringing a new chef and menu. The dining room is truly romantic with its floor-to-ceiling wood paneling, cozy alcoves, and huge hearth. The outdoor patio has views across the lawn to historic Granville. The inn has 27 rooms, 3 suites, and a tavern.

Hocking Hills

Hocking County Tourism Association
13178 State Route 664 S, Logan
(740) 385-9706, (800) HOCKING
www.hcta.org

The region just southeast of Columbus, known as Hocking Hills, beckons hikers and outdoorsmen into the foothills of the Appalachian Mountains. Mother Nature provides attractions in the form of 300-million-year-old hills, valleys, ridges, and cliffs.

Some 9,000 picturesque acres encompassing nine state parks and four nature preserves offer year-round outdoor activities. Try something different, like scouting for bald eagles or canoeing in the moonlight. In just an hour's drive you'll find hiking, fishing, horseback riding, rappelling, bird watching, and boating in some of Ohio's most remote areas.

ATTRACTIONS

The Hocking Hills Regional Welcome Center is located on U.S. Route 664 and U.S. Route 33 in Logan and can provide comprehensive information and detailed maps of the region.

Ash Cave is in the southernmost parts of the Hocking Hills and is the largest and most impressive cave in the state. At 700 feet wide, 100 feet deep, and 90 feet high, Ash Cave provided shelter to the earliest inhabitants and a resting place for weary travelers. Its cascading waterfall and Pulpit Rock offer great photo opportunities.

Early settlers mistook the hemlocks for cedars, therefore misnaming Cedar Falls. The cool, damp climate of this gorge favors hemlock growth, so it's no surprise Cedar Falls claims the largest tree in Ohio—a giant, 149-foot hemlock.

Cedar Falls is in a remote and austere part of Hocking Hills, 1 mile west of Route 664 on Route 374. Towering rock walls and grottoes surround this wild and lonely chasm. The falls, which plummet 50 feet into a pool below, is the greatest in terms of volume in the hills.

Conkle's Hollow is a rugged and rocky gorge, just off SR 374 on Big Pine Road. The 200-foot vertical cliffs surround the trail, which leads through a ravine overgrown with ferns, wildflowers, soaring hemlocks, and birch trees. Adventurous hikers can circle the gorge on the highest cliffs in the area by taking the Rim Trail. Stunning views are guaranteed, but caution is a must, as this trail can be dangerous in all seasons.

Old Man's Cave, located on SR 664, is the most visited area and the heart of Hocking Hills. This magnificent ½-mile gorge is divided into five sections: Upper Falls, Upper Gorge, Middle Falls, Lower Falls, and Lower Gorge. The Upper Gorge contains the Devil's Bathtub, a swirling natural pool that local legend contends reaches into the depths of Hades, where the devil resides. The 6-mile Grandma Gatewood Trail runs from Old Man's Cave to Cedar Falls to Ash Cave.

Rock House is the only true cave in the park. Nature has carved a 200-foot corridor into the sandstone, replete with gothic arches and massive columns. Native Americans used recesses in the rear wall as baking ovens. It is located on SR 374 and Thompson Road, north of Conkle's Hollow.

DINING AND LODGING

If you need a place to stay while exploring Hocking Hills, check out www.hocking-hills.com, or contact the Hocking County Tourism Association to find out who has vacancies or which places permit pets. State parks also offer lodging, which you can read more about in the Parks and Recreation chapter. There are loads of different cabins and cottages to choose from. Listed here are just a few of the reputable rental groups. From time to time, a restaurant comes with lodging, but most are self-contained cabins with fully equipped kitchens.

Four Seasons Cabin Rentals
14435 Nickel Plate Road, Logan
(800) 242-8453
www.hockinghills.com/fourseasons
This secluded house is located on 55 acres, where you can hike, mountain bike, fish, or use the paddleboat. You'll find an outdoor hot tub, deck, grill, and wood-burning stone fireplace.

Getaway Cabins
Various parts of Hocking Hills
(888) 587-0659
www.getaway-cabins.com
These private, secluded cabins are a perfect hideaway from reality and allow for uninterrupted romantic weekend getaways. Check out the Web site, or call for special packages.

The Inn at Cedar Falls
21190 Route 374, Logan
(740) 385-7489, (800) 65-FALLS
www.innatcedarfalls.com
Located less than ½ mile from its namesake, this 1840s cabin offers guests a chance to dine from a seasonal menu and stay in the romantic Cozy Cottages just across the lane. The cabins are decorated with antiques, have a whirlpool and king-size bed, but no TV or phone.

Old Man's Cave Chalets
18905 Route 664 South, Logan
(800) 762-9396
www.oldmanscavechalets.com
More guests stay at these wonderful chalets, log homes, and A-frame cabins than anywhere else in the Hocking Hills region. All are spacious one-, two-, or three-bedrooms and come fully furnished.

Lake Erie Islands and Sandusky

Sandusky/Erie County Visitor's and Convention Bureau
U.S. Route 250, 1 mile north of intersection at State Route 2
(800) 255-ERIE
www.visitohio.com
Many people think of Ohio as a landlocked Midwest state full of corn and cows. Not obvious are the plentiful beaches of northern Ohio and the Lake Erie Islands. Just one ride up Cedar Point's roller coasters and you'll have a different perspective, a bird's-eye view out over one of the nation's Great Lakes. While Cedar Point might be an easy day trip from Columbus, many opt to spend the night in Sandusky or plan a whole weekend around fun in the sun.

A two-hour drive north of Columbus will not only get you to one of the most popular theme parks in the country, but it will also land you at The Headlands Beach State Park near Mentor. It features the largest (mile-long) natural beach in the state and borders two state nature reserves. A third preserve in Mentor, the Lagoon Nature Preserve and Marina, encompasses 450 acres and includes 1.5 miles of shoreline, with 3 miles of hiking and biking trails.

Traveling along the Erie coast, there are no fewer than a dozen lighthouses, some of which are only visible from shore or accessible by boat, but several are located on the mainland and open to the public. The museum at Old Fairport Harbor Main Lighthouse (c. 1871), just east of Cleveland, houses Great Lakes artifacts. Farther west of Cleveland is the newly renovated Cedar Point Lighthouse and the Great Lake's oldest continuously operated Marblehead Lighthouse. Both are open for tours during the summer.

Visitors to northern Ohio can reach the Lake Erie Islands by ferry or plane, but if you're lucky enough to have your own boat, there are plenty of places from which to launch. Cars are permitted on all the islands, but you'll have the most freedom to explore if you rent a bicycle or golf cart. Rental facilities are located near all the ferry docks, and you can learn more about these services by contacting the ferry services included here.

THE ISLANDS

Ferries leaving Sandusky, Port Clinton, Marblehead, and Catawba go to most of the Lake Erie Islands.

Vacations magazine named Kelley's Island one of the "Top 10 Undiscovered Places" in 1992. It is still quite unspoiled. It helps that the entire island is on the National Register of Historic Places. The downtown area is most active in the summer months and has shops, restaurants, and bars within a few steps of the waterfront. The north side is less commercial, with an abundance of wildlife, beaches, and clean, clear water. Contact (419) 746-2360 or www.kelleysislandchamber.com for information on activities and cottage rentals.

Put-in-Bay on South Bass Island is a party place, but the festive atmosphere often overshadows its family-friendly side. Victorian-style housing, restaurants, boutiques, arcades, and a waterfront park give it a seaside resort atmosphere. The island is also home to two museums, a winery, and the towering, 352-foot Perry Monument, which can be ascended for panoramic views of Lake Erie. South Bass Island State Park offers waterfront camping and a lovely beach. Have a look at www.put-in-bay.com, or call (419) 285-2832 for more information on year-round activities, including ice fishing.

Middle Bass Island is covered with vineyards, old cottages, summer homes, and a campground. Most of the attractions are natural and include a rocky shoreline with expansive vistas and the Kuehnle Wildlife Area. The interior wetland's 20-acre pond is a favorite among bird-watchers and anglers.

i **_Kelley's Island is home to the world's largest prehistoric glacial grooves. Heavy glaciers carved out the soft island limestone, leaving a fossilized record of marine life from millions of years ago. Perimeter viewing of the grooves is possible._**

Ferry Information

Jet Express
3 Monroe Street, Port Clinton
(800) 245-1538
www.jet-express.com
Hydrojet catamarans whisk passengers to Put-in-Bay on South Bass Island. They also provide early-morning and late-night service. Children under 12 ride for free.

Kelley's Island Ferry Boat Lines
510 West Main Street, Marblehead
(419) 798-9763
www.kelleysislandferry.com
Boats depart every half hour, year-round, and run well into the evening. Automobile transportation is also available.

Miller Boat Line
State Route 53, off Route 2, Catawba
(419) 285-2421, (800) 500-2421
www.millerferry.com
Ferry service carries both cars and passengers every half hour to South and Middle Bass Island on a daily basis in the spring, summer, and fall.

Attractions

Cedar Point, Challenge Park, and Soak Park

1 Cedar Point Drive, Sandusky
(419) 627-2350
www.cedarpoint.com
The prestigious *Amusement Today* magazine voted this 364-acre family amuse-

ment park/resort the "Best Park in the World" for seven consecutive years. As home to the largest collection of roller coasters and rides, there is something here for everyone.

Four of the 16 coasters have hills more than 200 feet tall. Newer rides include the world's tallest (420 feet) and fastest (120 mph) coaster, the Top Thrill Dragster. Thrill seekers also swear by the 15-story, free-fall Skycoaster at Challenge Park. Parents can join their younger children on seven rides at Camp Snoopy, while scaredy-cats can play it safe in the self-paddle swan boats. Families can beat the heat on the inner-tube slides and wave pool at Soak City.

One- and two-day passes can be purchased and range in price from $22 to $64. Cedar Point offers a variety of lodging options within walking distance of the park. Some have their own private beaches. Guests staying at Cedar Point resorts receive discounted admission and early entry to the park. There is so much to do here that two days is not unreasonable, but be prepared to spend half the time waiting in line for the more popular rides.

Crystal Cave at Heineman's Winery
978 Catawba Avenue, Put-in-Bay
(419) 285-2811
www.ohiowine.com

One of the most popular attractions on South Bass Island is 40 feet below a winery. This massive rock is hollowed out and lined with sparkling crystals. You gotta see it to believe it. Tour both the winery and cave, but be sure to take a jacket, as this natural wine cellar maintains a cool 52° Fahrenheit year-round.

Ghostly Manor
3319 Milan Road, US 250, Sandusky
(419) 626-4467
www.ghostlymanor.com

This seasonal haunted house is certain to startle you with the best in ghostly technology. Wander through this old mansion every Thursday, Friday, and Saturday night from June through October.

Dining

Angry Trout Fish and Steakhouse
505 East Bayview Drive, Sandusky
(419) 684-5900
www.angrytrout.com

This full-service restaurant and bar specializes in fresh fish, steaks, and ribs. Eat in the rustic dining room or on a deck overlooking Sandusky Bay. Open seven days a week.

Beer Barrel Saloon
1618 Delaware Avenue, Put-in-Bay
(419) 285-BEER

Grab a bite to eat and check out one of the longest bars in the world. If you can't find a seat somewhere along the 405-foot bar, take your beer outside on the patio.

Cedar Point Dining
1 Cedar Point Drive, Sandusky

There is an endless assortment of amusement park fare, fine dining, and everything in between. If you want to indulge in fine steaks and seafood, try out the Bay Harbor Inn. It is open year-round and located in an elegant hotel overlooking the lake. Also open year-round is Dominic's, the Italian restaurant in the historic Hotel Breakers.

Kelley's Island Brewery
Lakeshore Drive, Kelley's Island
(419) 746-2314
www.kelleysislandbrewpub.com

This full-service restaurant and bar is known for its microbrews and handcrafted root beer. The dining room and outside patio offer a beautiful lake view. It is open for breakfast, lunch, and dinner and can be quite busy during peak season.

A final comprehensive source of vacation information on the Web is www.lakeerie vacations.com.

Mariner's Retreat Restaurant at Marina Del Isle
6801 East Harbor Road, Marblehead
(419) 732–2816
www.marinadelisle.com

This casual waterfront restaurant sits in a scenic harbor and specializes in seafood, steaks, and pasta. The nonsmoking facility is open mid-April through mid-October and is closed on Tuesday.

Lodging

In 2004, Cedar Point (419–627–2106; www .cedarpoint.com) expanded its lodging to include 14 lakeside cottages, 30 cabins, and 38 luxury RV campsites. A more classic option is the magnificent, 650-room Hotel Breakers, which first opened its doors in 1905. It has entertained such guests as Annie Oakley, John Philip Sousa, and several U.S. presidents and is a two-minute walk from the park. Cedar Point also has a half dozen resorts on the property, a few with their own private beaches.

The most comprehensive listing for hotels in the Cedar Point/Sandusky area can be viewed online at www.sandusky hotels.com. There are plenty of affordable family-friendly chains, including the Ramada Inn, Comfort Inn, and Amerihost Inn, located all along Lake Erie. Many are lakefront, have pools, and offer shuttle service to Cedar Point.

If you plan to stay on one of the Lake Erie Islands, contact the chambers of commerce or visitors' bureaus for each individual island for a listing of accommodations. Remember, most are only open seasonally.

RELOCATION

Most of the communities that make up Greater Columbus lie within the Interstate 270 beltway. When deciding where to live in Columbus, take time to explore different parts of town. Like many big cities, Columbus is made up of a string of neighborhoods, each with its own distinct identity.

The north and south sides of Columbus are like night and day, while the east and westsides are equally unalike. New luxury apartments are going up in the Arena District, while unique historic homes can be found in Victorian Village and Worthington. Suburban housing is becoming bigger as new developments sprawl farther and farther from the city. There is a great diversity in architectural styles and housing options all over Columbus.

In 2005, Columbus homes averaged $168,376, up 5.5 percent from the previous year, but still below the national median of $187,500. A variety of housing options is available in Columbus, but without waterfront property and scenic landscape features in central Ohio, developers rely heavily on golf courses, manicured green spaces, and private amenities to add value and aesthetic appeal to property.

Golf course communities are as popular as ever, and home buyers do expect to pay a premium for these homes, but because of a growing and more diverse market, golf club living has become much more affordable than it used to be. These homes cost anywhere from $200,000 to $2 million. People are also willing to pay for the extra amenities that come with a planned community, such as a clubhouse, swimming pools, and tennis courts.

If your preference is for older neighborhoods, downtown Columbus has several landmark districts with big, old Victorian and Italianate homes begging to be restored. Olde Towne East and Italian Village are works in progress, while German Village is much more established as a historic district but also much more expensive.

Falling somewhere in between are Victorian Village and Grandview. Both are safe residential areas, with many homes requiring updates rather than a total overhaul. Each of these urban neighborhoods has tight lots and often competitive street parking, but farther outside the metropolitan area one will find bigger lots and bigger homes.

The northern and western suburbs of Columbus were developed rapidly in the past 10 years. Worthington, Westerville, and Dublin are home to the quintessential suburban cul-de-sacs, good school districts, and plenty of country clubs. What differentiate these neighborhoods from other suburban sprawl are their restored old town centers with pubs, boutiques, and historic homes. While each city encompasses a huge area, their historic hubs, particularly in Olde Worthington, quite often define them.

Upper Arlington has a distinctly suburban feel to it, but it is adjacent to the university and only 10 minutes from downtown. The styles of homes are diverse, but most were built in the early to mid-20th century. Arlington has fantastic public schools, and the residents have a deep sense of community; because of this, Arlington homes sell rather quickly.

Looking for that one-of-a-kind, multimillion-dollar mansion? Then head east to the tree-lined streets of Bexley. Want a Georgian home of 5,000 square feet? New Albany is your place. It seems the farther east you go, the larger everything becomes, but rest assured more moderate-scale living can be found out east in Gahanna, Blacklick, and Reynoldsburg. Unfortunately, in between all these nice, livable neighborhoods are not-so-nice pockets of urban dwellings. Bexley, for

The Wyandotte building at 21 West Broad Street was built in 1898 and was Columbus's first steel-framed skyscraper. It was built by Chicago architect Daniel Burnham, who also built New York City's landmark Flatiron building and Columbus's Union Station.

example, is a distinguished "old money" community surrounded by some of the most run-down parts of the city.

While stereotypes are not always fair or accurate, there is no getting around the fact that certain generalizations are made about each neighborhood. Columbus is less racially segregated than other Ohio cities, but it has greater levels of economic segregation. This chapter attempts to be honest about the demographics and socioeconomic status without pigeonholing the residents into one category. It provides a synopsis of each neighborhood, while highlighting its interesting features.

There are plenty of real estate agencies to help with the search, and this chapter includes the contact details for several of the more reputable ones. If you want to do your homework before talking to an agent, request the free monthly publication titled *Columbus Homes Illustrated* (614-866-7878), or search the Web site www.columbushi.com for a comprehensive listing of properties in the region. Another good site to check out is www.noplacelikehome.com. Most real estate agents publish free magazines with their own listings.

DOWNTOWN

www.downtowncolumbus.com

Downtown Columbus is undergoing a renaissance; and the city has made urban living priority No. 1. Paving the way was the landmark Miranova condominiums built by developer Ron Pizzuti in 2001. This gleaming, crescent-shaped building occupies a piece of land between the Waterford Tower and Scioto River and has ushered in urban living for the 21st century. At starting prices of $400,000 for custom-designed condos with impeccable views of the city, One Miranova Place is downtown Columbus's premier address.

With a daytime working population of nearly 100,000, studies have proven that downtown residential living is in demand. Developers have wasted no time putting up loads of new apartment buildings and condominiums, including the large Market Mohawk complex on Grant Avenue and Parkview at Goodale Park. Housing more along the lines of lofts is being constructed along Rich and Front Streets, while the Columbus Landmarks Foundation has initiated a trend toward rehabilitation of old residential units.

Downtown Columbus tends to shut down pretty early, but with apartments and condos going up almost daily, this building boom anticipates an increase in city living and, hopefully, a lot more downtown activity in the near future. It is bringing about an influx of new restaurants, bars, and shops and is stimulating redevelopment of the south side of the city.

The newest addition to the downtown area is the Market Exchange. This area, which runs east along Main Street from Grant Avenue to the Interstate 70/71 split, was once the primary downtown neighborhood. The bustling 19th century Central Market, for which the Market Exchange is named, was located where the Greyhound Bus Station now sits. It totals just a few blocks in length, but it is being transformed into an upscale urban locale. It is now home to galleries, offices, boutiques, and restaurants. Various types of housing options are also being developed along East Main Street.

The Market Exchange District is conveniently located near the Columbus College of Art and Design and Franklin University. The area attracts a student crowd and businesspeople during the day. The nightlife in this little pocket is somewhat minimal, but there are a handful of bars and restaurants that stay open late enough to provide downtowners something to do.

This district may seem a bit incomplete right now, but what was a decrepit part of the city just a few years ago is quickly turning into the trendiest. This is one place to keep an eye on if you are considering making the move downtown.

The white art deco building that dominates the Columbus skyline is the LeVeque Tower. It was completed in 1927 and remained the tallest skyscraper in the city until 1973. The LeVeque Tower was added to the National Register of Historic Places in 1975.

THE "ORIGINAL" SUBURBS

Some of Columbus's earliest neighborhoods radiate around the city center; a few are renovated historic districts, while others are, unfortunately, very run down. Most of the neighborhoods, which are now considered downtown were the earliest "suburbs" of Columbus. During the mid-1800s, wealthy industrialists and bankers ventured eastward along Broad and Main Streets to build new mansions away from the hubbub of the city.

You will notice as you drive east out of the city that for every beautiful, renovated building, there are four or five desperate ones in need of repair. It takes a lot of vision to see beyond the crime and boarded up structures, but there is a glimmer of hope that this corridor between downtown and Bexley will someday be whipped into shape. While many of these near east communities have seen better days, some semblance of their former grandeur can be found in the majestic old homes lining the streets.

Historic Olde Towne East was once one of Columbus's wealthiest neighborhoods. The boundaries of this eclectic area are generally defined as East Long Street on the north, I-71 and I-70 to the west and south, and an eastern border of Winner, Miller, and Wilson Avenues. The population is a mix of different races, professionals, artisans, tradespeople, singles, couples, and families.

The buildings of Olde Towne East are, like its residents, a mixed bag, having both residential and professional functions. Over 50 architectural styles are represented in more than a thousand homes. Some of Columbus's oldest inhabited houses are in this part of town. They range from restrained Italianate to Victorian Queen Anne; a few even date to the 1830s.

Olde Towne East has experienced hard times, and many of its magnificent old homes have been subject to the wrecking ball. Plenty more are in dire need of TLC. Many of the ornate professional buildings have great potential, and, according to the *RetroMetro Real Estate News for Metropolitan Columbus,* Olde Towne East is the No. 1 spot for property appreciation.

The Old Towne East Neighborhood Association (866-234-0414; www.oldetowne.org) plays a big role in restoring many of the grand old houses while preserving what currently exists. This neighborhood organization offers an annual tour of homes and sells a publication titled *Historic Homes of Olde Towne East,* which details the 50 most notable houses.

Another near east side community, the Jefferson Avenue Historic District, has several landmark buildings and was added to the National Register of Historic Places in 1982. This small area is bounded roughly by I-71, East Broad Street, 11th Avenue, and Long Street. The architecture is primarily Italianate, and many of the buildings date to 1875-1899 or 1900-1924. The most notable historic structure in the area is the James Thurber House, but this 55-acre district also encompasses the Franklin House, Columbus Museum of Art, and Columbus College or Art and Design.

Until you reach Bexley, the east side of the city has only a scattering of safe neighborhoods. Statistics show high crime and low incomes in this part of town. There are, however, bright spots in the community. The Franklin Park neighborhood, also on the near east side, is situated to the south of Broad Street and north of Main, east of Wilson Avenue and west of Alum Creek. It encompasses Franklin Park, which is home to the city's beautiful conservatory, and it is surrounded by a variety of buildings.

The west side of downtown Columbus is a different, and somewhat sad, story. Franklinton, on the near west side, is the oldest part of Columbus, but few remnants remain of the early settlement. This area was nicknamed "The Bottoms" because of its low ground level and continual subjection to flooding of the Scioto and Olentangy Rivers. A new floodgate is expected to solve that 200-year-old problem.

It is hard to tell where the city of Franklinton begins and ends. The Scioto River to the east and north, I-70 to the west, and Greenlawn Avenue to the south roughly define the area. West Broad Street, which is the main corridor, is a clutter of shopping centers, apartment buildings, fast-food joints, and auto dealerships. Just to the west of Franklinton is a small group of neighborhoods referred to as "The Hilltop." Though steeped in history, this area is also steeped in crime.

There are, however, reasons to venture to the west side of Columbus. The Center of Science and Industry (COSI), Cooper Stadium, and Veterans Memorial are all situated on the near west side of town. History buffs seek out the ghosts of Columbus's past at West Gate Park, the site of a former Civil War prison camp cemetery. The Franklinton Post Office, built in 1807, is located at 72 South Gift Street. This dilapidated, boarded up structure was placed on the National Register of Historic Places in 1973 and, though not much to look at, is considered the city's oldest standing building.

Franklinton Cemetery was established in 1799 and is central Ohio's oldest burial ground, but most of the bodies have been removed to Greenlawn Cemetery, including Lucas Sullivant and many of Columbus's early families. Both cemeteries are on the west side, but, unfortunately, not much else remains of the original city.

THE BREWERY DISTRICT

www.brewerydistrict.org

The Brewery District is located on the south side of I-70 and is primarily centered along Front Street and east of High Street. This neighborhood is immediately south of downtown Columbus and was settled by German immigrants in the 1830s. It consisted of family homes, churches, and family-owned breweries that thrived until World War I, after which anti-German sentiment and Prohibition forced many of the Germans out of business—and out of town.

Many of the buildings lay abandoned until the end of the 20th century. New life was breathed into the derelict brick warehouses and breweries during the 1980s, and by 1992 this neighborhood was saved as the Brewery District Historical Preservation District. Thanks to the ongoing efforts of the Brewery District Business Association, development and restoration are ongoing.

Nightclubs, restaurants, and bars make the Brewery District more of an entertainment hot spot than a residential area, but this is changing. Brewer's Gate, a 35-unit condo on Front Street, is open for tenancy, while several other apartment buildings are under way. Construction is also planned for Columbus's first urban grocery store to be built in the Brewery District. This Kroger's will be a full-service grocery with a built-in Donato's pizzeria and a Starbucks Outlet.

The Brewery District supports a few professional offices, such as architects, attorneys, and accountants, but farther south along High Street are the many quaint homes of German Village and the contiguous neighborhoods of Schumacher Place, Merion Village, and Hungarian Village.

GERMAN VILLAGE

www.german-village.com
German Village is without a doubt one of the most popular downtown neighborhoods in which to live. For residents, much of German Village's appeal lies in its Old World atmosphere. Sturdy brick cottages and charming brownstones line the brick-paved streets. Window boxes spill over with flowers, and chimney pots add historical detail. Columbus doesn't get any more picturesque than German Village.

For visitors, the appeal lies in the variety of eateries, shops, and galleries. Locals will come from miles around to eat at the many fine restaurants, drink at the long-established watering holes, browse the bookshops, or see a show at Schiller Park. The Village is a completely self-contained community, with professional offices, dry cleaners, banks, and even a veterinary hospital.

German Village is situated 6 blocks south of downtown Columbus. It is bound by Pearl Alley on the west, East Livingston Avenue on the north, Jaeger and Bruck Streets to the east, and Thurman and Mithoff to the south. Prior to its settlement, sewers and tanneries made this property, just outside city limits, undesirable and cheap.

In the early 1800s, poor German immigrants settled "die alte sud ende" (the old south end), but they made the most of it. By 1865, schools, churches, and family-owned breweries were prospering. More than a third of Columbus's population was of German descent. Many of the wealthier residents moved east, and with all the anti-German sentiment during World War I, even more German Americans left the village (and Columbus). The neighborhood subsequently fell into disrepair.

In the 1960s, the German Village Society (www.germanvillage.org) was formed to rescue this once-thriving community. Members undertook a fundraising campaign that resulted in the largest restoration project in the country. Thoughtful renovations led to the entire neighborhood—all 233 acres—being placed on the National Register of Historic Places; it remains the largest privately funded historic district on the register and in the country.

The heritage and culture of the German immigrants who fashioned this neighborhood have been preserved in a few restaurants, German music choirs, and organizations that uphold traditions like Oktoberfest, but that's about it. Yes, the street names are good and guttural, but flip through the German Village directories and you won't come across many Deutsch names. As for cuisine, you'll probably find more pasta and burgers than you will brats and sauerkraut balls. I am respectful, but unapologetic, when I say German Village doesn't seem very German.

The demographics are predictable for such a popular (trendy) area. A majority of German Village residents are white professionals between the ages of 20 and 49. Plus, most residents of German Village don't speak a lick of German. But who cares? It's a lovely part of town, where homes average around $150,000. It's a living museum and a tribute to our city's heritage. A visitor center is located at the German Village Meeting Haus, 588 South Third Street.

ARENA DISTRICT

www.arena-district.com
The Arena District creates the transition from downtown to the Short North and is bordered by North High Street to the east, Neil Avenue to the west, Spring Street to the south, and railroad tracks to the north. This lively new part of town is a total boom-or-bust neighborhood, driven mostly by the throngs of hockey fans attending Blue Jackets games (or not).

The Arena District is situated around Nationwide Arena and was planned from the very beginning, so who better than the master urban planner Daniel Burnham to provide the symbolic gateway to this district? Columbus's last remaining limestone arch from Burnham's 19th-century Union Station now stands at the end of a landscaped park, McFerson Commons.

The Arena District is home to a few interesting chain restaurants and bars, several live music venues, and the Arena Grand movie theater. While the Arena District has a distinct warehouse feel to it, brick alleys provide pedestrianized zones between the restaurants and pubs. This coziness is occasionally interrupted by views of the Columbus skyline—a friendly reminder you are still downtown.

A not-so-friendly reminder is the parking. Locals are turned off by the parking situation in this area, particularly on the weekends and during Gallery Hop. There are, however, a few (pricey) surface lots and garages. If you park in the Arena Grand Garage, the theater will validate your ticket, so parking will only cost $1.00 for up to four hours. The street meters are free after 6:00 P.M.

Walking is the way to go if you are living or staying in this area. The Arena District is a five-minute walk into downtown or the Short North, and an easy jaunt to Victorian Village and Goodale Park. The newly created North Bank Park along the Scioto River will provide urbanites 14 acres of green space and bike trails right at their back door.

Luxury apartments and high-rise condos are being built in the Arena District as part of the downtown development campaign. Burnham Square Condominiums overlook McFerson Commons, while the Arena Crossing apartments are literally a few steps away from Nationwide Arena and the North Market. It is a high-rent district but is worth it for those who want to be in the heart of it all.

THE SHORT NORTH

www.shortnorth.org

The Short North begins just north of the Arena District and has pushed its boundaries to the edge of The Ohio State University. It runs along High Street from Goodale Avenue to the evolving "Garden District" at Fifth Avenue. This artsy neighborhood is both trendy and charming. One would never guess it was dilapidated and crime-ridden just 20 years ago.

After going through a complete overhaul in the 1980s, the Short North has become one of the most diverse, eclectic urban neighborhoods in Columbus. It's lined with trendy boutiques, art galleries, modern theatrical venues, and some of the best restaurants in town. Wander off onto the side streets, and you'll come upon brick town houses and clever little green spaces, called "pocket parks," tucked into unexpected places.

The community's socially conscious and creative side shows through in the variety of murals painted on the Short North buildings. Graffiti is given a new twist at 641 North High Street with a modern depiction of George Bellows *Cliff Dwellers,* a social commentary on urban living. Fresh interpretations of *American Gothic* can be found opposite R. J. Snapper's at 714 North High Street, and the *Mona Lisa* watches over the neighborhood from Warren Street. Not everyone likes them, but *Mona Lisa* has become synonymous with the Short North and, if nothing else, makes for a good photo op.

The Short North is known particularly for its culinary and artistic offerings and its residents for their alternative lifestyles. There is a large concentration of gay- and lesbian-owned businesses in this neighborhood, but there is also an awareness, and acknowledgment of the consumer base among those that are not. This part of town can be a little over the top with various forms of self-expression, but this has nothing to do with being gay or straight. Overall, it's just a colorful, offbeat, entertaining district.

VICTORIAN VILLAGE

www.victorianvillage.org

Victorian Village is another trendy historic district located between the OSU campus and the Arena District. Its primary road, Neil Avenue, runs all the way from the campus into downtown, making this a popular location for professors, students, and historic home lovers. Officially, the village lies to the north of Goodale Avenue, south of West Fifth Avenue, and in between North High Street and Neil Avenue.

Unlike the Short North, which is more of an arts and entertainment district, Victorian Village is truly residential. It's quite lovely to drive around and offers residents a handful of good restaurants and friendly neighborhood bars. Many of the homes are within easy walking distance of grocery stores, coffee shops, and bus stops. There's also Goodale Park, which is covered in the Parks and Recreation chapter.

Prior to 1870, this area was farmland owned by the Neil family, but as the university and city developed, Neil Avenue became one of the major thoroughfares into downtown Columbus. By 1879, Victorian Village was a thriving and growing community, but with the introduction of the automobile, residents began moving to suburbia. By 1920, the decline of this near north side community was under way. Fortunately, its architectural value was recognized, and Victorian Village was designated a historic district in 1973. Now, more than 80 percent of the neighborhood has been renovated.

Victorian Village's close proximity to the university keeps its social makeup economically, racially, and religiously diverse. The median household income is about $33,000, and more than 50 percent of residents have college degrees. In fact, 8 percent of Victorian Village residents have a graduate or doctoral degree, which makes sense since a large number of Ohio State faculty and staff live in this area.

Catering to the student population, many of the houses along Neil Avenue are split into rental units. The homes farther south of campus and off the side streets are private residences. Impressive examples of Italianate, Queen Anne, Tudor, Greek, and Gothic Revival can be found throughout the area, while the biggest and most prominent homes are situated around Goodale Park. Take some time in September to go on the Victorian Village Society's Annual Home and Garden Tour to see how beautifully these homes have been restored.

i

In 1851, Columbus's first physician, Dr. Lincoln Goodale, donated 40 acres to the city. Goodale Park, in Victorian Village, became the nation's first tract of land to be used as a public park.

ITALIAN VILLAGE

www.sjms.net/italianvillage

Tucked between highways, railroads, and two major thoroughfares is another historic district waiting to be resurrected. Italian Village is technically part of the Short North. It lies to the east of High Street and south of Fifth Avenue, picking up where OSU ends. Summit and Fourth Streets run right through Italian Village into downtown Columbus.

The housing options in Italian Village are truly "metro" in style: close together, minimal grass, and lots of pavement. They range from duplexes and row houses to town houses and apartments. Forty percent of Italian Village homes were built in the 1950s and '60s, and another 20 percent are pre-1939. After several historic homes were leveled, residents began working toward revitalization and preservation. A few parts of Italian Village are now on the National Register of Historic Places, and others are currently being considered.

Besides restoration projects, the Italian Village Society addresses panhandling, parking, traffic, and crime issues. The area is making slow progress, but with an average household income just shy of $25,000, it's no wonder the neighborhood is being restored at a snail's pace. Italian Village might be a slow work in progress, but the new Jeffery Place town homes, lofts, and single-family units being built on the site of the former Jeffery Manufacturing Company will provide a much needed facelift for this side of the neighborhood.

NEIGHBORHOODS AND SUBURBS

The Ohio State University Campus

www.osu.edu

If you read only the introduction to The Ohio State University chapter, you'll realize it's a big school. The heart of campus is loosely defined as lying between Indianola Avenue to the east and Neil Avenue to the west, Lane Avenue to the north and Ninth Avenue to the south. These boundaries include the Oval, with its peripheral buildings, the medical center, Ohio Stadium, and fraternity and sorority houses.

It also encompasses dormitories, off-campus housing, restaurants, bars, and shops. It's basically a concrete jungle. Like any university town, there are the nice parts and there are the not-so-nice parts, but the redevelopment of south campus has reclaimed several blocks of ramshackle buildings.

Students who attend OSU usually live in one of three places: on campus in the dorms, off campus within a few blocks of High Street, or in one of the nearby neighborhoods of Clintonville, Grandview, or the Short North. It's not difficult to envision the campus itself as a neighborhood, especially if you have tried parking on any of the side streets. The apartment buildings and rental properties situated east of High Street are exactly how one might picture student housing: porches crowded with ratty sofas, empty beer cans in the front yards, and a rowdy bunch of guys tossing a football around.

This isn't exactly a dangerous neighborhood, but it has its moments—quite often alcohol-related college stupidity. The university publishes an annual crime report, so students and parents can be aware of what is happening on this diverse and energetic campus.

i ***Locals are certain to differentiate between Clintonville and Old Beechwold proper. This wooded pocket of interesting early-20th-century homes was placed on the National Register of Historic Places in 1987.***

Clintonville

www.clintonville.com

More hippie than hip, Clintonville is a laid-back residential neighborhood to which OSU professors and postgraduate students migrate. Bungalow-style houses with big porches and tree-lined streets give it a suburban feel, but Clintonville is only 4 miles north of downtown and convenient to Ohio State, the main bus lines, and two major highways.

Having been established in 1847, many of Clintonville's unusual street names are derived from the earliest settlers' names, such as Brevoort, Chase, Whetmore, and Webster. It is tucked between Arcadia Avenue and Cooke Road and is bounded on the east and west by I-71 and Route 315. The main artery through Clintonville is High Street, and like many other parts of town, it is undergoing major redevelopment.

Clintonville is one of the first suburban neighborhoods in which you encounter true Columbus natives with families more than one generation deep. Bob Vila types will be in their glory, as more than half the homes in the community are pre-1940. There is no shortage of house projects here. Clintonville housing options are typically not for transients. Apartment complexes are few and far between, but they do exist.

While not a destination shopping or entertainment district, Clintonville has a decent number of eclectic boutiques, antiques shops, art galleries, and specialty stores. It does not offer the most upscale dining, but Columbus's oldest vegetarian restaurant and two of the city's finest diners are located here. Some people have the idea that Clintonville is dry because one small section forbids liquor sales, but this is not the case. In fact, it's rather heavy into neighborhood bars.

Worthington

www.worthington.org
Driving directly up High Street (Route 23) from downtown will put you right in the heart of one of Columbus's oldest suburbs. Worthington is located 8 miles north of the city between Route 315 and I-71. A group of New Englanders from the Farmington River Valley in Connecticut settled the Village of Worthington in 1803, the same year Ohio became a state.

The two names that are most frequently associated with Worthington are James Kilbourne, the man who purchased the property, and Thomas Worthington, the land agent who pointed him to this site and for whom the town is named. Interestingly enough, Worthington had little to do with the actual settlement of the village.

Under the leadership of Kilbourne, a New England-style village was developed around a central public square. Despite a losing bid to become the state capital, Worthington became well known for its religious diversity, emphasis on education, and antislavery position.

Some 200 years later, the city covers more than 5 square miles and is home to 1,400 businesses, 21 different religious congregations, and a population of 14,000. Its schools are always at the top of the heap, and despite the low crime, great parks, and excellent location, most locals still seem to define Worthington by 6 square blocks known as Olde Worthington, the original village.

Olde Worthington lies within Morning, Evening, North, and South Streets and has all the trappings of a lovingly restored New England village: antiques shops, a village green, brick paved walks, charming restaurants with street-side patios, and, of course, a pub or two. Many of Worthington's historic homes are in this area, and the Web site has a nice walking tour with points of interest.

Worthington homes range from $115,000 to $400,000, and various housing options exist. Ranch homes can be found in the Riverlea section of Worthington, while Cape Cod-style bungalows dot the neighborhood. Rush Creek Village, located just east of Morning Street, is a wooded pocket of ultramodern homes based on the architectural principles made famous by Frank Lloyd Wright. Worthington, though known for its colonial ambience, has a little bit of something for everyone.

Westerville

www.visitwesterville.com
Ten miles northeast of downtown Columbus is the vibrant middle-class suburb of Westerville. It is one of the few communities located outside the I-270 Outer Belt that has been included in this chapter. It is easily accessible from all parts of Columbus by I-270, I-71, and Route 3, also known as Cleveland Avenue and Westerville Road.

Westerville is an attractive place to live and work for several reasons. First and foremost, it is affordable. The city boasts one of the lowest income tax rates in the region, and the average home costs around $200,000. The area has its own electric and water division, which saves residents and businesses money. It is home to Otterbein College, Mount Carmel St. Ann's Hospital, and Polaris Fashion Place, one of Columbus's newest and biggest malls.

Families appreciate the excellent emergency response and community and city services. There is a large police presence in the area, making this a safe, family-oriented community. In 2000, Westerville was voted the "Best Place to Raise a Family" in central Ohio by *Columbus Parent* magazine.

Despite having a population of 37,000, Westerville retains a small-town feel. This is due largely in part to the historic "uptown" built around Otterbein College. B&Bs, landmark homes, antiques shops, galleries, and storefront eateries lend Uptown Westerville (www.uptownwesterville.org) a certain charm. To experience this side of the city, just park your car and wander around Main Street and College Avenue.

While you're wandering, have a look at the Anti-Saloon League Museum at the Westerville Public Library. You'll quickly learn that this small suburb, established in 1809, was once an epicenter of the Prohibition movement. Even more surprising is that Uptown Westerville only lifted the booze ban in late 2004 when The Old Bag of Nails Pub was approved to sell liquor. Alcohol or not, Westerville offers visitors and residents a good selection of eating and drinking—and even better shopping.

New Albany

www.newalbanychamber.com

What comes to mind when you think of planned housing developments? Now, put that out of your head and think Georgian manors. Think country estates. Think horse farms. The community of New Albany is a series of exclusive neighborhoods, each with its own distinct qualities, but all inspired by the American colonial and English Georgian style.

New Albany was founded in 1837 and until recently was just a small farming community. Development of this rural area began in the 1980s and is still going strong. In fact, the current population of 2,400 is projected to grow an impressive 35 percent between 2003 and 2008—not bad for the highest priced community in central Ohio.

With homes averaging $500,000, this suburb attracts well-educated, affluent residents with a median household income well over $100,000. Some of Columbus's best shopping and dining are just 10 minutes away at Easton Town Center, and its close proximity to the airport makes New Albany convenient for those who frequently travel.

Aside from location, there are many things that make this gentrified community so appealing, the obvious being the architectural cohesiveness among the homes, professional buildings, and schools. Every little detail has been planned, right down to the hand-molded bricks chosen for all the buildings.

Forty miles of white fencing and acres and acres of green spaces, meadows, and streams allow New Albany to retain an ambling countryside feeling though only 15 miles from downtown Columbus. Many miles of trails meander through the village and will eventually link all the neighborhoods and parks together. New Albany is home to the state-of-the-art Aquatic Center and a beautiful country club with a 27-hole championship golf course designed by Jack Nicklaus.

Retail boutiques, professional offices, and a branch of the Columbus Metropolitan Library are clustered around Market Square, which looks and feels like an old town square. With all the arts-, community-, and philanthropic-based events and organizations available to its residents, New Albany is well on its way to attaining similar renown as Chautauqua, New York.

While many Columbus natives aspire to live in New Albany, corporate relocation brings a large number of executives in (and out) of this community. One of the biggest draws is the school system. The New Albany-Plain public school district might be one of the fastest growing in Ohio, but its outstanding programs and beautiful campus rival that of any fine private school.

Most of the homes are detached, but new condominiums, apartments, town homes, and even retirement communities are being developed in the surrounding area. Several real estate agencies represent homes within a 5-mile radius of New Albany, but New Albany Realty has been the community's premier brokerage from the very beginning.

Gahanna

www.visitgahanna.org

Gahanna is located 8 miles northeast of downtown Columbus and only five minutes from Port Columbus International Airport. It offers easy access to I-270, I-70, and I-670. The main thoroughfare through Gahanna is Route 62, also known as Granville Street.

Gahanna was founded in 1849 along Big Walnut Creek, and its name is derived from an Indian word meaning "three creeks joining into one." You will find reference to this on the City of Gahanna's official seal that reads "Three in One" and depicts the confluence of three creeks.

Olde Gahanna (www.ganhanna.org) is currently the site of urban redevelopment that uses the natural waterway as a focal point for downtown activity and business. The polluted creek was cleaned up, and a waterfall and river boardwalk were added. This five-acre park is now a great place for picnics and fishing, and hosts many festivals and annual events.

The restored old town features antiques and collectible shops, restaurants, and pubs. The businesses along Mill and Granville Streets were given a facelift, while a few decks and patios helped pedestrianize the area. The Gahanna Historical Society offers a 1-mile walking tour of the town's 16 historic landmarks, which include a log house, two historical churches, and several historic homes.

Olde Gahanna is quaint, but it's just a small part of the overall city. Currently home to more than 33,000 people, Gahanna is one of the fastest-growing suburbs in the Columbus area. Statistically, it has a low crime rate and is the most diverse suburb in central Ohio. Homes average around $175,000, making this an affordable and very family-oriented neighborhood.

With more than 700 acres of parkland, Gahanna has more park space per capita than anywhere else in central Ohio. Bikeways and nature paths run throughout the community, and there are a number of excellent golf courses located in the vicinity.

In 1972, Gahanna was named the "Herb Capital of America" and subsequently established the Ohio Herb Education Center, at which gardening classes and cooking and craft demonstrations are available. Call (614) 428-9255, or visit the Gahanna Web site for more information.

Whitehall

www.whitehallchamber.org

Six miles east of downtown Columbus, tucked between Gahanna and Bexley, is the urban community of Whitehall. This small municipality was designated a village in 1947 and a city in 1950. It was named for a local landmark, the White Hall Tavern.

The heart of Whitehall is around East Broad Street and Hamilton Road, but, unfortunately, this section of town can be a little rough at times. Statistics have shown that its property and violent crime levels are higher than Ohio's average, but Whitehall seems to get a far worse rap than it deserves. The residents of this community take a lot of pride in their city and are doing what they can to make it a better place.

Whitehall homes average between $65,000 and $200,000, and while many of them were built in the 1950s, several housing options do exist. Just drive along East Broad Street and you'll find apartment complexes and town houses in between the shopping centers and strip malls; you'll also find a lot of low-income housing in this part of town.

Whitehall's median household income is around $32,000. Its population of 20,000 is 74 percent white, 19 percent African or African American, and the rest a mix of Hispanic, Asian, and other races. Because of this diverse population, Whitehall has some of the most authentic ethnic eateries in town. Wander over to these parts for some Vietnamese or Ethiopian cuisine, and you won't be disappointed.

Bexley

www.hyperactiveinc.com/bexley

Whether you drive east out of Columbus on Broad or Main Street, you will eventually enter the "old money" city of Bexley, and quite frankly, all 2.5 square miles of it is beautiful. A small population of 13,000, outstanding schools, and excellent city services make this one of the most desirable (and expensive) parts of the city to live in.

This quiet, dignified community is bordered by Alum Creek on the west, Livingston Avenue on the south, Chelsea Avenue on the east, and Delmar Avenue on the north. It is situated 4 miles east of downtown, and trust me when I say you'll know when you've entered Bexley and you'll know when you've exited it.

Urbanization of this area began around 1875 when Capital University moved from Goodale Park to its present location on Main Street. By 1905, several prominent families made an exodus from Columbus and built magnificent mansions in this new suburb. Bexley became a village in 1908, but not without having to wrestle with Columbus for that status. Bexley formally became the City of Bexley in 1932.

The prices of homes vary dramatically between $100,000 and upwards of a million dollars. Starter homes are located on beautiful tree-lined streets south of East Main Street, some of which can be quite large but are dwarfed in comparison to many of the Bexley estates. Multimillion-dollar mansions are concentrated north of Broad Street. Even if you can't afford to buy one, take a drive through the area just to gawk.

Families move here for the school system. Bexley's public schools are exceptional, and two of Columbus's best private schools are located here. The fact that 90 percent of Bexley high school graduates pursue some sort of higher education says a lot. The library, parks, and proximity to hospitals and major highways also add to Bexley's appeal.

While most of the city is residential, East Main Street (www.bexleymain.com) contains a small business district, with restaurants, professional services, and loads of galleries and boutiques. It is within walking distance of most residents. Despite being surrounded by some of Columbus's most run-down areas, Bexley remains safe and relatively self-contained. It is truly a one-of-a-kind neighborhood.

Hilliard

www.cityofhilliard.com

Geographically situated outside I-270 between Big Darby Creek and the Scioto River is the suburb of Hilliard. Originally settled by John Reed Hilliard in the 1850s, Hilliard's Station grew around the rail station. Main Street remained the center of town until the 1960s, when rail service ceased and the completion of the Outer Belt shifted the city's focus to newer residential subdivisions and commercial development.

Hilliard now covers 12 square miles and is home to approximately 60,000 very diverse people. The housing options vary dramatically, from small starter homes to elegant stone houses, costing anywhere from $100,000 to $1 million, the average being $200,000.

Depending on where one lives, it could be very close to the west side of Columbus, or it could be very close to Dublin; it could be near the railroad tracks or nestled along the banks of the Scioto River. If you don't like what you see, drive a few miles, and there will be a complete change of scenery, but no matter where you live in Hilliard, it is only 13 miles from downtown Columbus and 18 miles from the airport.

Aside from location, Hilliard can boast one of the healthiest tax bases in the city, as 40 percent of its tax revenue comes from businesses. This translates to an ever-growing number of office, manufacturing, and warehouse facilities. It also means there are a lot of strip malls and shopping centers on this side of town, including Tuttle Mall, which is only 10 minutes away.

In the past few years, Hilliard has become one of the fastest-growing suburbs, primarily due to its good public schools. Encompassing 60 square miles, Hilliard is the ninth-largest school district in the state and is reputable both academically and athletically. The city has upward of two dozen churches and an abundance of social and civic organizations, 18 parks, and a community center. The revitalization of Old Hilliard has helped the city retain a small-town feel amid the sprawl of suburban development.

Grandview Heights

www.grandviewheights.org

Locals tend to shorten this small suburb's name to Grandview. Its location just west of The Ohio State University and less than 3 miles from downtown Columbus makes it one of the more popular urban neighborhoods for young professionals and students.

Grandview Heights was once part of the neighboring Village of Marble Cliff but became its own separate entity in 1906. Annexations expanded the city to its present-day boundaries, which are defined by Cambridge Boulevard to the west and the Olentangy River to the east. The northern boundary is around King Avenue, while the southern edge runs along Goodale Boulevard.

The homes in this predominantly residential neighborhood average $145,000. Grandview's population of 7,500 is a healthy mix of singles and families, professionals, and students, with a median age of 35. It is a safe community with good public schools, pretty churches, and a deep sense of community and history.

The most popular aspect of Grandview for nonresidents is its downtown commercial area. While not as artsy as the Short North, it certainly rivals the amount of good eating and drinking to be had in a concentrated area. Several trendy restaurants, bars, galleries, and shops line Grandview Avenue, while others straggle out along First, Third, and Fifth Avenues. Grandview is also home to one of the "old fashioned" Drexel movie theaters. It's a great part of town to go on a date or people watch from a sidewalk patio. Grandview Heights is a classic community that has, luckily, remained unspoiled for the past century.

Marble Cliff

www.marblecliff.org

Consisting of only 175 acres and fewer than 700 residents, this tiny village is one of three "bedroom communities" that make up the Tri-Village area. Marble Cliff is tucked between the other two, Grandview Heights and Upper Arlington.

It was settled in 1890 and incorporated as the Hamlet of Marble Cliff in 1901 (then including Grandview Heights). It detached from Grandview in 1902 and has remained its own picturesque neighborhood ever since. With only a handful of tree-lined streets, Marble Cliff is lovely, wooded, and private. One would never suspect it is less than 3 miles from downtown Columbus.

Marble Cliff residents have access to the Grandview Heights swimming pool and are allowed to participate in Grandview recreation programs at residential rates. Dogs are not permitted in Marble Cliff parks, and it's a dry community. The Web site for Grandview Heights Marble Cliff Historical Society (www.ghmchs.org) provides an interesting virtual walking tour of sights that may or may not still exist in this area.

Upper Arlington

www.ua-ohio.net
This bedroom community is one of the oldest and most prestigious suburbs of Columbus. It was established in 1913 by Ben and King Thompson as an idealistic country club district and was incorporated in 1918. Neighboring Marble Cliff was, at the time, named Arlington, so the area north of Fifth Avenue became Upper Arlington.

The original 840-acre village was developed (south of Lane Avenue) using the distinctive Pitkin Plan, which is seen to this day in the wide, curving, tree-lined streets and balanced layout of municipal, educational, retail, and residential buildings. The plan was tweaked in the 1920s to include the Mallway business district, and, after substantial population growth, Upper Arlington became a city in 1941. In 1985, the Upper Arlington Historic District was placed on the National Register of Historic Places. A book entitled *History of Upper Arlington* can be purchased from the Upper Arlington Historical Society (614-470-2610) or the city.

Over the years, Upper Arlington grew to encompass almost 10 square miles. Its current boundaries stretch from Riverside Drive (Route 33) in the west to Kenny Road in the east, Fifth Avenue in the south to Henderson Road in the north. It is convenient to most of the city's major highways and two hospitals and is literally a stone's throw away from The Ohio State University.

You'll also find medium-sized shopping centers, small plazas, exclusive boutiques, and fine restaurants throughout the predominantly residential neighborhood. Though adjacent to the university, traditional student housing is not common in Upper Arlington. Most of the homes in this neighborhood are private residences, with the occasional town house for rent.

The cost of Arlington homes ranges from $100,000 to well over $1 million, but don't expect to find many at the lower end. The average price range is between $200,000 and $400,000. It is also well known that Arlington has one of the largest higher-priced markets with homes over $500,000.

South of Lane Avenue is where to find the most dramatic stone houses, many of which are landmark buildings and all of which are expensive. South of Lane is where most of the oldest homes are situated. As you venture north along Tremont, Redding, and Reed Roads, the homes will vary in style, from two-story colonials and Tudors to Cape Cods and ranch style. There is, however, so much more to Upper Arlington than beautifully maintained homes and well-tended lawns.

It is a family-oriented community with several public swimming pools, 180 acres of parks (dogs are allowed!), tennis courts, and excellent city services. It is extremely safe and has one of the best public school systems in central Ohio. Upper Arlington puts a strong emphasis on developing an already highly esteemed school system, and the proof is in the pudding. Ninety-five percent of UA high school graduates pursue higher education.

UA, as it is referred to, has a population of around 34,000. The residents' deep sense of community is reflected in the strong civic association and numerous volunteer, cultural, and recreational organizations. The city puts on a very reputable Labor Day Arts Festival, but its biggest community celebration is the Fourth of July parade and fireworks. From the very beginning, Upper Arlington has been fortunate enough to have people who care tremendously about the community—and it shows.

Dublin

www.dublinvisit.org

Money magazine got it right when it commented, "Here's where people are moving." With a population topping 36,000, Dublin is one of Columbus's fastest-growing suburbs. An average household income close to $90,000 and homes from $150,000 to $800,000 make it one of the more prestigious neighborhoods as well. It is located 20 minutes northwest of downtown and is easily accessible by Route 33 and I-270.

What we currently refer to as Historic Dublin was originally platted as Sells Mills by John Sells in 1810 and renamed Dublin by an Irish surveyor in 1815. Dublin was incorporated in 1881. It remained a rural village with a population of only 681 until the completion of the I-270 Outer Belt, after which people flocked to this new suburb in droves. An influx of big businesses transformed farmland into a suburban commercial center.

The development of the prestigious Muirfield Golf Club and its surrounding subdivisions put Dublin on the map as one of the Midwest's premier golf and residential communities. Muirfield Village is quintessential suburbia: big homes on quiet cul-de-sacs, golf course views, excellent recreational facilities, and private lakes. The annual Memorial Tournament draws the biggest names in golf to Columbus once a year.

Tourism has become one of the major underpinnings of Dublin's local economy. Its significant Irish heritage and charming historic district attract a lot of attention. The annual Irish Festival and St. Patrick's Day Parade draw more than 100,000 people to Dublin, while Columbus's most popular attractions, the Columbus Zoo and Six Flags Wyandot Lake Park, are both just a few minutes' drive north.

Historic Old Dublin is situated around the intersection of Bridge Street (Route 161 West) and High Street (not Route 23). As one of central Ohio's oldest communities, it has more than 30 landmark buildings, many of which house pubs, restaurants, shops, and galleries. This a perfect place to stroll the brick-paved streets and admire some of the finest examples of 19th-century architecture in Columbus.

The city is well known for its excellent park system, good golf courses, shopping malls, and extensive community programming. The Dublin City school system has a reputation for superior academics. Its rapid growth necessitated the opening of a third high school, but size has not detracted from the quality of education, as more than 85 percent of Dublin graduates move on to a four-year institution.

Now covering more than 23 square miles around the Scioto River, Dublin is one of the best-known suburbs in Columbus and one of the most progressive communities in central Ohio. The Dublin Convention and Visitors Bureau, located at 9 South High Street, offers extensive travel and planning services. Call (800) 245-8387 for information, or download a very nice walking tour of Old Dublin from the Web site.

Two famous Jacks call Dublin home: golf legend Jack Nicklaus and "Jungle Jack" Hanna, director emeritus of the Columbus Zoo.

THE OUTSKIRTS

To the east of Columbus, outside the I-270 beltway, are the cities of Reynoldsburg (www.visitreynoldsburg.com) and Pickerington (www.ci.pickerington.oh.us). Both were settled in the early 1800s and remained rural communities into the 20th century.

Naturally, Reynoldsburg was developed first because it is closer to the city. It has a decent number of shopping centers, strip malls, and several parks. The average cost of a home here is $140,000, and the population is a mixed bag. Pickerington is a bit farther east and remains a distinctively rural community. Both areas have a

Popular Science magazine ranked Columbus the seventh "Best High-Tech City" in the United States. The results were based on 36 technology indicators, such as robotic surgery, WiFi hotspots, and R&D budgets at local universities.

variety of housing developments, affordable golf course communities, and large but decent school districts. In between the two is the small suburb of Blacklick, with several new developments and homes averaging $250,000.

Grove City (www.visitgrovecityoh.com) is located 8 miles southwest of Columbus's Outer Belt and is a quiet little suburb with a population of 30,000 and homes averaging $150,000. It is considered the Southern Gateway into Columbus and is typical small-town America, with affordable family homes, low taxes, and relatively low crime. Grove City has been around for over 150 years, and its town center has been redeveloped to include specialty shops, pubs, and restaurants. It is home to the Beulah Park horse racing track, and green thumbs particularly enjoy the 27-acre Gardens at Gantz Farm.

To the north of Columbus is the sprawling Delaware County community of Powell. Homes vary from $80,000 to well over a million dollars. In 2005 *Money* magazine named Powell the top small city in Ohio and the 18th best place to live in the United States.

The main post office for the city of Columbus is located at 850 Twin Rivers Drive and can be reached at (614) 722-9600. To find the post office closest to your community, call the United States Postal Service at (800) 275-8777, or look it up online at www.usps.com.

REAL ESTATE

Each year, *Columbus Business First* ranks the top 25 greater Columbus residential real estate agencies based on sales volume and local transactions (listing and selling properties). This section lists the top-rated agencies and gives an overview of their services and specialties.

Century 21 Joe Walker and Associates
409 West Main Street, Westerville
(614) 899-1400
www.c21joewalker.com

Century 21 is one of the largest real estate companies in central Ohio. It lists homes in the Columbus metropolitan area and provides the usual relocation and mortgage services. Other branch offices are located in Reynoldsburg, Delaware, and northern Columbus.

Coldwell Banker King Thompson
5500 Frantz Road, Dublin
(614) 792-0808
www.kingthompson.com

King Thompson was started by the original developers of Upper Arlington and is now part of the nation's largest residential real estate brokerage. The 800+ sales associates sold nearly 8,000 homes in the Columbus area. They specialize in luxury homes, new construction, land, and commercial properties. Check out the *Sunday Morning Home Show* (Channel 4), which highlights property all over central Ohio.

HER Real Living, Inc.
77 East Nationwide Boulevard
(614) 459-7400
www.realliving.com

Real living sold well over 10,000 homes last year and made $2.82 billion, earning themselves top spot on the list. Central Ohio's premier residential real estate company has offices all over central Ohio with hundreds of award-winning agents. They specialize in every sort of home you can imagine and offer a variety of financing, mortgage, title, and relocation services.

Keller William Capital Partners Realty
500 West Wilson Bridge Road
Worthington
(614) 888-1000
www.housecolumbus.com
This smaller agency specializes in residential property in northern Columbus and southern Delaware County.

Re/Max Associates Realty
5975 Cleveland Avenue
(614) 899-2600
www.realtycolumbus.com
This well-known agency has 25 offices in the Columbus area and specializes in residential homes, prestigious homes, and new builds. It also lists commercial properties and provides the usual variety of services related to mortgages. Given its national network, Re/Max can help make relocation to or from the Columbus area a lot easier.

APARTMENT LIVING

The following Web sites are good online resources for sifting through the countless number of rental properties available in the Columbus area: www.columbus-apartments.com, www.columbus.apartments.com, and www.columbus.rentnet.com. Some of the bigger real estate agencies mentioned in this chapter also have rental divisions.

An alternative for those who do not need a 12-month lease is to check out columbus.sublet.com, which lists apartments and rooms to rent.

Brixton Properties (614-486-8669) lists rentals around Ohio State, Clintonville, and the Grandview areas. Also popular with Ohio State students are pet-friendly Fox and Hound Apartments (888-871-4871; www.foxandhoundapts.com) on Kenny Road, Heritage Apartments (614-486-5232) off King Avenue in Grandview, and Olentangy Commons (614-451-6512) and University Village (614-261-1211), both located off Olentangy River Road.

Even if you don't attend Ohio State, it may be worth looking at the school's list of off-campus housing and sublet opportunities (offcampus.osu.edu). The Web site offers the names of local landlords and gives perspectives on rental prices in different parts of town. Another suggestion for potential students is to drive around the campus and look for rental property signs. While companies manage certain apartment buildings, others are privately owned and not listed through an agency.

Those of you wanting to live a bit more upscale, the Edwards Communities (www.edwardscommunities.com) offer six exclusive, gated apartment complexes in convenient parts of Columbus and Dublin. They promote "resort-style living" with on-site amenities such as pools, gyms, a movie theater, boating, a clubhouse, and much more. The Quarry, which is closest to downtown Columbus, has a variety of one- and two-bedroom apartments, as well as furnished corporate units.

UTILITIES

Columbus's Department of Public Utilities can be reached at (614) 645-6141 with general questions about the individual divisions of electricity, water, sewerage, and drainage. When it comes to electricity, most Columbus residents use American Electric Power (AEP). To begin new service, call (614) 716-1000, or go to the AEP Web site: www.aep.com. Some folks do, however, have the choice of using the Columbus Division of Electricity; it just depends on where you live. Contact the city at (614) 645-7038 to find out if you have options.

Columbus has been pumping water since 1871. To sign up for new water service, call the customer service line at (615) 645-8270. Water is slightly cheaper for those living in Columbus proper versus those living in suburban neighborhoods.

CLOSE-UP

Columbus Metropolitan Library

In 2004, 1.2 million questions were asked and 16 million items were borrowed during the course of 8.2 million visits, making Columbus's one of the most used library systems in the country. According to Hennen's American Public Library Ratings, the Columbus Metropolitan Library (CML) was ranked first among the nation's public libraries serving a population of more than 500,000. Among other things, this ranking is based on circulation and the number of volumes owned.

The CML system includes the downtown main library, 22 branches, and an Outreach Services Division, and jointly operates the Northwest Library with the Worthington Public Library. Holding a library card from any one of the libraries in the system allows you to borrow from any branch, return to and request items from any branch, and reserve books online.

The multistory main library houses a diverse collection of three million books, periodicals, maps, CDs, audio- and videotapes, and more. The variety of videos and DVDs available to borrow rivals Blockbusters. A coffee shop and gift shop are located on the ground level of the main library. Branches are located in just about every neighborhood, but Bexley, Grandview, and Upper Arlington libraries are not part of the city system. They operate their own independent libraries, which are discussed elsewhere.

Libraries are becoming much more than just a book-lending service. Having entered the information age, there is now a huge focus on electronic resources. On the most fundamental level, the library catalogues are now digitized and available online. No more manually searching through drawers of index cards! Self-check kiosks allow you to scan your card and check out the items you are borrowing.

Library users have access to other online services, such as Internet 101 classes and downloadable e-books. The main and branch libraries have dozens of computers on which to surf the Net or do your homework, free of charge. Philosophically, libraries are bridging the digital divide by making computers available to those who may not otherwise have access to them. Special computers are also available for the visually impaired.

The depth and breadth of Columbus's library services are staggering and vary from branch to branch. Many of the libraries offer programs for toddlers, large-print books for seniors, and multilingual books and services for the growing non-English-speaking population. The main library and a few branches provide Homework Help programs for children in the Columbus school system. They also have outreach programs that will deliver books to nursing homes, hospitals, and private residences.

All these services mean growth, and all this growth means it takes a lot more money to run a library than it used to.

Columbus Metropolitan Main Library. RYCUS ASSOCIATES

The state of Ohio's funding is gradually shrinking. Thankfully, Columbus residents recognize the new role of the libraries and understand the need for these institutions in supplementing and supporting the community. This is why library levies do well at the polls with all age groups.

The Columbus Metropolitan Main Library (614–645–2ASK; www.columbuslibrary.org) is located downtown, across the street from Grant Hospital, at 96 South Grant Avenue. The classic Vermont marble-and-granite building was constructed in 1904 through a gift from Andrew Carnegie, the father of public libraries. The attached parking garage is free for the hour and 50 cents for each additional hour up to a maximum of $3.00. The library is open seven days a week, Monday to Thursday, from 9:00 A.M. to 9:00 P.M., Friday and Saturday from 9:00 A.M. to 6:00 P.M., and Sunday from 1:00 to 5:00 P.M. The hours for the branch locations vary.

Sanitation services vary, depending on where you live. Contact the city to find out about recycling laws, trash pickup, tree-trimming schedule, and leaf collection.

LIBRARIES

Bexley Library
2411 East Main Street
(614) 231-2793
www.bexlib.org
The Bexley library has been at its current location since 1929 and has undergone several expansions and renovations. Anyone who resides, attends school, or is employed within Franklin County may obtain a library card. Cardholders have access to a collection of 300,000 items, including 65,000 audiovisual items. Workstations and walk-in Internet service is available free of charge. A 24-hour drive-up repository is provided for convenient return of the material.

Grandview Heights Library
1685 West First Avenue
(614) 486-2952
www.ghpl.org
If this small, friendly neighborhood library doesn't have what you are looking for, staffers can probably track it down through the Central Ohio Library Consortium. Between the seven libraries, five branches, and two bookmobiles you'll have more than 450,000 titles and a million holdings to choose from. There is no limit to the number of items you can borrow from the library, but you are limited to 20 DVDs. Computers are available to surf the Internet, and a quiet room is available for serious work. The Grandview Heights Library has been in this same building since 1923.

Upper Arlington Library
Tremont Road
(614) 486-9621
www.ualibrary.org
Once again, Columbus libraries are doing great things. Hennen's American Public Library Ratings ranked the Upper Arlington Public Library No. 1 among the nation's public libraries serving a community of its size (25,000–49,999). The UAPL system includes the main library and two small branches at Lane Road and Miller Park.

There are lots of things that set this library apart from others. Aside from the primary collection of 450,000 items, the library houses special collections of works by local authors, the Older Adults Collection, the Ohio Reference Room, and an impressive media services department. The children's area is equipped with computers, plenty of tables, and a play space.

Patrons can use the libraries' PC and Mac computers free of charge. If one of the Internet workstations is not available on the ground level, try going downstairs, where there are a few dozen. If you bring your own laptop, free plug-in data ports and wireless Internet are also available in the reference department. Your library card gives remote access to online reference databases and homework tutors and the ability to reserve books via the Web site.

In keeping with the city's deep sense of community, the library's Outreach Service will deliver books to homebound residents, care centers, senior residences, and children's day care centers. Adult and youth classes, author lectures, and book clubs are just a few of the library's year-round offerings.

EDUCATION AND CHILD CARE

Education was among the first institutions dealt with when Ohio became a state. Two hundred years later, many are left to wonder where it ranks next to new arenas, stadiums, highways, and shopping malls. It's no big secret that, not so long ago, Ohio was at the absolute bottom of the barrel when it came to the quality of public school education.

Ohio public schools are funded largely by local property taxes, which in Columbus's case vary drastically across the city, as does the caliber of education students receive. The Columbus area has 16 public school districts serving more than 160,000 students. Like any big city, some of the schools are very wealthy and capable of providing the best educations, while others leave a lot to be desired.

The city has tried shifting the demographics around by busing students to other schools, starting community (charter) schools, and allocating tuition vouchers to low-income students so they can attend their school of choice, but change isn't happening on the scale that it needs to. Lobbyists and politicians have been working for years to bring about reform through budget and constitutional amendments, anticipating the day low-income, urban school districts gain equal footing with the wealthier suburban districts. In the meantime, the state of Ohio is forcing schools to take accountability for the quality of education provided to their students.

The Ohio Department of Education has implemented an annual "report card" that assesses each school district by measuring attendance, graduation rates, various academic proficiencies, and funding. Fourth-, 6th-, and 10th-grade students from all Ohio public schools are given standardized tests through which progress can be tracked. Twenty-two performance indicators are used to designate a "grade" of excellent, effective, continuous improvement, academic watch, or academic emergency.

Three additional measures are looked at when determining the "grade" for each school. The Performance Index Score measures the achievements of *every* student who takes the standardized tests (whereas in the past, it included only students who scored proficient or higher). The Performance Index Growth takes into consideration the improvement low-scoring schools have made. Adequate Yearly Progress (AYP) measures the achievement of various target groups, such as ethnic minorities, the economically disadvantaged, and disabled students.

If a school fails to meet AYP goals for two or more years, it is classified as a school in need of improvement and faces consequences. Parents of students in these schools may be eligible to send their children to a different school or be given access to supplemental services, including tutoring.

Ohio, in general, has shown steady improvement in many areas. Several urban, low-income school districts have moved out of academic emergency, sixth graders are reading better, and 89 percent of Ohio's schools earned overall grades of excellent, effective, or continuous improvement. But how does Columbus fare when compared with the rest of Ohio?

Bexley, Dublin, New Albany-Plain, Upper Arlington, and Worthington public schools received an overall grade of excellent for meeting all 18 standards, except for Dublin, which met 17. Six school sys-

The Ohio Department of Education is the most comprehensive source of information related to all levels of education. View your school district's report card online at www.ode.state.oh.us/report card, or call (877) 644-6338 for a copy.

tems in Franklin County received a grade of effective; two school districts are showing continuous improvement; while three, including the Columbus Public School District, are on academic watch. None received the lowest score of academic emergency, which is a good thing.

The section on public schools presents a brief overview of each public school district and highlights a few statistics from its 2003–2004 report card, such as the percentage of 10th-grade students who scored at or above proficiency in several areas and the district's overall attendance and graduation rates. The Ohio Department of Education's Web site provides far more report card stats than are included here.

PUBLIC SCHOOLS

Columbus Public Schools

270 East State Street
(614) 365–5000
www.columbus.k12.oh.us

The Columbus Public School (CPS) system is the nation's 16th largest urban school district. CPS had an enrollment of over 62,000 students in 2003–2004. Demographically speaking, it is an even 50–50 breakout of males to females, but the racial distribution is 62.5 percent black, 31.5 percent white, with the rest Hispanic, Asian, and Native American. An interesting statistic is that almost 20 percent of public school students are considered gifted, while 13 percent are receiving some sort of special education.

CPS is made up of 87 elementary schools, 26 middle schools, and 18 high schools, including 1 for adults. Four additional special schools and four career centers are also in the system. Most of the 142 schools are urban in location and face the usual problems of inner-city schools. Aside from many of the top teachers being lured away to the suburban school districts, city teachers have to deal with issues that go beyond the classroom.

A large number of students that attend the city schools come from lower-income families or broken homes, and many of these kids simply don't have a proper diet (66 percent are eligible for free or reduced meals), let alone access to modern technology and current educational tools. These circumstances may not justify but they certainly explain why a large percentage of students in the city school system aren't yielding proficient academic results.

Despite having met only 5 of the 18 required measuring standards, CPS was elevated from the lowest grade of academic emergency to its current status of academic watch because of its (albeit slow) progress. The two other urban public school systems on academic watch are Hamilton and Whitehall.

Like most urban school districts, the two major funding sources for CPS are state funding and property taxes. Unlike other urban districts in Ohio, Columbus is considered property rich, so 60 percent of the district's revenue comes from property taxes, while only 40 percent comes from state revenue. It is the reverse for most other urban areas.

State funding, simply put, is directly related to the district's enrollment numbers. With a decline in enrollment, state funding was cut for the 2005 fiscal year (as were 604 jobs), but despite funding woes, teachers average around $52,000, and the district spent a very respectable $10,356 per student.

On a more positive note, the community has continued to support education

levies. Schools have developed special task forces to help students overcome learning barriers. City schools have created programs to help those who may have quit school earn credits to graduate and implemented several initiatives to help students make the transition beyond high school. Parents, too, have wider options as to where they can send their children to school.

The state of Ohio and the Columbus Public School system have also approved a plan to modernize 144 schools during the next 15 years. Many of these buildings are over 100 years old, overcrowded, and are in desperate need of updating. In most cases, the buildings will be built anew in order to accommodate physically challenged students and integrate the newest technologies.

Report Card: Academic watch; 88.4 percent of CPS 10th graders scored at or above proficiency in citizenship, 71.6 percent in math, 93 percent in reading, 95.1 percent in writing, and 77 percent in science. They had an attendance rate of 93 percent attendance and a 59.9 percent graduation rate.

Bexley City School District

348 South Cassingham Road
(614) 231-7611
www.bexley.k12.oh.us

People often move to Bexley for its outstanding public schools. In 2003–2004, 2,133 students were enrolled across three elementary schools, a middle school, and a high school. In fact, according to the National Association of Secondary School Principals, Bexley Middle School was dubbed one of the 100 Highly Successful Middle Level Schools in the Nation. The student/teacher ratio is 15:1 and 8 percent of the students are minorities. The facilities in this well-to-do neighborhood have recently undergone ambitious renovations.

Beginning with the class of 2007, students in Ohio will be required to pass the Ohio Graduation Test in order to graduate. The standardized test will measure how well students master specific skills as defined by the state of Ohio.

Bexley High School offers its 764 students a rich and varied curriculum; their academic programs of distinction include French, Spanish and Latin classes as well as physical education and social studies. Bexley City School District is currently implementing a variety of "Best Practices," including an International/Multicultural Education Program. While academic excellence is their primary focus, Bexley athletics draws an 80 percent participation in more than 54 sports teams and students also produce an award-winning yearbook and newspaper. Interestingly, the average expenditure per pupil is $10,178, not much more than Columbus Public Schools.

Report Card: Excellent; 97.1 percent of Bexley 10th graders scored at or above proficiency in citizenship, 95.4 percent in math, 98.3 percent in reading, 98.9 percent in writing, and 97.7 percent in science. They showed a 95 percent attendance and 96.9 percent graduation rates.

Dublin Public Schools

7030 Coffman Road
(614) 764-5913
www.dublinschools.net

As one of the larger public school systems in Columbus, Dublin City Schools encompass almost 50 square miles and have 19 schools in operation: 3 high schools, 4 middle schools, 11 elementary schools, and 1 preschool. A levy was recently passed to build another elementary school.

As one of the fastest growing school districts in Franklin County, it isn't surprising to learn the enrollment has increased for 27 straight years, bringing the total student population to 12,755. This growth also attracts highly qualified faculty. The pupil to teacher ratio is 19:1, and the average salary is just over $56,000. The 2004 fiscal year per pupil expenditure was $9,511. The school district had a record year, producing 15 National Merit Scholar Semifinalists; while 93 percent of the graduates went on to pursue higher education.

Report Card: Excellent; 10th graders at Dublin schools scored 97.8 percent at or above proficiency in citizenship, 95.3 percent in math, 98.7 percent in reading, 98.7 percent in writing, and 96.3 percent in science. The attendance rate was over 96 percent, and graduation rate was 97.1 percent.

Gahanna-Jefferson Schools

160 South Hamilton Road
(614) 471-7065
www.gahannaschools.org

The Gahanna-Jefferson Public School System includes the city of Gahanna and parts of Jefferson and Mifflin townships. The 6,803 culturally diverse students were enrolled in kindergarten through 12th grade at the district's seven elementary schools, three middle schools, and one high school. Approximately 1 percent of the students are Hispanic, 3 percent are Asian, 12 percent are African American, and about 3 percent are multiracial.

The elementary schools have approximately 450 students in each building, while the middle schools have around 550 students per building. The high school is quite large, with a population of around 2,100 students. Approximately 86.5 percent of students graduating from Gahanna Lincoln High School pursue two- or four-year postsecondary education. The average expenditure per pupil is $8,402, and the classes are capped at 25 students.

Report Card: Effective; 95.2 percent of the 10th graders scored at or above proficiency in citizenship, 91.4 percent in math, 97.8 percent in reading, 94.6 percent in writing, and 92.8 percent in science. The district showed over 96 percent attendance and 94.6 percent graduation rates.

Grandview Heights

1587 Third Avenue
(614) 481-3600
www.grandviewschools.org

Having to overcome the loss of major businesses from the community (therefore the loss of tax revenue for the school district), this school district continues to turn out high-performing students from both Grandview Heights and Marble Cliff. Academic achievement, coupled with a strong sense of community service, makes for well-rounded graduates. This small district had a total of 1,133 students enrolled at two elementary schools, one middle school, and one high school during the 2003–2004 school year.

Report Card: Effective; 98 percent of 10th graders scored at or above proficiency in citizenship, 96.1 percent in math, 99 percent in reading, 99 percent in writing, and 96 percent in science. They showed an attendance rate of 95 percent and a 96.9 percent graduation rate.

Hilliard City School District

5323 Cemetery Road
(614) 771-4273
www.hilliard.k12.oh.us

An enrollment of 14,529 students at 2 high schools, 3 middle schools, 2 sixth-grade schools, and 13 elementary schools makes Hilliard the largest public school system outside of Columbus Public Schools and the ninth-largest district in the state of Ohio. The sprawling Hilliard City School

District encompasses 60 square miles, and its students come from Columbus, Dublin and five surrounding townships. For being such a huge school system, the student/teacher ratio is 16:1, and the average spending per pupil is $8,759.

Report Card: Effective; 95.5 percent of Hilliard's 10th graders scored at or above proficiency in citizenship, 91.2 percent in math, 95.9 percent in reading, 97.2 percent in writing, and 94.2 percent in science. Attendance rates were at 95 percent, and 91.7 percent graduated.

New Albany-Plain Local School District

99 West Main Street
(614) 855-2040
www.new-albany.k12.oh.us

New Albany-Plain isn't just a school district; it is a "learning community." The beautiful campus consists of eight magnificent buildings on more than 200 acres. All the facilities are new and state-of-the-art. The school, local government, and community organizations work collaboratively to create a learning environment that treats children as active participants in the community.

Development of the New Albany Library/Information Center, Health and Wellness Center, the Wetlands Nature Preserve, and Kinko's for Kids within the school grounds puts unique learning tools and resources at the students' fingertips. It's much akin to a college campus—maybe even better than some.

In just 12 years, the schools have grown from 650 students to more than 3,000. The 2004 test scores placed New Albany-Plain school district in the top 3 percent in the state. At the rate it is progressing, New Albany is well on its way to becoming a nationally recognized school system.

Report Card: Excellent; 98.3 percent of the 10th graders scored at or above proficiency in citizenship, 97.8 percent in math, 98.3 percent in reading, 97.2 percent in writing, and 97.2 percent in science. New Albany showed over 96 percent attendance and 96.5 percent graduation rates.

Upper Arlington City School District

1950 Mallway North
(614) 487-5000
www.uaschools.org

The district's 5,388 students were enrolled in the award-winning Upper Arlington School District, which consists of four elementary schools, two middle schools, one high school, and an alternative school. Upper Arlington High School also offers the International Baccalaureate Diploma Program, a rigorous, two-year curriculum that earns 11th and 12th graders advanced college credit.

UA students participate in cultural and performing arts and competitive sports. They are also given the opportunity to take part in business- and service-related activities. Academics, however, is the primary focus within this school system. Standardized tests scores generally place UA students among the top 5 percent in the nation. The state-issued report card is testimony to the district's philosophy that its primary responsibility is quality education.

Report Card: Excellent; 98.5 percent of UA 10th graders scored at or above proficiency in citizenship, 98.1 percent in math, 98.9 percent in reading, 99.6 percent in writing, and 98.1 percent in science. The district shows over 96 percent attendance and a 98.1 percent graduation rate.

Worthington City Schools

200 East Wilson Bridge Road
(614) 883-3000
www.worthington.k12.oh.us

The city of Worthington was built around education. What began as a log cabin school in 1802 has evolved into a dozen elementary schools, four middle schools, two high schools, and one alternative school. This school system, which engulfs 20 square miles, is well known for solid academics and very good athletic and cocurricular programs.

Despite a declining enrollment, almost 10,000 students are enrolled in Worthington schools. They also constitute one of the most ethnically diverse student populations in central Ohio. Approximately 7 percent of the students are Asian, 5.9 percent are African American, 2.1 percent are Hispanic, and about 0.2 percent are American Indian. Worthington also gets bragging rights as the largest school district in Ohio to meet all 22 standards on the state report card.

Report Card: Excellent; Worthington 10th graders scored 97.2 percent at or above proficiency in citizenship, 95 percent in math, 98.6 percent in reading, 98.6 percent in writing, and 95.8 percent in science. They had over 95 percent attendance and 93.4 percent graduation rates.

COMMUNITY SCHOOLS

These pseudo-independent public schools, also known as charter schools, were developed primarily for urban students as an alternative choice to public and private school education. They have been around in Ohio for quite a few years now, and the number of charters continues to grow. Some states have capped their growth because state funding is diverted into the charter schools away from the public schools, where it is still very much needed.

What differentiates charters from traditional public schools? The school board is appointed by the founder of the charter school rather than elected. The state can also revoke funding if educational standards are not met. Most of Columbus's community schools are grouped by grades. Very few schools accommodate kindergarten through 12th grade, but there are almost 20 to choose from that focus on grades kindergarten through third or fifth. To learn more about the 35 charter schools in Columbus, check out www.ohiocharterschools.org, or call (614) 221-3992.

Electronic Classroom of Tomorrow

3700 South High Street
(614) 492-8884
www.ecotohio.org

The Electronic Classroom of Tomorrow is an online community school that provides students grades K-12 with a tuition-free alternative to traditional public education. This charter school is sponsored by the Lucas County Educational Service Center and has been providing students throughout the state with an online education since 2000. ECOT students are mostly nontraditional. This type of schooling accommodates those who may need to remain at home due to or illness, pregnancy, house arrest, or foster care. Students are required to take proficiency exams and will earn a regular high school diploma.

ALTERNATIVE PUBLIC EDUCATION

The Columbus Public School district has 21 alternative elementary schools, 4 alternative middle schools, 4 alternative high schools, and 2 kindergarten through eighth-grade schools. Alternative schools differ from traditional public schools in how the subjects are taught or in the focus of the instruction. Some schools engage students in their education by giving them higher levels of responsibility or having students apply what they have learned in "real world" settings.

The French immersion school, Ecole Kenwood (614-365-5502), and The Columbus Spanish Immersion Academy (614-365-8129) are both tuition-free schools within the Columbus Public School District. Admission is by lottery. Children fortunate enough to be chosen won't just learn a foreign language, they will be taught in French or Spanish until the eighth grade, making them truly bilingual by the time they get into high school.

Also part of the Columbus Public School system are two Africentric Alternative Schools that provide an African-centered education using traditional and cultural guidelines, holistic perspectives, Kemetic principles, and historical knowledge as guiding tenets for teaching and learning. The elementary school (614-365-6517) with grades K-5 and the secondary school (614-365-8675) with grades 6-12 are both located at 300 East Livingston Avenue. The secondary school has an early college program that allows students to gain 45 to 90 hours of college credit. Admission to these schools is by lottery.

The Columbus Alternative High School at 2632 McGuffey Road (614-365-6006; www.cahs1.org) was recognized as one of 200 outstanding high schools in the nation by the U.S. Department of Education. It was also recently named an International Baccalaureate School, where students who fulfill program requirements can earn advanced credits for college. There are bright spots in the Columbus Public School system!

Other school districts have their own alternative schools. Linworth Alternative Program (614-883-3700) is an option for high school students in the Worthington City Schools but is not a separately chartered program, while Wickliffe Alternative (614-487-5150) is part of the Upper Arlington district.

PRIVATE SCHOOLS

Columbus has 30 private and non-Catholic parochial schools. Most of them charge some sort of tuition, have very small classes, and provide a broader and more balanced cultural and ethnic diversity than many of the public schools.

There are 24 Catholic elementary schools and 5 high schools. To find out more information about Catholic education in Columbus, contact the diocese's Department of Education at (614) 221-5829. Following is a list of the direct contact numbers and Web sites for the high schools only:

Bishop Hartley
1285 Zettler Road
(614) 237-5421
www.bishop-hartley.org

Bishop Ready
707 Salisbury Road
(614) 276-5263
www.brhs.org

Bishop Watterson
99 East Cooke Road
(614) 268-8671
www.bishopwatterson.com

St. Charles Prep
2010 East Broad Street
(614) 252-6714
www.stcharlesprep.org

St. Francis DeSales
4212 Karl Road
(614) 267-7808

Columbus Academy
4300 Cherry Bottom Road, Gahanna
(614) 475-2311
www.columbusacademy.org
One thousand students in prekindergarten through 12th grade come from all over to attend Columbus's premier coeducational day school. This prep school began as an all-boys institution in 1911 and became coed in 1991. Female enrollment now equals almost half the student body.

The campus is located on 233 wooded acres and feels very college-like with its 3 libraries, 10 laboratories, a fine arts complex, and extensive indoor/outdoor athletic facilities. Many of the buildings and athletic fields have recently undergone renovations, so the facilities are updated.

With a pupil to teacher ratio of 9:1, the small classes allow for more unique academic offerings. Students receive foreign language instruction from prekindergarten onward; Columbus Academy is one of the few schools in central Ohio to offer instruction in Chinese. Small classes also afford the middle school children a chance to "learn by doing." Upper-level students have the opportunity to take over 20 advanced placement courses, which seems a good idea since 100 percent of the graduating class went on to four-year institutions.

Columbus Academy students consistently place high in artistic, music, and choral competitions, and let's not forget the women's field hockey team, who took the 2003–2004 state championship. The tuition isn't cheap, but need-based scholarships are available.

Columbus School for Girls
56 South Columbia, Bexley
(614) 252–0781
www.columbusschoolforgirls.org

Studies show that women who attended all-girl schools grew up more confident, are accepted into top colleges, and earn higher salaries than their coed counterparts. Columbus School for Girls is an independent college preparatory school founded over 100 years ago in Bexley. It is made up of an upper, middle, and lower school and has a Program for Young Children.

The school is known for it rigorous curriculum and extremely small classes. With only 650 students in prekindergarten through 12th grade and a pupil to teacher ratio of 9:1, the instruction is extremely personalized. Typically, 100 percent of the graduates attend college. The school offers its girls a dozen sports programs and a broad selection of music, theater, and fine arts classes, as well as extracurricular activities to choose from. Tuition ranges from $8,000 to almost $16,000, but three payment options are available, and the school will make other suggestions on how to fund your child's education.

Montessori Schools
Various locations
www.montessori.org

The Montessori schools stress individual instruction to help children work at their fullest potential in all areas of life, and particularly emphasize the first six years of life. In Columbus, the Montessori schools offer programs for children from birth through eighth grade, after which they transfer to a high school. The two more popular locations are The Columbus Montessori Education Center at 979 South James Road (614–231–3790) and St. Joseph Montessori School, located at 933 Hamlet Street (614–291–8601).

St. Charles Preparatory School
2010 East Broad Street, Bexley
(614) 252–6714
www.stcharlesprep.org

Bexley covers only 2 square miles but is loaded with excellent private schools. St. Charles is Columbus's premier private all-boys' school and has been providing 9th through 12th graders an exclusive foundation for college since its establishment in 1923. This school seems to have it all: a beautiful campus with a chapel, theater, and top-notch athletic facilities, 13 interscholastic sports, and a student body made up of 585 smart boys who end up at schools like Harvard, Yale, and West Point. Though affiliated with the Roman Catholic diocese, students of all faiths are welcome here. Tuition is around $5,590 for members of the parish and slightly more for nonmembers.

Sunrise Academy
5657 Scioto Darby Road, Hilliard
(614) 527–0465
www.sunriseacademy.net

Sunrise was founded in 1996 and is the only full-time Islamic school in central Ohio. It is owned and operated by the Islamic Society of Greater Columbus and offers education to more than 200 kindergarten through 10th graders. The school's curriculum is that of any Ohio public school, only with Islamic studies and Arabic integrated into each class. Sunrise also offers a Saturday program of Qur'an, Islamic studies, and Arabic language for children at a different site, which is not part of the school's full-time program.

Torah Academy
181 Noe Bixby Road
(614) 864-0299
www.torahacademy.org
Columbus Torah Academy sits on a wooded campus of 42 acres and provides students with a dual curriculum of secular and Judaic education, within a modern Orthodox Zionist framework. The students, however, come from various cultural and economic backgrounds and from Reform, Conservative, Orthodox, and unaffiliated families. The campus includes a library and computer and chemistry labs, as well as a state-of-the-art gymnasium, athletic fields, and more than 30 classrooms.

Wellington School
3650 Reed Road, Upper Arlington
(614) 457-7883
www.wellington.org
Wellington was founded in 1982 as the first independent coeducational college prep school in Columbus. Some 600 students are enrolled in grades pre-K through 12th grade, and the student to teacher ratio is only 8:1. Wellington has developed a challenging curriculum that includes accelerated, honors, and advanced placement courses, and 100 percent of Wellington graduates attend four-year colleges and universities. Students begin receiving college counseling in ninth grade.

But it's not all about academics. More than 80 percent of upper-level students participate in one of eight sports, and the school boasts a national award-winning drama program. An education at Wellington is a serious investment, as tuition ranges from $7,600 to $15,000. There is a modest financial assistance program available.

Worthington Christian Schools
6670 Worthington Galena Road
Worthington
(614) 431-8210
www.worthingtonchristian.com
Worthington Christian Schools provide a biblically based education for students in preschool through 12th grade. It currently consists of a preschool, elementary, middle, and high school and has a student population totaling close to 1,200. The school is partially underwritten by Grace Brethren Church of Columbus, and new facilities are being built to accommodate a 37 percent increase in enrollment. Students have access to technology and art resources, internships, and 10 sports programs. WCS students are often found taking their ministry out into the community, and 93 percent of Worthington Christian graduates attended postsecondary schools. Tuition ranges from $3,200 to $7,092. Tuition payment plans are available.

HIGHER EDUCATION

The Ohio State University isn't the only academic game in town. There are 16 universities in the Columbus metropolitan area, not to mention several dozen vocational and technical schools. The phone book is a great place to get a feel for what is available. The Ohio Department of Education can also help you find a postsecondary school suited to your needs.

Colleges and Universities

Capital University
1 College and Main, Bexley
(614) 236-6011, (866) 544-6175
www.capital.edu
Capital University was founded by the Lutheran Church in 1830 and is one of the largest Lutheran-affiliated universities in North America. This liberal arts school is known primarily for its conservatory of

music, law school, and Center for Professional Development, which offers working professionals the opportunity to further their education. CU's 4,000 students can choose from 50 undergraduate majors and 8 graduate degrees in 6 schools of study. Students can get involved in a variety of campus organizations or become a Capital Crusader in 18 different athletic programs. A new Center for Lifelong Learning provides affordable undergraduate education to adult students in centers throughout Columbus. Capital's tuition is $24,100 for a first-year student.

Columbus College of Art and Design
107 North Ninth Street
(614) 224-9101
www.ccad.edu
CCAD is one of the oldest and largest private art colleges in the United States. It recently celebrated its 126th anniversary and is a recognized leader in visual arts education. More than 1,300 national and international students are enrolled in four-year programs of study resulting in a bachelor of fine arts degree in one of the seven majors. Students study everything from advertising and fashion design to traditional fine arts and industrial design. Students of photography, digital imaging, and film are also right at home at CCAD. Liberal arts courses are integrated into the curriculum to provide a well-rounded education. Tuition costs $9,864 per term, which doesn't include art supplies. CCAD is a great place for the general public to attend special events and art exhibitions or to meet many up-and-coming artists.

Columbus State Community College
550 East Spring Street
(614) 287-5333, (800) 621-6407
www.cscc.edu
Columbus State is the city's only community college, and the main campus is conveniently located downtown. Students can attend classes on a full- or part-time basis while working toward a career or technical degree in more than 40 fields. Many graduates receive an associate's degree in applied science or technical studies and go directly into the workforce. Others choose to transfer their credits to a four-year institution and continue on for a bachelor's degree. Community college is a great way to explore your options if you aren't sure what you want to study or to get the fundamental classes out of the way at a much cheaper rate than a four-year college. CSCC has about a dozen additional campuses, but those closest to Columbus are located in Dublin, Delaware, Gahanna, and Westerville. Tuition is around $2,600 for an academic year.

Dennison University
100 South Road, Granville
(800) DENNISON
www.dennison.edu
This posh little school is situated on 1,200 rolling acres 20 minutes east of Columbus. It is located in the charming village of Granville and has close to 2,000 students. The Ohio Baptist Society founded Dennison in 1831 as a theological institution for men only, but shortly after it became a private coeducational university and has since earned a reputation as one of the top 50 liberal arts colleges in the country. According to *U.S. News and World Report*'s annual rankings, Dennison placed 50th among 217 schools.

Dennison offers only undergraduate programs, and admission is extremely competitive. Its small student body, along with an 11:1 student to teacher ratio, allows for very personalized education. Students have 45 majors to choose from and a variety of clubs; Greek life, religious groups, student government, and multicultural events enhance campus life. Big Red athletics make 11 varsity sports available to both men and women. Dennison's excellent academic programs and New England-style campus don't come cheap. The 2005-2006 tuition is $26,600, but you get what you pay for at DU.

DeVry University
1350 Alum Creek Drive
(614) 253-7291, (800) 426-2206
www.devrycols.edu

DeVry University, which was originally called DeVry Institute, is one of the largest private higher education systems in the country. DeVry Columbus provides technology-based, career-oriented undergraduate programs in business and technology. The curriculum integrates general education with industry-specific coursework and offers both bachelor's and associate degrees in biomedical and computer fields. One might scoff at a school that has normally advertised on television, but it is much akin to a community college with full degree programs and top-notch instruction. One can also get a master's degree in seven different fields from DeVry's Keller Graduate School of Management. Tuition varies depending on the program.

Franklin University
201 South Grant Avenue
(614) 797-4700, (877) 341-6300
www.franklin.edu

Franklin University originally focused on prelaw and law school but now offers 15 business-related undergraduate majors and three master's degree programs. Though 9600 students are enrolled, the class size only averages about 18 students. Franklin is a good choice if you are a working professional wanting to continue school. It has concentrated on adult education by expanding night course offerings and giving "life experience" credit to mature students.

Franklin is conveniently located on 14 acres in the heart of downtown Columbus and has two additional suburban campuses in Dublin and Westerville. Franklin has one of the largest MBA programs in central Ohio. It can be completed at any of the three campuses or online via the Virtual Campus. Franklin University was one of the original 29 institutions selected by the U.S. Army to deliver online education to eligible enlisted soldiers. Undergraduate tuition begins at $244 per credit and graduate classes at $376.

Muskingum College
163 Stormont Street, New Concord
(740) 826-8211
www.muskingum.edu

Located an hour east of Columbus and founded in 1837 by a group of Scotch-Irish citizens in New Concord, Muskingum, meaning "a town by the river," retains its original affiliation with the Presbyterian church. The college's 1,584 students can attain a bachelor's degree in 42 majors, while graduate students can earn a master's degree in education or teaching. The school's low student to teacher ratio and solid curriculum, combined with a very low cost (as private colleges go), assures Muskingum graduates an exceptional education at an exceptional value. Tuition is less than $15,000 and student life consists of more than 90 clubs and organizations, 6 sororities, 5 fraternities, and 17 men's and women's collegiate sports teams. The most famous Muskies include astronaut and former Ohio senator John Glenn, his wife Annie Castor Glenn, and the Columbus Zoo's beloved Jack Hanna.

Ohio Dominican University
1216 Sunbury Road
(800) 955-OHIO
www.ohiodominican.edu

Ohio Dominican University is a four-year, coeducational liberal arts college, founded in 1911 as an all-women's college. It became a university in 1968 and retains its Catholic and Dominican tradition. The university has approximately 3,000 students and is located in a residential suburb of Columbus. Ohio Dominican offers undergraduate degrees in 50 majors as well as 5 graduate degree programs. Students can participate in seven intercollegiate sports teams, and a number of campus organizations, ministry, and outreach groups. Tuition is $18,000 per year.

Ohio Wesleyan University
South Sandusky, Delaware
(740) 369-4431
www.owu.edu

Ohio Wesleyan was founded in 1842 by the Methodist Church to educate missionaries. It is a now a private, coeducational liberal arts college associated with the Methodist Church only on paper. Its high selectivity and rigorous curriculum rank it among the best liberal arts colleges in the nation. OWU is nationally known for its blend of scholarship, teaching, and service. Graduates are no longer serving abroad as missionaries, but the university has been recognized for its extraordinary number of alumni who have served in the Peace Corps and are active in volunteer work within their own communities.

The campus is located 20 minutes north of Columbus in Delaware, and the facilities range from 19th-century landmark buildings to state-of-the-art science centers and labs. Around 1,800 students are enrolled, half of whom come from Ohio. The school has more than 85 student organizations and 19 fraternities and sororities, and the Battling Bishops compete in a whole gamut of intercollegiate sports. The women's and men's soccer teams are the most recent teams to earn national titles. The 2005-2006 tuition is $26,460.

Otterbein College
One Otterbein College, Westerville
(614) 890-3000
www.otterbein.edu

Founded in 1847, Otterbein was the first educational institution founded by the Church of the United Brethren in Christ, which later joined with the Methodist Church to form the United Methodist denomination. It was the first college to admit women without restrictions on what they could study, the first to include women on its faculty, and one of the first colleges to admit students of color.

This liberal arts school has about 3,100 students, and its program balances a classical liberal arts education with practical training, so it's no wonder *U.S. News and World Report*'s *2004 Guide to America's Best Colleges* ranks Otterbein eighth among the Midwest's comprehensive colleges. It offers 49 undergraduate majors and can boast a 13:1 student to faculty ratio, but it is particularly strong in the performing arts. Student can choose from 12 fraternities and sororities, a number of service clubs, and Cardinal athletics. Those looking for a small-town college but want access to a big city will appreciate this school's location 20 minutes north of downtown Columbus. The 2005-2006 tuition is $22,518.

The Pontifical College Josephinum
7625 North High Street, Worthington
(614) 885-5585
www.pcj.edu

The Pontifical College Josephinum is an international seminary that prepares Roman Catholic priests and missionaries. It is subject directly to the Holy See and is the only pontifical seminary outside Italy. The church requires a minimum of four years of theological study to enter the priesthood. Josephinum students can choose from two tracts: the College of Liberal Arts and the School of Theology. A master's of divinity is the highest degree offered. Resident seminarians should expect to pay $13,750 per year for tuition, room, and board.

University of Dayton
4807 Evanswood
(614) 785-1801
www.udayton.edu

The University of Dayton has a very small satellite campus in north Columbus, largely to service correspondence and online students, but graduate classes in counselor education and human services are also taught here. View the university's main Web site to see what programs you can attend at this branch.

Wittenberg University
200 West Ward Street, Springfield
(937) 327-6231, (800) 677-7558
www.wittenberg.edu

Wittenberg is located on a rolling 100-acre campus just 45 minutes west of Columbus in Springfield, Ohio. This nationally recognized college is affiliated with the Evangelical Lutheran Church. It was established in 1845 to train Lutheran ministers, and by the turn of the 20th century arts and sciences were integrated into the curriculum. Thanks to a sizeable gift from Andrew Carnegie, Wittenberg's first science hall was built in 1908.

Until recently, the school's traditional strengths have been in the liberal arts, but the sciences, management, and education are becoming more popular majors for students. WU has also developed strong interdisciplinary programs in East Asian studies and Russian area studies. With more than 50 majors, including 8 preprofessional programs, Wittenberg students are exceptionally well prepared for post-graduate education, and it shows. About 70 percent eventually pursue graduate studies.

Campus life thrives, with more than 125 student organizations, 15 fraternities and sororities, and 22 varsity teams. Thirty-six percent of the student body partakes of varsity sports, making athletics the most popular campus activity. The Tigers will be able to continue their tradition of athletic success in a sports complex that is undergoing a multimillion-dollar facelift. The 2005-2006 tuition is $27,542.

Technical and Vocational Schools

If college isn't your cup of tea, there are plenty of vocational, trade, and technical schools to choose from in the Columbus area. Listed here are a few of the more popular ones.

i

Students at the Aveda Institute provide discounted hair, skin, nail, and waxing services to the public. Haircuts range from $15 to $18 and include a consultation with aromatherapy, a stress-relieving experience, and mini-facial, blow dry, and makeup touch-up. All services are supervised, and tipping is not accepted.

Aveda Institute
1618 Neil Avenue, near OSU
(614) 291-2421
www.avedacolumbus.com

Columbus's newest beauty school offers two programs in beauty and personal care. The 42-week, $12,300 cosmetology program goes well beyond the study of hair and makeup. Classes in anatomy and physiology, aromatology, and skin care are also part of the curriculum. The esthiology program, which lasts 25 weeks and costs $8,300, teaches skin and body care and makeup training, with an emphasis on pure flower and plant essences in treatments.

The Bradford School
2469 Stelzer Road
(614) 416-6200, (800) 678-7981
www.bradfordschoolcolumbus.edu

This school offers career-focused programs in business, technology, and health care. The courses last a few months to two years. Diplomas and associate degrees are offered in various administrative, legal, and secretarial fields, graphic design, medical assisting, paralegal, travel, and hospitality. Tuition rates vary, and federal financial aid is available.

Bryman Institute
825 Tech Center Drive, Gahanna
(614) 322-3414, (888) 741-4271
www.go-bryman-inst.com

This Boston-based technical school trains students in health care and business-related fields. Massage therapy, medical assisting, and medical insurance billing are the three career-specific programs available at the Gahanna campus. The school also helps with job placement, and financial aid is available.

ITT Technical Institutes
3871 Park Mill Run Drive, Hilliard
(614) 771-4888
www.itt-tech.edu
This "chain-like" private college system offers technology- and career-oriented degree programs. Both traditional campus programs and online programs are available to students. Most of the courses blend traditional academic studies with applied learning concepts, while a significant amount of time is spent in practical study in a lab environment. Associates and bachelor degrees are available in schools of information technology, electronics, drafting, and criminal justice, and an MBA is available through the business school.

Professional Bartending Institute of Columbus
5354 North High Street, Clintonville
(614) 885-9610, (800) BARTEND
It is likely we have all encountered one of the 5,000 graduates from the Professional Bartending Institute of Columbus. PBI has been turning out professional mixologists since 1978. This fully licensed school teaches the art of bartending through "classroom" experience—the classroom being a simulated full-service bar. The course teaches you how to make everything from ice-cream and coffee drinks to the more traditional cocktails. Class times are flexible, and nationwide job placement is available.

CHILD CARE

Choosing child care is no doubt one of the most important and difficult tasks parents undertake. Child care services in Columbus vary in quality, price, and structure, but the average cost of child care in central Ohio is $800 to $900 per month for one child.

The two Web sites parents might find particularly useful are the National Child Care Information Center (www.nccic.org) and the National Network for Child Care (www.nncc.org). The former is a national clearinghouse and technical assistance center that links parents, providers, and researchers to early care and education information. The latter provides articles, e-mails lists, and forums related to early childhood issues.

The Ohio Department of Job and Family Services can also offer insight on how to choose child care. The key is to find the type of care that is best for your family. Once you identify your personal needs and the needs of your child, try contacting one of the many local services to help you find qualified child care or point you to up-to-date resources.

Some parents prefer having total control of their child's care and environment and want a family member, friend, or nanny to watch their child at home. The weekly cost for this type of child care varies from a devoted relative charging nothing to more than $400 per week for a full-time nanny. Some of the local agencies listed in this section can help sort out financial matters such as taxes and compensation.

Some care providers work directly from their homes, and the cost averages between $75 and $200 weekly. These child care centers are regulated by state or local laws and vary in quality and price. Make sure to evaluate family child care homes carefully so your child is placed in an optimal situation. The skills of these care providers vary dramatically. Some have extensive early childhood training, while others may lack basic first-aid skills. One potential problem to consider with home day care centers is what happens when the regular care provider is ill. In this situation, you may not have child care available for your child. Questionnaires and checklists are available from various sources to help you ask the hard questions and know which qualifications should be reviewed.

Finding and affording quality child care has been a pressing need for lower-income working families in Columbus. Recent changes in income eligibility guidelines found that more parents

earned too much to qualify for child care assistance. The Columbus Foundation (614-251-4000; www.columbusfoundation.org) undertook initiatives to raise money to help working families afford licensed, quality child care. These efforts resulted in hundreds of thousands of dollars being granted to the Champion of Children Fund and subsequently helping lower-income families reduce their annual cost of full-day child care by approximately $4,000.

The City of Columbus's Office of Education is developing a database of resources related to after-school programs. For more information regarding the latchkey programs at many of the Columbus public elementary schools, call (614) 365-5891.

Other school systems offer child care before and after school on school days. Student in grades 1 through 5 from all seven of Gahanna-Jefferson elementary schools are eligible for the afternoon YWCA child care program (614-224-9121) from 2:30 to 6:00 P.M. Hilliard Schools (614-771-2267), likewise, provides child care services on school days from 7:00 to 9:00 A.M. and 3:30 to 6:00 P.M. The Upper Arlington School-Age Child Care Program (614-487-5133) is provided both before and after school. Check with your own school district to see if it provides these services.

Child Care Referral Services

Local groups can help sort through the types of services available within the large, diverse child care industry. This section will point you to a few referral services in the Columbus area.

Columbus Metropolitan Area Community Action Organization (CMACAO)
700 Bryden Road
(614) 324-5100
www.cmacao.org

To report suspected child abuse in Ohio, call the county Children's Services Board (614-275-2571) or Prevent Child Abuse at (800) CHILDREN. For national child abuse information, contact the 24-hour National Child Abuse Hotline at (800) 4-A-CHILD.

A variety of services ranging from emergency assistance with utility and rent payment, food and clothing, employment opportunities, and transitional housing are provided through a decentralized network of six Action Centers and two Teen Drop-In Centers throughout the county. As Franklin County's community action organization, CMACAO focuses on creating self-sustaining, long-term economic stability for low-income individuals. CMACAO offers a broad array of services and opportunities, including Human Services, Head Start, and Early Head Start.

Ohio Action for Children
78 Jefferson Avenue
(614) 224-0222
www.actionforchildren.org

This resource and referral agency can help you find affordable, quality care and early education for your child. Action for Children maintains a database of over 1,300 child care providers, and specialists assist you in finding a provider who meets your criteria. The agency also offers courses on parenting skills and has a satellite branch at 39 West Winter Street in Delaware, Ohio.

Ohio Child Care Resource and Referral Association
80 Jefferson Avenue
(614) 849-0500
www.occrra.org

Child Care Resource and Referral agencies are community-based services that work to make higher-quality child care more accessible to everyone. There are currently 21 CCR&Rs in Ohio, serving all 88 counties. Each agency maintains a database of regional child care providers and helps families select the right one. The association also offers professional development opportunities to early childhood professionals and relays information to policy and decision makers. Ohio CCR&Rs provide direct services to over 40,000 Ohio families each year.

Ohio Child Care Resource and Referral Information in neighboring counties:

Delaware	**(740) 369-0649**
Fairfield	**(740) 687-6833**
Licking	**(740) 345-6166**
Madison	**(740) 852-0975**
Pickaway	**(740) 477-1602**
Union	**(937) 644-1010**

Child Care Choices
120 Harding Way E, Suite 107, Galion
(419) 468-7581, (800) 92-CHILD
www.childcarechoices.org
Child Care Choices is a community-based, nonprofit child care resource and referral agency regarding child care and educational services in Crawford, Marion, Morrow, and Richland counties. Child Care Choices lists only those facilities and providers who have successfully completed a rigorous screening process

Care Centers and Preschools

These commercial centers provide child care for up to 120 children per day. They are regulated by state or local laws with regard to the number of children per staff member, immunization of children, and cleanliness of the environment. All child care center staff members must be at least 18 years old and have a high school education. Many have completed training programs approved by the Department of Human Services. The cost for this type of child care varies but is more expensive than a home day care facility. You can contact the Child Care Licensing Agency at (614) 466-1043 to get more information about the licensing procedures or to find accredited day cares in your area.

National Guard and Reserve members (or spouses) who are on two-week leave from Operation Iraqi Freedom or Operation Enduring Freedom are eligible for a minimum of four hours' free child care. Go to www.occrra.org, or call (800) 424-2246 to find participating care providers and registration forms.

City Kids Daycare
274 Marconi Drive, downtown
(614) 464-1411
www.citykids.columbus.oh.us
Downtown working professionals have been taking their children to this locally owned and operated day care facility since its opening in 1989. It is a fully licensed kindergarten as well as a child care facility. Parents appreciate the "drop-in anytime" philosophy, and daily reports are sent home with children. The center is open daily from 6:45 A.M. to 6:30 P.M. A suburban City Kids is located at 4940 Scioto-Darby Road in Hilliard (614-777-4320). This facility has a before- and after-school program rather than a kindergarten.

Dublin Community Preschool
81½ West Bridge Street, Old Dublin
(614) 889-0052
www.dublincommunitypreschool.org
Children ages 3 to 5 are taught the alphabet, numbers, creativity and social, language, and science skills through structured hands-on learning. This preschool has been around for nearly 30 years, and its tuition remains well priced at $100 to $195 per month.

The Goddard School
Various Locations
www.goddardschool.com
These learning centers accept children between the ages of 6 weeks and 10 years.

The kids are placed in age-appropriate programs, and indoor and outdoor activities are fully supervised by qualified teachers. The school has created a fully accredited continuing education program to support the ongoing training of its teachers. There are several locations in Dublin, Gahanna, Hilliard, Westerville, and Worthington.

La Petite Academy
Various Locations
www.lapetiteacademy.com
La Petite's curriculum is designed to develop children's social and educational skills through activities and a lot of interactive playtime. This Chicago-based chain offers well-staffed programs for seven different age groups for children ages 6 weeks to 12 years. Many of the academies are affiliated with Montessori schools and strategically located near corporate complexes to make pickup and drop-off easy for the working parents. A checklist is available on the Web site to help parents determine which facility is best for their children. There are nine centers in the Columbus area, including Hilliard, Westerville, and Dublin.

HEALTH CARE AND WELLNESS

If you're going to get sick, Columbus is a good place to do it. The greater Columbus region supports 19 hospitals with a total of more than 6,000 beds. Many of the city's hospitals are well known regionally and nationally for offering the highest quality care and specialty services.

In fact, midwestern hospitals dominated Solucient's 12th annual list of the "100 Top Hospitals." This reputable study objectively identifies hospitals that are the highest performers in the nation and uses them to set the bar for national health care standards. Two of Columbus's hospitals, Riverside Methodist and Grant Medical Center, made the 2004 list for best teaching hospitals. *U.S. News and World Report* has ranked Riverside among the nation's top 50 hospitals for cancer care and heart surgery and top 35 for neurosciences. It also ranks in the top 100 hospitals for cardiovascular and orthopedic programs.

The past few decades has seen the merger of several hospitals into one health care alliance. OhioHealth (www.ohiohealth.com) is the organization with which Grant Medical Center in downtown Columbus, Riverside Methodist Hospital in northwestern Columbus, and both locations of Doctors Hospital are affiliated. The network includes 10 other regional hospitals, as well as many outpatient and urgent care centers and the McConnell Heart Health Center.

Columbus's other major hospital consolidation is the Mount Carmel Health System, which has three locations throughout the metropolitan area, including St. Ann's Hospital in nearby Westerville. It too has a network of outpatient surgery centers and family practices.

When it comes to size, Columbus breeds some big health care facilities. Doctors Hospital has two locations and is the largest osteopathic teaching facility in the nation. Columbus Children's Hospital is the second-largest pediatric health care institution in the country. The new R. David Thomas Asthma Clinical Research Center at Children's Hospital will be one of only five such research centers in the country.

The Ohio State University Medical Center is gargantuan. It contains the university's College of Medicine, College of Public Health, five hospitals, two research institutes, and a network of more than 30 community-based specialty and primary care facilities. Ohio State's three-part mission of patient care, teaching, and research makes it the only academic medical center in the area. To obtain a physician referral from The OSU Care Connection, call the toll-free number at (800) 293-5123.

If you're looking for a pediatric or family doctor, check out the Children's Hospital Web site, or call (614) 722-KIDS for the free referral and service hotline. The Web site allows you to search for doctors by a variety of criteria. Special notations have been made when a doctor has been voted by his or her peers as one of the "Best Physicians in America."

This chapter offers a brief overview of the city's major hospitals and urgent care facilities. Hospital Web sites are extensive and offer links to all sorts of health care resources. This chapter also provides information on some of the more interesting alternative health care options available in Columbus, along with a few ideas for rejuvenating your mind and body.

HOSPITALS

Children's Hospital
700 Children's Drive
(614) 722-2000
www.columbuschildrens.com

Children's hospital was founded in 1892 as a charity organization to help sick children. It has since grown into one of the nation's most sophisticated health care institutions. Columbus Children's is one the country's biggest hospitals and pediatric research centers. With more than 700,000 visits per year, Children's is also one of the busiest emergency rooms in the country. Parents should feel good knowing the Midwest's premier provider of pediatric health care is right on their doorstep.

The vast campus of the main hospital includes the emergency rooms and trauma center, the Outpatient Care Center, Children's Heart Center, Children's Research Institute, Children's Hospital Foundation, and the Center for Child and Family Advocacy. Children's also provides a multitude of services ranging from radiography to nuclear medicine and transplants.

For those who live in the suburbs, Children's has 16 Close to Home Health Care centers. These facilities provide community-based treatment and care, while four of them are urgent care centers. At the opposite end of the spectrum, the hospital will work with out-of-town families to find somewhere to stay in Columbus while their child is being treated. The Welcome Center (800-792-8401) is a good place to start organizing clinical arrangements, housing, and transportation.

Doctors Hospital
5100 West Broad Street
(614) 297-4000
www.ohiohealth.com/facilities/doctors

With more than 70,000 visits in 2003, Doctors Hospital has one of the busiest emergency rooms in Columbus, but it is much better known for its position in the field of osteopathic medicine. Doctors has recently received an $18 million grant from the Osteopathic Heritage Foundation, the nation's preeminent foundation supporting osteopathic health care and research, for the advancement of patient care and osteopathic education.

Doctors Hospital is one Columbus's three hospitals to be a designated Chest Pain Center. With heart attacks being the leading cause of death in the United States, their goal is to have an artery open within 90 minutes of the patient's arrival. One of the hospital's unique features is its customer service hotline (614-297-HELP), which gives patients and families direct access to the hospital administration so that complaints can be handled prior to the patient's leaving the hospital.

Grant Medical Center
111 South Grant Street
(614) 566-9000
www.ohiohealth.com/facilities/grant

If you are ever in a serious accident, get to Grant. It is known throughout the community as a level 1 trauma center and offers the highest caliber of technology and staff for the worst injuries. There are several other reasons Grant has been recognized as one of the country's top 100 hospitals, including but not limited to its orthopedics program, which ranks among the top 100 in the nation, and its excellent reputation as a teaching hospital.

Grant provides the whole gamut of services, from laser surgeries to women's health services. Having been founded on the philosophy of charitable care, many of the hospital's outreach and community programs provide prenatal care for at-risk teens and wellness programs to seniors. Grant's urban location, right in the heart of downtown Columbus, often poses traffic and parking problems, but there is valet parking available for $4.00.

Mount Carmel Health
6001 East Broad Street, Whitehall
(614) 234-6000
www.mountcarmelhealth.com

Mount Carmel was founded in 1886 by nuns from Indiana. It is now one of the largest health care systems in central

Ohio. Aside from Mount Carmel East, there are two other hospitals and a dozen more outpatient, family practice, and wellness centers throughout Columbus. The system has a very strong community outreach program that provides free health care, exams, screenings, and social services to the neighborhoods with the greatest need. All parking at Mount Carmel Hospital East is free.

Mount Carmel Hospital West, the second hospital in this system, is located in a much more urban location at 793 West State Street (614-234-5000). Parking garages near this hospital range in price from $1.50 to $4.00, while surface lots cost $3.00. Valet parking is also available.

The third hospital is officially known as Mount Carmel St. Ann's, but most locals shorten it to plain old St. Ann's. The Sisters of St. Francis founded St. Ann's Infant Asylum (orphanage) in 1908, but in the 1920s it became a hospital for women. Men didn't step foot in the door until 1972. St. Ann's became part of the Mount Carmel Health System in 1995, but St. Ann's is still viewed as a women's health and maternity hospital. It is located at 500 West Cleveland Avenue in Westerville (614-898-4000).

New Albany Surgical Hospital (NASH)
7333 Smith's Mill Road, New Albany
(614) 775-6600
www.newalbanysurgicalhospital.com

Columbus's newest hospital is focused specifically on in- and outpatient orthopedic, neurological, and musculoskeletal care. NASH, a for-profit hospital, was born out of the need for space to perform orthopedic surgeries. A number of orthopedic groups and physicians came together with this idea for a specialty hospital, but it wasn't without a lot of resistance that it opened in 2003. Many believe that specialty hospitals somehow deprive nonprofit community hospitals of revenue, which resulted in a bill being passed in the Ohio House that placed a moratorium on the development of any more specialty hospitals until certain issues can be studied further.

The Ohio State University Hospital
410 West 10th Street
(614) 293-5123, (800) 293-5123
www.medicalcenter.osu.edu

The University Hospital, OSU's flagship patient care facility, has been rated one of America's best hospitals by *U.S. News and World Report* in a record 13 specialties and been on the list for the past 12 years. Its recent designation as a magnet hospital means the nursing services are among the best anywhere, and 145 OSU doctors are listed in the book *America's Top Doctors.*

The hospital specializes in cardiac care, organ transplantation, women's health, digestive diseases, minimally invasive surgery, rehabilitation, and neurosciences. The facilities include Doan Hall Maternity Center, with its level 3 neonatal intensive care unit, Dodd Hall Rehabilitation Hospital, and a level 1 trauma center. It has 900 beds and offers the most sophisticated surgical intensive care units in the area. Parking garages can be found on 12th Avenue and West Park Street just off Medical Center Drive. The garages charge an hourly rate, while valet parking is a flat fee.

The University Hospital East (614-293-8000), referred to as OSU East, is located at 1492 East Broad Street. It provides a full spectrum of health care services in an urban, community hospital-type atmosphere.

Ohio State's Harding Hospital (614-293-9600) is more or less a psychiatric hospital. Doctors provide behavioral health care services to people of all ages who may be suffering from depression, schizophrenia, or various forms of abuse. The facility is located at 1670 Upham Drive on Ohio State's campus.

Also located on the OSU campus is the Richard M. Ross Heart Hospital, a 100-bed state-of-the-art facility focused on all matters of the heart. Cardiovascular medicine, thoracic surgery, and transplant surgery are just a few of the procedures performed at this hospital. Educational, preventive, and diagnostic services are also available. The address is 452 West 10th Avenue, and the phone number is (614) 293-5123.

Last but not least is the James Cancer Hospital, one of only 39 National Cancer Institute-designated comprehensive cancer centers in the country, which means you get the highest levels of diagnostics, treatment, and prevention education all under one roof. The James Cancer Hospital, located on the west side of campus, is the only freestanding cancer hospital in the Midwest. It is located at 300 West 10th Avenue, and the phone numbers are (614) 293-5066 and (800) 293-5066.

Riverside Methodist Hospital
3535 Olentangy River Road, Upper Arlington
(614) 566-5000, (800) 837-7555
www.ohiohealth.com/facilities/riverside

Riverside, which was established as the Protestant Hospital in 1892, has been at its current location since 1961 and is now part of the Ohio Health network. Many of the reasons for which this hospital has bragging rights have been pointed out in the introduction to this chapter. Aside from national recognition, it is by far the most popular hospital with locals living on the west side of Columbus.

It's a great place to have a baby. Riverside's maternity services are state of the art, and its on-site neonatal special care unit is provided in conjunction with Children's Hospital. Its cancer services are nationally recognized, and the new McConnell's Heart Hospital, which opened in 2004, delivers the highest quality, innovative heart and emergency care around. Parking isn't even a pain! There are secured garages, lots, and valet services to choose from. The parking lots cost $3.50 a day for unlimited in-and-out privileges.

i

Riverside is one of only 20 hospitals in the country using a new therapy to remove blood clots in patients suffering from stroke. This extends the length of time available for successful treatment.

URGENT CARE

While all of the community hospitals included in this chapter have emergency rooms, the ER isn't necessarily the best choice for all incidents. Urgent care centers are good for accidents like broken bones and twisted ankles and flu visits. They also require proof of insurance.

Columbus Children's Hospital Emergency Department (614-722-4300), at 700 Children's Drive, is open 24 hours a day, 7 days a week. The on-site urgent care facilities are open from noon to 10:00 P.M., seven days a week. Children's Hospital also has urgent care centers that provide after-hours urgent care, lab, radiology, guidance services, and community education in three suburban neighborhoods.

The Children's Hospital Close to Home Health Care Centers are located in:

Northwest Columbus
5675 Venture Drive
(614) 355-8400

East Columbus
6435 East Broad Street
(614) 866-7353

Northeast Columbus
433 North Cleveland Avenue
(614) 839-2800

Grant, Riverside, and Doctors hospitals each have their own on-site emergency rooms, but Ohio Health also operates a network of neighborhood urgent care offices:

As a community service, the City of Dublin and the Franklin County Board of Health offer immunizations against all childhood and some adult diseases the first Wednesday of every month at the Dublin Municipal Building.

Victorian Village Health Center Urgent Care
1132 Hunter Avenue
(614) 298-7940

America's Urgent Care
6955 Perimeter Loop Road, Dublin
(614) 923-0300

America's Urgent Care
765 Hamilton Road, Gahanna
(614) 566-0520

America's Urgent Care
6200 Cleveland Avenue
(614) 566-0590

Mount Carmel Health also has three urgent care facilities around the city that are open regular business hours seven days a week:

Mount Carmel East Adult Urgent Care
6435 East Broad Street, Whitehall
(614) 861-7001

Mount Carmel Urgent Care
5677 Scioto Darby Road, Hilliard
(614) 921-0648

Westar Urgent Care
444 North Cleveland Avenue, Westerville
(614) 839-1118

ALTERNATIVE HEALTH CARE AND BODYWORKS CENTERS

Alternative health care practitioners treat the body and mind on a very integrated level. This section provides information about wellness centers and therapies that offer a more holistic approach to medicine.

A good source of information is *The Wellpoint* (www.thewellpoint.com), a free quarterly publication distributed at various health stores, healing centers, and libraries in the Columbus area. It is a centralized hub for news, articles, and advertisements related to holistic and alternative medicine in central Ohio. The Holistic Health Network (www.holisticnetwork.org) maintains a national, up-to-date listing of practitioners of alternative therapies.

American Institute of Alternative Medicine
6685 Doubletree Avenue, Worthington
www.aiam.edu
Functioning as both a training center and clinic, the AIAM began as a massage school but has grown to teach acupuncture and tui na, a form of Oriental massage using soft-tissue manipulation techniques and acupressure points. The student clinic provides discounted massages, while professional massage and acupuncture are also available.

Columbus Center for Movement Studies
3003 Silver Drive, Clintonville
(614) 263-1111
www.being-in-movement.com
One can develop better breathing, body alignment, muscle tone, and flow of energy through the shapes and quality of one's movements. This center offers a variety of body and movement awareness training, including the nonviolent martial art of aikido and three other movement disciplines. Classes are available for adults and children

Columbus Polarity Institute
170 West Fifth Avenue, near OSU
(614) 299-9438
www.columbuspolarity.com
Life in many cultures is based on the principles of energy, and this center helps keep the energy flowing freely through the

body via a variety of energy-balancing, stress-relieving services. Touch, reflex, and acupressure are among the therapies. Services include lymphatic, deep tissue, and relaxation massage, Rolfing, cranial sacral therapy, and aromatherapy. Students and seniors are given discounted rates.

Feng Shui
(614) 258-3299
One can derive healing environments by using the feng shui practices of balance and harmony. Two reputable local feng shüi masters, Connie Spruill and Sylvia Watson, can provide consultations for your home, office, and gardens. They teach workshops at various learning centers and present at expos and conferences.

Gentle Wind Center for Conscious Living
4695 Morse and Hamilton Road, Gahanna
(614) 471-2281
www.gentlewind.net
This center offers an extensive and interesting mix of holistic, metaphysical, empowerment, and movement classes. Workshops are offered on chakras, tarot reading, shamanism, and energy sensing. Swedish, shiatsu, and lomilomi (Hawaiian) massage services are also available. A second location is at 1516 West First Street in Grandview Heights

Harmony House Wellness Center
420 West Olentangy Street, Powell
(614) 436-0182
www.harmonyhousewellness.com
Programs and workshops leading to a more balanced life are taught at this holistic health center. A broad range of yoga classes, such as hatha, yin, vinyasa, and yoga for golfers, are offered, as well as more than a dozen holistic health care services, including hypnotherapy, light therapy, and reflexology.

Inner Connections
1196 Neil Avenue, near OSU
(614) 560-9069
www.innerconnect.biz
Inner Connections provides both familiar alternative bodywork, such as sports, pregnancy, and infant massage, and lesser-known forms of massage, like craniosacral therapy and polarity therapy, which integrate acupressure, reflexology, and meditation into massage sessions.

Wellcare Center for Health
3620 North High Street, Clintonville
(614) 220-9355
www.wellcareonline.com
Wellcare treats both your mind and body through traditional and cranial osteopathy, medical acupuncture, therapeutic medical massage, Reiki, and movement therapy using the Feldenkrais Method. These practitioners take a more multidimensional/multipractitioner approach to healing.

Wellness Works
1000 Old Henderson Road
Upper Arlington
(614) 451-9355
www.healthchanges.com
This holistic health and education center provides homeopathic and naturopathic health care. Among the massage offerings are therapeutic massage, Thai massage, and Reiki. Other therapeutic offerings include reflexology, hypnotherapy, and craniosacral therapy. Couples massage, yoga, and health-related classes are on the calendar.

Health and Holistic Stores

Clintonville Community Market
200 Crestview Road, Clintonville
(614) 261-3663
www.communitymarket.org
This is a co-op market for the people, by the people. CCM is a community-owned

and operated natural foods store that carries a great selection of organically grown produce, herbs, supplements, and natural and bulk food items. The dairy department has a variety of milk, cheese, and soy products, while a deli serves up all-natural breakfast burritos. Vegetarians and vegans will be in their glory here. The market shares a space with and works in conjunction with Simply Living, a non-profit organization dedicated environmental and other issues.

Feed Your Spirit
3292 North High Street, Clintonville
(614) 262-4277
This shop carries whimsical art and jewelry, aromatherapy products, journals, and other spirit-nurturing goods. You can also have a tarot reading or take meditation classes on-site.

Momentum98
3509 North High Street, Clintonville
(614) 262-7087
www.momentum98.com
Looking for an infrared sauna or a knowledge decoder chart? You've found your place! This unique store carries a huge selection of holistic health products. In fact, it has a thriving Internet business, but we are fortunate enough to have the physical store right here in Columbus. Some of the best sellers are color therapy glasses, neti-pots, seabands, and Hitachi magic wands. Momentum98 also carries a variety of enzymes, Chinese herbs, and probiotics.

COLUMBUS THE BEAUTIFUL

Salons and Day Spas

Charles Penzone
1356 Cherry Way Drive, Gahanna
(614) 476-8200
www.charlespenzone.com
The seed of Charles Penzone's innovative concept of the grand salon was planted in Upper Arlington almost 40 years ago. It has since grown into six concept salons with a variety of atmospheres, including the Grand Salon in Dublin, the industrial Q Salon and Day Spa in Upper Arlington, and trendy Max the Salon in German Village. You'll find all the traditional hair and nail services, along with massage, hydrotherapy treatments, and spa packages. Plus, they carry more than a dozen different types of products.

Kenneth's Hair Salons and Day Spas
3610 Fishinger Boulevard, Mill Run
Hilliard
(614) 538-5800
www.kenneths.com
Locals consistently rank Kenneth's as the best hair salon in Columbus, and it has received quite a few accolades in several fashion and spa magazines. These salons are slightly less expensive than the others listed here, but it's not because they skimp on services, which are rather extensive. They're just a good value. You'll find as many men as women indulging in hair care and the wide range of body treatments and spa packages. They do, however, primarily carry Kenneth's hair and body products. The Ageless MedSpa at the Hilliard and New Albany Salons offers botox, chemical peels, and laser hair removals. There are five Kenneth's locations, including salons in Westerville and Dublin

Marengo Institute
Westin Great Southern Hotel
310 South High Street
(614) 224-6640
www.marengoinstitute.com
The originators of the day spa have found their way from Beverly Hills to Columbus. The clientele are mostly women looking to pamper themselves in a high quality spa. It is by no means cheap, but the atmosphere is elegant and tranquil. You'll get what you pay for, which is high-end hair and nail care and luxurious massage and body treatments (rather impressive for being located in a hotel and a mall). Marengo offers a variety of interesting packages for couples, rejuvenating

overnight retreats, and even bachelorette spa parties. A second location is in the Polaris Fashion Place, Westerville.

Mario Tricoci Salon and Day Spa
3934 Townsfair Way, Easton Town Center
(614) 428-1000
www.tricoci.com
Famed as a cutting-edge salon and spa, Mario Tricoci offers all the classic hair and nail care services as well as innovative and customized facials. Pamper yourself in luxury at this Chicago-based salon for a day or a weekend. On-site body treatments range from massages and wraps to hydrotherapy and aromatherapy or you can arrange for a spa weekend at the Pheasant Run Resort location near Chicago. A second Columbus location is near Tuttle Mall in Dublin.

Tanning Salons

Columbus has several locally owned and operated tanning salons that offer traditional tanning, mega-super-beds, and the ever-popular spray-on tans. Most sell tanning lotions and protective eyewear on-site.

Dolphin Beach Tan
www.dolphinbeachtan.com
4510 Kenny Road, Upper Arlington
(614) 457-7786

2394 North High Street, OSU Campus
(614) 262-4826

8286 Sancus Boulevard, Westerville
(614) 840-0730

6215 Perimeter Loop Drive, Dublin
(614) 734-9349

5585 North Hamilton Road, Gahanna
(614) 418-9506

Express Tan
www.expresstanusa.com
1317 Stoneridge Drive, Gahanna
(614) 899-6212

1254 West Fifth Avenue, Grandview
(614) 486-5162

1238 East Powell Road, Polaris
(614) 885-8267

630 West Schrock Road, Westerville
(614) 899-6211

7170 High Street, Worthington
(614) 985-6660

Polo Tan Incorporated
545 South Front Street
(614) 628-0068

1372 Cherry Bottom Road, New Albany
(614) 337-8430

Savage Tan
18 East 13th Avenue, OSU Campus
(614) 299-0400

RETIREMENT AND SENIOR CARE

Let's face it, people aren't exactly retiring to central Ohio, but given that the 55 and over age group is the fastest growing segment of the country's population, Columbus has its fair share of seniors and retirement-age baby boomers. The 2000 census showed that Columbus has more than 63,000 seniors, 8 percent of whom are considered elderly, but age isn't slowing them down. All levels of independent and assisted living are available within the city, but the average age at which Columbus seniors go into a nursing home is 85. Impressive.

Until then, all you active seniors should get your hands on a Golden Buckeye card. This statewide discount card is honored at 18,000 restaurants, attractions, and retailers throughout Ohio. There are hundreds of places in the Columbus area alone that offer discounts (sometimes laughingly small) on everything from pet grooming and dry cleaning to oil changes and dental care. Call (800) 422-1976, or stop in at any of the Columbus Metropolitan Libraries to get your free card. You can view all participating organizations on the Web site www.goldenbuckeye.com.

To stay abreast of the issues facing our seniors, a number of publications are available free of charge at libraries, senior centers, and retailers. *The Senior Times* (614-337-2055) is Ohio's foremost magazine for the over 55 set. This monthly newspaper features articles about aging, laws, medicine, and health insurance.

You can request the* Franklin County Senior Citizen Handbook *by calling (614) 462-5230, or view it online at the Franklin County Office on Aging Web site: www.officeonaging.org.

Seniors will find plenty of advertisements and discounts for restaurants, activities, and services.

Senior Outlook (614-760-5590; www.senioroutlook.com) is a free monthly housing and real estate resource guide. It can be found at most supermarkets, senior centers, and libraries. It has a fairly comprehensive listing of retirement communities, apartments, and independent living villages. It will also point you toward more specialized living, such as respite care and Alzheimer's and skilled care facilities.

Senior Source (614-985-4659; www.seniorsource.com) is a glossy lifestyle magazine featuring travel, financial, and health articles, many of which are directly related to central Ohio. The free publication comes out quarterly and can be picked up at libraries or retailers around town.

This chapter provides a brief overview of various services and activities directed toward seniors and offers resources that might help make your transition into "maturity" a little easier.

SENIOR SERVICES

The Alzheimer's Association of Central Ohio
3380 Tremont Road, Upper Arlington
(614) 457-6003
www.alzheimerscentralohio.org

This free support group is open to those suffering from the disease, as well as family members, caregivers, and friends. The group meets on a monthly basis.

Care Choice Ohio
174 East Long Street
(614) 645-7250, (800) 589-7277
www.coaaa.org

The Central Ohio Area Agency on Aging

offers free advice, referrals, and recommendations about retirement, lifestyle changes, and long-term care to anyone of any age. This is a free statewide program.

The Franklin County Office on Aging
280 East Broad Street
(614) 462-5230
www.officeonaging.org
The Franklin County Office on Aging is responsible for planning services and programs that assist older citizens in independent living. The Office on Aging administers Franklin County Senior Options, a program that provides "one-stop shopping" for those in need of information, advocacy, or direct access to a range of community-based services.

It also administers the following services: Adult Protective Services (614-462-4348), for those who may be abused or neglected; Property Tax Assistance Program (614-462-5230), for lower income individuals unable to pay their property taxes; and the Widowed Support Program (614-462-5230), to aid in grieving. The FCOA also maintains lists of senior centers and volunteer opportunities. This is the overall best starting point if you are a newcomer to Columbus or are beginning to look for a new place to live.

Counseling Services
A handful of agencies in Franklin County will provide support groups, in-home counseling, and enrichment workshops for Columbus's older adults. Among them are Catholic Social Services (614-221-5891; www.colscss.org), The Ohio State University Hospital Psychiatry Department (614-293-8039), The John J. Gerlach Center for Senior Health at Grant/Riverside Hospitals (614-566-5858), and Elder Focus (614-421-3112) on West Fifth Avenue.

Franklin County Senior Options
(614) 462-6200
www.officeonaging.org
Residents of Franklin County 60 years and older qualify for Senior Options services. This referral service puts seniors in contact with companies and agencies that provide personal care, home-delivered meals, adult day care, transportation to and from medical appointments, and other services that help maintain their independent living.

Senior discount cards are issued to people ages 65 and older entitling them to ride any COTA bus for 55 cents each way. Transit cards are issued at 177 South High Street (614-228-1776), and photo ID is required.

Geriatric Dental Clinic
The Ohio State University College of Dentistry
305 West 12th Avenue
(614) 292-8802
The OSU Geriatric Dental Clinic provides comprehensive dental services to seniors ages 60 and older. Dental insurance, Medicaid, and fees are accepted at the weekly half-day clinic. Homebound seniors may also be eligible for visits through the Geriatric Home Nursing Dental Program.

Golden Age Passport
U.S. Department of the Interior
18th and C Street, Washington DC
American citizens ages 62 and older can purchase a lifetime pass to most national parks, monuments, wildlife refuges, and historic sites for a one-time fee of $10. You will not receive the pass by writing to the above listed address, but you can purchase it at any national park or monument. The closest national parks to Columbus are Hopewell Culture National Historic Park in Chillicothe and the Aviation Heritage National Historic Park in Dayton. It also gets you a 50 percent discount on federal fees charged for parking, camping, boat launching, and other park services.

Residents of Franklin County can call (614) 462-6200 to access a network of services and information about community- and home-based care for frail seniors.

Goodwill Columbus
1331 Edgehill Road
(614) 294-5181
www.goodwillcolumbus.com
Seniors with developmental disabilities and mental retardation are given opportunities to work, socialize, and participate in volunteer work and community service through the Senior Additional Growth Experiences (SAGE) program. Goodwill also provides seniors with a list of retirement options.

Meals-on-Wheels
1699 West Mound Street
(614) 278-3152
www.lifecarealliance.org
Homebound, chronically ill, and disabled people over the age of 60 are eligible for hot lunch delivery seven days a week. Frozen meals and cold dinners can also be provided. Make certain to tell them of your special dietary requirements.

Northwest Older Adults Program
1945 Ridgeview Road
(614) 457-7876
Social workers will assist older adults and their families in finding various resources and dealing with family problems, money management, and health care issues. The program offers links to community resources such as home-delivered meals, household assistance, and specialized counseling issues.

Active single seniors meet for swing dancing each Monday night at Bowties Drinkery, at 4900 Sinclair Road, near Worthington (614-846-0300). Lessons are given at 7:00 P.M. and open dancing begins at 8:00 P.M. Wednesday is oldies night.

Riverside Adult Day Program
3724 Olentangy River Road
(614) 566-4063
www.ohiohealth.com
Riverside Methodist Hospital provides an alternative to nursing homes for seniors who want to maintain their independent living but need intermittent supervision or occasional medical attention. Activities, exercises, support groups, rehab, and other services, as well as door-to-door transportation, are available. Beauticians and massage therapists can also be scheduled.

United Cerebral Palsy Grace Kindig Adult Day Center
440 Industrial Mile Road
(614) 279-0109, (800) 670-9146
Adults afflicted with cerebral palsy can maintain their independence while engaging in music, arts, crafts, discussion, and exercise in a monitored environment with health care professionals on-site. Door-to-door transportation is available, and the center is open business hours on weekdays only. The Reese Adult Day Center (740-345-4771) in Newark only accepts adults 35 and older.

SENIOR CENTERS

There are dozens of senior citizen recreation centers operating within Franklin County. The activities and amenities vary, but most offer art workshops, dance classes, and exercise facilities geared specifically toward the 50-plus age group. Some have theaters, on-site social services, and lunch programs. A detailed list of these centers can be found on the Franklin County Office on Aging Web site or by calling them directly.

The Columbus Department of Recreation and Parks operates four senior (50+) centers.

Barber Roselea Senior Center
4048 Roselea Place
(614) 645-3243

Gillie Senior Center
2100 Morse Road
(614) 645-3106

Martin Janis Senior Center
East 11th Avenue
(614) 645-5954

McDowell Senior Center
275 McDowell Street
(614) 645-3176

Other municipalities have senior centers and arts or educational programs. The following is a brief list of the bigger community centers or cities with extensive programming for older adults.

Bexley Parks and Recreation Department
(614) 258-5755
www.bexley.org

Blendon Township Senior Center
Westerville
(614) 882-1260

Dublin Community Recreation Center
(614) 410-4550
www.dublin.oh.us

Gahanna Senior Center
(614) 471-6968

Grandview Heights Senior Center
(614) 488-8792

Hilliard Happiness Senior Center
(614) 876-0747

Upper Arlington Senior Center
(614) 583-5320

Westerville Senior Center
(614) 901-6560

Whitehall Senior Center
(614) 501-8593

Worthington Senior Center
(614) 842-6320

Adult day services and home-delivered meals are assessed on a sliding fee basis for those who are over 60.

EMPLOYMENT, VOLUNTEER, AND COMMUNITY SERVICES

Most of the previously mentioned organizations will be able to help you if you are interested in working with the elderly or are a senior looking for employment opportunities. Don't overlook the churches, youth groups, and cultural and educational organizations mentioned elsewhere in this book as places to lend a helping hand.

Employment for Seniors, Inc.
5 East Long Street, Suite 701
(614) 228-2915
www.employseniors.org
This free service puts people ages 50 and older in touch with employers who might need their skills.

Seniors Community Service Employment Program
1393 East Broad Street
(614) 252-0210
The American Association of Retired Persons sponsors this free program to help Franklin County residents ages 55 and older secure employment. It also provides career counseling and on-the-job training.

The Senior Citizens Bureau is a national community resource for the elderly, children of the elderly, and caregivers. It provides information and services via a 24-hour user-friendly Web site, www.seniorcitizensbureau.com, or the 24-hour toll-free Elder Info Hotline, (866) 847-4415.

Senior Companion Program
35 Midland Avenue
(614) 274-0172
Healthy, active older volunteers provide respite care, meal preparation, and peer support and friendship to older seniors throughout Franklin County.

Upper Arlington Commission on Aging
1945 Ridgeview Road
(614) 583-5326
The UA Commission on Aging has set up an In-Kind Call program that offers a daily telephone or computer check-in service for residents who are older or living alone. Calls are made to members' homes daily at a specified time. If the member does not respond to a second contact attempt, a key holder is notified to respond to the home.

HOUSING

Choosing where to live is a very serious matter, and many of the aforementioned organizations act as referral services. They can give you endless amounts of literature on housing in Columbus.

There are three different types of living options seniors need to consider. Independent living, which is more or less condo or apartment living, covers indoor and outdoor maintenance and sometimes provides structured community events, while offering a high degree of freedom. Assisted living can vary from minimal daily help to full 24-hour nursing care. A nursing home provides full medical care, and residents typically have one-room living quarters.

Prices vary, and, like anywhere, location and quality of care drive the cost. Seniors should also be aware than heavy discounts are given at many of the apartments and condos that are not traditionally senior-oriented. Home Sharing (614-221-4663), at 1560 Fishinger Road in Upper Arlington, will screen and match people who have room to spare with others who are seeking affordable housing. One of the two parties is typically over the age of 55 or has a disability. It does background and reference checks on everyone.

This section is by no means an exhaustive list of options; rather, it provides contact details for a few of the senior-oriented communities in Columbus.

Abbington of Arlington
1320 Old Henderson Road
Upper Arlington
(614) 451-4575
www.abbingtononline.com
Abbington provides assisted living accommodations that emphasize independence, but it can also provide help with daily personal hygiene, medication, and housekeeping. There are two other nearby locations in Pickerington and Powell.

The Enclave at Albany Park
4955 Enclave Boulevard, Westerville
(614) 476-8579
This pet-friendly apartment building is located just a few minutes away from Easton. A membership to a health club is included, and seniors are given discounted prices. It is totally independent living.

First Community Village
1800 Riverside Drive, Grandview Heights
(614) 324-4455
www.firstcommunity.org
Central Ohio's first continuing care retirement community has everything you need on-site: a bank, library, chapel, beauty services, and a store. It offers independent living in garden apartments and manor homes, or assisted living with skilled nursing and respite care.

Friendship Village of Dublin
6000 Riverside Drive, Dublin
(614) 764-1600
www.fvdublin.org
This is a comprehensive retirement community that offers all three levels of living: independent living, assisted living, and a nursing home. One of the benefits to this is that you can enter into independent liv-

ing but move within the same community as your needs change. The rates stay the same as your needs change, so you can potentially pay independent living rates while living in the nursing home.

Heartland Victorian Village
920 Thurber Drive West
(614) 464-2273
This skilled nursing facility has 148 beds and can accommodate those needing short-term rehabilitation. It accepts both Medicare and Medicaid.

The Ravine at Central College
630 Sunbury Road, Westerville
(614) 794-1333
Seniors age 55 and older live in luxury here. This brand-new apartment complex has two-bedroom apartments with private patios and two-bedroom condo homes with attached one-car garages. The facility also has a community computer room, business center, and gym.

Residences of Gahanna
1350 Underwood Farms Boulevard
Gahanna
(866) 507-0623
These one- and two-bedroom apartments have been designed with seniors in mind. The building is close to shopping and restaurants and is a good location for active, independently living seniors.

Wesley Glen Retirement Community
5155 North High Street, Worthington
(614) 888-7492
www.wesleyglen.com
The Methodist Eldercare Services operates these quality and comfortable homes for seniors, along with health care, daily housekeeping, and personal grooming services. A second retirement community, Wesley Ridge, is in Reynoldsburg (614-759-0023).

Whetstone Gardens and Care Center
3710 Olentangy River Road, Clintonville
(614) 457-1100
www.whetstonegardensandcarecenter.com
Clintonville's skilled care center has only 54 beds and can provide short-term rehabilitation. It accepts both Medicare and Medicaid. Whetstone is part of the larger MacIntosh Company, which manages five more care centers around Columbus.

The Woodlands
5380 East Broad Street, Whitehall
(614) 755-7591
www.columbuswoodlands.com
This senior care facility offers independent, assisted living, and Alzheimer's care in one- and two-bedroom apartments.

The Worthington
1201 Riva Ridge Boulevard, Gahanna
(614) 933-8640
www.holidaytouch.com
This gracious retirement residence offers studios and one- and two-bedroom plans. Indoor and outdoor maintenance, meals, and laundry service are among the amenities.

Worthington Christian Village
165 Highbluffs Boulevard
(614) 846-6076
www.wcv.org
Seniors have a choice between apartments, cottages, and assisted living and various levels of health care. The complex hosts family events, activities, and group outings.

MEDIA

Columbus residents have been referred to as "media savvy," "breaking-news obsessed," and "weather crazy." We tune into what is referred to as "smart shows," such as *Dr. Phil* and *Oprah. The West Wing* and reality shows like *The Apprentice* are also considered "smart shows"; we watch them, too. With such an educated, diverse, news-hungry populace, you'd think Columbus might have more than one daily newspaper. Not so.

When it comes to daily printed news, it is slim pickings. Columbus has one daily newspaper called the *Columbus Dispatch.* It is owned by media mogul Wolfe Enterprises, which also just happens to own the television station WBNS Channel 10 (the CBS affiliate), ONN (Ohio News Network), *CityScene Magazine, Columbus Parent, ThisWeek* community newspapers, and radio stations WBNS 97.1 FM and 1460 AM.

Most of the other well-known local papers (*The Other Paper, Mid-Ohio Golfer,* and the 21 Suburban News publications) and magazines (*Columbus Monthly* and *Columbus C.E.O.*) are owned by CM Media. With just a few independent weekly papers, there seem to be too much media owned by too few people.

That goes for Columbus television stations, too. While Wolfe owns the CBS affiliate and the NBC network owns its own local station, another company owns both the ABC and Fox station affiliates. It's no wonder the Federal Communications Commission has rules in place preventing one company from owning all the airwaves. In order to protect the diversity of viewpoints, the FCC limits the number and type of media any one person or group can own in a given market.

In addition to the "big three" television networks, Columbus has WOSU, UPN, and WB networks and a few independent stations that broadcast local access shows and religious programming. There are six privately owned television stations in our city. These smaller, low-powered stations are seldom carried by cable systems and are often owned by community groups or churches. Of the six, two are owned by religious broadcasters, one by a major national broadcaster, and the remaining by a mix of people.

The public broadcasting stations of The Ohio State University are quite good and include a television station and both AM and FM radio stations. WOSU TV reaches 500,000 viewers each week with educational and cultural programming. Their local radio hosts are talented and knowledgeable and bring classical music, international news, and National Public Radio to Columbus airwaves.

Radio is probably the most diverse medium in Columbus, but Clear Channel owns seven stations, making them one of the dominant broadcasters. The average listener in Columbus also seems to like many of these stations, as they consistently rank high in the Arbitron surveys.

In general, Columbus's radio market is large, but most of the stations run "programmed" music. Some "purists" have gone as far as to say that Columbus is devoid of alternative radio, but this is a matter of opinion. We might not have a cutting-edge college station, but there is at least a little something for everyone on the air.

Columbus may be a one-paper town, but we do have at least three cable companies and a good selection of broadband Internet services to choose from. This chapter includes contact details, along with a little bit of information about each local publication and the call numbers and channels for television and radio stations. Check out the Kidstuff chapter to find out about *Columbus Parent* and the Retirement and Senior Care chapter for publications directed toward seniors.

DAILY NEWSPAPERS

The Columbus Dispatch
(614) 461-5000
www.dispatch.com
This is the city's only daily newspaper, which probably explains the 500,000 weekday and 750,000 Sunday paper home deliveries. With numbers like that, the *Dispatch* ranks among the country's leaders in household distribution. It has award-winning reports on local and global news and was recently named "Best Newspaper in Ohio." The Sunday paper has additional sections—Sports, Metro and State News, Travel, Lifestyle—and classifieds. You can subscribe online or by calling (877) 7-DISPATCH. Daily delivery for 10 weeks will cost around $30.

The Daily Reporter
580 South High Street
(614) 228-NEWS
www.sourcenews.com
This paper is published Monday through Friday. It focuses on business, legal, and real estate issues around central Ohio and publishes the annual *Central Ohio Business Resources Guide*. Prospective entrepreneurs, small business owners, attorneys, and real estate agents will probably get the most from this newspaper. Subscription runs about $90 a year.

COMMUNITY AND SPECIALIZED NEWSPAPERS

Business First of Columbus
303 West Nationwide Boulevard
(614) 461-4040
www.columbus.bizjournals.com
In-depth local business, industry, and enterprise articles make up this weekly newspaper. A one-year subscription costs $89 and gives you access to Columbus First online as well as 41 other cities' business newspapers owned by the same parent publishing company, American City Business Journals.

The Catholic Times
197 East Gay Street
(614) 224-5195
www.ctonline.org
The official newspaper of the Catholic Diocese of Columbus is published weekly, 49 times a year. The articles cover local, national, and international Catholic news. Each issue includes regular columns and a listing of events at the different parishes. Home delivery costs $25 for a year's subscription.

Columbus Alive
1079 North High Street
(614) 221-2449
www.columbusalive.com
This free newspaper has a bit of an alternative slant, but I wouldn't go as far as to say it is a strictly "gay" publication. The articles focus on everything from the local arts scene and politics to gay pride and music reviews. It offers a fairly comprehensive listing of the goings-on in Columbus, including restaurant and film reviews. *Alive* comes out every Thursday and is distributed in libraries, grocery stores, and coffee shops.

The Columbus Call and Post Newspaper
109 Hamilton Avenue
(614) 224-8123
www.callandpost.net
This newspaper has been reporting the black experience for 78 years and is published by Don King Productions. Stories highlight education, religion, history, business, and health. A yearly subscription is $39 for the year, and individual issues are carried in just about every Kroger's and major bookstore in Columbus.

The Columbus Post
172 East State Street
(614) 224-6723
www.columbuspost.com
Serving Columbus's African-American population, this weekly newspaper is published by Freedom Media Group, Inc. and can be delivered to your door for $25 a year. The articles focus on lifestyles, health, fashion, business, and entertainment.

The Free Press
1240 Bryden Road
(614) 253-2571
www.freepress.org
Since its birth in 1970, this left-wing paper has gone through several incarnations and is currently a monthly publication. One thing that hasn't changed is its dedication to publishing new, progressive works by local and national writers. *The Free Press* is distributed in the campus, downtown, and arts districts and is subsidized by dedicated home subscribers, donations, and fundraising events.

Mid-Ohio Golfer
5255 Sinclair Road
(614) 848-4653
This newspaper features golf articles, reviews of local courses, and a calendar of events. It is a good resource for golfers in central Ohio, with its annual directory of all the courses in the region, along with their costs, par, and contact details. The annual subscription costs $35 for 18 issues.

The Other Paper
5255 Sinclair Road
(614) 847-3800
www.theotherpaper.com
If you prefer news of the weird, liberal editorials, and page after page of upcoming events, you'll enjoy this free weekly paper. Quirky articles and a listing of live music, art exhibitions, and happy hour specials are included in *TOP*. Ultraconservatives probably shouldn't read the editorials or personals too closely, because they can be a bit graphic at times. You will also find the whole gamut of adult entertainment options advertised here. *The Other Paper* comes out every Thursday and is carried at retail, dining, and drinking establishments.

Outlook News
406 East Wilson Bridge Road
(614) 268-8525, (866) 452-6397
This weekly paper is Columbus's most widely circulated gay publication. It is sectionalized into news, entertainment, lifestyle, and features focused on gay and lesbian issues, music and film reviews, and events in the community. The advertisements are visually provocative (to say the least). *Outlook* manages Network Columbus, a chamber of commerce for gay-owned and -allied businesses and straight friends of the gay community.

Short North Gazette
404 Thurber Drive
(614) 464-0103
www.shortnorth.com
This free independent newspaper has an artsy slant to it. Articles cover the visual and performing arts community in the Short North and surrounding neighborhoods. Regular restaurant reviews and columns about James Thurber are also part of this monthly paper. It can be found free in libraries, stores, bars, and restaurants.

Suburban News Publications
5257 Sinclair Road
(614) 847-0085
www.snponline.com
This community paper owned by CM Media features local news, sports, government, and classified ads. It is published for 22 suburban neighborhoods, including Gahanna, Hilliard, Reynoldsburg, and Westerville. For $40 a year, you can have it delivered to your home.

ThisWeek Community Newspapers
670 Lakeview Plaza Boulevard
Worthington
(614) 841-1781
www.thisweeknews.com
This simple, 20-page newspaper is published every Thursday in 21 neighbor-

hoods. The stories cover community business and sports, local government and school issues, and special events. It can be delivered to your home or found free at libraries.

MAGAZINES

CityScene Magazine
4500 Mobile Drive
(614) 572-1240
www.columbuscityscene.org
This glossy magazine showcases Columbus's shopping, dining, and other attractions and is a good source to check for visual and performing arts events. It is published in partnership with WBNS Channel 10 and features a daily segment at 5:30 P.M. on that station. CityScene comes out once a month and can be delivered for free to your home.

Columbus CEO
5255 Sinclair Road
(614) 221-7995
This free monthly business magazine features articles on the business climate of central Ohio, including analysis of various sectors, management advice, and job listings. Libraries maintain current and back issues.

Columbus Monthly
5255 Sinclair Road
(614) 888-4567
www.columbusmonthly.com
Columbus Monthly has been the city's premier monthly magazine for 30 years now. It features restaurant reviews, business profiles, and articles on a variety of subjects, including political and civic issues. It continues to provide an alternative voice to the daily newspaper and is known for its well-written and heavily researched service pieces, like the "Best of . . . " series and school ratings. The individual issues can be purchased at most local news and magazine sellers or delivered to your home. Libraries also maintain back issues.

TELEVISION STATIONS

Channel 4—WCMH
3165 Olentangy River Road
(614) 263-4444
www.nbc4i.com
The Nielsen Survey has recently rated this NBC affiliate's newscasts at 6:00 A.M. and at 5:00, 6:00, and 11:00 P.M. No. 1 in the city, making anchors Colleen Marshall and Cabot Rea "the most watched news team in central Ohio." On top of these growing achievements, the station has won several awards, including "Best Web site in Ohio" by the Ohio Society of Professional Journalists and the Ohio Associated Press. Channel 4's motto, "Working for you," is reflected in much of what it does, from breaking news and consumer reports to strong community outreach events that tie in with local organizations. The station works with both the Columbus Dog Connection and Franklin County Shelter to find homes for pets-to-be. Chief meteorologist Jym Ganahl, "The Dean of Central Ohio Weather," is one of the station's best-known faces, but it is weatherman Ben Gelber who has a song and dance named for him and has recently celebrated 25 years with the station. Ask anyone who has lived in Columbus for a while how to "do the Ben Gelber," and see what you get! In 2006, the station is opening a *Today* show-style satellite studio at Broad and High Streets.

Channel 6—WSYX
1261 Dublin Road
(614) 481-6666
www.wsyx6.com
This ABC affiliate is owned by the Maryland-based Sinclair Broadcast Group. Many people find the points of view, news, and censorship of this station one-sided and right wing, but you can't blame the local affiliate for the big dog's decisions. One of the more recent scandals this channel endured was when the Sinclair Group ordered its ABC affiliates in 2004 not to run a *Nightline* segment that listed the names of all the servicemen and women

i ***Columbus has very strong affiliates of both CBS and NBC, so the networks' national ratings can be significantly affected by Columbus viewers—especially when they decide to air sporting events that involve local teams.***

killed in Iraq to that point. Whether a political move or not, WSYX muddled through by covering the story in a somewhat round-about way. Many folks—including myself—thought *The Point,* an extreme right-wing commentary by Mark Hyman, was a local production, when in reality it is produced at corporate headquarters in Baltimore. All Sinclair affiliates must air it as part of their local news. Whether or not you agree with Hyman's comments, you won't be bumping into him here in Columbus anytime soon. You might, however, come across the station's chief meteorologist, Chris Bradley (and his "Weather Hound," Boswell). He gives his viewers "a three-degree guarantee" and does interesting gardening segments.

Channel 8—WINJ
363 Reeb Avenue
(614) 444-8872
www.winj.com
This independent, low-powered station features a hodgepodge of news, business, gospel, and music programming. The small station is licensed to the Newlife Fellowship of Churches and broadcasts Columbus Clippers games, vintage films, and reruns of *The Beverly Hillbillies* and *I Love Lucy.*

Channel 10—WBNS
770 Twin Rivers Drive
(614) 460-3700
www.wbns10tv.com
This TV station, more commonly known as 10TV, is Columbus's CBS affiliate and was founded in 1949. It is owned by Wolfe Enterprises, and the call letters actually stem from the Wolfe family businesses: books, news, and shoes. It is touted as the most-watched news channel in central Ohio, and early birds appreciate the 10:00 P.M. local news broadcast. Many famous personalities got their television start at this station: Rod Serling, Jonathan Winters, and Jack Hanna, to name a few. Aside from 24-hour news coverage, 10TV investigates consumer issues and is the station to catch The Ohio State University's men's basketball games and Big Ten sports. *Wall to Wall Sports* is a popular sports talk show covering the latest hot topics on weekend nights.

Channel 28—WTTE
1261 Dublin Road
(614) 895-2800
www.wtte.28.com
There is no shortage of sitcom reruns, trashy prime-time shows, and Ohio's very own Jerry Springer on this Fox affiliate. WTTE is owned by the same folks who own the ABC affiliate, the Sinclair Broadcast Group.

Channel 34—WOSU TV
2400 Olentangy River Road
(614) 292-9678
www.wosu.org
The Ohio State University television station reaches 500,000 viewers each week with educational and arts programming. The prime-time lineup (8:00 to 11:00 P.M.) can be viewed the following night as part of the late-night lineup (1:00 to 4:00 A.M.). Episodes of *Nova* and *Are You Being Served?* are aired, as well as history, theatrical, and cultural shows. Like all public broadcasting stations, it has its fair share of televised fundraisers. WOSU TV went digital in February 2004, which means you get more than just a pretty image on your television. Special high-definition and wide-screen programming is broadcast throughout the week, and several other multibroadcasting options are available. The Web site lists the up-to-date broadcast schedule.

Channel 48—WCPX-LP
(877) 296-7744
www.worship.net
This Christian network, based in Florida, propagates a Christian message 24/7 through religious programming, which they refer to as "worship and praise TV." One of the recently appointed hosts is from Columbus.

Channel 51—WSFJ
3948 Townsfair Way
(614) 416-6080
www.wsfj.org
This nonprofit, Christian-based station has been providing cable programming since 1976. It airs high-quality inspirational and children's programs and family-friendly movies. The network embodies strong family values and is free of excessive violence, explicit sex, or foul language.

Channel 53—WWHO
1160 Dublin Road, Dublin
(614) 485-5300
www.upn53.com
This Viacom-owned station has recently been purchased by the Indianapolis-based Lin TV, which plans to keep much of its UPN and WB programming the same. Currently, you can catch a variety of goofy comedies, like *That 70's Show* and *King of the Hill,* and endless reruns of '80s flicks and *Fear Factor.* As a service to central Ohio, WUPN-Columbus has developed *Spotlight,* a public affairs show that focuses on community issues.

ONN (various channels)
175 Third Street
(614) 280-3600
www.onnnews.com
The Ohio News Network offers exclusive, 24-hour, Ohio-related news and stories. It delivers full news coverage at the top and bottom of every hour, with news headlines every 15 minutes. The Ohio weather forecast is offered every 10 minutes around the clock, while political talk shows, Worldwide Kids News, and postgame live shows air at scheduled times. ONN can be viewed on channel 14, 58, or 119, depending on your cable provider.

RADIO

AM Stations

610 AM—WTVN
(614) 821-WTVN
www.610wtvn.com
This Clear Channel station provides news coverage, talk radio, and Buckeye sports coverage. Its newsroom and Bob Conner's morning show helped it reach the top of the heap in Arbitron's 2005 ratings.

820 AM—WOSU
(614) 292-9678
www.wosu.org
This station is referred to as NPR 820 and offers high-quality news, "intelligent talk," public affairs, and world music programming 24 hours a day. It is here you'll find National Public Radio, BBC World Service, and even a little bluegrass.

920 AM—WMNI
(614) 232-0289
www.wmni.com
This station offers a mix of talk, news, and light music. Every weekday morning at 9:30, *The Senior News Network Update* is hosted by an expert in elder law and focuses on issues for the aging. Another popular show is *Plant Talk,* a live, interactive gardening show on Saturday morning at 8:00 A.M. It also airs a syndicated program called *Swingin' with Sinatra.*

1230 AM—WTPG
(614) 486-6101
www.progressive1230.com
This former oldies channel now broadcasts in the new liberal-progressive talk format. You'll find syndicated talk radio and sports on yet another station owned by Clear Channel. Tune into 1230 when you need a dose of Al Franken or want to catch America's most listened to home-improvement show, *At Home with Gary Sullivan.*

1460 AM—WBNS
(614) 821-1460
www.1460thefan.com
It is sports everything on this channel: call-in radio shows, local and nationally syndicated programs, and live broadcasts of Buckeye and Blue Jacket games. You can also catch Upper Arlington's very own Kirk Herbstreit weekdays from 3:00 to 7:00 P.M. cohosting *The Big Show.* If you happen to miss your favorite show, you can listen to it on demand online, but keep in mind that most of the sports coverage is local.

FM Stations

89.7 FM—WOSU
(614) 292-9678
www.wosu.org
This Ohio State University station features classical and jazz music, with a little arts and culture programming in the mix.

90.5 FM—WCBE
(614) 365-5555
www.wcbe.org
WCBE is central Ohio's NPR station and provides a broad mix of local news coverage and cultural and world music programming. It is an eclectic station where you will find shows like *Fresh Air, All Things Considered,* and BBC World Services.

92.3 FM—WCOL
(614) 486-6101
www.wcol.com
This country music station is owned by Clear Channel, and while country music has dropped in Columbus's ratings, *Woody and the Wake-Up Call* is still a reliable and popular morning show.

94.7 FM—WSNY
(614) 451-2191
www.wsny.com
Sunny FM plays your standard elevator music: Elton John, Celine Dion, and The Eagles. But apparently we ladies totally dig it! This station has ranked first with adult female listeners for 24 rating periods in a row, and women ages 35 to 54 like the *Dino & Stacy* morning show 36 percent better than any other. Beginning late November it plays holiday music 24/7 through Christmas Day. This light station is owned by Franklin Communications.

96.3 FM—WLVQ
(614) 821-9696
www.qfm96.com
Infinity Broadcasting owns Q-FM. It plays album-oriented rock music and, despite having a limited promotional budget, ranked first among men ages 35 to 54.

97.1 FM—WBNS
(614) 460-3850
www.971moremusic.com
This station is playing mostly programmed top 40 and adult-contemporary tunes. It also gives school closings and delays as necessary. Friday is '80s night, and deejay Buzz Fitzgerald plays an hour worth of new music every Monday night between 11:00 P.M. and midnight.

97.9 FM—WNCI
(614) 821-WNCI
www.wnci.com
The top 40 music broadcasted from this Clear Channel station appeals to a broad age group. According to a recent Arbitron survey, WNCI ranked first among age groups 18 to 34 and 25 to 54. The Morning Zoo is the popular morning crew, and you'll find the station's crazy deejays broadcasting live from various bars and nightclubs on the weekends.

99.7 FM—WBZX
(614) 821-9970
www.wbzx.com
"The Blitz" plays rock with a heavier slant. Since its founding in 1992, it has remained a popular station with the headbangers of Columbus. It is owned by the North American Broadcasting Company and broadcasts from the highest radio antenna in Columbus.

101.1 FM—WWCD
(614) 221-1011
www.cd101.com
CD101 has made a name for itself as Columbus's alternative rock station and the official FM station of the Columbus Blue Jackets. Some people will disagree with its claim to being a true alternative station, but it is not as mainstream as other channels. Community involvement is high on the list for this station, too. The annual Andyman-A-Thon raises money for the Kids Charity, while the Green Team is a volunteer group dedicated to keeping Columbus beautiful.

104.9 FM—WCVO
(614) 479-1049
www.1049theriver.com
Programming consists of positive, uplifting music with a Christian message. Artists like Steven Curtis Chapman and Jars of Clay are played at this station owned by The Christian Voice of Central Ohio.

107.5 FM—WCKX
(614) 487-1444
This station owned by Radio One, cranks out hip-hop and urban music and is rated the second most popular station among listeners ages 18 to 34.

107.9 FM—WODB
(614) 573-8400
www.oldies1079columbus.com
Sagg owns this oldies channel. Feel-good music by the Beach Boys, Temptations, and Four Tops is on the playlist, along with Eagles, Rolling Stones, and Creedence.

Other Radio Stations

95.5 FM—WHOK
Country classics

98.9 FM—WXMG
Urban contemporary

103.9 FM—WTDA
Classic hits

105.7 FM—WFJX
Classic rock

106.3 FM—WJYD
Gospel

CABLE AND INTERNET PROVIDERS

Adelphia
15 North Third Street, Newark
(740) 345-1909
www.adelphia.com
Adelphia cable and Internet services are available in areas to the east and southeast of Columbus.

Insight Communications
3370 East Livingston Avenue
(614) 235-6157
www.insight-com.com
This local cable company offers basic, classic, and digital cable, as well as Road Runner broadband Internet access.

Time Warner Cable
(614) 481-5050
www.twcol.com
As one of the biggest cable providers in Columbus, Time Warner serves 320,000 customers in the Columbus area. Video on Demand, high-definition television, and Road Runner, a high-speed Internet service, are just a few of the products it offers beyond basic cable.

WOW! Internet and Cable
(866) 4-WOW NOW
www1.wowway.com
Denver-based Wide Open West is another competitive provider of high-speed Internet access and advanced cable services. It is available in most of Columbus.

WORSHIP 

Regardless of one's religion, Columbus has a place for everyone. Naturally, as the city becomes more and more of a melting pot, a larger number of religions and religiously affiliated social groups are represented. It would be impractical to list the thousands of churches, temples, synagogues, and mosques in central Ohio, so this chapter just presents an overview of the religious scene in Columbus.

---

i ***When looking for a new church, try the yellow pages. Churches are neatly divided into religious denominations and broken down even further into different sects. Also check the Saturday* Columbus Dispatch *or community papers in which service times are published for many congregations.***

THE CATHOLIC COMMUNITY

A good place to begin a synopsis is with Columbus's Catholic population, which is around 250,000, making it the largest religious group in the city. The Diocese of Columbus (www.colsdioc.org) was established in 1868. Sylvester Rosecrans, the first bishop of Columbus, created many institutions within the new diocese, including parishes, schools, and its first newspaper, *The Catholic Columbian.*

During this time, he oversaw the construction of Columbus's first Catholic church, St. Joseph's Cathedral, on East Broad Street. It was consecrated October 20, 1878, and Bishop Rosecrans died a day later. The diocese now encompasses 11,310 square miles and has 121 active priests and 107 parishes.

Education is discussed in a separate chapter, but this seems a logical place to mention that Columbus has 24 Catholic elementary schools and 5 high schools. To find out more about Catholic schools, contact the Department of Education at (614) 221-5829.

Several institutions of higher education are directly affiliated with the church, the best known being the Pontifical College Josephinum in Worthington, which trains Roman Catholic priests. This beautiful monastery is often home to art shows and classical music concerts, which give the public opportunities to visit the campus and chapels.

Capital University was founded as a Lutheran seminary in Canton and moved to Columbus in 1832. In 1959, the Evangelical Lutheran Theological Seminary and Capital University were separated. Capital is now one of the largest Lutheran-affiliated colleges in the nation, while Trinity Seminary continues to train church leaders. Unlike the Josephinum, Trinity admits women to the seminary.

Women also have a part in Columbus's monastic community. When the Diocese of Columbus was formed in 1868, the Dominican Sisters of St. Mary's of the Springs were given property in northwestern Columbus from which they continue to preach, teach, and reside. The Ohio Dominican University, a four-year liberal arts and coeducational college, was established by the Dominican community on property adjacent to the motherhouse.

THE NON-CATHOLIC CHRISTIAN COMMUNITY

While Catholicism claims the most members in Columbus, the evangelical Christian churches pack the most people in under one roof. Every Sunday, Pastor Rod

Parley fills his 5,200-seat state-of-the-art World Harvest Church in Canal Winchester. His sermons are televised from an on-site studio. The networks and times are listed online at www.breakthrough.net, or call (614) 837-1990. World Harvest also has a prep school and Bible college affiliated with it.

Charismatics and Pentecostals might appreciate the old-fashioned preaching style at The Vineyard Church (614-890-0000; www.vineyardcolumbus.org) in Westerville. It is one of the fastest-growing congregations and has seating for more than 3,000 people. This church is known for its orthodox ministry and extensive musical worship.

In general, there are a lot of resources available for the Christian population of Columbus. The Christian Blue Pages (614-890-9006; www.christianbluepages.com) is based in Dayton and offers a free printed and Internet listing of Christian-owned or -operated businesses in the Columbus area. It is laid out like a telephone book and contains advertising as well.

Coming in a very distant second place to the Catholics, Methodists are the next largest religious group in Columbus. Just flip through the phone book and you'll find a substantial number of United Methodist churches, as well as Free Methodist, Korean Methodist, and African Methodist Episcopal.

Again, open the phone book and you'll find every variation on the Baptist church you can imagine. Each church is an individual entity, having no council or higher ecclesiastical body. There are about 300 Baptist churches in the Columbus area to choose from, too many to list in this chapter.

The Lutherans, Presbyterians, and Episcopalians make a strong showing, but, like the Baptists, there are too many to list here. Some of the architecturally interesting churches within these denominations are described later in this chapter. Bible churches, Assemblies of God, Mennonite, Jehovah's Witness, and Eastern Orthodox churches, though not plentiful, do have a presence in Columbus.

The temples of the Church of Jesus Christ of Latter-day Saints are separate and distinct from their Mormon meetinghouses. There are thousands of Latter-day Saint churches and meetinghouses in the world but relatively few temples, and Columbus is fortunate enough to have one. Hilliard is home to the Columbus Ohio Temple (614-351-5001), which includes 11 stakes, 4 missions, and more than 53,000 members.

Quakers have a number of options in central Ohio. Meetings are held every Sunday at 1954 Indianola Avenue (614-291-2331), just north of the OSU campus. If you don't mind venturing out of Columbus, meetings are also held at the Andrews' House in Delaware (740-362-8921) and in Slayter Hall at Denison University (740-344-4656).

Columbus has several churches that not only accept but also advocate and openly support their gay, lesbian, and bisexual members. Gay-friendly churches will sometimes run advertisements in the free weekly papers, but a good place to start your search is with Stonewall Columbus (614-299-7764; www.stonewallcolumbus.com). A list of churches that welcome gay Christians can also be found at www.gaychurch.org.

An increasing need for tolerance and compassion in our society is leading to the formation of several interfaith organizations. Students can get involved with religious organizations at their campus. The Office of Student Affairs (studentaffairs.osu.edu) supports the University Interfaith Association. Representatives of two dozen different faiths and churches come together to collaborate on the spiritual needs and issues of the student population.

The Spirituality Network (614-228-8867; www.spiritualitynetwork.org) is located at 444 East Broad Street and maintains a referral list of spiritual guidance counselors within numerous

Build It Again Center (614-414-0427) is Habitat for Humanity's local retail store. The center accepts donated goods and building materials, which are in turn sold to the public at highly reduced prices. Drop off good-quality cabinets, doors, sinks, windows, and leftover remodeling supplies at 3140 Westerville Road in Westerville to help out the community.

Christian denominations. Some are ordained ministers, some are affiliated with specific religious orders, and others are laypeople. The network sponsors classes and retreats on spiritual transformation. This is the sort of place you can explore the "Sacred Feminine."

Many of the ecumenical and interfaith groups put their beliefs into action. Habitat for Humanity is one of them. This nonprofit Christian housing ministry brings together volunteers of all faiths to help eradicate substandard housing in poverty-stricken and low-income areas. Volunteers help build affordable homes. To get involved with Habitat for Humanity, call (614) 414-0427, or check out the Web site www.habitat-columbus.org.

THE JEWISH COMMUNITY

Columbus has a Jewish population of 150,000, and their heritage runs deep, particularly in Bexley. Founded 155 years ago, Temple Israel in Bexley was the first Jewish organization to be established in Columbus. There are now eight synagogues in the city, most of them located in or around Bexley. Beth Tikvah is the only synagogue on the northwest side of Columbus, and Temple Beth Shalom is in New Albany.

The Columbus Jewish Historical Society is dedicated to documenting the history of the Jewish communities of Columbus and central Ohio. Aside from archiving the collections of local Jewish families, it maintains a library of oral histories, Jewish history books, and genealogies. You can contact the society at (614) 238-6977, or check out the Web site, www.columbusjewishhistoricalsociety.org.

The Leo Yassenoff Jewish Community Center (614-231-2731; www.columbusjcc.org) is located at 1125 College Avenue and hosts a variety of recreational, cultural, and educational activities, as well as fundraising and outreach programs, that support the Jewish community.

If you are planning to relocate to Columbus and are looking to integrate into the Jewish community, a good source of information is the Columbus Jewish Federation, which has been around since 1926. Its extensive Web site (www.jewishcolumbus.org) offers a comprehensive listing of community and educational services, volunteer and advocacy opportunities, and synagogues throughout the city. It also provides links to national and international organizations.

OTHER RELIGIOUS COMMUNITIES

The Muslim community of Columbus is growing. The Islamic Society of Greater Columbus (ISGC) is a nonprofit organization that conducts religious, educational, cultural, and social activities in the best traditions of Islam. It also provides philanthropic and community services to those in need. The ISGC is based at Omar Mosque on Riverside Drive (614-262-1310; www.isgc.org). It also operates the only full-time Islamic school in central Ohio, with kindergarten through 10th grade. Sunrise Academy is discussed in the Education and Child Care chapter.

Buddhists will find about a half dozen meditational centers and groups that meet at various places around Columbus. The Shambhala Meditation Group of Columbus can be reached at (614) 562-4012 or viewed online at www.shambhala

.org/center/columbus. Mindfulness Meditation of Columbus offers meditation in the Vipassana tradition. Two groups meet weekly at 870 North High Street and at the First Community Church in Grandview (614-841-1908; www.geocities.com/mindfulnesscolumbus). A statewide listing of Buddhist groups can be viewed at www.buddhanet.net.

Hindus from all over central Ohio worship at the Bharatiya Hindu Temple at 3671 Hyatts Road in Powell. It serves those who wish to live life in accordance with the Vedic dharma philosophies and traditions. For more information, call (740) 369-0717, or check out www.columbushindutemple.org. There are a few more Hindu temples in nearby Dayton, Cincinnati, and Cleveland.

The International Society for Krishna Consciousness (ISKCON), better known as the Hare Krishna movement, was started in 1966. The Columbus Krishna House (614-421-1661; www.columbuskrishnahouse.com) was founded in 1969 as an all-female congregation. Men are now welcome in the temple, which is located on the OSU campus.

Pagans and witches are right at home in Columbus, too. The Pagan Community Council of Ohio (614-470-3280; www.mypcco.com) provides liturgical classes and educational workshops on the beliefs of witches, pagans, and spiritual healers. Members of this group follow the principles of Wiccan beliefs and promote earth-based religions. Pagan Nation (www.pagannation.com) is more of a social organization. The Web site has links to everything pagan, and it hosts the annual Real Witches Ball.

RELIGIOUS ARCHITECTURE

You don't have to go to church to agree that places of worship make for some of the most interesting architecture in any city. Columbus is no different. Included here are a few of the more outstanding and unique religious structures in the city. They have been singled out for a variety of reasons including, beautiful mosaics, a famous architect and special gardens.

If you travel through Port Columbus International Airport, the Interfaith Meditation Room is available to travelers of all faiths. It is located near the baggage carousel in Concourse C.

Annunciation Greek Orthodox Cathedral
(614) 228-6245
30 Spruce Street, Short North
www.greekcathedral.com

Columbus's piece de résistance as far as church architecture goes is the Annunciation Greek Orthodox Cathedral. This hulking building is situated in the Short North and belongs to the Greek Orthodox Metropolis of Pittsburgh. The current church was built in 1990 on the site of the original church, which was founded in 1922. You will never know from the austere exterior how lavish and impressive the interior is—unless you go in.

Built in the traditional Byzantine style, its Greek cross floor plan dates back to the sixth century. The place is filled with symbolism, both within the architecture of the cathedral and its decoration. The floor symbolizes the earth, and the ceiling and chandelier represent the celestial universe with all its stars. Christian or not, you can't help but be moved by the powerful image of Christ looking down at you from the central dome.

The interior is covered with mosaics created by an Italian artisan from five million pieces of Venetian glass. If that isn't lavish enough, marble and 24-carat gold add to the glowing ambience. The choir screen is covered with icons, and the stained-glass windows depict scenes from the life of Christ and various saints. The church's Web site is beautifully done and provides an extensive explanation of the symbolism throughout the building. This is a must-see if you are staying in the downtown area. The church hosts the annual Labor Day Greek Festival and supports a variety of Greek cultural organizations and outreach ministries within the Columbus community.

Broad Street First Presbyterian Church
760 East Broad Street, Near East Side
(614) 221-6552
www.bspc.org

There are a number of interesting stone churches built along East Broad Street. The First Presbyterian Church is included here because it was designed by the famous architect Frank Packard in 1887 for the growing east side community. The church was completed in 1888, and like many of Packard's buildings it is a Victorian's interpretation of Gothic architecture.

In celebration of Columbus's diversity, Broad Street Presbyterian unconditionally welcomes anyone into its congregation and emphasizes social outreach. Practicing what it preaches, the church gifted 300 acres of Broad Acres land to Buckhorn Children's Center for at-risk children in 1989. Members also hand out food and provide day care for low-income families in the neighborhood and sponsor Habitat for Humanity projects.

First Unitarian Universalist Church of Columbus
93 West Weisheimer Road, Clintonville
(614) 267-4946
www.firstuu.columbus.org

The First Unitarian Universalist Church of Columbus ranks among the top 25 largest congregations of this more liberal religion. Combining reason in their approach to scripture and teaching freedom, tolerance, and unconditional love, Unitarian Universalist churches welcome all people regardless of race or sexual orientation. First Unitarian is located in the heart of Clintonville and has two lovely gardens onsite. The Memorial Garden is a tribute to life, while the walls containing the garden commemorate the church members who have died of HIV-related diseases. The Japanese Garden offers people a place to reflect and imagine.

Liberty Presbyterian Church
7080 Olentangy River Road, Delaware
(740) 548-6075
www.libertybarnchurch.com

This laid-back Presbyterian church looks a lot older than it really is. A church was built on this site just after the War of 1812 as a tribute to the landowner's deceased sweetheart. In 1993, Amish barn-raising legend Josie Miller was hired to erect a duplicate of the original church, which is believed to be the largest bank barn in the country.

The church is constructed of hickory and hemlock. A 300-year-old oak (struck by lightning) was recycled into a beautiful pulpit. The sanctuary is decorated with Amish quilts and can accommodate 1,100. You'll find no pipe organ here, only string quartets playing Bach and a congregation clapping while they sing. The services are so informal that many members wear shorts to church. Come as you are!

You'll find the Liberty Barn situated at a very scenic corner of Olentangy River Road (Old Route 315) and Home Road, slightly north of Worthington. If the church is not open, it is still worth checking out the gardens and wandering through the old cemetery, where you'll find Lydia Sackett buried in the churchyard alongside her sweetheart, John Flanagan.

St. John's Episcopal Church
700 High Street, Worthington
(614) 846-5180
www.stjohnsworthington.org

There's no mistaking the Connecticut roots of this church's founder. When you visit the first Episcopal church west of the Alleghenies, you'll swear you've made a wrong turn and ended up in New England. The present building was completed in 1831, but a church has been on this site since 1802.

James Kilbourne founded St. John's shortly after establishing Worthington. Its bell was rung for the first time on Christmas Eve in 1822. The exterior is of handmade brick and the interior of hand-hewn wood making St. John's well deserving of its inclusion on the National Register of Historic Places.

Worth noting is the labyrinth garden and cemetery located behind the church. The cemetery was once a community burying ground and includes five Revolutionary War veterans and seven veterans of the War of 1812.

St. Joseph's Cathedral
212 East Broad Street
(614) 224-1295
www.saintjosephcathedral.org

This beautiful cathedral was started in 1866 and is built in the Gothic style. The glowing yellow stone of this bulky church helps it to hold its own amid the skyscrapers surrounding it. The cathedral was consecrated in 1878 and was the first Catholic church built in Columbus. Its Web site has a very nicely written history and listing of who's who on the stained-glass windows. There are three entrances from Broad Street and one from Fifth Avenue. The current seating capacity is around 700.

INDEX

ABOUT THE AUTHOR

Shawnie Kelley lives in Upper Arlington with her fiancé, Kevin Foy, their two dogs, Riley and Brooklyn, and their cat, Freddie. She has traveled extensively through Europe, Scandinavia, North America, and the Caribbean. Shawnie teaches travel- and architecture-related classes through Upper Arlington's Department of Lifelong Learning and Leisure. Aside from travel writing, she enjoys photography, golfing, gardening, and collecting wine.

KEVIN FOY